How Am I Going to Grow Up?

An Exploration of Congregational Transition among Second-Generation Chinese Canadian Evangelicals and Servant-Leadership

Enoch Wong

MONOGRAPHS

© 2021 Enoch Wong

Published 2021 by Langham Monographs
An imprint of Langham Publishing
www.langhampublishing.org

Langham Publishing and its imprints are a ministry of Langham Partnership

Langham Partnership
PO Box 296, Carlisle, Cumbria, CA3 9WZ, UK
www.langham.org

ISBNs:
978-1-83973-226-3 Print
978-1-83973-636-0 ePub
978-1-83973-637-7 Mobi
978-1-83973-638-4 PDF

Enoch Wong has asserted his right under the Copyright, Designs and Patents Act, 1988 to be identified as the Author of this work.

All rights reserved. No part of this publication may be reproduced, stored in a retrieval system or transmitted, in any form or by any means, electronic, mechanical, photocopying, recording or otherwise, without the prior written permission of the publisher or the Copyright Licensing Agency.

Requests to reuse content from Langham Publishing are processed through PLSclear. Please visit www.plsclear.com to complete your request.

All Scripture quotations, unless otherwise indicated, are taken from the Holy Bible, New International Version®, NIV®. Copyright ©1973, 1978, 1984, 2011 by Biblica, Inc.™ Used by permission of Zondervan.

British Library Cataloguing-in-Publication Data
A catalogue record for this book is available from the British Library

ISBN: 978-1-83973-226-3

Cover & Book Design: projectluz.com

Langham Partnership actively supports theological dialogue and an author's right to publish but does not necessarily endorse the views and opinions set forth here or in works referenced within this publication, nor can we guarantee technical and grammatical correctness. Langham Partnership does not accept any responsibility or liability to persons or property as a consequence of the reading, use or interpretation of its published content.

With an appreciative understanding of the idea of service in the tradition of Robert Greenleaf's *Servant-Leadership*, Dr. Enoch Wong sets out to comprehend the transitioning experiences of the second-generation Chinese Canadian Evangelicals (SGCCE) in the areas of ethnicity and religiosity. His research also surveys the Chinese Christian churches and their leaders' handling of the transitional experiences of the SGCCE. The meanings of these experiences are revealed through Dr. Wong's use of the qualitative case study method rather than the classical use of the phenomenological methodology. His work implies that Greenleaf's philosophy of the idea of being the "servant first" could be realized and embraced with appreciation by individuals and communities so that all can "become freer and wiser and become servant-leaders." (p452)

Peter L. Lim, PhD
Headington Chair of Global Leadership Development,
School of Intercultural Studies, Fuller Theological Seminary,
Pasadena, California, USA

Surely one of the greatest challenges and responsibilities of the church is "passing on the faith" from one generation to the next. This is always a challenge and always a responsibility, but it is particularly so for relatively new immigrant communities, whether it is Russian Mennonites or Cantonese Chinese, Filipino or Somalian. In this publication, Dr. Enoch Wong focuses on the Chinese diaspora communities in Canada; however, what emerges in this study is invaluable for all communities and churches that are keen to foster the capacity of the church to nurture faith in the children of the church.

Gordon T. Smith, PhD
President,
Ambrose University and Seminary, Calgary, Alberta, Canada
Author, *Beginning Well*

Research on the "silent exodus" of second generation Chinese Christians in North America is long overdue despite the common recognition of its seriousness. Dr. Wong's research is a real breakthrough. Grounded on solid socio-cultural understanding, all the data point to the complexity of the issue. Other than ethnic identity and a cultural paradigm shift, personal interviews of members who are a part of the exodus and reflective pastors reveal a deeper problem, the style of leadership is affected by an unconscious immigrant mentality. Reflection on leadership is therefore considered to be vital. By this research, Dr. Wong has indeed done a great service to the Chinese Church in North America.

Carver Yu, PhD
President Emeritus,
China Graduate School of Theology, Kowloon Tong, Hong Kong

This work is dedicated to the loving memory of my
parents, Kwing Wong and Yuk Oi Law,
*whose selfless sacrifice and incredible support shaped
the lives of their three children and
made it possible for me to study and lead a new life in Canada.*

Contents

Acknowledgments xiii

Abstract xv

Chapter 1 1
Introduction
    Background 3
    Significance of the Study..7
    Personal Reasons for This Study..8
    Purpose Statement...9
    Conceptual Framework 9
        Ethnicity, Religion, Incorporation, and Congregational
            Transition Pathways for the "New" Second-Generation............10
        Leadership..16
    Research Questions 23
    Overview of Research Method 23
    Definition of Terms 24
    Overview of the Study..25

Chapter 2 27
Literature Review
    Chinese Evangelical Churches in Canada 29
        The Era of Chinese Evangelical Church (1967–Present) 40
        Second-Generation Chinese Canadian Evangelicals (SGCCE) 51
        Summary 61
    Ethnicity, Religion, and Incorporation 62
        Ethnicity 62
        Ethnicity, Religion, and the Incorporation Process 82
        Incorporation Process..88
        Canadian Multiculturalism and Incorporation............................94
        Summary 101
    Congregational Transition of Second-Generation Asian
        American Evangelicals in the Ethnic Churches..................................101
        Silent Exodus: The Emergent Phenomenon of Departure
            and Transition of the Asian North American Second-
            Generation from Their Parents' Church.....................................101
        Congregational Transition at the North American Ethnic
            Churches..104
        Summary 124
    Leadership 125

    Evolution of Modern Leadership Studies 125
    Greenleaf's Servant-Leadership 133
    Limitations and Challenges of Servant-Leadership 138
    Servant-Leadership Characteristics 143
    Foresight and Servant-Leadership 148
    Greenleaf's Servant-Leadership and Foresight 154
    Absence of Leadership Foresight 164
    Summary 168

Chapter 3 169
  Methods
  Research Methodology 169
    Epistemology and Theoretical Perspectives for
      Social Research 169
    Qualitative Research 174
    Research Approach 177
    Research Design 178
  Research Participants 185
  Data Collection 186
  Data Analysis 191
    Triangulation 193
  Bias and Bracketing 194
  Limitations of the Study 196
  Ethical Considerations 196
    Right of Privacy and Confidentiality 197
    Do No Harm 197
    Informed Consent 198
    The Right to Access the Results of the Study 198

Chapter 4 201
  Data Collection and Analysis
  Research Questions and Methodology 201
  Data Collection Summary 203
  Case One – Participants Attending Worship in a Second-
    Generation Chinese Canadian Church Setting 206
    Synopsis of Interview with First Participant: Martha Yeung 206
    Synopsis of Interview with Second Participant: Peter Fai 213
    Synopsis of Interview with Third Participant: James Chiu 219
    Themes for Case One 225
    Summary 234
  Case Two – Participants Attending Worship in a Pan-Ethnic
    Asian Church Setting 234

  Synopsis of Interview with First Participant: Eunice Chu 235
  Synopsis of Interview with Second Participant: Phoebe Lee.......242
  Synopsis of Interview with Last Participant: Lois Yung...............249
  Themes for Case Two..253
  Summary 261
 Case Three – Participants Attending Worship in a Multiethnic Setting...261
  Synopsis of Interview with First Participant: John Yang...............262
  Synopsis of Interview with Second Participant: Nathaniel Lam....268
  Synopsis of Interview with Third Participant: Mariam Yeung....274
  Themes for Case Three 283
  Summary 295
 Case Four – Participants Attending Worship in a Mainstream Caucasian Church Setting 295
  Synopsis of Interview with First Participant: Mark Luk 296
  Synopsis of Interview with Second Participant: Matthew Ly 302
  Synopsis of Interview with Third Participant: Paul Ling 307
  Synopsis of Interview with Fourth Participant: Luke Lau 313
  Themes for Case Four..319
  Summary 327
 Church Leaders From the Chinese Immigrant Church (Triangulation Group One)..327
  Synopsis of Interview with First Chinese Immigrant Pastor: Silas Wong..327
  Synopsis of Interview with Second Chinese Immigrant Pastor: Adam Wang...334
  Triangulation Analysis: Group One..339
  Summary 345
 Church Leaders From the Congregations (Triangulation Group Two)...345
  Synopsis of Interview with First Pastor: Tim Conrad 346
  Synopsis of Interview with Second Pastor: Charles Ho 353
  Synopsis of the Interview with the Third Pastor: Isaac Gregorcic..360
  Triangulation Analysis: Group Two..366
  Summary 377

Chapter 5 379
 Findings and Conclusion
 Cross-Case Analysis..380
  Cross-Case Theme #1: Dysfunctional and Inept Immigrant Church Leadership..382

- Cross-Case Theme #2: Mutuality between Ethnic Salience and Boundary of Congregation 392
- Cross-Case Theme #3: Relationship 396
- Cross-Case Theme #4: Stagnation, Solid Teachings, and Growth 398
- Cross-Case Theme #5: Indictment of Ethnic Culture and Values 402
- Cross-Case Theme #6: Social Construction of Identity 410
- Outlier #1: Abuse as the Trigger to Find a New Church 414
- Outlier #2: Meeting Spiritual Needs of Children Is Paramount 415

Findings 416
- Finding #1: Ethnicity retention and congregational affiliation: A function of cultural incorporation (Ethnicity and Socialization; RQ #1) 416
- Finding #2: Ethnic identity for SGCCE is an experiment in social construction and a function of the socialization process (Ethnicity and Socialization; RQ #2) 423
- Finding #3: All things being equal, SGCCE placed a high premium on relationship, and ethnicity played a significant role in it (Ethnicity and Socialization; RQ #1) 426
- Finding #4: Ethnic exclusivity and internecine conflicts contributed to the silent exodus (Ethnicity and Socialization; RQ #3) 430
- Finding #5: Stagnation and a yearning for growth and freedom motivated SGCCE to engage in the transition (Religious Identity; RQ #1) 433
- Finding #6: Religious identity reigns supreme (Religious Identity; RQ #2) 435
- Finding #7: Dysfunctional leadership and lack of vision and foresight at the Chinese immigrant church thwarted the SGCCE's growth and search for autonomy (Presence/Absence of Leadership; RQ #3) 439
- Finding #8: Compelling vision, explicit foresight, and a narrative of inclusivity over ethnicity were big draws for the SGCCE (Presence/Absence of Leadership; RQ #4) 444

Conclusion..449

Limitations of This Study and Future Research.............................452

Personal Reflection..453

Appendix 455
Semistructured Interview Guide

Bibliography 459

List of Tables

Table 1: Chinese Canadian and Chinese Canadian Evangelicals (Immigrants and Non-Immigrants) and Their Locations of Residence (Statistics Canada, 2014) 52

Table 2: Second- and Third-Generations of Chinese Canadian and Chinese Canadian Evangelicals (Statistics Canada, 2014) 53

Table 3: Servant-Leadership Characteristics and Attributes 145

Table 4: Participant Profile 204

Table 5: Ethnic Identity: Case One Participants 234

Table 6: Ethnic Identity: Case Two Participants 260

Table 7: Congregation Selection: Case Two Participants 261

Table 8: Ethnic Identity: Case Three Participants 295

Table 9: Ethnic Identity: Case Four Participants 321

Table 10: Congregation Selection: Case Four Participants 322

Table 11: Summary of the Analysis of Cross-Case Themes 384

Table 12: Triangulation Analysis 385

Table 13: Cross-Case Themes and Outliers 385

Table 14: Identity Comparison 412

Table 15: Findings, Arbitrating Factors, and Research Questions 417

List of Figures

Figure 1: A conformity-pluralist conceptual model (Driedger, *Ethnic Factor*, 51, figure 2.2) 99

The Archaeology of Daily Life

The Archaeology of Daily Life

Ordinary Persons in Late Second Temple Israel

DAVID A. FIENSY

CASCADE Books · Eugene, Oregon

THE ARCHAEOLOGY OF DAILY LIFE
Ordinary Persons in Late Second Temple Israel

Copyright © 2020 David A. Fiensy. All rights reserved. Except for brief quotations in critical publications or reviews, no part of this book may be reproduced in any manner without prior written permission from the publisher. Write: Permissions, Wipf and Stock Publishers, 199 W. 8th Ave., Suite 3, Eugene, OR 97401.

Cascade Books
An Imprint of Wipf and Stock Publishers
199 W. 8th Ave., Suite 3
Eugene, OR 97401

www.wipfandstock.com

PAPERBACK ISBN: 978-1-5326-7307-8
HARDCOVER ISBN: 978-1-5326-7308-5
EBOOK ISBN: 978-1-5326-7309-2

Cataloguing-in-Publication data:

Names: Fiensy, David, author.

Title: The archaeology of daily life : oridinary persons in late second temple Israel / David Fiensy.

Description: Eugene, OR: Cascade Books, 2020 | Includes bibliographical references and index.

Identifiers: ISBN 978-1-5326-7307-8 (paperback). | ISBN 978-1-5326-7308-5 (hardcover). | ISBN 978-1-5326-7309-2 (ebook).

Subjects: LCSH: Jews—Social life and customs. | Jews—Economic conditions. | Palestine—History— To 70 AD. | Bible—Antiquities.

Classification: DS121.65 F54 2020 (print). | DS121.65 (ebook).

Manufactured in the U.S.A.   JULY 24, 2020

All scripture translations are my own except in two places where I refer to the New Revised Standard Version for comparative purposes.

Contents

List of Maps | vi
List of Tables | vii
List of Figures | x
Acknowledgments | xiii
Abbreviations of Secondary Sources | xiv
Abbreviations of Primary Sources | xvii

Introduction | 1
1. What Were The Climate and Topography of Palestine/Israel? | 9
2. What Was City Life Like? | 21
3. What Was Village Life Like? | 57
4. What Kind of House Would You Have Lived In? | 78
5. What Would Your Family Dynamic Have Been Like? | 98
6. What Would Be Inside Your House? | 132
7. What Would You Do for a Living? | 161
8. What Would Your Bones Tell Us? | 186
9. What Chronic Disease(s) Would You Probably Have Contracted? | 199
10. How Long Would You Have Lived? | 229
11. How And Where Would They Bury You? | 249
12. How Would You Practice Your Religion? | 270

Appendix A: Why Did Jesus not Marry? | 303
Appendix B: Archaeological Periods of Palestine | 316
Bibliography | 317
Subject Index | 355
Scripture Index | 361

List of Maps

1.1 Topographical map of Israel | 11

2.1 Palestine in the late Second Temple period | 22

2.2 Jerusalem in the first century CE | 24

2.3 Galilee in the first century CE | 42

3.1 Khirbet Karqush village plan | 67

3.2 Dead Sea Area (plus Herodium) | 76

4.1 Galilee and Northern Samaria | 81

5.1 The Dead Sea region | 118

7.1 Khirbet el-Buraq | 163

7.2 Galilee and the Golan (Meiron and Gamla) | 178

9.1 Galilee with malarial zones | 218

12.1 Lower Galilee (with Shikhin) | 290

List of Tables

Intro.	Top archaeological discoveries for interpreting the historical Jesus	3
1.1	Average annual rainfall by zones	15
1.2	Average temperatures by zones	18
3.1	Villages sizes	62
3.2	Settlement categories	63
3.3	Village/city contrasts	73
3.4	Features in villages	75
	Appendix—Synagogue Sizes from the First Century CE	77
5.1	Childhood phases	103
5.2	Age at marriage	109
5.3	Values of dowries at Elephantine	115
5.4	Marriage/Divorce contracts	120
5.5	Views of divorce and polygamy in the late Second Temple period	125
6.1	Inventory of house items Masada/Naḥal Ḥever	135
6.2	Clothing samples	137
6.3	Food rations according to the Mishnah	145
6.4	Cooking vessels	149
6.5	Faunal remains	154
6.6	Plant remains	155

List of Tables

7.1	Gezer calendar	167
7.2	Agricultural year	168
7.3	Daily wages	173
7.4	Annual wages	174
7.5	Cost of bread	175
7.6	Estimates of necessary farm sizes	176
7.7	Women's daily tasks	185
8.1	The working class according to the skeletal remains	192
8.2	Stature in the late Second Temple period	193
8.3	Greek stature in the classical and Hellenistic periods	194
8.4	Jewish stature, ancient and modern	195
8.5	Stature comparisons (men)	195
8.6	Stature comparisons (women)	195
9.1	Major diseases in the ancient world	201
9.2	Diseases of Deuteronomy 28	204
9.3	Intestinal parasites in the Roman Empire	210
9.4	Agrippa I's death	211
9.5	Seasons of mortality	220
9.6	Malarial infections	222
9.7	Skull pitting in ancient Israel	225
9.8	Cribra orbitalia in the Roman empire	225
10.1	Child mortality	231
10.2	Infant mortality at Parvum Gerinum (Tel Jezreel)	232
10.3	Youth mortality	233
10.4	Youth mortality in the Greco-Roman world	234
10.5	Life expectancy from birth	236

10.6	Life expectancy from adulthood	238
10.7	Life expectancy according to various findings	239
10.8	Population percentages	246
12.1	Archaeological distinctives of household Judaism	270
12.2	Rules of uncleanness in the Torah	274
12.3	Levels of uncleanness	277
12.4	Levels of holiness	277
12.5	Chemical analysis of clay lamps	288
12.6	Further chemical analysis of clay lamps	289
12.7	Grades of Purity in first century Judaism	291

List of Figures

1.1	The Judean hill country	14
1.2	Wilderness east of Jerusalem	15
1.3	Sea of Galilee	17
1.4	The Dead Sea	18
2.1	The Tyropoeon street, Jerusalem	25
2.2	Artist's reconstruction of Jerusalem	26
2.3	Inside a wealthy family's house, Jerusalem	28
2.4	Artist's reconstruction of the wealthy family's house	29
2.5	The Pool of Siloam, Jerusalem	33
2.6	Theater of Caesarea Maritima	36
2.7	Promontory palace, Caesarea	38
2.8	The circus of Caesarea	39
2.9	Artist's reconstruction of Caesarea Maritima	40
2.10	The Aqueduct of Caesarea	41
2.11	Decumanus street, Sepphoris	45
2.12	Theater, Sepphoris	46
2.13	Sepphoris aqueduct	50
2.14	Artist's reconstruction of Tiberias	52
2.15	Mikveh at Magdala	54

List of Figures

3.1	Village model	65
3.2	Gamla synagogue	69
3.3	Hill where Khirbet Qana located	70
3.4	Cistern opening	74
4.1	House at Umm Rihan	80
4.2	"Mansion" of Jerusalem	83
4.3	"Villa" of Sepphoris	84
4.4	Capernaum house with communal courtyard	85
4.5	Mansion at Ramat ha-Nadiv	87
4.6	Underground stable	91
4.7	Courtyard	96
6.1	Inside Arab house	134
6.2	Mediterranean diet pyramid	145
6.3	Wine press	147
6.4	Cooking pots	148
6.5	Casserole bowl	150
6.6	Arab men drinking coffee	159
7.1	Terraces	165
7.2	Olive crusher	168
7.3	Threshing floor	171
10.1	Mortality curve	246
11.1	Tomb niches	255
11.2	Herod family tomb	256
11.3	Tomb niches	259
11.4	Ossuaries	261
11.5	Rolling stone tomb	263

LIST OF FIGURES

    11.6   Façad of Beth She'arim catacombs | 267

    12.1   The oral Torah | 271

    12.2   *Mikveh* (Qumran) | 280

    12.3   *Mikveh* (Yodefat) | 283

    12.4   *Mikveh* (Jerusalem) | 285

    12.5   Stoneware | 287

    12.6   Herodian lamp | 288

    12.7   Replica lamps from Briton and Asia | 292

    12.8   Magdala synagogue | 293

Acknowledgments

No work is ever done entirely alone. I owe a debt to many who have written on these topics before me, to those who helped in a specific way to understand and clarify the issues, and to those who assisted me in securing resources for this research. Special thanks go to Professors David Instone-Brewer, Hanna Cotton, Mordechai Aviam, and Andrea Berlin for reading portions of this manuscript and offering advice. I have benefitted greatly from their counsel. I also thank the library staff of Kentucky Christian University for their eager assistance in securing many resources through interlibrary loan. They have made this endeavor more enjoyable by their timely help.

Further, I wish to thank those who gave permission to use their figures or maps gratis in this volume:

- Shimon Dar gave permission for Map 3.1, Figure 4.1, and Map 7.1
- Balage Balogh gave permission to use Figure 4.6
- Bertelsman Unternehmensarchive gave permission to reuse Figures 6.1 and 6.6
- Danny Syon, Andrea Berlin, and the Israel Antiquities Authority allowed Figure 6.4
- Yossi Nagar and Hagit Torgeé gave permission for Figure 10.1
- Fortress Press graciously allowed the reuse of my previous publications that became Chapters 3, 4, and 10 in this volume.

Many thanks for these permissions.

Most importantly, I thank Molly, the love of my life, for her support during my research time and her tolerance of my purchasing "yet another book" to read for this project.

Abbreviations of Secondary Sources

ABD   David Noel Freedman, ed. *The Anchor Bible Dictionary*. 6 vols. New York: Doubleday, 1992

ANRW   *Aufstieg und Niedergang der römischen Welt*

BA   *Biblical Archaeologist*

BAIAS   *Strata; Bulletin of the Anglo-Israel Archaeological Society*

BAR   *Biblical Archaeology Review*

BASOR   *Bulletin of the American Schools of Oriental Research*

Bib   *Biblica*

BNP   Hubert Cancik and Helmuth Schneider, eds. *Brill's New Pauly: Encyclopedia of the Ancient World*. 15 vols. Leiden: Brill, 2006

BTB   *Biblical Theology Bulletin*

DDL   Edwin M. Yamauchi and Marvin R. Wilson, eds. *Dictionary of Daily Life in Biblical and Post-Biblical Antiquity*. 4 vols. Peabody, MA: Hendrickson, 2014

EncJud1   Cecil Roth, ed. *Encyclopedia Judaica*. 16 vols. Jerusalem: Keter, 1972

EncJud2   Fred Skolnik, ed. *Encyclopedia Judaica*. 22 vols. 2nd ed. Detroit: Thomson/Gale, 2007

ESA   Eastern Terra Sigillata A (ceramic ware)

GLSTMP   David A. Fiensy and James Riley Strange, eds. *Galilee in the Late Second Temple and Mishnaic Periods*. 2 vols. Minneapolis: Fortress, 2014–2015

ABBREVIATIONS OF SECONDARY SOURCES

HTR	*Harvard Theological Review*
IDB	George Arthur Buttrick, ed. *The Interpreter's Dictionary of the Bible.* 4 vols. Nashville: Abingdon, 1962
IDB (New)	Katharine Doob Sakenfeld, ed. *The New Interpreter's Dictionary of the Bible.* 5 vols. Nashville: Abingdon, 2006–2009
IEJ	*Israel Exploration Journal*
IJO	*International Journal of Osteoarchaeology*
IJP	*International Journal of Paleopathology*
JBL	*Journal of Biblical Literature*
JJS	*Journal of Jewish Studies*
JRA	*Journal of Roman Archaeology*
JRS	*Journal of Roman Studies*
JSHJ	*Journal for the Study of the Historical Jesus*
JSJ	*Journal for the Study of Judaism*
JSOT	*Journal for the Study of the Old Testament*
LCL	Loeb Classical Library
LSJM	Henry George Liddell, Robert Scott, Henry Stuart Jones, and Roderick McKenzie. *A Greek-English Lexicon.* Oxford: Clarendon, 1968
NEA	*Near Eastern Archaeology*
NEAEHL	Ephraim Stern, ed., *The New Encyclopedia of Archaeological Excavations in the Holy Land.* 4 vols. Jerusalem: IES, 1993 (Volume 5, Supplementary, 2008)
NH	Marvin W. Meyer, ed., *The Nag Hammadi Library in English.* San Francisco: Harper & Row, 1977
NovT	*Novum Testamentum*
NRSV	New Revised Standard Version
NTS	*New Testament Studies*

ABBREVIATIONS OF SECONDARY SOURCES

OCD	N. G. L. Hammond and H. H. Scullard, eds. *Oxford Classical Dictionary*. Oxford: Clarendon, 1970
OCD3rev.	Simon Hornblower and Antony Spawforth, eds. *The Oxford Classical Dictionary*. 3rd ed. Oxford: Oxford University Press, 2003
OEANE	Eric M. Meyers, ed. *The Oxford Encyclopedia of Archaeology in the Near East*. 4 vols. New York: Oxford, 1997
OEBA	Daniel M. Master, ed. *The Oxford Encyclopedia of the Bible and Archaeology*. Oxford: Oxford University Press, 2013
OHJDL	Catherine Hezser, ed. *The Oxford Handbook of Jewish Daily Life in Roman Palestine*. Oxford: Oxford University Press, 2010
PEQ	*Palestine Exploration Quarterly*
POT	James H. Charlesworth, ed. *The Pseudepigrapha of the Old Testament*. 2 vols. New York: Doubleday, 1983, 185.
RevExp	*Review and Expositor*
RevQ	*Revue de Qumran*
TDNT	Gerhard Kittel et al., eds. *Theological Dictionary of the New Testament*. 10 vols. Translated by Geoffrey W. Bromiley. Grand Rapids: Eerdmans, 1964–1976
TZ	*Theologische Zeitschrift*

Abbreviations of Primary Sources

1QS	Qumran Community Rule
1QSa	Qumran Rule of the Congregation
11QT	Qumran Temple Scroll
4QMMT	Qumran Miqṣat ma'aseh ha-Torah (or Halakhic Letter)
4QSam[a]	Qumran manuscript "a" of the Book of Samuel
Abod. Zar.	Abodah Zara
Ahil.	Ahilot
Ant.	Josephus, *Antiquities*
Apion	Josephus, *Against Apion*
'Arak.	'Arakin
Arist.	Letter of Aristeas
b.	Babylonian Talmud
B. Batra	Baba Batra
Ber.	Berakot
B. Metzia	Baba Metzia
B. Qama	Baba Qama
Cant. R.	Canticles (or Song of Solomon) Rabbah
Clem.	Clement
Congr.	Philo, *de congressu eruditionis gratia*

Abbreviations of Primary Sources

CD	Cairo Damascus Document
Eccl. R.	Ecclesiastes Rabbah
ʿEd.	Eduyyot
ʿErub.	Erubin
Exod. R.	Exodus Rabbah
Gen. R.	Genesis Rabbah
Gitt.	Gittin
Gos. Ebion.	Gospel of the Ebionites
Gos. Mary	Gospel of Mary
Gos. Phil.	Gospel of Philip
Gos. Thom.	Gospel of Thomas
Haeres	Epiphanius, *Haereseis*
Ḥag.	Ḥagigah
Ḥall.	Ḥallah
H.E.	Eusebius, *Ecclesiastical History*
Ḥev.	Text from Naḥal Ḥever
Ḥull.	Ḥullin
Hypoth.	Philo, *Hypothetica*
j.	Jerusalem (or Palestinian) Talmud
Jdt.	Judith
Jos. Asen.	Joseph and Asenath
Jub.	Book of Jubilees
Kel.	Kelim
Keri.	Keritot
Ket.	Ketubbot
Kil.	Kilayim

Abbreviations of Primary Sources

L.A.E.	*Life of Adam and Eve*
Lam. R.	Lamentations Rabbah
Lev. R.	Leviticus Rabbah
Liv. Pro.	The Lives of the Prophets
LXX	The Greek translation of the Old Testament
m.	Mishnah
Ma'as.	Ma'aserot
Ma'as. S.	Ma'aser Sheni
Macc.	Book of Maccabees
Maksh.	Makshirin
Meg.	Megillah
Mikv.	Mikva'ot
Mo'ed Qat.	Mo'ed Qatan
Mur	Text from Wadi Muraba'at
Ned.	Nedarim
Nidd.	Niddah
Ohol.	Oholot
Pan.	Epiphanius, *Panarion*
Pes.	Pesaḥim
Pliny, *N.H.*	Pliny, *Natural History*
POxy.	Papyrus Oxyrhynchus
Ps. Philo	Pseudo Philo (also called *Liber Antiquitatum Biblicarum*)
Ps.-Phoc.	Pseudo-Phocylides
Qidd.	Qiddushin
Rosh H.	Rosh Ha-Shanah
Sanh.	Sanhedrin

Abbreviations of Primary Sources

Se	Text from Naḥal Ṣe'alim
Sem.	Semaḥot
Shabb.	Shabbat
Sheb.	Shebi'it
Sib. Or.	Sibylline Oracles
Spec. Leg.	Philo, *de Specialibus Legibus*
Sheq.	Sheqalim
Sir.	The Wisdom of Jesus ben Sirach
Sukk.	Sukkah
Sus.	Book of Susanna
Syr. Men.	Syriac Menander
t.	Tosephta
Ta'an.	Ta'anit
Test. Iss.	Testament of Issachar
Test. Jud.	Testament of Judah
Tohor.	Tohorot
T. Yom	Tevul Yom
Virt.	Philo, *de Virtutibus*
War	Josephus, *War*
Yad.	Yadayim
Yebam.	Yebamot

ABBREVIATIONS OF SCRIPTURAL BOOKS

1 Chr	1 Chronicles
1 Cor	1 Corinthians
Deut	Deuteronomy

Abbreviations of Primary Sources

Eccl	Ecclesiastes
Ezek	Ezekiel
Exod	Exodus
Gen	Genesis
Hab	Habakkuk
Isa	Isaiah
Jas	James
Jer	Jeremiah
Lam	Lamentations
Lev	Leviticus
Mal	Malachi
Matt	Matthew
Neh	Nehemiah
Num	Numbers
Prov	Proverbs
Pss	Psalms
Rev	Revelation
Sam	Samuel

Introduction

THE PURPOSE OF THIS monograph is to reconstruct the world of the Jesus Movement in order to meet the ordinary people with whom it interacted. What experiences played a role in their lives that would influence the way they heard the teachings of Jesus? How can archaeology play a role in a new way in answering this question?

Two continental New Testament scholars recently lamented the lack of interaction with archaeological remains on the part of their colleagues. They complained that, for many, New Testament studies were an "archaeology free zone." Although Old Testament scholars and church historians use material remains freely in reconstructing their respective histories, New Testament scholars mostly focus exclusively on the texts.[1] The lack of experience with archaeology (with the methods of excavation and dating) leads to the inability to use it in interpreting the New Testament.

On the other hand, the popular blogs about archaeological finds often make absurd and exaggerated claims and leave a false impression with their readers. These websites seem to have one agenda: using archaeology to "prove the Bible." Although they are to be commended for calling the attention of the average reader to some archaeological finds, they usually press the inferences one can draw from them beyond reason.[2] If New Testament scholarship will make use of the increasingly vast source of data in the undertaking of exegesis, it must neither neglect archaeology nor assume that every potsherd "proves" yet another biblical chapter.[3]

---

1. See Alkier and Zangenberg, "Zeichen aus Text und Stein." The expression "archaeology free zone" originated with Peter Pilhofer (x).

2. E.g., Leap, "Archaeology Proves."

3. For ideas in utilizing archaeology in interpreting texts, see: E. M. Meyers and J. F. Strange, *Archaeology, the Rabbis, and Early Christianity*, 28–29; Charlesworth, "Archaeology," 8–9; E. M. Meyers and C. Meyers, "Holy Land Archaeology"; Hoppe, *Biblical Archaeology*, 4–8; Starbuck, "Things Forbidden?"; James F. Strange, "Sayings of Jesus and Archaeology," 296–97; Reed, *Archaeology*, 18; McRay, *Archaeology*, 17–19; Levine, "Archaeological Discoveries," 76; Dever, *Recent Archaeological*, 32–35; Dever, *Biblical Writers*, 124–28; Dever, *Ordinary People*, 189–91; Moreland, Burkes, and Aubin, "Introduction," 1–2. See also the table in Fiensy, *Insights*, 21.

TOP ARCHAEOLOGICAL FINDS IN THE STUDY OF THE HISTORICAL JESUS: THREE VIEWS[4]

Although the use of archaeology on the European continent has been limited, it has found a bit more interest in North American New Testament scholarship.[5] There have been a few voices in the last decades challenging us to consider the material remains as informants in our attempt to understand the world of Palestine/Israel in the late Second Temple Period. We will here survey the "top archaeological discoveries" cited by two prominent monographs—one in 1988 and one in 2001—and a seminal journal article from 2003. The three lists of the most important material remains—especially in interpreting the life and words of the historical Jesus—are rather similar in many places with a couple outliers thrown in:

	Charlesworth[6]	Crossan and Reed[7]	Witherington[8]
1		Caiaphas' ossuary	Caiaphas' ossuary
2	Bones of the crucified man	Bones of the crucified man	
3		Peter's house	House of Peter
4		Monuments of Jewish Resistance (Masada and Qumran[9])	Dead Sea Scrolls
5	Temple mount		Herodian sites (Masada, Herodium, Temple Mount)
6		Cities of Herod the Great (Caesarea Maritima and Jerusalem)	
7		Cities of Antipas (Sepphoris and Tiberias)	Scythopolis and Sepphoris
8		First-century Jewish villages in the North (Yodefat and Gamla[10])	
9	(stone vessels)	Stone vessels and *miqvaot*	
10		The Galilee boat	Jesus boat

---

4. For another, more popular view see, e.g., Shogan, "Favorite New Testament Archaeological Discoveries."

5. See the recent jointly authored essay by Charlesworth and Aviam, "Reconstructing First-Century Galilee."

6. Charlesworth, *Jesus within Judaism*, 103–30.

7. Crossan and Reed, *Excavating Jesus*, 2.

8. Witherington, "Top Ten New Testament Archaeological Finds."

9. Including Qumran in this category (Jewish resistance) seems odd to me although the site was destroyed by the Romans in c. 68 CE.

10. Again, an odd designation. These were not just any villages but those destroyed completely by Rome in the war.

11		The Pilate inscription	Pilate inscription
12	Church of the Holy Sepulchre		
13	Place of the Praetorium		
14	Pools of "Bethesda"		
15	Walls and gates of Jerusalem		
16	First-century synagogues of Palestine		
17			Rylands fragment of the Gospel of John
18			Shroud of Turin
19			James ossuary

Introduction Table 1: Top Archaeological Finds for Interpreting the Historical Jesus

Charlesworth, after presenting the "Burnt House"[11] and the stoneware vessels as significant in the study of the historical Jesus, lists seven discoveries that have made an impact on this research. His conclusion is that the Church of the Holy Sepulchre as the site of the crucifixion is the most important "discovery" to date. Of his seven top discoveries, six of them are in Jerusalem. Only the synagogues from the first century (just Masada, Herodium, and Gamla at his time of writing, but see Chapter 3) lie outside the holy city. All of the significant discoveries, except for the bones of the crucified man, are monumental ruins. In a later publication, in 2006, Charlesworth adds to these original seven top finds the excavations at Nazareth, at Cana, of the mansion at Ramat Ha-nadiv (see Chapter 4), at Herodium, at Caesarea Maritima (Chapter 2), and at Bethsaida. He also adds the Galilee boat, making his more complete list of fourteen items even more similar to the other two lists.[12] His expanded list also takes us farther from Jerusalem.

Crossan's and Reed's list is similar to Charlesworth's in its selection of sites and items. Most of their top ten finds (as opposed to Charlesworth's seven finds) are of large ruins: cities, houses, boats, and monasteries. Only the bones of the crucified man, the ossuary of Caiaphas, and the fragments of stone vessels (and of ritual baths) are small(er) finds. Unlike Charlesworth's original list, however, is their geographical variation. Of the ten discoveries, only two and one half are in Jerusalem. The rest are in Galilee, the Golan, and elsewhere in Judea.

---

11. Charlesworth, *Jesus within Judaism,* 106. The Burnt House was destroyed when the Romans overran Jerusalem in 70 CE.

12. Charlesworth, "Jesus Research and Archaeology."

Witherington's list is much like that of Charlesworth and Crossan/Reed. He lists the monumental ruins of cities along with the ossuary of Caiaphas, the "Jesus boat," and the Pilate inscription. So far there is nothing unusual here. But he adds to this list the Rylands papyrus fragment of the Gospel of John, the oldest scrap of the New Testament found thus far. This can certainly be justified as an entry onto the list. But then he adds the Shroud of Turin and the James ossuary, both of which are considerably dubious with respect to provenance and date.

Still, apart from the Shroud of Turin and the James ossuary, the three lists are rather similar. They want to use mostly large, monumental ruins to interpret the life and teachings of Jesus. If we can just picture Jesus walking down the streets of Sepphoris, for example, perhaps we can understand his aims and his teachings a little better. If we can find the actual spot of Jesus' crucifixion or construct an accurate model of the Temple, maybe we can answer some lingering questions about events that took place at those sites.

The excavation of these large ruins has given the New Testament interpreter much to chew on in reflecting on the world of late Second Temple Israel. Certainly, these finds have helped us construct some of the context for Jesus' life and teachings. We have a much clearer understanding of the geography, economy, and culture because of these excavations. Every New Testament historian can be excited about those material remains and the insights they bring to the exegetical task of the New Testament interpreter. We must not now ignore these results. Indeed, Chapters 2–4 of this volume will describe some of them.

But should we remain fixed on the monuments? Is it time now also to push on and ask further questions? Where can one go from here to gain insights? After all, did most village residents visit the big cities that much? Did the large monuments really influence their lives? Apart from the bones of the crucified man, the fragments of the stone vessels, and the James ossuary—if one agrees that this relic actually is the ossuary of Jesus' brother—there is very little here in these lists about ordinary people. The monuments were built by the elites, the wealthy, and the powerful—though they may have used lower-class labor and taxes to accomplish their task. But most of the population of late Second Temple Israel was not from that class. How can we hear from them?

Thus, while North American scholars have shown more interest in archaeology, there is still need to push forward beyond the "monuments."

THE NEED FOR A HOLISTIC APPROACH

Seeking to reconstruct the context for Jesus' life and ministry based solely on the monumental remains is like an American tourist visiting China. He/she sees the Forbidden City and the Great Wall. Our tourist views some of the ancient palaces and the "Terra Cotta Army." The visitor then returns home and announces that he/she now knows and understands China. We would all smile indulgently but not be convinced. Although viewing those sites would be important, it would not be adequate. If one has not met at least a few of the people, one does not "know China." And the people one meets cannot be limited to the wealthy upper one per cent.

Likewise, believing that we know Jesus' life and times because we have seen the ruins of Sepphoris, is not convincing. They are important; we must see them but they must not satisfy us. It is a bit more convincing to find information on his life and times in the remains of religious practices such as the ritual baths and stoneware vessels. But even they do not bring us to the people themselves. Nor can one, in meeting the people, focus on Herod the Great and his descendants, on the religious sects, or on the exciting manuscripts found near the Dead Sea. All of these elements must be a part of a complete investigation but we need more. Our task in this monograph is not to describe the Pharisees and Essenes, not to analyze the Dead Sea Scrolls, not to give a complete account of major events of the first century CE, although, at times, these things may enter peripherally into our quest.

In the pursuit of information beyond these issues, archaeologists have begun to examine remains that were not even considered some decades back. They microscopically look at latrine remains to understand ancient diets (there are clues in the pollen) and ancient diseases (eggs of parasites). They look at bones and teeth to check for signs of chronic illness and to determine demographics and longevity. They check out data on tombstones and ossuaries to sketch mini-biographies of ordinary persons. I hope to capitalize on all of these methods in this volume.

Our task, in so far as one can achieve it, is to meet the ordinary people. I want to visit the ordinary people in all their poverty, sickness, and pain. The biblical world was a "third world" country where daily suffering and horrible illness were taken for granted. If we can get a clearer view of the ancient persons who heard Jesus' parables and Jesus' Beatitudes, for example, it might give us insight and nuance in our modern reading of these texts. We surely do not hear them now as the ancients did.

Although I appreciate and have learned from the other studies on "daily life," I also hope to add a dimension—not to mention topics—untouched in most of the other works. I want my portrayal of first-century Palestine/Israel to be a grittier story. Thus, I discuss unhappy topics like morbidity and mortality. I will talk about the treatment of children and women. The result may be disturbing in places but ultimately more satisfying in terms of the exegetical payoff for those interpreting the New Testament and/or the Mishnah. At least, that is my goal.

Other historians have made and are making similar attempts.[13] Such a task is a growing area of interest in scholarship. The study of ancient history is no longer just

---

13. E.g., see: Dever, *Ordinary People*; Borowski, *Daily Life*; Nakhai, "Embracing the Domestic"; Hezser, ed., *OHJDL*; King and Stager, *Life in Biblical Israel*; Yamauchi and Wilson, eds., *DDL*; Evans, *Remains*; Collins and Harlow, eds., *Dictionary*; Rousseau and Arav, *Jesus and His World*; Magness, *Stone*; Master, ed., *OEBA*; Gurtner and Stuckenbruck, eds., *Encyclopedia*.

about the great politicians and military conquerors. As Richard Horsley and John Hanson observed in their groundbreaking work of 1985:

> Until very recently, the modern Western assumption has been that the common people have had little to do with the making of history... Standard treatments of Jewish history and the background of Jesus... Almost always discuss groups and figures from the ruling class and the literate stratum.[14]

In other words, Richard Horsley and John Hanson challenged, rightly so, the focus and near obsession with previous investigations into the great and wealthy people, the "beautiful people." Horsley and Hanson, on the other hand, were interested in the ordinary people, for the upper class—the elites of antiquity—comprised a mere one to two percent of the population. Clearly, focusing on them was presenting a skewed view of history.

Likewise, and more recently, the classical historian Thomas Grünewald has written: "Historians are recognizing that those on the margins of the community... have a significant effect on the historical process."[15] Thus, social historians are now paying greater attention to those of lower social standing. He then explores the topic of banditry, the low-class version of politics, in the Roman empire. In my monograph, one could say, I will look at mostly those of that social stratum: the low-class, the poor, the working class, and non-famous—not necessarily infamous—persons of Palestine/Israel in the late Second Temple Period.

OUR SOURCES

How will we get into this information? In the following chapters, we will freely use the ancient literary sources to supplement the archaeological finds (and, indeed, to interpret the finds). But here a word of caution is in order. Most of the literary sources are from the upper class, the elites, or aristocracy. This is true of Josephus, a priest from the wealthy Hasmonean family, and it is true of much of the rabbinic literature. The rabbis were educated, literate, and often wealthy persons. They were religious authorities and often large landowners. Their take on "reality" for the ordinary person might not have been accurate.

David Kraemer writes of this concern in his essay: "(the rabbinic literature) is a literature which speaks for a small segment of the Palestinian Jewish population,

---

14. R. A. Horsley and J. S. Hanson, *Bandits, Prophets, and Messiahs,* xii. Cf. also: C. Meyers, ("Women's Culture," 427), who asks for a bottom to top perspective instead of the top down perspective "that has dominated Syro-Palestinian archaeology"; Donaldson ("Rural Bandits," 19), who observes that the peasants comprised 90% of the population but most historical studies ignore them and focus on the ruling aristocracy; and R. A. Horsley (*Sociology,* 3): "we are no longer satisfied with such an idealist individualist theological understanding of the biblical texts... biblical literature is about the problems and experiences of real people."

15. Grünewald, *Bandits in the Roman Empire,* 1.

motivated by its own particular elitist, polemical, and even sectarian concerns."[16] Kraemer offers three checks on the bias of the use of the rabbinic literature: First, one may assume that details that are not directly in service of polemical rabbinic goals are accurate. Second, evidence from the rabbinic literature that is confirmed by contemporaneous literature—Josephus, the New Testament, and Greco-Jewish sources—has a good chance of accurately representing the ordinary people. Third, archaeology should be used to confirm or contradict the rabbinic evidence.[17]

These are helpful safeguards in our use of rabbinic sources to construct daily life in the late Second Temple Period. But to these I would add a fourth. In addition to the material remains mentioned by Kraemer, many archaeologists use cultural anthropology in order to understand the ruins they are looking at. They also will use demographic data from pre-modern societies to help interpret the remains. Lawrence Stager, an archaeologist investigating the Hebrew Bible era, wrote: "ethnoarchaeological models forged from many of the same cultural and ecological constraints operative in the past, provide guidelines within which the archaeologist can reconstruct aspects of everyday life from the patterns of material remains."[18] Likewise, Brent Shaw, a classical historian, maintained that the "most reasonable guide remains comparative data from the same physical environments" as the material remains under discussion.[19] We will, then, make free use of ethnographic studies (traditional Arab villages in the modern era) as well as comparisons of morbidity in roughly similar environments and situations to help us interpret the material remains and literary sources.[20] If a custom referred to in the rabbinic literature is also found in some form in the contemporary Arab villages of Palestine and the wider region, it may have represented not just the elites but the common people as well.

THE CHAPTERS

After a brief look (chapter 1) at the climate and topography of Israel, the monograph will summarize what has been found, archaeologically, in the Jewish cities and villages of Palestine, also giving an accounting of housing types in the Hell II–ER II periods (Chapters 2–4). From there, we turn to a discussion of family (Chapter 5), home furnishings (Chapter 6), and daily labor (Chapter 7). Along the way, we discuss

16. Kraemer, "Food, Eating, and Meals," 404. See also Hamel, "Poverty and Charity"; and Martin, "Slavery," 117.
17. Kraemer, "Food, Eating, and Meals," 404–5.
18. Stager, "Archaeology of the Family," 18.
19. Shaw, "Seasons of Death," 131.
20. The following ethnographies were consulted for this monograph: Amiry and Tamari, *Palestinian Village Home*; Canaan, "Arab House"; Dalman, *Haus*; Fuchs, "Arab House"; Fuller, *Buarij*; Hirschfeld, *Palestinian Dwelling*; Kramer, *Village Ethnoarchaeology*; Lutfiyya, *Baytin*; Sweet, *Tell Toqaan*; Tannous, "Arab Village"; Lancaster and Lancaster, "Jordanian Village Houses"; and Thompson, *Land*.

childhood, marriage, clothing, food, and the annual cycle for agricultural villages. We then turn to rather unhappy topics, based largely on the examination of ancient bones (Chapters 8–10). These chapters will indicate things such as stature and facial looks, diseases, and life-spans and mortality. We end the volume with two chapters on religion, one (Chapter 11) on death and burial, and the last (Chapter 12) on ritual purity and aniconic decorations. In each of these chapters, archaeology will play a crucial role.

1

What Were The Climate and Topography of Palestine/Israel?

WHAT WOULD YOUR DAILY life have been if you lived in Palestine in the late Second Temple Period (c. 37 BCE—70 CE)? Would you have been a farmer? Artisan? Lived in mountains? On a plain? In the desert? You could have done any of the above.

Herodian Palestine was about the same size as the state of Vermont in the United States. From the ancient city of Dan to the city of Beersheba, the boundaries in the Old Testament period, it is 150 miles (241 km.).[1] Although Palestine is geographically a small land area, it had and has three distinct topographical and climatic regions[2] (if we add the Transjordan area, then four regions). Let us look at each of these in three narrow strips running from north to south:

- Region 1 is the Coastal Plain.
- Region 2 is the Hill Country.
- Region 3 is the Jordan Rift.

THE TOPOGRAPHY OF PALESTINE/ISRAEL: THE THREE ZONES

In spite of the small land area of Palestine, there is an interesting variety of topography and climate. One has the feeling of a larger country when one is there perhaps because of these differences. Certainly, a person's life and yearly experiences would vary greatly depending on which of these zones he/she lived in.

1. Coogan, "Geography."
2. One can also analyze Israel based on "geomorphic or physiographic provinces." See Bullard, "Geological Studies," who gives seven zones based on topography and petrology.

The Archaeology of Daily Life

The Coastal Plain

The coastal plain is that narrow strip of land that borders the Mediterranean Sea on its west. The northern part of the coast was called in the Old Testament the Plain of Sharon, the southern area the Philistine Plain. It is made of mostly alluvial soil and ranges from 10 to 15 miles (16–24 km.) wide. Its temperatures range from an average of 54 degrees Fahrenheit in the month of January to an average of 77 degrees Fahrenheit in the month of August. The average rainfall on the coast in November (as the rainy season begins) is one inch; in January (the height of the rainy season) five inches; and in April (as the rainy season ends) one inch. Snow and frost are rare on the coast, but the scorching east winds called the *sirocco* or *khamsin* are also less frequent.[3] If you lived on the coast, you would be used to relatively mild weather all year round. On the coast were cities with large Gentile populations such as Caesarea (Map 2.1), Lydda, Ptolemais, and Joppa (Map 1.1). A major highway for international travel and commerce, the Via Maris ("way of the sea"), ran up the coast of Israel, turned eastward through the Great Plain (Map 4.1), turned again north around the Sea of Galilee and on to Damascus.

The Central Highlands

Running from Upper Galilee south to the Negev is a range of mountains. This is the second region or climate zone of Palestine/Israel. In these low mountains (reaching 3,000+ feet, or 914 m., in places) it often snows in winter. They are mostly composed of limestone making numerous caves, hideouts for bandits in antiquity.[4] Let us discuss Galilee first and then move southward.

The Region of Galilee

The Jewish historian, Josephus (first century CE; *War* 1.22; 3.35–39) divided Galilee into two sections: Upper Galilee and Lower Galilee. The rabbinic collection called the Mishnah (collected in 200 CE; m. Sheb. 9:2) divided Galilee into three parts: Upper Galilee, Lower Galilee, and the Great Plain. A steep slope separates the Upper and Lower Galilee. To determine where the one ended and the other began, the reader may draw an imaginary line from the northern end of the Sea of Galilee westward toward the Mediterranean Sea.[5] The mountains of Upper Galilee reach a height of

---

3. See Rainey and Notley, *Carta's New Century*, 19; and Frick, "Palestine, Climate," 120–22.
4. Herr, "Geography," 103.
5. This is only an approximate division. For a more precise dividing of the two Galilees, see Avi-Yonah, *Holy Land*, 133–35.

What Were The Climate and Topography of Palestine/Israel?

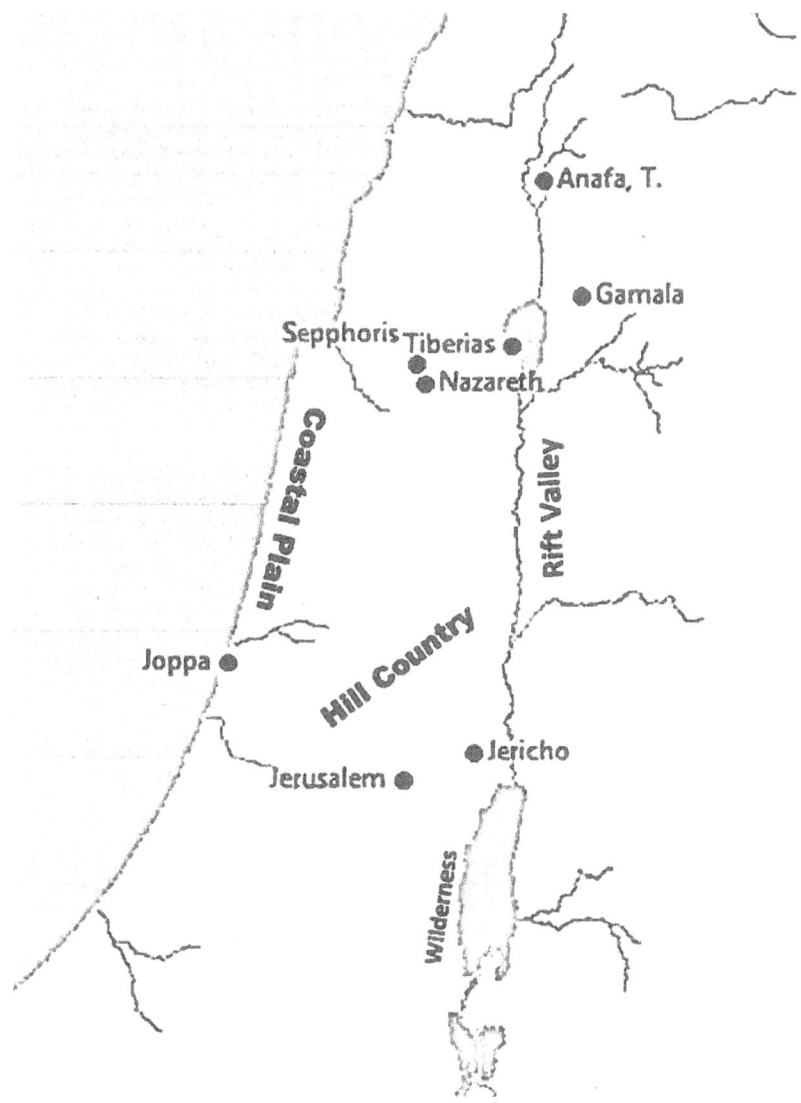

Israel showing topographical regions (from west to east)
1. The Coastal Plain
2. The Hill Country
3. The Rift Valley from the north to the Dead Sea in the south, including the Judean Wilderness

Map 1.1: Topographical map of Israel (created with Accordance)

3,900 feet (1188 m.) while those of Lower Galilee rise to just under 2,000 feet (609 m.). Lower Galilee is intersected by four valleys running east to west and finally drops in the south from a height of 1,500 feet (457 m.) at Nazareth to the Great Plain which is 492 feet (149 m.) above sea level. Upper Galilee extended over 180 square miles (466 sq. km.); Lower Galilee 470 square miles (1217 sq. km.).[6] Upper Galilee averages 40 inches of rain per year; Lower Galilee averages 24 inches.[7] The eastern part of Galilee is made of mostly hard, basaltic (volcanic) rock; the western of limestone, not as hard and more useful for building.[8] The valley called by Josephus the Great Plain (called in the Old Testament the Valley of Jezreel and by the Greek writers, the Plain of Esdraelon) is made of alluvial soil and is very fertile.[9]

Archaeologists have confirmed that there was also a bit of a cultural divide between Upper Galilee and Lower Galilee. Upper Galilee was more conservative and isolated, speaking mostly Hebrew and Aramaic (as evidenced by the inscriptions found so far). It had only villages and small towns and no major trade routes dissected its region. Lower Galilee has produced more Greek inscriptions, had two fair-sized cities, Sepphoris and Tiberias, and one small city, Magdala/Taricheae (see Map 2.3).[10] It was more open to outside influences because important trade routes (such as the Via Maris) ran through it. The differences between the two Galilees have sometimes been exaggerated but that there were differences few would deny today. Jesus' home town, Nazareth, was located in Lower Galilee.

There are today three hypotheses as to the origin of the citizens of Galilee. Some suggest that they were the remnants of the old Israelites, that is, those left over after the deportations in the eighth century BCE. Others offer that these folk were converted Iturians, that is, Gentiles, who became Jews when Alexander Jannaeus conquered the territory (first century BCE). Finally, others posit that the people were Jewish colonists who settled in Galilee after Alexander Jannaeus annexed the territory for Judea.

Which view does archaeology support? Jonathan Reed has done an effective job of presenting the data, pulled from archaeological surveys of Galilee. A survey involves having a team visit a site, randomly collect ceramics (potsherds) from the surface (no excavating), and then record the dates of the finds.[11] He points out that there was an absence of any Galilean settlements for over a century after the conquest of the Assyrians (thus hypothesis 1 seems improbable). Further, the rule of Alexander Jannaeus (103–77 BCE) coincides with an increase of population. This looks to Reed like Jewish colonization not forced conversion of Gentiles. Reed suggests that the Galilean Jews originated as colonists from Judea. This view seems to be the consensus today.[12]

---

6. See Lawrence, *IVP Atlas*, 50; Aharoni, *Land of the Bible*, 27–28; E. M. Meyers, "Cultural Setting of Galilee"; and Reed, *Archaeology*, 115.

7. See Longstaff and Hussey, "Palynology," 153; and Herr, "Geography," 106.

8. Rainey and Notley, *Carta's New Century*, 19.

9. Aharoni, *Land of the Bible*, 24.

10. See E. M. Meyers, "Galilean Regionalism"; E. M. Meyers, "Jesus and His Galilean Context"; and Vale, "Literary Sources."

11. See Herr and Christopherson, *Excavation Manual*, 51.

12. Reed, "Galileans." See also Meyers et al., "The Meiron Excavation Project." Aviam, "Galilee"; Freyne, "Archaeology and the Historical Jesus," 133–34; Root, *Galilee*, 99, 112–13, 148–50 (who also gives New Testament evidence); and Jensen, "Political History," 52–57.

The Great Plain (Map 4.1)

The large valley just below Lower Galilee (or, by some accounts, part of Lower Galilee), the Great Plain, called the Jezreel Valley in the Old Testament, was a very fertile, and thus, very desirable land. It forms a rough triangle measuring 20 miles (32 km.) on the south, and 17 miles (27km.) running from the south to the northeast and from the south to the northwest. It receives around 28 inches of rainfall on average each year.[13]

The Hill Country of Samaria (Mount Ephraim or the Northern Highlands):

Moving further south but staying within the borders of our middle "strip," we come to the mountains of Samaria (called Mt. Ephraim in the Old Testament), an area 37 miles (60km.) long and 25 miles (40 km.) wide. Elevations here reach 3,000 feet (914 m.) and annual rainfall is around 25 inches. This region was controlled by the Samaritans in the New Testament period. The hills are so steep in Ephraim (Samaria) and Judah, that they learned a long time ago to use terraces. Constructing terraces on steep hillsides forms an artificially level field for planting crops (see Figure 7.1 in Chapter 7).

Judea (or the Southern Highlands)

As one moves from west to east in the Southern Highlands, from the Mediterranean Sea to the peaks of the "Hill Country," one first encounters a series of low hills called in Hebrew the "Shephelah." These hills top out at 656 feet[14] (200 m.) and lead into the higher elevations of Judea. The area of the Shephelah stretches from north to south for 27 miles (43 km.) but is only 10 miles (16 km.) wide.

As we continue to move a bit eastward, still on our middle strip, we next climb to the higher hills of the Hill Country. These hills (or mountains as the Bible calls them) are formed of limestone and reach, at their highest point around 3,000 feet (914 m.) . Jerusalem, sitting on the watershed of our middle strip, is around 2,500 feet (762 m.) above sea level.[15] The Hill Country of Judah is a bit drier than the Northern Highlands of Samaria. Here rain averages 19 inches per year.[16] It averages 50 degrees Fahrenheit in January and 78 degrees in August.[17] If you lived in the Samaritan or Judean Hill Country, you would enjoy relatively mild temperatures and adequate rainfall.

---

13. Herr, "Geography," 106.
14. Rainey and Notley, *Carta's New Century*, 122.
15. See Rainey and Notley, *Carta's New Century*, 121; Lawrence, *The IVP Atlas,* 50; and Coogan, "Geography."
16. Coogan, "Geography"; Herr, "Geography," 108.
17. Frick, "Palestine, Climate," 121–122.

Figure 1:1: The Hill Country of Judah (photo by the author)

The Eastern Slope

Just east of Jerusalem and east of the watershed generally, in the Southern Highlands, begins the Judean wilderness. Some geographers divide this area into two sub-zones: Semi-desert and Desert.[18] The former is an area of diminished rainfall. It is a place of no forests and little rain because these hills are in the weather shadow of the hills to the west. The Eastern Slope runs from Jericho in the north to the southern end of the Dead Sea to the south, a distance of 60 miles (97 km.) but only 10 miles (16 km.) in width. This area averages around 4 inches of rain each year.[19] Few people lived here because the soil and lack of rain made agriculture difficult but it was a refuge for outlaws, rebels, and religious sects. Further east, begins the "Desert," where rainfall averages less than four inches per annum.

18. See Finkelstein and Langgut. "Climate," 155.
19. Herr, "Geography," 109.

What Were The Climate and Topography of Palestine/Israel?

Figure 1.2: Wilderness just east of Jerusalem (photo by the author)

The Negev

Moving farther south (and still remaining in the middle topographic strip) we come to the Negev ("desert land"). Here the land receives only marginal annual rainfall. On farther south is the subtropical steppe, or treeless, flat landscape.[20]

Coastal Plain (Lydda)	26 inches
Hill Country	Upper Galilee: 40 inches Lower Galilee: 24 Inches Samaria: 25 inches Judea: 19 inches Eastern Slope: 4 inches
Rift Valley	Lake Huleh area: 25 inches Wilderness: less than 4 inches

Table 1.1: Average annual rainfall by region[21]

20. Rainey and Notley, *Carta's New Century,* 21.
21. See Frick, "Palestine, Climate," 121–22; Longstaff and Hussey, "Palynology," 153; Herr,

The Rift Valley

The rift begins all the way north to Mount Hermon. It is the highest mountain in Israel, reaching a height of 9230 feet (2813 m.). At its base lay ancient Caesarea Philippi (Map 2.1), one of Herod Philip's cities, and the Old Testament city of Dan. Here begins the Jordan River which will flow through Lake Huleh (the small body of water north of the Sea of Galilee in Map 4.1), through the Sea of Galilee, and on toward the Dead Sea.

At Lake Huleh, the elevation is 220 feet (67 m.) above sea level[22] but by the time the Jordan River reaches the Sea of Galilee, the shoreline is 656 feet (200 m.) below sea level.[23] While the actual "Lake" Huleh remained around three miles long and two and a half miles wide year round, there was a large swath of marsh area north of it running three and a half miles wide and nine miles long. Ancient settlement patterns show that no one wanted to live near this swamp. This was probably because in ancient times the region around Lake Huleh was malarial.[24] In the 1950s the Israelis began draining the swampy areas and the malarial infestation disappeared. This region receives around 25 inches of rain each year.[25]

The Sea of Galilee averages 13 miles (21 km.) long (depending on water levels) and 8 miles (13 km.) wide at its widest point. Its average depth is 150 feet (46 m.).[26]

"Geography," 108; Coogan, "Geography."

22. Lawrence, *The IVP Atlas*, 50; Aharoni, *Land of the Bible*, 33.

23. This figure is from Rainey and Notley, *Carta's New Century*, 21. But Aharoni (*Land of the Bible*, 33) writes that the shoreline is 630 feet below sea level. Lawrence (*The IVP Atlas*, 50) offers 689 feet below sea level. The shoreline will fluctuate, of course, depending on the amount of rainfall during the year.

24. See Zwickel, "Huleh Valley"; and Chapter 9 of this volume.

25. Herr, "Geography," 109.

26. Rousseau and Arav. *Jesus and His World*, 246.

What Were The Climate and Topography of Palestine/Israel?

Figure 1.3: Sea of Galilee from Mount Arbel (photo by the author)

The river then proceeds another 65 miles (105 km.) until it empties into the Dead Sea, a large lake with no outlets, no fish or marine life, and unusually high salt and mineral content. The shoreline is around 1310 feet (399 m.) below sea level[27] and the sea has a depth of 1420 feet (433 m.), making it the lowest spot on earth. The Dead Sea measures approximately 47 miles (76 km.) by 10 miles (16 km.) across. It is 25% salt and minerals (compared to the 6% salt of the Atlantic Ocean).[28] In spite of this harsh environment, several important sites are found on its western shore (see Maps 3.2 and 5.1) and we will refer to these sites throughout this volume.

As the rift moves from the Sea of Galilee toward the Dead Sea, it becomes wilderness. The high hills of Samaria and Judea block most of the winter rains making for arid conditions. Annual precipitation here averages less than 4 inches. The temperatures

---

27. Rainey and Notley, *Carta's New Century*, 22.
28. Lawrence, *The IVP Atlas*, 50.

also reach their highest level in Palestine along the Dead Sea. See the table below for average temperatures for each of the three zones or topographical strips:

Zone	January average temperatures	August average temperatures
Coastal plain	54	77
Hill country	50	78
Jordan valley	54	88

Table 1.2: Average temperatures (Fahrenheit) of the three topographical zones[29]

The reader should bear in mind that these are average temperatures, taking into the calculation both the day time and night time measurements. At night in the desert, the temperature often drops considerably. Still, the average temperature in the Rift Valley is more than ten degrees higher than the other two zones. As a matter of fact, the highest temperature recorded at the south end of the Dead Sea was 124 degrees Fahrenheit. Temperatures regularly reach 120 degrees.[30]

Figure 1.4: The Dead Sea from Masada (photo by the author)

29. See Frick, "Palestine, Climate," 120.
30. Herr, "Geography," 110.

CLIMATE

People use the terms summer and winter for Israel but actually there are only the dry season and the wet season as Gen 8:22 summarizes: "seedtime and harvest." The rainy season runs from Tishri to Nisan (from late September/early October to late March/early April). Rainey and Notley observe about the Palestinian/Israeli weather: "There is never an infertile season."[31] There are either crops to be planted (in winter or rainy season) or harvested (in summer or dry season; see Table 7.2).

The rain comes in three phases (Deut 11:13–17): Early rain comes in late September-early October. The main rainy period occurs from December to February. During this time 75% of the annual moisture falls. This interval is the main planting season. The late rain comes in April.[32]

In addition to the two seasons (summer or dry season and winter or rainy season), there are two brief transitional periods. These are at the close of one season and the start of the next. During this time, east winds come from the desert—called *khamsin* or *sirocco*—bringing hot and dry air. They last for anywhere from a couple of days to three weeks.[33] It is during this time that the flower can so quickly fade and the grass can so easily wither, as the scriptures tell us (Isa 40:7; Jas 1:11).

CONCLUSION

What would your life have been like had you lived in Palestine/Israel in the late Second Temple Period? To a great extent, it depended on where you lived. If you lived around the Lake Huleh region and even around the Sea of Galilee, you might have been part of a fishing family. But you would also fear "pestilential air" (malaria). Chances are you would have been infected and carried around this disease for decades.

If you lived in the highlands of Judea or Samaria, you might have avoided this illness but other ones awaited there. You would have farmed a small farm probably on a rather steep hillside and kept goats and sheep. If you lived on the coast, again, you might have lived in a fishing family. If you lived in one of the cities, you would probably have been engaged in a craft of some kind. Had you lived in the southern part of the Rift Valley (especially around the Dead Sea), your life would have involved trying to escape the intense heat and store enough water.

Your location (and climate) would have influenced your occupation and your diet. If, for example, you lived in the small city of Magdala (also called Tarichaea; see Map 2.3), you would have fished for a living in the Sea of Galilee or engaged in fish processing (pickling in salt) to transport them to far away places. You would have had an abundance of fish for food and an abundance of water from the lake. If you

---

31. Rainey and Notley, *Carta's New Century*, 23.
32. Rainey and Notley, *Carta's New Century*, 23.
33. Frick, "Palestine, Climate," 125.

lived in the tiny village of En Boqeq (eight miles south of Masada on the western shore of the Dead Sea; Map 3.2), you would have worked in a perfume, cosmetics, and pharmaceuticals craft shop (boiling desert fruits, seeds, resins, twigs, and bark) and would have dined on the salted fish imported from Magdala 118 miles away. Your only source of water in this hostile desert would have been the precious natural spring (the "En") nearby.[34] Location and climate: these factors determined one's occupation and well-being.

Let us now visit life in the cities and villages. We will explore the types of houses you might have lived in and the family life you might have enjoyed. We will look at the occupations you might have pursued and what a woman's daily labor involved. All this we will consider before we begin discussing even more personal investigations such as the chronic diseases you might have contracted, your probable stature and features, your expected life span, and, alas, where and how they would bury you.

---

34. See for distances Rousseau and Arav, *Jesus,* 356; Gichon, "Ein Boqeq," 395; and Bauckham, *Magdala,* 8. For the fish diet of En Boqeq, see Chapter 6.

2

What Was City Life Like?

MOST OF THE JEWISH inhabitants of Palestine—from one million to 1 ½ million of them[1]—lived in rural villages. Yet around ten percent of the population resided in one of the five Jewish cities: Jerusalem in the Judean hill country, Caesarea (with a significant Jewish minority) on the coast, and Sepphoris, Tiberias, and Magdala in Galilee.[2] These cities were not equal in size or influence. The population of Jerusalem alone was three or four times that of Sepphoris and Tiberias combined. It was a major eastern Mediterranean city. What would life have been like if you had lived in one of these cities? Let us take a brief look at each of them.

---

1. See Hammel, "Poverty and Charity," 311, and Broshi, *Bread, Wine,* 106, 135, for the estimate of one million. Avi-Yona (*Holy Land,* 219) argues for two and one-half million. He also notes that estimates have ranged from 700,000 to five million. Sanders, however, (*Judaism,* 127) suggests a population of between one-half million to one million. My figure seeks to capture the average of these estimates.

2. There were certainly other cities in first-century Palestine. Scythopolis, Gadara, and Gerasa (Map 2.1 above) were Decapolis (Gentile) cities (along with Philadelphia, Pella, and Hippos). They were under independent administration and had no or slight Jewish influence. Likewise, Sebaste (in Samaria) and Caesarea Philippi, although built by the Herods, were mostly Gentile (Rousseau and Arav, *Jesus and His World,* 35). I will handle in this chapter only the mostly Jewish cities or those with a significant Jewish minority (i.e. Caesarea Maritima). For a complete list of the Decapolis cities, see Rey-Coquais, "Decapolis."

The Archaeology of Daily Life

Map 2.1: Palestine/Israel in the First Century CE Showing Jerusalem, Caesarea, Sepphoris, and Tiberias

Z. Safrai[3] has sought to define a city, πόλις (*polis*), by identifying three categories:

1. The metropolis
2. The important city
3. The smaller city

Adhering to these categories, we would characterize Jerusalem as the metropolis of Palestine/Israel in the late Second Temple Period. Caesarea (as the capital city) and Sepphoris and Tiberias (as capital cities of Galilee) were the "important cities." Magdala was a "smaller city."

JERUSALEM

Jerusalem was called in the first century CE the "most illustrious city in the east."[4] A city of sixty thousand to one hundred thousand inhabitants,[5] Jerusalem was twice the

---

3. Z. Safrai, *Economy*, 18.
4. Pliny, *N.H.* 5.70.
5. This figure is in line with the estimates of Wilkinson, "Ancient Jerusalem"; Broshi, "Estimating

size of the city of Corinth in Greece and one half the size of Ephesus in Asia.[6] It was a very significant city. In the early Roman period, Jerusalem contained the fabulously rich as well as the unbearably poor. Most of the inhabitants were probably Palestinian natives but the city also had a sizeable minority of Jews from the Diaspora (and of course a few Gentiles as well).

What were the features of a "city" in the ancient world? Again, Z. Safrai offers a list of structures and characteristics that he believes could be found in virtually every population center calling itself a city or *polis*. We will select only the most important and helpful items from his lengthy list:

1. Large population

2. Institutional structure (some sort of city council)

3. Architectural distinctives (public buildings, theaters, stadia, gymnasia, aqueducts, baths, walls, sewage systems, etc.)

4. Social stratification (an elite class of very wealthy, a working class, and a class of desperately poor)

5. More Gentiles living among the Jews than in a village[7]

These features appeared in all five[8] of the cities of Palestine during our period, even in the small city of Magdala/Taricheae. Let us now look at the individual urban centers.

---

the Population"; King, "Jerusalem"; Mazar, *Mountain of the Lord,* 210; Geva, "Jerusalem," 721; and Reinhardt, "The Population Size of Jerusalem," 263. Wilkinson estimates that at the time of Herod the Great there were 36,280 residents and in the time of Agrippa II there were 76,130. Broshi estimates 40,000 residents for Herod's time and 80,000 just before the war. Reinhardt likes a figure of 100,000 to 120,000 in the first century. But see many more population estimates quoted by Reinhardt (241–43).

6. For Corinth, see Engels, *Roman Corinth,* 181. For Ephesus, see Trebilco, *Ephesus,* 17.

7. Safrai, *Economy,* 30–32.

8. But there is debate concerning Sepphoris. See Weiss, "Josephus and Archaeology," and below.

The Four Zones of Jerusalem

Map 2.2: Jerusalem in the First Century CE[9]

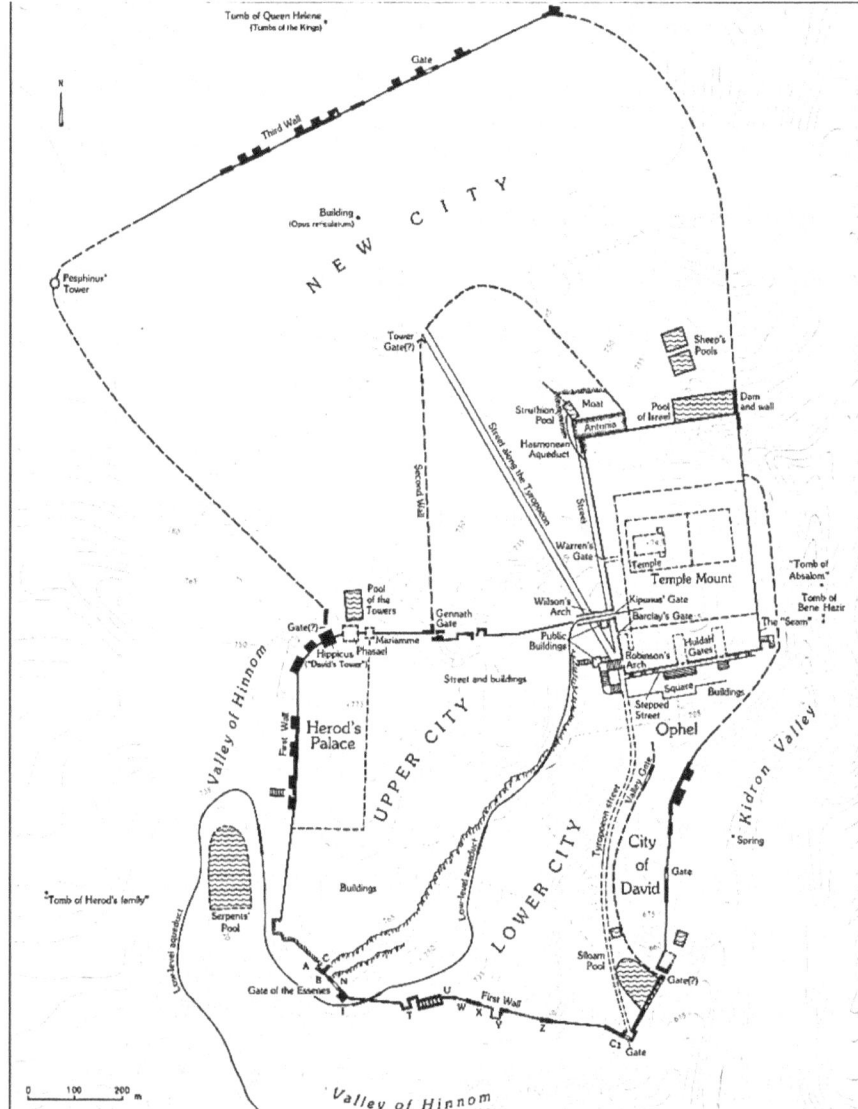

We can clarify the topography of Jerusalem by describing in order:[10]

1. The Lower City
2. The Upper City
3. The "New City"
4. The Temple Mount

9. From Geva, "Jerusalem," 718. Used with permission
10. See the description of Geva, "Jerusalem," 720.

Jerusalem is described by Josephus as consisting of two main parts (*War* 5.136–137): the Lower City and the Upper City. The Lower City, also called the Acra (*War* 5.253), included the Ophel, the City of David, and the Tyropoeon Valley, through which the Tyropoeon Street ran. The Tyropoeon Street—following the Tyropoeon Valley—follows the present el-Wad street extending from the Damascus Gate to the Dung Gate, whence it leaves the walls of the Old City and ends up at the Pool of Siloam (Map 2.2) which in the first century was still inside the southern wall.

Figure 2.1: Street west of Temple Mount, possibly Tyropoeon Street (photo by the author)

The Upper City covered the Jewish and Armenian quarters of today's "Old City" and stretched to the south over the hill now called Mt. Zion (*War* 2.422). This area was not only elevated topographically from the Lower City but also socially and economically. Here the wealthiest of the wealthy lived in the first century CE.

Josephus also writes of an area just north of the Lower and Upper Cities which he calls New City (*War* 2.530; 5.149–151, 246, 331). By the time of the war in 66 CE this last area was encompassed by the third north wall. But within most of our time frame (37 BCE—70 CE) only a small part of that suburb was enclosed by the second north wall.

Finally, the Temple mount formed one of the significant districts of ancient Jerusalem. The trapezoidal platform, built up by Herod the Great, measured 910 feet at its southern wall and 1,575 feet along its western wall. This sacred precinct, then, covered a significant amount of space within the city's walls (see Map 2.2).[11]

---

11. Ben-Dov, *Shadow*; Geva, "Jerusalem."

The Archaeology of Daily Life

Figure 2.2: Artist's Reconstruction of First-Century Jerusalem Aerial View (Looking from the NW toward the SE)[12]

The Social Groups In Jerusalem[13]

L. Finkelstein[14] has sketched the social situation in Jerusalem which, when informed by the sociologically sensitive work of G. Sjoberg,[15] can serve as a model for us.

The upper class of Jerusalem lived mainly in the Upper City and consisted of the Temple nobility and the lay nobility. Most of these, even the wealthy priests, were probably large estate owners though some may have been wealthy merchants. Literary and archaeological sources[16] have identified many medium to large estates[17] in Judaea and even around Jerusalem itself. Since large landowners tended in antiquity to live in the city as absentee landlords and leave the administration of their estates to bailiffs, these land holdings may well have belonged to the members of the Jerusalem

---

12. The "Third Wall" is not shown in this reconstruction. Reconstruction by Balage Balogh/www.archaeologyillustrated.com/. Used with permission. Notice the wilderness and then the Dead Sea to the east.

13. For a detailed presentation of this section, see Fiensy, *Christian Origins,* 161–75.

14. Finkelstein, *Pharisees,* 1:4.

15. Sjoberg, *Preindustrial City,* 118–33.

16. See Applebaum, "Problem of the Roman Villa," 1–5; Applebaum, *Judaea*; Applebaum, "Judaea as a Roman Province." See also Fiensy, *Social History,* 21–73.

17. See K. D. White, *Roman Farming,* 385–87, for the categories of small, medium and large estates in antiquity.

upper class. Probably the most significant class of wealthy landowners was the group of aristocratic priests, especially the High Priestly families.[18]

The archaeological excavations of the Jewish quarter of Jerusalem confirm the impression we get from the literary sources that a significant wealthy class resided in Jerusalem before the war. The excavation team of Nahman Avigad[19] discovered in the Upper City large mansions owned obviously by very rich people. The "Herodian house" from the first century BCE covered 200 square meters (c. 2,100 sq. ft.), had several rooms, a *mikveh* (ritual bath), and used imported fine ceramic ware (ESA). The "Burnt House"[20] from the first century CE had a small courtyard, four rooms, a kitchen, and a small *mikveh*. Most impressive was the so-called "Palatial Mansion." It covered 600 square meters but had a second story—hence 1,200 square meters total (c. 13,000 sq. ft.). Inside this large "villa like" house were stone tables, stone vessels (attesting to care in ritual purity), several *mikva'ot*, a large hall, frescoed walls, and floor mosaics with geometric (not animal or human) figures, indicating adherence to the commandment against graven images (Exod 20:4; See Figures 2.3, 2.4). These were strict Jews—and wealthy ones.[21]

---

18. Stern, "Aspects of Jewish Society," 586–87.

19. Avigad, *Discovering Jerusalem*, 83–137; and Avigad, "How the Wealthy Lived."

20. The Burnt House apparently, from an inscription found in it, belonged to a member of the house of Kathros, a priestly family. See Avigad, "The Burnt House."

21. See Avigad, "Upper City."

The Archaeology of Daily Life

Figure 2.3: One of the rooms of a house of a wealthy family in Jerusalem. Stone tables, stone vessels, and mosaic floor with geometric pattern. See artist's reconstruction of this room below, Figure 2.3 (photo by the author)

But just as interesting for our purposes are not only the huge mansions but the rows of slightly more modest houses which still, according to Avigad, "belonged to upper class families."[22] These houses are not only distinguished by their size from other houses of the same period, but by their furnishings and decorations. The costly pottery, the wine imported from Italy, the elaborate frescoes and floor mosaics, and the many water installations—among other items—point to the wealth of the occupants. That these people were Jewish is evident from the *mikva'ot* found in many of the houses.

The lower classes consisted of the poorer priests and Levites, the small merchants, the craftsmen, and the unskilled laborers.[23] The lower-class priests, divided into twenty-four weekly courses (*Ant.* 7.365), lived in villages throughout Judaea and Galilee.[24] But many priests resided in Jerusalem. The priests in Jerusalem at the time of

---

22. Avigad, *Discovering Jerusalem*, 95.

23. Cf. Finkelstein, *Pharisees*, 1.4 and Sjoberg, *Preindustrial City*, 121–25. Finkelstein actually lists both a middle class and a lower class, but most sociologists would be reluctant to identify a true middle class until the industrial age.

24. See Hachlili, "The Goliath Family in Jericho" (on a priestly family in Jericho); b. Ber. 44a; b. Ta'an. 27a; t. Yebam. 1.10; Luke 1:39; t. Sota 13.8; *Ant.* 17.66; and Stern, "Aspects of Jewish Society," 584.

Nehemiah numbered 1,192 (Neh 11:10–14; but cf. 1 Chr 9:13).²⁵ E.P. Sanders surmises reasonably from this figure in Nehemiah's time that by the first century CE there were probably "a few thousand priests and Levites" in Jerusalem.²⁶

Figure 2.4: Artist's reconstruction of the room of Figure 2.3.²⁷

The lower class also included craftsmen and small merchants. One of the main sources of income was the Temple, which required bakers, weavers, goldsmiths, washers, merchants of ointments and money changers.²⁸ Further, the Temple was still in the process of being built. This labor force employed a large number of carpenters and stone masons. Josephus reported that when the Temple was completed in the procuratorship of Albinus (62–64 CE), it put 18,000 workers out of a job (*Ant.* 20.219). Thus, the Temple required a large force of craftsmen throughout most of the first century CE. Two of those that worked on the Temple identified themselves in their ossuaries (bone

---

25. See Stern, "Aspects of Jewish Society," 595 who notes that Hecataeus writes of 1,500 priests, evidently referring to priests of Jerusalem (*Apion* 1.188).

26. Sanders, *Judaism,* 170. Jeremias, *Jerusalem,* 200 estimated that the total number of priests in Palestine was 7,200 and the total number of Levites was 9,600. Sanders (78) accepts that Josephus' (*Apion.* 2.108) total figure of 20,000 for the priests and Levites in Palestine is probably close to correct. See Frey, *Corpus* 2, nos. 1221, 1317, and 1400 and Naveh, "A New Tomb Inscription," 73 for inscriptions in Jerusalem referring to priests.

27. Reconstruction by Balage Balogh/www.archaeologyillustrated.com. Used with permission.

28. See Avi-Yonah, *The Holy Land,* 194 and his references.

boxes). There is an ossuary holding the bones of "Simon the Temple builder" and another "the bones of Alexander who made the gates (of the Temple)."[29]

But in addition, there were markets both in the Upper and Lower Cities where wares were sold (*War* 2.305, 315). Jerusalem was famous for jewelry, spinning, weaving, dyeing, tailoring, shoemaking, perfume and incense but also produced oil, pottery, ossuaries, stoneware and woodwork.[30] In the Lower City was the Tyropoeon Valley with a main street running through it lined by shops on both sides of the street. The name suggests that a cheese market stood there,[31] but we should expect that other goods were found there as well. Archaeologists have found remains of the street (see Figure 2.1), its large drain, and some shops from Robinson's Arch next to the Temple all the way south along Tyropoeon street.[32]

Archaeology can now supplement the literary evidence on the crafts of Jerusalem. Excavators have found evidence of stone furniture manufacturing (tables; see Figure 2.3), stone vessels such as jars (Figure 2.3), cups and bowls (see Chapter 12, Figure 12.5), fine ceramic ware (painted bowls, jugs, and juglets), and glass (bowls and flasks).[33] In addition, ossuaries—when they name the occupation of the deceased—inform us of their trade. There are bone boxes celebrating workers who were potters, priests, scribes, and artisans.[34] Sometimes the ossuaries list the religious distinctiveness of the deceased: Nazarite, proselyte, pious, or just. Other inscriptions on the ossuaries note a person's social rank: rabbi, ruler of the synagogue, sage, or elder.[35]

There was also a market center in the New City district, north of the first wall. The Mishnah refers to a weavers' and wool-dealers' market in Jerusalem (m. ʿErub. 10:9; m. ʿEd. 1:3). Josephus writes that metal workers, tailors, fullers, wool dealers, and timber merchants had a market in the New City district (*War* 2.530; 5.147, 331).

Also, in the lower class were the unskilled day laborers. Laborers could work in the fields or olive groves around Jerusalem plowing, weeding, harvesting, threshing, picking fruit and doing other seasonal jobs.[36] The unskilled worker was apparently paid on average one denarius per day (Chapter 7).[37] But many were certainly paid

---

29. Puech, "Palestinian Funerary Inscriptions," 132; Naveh, "Ossuary Inscriptions," 33–37.

30. See Mazar, *Mountain of the Lord*, 210; Jeremias, *Jerusalem*, 4–9 and their citations.

31. Its name in Greek means "Valley of the cheese makers," but Avi-Yonah suggests it is a corruption of some unrecognizable Hebrew term. See *Holy Land*, 193.

32. Bliss and Dickie, *Excavations*, 133; Mazar, *The Mountain of the Lord*, 205–6.; Ben-Dov, *Shadow of the Temple*, 114.

33. Avigad, "Jerusalem Flourishing."

34. Puech, "Funerary Inscriptions," 5.132; Evans, *Jesus and the Ossuaries*, 53–58.

35. Evans, *Jesus and the Ossuaries*, 53–58. Evans also cites a few ossuaries that indicate physical features: midget, giant, a "cow."

36. T. Maʿas. 2.13, 15; t. B. Metzia 7.5f.; m. B. Metzia 7:5, 7:4, 7:7, 6:1, 8:8; m. Peʾah 5:5. See Krauss, *Talmudische Archäologie*, 2:105; and Goodman, *State and Society*, 39.

37. See Matt 20:2,9,13; Tobit 5:14; y. Sheb. 8:4; b. B. Batra 87a; b. Abod. Zar. 62a; Ben-David, *Talmudische Ökonomie*, 66; and Sperber, "Costs of Living."

less. We should expect that most of the craftsmen and small merchants lived near the Tyropoeon market and thus in the Lower City or in the less populated New City.

The City of David (the southern part of the Ophel spur) was the oldest inhabited area in Jerusalem. Even in the Hellenistic period the evidence is that most residents lived there. Only in the first century BCE did people begin moving up the slope towards the Upper City.[38] But even though most of the lower class lived in the older district of the City of David, Jews from the Diaspora and proselytes were also drawn to this area.

Archaeological evidence shows that many residents of the City of David grew up in Greek centers of the Diaspora. We infer this because their tomb and ossuary inscriptions were chiseled in Greek. Martin Hengel reported at his time of writing that of all the ossuaries from Jerusalem with inscriptions (many ossuaries are not inscribed), the Greek inscriptions made up 39% of the total. Most of the rest were in a Semitic language only, but some were bilingual. Hengel concluded that those people inscribed their ossuaries in Greek whose family used Greek as the vernacular. Thus, he suggested (conservatively) that the Greek-speaking population of Jerusalem was 10% to 20% of the total population.[39] Based on our figure for the total population of Jerusalem (60,000–100,000 residents) the Greek-speaking Jews numbered anywhere from 6,000 to 20,000.

There is evidence that many if not most of the Jews buried in Jerusalem whose epitaphs are in Greek grew up in the Diaspora. There are ossuary and epitaph inscriptions in Greek of a man called Africanus Furius, of Justus the Chalcidian, of Nicanor from Alexandria, of Maria wife of Alexander from Capua, of Rabbi Samuel from Phrygia, of Anin from Scythopolis, of Eleazar of Beirut, of Ariston of Apamea, and of a family from Cyrenaica.[40] Further, an ossuary inscription seems to state clearly that a family has immigrated to Jerusalem: "The bones of those who immigrated . . . the house of Izates" (in Greek).[41] There were, evidently, many repatriates in the city.

P. Thomsen maintained that at least some of these were brought to Jerusalem after their deaths to be buried in the holy city.[42] This suggestion is certainly possible as the evidence, both archaeological and literary, indicates. We know for sure of at least one case of this, a man named Abba, whose tomb tells his story.[43]

---

38. Shiloh, *Excavations*, 30.

39. Hengel, *Hellenization of Judaea*, 10. His work appeared in 1989.

40. See Frey, *Corpus* 2, nos. 1226, 1227, 1233, 1256, 1284, 1372, 1373, 1374, 1414; Avigad, "Depository of Inscribed Ossuaries"; Sevenster, *Do You Know Greek?* 147; Hengel, *Between Jesus and Paul*, 17; Avni and Greenhut, "Resting Place."

41. Frey, *Corpus* 2, no. 1230.

42. P. Thomsen, "Inschriften," 116. See Sevenster's discussion, *Do You Know Greek?* 146–47.

43. See the Abba inscription in which the deceased boasts of bringing back the bones of Mattathiah to be buried in Jerusalem. Yet Abba also illustrates the other position. He was born in Jerusalem, had gone into exile in Babylonia, and had returned. See Naveh, "New Tomb Inscription," 73; and Chapter 10.

We also have plenty of literary evidence of Jerusalem residents having come from the Diaspora. Ananel the priest came from Babylonia (*Ant.* 15.22, 34, 39–51), and Boethus the priest came from Alexandria (*Ant.* 15.319–22; 17.78, 339; 18.3; 19.279f.). The New Testament refers to other Jerusalem residents that came from the Diaspora: Simon of Cyrene (Mark 15:21[44]), Barnabas of Cyprus (Acts 4:36), and Nicolas a proselyte from Antioch (Acts 6:5). Indeed, we assume that all seven of the so called "Hellenists" of Acts 6 were immigrants or children of immigrants from the Jewish Diaspora (Acts 6:1, 5). Acts 6:9 may be referring to no less than five synagogues: one for freedmen, one for the people from Cyrenaica, one for Alexandrians, one for those from Cilicia and one for those from Asia. The synagogue of the Alexandrians is referred to in the rabbinic sources (t. Meg. 3.6; j. Meg. 3.73) and possibly a synagogue for people from Tarsus is named (b. Meg. 26a).[45] There is also speculation that the synagogue called the 'synagogue of the freedmen' alluded to in Acts 6:9 has been discovered.[46] We may presume, then, that the "Seven" of Acts 6 came from these synagogues.

There were also proselytes in Jerusalem, former non-Jews who had grown up in Greek culture. One of the Seven in Acts was Nicolas the proselyte from Antioch (Acts 6:5). The ossuaries tell of others: "Judas, son of Laganio, the proselyte" (in Greek).[47] In addition, the royal family of Adiabene, which had converted to Judaism, had palaces and monumental tombs in Jerusalem. Queen Helena, her son Menobazus, and Grapte, another relative, had residences (*War* 4.567; 5.55, 119, 252f.; 6.355; *Ant.* 20.17–37, 75–80). These palaces were located in the Lower City not far from the Siloam pool (see John 9:7 and Map 2.2 above). B. Mazar believed that a large building excavated on the southeast edge of the Ophel was one of these palaces. He suggested that this area was the popular place of residence for the highly-placed Jewish proselytes from abroad.[48]

Therefore, we conclude that a considerable number of Diaspora Jews had immigrated to Jerusalem by the first century CE. As Hengel maintained, we have to assume an independent, Jewish-Hellenistic culture in Jerusalem. Jerusalem was the "most important center of the Greek language in Jewish Palestine . . ."[49]

---

44. The ossuary of his son, Alexander (mentioned in Mark 15:21), may have been found. See Evans, *Jesus and the Ossuaries,* 94–95. The inscriptions on the ossuary read on one side: "Alexander son of Simon"; and on the other side: "Alexander the Cyrenian."

45. See Strack and Billerbeck, *Kommentar*, 2:663 and Jeremias, *Jerusalem*, 5, 66. Conzelmann, *Acts*, 47 maintains that there is only one synagogue in mind in Acts 6:9 as did Bruce, *Acts*, 133. On the other hand, Marshall, *Acts*, and Haenchen, *Acts*, 271 maintain that there are two synagogues in view.

46. See Hengel, *Between Jesus and Paul*, 18. This is based on the Theodotus inscription. But contrast Deissmann, *Light*, 441. Compare the Goliath family in Jericho. One of them was a freedman who returned to Palestine after many years. See Hachlili, "The Goliath Family," 33.

47. Frey, *Corpus* 2, no. 1385. But see also no. 1386: "Maria the fervent proselyte" (in Hebrew).

48. Mazar, "Herodian Jerusalem," 230–37; Mazar, *Mountain of the Lord*, 213; and Ben-Dov, *Shadow of the Temple*, 155. Queen Helena's tomb was north of Jerusalem. See Map 2.2.

49. Hengel, *Hellenization of Judaea*, 9, 11.

Figure 2:5: Pool of Siloam in Jerusalem, a large ritual bath?
Where Jesus told the blind man to wash his eyes, John 9:7 (photo by the author)

Archaeologists have discovered the ruins of some houses in the Lower City. M. Ben-Dov had described the area in the lower City known as the City of David as "slums" and termed it "run-down."[50] This assessment of the quality of housing in the Lower City is now being revised, however. Recent excavations have uncovered monumental building activity in this area during the first century CE. One hypothesis is that well-to-do Jews from the Diaspora were returning to Jerusalem in the first century, finding that housing in the elite Upper City was limited, and building in the older section of the city: i.e. the Lower City. Thus, the description of the Lower City as "slums" may be inaccurate for the first century CE.[51] Still, the poor had to live somewhere; they probably lived further from the center of the city.

At the very bottom of the social and economic scale was the "submerged" class or the class of "outcasts."[52] This class included slaves, beggars, those from unapproved occupations, the diseased, and those from questionable births. In the ancient cities the submerged class, especially the destitute, the beggars, and the terribly ill, usually

50. Ben-Dov, *Shadow of the Temple*, 155. Cf. Finkelstein, *Pharisees*, 1.14.

51. See Ben-Ami and Tchekhanovets, "Lower City."

52. Finkelstein, *Pharisees*, 1.4 used the term "submerged," and Sjoberg, *Preindustrial City*, 133 used the designation "outcasts." See also Fiensy, *Social History*, 164–67.

lived on the outskirts of the city.[53] The farther one was from the center socially and economically, the farther one lived also from the center geographically. Thus, the wealthy lived mainly in the Upper City in nice houses ranging from huge mansions to up-scale smaller residences; the lower classes lived in the Lower City—but there were also well-to-do Diaspora Jews moving into this area and building impressive constructions—and in the New City; the outcasts lived on the fringes of the city in tents and hovels, if, indeed, they had a roof over their head at all.

Had you lived in Jerusalem during our time period, where would you have resided? That depended on your economic status, your national origin (native born or Diaspora Jew), and how long your family had been resident in the "most illustrious city of the East." You might have lived in the Upper City if you came from a wealthy and old-moneyed family; but you also might have huddled with the destitute masses on the edge of the city, sleeping under old urns and begging for your daily bread. Most likely you would have lived in the Lower City or New City and practiced a craft of some sort.

CAESARIA (MAP 2.1)

The second most important city in Judea was Caesarea on the Mediterranean Sea coast (called by modern historians "Maritima"). Jerusalem was much larger in population, but Caesarea was the administrative capital. Here the Roman governors resided most of the year; here the military were garrisoned; and here a thriving sea trade took place. Caesarea was significant in Christian history as well.

The History of the City

Herod the Great (reigned 37 BCE—4 BCE) had a problem with his economic situation: he had no good harbor on the Mediterranean Sea. To solve his problem, he built an artificial harbor at a place formerly called Strato's Tower. Josephus writes that he sank huge blocks of stone (transported in from afar at great expense) out from the shore to form a breakwater two hundred feet wide on the south side of his artificial harbor. Underwater archaeologists (the harbor is now submerged) have also discovered that Herod's engineers employed hydraulic concrete in making the harbor, some concrete blocks being 49 x 39 feet and preserved today to a height of five feet.[54] He followed this construction with a mole on the north side of the harbor leaving a sixty feet gap between the two constructions for the ships to enter. The entire area of the harbor covered three and one-half acres.[55] Then he built on top of the blocks various

---

53. See Sjoberg, "Preindustrial City," 15–24; MacMullen, *Roman Social Relations*, 48–87; and Rohrbaugh, "Pre-Industrial City in Luke–Acts," 125–49.
54. Vann, "Herod's Harbor."
55. Bull, "Caesarea," 108.

buildings. His building efforts resulted in one of the largest two or three ports on the Mediterranean.[56]

But the harbor was only one of the engineering feats of this city. Herod also had built an aqueduct system, warehouses, and, under the streets, sewers flushed daily by the tides (see below).[57] Just ashore inside the harbor he constructed a temple dedicated to Augustus and to Roma (see Figure 2.9). He laid out his new town with orthogonal streets (a Hippodamian grid pattern). He built a race track (a *circus* in Latin, a *hippodrome* in Greek) for chariots, a theater for plays, and a palace complex for himself and for his bureaucrats. The entire project took twelve years according to Josephus (*War* 1.408–414; *Ant.* 15.331–341). Historians calculate the building time from 22–10/9 BCE.[58] Herod called his new city, Caesarea after emperor Caesar Augustus.[59]

Caesarea on the sea, or Maritima,[60] became the capital city of Judea, the residence of the Roman governor after 6 CE (when Herod's son, Archelaus was deposed), and the headquarters of the Roman garrison stationed in Palestine.[61] The city covered, during Herod's time, around 91 acres[62] and would have had—according to the way we have been calculating population—around 14,500 persons residing in it. Thus, Caesarea Maritima, was a bit larger than the Galilean cities of Sepphoris and Tiberias (8,000–10,000; see below).

56. Bull, "Caesarea," 108.
57. Hoppe, "Caesarea," 516; Bull, "Caesarea," 109.
58. Holum, "Combined"; Patrich, "Chapter 1"; Porath, "Vegas."
59. To be distinguished from Caesarea Philippi, a later construction by one of Herod's sons.
60. It was not called Maritima in antiquity. See Hoppe, "Caesarea," 516.
61. Stern, "Herodian Dynasty," 174.

62. So Patrich, "Chapter 1," 1 who notes that at its apogee, the city covered 111.5 hectares (= 275.5 acres) and an estimated population of between 35,000 and 100,000. He further calculates that, under Herod the Great, the urban space was about one third that size, thus 91 acres. That would make, using his figures, a population of between 11,000 and 33,000 at the time of Herod. My figure of 14,500 fits within his parameters. But Bull, "Caesarea," 109, writes that the city at the time of Herod covered 164 acres, nearly twice larger. That would make the population in Herod's day around 26,000 persons. I have opted to follow the more recent estimate of Patrich since I suspect that much of what Bull described was Byzantine.

The Archaeology of Daily Life

Figure 2.6: The Theater at Caesarea Maritima (restored)
Photograph by the author

Caesarea was populated mostly by gentiles but there was also a significant Jewish minority. Tensions between the Jews and non-Jews festered at various times approaching the Jewish war. Under Felix (governor of Judea from 52–60 CE), the Jews and Syrians quarreled. Felix, according to Josephus, killed many Jews, arrested others, and in general gave permission to his men to plunder Jewish houses (*Ant.* 20.173–178). Some years later, under the governorship of Gessius Florus (64–66 CE), Jews and pagans clashed over the Jewish synagogue and their right to worship in safety and peace. Still later, also under Florus, several thousand (Josephus alleged twenty thousand) Jews were killed at Caesarea and the city was emptied of Jews. Those that had fled were captured and put in chains (*War* 2.285–292, 457).

Caesarea played an important role in early Christianity. It was there that Philip, one of the Seven Evangelists or Deacons of Acts 6, settled along with his prophesying daughters (Acts 8:40, 21:8–9). The first gentile convert to the new faith, Cornelius the Centurion, lived in Caesarea Maritima (Acts 10). Paul visited there on some of his travels and greeted the church (Acts 18:22, 21:8). Finally, it was in Caesarea, the capital city of Judea, seat of the Roman government and headquarters of the Roman army in Judea, that Paul was imprisoned for two years (Acts 23–27). Here Paul was tried and from here, after appealing to Caesar, sent to Rome.

The City's Features

The Temple

Yosef Porath describes Caesarea as "the pagan counter weight to Jewish Jerusalem."[63] The city not only had a predominantly gentile population but a pagan temple—"the center" of the city—built by Herod the Great, a temple dedicated to Emperor Augustus and to Roma. This was one of three pagan temples Herod built in honor of Augustus (here at Caesarea, at Sebaste/Samaria, and at Paneas/Caesarea Philippi; see Map 2.1).[64] All three temples were built at approximately the same time (between 25–10 BCE)[65] and all three were dedicated to Augustus and Roma. All three cities eventually were named after the emperor.[66]

The temple in Caesarea measured 90 x 100 m. (295 x 328 feet).[67] In the temple stood a colossal statue of the emperor similar in size to that of Olympian Zeus, and a statue of Roma (patron goddess of Rome) similar to the Greek goddess Hera, according to Josephus. Nothing remains of these colossal statues except a three feet long white marble foot from one of them.[68]

The Streets

The streets were laid out in a Hippodamian grid pattern. The Cardo street was 4.9 meters wide (16 feet). The Decumanus streets ranged from 4.25m to 4.7m (14 to 15 feet) wide. There were sewer canals under each street which were flushed by sea water. The streets were not colonnaded.[69]

---

63. Porath, "Vegas," 26.

64. J.F. Wilson, *Caesarea Philippi*, 12. See *War* 1.404–406//*Ant.* 15.364 (Caesarea Philippi) and *Ant.* 15.296–298 (Sebaste).

65. J.F. Wilson, *Caesarea Philippi*, 12.

66. I.e., eventually, because Herod named Caesarea Maritima after Augustus Caesar as well as Sebaste (the Greek form of Augustus). But the city eventually called Caesarea Philippi (built by Herod's son, Philip) was still called Paneas until the early first century CE. Later in the first century (61 CE) the named was changed again to Neronias. See J.F. Wilson, *Caesarea Philippi*, 28.

67. Holum, "Combined."

68. Rousseau and Arav. *Jesus and His World*, 31.

69. Patrich, "Combined"; Patrich, "Chapter 1."

The Archaeology of Daily Life

Figure 2.7: The Promontory Palace, looking northwest.
Was the Apostle Paul held prisoner here? (photo by the author)

The Promontory Palace

Southwest of his circus or racetrack (see below), Herod built himself a palace with bureaucratic offices which extended partly into the sea (Figure 2.7). This complex measured 175 x 54 meters (574 x 177 feet). In the center of the complex was a pool measuring 35 x 18 m (115 x 59 feet) and ringed by a peristyle.[70] Later the Roman governors used this renovated palace as their usual residence and called it the "Praetorium" (Acts 23:35). East of the palace were the government offices. After the Jewish war of 66–73 CE, they built a second government complex elsewhere in the city.[71] Evidently, the Apostle Paul was held prisoner in this complex for two years (Acts 24:27).

The Entertainment Complex

Herod built, first of all, a Roman style theater (semicircle rather than a circle) for producing Greek and Roman plays (Figure 2.6 above). The theater was 100 m (328 feet) in diameter and held originally 5,000 spectators. It was later expanded several times.[72]

70. Netzer, Promontory Palace," 158–59.

71. Patrich, "Combined"; Patrich, "Chapter 1," 6; Patrich, "Caesarea," 148; Porath, "Caesarea."

72. Porath, "Vegas"; Patrich, "Caesarea," 153. But see Bull, "Caesarea," 113 who writes that the theater only held four thousand persons.

WHAT WAS CITY LIFE LIKE?

More important to New Testament students than the entertainment value of the theater is the inscription found in one of the stones used to repair its steps. A stone had been moved from its original place and re-used in a late repair of the theater. But the stone contained a Latin inscription that read:

> Pontius Pilate, the Prefect of Judea, has dedicated to the people of Caesarea a temple in honor of Tiberius.[73]

It had been, then, a dedicatory inscription for a structure, a temple, in honor of the emperor Tiberius (reigned 14–37 CE). Later, when the theater needed repairs, the workers pulled up the stone and moved it to the steps of the theater. Thus, the Judean governor, who sentenced Jesus to death, is attested archaeologically.

Figure 2.8: The Circus or Hippodrome (looking north).
The seating is on the right; the starting gates are at the top of the photograph.
(photo by the author)

But his main offering for entertainment was his race track (*circus*). The external dimensions of the circus were 63.5 x 313 m. (208 x 1026 feet). The race track ran north to south. The interior dimensions were 50.3 x 301 m. (164 x 987 feet), approximately the dimensions of two other hippodromes in the region: in Neapolis and in Gerasa.[74]

---

73. Translation in Bull, "Caesarea," 113. See also Rousseau and Arav. *Jesus and His World*, 225–27.

74. See Porath, "Herod's 'Amphitheatre,'" 24. The dimensions of the hippodrome at Gerasa (in modern Jordan) were 50 m. x 244 m.; of that in Neapolis, 48 m. x 280 m. Porath concludes that this was evidently the size of hippodromes "in moderate-sized cities" in the Near East.

The Archaeology of Daily Life

The seating for the race track (used for chariot racing) was on the eastern side of the oblong (see Figure 2.8). The starting gates could accommodate twelve chariots. The circus (or hippodrome) held at first 7,500 spectators and, then, later, after expansion, 12,500.[75]

Of interest, was the shrine discovered at the southern end of the hippodrome/circus. The shrine consisted of three small rooms with niches cut into bedrock. There were still lamps in place in the niches when discovered. In the rooms were found also "votive feet" (carvings of feet) made of marble (all right feet). There was one inscription which read "Merismos charioteer." Four stone altars were found nearby.[76] Was this the place the charioteers came to pray and beseech the safety of the gods before a race? Chariot racing was enormously dangerous.

Also of interest was the fish-kiosk discovered attached to the hippodrome. This was a small business selling snacks and refreshments to the spectators much the way a hotdog stand does today at American baseball parks. Chapter 6 will present the details of this kiosk and the fish remains discovered at the site. The remains of the many species of fish indicate the wide variety of aquatic food available to the residents and visitors of Caesarea.

Figure 2.9: Artist's Reconstruction of Caesarea Maritima. In the center, the harbor; just to the left of the harbor, the Temple to Augustus and Roma; in the upper center, the Circus, to the right of the Circus is the Promontory Palace; to the left of the Circus and above it is the Theater. (view looking south)[77]

---

75. Porath, "Caesarea," 1659; Porath, *Caesarea,* 33–68; Patrich, "Chapter 1," 6; Patrich, "Caesarea," 153.

76. Porath, "Herod's 'Amphitheatre,'" 21–23.

77. Artist's reconstruction by Balage Balogh, *Archaeology Illustrated.* Online: www.archaeologyillustrated.com Used with permission

The Aqueduct

The city was watered by an aqueduct, built by Herod the Great, and originating thirteen miles north at the base of Mt. Carmel. Later, Emperor Hadrian (reigned 117–138) added a second channel beside Herod's original so that today the "high-level" aqueduct[78] is doubled-channeled. The channel on the eastern side is Herodian.

Figure 2.10: The aqueduct, eastern side, dating from the time of Herod the Great
(photo by the author)

Caesarea was a true Greco-Roman city. It was laid out in a grid pattern; it had pagan temples, a theater, and a race track. It did not yet have an amphitheater for gladiatorial combats but that would come in the second century CE. The majority of the population was gentile with a significant minority of Jews.

It played a growing role in the spread of Christianity. As related above, several key New Testament figures lived there or visited there. Later Christian leaders (e.g., Origen and Eusebius) spent considerable time in this city.

We do not know about the social classes of this city. There would have been a large number of government bureaucrats (such as the Jewish tax collector, John, *War* 2.287, 292), soldiers and military leaders (such as the Christian centurion, Cornelius,

---

78. There is also a low-level aqueduct which was built in the fifth century CE. See Bull, "Caesarea," 111.

The Archaeology of Daily Life

Acts 10), pagan religious leaders of the temple dedicated to Augustus, entertainers such as actors, charioteers, pantomimes, etc., and doubtless many who worked on the docks loading and unloading the ships. In addition, there could be found a not inconsiderable number of sailors temporarily staying there waiting for their ship to sail. We would also, as anywhere, expect certain craft persons making pottery, jewelry, leather goods, wooden objects, and metal goods. Someone had to sell the food brought in from the countryside. But the mix would have been quite unique for Palestine. It would have necessarily included a larger number of aristocrats and their bureaucratic retainers than in other cities plus those of the lowest classes in terms of honor (actors and charioteers) but not necessarily the poorest. Doubtless one could hear on the streets four different languages: Aramaic, Hebrew, Greek, and Latin. It was a very cosmopolitan city, a true Hellenistic *polis*.[79]

THE GALILEAN CITIES

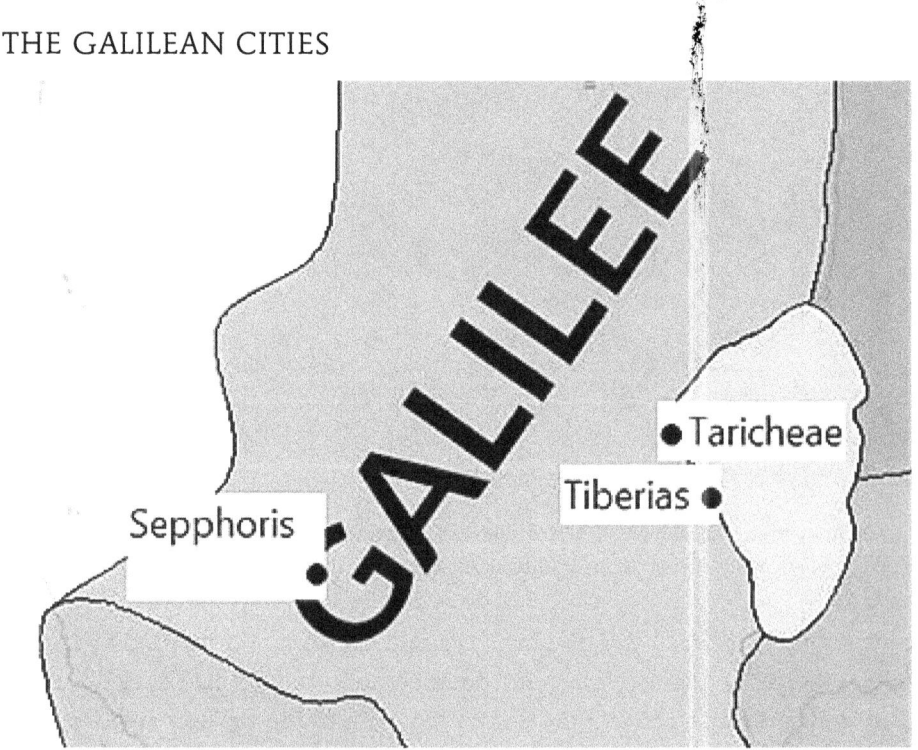

Map 2.3: The three cities of Galilee
(Map created with Accordance)

Compared to Jerusalem, which was a major, eastern Mediterranean city, two of the cities of Galilee—Sepphoris and Tiberias—were of modest size though the largest cities in Galilee (*Life* 346) and a third, Magdala/Taricheae, was smaller still. Yet they still exhibit the features of small cities such as large, public buildings, gridded streets,

---

79. Patrich, "Caesarea," 149.

theaters, and, in the case of Tiberias, a stadium. They were, like Caesarea Maritima, more recently founded than Jerusalem and much less important religiously. But their economic influence on the region was substantial.

Sepphoris was in existence in some form as early as the Persian period and continued until the early Arab period.[80] But by the advent of Pompey of Rome (63 BCE) it was a Jewish city. Destroyed (or at least damaged) in 4 BCE and its inhabitants reduced to slavery, it was rebuilt immediately by Antipas and became, according to Josephus, the "ornament of all Galilee," (*Ant.* 17.289//*War* 2.68; *Ant.* 18.27). This was the city of Jesus' day. Tiberias was founded sometime between 19 and 21 CE and became the new capital of Galilee. After 61 CE Sepphoris once again was named the capital city of this region.[81]

It appears from the literary evidence that both Sepphoris and Tiberias had basically three social classes: upper class, working class, and destitute class. A Talmudic text refers to three socio-economic classes in Sepphoris in the third century CE: 1) as "the great ones" and the "great of our generation" meaning the upper class; 2) as the *am ha-aretz* (people of the land, i.e. farmers) in the second class; 3) and as the "empty ones" or the very poor in the lowest class (b. Hull. 92a).[82] One can surmise that these three classes would have persisted since the city's founding three centuries earlier, especially since we find the same three in evidence at Tiberias (and based on archeological evidence, in Magdala) in the first century.

Likewise, Josephus reports three classes in Tiberias at the outbreak of the war (c. 66 CE): 1) the "respectable citizens," in the upper class; 2) a group led by one Justus, evidently the working class persons (for Tiberias perhaps fishermen);[83] 3) and the "most insignificant persons" in the lowest class (*Life* 32–39).

Doubtless a sociologist who wandered the streets of these two cities would have sketched a more nuanced outline of the social classes. We would expect that most of those social and economic groups we referred to with respect to Jerusalem also existed in Galilee in the two cities of Sepphoris and Tiberias. But these three levels seem to catch the essence of the situation. In the ancient cities there were the rich, the working poor, and the destitute poor.

Economic Level of the Elite Class of Sepphoris

The houses of some of the elites may have been discovered in Sepphoris in the domestic quarter on the western slope of the acropolis. Eric Meyers, one of the excavators of

---

80. E. M. Meyers and C. Meyers, "Introduction."

81. See J. F. Strange, "Sepphoris"; E. M. Meyers, C. L. Meyers, and Gordon, "Residential Area"; Weiss, "Galilean Town to Roman City, 100 BCE–200 CE."

82. See Büchler, *Political and Social Leaders* 35.

83. See Rajak, "Justus of Tiberias."

Sepphoris, believes that it was inhabited by "well-to-do aristocratic Jews."[84] The houses in this quarter date from the early first century CE (therefore from the time of Jesus). These were multi-room dwellings with courtyards (see the "Villa", Figure 4.3). Many of the houses were furnished with fresco paintings on the walls with floral scenes (no animals or human depictions) and a few had mosaic floors. Several of the houses were multi-storied and many of them had ritual bath installations (stepped pools). By the size of houses and by the furnishings, we know that these were houses of the well-off.[85]

They are the houses of the "well-to-do aristocratic Jews"[86] but not the extravagantly rich. They do not, for example, compare with the large and elaborately furnished mansions found in the Jewish Quarter of old Jerusalem[87] and dating to the same time period (see above). They were impressive for their time and place. But compared with the Jerusalem houses they were modest. For example, the "Palatial Mansion" of Jerusalem (referred to above) had a living area of 1,200 square meters (13,000 sq. ft.) while a large house of Sepphoris (labeled 84.1) had an area of 300 square meters (3,200 sq. ft.). The size difference of the largest houses alone is remarkable. The excavators did produce fifteen fragments of large stone jars (*kallal* vessels) which were expensive.[88] Thus, one can find some evidence of wealth.

On the other hand, the residences of the moderately sized houses with courtyard measured on average 10 x 18 meters (2,000 sq. ft.). Only one unit displayed finely worked masonry of the "Herodian" style.[89] Further, the small finds in the aristocratic houses of Sepphoris indicate modest wealth. They used bone instead of ivory for cosmetic applications; they employed common pottery, not fine ware; they imported no wines.[90] By comparison of the houses alone, we would say that these are modestly rich persons for the most part. Thus, based on the evidence of the houses from first century Sepphoris discovered so far (Tiberias has not been excavated adequately for such an assessment[91]), we would have to say that the extreme distance between the elites and lower class, found elsewhere in the Roman empire and even in Jerusalem, was diminished in Galilee. While there certainly was an economic distance between these two groups, it was not as great as in other regions. We will find the same evidence below with respect to Magdala.

---

84. Meyers, "Roman Sepphoris," 322.

85. See Netzer and Weiss, *Zippori,* 21–23; E. M. Meyers and C. Meyers, "Sepphoris"; Reed, *Archaeology and the Galilean Jesus,* 126; and Weiss and Netzer, "Hellenistic and Roman Sepphoris"; Hoglund and E. M. Meyers, "The Residential Quarter," 40.

86. E. M. Meyers, "Roman Sepphoris," 322.

87. See Avigad, "How the Wealthy Lived"; E.M. Meyers, "Gendered Space," 51 and 67.

88. E. M. Meyers, C. L. Meyers, and Gordon, "Residential Area."

89. E. M. Meyers, C. L. Meyers, and Gordon, "Residential Area."

90. See E. M. Meyers, "Gendered Space"; Avigad, "How the Wealthy Lived"; Reed, *Archaeology and the Galilean Jesus,* 126.

91. See Hirschfeld, "Tiberias."

Figure 2.11: The Decumanus street, Sepphoris.
Was it there in the early first century CE?
(photo by the author)

How many rich persons were there in ancient Galilee? It is important to emphasize that ancient agrarian societies, with poor agricultural technology, could support only a small group of elites.[92] The surplus was simply too meager. Thus, the elite groups, although highly significant in wealth and power, were only a very small percentage of the population. There was not enough "surplus" to keep very many absentee landowners. R. MacMullen, G. Alföldy, and R. Rillinger estimate that the upper classes of the Roman empire (the senators, knights, and decurions) comprised no more than one per cent of the total population.[93] One would expect this percentage roughly to hold true in Galilee, for the nature of agrarian societies, as Kautsky observed, prevented a large elite class. We obviously are not bound to this percentage, but we should be cautious about estimating too far over it. Thus, if we assess the population of first-century Galilee at 175,000 persons,[94] we would expect no more than, say, 1,500 to 2,000 elites living mostly in Sepphoris and Tiberias.

92. Kautsky, *Politics*, 79f.

93. MacMullen, *Roman Social Relations*, 89; Rillinger, "Moderne und zeitgenössische Vorstellungen," 302; Alföldy, *Römische Sozialgeschichte*, 130. Cf. Lenski, *Power and Privilege*, 228, who gives a similar figure for other agrarian societies.

94. See E. M. Meyers, "Jesus and His Galilean Context," 59; and Hoehner, *Herod Antipas*, 53.

The Archaeology of Daily Life

Figure 2.12: Theater of Sepphoris, partly restored. It could seat 4,000 persons.[95]
Did it exist in the first century CE? (photo by the author)

Likewise, we should probably expect that 15,000 to 20,000 persons combined lived in the two Galilean cities. Estimates range for Sepphoris from 2,500 to 30,000 and for Tiberias from 12,000 to 40,000. On the other hand, one scholar has offered that both cities together had a population of only 15,000. Thus, the estimates vary. My view is—taking a figure of ten percent of the population living in the cities—that a total population of 175,000 for Galilee only allows for the sum of 15,000–20,000 for the cities.[96] Thus, the overwhelming majority (155,000 at a minimum) lived in rural villages.[97]

Hoehner prefers the figure 200,000 and Meyers prefers 150,000 to 175,000.

95. Chancey and E. M. Meyers, "Sepphoris," 26.

96. These are the figures of Reed, *Archaeology and the Galilean Jesus*, 117. E. M. Meyers suggests 18,000 for Sepphoris and 24,000 for Tiberias ("Jesus and His Galilean Context," 59). Overman, "Who Were The First Urban Christians?" offered 30,000 to 40,000 for Tiberias and 30,000 for Sepphoris. R. A. Horsley, *Archaeology, History and Society in Galilee*, 45, maintained that both cities together had a population of 15,000. More recently, Schumer, "Population Size of Sepphoris," has argued for a population of Sepphoris from 2,500 to 5,000. If we adhere to the general rule of 10% of the population in the ancient world lived in the cities then a population of 175,000 for Galilee, accepted above, needs around 10,000 or less in each of the two cities.

97. De Ste. Croix, *Class Struggle*, 10; and L. White, "Die Ausbreitung," 92. See also Sjoberg, *The Preindustrial City*, 83, who affirms that no more than 10% of agrarian populations usually lived in

Was Lower Galilee Hellenistic or Jewish?

Great stress has been placed on the Hellenistic nature of the cities of Lower Galilee in the time of Jesus and Antipas. James F. Strange had spoken of Rome's imposing "a distinctive urban overlay" over a Jewish base.[98] This measured statement may have been exaggerated in subsequent works by other authors. Thus one can call Sepphoris a "Greco-Roman-style city;"[99] another can maintain that Galilee was "semi-pagan;"[100] yet another that Jesus might even have read the works of a Cynic philosopher alongside his reading of the Torah: "Galilee was in fact an epitome of Hellenistic culture on the eve of the Roman era."[101]

The response on the part of some archaeologists has been to cite the material remains as evidence that throughout Galilee, even in Sepphoris and Tiberias, the Jewish residents were Torah observant and were not assimilating as much Hellenism as one might think. The evidence is:

1. Numerous stoneware vessels have been found in many Galilean villages and in both of the above named Galilean cities as well as Magdala (see Chapter 12).

2. Many villages have ritual baths. Even Sepphoris had around thirty stepped-pool installations[102] that were probably used for ritual bathing. Both stone vessels and ritual baths have to do with maintaining ritual purity (see Chapter 12). Jews meticulous about ritual purity did not give up their Jewishness in favor of Hellenism.

3. There is an absence of pig bones (Lev 11:7). In most sites, including Sepphoris, the occurrence of pig bones is so slight as to be statistically non-existent.

4. None of the coins minted in the reign of Antipas the tetrarch of Galilee had images of humans, pagan gods, or animals[103] (see Chapter 12).

5. These clear Jewish markers contrast with what was not in Sepphoris: There were no hippodromes (for chariot racing), no amphitheaters (for gladiatorial combats), no pagan temples, and no gymnasia.[104] Most of these things, however, can be found in Scythopolis (Map 2.1), Gerasa (Map 2.1), and Caesarea (Map 2.1).

---

cities. Sometimes it was less than 5%. Lenski estimates between 3 and 10% (*Power and Privilege*, 199–200, 279).

98. J. F. Strange, "Some Implications of Archaeology, 31.
99. Kee, "Early Christianity in the Galilee," 15.
100. Funk, *Honest to Jesus*, 58.
101. Mack, *Myth*, 64, 66.
102. Each house in the "western domestic quarter," had "at least two" ritual bath installations. See E. M. Meyers, C. Meyers, and Gordon, "Residential Area," 47.
103. See Reed, *Archaeology and the Galilean Jesus*, 49–51; Chancey and E. M. Meyers, "How Jewish"; E. M. Meyers, "Jesus and His World," 191–95; Chancey, *Myth*, 79–90.
104. Actually, a gymnasium may have been found at Hamat Tiberias just south of ancient Tiberias and dating from the first century. See T. Dothan, *Hamat Tiberias*, 16.

These were the truly Hellenized cities, not Sepphoris and evidently not Tiberias.[105] Yet, one must be careful in making these affirmations since Magdala, a smaller city, did have a hippodrome and a Roman *palaestra* (the equivalent of the Greek gymnasium). See below. Perhaps Magdala was more Hellenized than Sepphoris (and maybe Tiberias).

Local folk do not usually accept more than the outward forms of the occupying culture. They may dress like the dominant culture, build their buildings like the dominant culture, and even learn the language of the dominant culture, but they do not readily think like the dominant culture. Cultural anthropologists speak of deep culture and procedural culture.[106] The former concerns a people's core values; the latter the vehicle of expression of these values. In other words, one can be a very conservative Jew and still dress like a Greek, speak Greek and live in a Greek styled house. But at Sepphoris (less so in Magdala) the core values seem to be clearly expressed by the above five items. As Eric Meyers has maintained, Hellenism need not have competed with Judaism but could have been the vehicle to express one's Jewishness.[107]

What Was in Sepphoris in the First Century CE?

The visitor to the site of Sepphoris today will see many ruins of what must have been fabulous constructions. Most of these did not exist in our time period. The following have been suggested to have been there.

1. The western domestic quarter (everyone agrees on this dating)
2. A "villa"[108]
3. The basilical building (debated)
4. The theater (debated)
5. Streets laid out in a Hippodamian grid (with *Cardo* and *Decumanus*; debated)
6. An aqueduct bringing fresh water to Sepphoris from two springs.

---

105. I say "evidently" because not enough of Tiberias has been excavated to get a clear picture of what the city was like in the first century CE. The reader should be aware that most of the architectural items listed above as found in Scythopolis and Gerasa are from the second century CE or later. We presume that these are replacements of earlier structures but these are not the structures the first-century traveler would have seen. See Foerster, "Beth-Shean"; and Ulama, *Jerash*. Caesarea, however, does have ruins of a theater and hippodrome/circus from the first century. See above.

106. The terminology is taken from Stewart and Bennett, *American Cultural Patterns,* 149. See also Samover and Porter, *Communication Between Cultures,* 90, who use the term "deep structure."

107. See E. M. Meyers, "Jesus and His Galilean Context," 64; and E. M. Meyers, "The Emergence of Early Judaism and Christianity." The wisdom of Freyne on this issue is, in my judgment, beyond question. See "Town and Country Once More."

108. See Chancey, "Cultural Milieu," 134 and Figure 4.3.

The city of Sepphoris had a large public building built in basilica fashion (i.e. with a nave and apse) measuring 35 x 40 meters (15,000 sq. ft.) in the interior area. This building, according to James F. Strange, was probably where the bureaucrats had offices and ran the government, the tax system, and the courts. In addition, some of the rooms were undoubtedly shops; in other words, it was a forum. The question, debated by archaeologists, is whether this building was built by Antipas or toward the end of the first century CE.[109] There may have been (gravel) *Cardo* and *Decumanus* streets in Sepphoris in the early first century, but this is debated.[110] There may have been a theater built in the time of Antipas and Jesus, but the date of this structure is also disputed.[111] An aqueduct was also necessary in the early first century to provide adequately for the large populace. One was constructed to bring water from the Ein Genona and Amitai springs.[112]

---

109. For the argument that this building existed only in the later part of the first century, see Weiss, "Josephus and Archaeology," 397–400. See also the discussion in Schumer, "Population Size of Sepphoris." On the other hand, Chancey, *Myth,* 76; Chancey, "Cultural Milieu," 134; and J.F. Strange, "The Eastern Basilical Buildling," say it was there in the early part of the century (and thus during the time of Jesus). See additionally on the basilica, J. F. Strange, "Sepphoris: The Jewel of the Galilee." The building consisted of rows of offices or shops all with floor mosaics. One room had a stepped pool.

110. See Weiss, "Josephus and Archaeology," 397 who maintains that the Cardo and Decumanus streets, the Hippodamian grid pattern of city planning, was a late first-century–early second-century CE innovation. For a contrary view, see Chancey, "Cultural Milieu," 134; Chancey, *Myth,* 76; and Crossan and Reed, *Excavating Jesus,* 104.

111. For a date in the early first century (thus the time of Antipas and Jesus), see J. F. Strange, "Six Campaigns at Sepphoris," 342; J. F. Strange, "Sepphoris: the Jewel," 28; and Batey, *Jesus and the Forgotten City*, 83–103. For a date of late first century or early second century for the theater see: Weiss and Netzer, "Hellenistic and Roman Sepphoris," 400–402; C. L. Meyers and E. M. Meyers, "Sepphoris"; E. M. Meyers, "Jesus and His World," 188–90; Weiss, "From Galilean Town to Roman City"; and Weiss, "Josephus and Archaeology," 400–402.

112. See Tsuk, "The Aqueducts of Sepphoris"; Tsuk, "Bringing Water to Sepphoris"; and J. F. Strange, "The Sepphoris Aqueducts."

THE ARCHAEOLOGY OF DAILY LIFE

Figure 2.13: The Sepphoris Aqueduct;
compare with the aqueduct at Caesarea, Figure 2.10 (photo by the author)

What Was in Tiberias in the First Century CE?

Antipas, in order to found his new city, settled people from all social stations, including persons of high standing, riffraff, poor people, criminals, and freed slaves (*Ant.* 18.36–38). He was desperate for population and took them where he could find them. He established the city amid controversy because he built it over graves, a religiously unclean location (see Chapter 12).

Tiberias played a small role in the ministry of Jesus. The Gospel of John (6:23) states that people from the city followed Jesus' prophetic/ministerial itinerary on one occasion by sailing in boats from the city to the other side of the lake.

So far, no ruins of lavish palaces from Antipas' day have been discovered at Sepphoris, the first capital of the region (from around 4 BCE until sometime around 20 CE). It is possible, however, that one has come to light at the later capital, Tiberias. Josephus, the Jewish historian of the first century CE, reports that Antipas had a palace in Tiberias in which there were animal representations, painted or carved, which was a breach of Exod 20:4. One would expect that Antipas had several palaces and retreats if he imitated his father, Herod the Great. Josephus also alludes to an athletic stadium for foot races and the like (now perhaps discovered archaeologically; see below). One can retrieve a list of structures that existed in the first century CE from Josephus and rabbinic sources.[113] Those items on the list that are attested at least partially archaeologically have an asterisk:

1. *A stadium (*War* 2.618; 3.539; *Life* 92)
2. Synagogue(s) (*Life* 277, 280; m. ʿErub. 10:10)
3. A fortified wall (*War* 2.573; 3.449)[114]
4. *Antipas' palace (*Life* 65)
5. Royal treasury (*Life* 38)
6. Public archives (*Life* 38)[115]
7. Markets (*Ant.* 18.149; b. ʿErub. 29a)
8. *Near hot springs (*Life* 85; *Ant.* 18.36)

What can we say with some confidence was standing in Tiberias during our time period based on the archaeological remains discovered to date? So far there are only a few structures that one can possibly date to the first century. Even the Cardo or main street is primarily a second-century feature though some maintain that parts of it date to the first. But the following may give us an idea of the possible first-century features of this lake-side city:

1. A theater (upper left corner in Figure 2.9 below)[116]
2. A lavish palace (with *opus sectile* floor, and painted plaster. Not depicted below.) Was this Antipas' palace?[117]
3. Perhaps the double-tower gate (lower left-hand corner Figure 2.9)[118]
4. Part of the stadium may have been discovered (on the north side of the city, not depicted below)[119]

---

113. See Hirschfeld, *Roman, Byzantine, and Early Muslim Tiberias*, for primary references to Tiberias.
114. Weiss, "Josephus and Archaeology," 388.
115. See S. Miller, "Tiberias," 430.
116. Bonnie, "Tiberias," concludes that the theater was possibly built in the first century.
117. So Hirschfeld and Galor, "New Excavations," 214, 223. But see Bonnie, "Tiberias."
118. Cytryn-Silverman, "Tiberias"; Hirschfeld, "Tiberias"; Foerster, "Tiberias." But see Bonnie, "Tiberias."
119. Miller, "Tiberias," 430. Bonnie ("Tiberias") maintains that this structure is actually part of a harbor.

The Archaeology of Daily Life

5. Part of the first-century Cardo may have been excavated (begins at the gate)[120]
6. The hot springs would be the Hamath Tiberias just south of the city.[121]

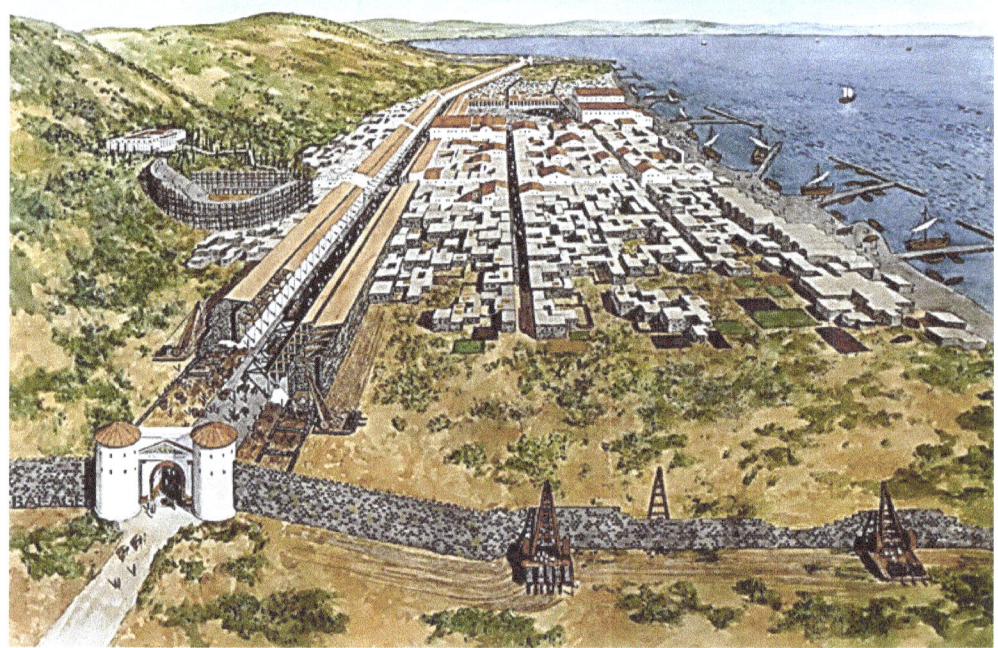

Figure 2.14: Tiberias in First Century CE.[122] Note the gate (round towers) and theater

What was in Magdala/Taricheae in the First Century CE?

Magdala, "the Tower" in Aramaic (also called Taricheae[123] in Greek), was located on the western shore of the Sea of Galilee, approximately 3.5 miles north of Tiberias (see Map 2.3). Uzi Leibner informs us that the area covered 22.5 acres.[124] That area would calculate to 3,600 persons populating this town/small city. The figure that seems to me about right for this small city would be four to five thousand.[125] It was not as large

---

120. Miller, "Tiberias," 431. But see Bonnie, "Tiberias," who maintains that this street is second century.

121. Savage, "Hamath Tiberias."

122. Artist's reconstruction by Balage Balogh/www.archaeologyillustrated.com. Used with permission. Some of these features are second century and later. See Bonnie, "Tiberias."

123. For a challenge to the identification of the two names, see Kokkinos, "Location"; and Taylor, "Magdala."

124. Leibner, *Settlement and History,* 214.

125. One might also hazard a guess of population based on one of Josephus's references to there being 230 fishing boats (*War* 2.635; *Life* 163) available for his use in the Jewish war. Bauckham observes that these boats required five persons to maneuver them (four to row and one to steer). If, in turn we multiply these five adults per boat times six (assuming six persons per family which is our standard in this volume) we get a total of thirty persons living off the produce of one boat. If we then multiply this figure times the total of 230 boats (Josephus's number) we arrive at 6,900 persons. But

at Sepphoris or Tiberias (8,000–10,000 according to my calculations), but larger than the average village. Magdala, then, would be in Z. Safrai's third category: "smaller city."

If its population was that low, why would one insist that it was a real city? Scholars point to the monumental buildings and other urban features. Here is a summary of them:

1. The city was laid out in an organized manner (Hippodamian grid) with a *Cardo* (10 m. wide) and several *decumani*.
2. There were urban buildings: fountains, baths, a *stoa*-shaped fountain house,[126] a *palaestra* (exercising building), and a hippodrome (horse race track). See Josephus, *War* 2.599 and *Life* 132, 138.
3. There was a water system bringing fresh water into the city and a latrine system.
4. There was a large Jewish population but gentiles as well.[127]

With these features, one is hard pressed to call Magdala a village. The reader will see in Chapter 3 that villages and cities were culturally differentiated based on architecture, entertainment opportunities, and water facilities (Table 3.4). Magdala has many of the architectural features of a city.

Based on its Greek name, Taricheae (see Map 2.3), which means "fish salting factories,"[128] historians universally agree that the small city lived from the fish industry, both catching the fish and preparing them for shipment to the far reaches of Palestine and beyond. Not only do we have the literary references to the pickled fish of the Sea of Galilee (Strabo 16.2.45;[129] m. Abod. Zar. 2:6; m. Ned. 6:4), but we also have in the Magdala ruins two indicators of the importance of fishing: numerous lead weights for holding nets in the water and installations probably used in the salting process. It is possible that excavators have discovered some of the fish vats where the fish were pickled/salted as well as possible aquaria where live fish were kept until ready to be killed and processed.[130] The pickled fish were well known in antiquity. As the reader will learn in Chapter 6, fish bones from the Sea of Galilee turn up even in far-away places like the tiny village of En Boqeq on the south end of the Dead Sea. Sepphoris also consumed a lot of fish.

---

allowing for some boats to be rowed by father and son(s) and for day laborers unmarried, we reduce that number to 4,000 to 5,000. See Bauckham, "Magdala," 27.

126. See Bonnie and Richard, "Building D1."

127. Bauckham, "Magdala," 23–37; De Luca and Lena, "Magdala/Taricheae," 304, 327; Leibner, *Settlement and History*, 215; Bonnie and Richard, "Building D 1," 73–74.

128. De Luca and Lena, "Magdala/Taricheae," 283; and LSJM.

129. "At the place called Tarichæ, the lake supplies the best fish for curing." Translation of Strabo in *Perseus Digital Library* on line at: http://www.perseus.tufts.edu/hopper/text?doc=Perseus:text:1999.01.0239:book=16:chapter=2&highlight=.

130. De Luca and Lena, "Magdala/Taricheae," 309.

The Archaeology of Daily Life

The pagan historians considered Magdala/Taricheae an important small city. It is listed by Pliny the Elder alongside Tiberias, Hippos (one of the Decapolis cities), and Bethsaida Julius (in the Golan) as the principle towns around the Sea of Galilee (Pliny, *N.H.* 5.71). Both the archaeological remains and the literary references indicate the importance of this city.

Magdala was populated by a large number of Jews as indicated by three sorts of archaeological finds:

1. Four *mikva'ot* (see Figure 2.15)
2. Numerous fragments of stone vessels
3. A synagogue (see Figure 12.8 in Chapter 12)

Figure 2.15: One of the four *mikva'ot* at Magdala (photo by the author)

These "markers of Judaism" make it certain that most of the residents were Jewish, although a significant minority must have been gentile. This latter conclusion is based on iconic finds (lamps and other items with depictions of erotic and animal scenes).[131] Thus, it was a mixed population like Jerusalem, Sepphoris, and Tiberias. The Jewish villages were more homogeneous, however.

---

131. See De Luca and Lena, "Magdala/Taricheae," 329; Bauckham, "Magdala," 39–45; Reich and Zapata-Meza, "Domestic Miqva'ot"; Aviam, "Synagogue"; Zapata-Meza, "Domestic and Mercantile Areas."

As in the other cities where we have enough exposed to tell, there were ritzier sections of Magdala. Some of the houses were constructed of better materials and better workmanship than others. These houses also had mosaic floors similar to those in the up-scale houses of Jerusalem. The excavators emphasize, however—as we saw also with Sepphoris—that the size of the Magdala houses is "modest in comparison" with the Jerusalem dwellings of the wealthy.[132]

Thus, one is inclined to surmise that, as in the cities of Sepphoris and Tiberias, there were three socio-economic classes: the wealthy class (the owners of the ritzy houses); the working class (fishing families and those in the fish pickling business); and the destitute persons. The interesting question becomes, for those of us researching the New Testament, which class do you think Mary Magdalene came from (Luke 8:2; Mark 15:47; Mark 16:1//Matt 28:1//John 20:1; Luke 24:10; John 20:2, 11–18)?

CONCLUSIONS

Of course, there were many other constructions in these Galilean cities besides those listed above. We just have no archaeological record of them so far. There must have been shabby housing in abundance for the middling class of working poor. These houses were so weakly made that perhaps little if anything is left of them. Perhaps, also, these neighborhoods just have yet to stick their heads up from the two-thousand-year-old top soil. Tiberias is a modern city, like Jerusalem, which makes excavation difficult. Sepphoris and Magdala are now national parks with no one living on the original site.

What would you have done for a living had you lived in one of the two Galilean cities? One would expect that you would have been a craft person just as in Jerusalem. But perhaps you can also imagine yourself living in the ritzy western domestic quarter of Sepphoris with two or more *mikva'ot*, with comfortable rooms, and with a nice view of the lower city to the east and the Bet Netofa valley to the north. If you lived in Tiberias or Magdala/Tarichaeae, you probably would have also been a craft person or a fisherman. Tiberias, in addition to fishing, was known for its production of cloth, mats, leather (tanned), and glass.[133] Maybe you would have engaged in one of those industries. But maybe you would have lived in the luxurious building in Tiberias (Antipas' palace?) described above that had inlaid marble floors. If you had lived in the nicer houses or in a luxurious mansion, you would have been in the upper one to two percent of the entire population.

But for most, their houses were adequate but not luxurious; warm and dry in winter but not decorated in frescoes and mosaics; very small and yet roomy enough for those unused to anything more. For a few others—the bottom ten percent—there

132. Zapata-Meza, "Domestic and Mercantile Areas," 93; De Luca and Lena, "Magdala/Tarichaeae," 306.

133. Avi-Yonah, *Holy Land,* 205. See b. Sukk. 20b; Cant. R. 1.4; m. Kel. 8:9.

was either a shanty or no house of any kind. Many lived on the streets, slept in winter under whatever shelter they could find, and begged for their daily bread. It was this group featured in the parable of the banquet in which the master of the house commanded his servants to go out into the streets and bring in the poor, the maimed, the lame, and the blind (Luke 14:21).

3

What Was Village Life Like?[1]

IF YOU LIVED IN Palestine/Israel in the late Second Temple Period, you would most likely have lived in a village. In addition to Caesarea—with a significant minority of Jews—there were four predominantly Jewish cities: Jerusalem, Sepphoris, Tiberias, and Magdala. Of the five, only Jerusalem was very large. What was it like to live in one of the villages? How large were they? When you walked around, what would you see?

In a previous era of scholarship, we were dependent on Josephus and the Mishnah to describe for us life in Palestine/Israel in the time of Jesus. More recently, scholars have turned to the social sciences—ethnographies of traditional, contemporaneous villages—to inform their understanding of ancient Palestine/Israel. Also, in the last thirty years more and more archaeological work has been done in the region. This work sometimes confirms the older views and sometimes leads to a reassessment. The survey below relies mostly on the material remains to draw a picture of village life in the late Second Temple Period.

VILLAGE AND TOWN SIZES

Most residents lived in a village. Josephus wrote that there were 204 cities and villages (πόλεις καὶ κῶμαι) in all of Galilee and no village was smaller than 15,000 inhabitants (*Life* 235; *War* 3.43). Whether a figure of 204 villages represents an actual administrative count or merely his estimate is unclear but the unevenness of the number might suggest the former.[2] The size of the villages, of course, (15,000) is a gross exaggeration.

---

1. A previous version of this chapter appeared as Chapter 8, in *GLSTMP*, 1:177–207. Reused with permission of Fortress Press.

2. On this, see Edwards, "Identity and Social Location." Edwards notes (357) that a survey of Upper Galilee showed evidence for 108 Early Roman settlements. He further states (358) that a study of Lower Galilee lists over 400 sites (from all periods of antiquity). Edwards then concludes that

At any rate, if we calculate the Jewish population of first-century Palestine/Israel as 1½ million,[3] and if we calculate the populations of Jerusalem at 60,000 to 100,000, Caesarea at 14,500, the two middle sized cities, Sepphoris and Tiberias, as 8,000 to 10,000 persons each, and Magdala the "smaller city" at 4,000,[4] then that leaves between 1,405,500 and 1,361,500 persons living in villages and towns in Judea, Idumea, Samaria, Perea, the Golan, and the Galilee. Clearly, the overwhelming majority of persons lived in villages.

Terminology

The two Greek terms which, in the main, are found in Josephus and the Gospels—πόλις (*polis*), usually translated "city" and κώμη (*kome*) usually translated "village"—seem to have been used in a confusing way. Technically, a *polis* had its own constitution, coinage, territory and town council (βουλή; See Chapter 2).[5] But these texts sometimes refer to villages as cities. The New Testament gospels, for example, may use the term *polis* to refer to what must have been very small villages.[6] Thus, one must read cautiously when the New Testament uses the terms. The rabbinic terms for cities, towns and villages are: *kerak, qiryah, 'irah, 'ir,* and *kaphar*.[7] The middle three terms appear to have been roughly equivalent in size representing a median between *kerak*, the large walled city, and *kaphar* the small un-walled village.

Archaeological Surveys[8]

The most informed way to answer the question, "How large were most villages in Palestine/Israel during our time period?" is to consult the archaeological surveys. We

---

Josephus' figure of 204 villages "seems entirely plausible . . ."

3. See Chapter 2 on the total population estimates. For Galilee, see E. M. Meyers, "Jesus and His Galilean Context," 59; and Hoehner, *Herod Antipas,* 53. Hoehner prefers the figure 200,000 and Meyers prefers 150,000 to 175,000. Meyers accepts Josephus' figure of 204 villages in Galilee and multiplies this number by 500 residents per village. That number plus the populations of the two cities give his final population figure. McCown cites an older figure of 400,000 for Galilee ("Density of Population," 426). His own estimate was 100,000 (436) based on an estimate of 150 persons per square mile. This estimate he derives from comparing with other population densities in the modern period.

4. On the city population calculations, see Chapter 2.

5. See Schürer, Vermes and Miller, *History* II, 86f; A. H. M. Jones "Urbanization"; Ehrenberg, "Polis." Sherwin-White suggested that considering the city (*polis*) in both Josephus and the Gospels as a capital of a toparchy (or region), even if the place was not technically a city. See Sherwin-White, *Roman,* 129f. Cf. Schürer et al., *History,* II, 188. See also Goodman, *State and Society,* 27.

6. See Reed, *Archaeology,* 167.

7. כְּפָר קְרִיָה עִירָה עִיר כְּרָךְ

8. The Israeli scholars measure space in dunams (4 dunams = c. 1 acre). Europeans use hectares (1 hectare = 2.47 acres). I will usually convert all measurements into acres.

will compare villages surveyed in the territories of Galilee, the Golan, and Samaria and those excavated in Judea.

The number of inhabitants of a typical town and village is only now being clarified by archaeologists. D. Urman's[9] survey of the Golan discovered one site over 175 acres but also 87 sites of 5 acres or less which were either small villages/hamlets or single farms. S. Dar[10] gives the measurement of six villages in Samaria ranging from 2.4 acres to 10 acres.

The team of R. Frankel has made a survey of Upper Galilee.[11] Although the survey identified settlements from the Neolithic through the Ottoman periods, we can select out the settlements that are relevant to our study.[12] The survey indicates that of the 74 sites that relate to our inquiry, 37 were less than 2.5 acres; 27 were 2.5 to 5 acres; seven sites were 5 to 10 acres; and three sites were 10 to 30 acres.

Uzi Leibner surveyed sites in eastern Galilee, dividing them into six categories based on his estimate of their area. Most of them (27 sites) were less than 5 acres with thirteen of them over five acres in size.[13]

We add a few sites from Lower Galilee which have been excavated, some of them some time ago, others more recently. Nazareth is somewhat difficult to measure since the ancient village lies underneath two churches today. J.D. Crossan and J. Reed[14] suggest that the village covered 10 acres but that much of it was empty space because of gardens, orchards, and places for livestock. S. Loffreda calculates the size of Capernaum to have been between 10 and 12 acres.[15] P. Richardson has likewise estimated that Cana[16] (8 to 9 acres) as well as Yodefat (10 acres) were in this same size-range.[17] Further, Crossan and Reed estimate the size of Sepphoris at 100 to 150 acres.[18]

---

9. Urman, *Golan,* 87f, 93.

10. Dar, *Landscape and Pattern,* 51, 53, 42, 47, 36, 231.

11. Frankel, Getzov, Aviam and Degani, *Settlement Dynamics.*

12. I have selected only settlements that include Hellenistic and/or Roman occupation and that did not continue past the Byzantine period.

13. Leibner, *Settlement and History,* 102–306. He found 50 sites but did not give size estimates for 10 of them.

14. Crossan and Reed, *Excavating Jesus,* 34. On the other hand, J. F. Strange ("Nazareth") surmises that it covered an area of 60 acres.

15. Loffreda, "Capernaum," 292. Crossan and Reed, *Excavating Jesus,* 81 suggest 25 acres was the size of Capernaum and that it had a population of 1,000. But in another publication, Reed (*Archaeology,* 83) suggests that the population of Capernaum was 1,700. See my calculation below.

16. He means Khirbet Qana on the north side of the Bet Netofa valley and not Kefar Qana just east of Nazareth.

17. Richardson, *Building Jewish,* 81. Douglas Edwards gives the size of the upper village of Khirbet Qana as 5 to 7 hectares (12 to 17 acres) "at its zenith" i.e. in the Byzantine era and Yodefat as 4.7 hectares (11 acres). See Edwards, "Khirbet Qana," 106. McCollough prefers 7 hectares (17 acres). See "City and Village in Lower Galilee," 58.

18. Crossan and Reed, *Excavating Jesus,* 81.

The Archaeology of Daily Life

Finally, we can add a few villages from Judea that have been excavated. The three we list here show that the villagers lived in small population centers as well.

It appears from these findings that most people lived in towns or villages ranging from less than 2.5 acres to 10 acres (see Table 3.1).

Calculating City and Village Population

The population of these towns and villages may be figured by counting the number of houses and multiplying by five, for five inhabitants on average to a dwelling, then subtracting 25% to allow rooms for storage and animals. Yeivin has, in this manner, estimated the population of several towns in Galilee and the Golan.[19] Most of these towns appear to have flourished in the Mishnaic period and, thus, we must hesitate in affirming that they also give us an appropriate sample in size of a typical late Second Temple village or town. Further, the method of counting dwellings is not always appropriate since many villages are not preserved enough to identify the living quarters.

Another method of determining population is to multiply the number of acres of the site times the supposed number of people that on average lived on one acre in antiquity. This method appears to be the most common one used by historians.[20] This method too is problematic since, in the first place, we cannot always tell exactly the total the area an ancient village covered and, in the second place, the estimates of population density vary. Wolfgang Reinhardt, who has done a detailed study of ancient population calculations, notes that one should not expect all villages/cities to have had the same population density.[21] Nevertheless, calculating populations can be a helpful heuristic exercise to compare villages. I do not claim below to know the actual population—a literal head count—of these ancient villages. I only present these figures as a good guess in general to help the reader picture what an ancient village was like.

The figure accepted by both M. Broshi and Y. Shiloh is 160 to 200 people per acre.[22] The higher number seems to me too many persons per acre since there must have been, in most villages, spaces for threshing floors, perhaps gardens, and even areas where nomadic folk and travelers stayed in tents.[23] I incline, therefore, toward

---

19. Yeivin, *Survey of Settlements*, VI.

20. See Reinhardt, "Population Size," 214: "The most common method is calculation by means of the product of area and density."

21. Reinhardt, "Population Size," 214.

22. I.e. 40 to 50 persons per dunam. See Broshi, "Population"; Shiloh, "Population." Yet, William G. Dever, *Ordinary People,* 48–49 has calculated populations of 8th century BCE towns and villages using a slightly lower estimate of population density. His estimate appears to be 100 persons per acre. At the other end of the time spectrum, Z. Safrai (*Economy,* 65) speculates that ten families could live on a dunam (or 40 families on an acre) of ground in the Talmudic period (200–500 CE). Thus he arrives at a figure of 120 to 160 persons per acre (125). Thus, his upper limit matches Broshi's lower limit.

23. See the work on a modern village in the Middle East: Sweet, *Tel Toqaan,* 52.

the lower number of 160 persons per acre.[24] Certainly the population figures obtained by this method are speculative but they are often the only figures we have. At least they offer some comparisons among contemporaneous villages.

Thus, using the lower number, we obtain the population figures given in Table 3.1. Also using this calculation method, Sepphoris would have numbered around 16,000 persons.[25] But since Sepphoris had more open spaces than most villages—a market place, wide streets, much larger houses for the same number of family members as a village house—perhaps we should estimate it lower. Thus, 8,000 to 10,000 seems more feasible. One can easily discern the difficulty of simply using Broshi's and Shiloh's calculations.[26] We offer these figures here simply by way of comparing villages and towns using the most common method of determining population.

	Site in Acres	*Population (160 person/ acre)*
Urman (Golan)	1 site 175 acres (Caesarea Philippi)	28,000
	4 sites 30–50 acres	4,800–8,000
	14 sites 10–30 acres	1,600–4,800
	28 sites 5–10 acres	800–1,600
	54 sites 2.5–5 acres	400–800
	33 sites less than 2.5 acres	Less than 400
Frankel et al. (Upper Galilee)	3 sites 10–30 acres	1.600–4,800
	7 sites 5–10 acres	800–1,600
	27 sites 2.5–5 acres	400–800
	37 sites less than 2.5 acres	Less than 400
Leibner[27] (Eastern Lower Galilee)	5 sites .5 acre	80
	14 sites 1.7 acres	300
	8 sites 3.7 acres	592
	7 sites 7.5 acres	1200
	4 sites 12.5 acres	1900
	2 sites 18.7 acres	3000
	1 site 22.5 acres (Magdala)	3600

24. Reinhardt inclines toward a higher population density, at least for Jerusalem. See "Population Size," 253–55.

25. Compare the calculation given in Chapter 2. This figure is closer to that of E. M. Meyers. The size of Tiberias is yet to be determined since most of it lies now under the modern city.

26. Compare Reed, *Archaeology*, 152, who wants to assign a population of 150 to one hectare (not one acre) and perhaps even 100 persons per hectare. He is thinking here mostly of Capernaum which was spread out and not confined by city walls that tend to squeeze people together.

27. Leibner gives a range of sizes (e.g., .5–3 dunams). I have averaged his site sizes and converted them into acres. See *Settlement and History*, 313.

The Archaeology of Daily Life

Dar[28] (Samaria)	4–5 acres	640–800
	3.5 acres	560
	6 acres	960
	6–7.5 acres	960–1,200
	2.4 acres	384
	10 acres	1,600
Western Lower Galilee Sites	3 sites 10 acres[29]	1,600
	1 site 5–10 acres	800–1,600
	1 site of 100 to 150 acres (Sepphoris)	16,000–24,000 (8,000–10,000)
Judea[30]	2 sites of 2.5 acres	400
	1 site of 10 acres	1,600

Table 3.1: Villages in Galilee, Golan, Samaria, and Judea

The dates for most of the villages cited by Dar are Hasmonean through the Herodian (one through Byzantine) period. The towns in the Golan range from the early Roman to the Byzantine period. All of those selected from the Upper Galilee survey are Hellenistic or Roman. All of those from the eastern Galilean survey are Early Roman to Middle Roman. All of those listed from Lower Galilee are Herodian (or ER I= 37 BCE to 70 CE). The sites in Judea (Qiryat Sefer, Horvat Ethri, and En-Gedi) are also Early Roman. Thus, it appears that most persons in the two Galilees, the Golan, Samaria, and Judea during the Roman period lived in villages with less than 2,000 inhabitants.

Several historians have constructed settlement categories for the late Second Temple and Mishnaic periods. Here is a comparative table of their suggestions:

---

28. Dar often estimates the population, however, at more than these amounts. For example, the population of Hirbet Hajar would be, at most, 1,000 persons using Broshi's method, but Dar estimates the population at 1,500 to 2,000. See Dar, *Landscape and Pattern*, 51. The average village in Egypt may have been somewhat larger. Cf. Lewis, *Life in Egypt*, 68.

29. But Crossan and Reed (*Excavating Jesus*, 34) estimate the population of Nazareth at 200 to 400 persons in spite of their suggested 10 acre size for the village. J. F. Strange ("Nazareth") calculates the population of Nazareth at 480 or less. Richardson (*Building Roman*, 76) suggests that Yodefat had a population of 1,000.

30. See Qiryat Sefer and En-Gedi below. Also Magen, et al., "Qiryat Sefer"; Hirschfeld, "En-Gedi"; and Zissu and Ganor, "Horbat ʽEthri."

Village sizes/types	Zeev Safrai[31]	Shimon Dar[32]	Anne Killebrew[33]	Arieh Ben-David[34]
	Villa	Isolated farm	Farm house	
		Incipient village		Hamlet
	Village	Nucleated village	Small village	Village
	Small town		Large village	Country town
	Medium town			
	City (three tiers)		Urban settlement	City

Table 3.2: Settlement categories in the Late Second Temple Period according to four historians[35]

These observations seem to follow a fairly consistent pattern. There were, of course, the cities (see Chapter 2), but most residents lived in smaller population centers. These smaller centers were in various stages of development, from incipient village to medium sized town. Further, as most of these historians suggest, there were also isolated farms not associated with a village. We will return to these installations in Chapter 7. For now, we focus on the villages.

Thus, although Josephus states that even the smallest village in Galilee had over 15,000 inhabitants (*War* 3.43), the archaeological data indicate that most folk in Galilee, Golan, Samaria, and Judea lived in villages of only a few hundred to 2,000 persons.

WHAT WAS IN A VILLAGE OR TOWN?

We will describe a typical Palestinian small town or village by comparing first the hypothetical "medium-sized town" in the Mishnaic period which Z. Yeivin has constructed with five actual villages: Khirbet Karqush in Samaria, Gamla in the Golan, Khirbet Qana in Lower Galilee, Qiryat Sefer in Judea, and finally, the village of En Gedi on the west coast of the Dead Sea.

---

31. Z. Safrai, Economy, 17. He bases his categories on rabbinic literature.

32. Dar, "History." He bases his categories on his archaeological survey of the Hermon mountain ridge.

33. Killebrew, "Village and Countryside." See especially 195. She was influenced by both Safrai and Dar in her categories.

34. Ben-David, *Talmudische Ökonomie*, 49.

35. Cf. also Dever, *Ordinary People*, 48–49, who lists 8th century BCE cities and villages in four "Tiers." He offers: 1. capital cities/administrative centers; 2. cities (with over 1,000 persons); 3. towns (300–1,000 population); and 4. villages (50–300 population). It is interesting to compare these categories with the Madaba Map which seems to divide settlements into four groups based on size. See Avi-Yonah, *Madaba Mosaic Map*, 21–22.

The Archaeology of Daily Life

A Composite Town of the Mishnaic Period

Yeivin[36] has put together a composite of town of medium size based on the plans of Chorazin and Einan in Galilee, Nahef and Naaran in the Golan, and Horvat Susia in Judea. Although these towns flourished in the late second century CE, they do not seem to differ markedly from the late Second Temple villages as far as their layout and the type of buildings are concerned.

First, Yeivin's composite town indicates no street planning. The streets were haphazardly determined, often leaving open areas which became public domain. Contrast Caesarea, Sepphoris, Magdala (and, presumably, Tiberias) which had streets running parallel and perpendicular in an orthogonal grid pattern, often called a "Hippodamian grid." This haphazard village arrangement can be observed in several of the villages in Palestine/Israel[37] and is often noted by observers of modern Middle Eastern villages. The description by Tannous of such villages is common:

> A compact, nucleated form of structure is the first striking impression one gets of the Middle Eastern village. It is a conglomeration of houses standing close to each other, divided by winding alleys and paths that do not seem to have any regular design.[38]

Second, Yeivin's composite village had no gates or fortified walls, but the houses were often built touching each other so that they formed a kind of *de facto* protective outer wall. Third, Yeivin's hypothetical small town or village had a synagogue and a public building. Probably many of the towns also had commercial buildings.[39] Fourth, also nearby the town was the cemetery. Although the composite village is Mishnaic, the buildings and their arrangement surely did not change that much from the late Second Temple to the Mishnaic period.

The one public building we cannot be sure existed in most first-century CE Galilean villages was the synagogue. Certainly, there were synagogues in the Herodian period, but that most villages had a separate building for them is unproven so far. Most

---

36. Yeivin, "Medium-Sized City."

37. E.g., in Capernaum. See Crossan and Reed, *Excavating Jesus*, 81. Cf. Killebrew, "Village and Countryside," 196, "Natural topography, and not a master plan that typified the *polis*, played a key role in the general layout and network of streets of these unfortified 'medium-sized cities.'" Cf. also Z. Safrai, *Economy*, 46: "The Jewish city or town was not planned. Therefore its streets and thoroughfares often meandered with no clear purposes." For open areas as public domain, see also Sweet, *Tell Toqaan*, 55. But contrast Loffreda, "Capernaum," who sees some order to the streets of Capernaum.

38. Tannous, "Arab Village Community," 528. For other ethnographic references to the haphazard arrangement of streets and alleys in Middle Eastern villages see: Kramer, *Village Ethnoarchaeology*, 85, 88; McGarvey, *Lands of the Bible*, 105, 108; Lutfiyya, *Baytin*, 20; Sweet, *Tell Toqaan*, 51, 54 (The streets [of contemporary Palestinian villages] are mere "cow paths."). These authors speak of "winding alleys"; crooked and narrow streets; and of paths in the village "twist(ing) around corners of long blocks of compounds."

39. Such as the building found at Nabratein by E. M. Meyers, J. F. Strange, and C. L. Meyers. See E. M. Meyers et al., "Second Preliminary Report on the 1981 Excavations at en-Nabratein, Israel."

of the remains of the synagogues in village ruins in Palestine/Israel are from the end of the second century or beginning of the third century CE.[40] The exceptions to these archaeological *realia* are synagogues listed in the Appendix at the end of this chapter. Among this growing list is the synagogue at Jericho, which the excavators think was first built in the first century BCE (one of the earliest synagogue buildings) and then expanded in the first century CE.[41] Some excavators also think that a building at Khirbet Qana (the biblical Cana?) was a synagogue and others surmise that under the fourth-century synagogue at Capernaum lies today the foundation for the first-century synagogue, the one in which Jesus preached. In addition, there are the late Second Temple buildings at Herod's palaces, which are presumed to be synagogues: Herodium (a synagogue fashioned out of a triclinium) and Masada. There may have been others but one cannot affirm with certainty yet. There does seem to be a growing list of early synagogue buildings but one should not yet confidently affirm that every village had one.

In the photograph below of a model of a typical Mishnaic Galilean village, the reader is urged to note how closely the houses were situated, how narrow the streets look,[42] and how unplanned the entire village seems.

Figure 3.1: Model of a Galilean Village in the Mishnaic Period[43]

40. On this subject see Levine, "Common Judaism"; Shanks, *Judaism in Stone,* 17–30; and Rousseau and Arav, *Jesus and His World,* 271.

41. Netzer, "Jericho."

42. For narrow streets, see Yavor, "Architecture," 27 where a street he calls an alley was between 1 and .7 meters wide; and Hirschfeld, "Architecture," 31 where an "alley" measured 1.4 to 1.2 m. wide. The Mishnah refers to narrow streets in villages as four cubits (6 ft. or 1.8 m.). See S. Safrai, "Home," 728.

43. The model is in the museum of the Galilee Boat, Kibbutz Ginosar, Israel. The photo is by the author.

THE ARCHAEOLOGY OF DAILY LIFE

Khirbet Karqush

The village in Samaria known as Khirbet Karqush will serve as our second example, this one of an actual village from the late Second Temple Period. This village is a helpful model because so many of its structures are well preserved. Shimon Dar[44] was able to date the village from the tombs in the nearby cemetery. The village covers an area of 3.5 acres and, thus, would have had a population of 560 people, according to Broshi's method of computing population, a typical size for the Herodian period. Dar used Yeivin's method of determining the population and concluded that the village held around 600 people.

Dar divides the village structures into two main blocks: Blocks A and B. Block A, which may be a later (Byzantine) section of the village contained several courtyard houses. Across the street from Block A, in Block B (the ER section), were several more courtyard houses (numbers 6, 9, 16, 18 and probably also 12 and 13). Dar believes that building 11 was a water reservoir. Another building (10) had an unknown function and was built in the Hellenistic period. There were also several parts of an oil press found in the village which were not *in situ* (numbers 20, 23, and 24).

Dar believes that two of the buildings (7 and 8) were public buildings. He found several other examples of such buildings in Samaritan villages[45] and from other evidence we know that many villages in Syria, even small ones, had public buildings of some sort.[46] The buildings were not evidently financed from taxes but from donations of wealthy families when such families lived in or near the village, and perhaps also from the revenues of village owned land.

---

44. Dar, *Landscape and Pattern*, 42–46.
45. E. g., Dar, *Landscape and Pattern*, 49.
46. Harper, "Village Administration"; and A.H.M. Jones, *Greek City*, 286.

WHAT WAS VILLAGE LIFE LIKE?

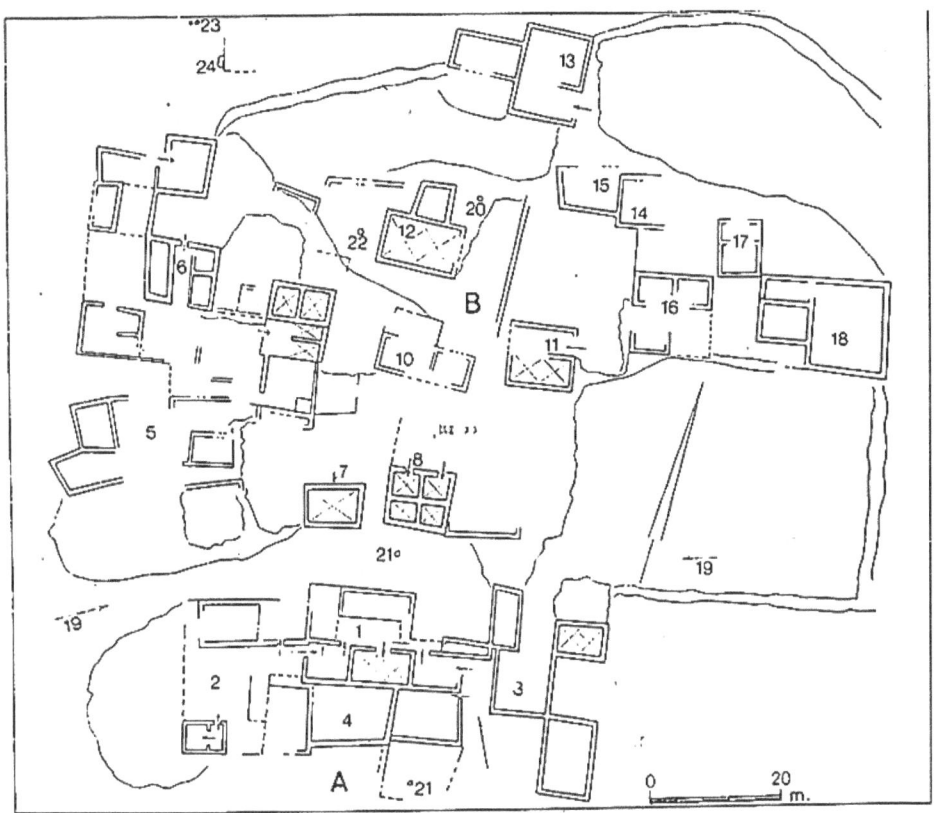

Map 3.1: Khirbet Karqush[47]

Southeast of the village of Khirbet Karqush lay the cemetery with both *kokh* (or *loculus*) type of burial and open cist graves. Dar found sixteen systems of *kokhim* tombs and twenty dwelling units in the village. Thus, he concludes that most families had a rock-cut tomb. Evidently, however, the poorer families did not (see Chapter 11).

There was some evidence that one family was wealthier than the others. Dar found an ornamental tomb in the cemetery and a larger than usual courtyard house. Yet the difference in economic status must have been small, argues Dar, so that this family is only *primus inter pares*. In other words, this family probably did not own the village.

This phenomenon was common in the villages. Several villages had larger, better constructed (with rectangular ashlar stones), or more richly decorated (with painted frescoes) houses. The villages of Yodefat, Gamla, and Khirbet Qana had such houses. In addition, the Judean village of Qiryat Sefer had a nicely constructed house-complex (where coin hoards were found) and a poorly constructed complex (see below). One concludes that not everyone in the village, then was of the same economic level. But if there were families more prosperous than the average of the village, then there were

---

47. Dar, *Landscape and Pattern*, II, Figure 32. Used with permission.

also, one would think, families poorer than the rest. The commonly quoted observation concerning villages ("There was limited economic stratification in the villages . . . there were no extremely wealthy residents"[48]) may need rethinking.

Just north of the supposed water reservoir was a large open square. One wonders if this area had a specific purpose such as a village market place, the center for exchange in ancient Palestine.[49] The Synoptic Gospels indicate that most small towns and villages had markets (Mark 6:56; 7:4; 12:28; Matt 11:16=Luke 7:32; Matt 20:3; Matt 23:7=Luke 11:43) in addition to major market centers such as Sepphoris, Shechem, Lydda, and Antipatris.[50] It is possible that such open areas served as temporary marketplaces in villages on the market day.[51] Alternatively, open areas may have been tent cities for seasonal nomadic visitors. Such village areas are known in modern Middle Eastern villages.[52]

This village, I believe, is a good example of what was in a Palestinian village during our time period.

Gamla (Maps 1.1 and 7.2)

The third village we will consider is Gamla, six miles northeast of the Sea of Galilee. This town is appropriate for our purposes since it certainly was active in the first century CE and was destroyed in 67 by the Romans. Thus, the last remains on the site have frozen for us the life of the ordinary people. Gamla is especially interesting because it had a first-century CE synagogue (65 x 52 feet; Figure 3.2) with a *mikveh* just outside the front door (the town had four ritual baths discovered so far). In addition to the synagogue, the town had a large public building—termed a Roman basilica by the excavators—on the western side (measuring 52 x 49 feet[53]) consisting of three aisles, like a medieval church.

In the middle of the town was an industrial olive pressing installation. Nearby this olive press was one of the more up-scale houses, this one with colored frescoed

---

48. Safrai, *Economy,* 357. If one, however, emphasizes his word "extremely," the quote is acceptable.

49. The market place was called שׁוּק in the rabbinic literature (see Jastrow, *Dictionary*) and ἀγορά in the Gospels (Mark 6:56). See also Goodman, *State and Society,* 54.

50. Applebaum, "Economic Life", 687.

51. The pre-Mishnaic market day was Friday. See Applebaum, "Economic Life", 687; and Goodman, *State and Society,* 54.

52. Sweet, *Tel Toqaan,* 52.

53. Compare with the basilica of Sepphoris which was 130 x 115 feet. See Chapter 2.

Figure 3.2: Synagogue at Gamla (photo by the author)

walls. Farther to the west was a large two-story mansion with multiple rooms (dating from the first century CE). The house was built from finely dressed stones (chiseled and not just stacked from the field).[54] Thus, Gamla, although a large village and not a big city, had some residents who could exhibit a bit of their wealth in their house construction. Also interesting was the large number of jewelry items found at Gamla (rings, pendants, beads, intaglios, and insets).[55] These were not starving peasants but they had the means to buy luxury goods on occasion.

Khirbet Qana (Map 4.1)

The fourth village we will consider is Khirbet Qana, which lies on the northern edge of the Bet Netofa valley in Lower Galilee (considered by some to be the Cana of the Gospel of John 2:1[56]). This village, as stated above, covered 8 or 9 acres.[57] Like Yeivin's

---

54. Syon, "Gamla"; Gutman, "Gamala"; Syon and Yavor, "Gamala."

55. See Amorai-Stark and Hershkovitz, "Jewelry." There was a total of 379 pieces, most of which were beads and insets.

56. See the discussion in: Alexandre, "Karm er-Ras"; McCollough, "Khirbet Qana"; and Luca, "Kafr Kanna."

57. But see above. Edwards, "Khirbet Qana," 106, gives the site dimensions as 12 to 17 acres for Khirbet Qana "at its zenith," i.e. in the Byzantine era.

The Archaeology of Daily Life

composite village and like Khirbet Karqush, Khirbet Qana had no wall (in our period of occupation). There has been found, so far, one olive press, a water reservoir, over 60 cisterns, and one "industrial complex" near a *mikveh*, identified by Peter Richardson as a wool dyeing installation.[58] There were also two *columbaria* (dovecotes[59]). Of the two constructions identified as "public buildings," one may have been a synagogue. The village was surrounded by thirteen tombs.[60] Douglas Edwards, the lead excavator of this site, estimated that the total population by the second century (the Mishnaic period) was between 750 and 1400 persons.[61]

Peter Richardson thinks that in Khirbet Qana (as well as in parts of Yodefat and Gamla) some of the streets on the acropolis were arranged in an "informal or quasi-Hippodamian" grid, that is, running north to south and east to west as opposed to meandering and winding.[62] Thus, if Richardson is correct, these villages/towns may have had a bit more planning, at least in some areas of them, than most.

Figure 3.3: Hill (in front) on which ruins of Khirbet Qana lie (photo by the author)

58. Richardson, "Khirbet Qana." McCollough also offers that the installation could have been used for tanning leather or as a fullery. See "City and Village in Lower Galilee," 65.

59. For other dovecotes in Israel in the late Second Temple, see Lipschits, Gadot, Arubas, and Oeming, "Palace and Village," 38; Aviam, *Jews, Pagans and Christians*, 31–40; and Zissu, "Two Herodian Dovecotes." As Aviam points out, so far nine *columbaria* have been found in Galilee. For dovecotes in general, see Z. Safrai, *Economy*, 174–79.

60. Richardson ("What has Cana to do with Capernaum?" 327 estimates that the tombs could have held around "100 loculi." Thus, there must have been other graves (cist or trench graves?) elsewhere if the population of the village approached anything like the estimate given above (i.e. around 1,600 persons). On this issue, see Magness, *Stone*, 155–64 and Chapter 11 of this volume.

61. Edwards, "Khirbet Qana," 101–132; see especially his maps on 106, 108. Also Richardson, "Khirbet Qana." McCollough, "City and Village in Lower Galilee," 58, estimates the population in the first century CE at 1200.

62. Richardson, "Khirbet Qana," 123. Stanislao Loffreda saw a similar possibility of town planning at Capernaum. See Loffreda, "Capernaum." But contrast Crossan and Reed, *Excavating Jesus*, 81; and Reed, *Archaeology*, 152–53 who think that Capernaum shows no evidence of planning at all.

Qiryat Sefer

Moving south, we will look at the Judean village of Qiryat Sefer, located fourteen miles northwest of Jerusalem. The village was constructed in the ER period and survived until the time of Bar-Kokhba (early second century CE). The entire village site covers 2.5 acres. It has numerous oil processing installations and several wine presses. There are cisterns, ritual baths, stone vessels, and a synagogue demonstrating that the village was clearly Jewish. The synagogue (31 feet x 31 feet[63]) follows the basic pattern of other first-century CE synagogues according to the excavators. Near the synagogue—as in the case of the synagogue of Gamla—was a community *mikveh*. South of the village several burial caves were identified but not excavated.[64]

Qiryat Sefer is situated on two sides of a hillock, with a Northern Complex on one side and a Southern Complex on the other. At the top of the hillock were a few constructions: two winepresses and a *mikveh*.

Of note is that the Northern Complex was constructed with more care and craftsmanship (with "arches and ashlars," i.e. squarely chiseled stones) than the Southern. The Southern Complex was mostly built using stones found lying in the field and simply stacked as securely as possible to form the walls. Was this practice due to the fact that the Southern Complex was only used for storage and industry while the Northern Complex was the principal residential section or was it due to the fact that the poorer residents lived in the Southern Complex? Did people live in the Southern Complex—the lower class crowd—or did they only use these buildings to store their produce (oil and wine) and for the processing of the produce (oil presses and wine presses)? The excavators offer both hypotheses.[65]

How may we decide which hypothesis is correct? The Northern Complex had several oil presses scattered in it and rooms labeled by the excavators as storerooms. That fact seems to argue that they mixed living quarters with industrial processes and storage. If so, then I would conclude that the Southern Complex was also mixed. Other finds argue for a well-to-do population in the Northern Complex. Excavators found two coin hoards: one numbered 45 coins, mostly bronze and one silver coin, and the other consisted of 144 coins including many silver and gold. These were prosperous people in the Northern Complex (on the north side of the hill, removed in distance and sight level from the Southern Complex). Consequently, we may have a two-tiered village: one part for the comfortable residents and the other (the Southern Complex) for the poor.

---

63. Compare with the dimensions of the synagogue of Gamla: 65 x 52 feet.
64. Magen, et al., "Qiryat Sefer."
65. See Magen, et al., "Qiryat Sefer."

En-Gedi (Maps 3.2 and 5.1)

Situated on the western coast of the Dead Sea was the ancient village of En-Gedi, the sometime haunt of the refugee, King David (1 Sam 24:1). The ten-acre site would have had, according to our method of calculating, a population of around 1,600 persons. How could such a large village survive in such a hostile region? It enjoyed the irrigation of ten fresh water springs.

In order to farm the area (the literary sources say they raised dates and the valuable balsam oil[66]) they had to build terraces on the steep hillsides (see Chapter 7 for terraces) and channel the ten springs into the fields to irrigate their trees. The *mikveh* found in the village along with the numerous fragments of stoneware vessels indicate that this was a Jewish village. Thus, this was a good sized village that could thrive in the wilderness because of the fresh water springs and the technology of terraces.

Interestingly, it looks like the Essenes may also have had a part of this village. One area contained several spartan, small cells which the archaeologists surmise might have been used for such a purpose. Pliny the Elder (*N.H.* 5.75) had written that some of the Essenes lived in En-Gedi.[67]

Common Patterns

The hypothetical medium-sized town of Yeivin, the village in rural Samaria described by Dar, Khirbet Qana (in Galilee), Gamla (in the Golan), Qiryat Sefer (in Judea), and En Gedi (on the western shore of the Dead Sea) indicate common patterns. Most villages of any size had not only residences but agricultural structures (oil or wine presses) and cemeteries outside the village. They might have water reservoirs but most used individual cisterns for their water supply. En-Gedi, however—being located in the Judean wilderness—depended on the ten natural springs for drinking water as well as for irrigation of their crops. There might be a public building but the smaller the village, the less likely that was. Finally, there were a few specially constructed synagogues but not many buildings excavated so far have been conclusively determined to have been synagogues.[68]

Yeivin's composite village and the village in Samaria had an open space perhaps used on market days as temporary markets; none of the Galilean and Judean villages has exhibited such space for temporary markets. They also had narrow, unpaved streets arranged in haphazard patterns and no gates or walls.[69] The exception to the

---

66. According to Dar ("Agrarian Economy," 309), a pint of balsam oil cost 1,000 denarii. See Pliny *N.H.* 12.123.

67. Hirschfeld, "En-Gedi"; and Hadas, "En-Gedi."

68. One in Galilee; one in the Golan; two in Judea. In addition, there are the two Herodian fortresses. Of less certainty are Capernaum, Khirbet Qana, Wadi Hammam, and Jericho. Of the cities, only Magdala so far has one. See Appendix at the end of this chapter.

69. See, e.g., Capernaum (Crossan and Reed, *Excavating Jesus*, 81); and Nazareth (Reed,

haphazard streets may have been some parts of Khirbet Qana and Yodefat. One Galilean town—Yodefat—in addition, was fortified (given walls) in preparation for the revolt of 66–73 CE as was Gamla.[70] But these were special preparations and not the usual feature for villages.

By way of contrast, the cities, Caesarea, Sepphoris, Magdala, and probably Tiberias, were planned with streets in a grid pattern and with a wide *Cardo* or main street in each. Jerusalem had a theater, hippodrome, and paved streets. Caesarea had a theater and hippodrome. Tiberias had a theater, a stadium for athletic games, a monumental gate and possibly a gymnasium and a hippodrome. Magdala had a hippodrome, baths, and a *palaestra*. Sepphoris had a large basilica (115 x 130 feet), i.e. a building used for government purposes (administration or law courts).[71] Finally, there may have been a theater built in Sepphoris in the first century CE, but the date of this structure is now debated (see Chapter 2). The cities had spacious streets, formally designated market places, large public buildings, large domestic quarters, and more comforts of life such as entertainment. To go from village to city was to cross into a new subculture.

The following table contrasts the Galilean cities and villages:

Villages	Cities
Most were un-walled. Exceptions: Yodefat and Gamla	Walled
No formal market places but open spaces may have served informally	Clearly designated market places
Topography determined how the streets were laid out. They were done in "traditional ways."	The cities were laid out in Hippodamian grids.
Cisterns were the main source of water but there were some water reservoirs (at Khirbet Qana and Yodefat)	The cities had aqueducts.
There was no architecture for entertainment.	There were theaters, stadiums, and hippodromes.

Table 3.3: Village and City Contrasts[72]

Archaeology, 131, 152–53).

70. Adan-Bayewitz and Aviam report that the excavations of Yodefat revealed that its walls were begun in the Hellenistic period but strengthened by Josephus. Thus, this town had walls—at least in some areas—from the beginning. See Adan-Bayewitz and Aviam, "Iotapata." Gamla, in the Golan, was also fortified during the revolt.

71. See Crossan and Reed, *Excavating Jesus*, 60–67; Dothan, *Hamath Tiberias,* 16; and Weiss, "Theatres, Hippodromes, Amphitheatres, and Performances." See on the basilica in Sepphoris: J. F. Strange, "The Eastern Basilical Building," 117–21. The building consisted of rows of offices or shops all with floor mosaics. One room had a stepped pool.

72. The table was constructed based on ideas in Richardson, "Khirbet Qana," 127–28.

THE ARCHAEOLOGY OF DAILY LIFE

Figure 3.4: Cistern Opening, Khirbet Qana[73]

What, then, was in the typical village? We may summarize our results for this section in the following table (Table 3.4). This table must be read with discretion. I have marked only those features attested archaeologically. But common sense will tell us that virtually all of the villages planted grain, olives, and grapes and most of them (except for those located on the Sea of Galilee) must have had cisterns. And, of course, they all must have had cemeteries. They simply have not all been located yet. There are probably ritual baths (*mikva'ot*) in all villages but may not yet have been uncovered. Capernaum, located on the Sea of Galilee, would have little need of them (yet Magdala had them). Thus, the table only indicates what has been discovered and cannot be used to demonstrate what was not in the villages. At most, it can only show what has (not yet) been excavated.

In addition to the villages discussed above, we add data for several others to enrich our profile. Some of these villages will receive further treatment in Chapter 7.

---

73. Photograph by the author.

Features	1	2	3	4	5	6	7	8	9	10	11	12	13
1st cent. Synagogue		Perhaps 1st	Perhaps				X			X	X		
House(s) of the wealthy	X		X	X			X			X	Herodian winter palaces		
Olives	X	X	X	X	X	X	X		X	X			
Vines			X	X	X	X			X	X			
Other crops											Dates, balsam	Dates, balsam	
Pottery production				X	X			X					
Grain production	X	X		X	X	X		X					
Wool (loom weights)		X		X				X					
Other Industry	Cooperage		Dyeing, Glass production								Date wine, balsam oil		Perfumes Pharmaceuticals
Quarries			X	X	X	X							
Columbaria			X										
Tombs	X		X		X	X	X	X	X	X	X		X
Ritual Baths	X		X	X	X	X	X	X	X	X	X		X
Stone vessels	X	X	X	X	X	X	X	X	X	X	X		X
Water Reservoir			X	X								X	
Cisterns	X		X	X	X	X	X			X			
Public Building			X				X						X

Table 3.4: Features in Ancient Palestinian Villages[74]
Key: 1=Meiron (Upper Galilee); 2=Capernaum; 3=Khirbet Qana; 4=Yodefat; 5=Shikhin; 6=Nazareth; 7=Gamla; 8=Karm er-Ras; 9=Ḥuqoq; 10=Qiryat Sefer; 11=Jericho; 12=En Gedi; 13=En Boqeq

74. The table has been constructed based on information from: Edwards, "Khirbet Qana"; Richardson, "Khirbet Qana," 120–44; McCollough, "City and Village in Lower Galilee"; Bagatti, "Nazareth"; Adan-Bayewitz and Aviam, "Iotapata"; Reed, *Archaeology*, 131–32, 143–59; Pfann, Voss, and Rapuano, "Nazareth Village Farm"; E. M. Meyers and C. L. Meyers, "Digging the Talmud"; E. M. Meyers et al., *Excavations at Ancient Meiron*, xviii, 44, 107–20; Loffreda, "Capernaum"; no author, "Capernaum: The Town of Jesus"; J. R. Strange, "Report of the 2011 Survey and 2012 Excavation Seasons at Shikhin"; Magen, Tzionit, and Sirkis, "Qiryat Sefer"; Gichon, "Ein Boqeq"; Hirschfeld, "En-Gedi"; Netzer, "Jericho"; Alexandre, "Karm er-Ras"; Grey and Spigel, "Ḥuqoq"; Magness et al., "Ḥuqoq"; Aviam, "Distribution Maps"; Adler, "Archaeology of Purity," 321–43; Magen, *Stone Vessel*; Aviam, "Socio-Economic Hierarchy."

The Archaeology of Daily Life

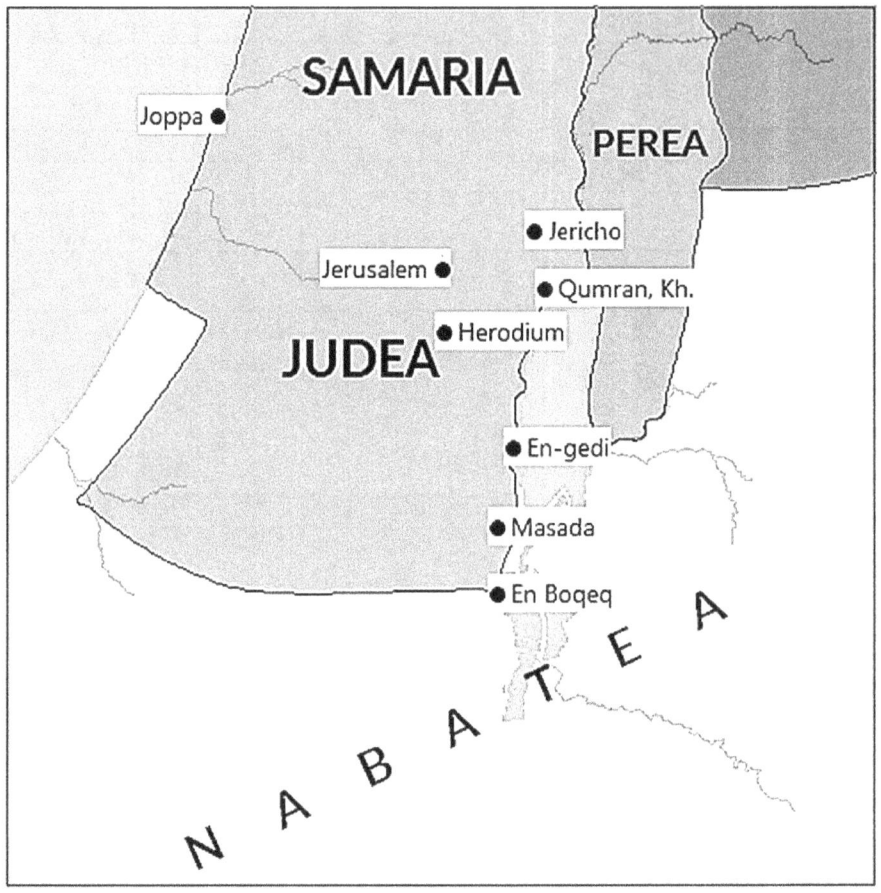

Map 3.2: Showing Jericho, Herodium, En-Gedi, Masada, and En Boqeq, west of the Dead Sea[75]

CONCLUSION

If the reader had lived in Palestine/Israel in the first century CE, chances are he/she would have lived in a village of less than 2,000 inhabitants. The village would have consisted mostly of simply made houses; haphazardly planned, unpaved streets; perhaps a public building or two; and a few open areas used on market day or by nomadic persons for pitching their tents. You might have had a building dedicated exclusively to synagogue study and prayer, but probably not. So far, it appears that a relatively small—but growing—list of villages had them. If you were fortunate enough to have lived in one of the five cities discussed in Chapter 2, you would have known wide thoroughfares, impressive architecture, and various forms of entertainment. If you had

---

75. Map created with Accordance.

lived in a village, you would probably have been engaged in agriculture, but certain kinds of industry would also not have been out of the question (see Chapter 7).

APPENDIX TO CHAPTER 3

Synagogue location	Size in square meters	Size in square feet
Capernaum (Map 4.1)	485.15	4,931
Gamla (Map 7.2)	376.25	4,050
Khirbet Qana (Map 4.1)	300	3,229
Jericho (Map 3.2)	189.75	2,042
Herodium (Map 3.2)	164	1,765
Masada (Map 3.2)	131	1,410
Magdala (= Tarichaea; Map 2.3)	120	1,291
Qiryat Sefer (NW of Jerusalem)	92.16	992
Umm el-'Umdan (near Modi'in in Judea)	84	904
Tel Rekhesh (near Mt. Tabor in Valley of Jezreel)	72	775
Khirbet Wadi Hamam (near Magdala)[76]	?	?

Synagogue Sizes from the First Century CE (in descending order of size)[77]

76. There was a public building, similar to the synagogue at nearby Magdala, but whose dimensions could not be ascertained since one end of it was destroyed and removed. See Leibner, "Hamam," 348–49.

77. See Bauckham, "Magdala," 42–44; Tessler, "Ancient Synagogue"; Levine, "Synagogues of Galilee"; Onn et al., "Umm el-'Umdan"; Netzer, "Masada"; Foerster, "Herodium"; Netzer, "Jericho"; Leibner, "Hamam." But compare the dimensions given by Haber, "Common Judaism, 67 for four of these synagogues: Jericho: 180 m²; Masada: 180m2; Gamla: 320m2; Herodium: 158m2. For a map of all synagogues excavated up to the year 1995, see Rousseau and Arav, *Jesus and His World,* 271. These synagogues date from the first to the fifth centuries CE.

4

What Kind of House Would You Have Lived In?[1]

IF YOU LIVED IN Israel in the late Second Temple Period, what sort of house would you have had? To a great extent that would depend on your means, your location, and your own skills. The situation cannot have been much different from the pioneers in the old American frontier. Materials for building were at hand, free for the taking (wood or sod) but the wealthier could hire professionals to do it for them. Likewise, in the first century BCE through the first century CE in Palestine/Israel, there were plenty of materials (stone, plaster, and mud) that could have been accessed presumably free of charge, but some wanted and could afford to hire professional carpenters and stone masons to build their house for them, or at least to direct its construction by volunteer laborers.

When we speak of a "house," what do we mean? We are here referring to the total domestic area: the buildings under roof, the open air courtyard, and the subterranean silos and animal stalls. Most houses in the ancient Near East and Mediterranean world were associated with an outdoor courtyard.[2] Likewise, many, if not most, houses contained underground passageways that led to their store of goods or even to their accommodations for livestock.[3]

---

1. A previous version of this chapter appeared as Chapter 10, in *GLSTMP*, 1:216–41. Reused with permission of Fortress Press.

2. See Beebe, "Domestic Architecture," 91: From the Middle Bronze period on the courtyard was the central feature of houses in Palestine.

3. See the excavations at Nazareth which are visible today under the courtyard of the Church of the Annunciation and under the Church of St. Joseph. See also Figure 4.6 below.

HOUSE TYPES

Those scholars studying Palestinian houses have organized them into architectural styles. The village house underwent a change from the typical four-room house (or "pillared" house) of the Israelite period, in which an extended family lived, to the "courtyard house" of the Hellenistic and Roman periods.[4] The four-room house consisted of "a back room the width of the building, with three long rooms stemming from it.[5] The house style which succeeded the four-room house usually had an internal courtyard and probably developed due to foreign influence.[6]

Z. Yeivin,[7] examining excavation and survey reports for Galilee and the Golan, places houses into four categories. Yizhar Hirschfeld[8] also found four types, though his four types were somewhat different from Yeivin's. Both Santiago Guijarro[9] and Pieter J.J. Botha[10] find five house types. Peter Richardson[11] has discovered nine forms of housing in rural areas and eleven in urban settings. We will below combine several of these forms and seek to explore the following housing styles:[12]

- The simple house
- The complex house (both urban apartments and rural farmhouses)
- The courtyard house (both side and central courtyard types and the peristyle house)
- The terrace house
- The "insula"
- Miscellaneous types (caves, tents, fortress-palaces, villas-rural mansions, monasteries, etc.)

---

4. Dar, *Landscape and Pattern,* 80f.

5. Shiloh "The Four-Room House." See also Rösel, "Haus," 138–41.

6. As Dar suggests (*Landscape and Pattern,* 80).

7. Yeivin, *Survey of Settlements,* XIf; for floor plans, see 186–89. His four types are: houses whose entrance is directly on the street and whose courtyard is usually in the back of the house; houses with exterior courts that open out into the street (see t. B. Batra 3:1); houses whose courtyards are inside the house (The rooms then are built around the court. This style is parallel to the buildings at Ostia, Pompeii and Herculaneum); non-symmetric buildings compiled from two squares or more. All of Yeivin's house types are courtyard houses.

8. Hirschfeld, *Palestinian Dwelling,* 21–107. Hirschfeld lists: the simple house, the complex house, the courtyard house, and the peristyle house.

9. Guijarro, "The Family." His housing types are: simple house, courtyard house, mansion, farmhouse, and house with a shop.

10. Botha, "Houses in the World of Jesus."

11. Richardson, "Typology." Richardson's typology has been by far the most comprehensive. The nine rural types are: cave, tent, beehive house, workshop house, farmhouse, villa, fortress-palace, apartment, and monastery. His urban typology includes: one room house, shop-dwelling, row shop, terrace house, side courtyard house, central courtyard house, peristyle house, axial peristyle house, communal courtyard house, apartment, and insula.

12. We will omit types that are not actually relevant to our time period and location. For example, Richardson notes that the beehive house is found in Syria, that urban apartments were rare, and that the shop dwelling and row-shop house were not part of villages in the late Second Temple Period.

The Archaeology of Daily Life

The Simple House

The simple house is "the most basic and commonly found of the Roman-Byzantine dwelling types."[13] It is basically a one-room building (or sometimes a building divided into two or more small rooms) attached to a courtyard. This domestic space minimized the amount of roofed area but still maintained a significant barrier from the public by way of its open-air courtyard. In the example below (Figure 4.1), two series of rooms enclose the courtyard (10 x 15 m.: 1,614 sq. ft.). On the north east there is a living room and two storage rooms or closets and on the southwest, a tower. Based on the pottery, Dar dated the dwelling to the first century BCE.[14]

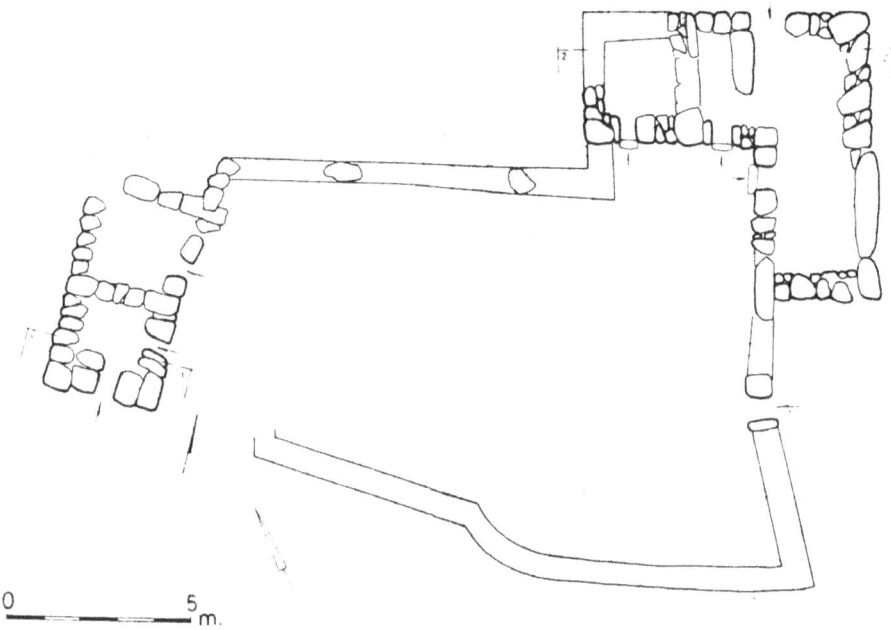

Figure 4.1: Plan of Farmhouse near Umm Rihan (Map 4.1) first century BCE.[15]
The large area is the open-air courtyard.

There would be virtually no personal or individual privacy in such a house but a great deal of family privacy behind the walls of the courtyard. The total area of the domicile tended to be smaller than most of the other types of houses.[16]

---

13. Hirschfeld, *Palestinian Dwelling*, 21.
14. Dar, *Landscape and Pattern*, Part I, 8–9.
15. Dar, *Landscape and Pattern*, Part II, Figure 10. Figure used with permission.
16. Hirschfeld, *Palestinian Dwelling*, 21; Guijarro, "The Family" 50–51.

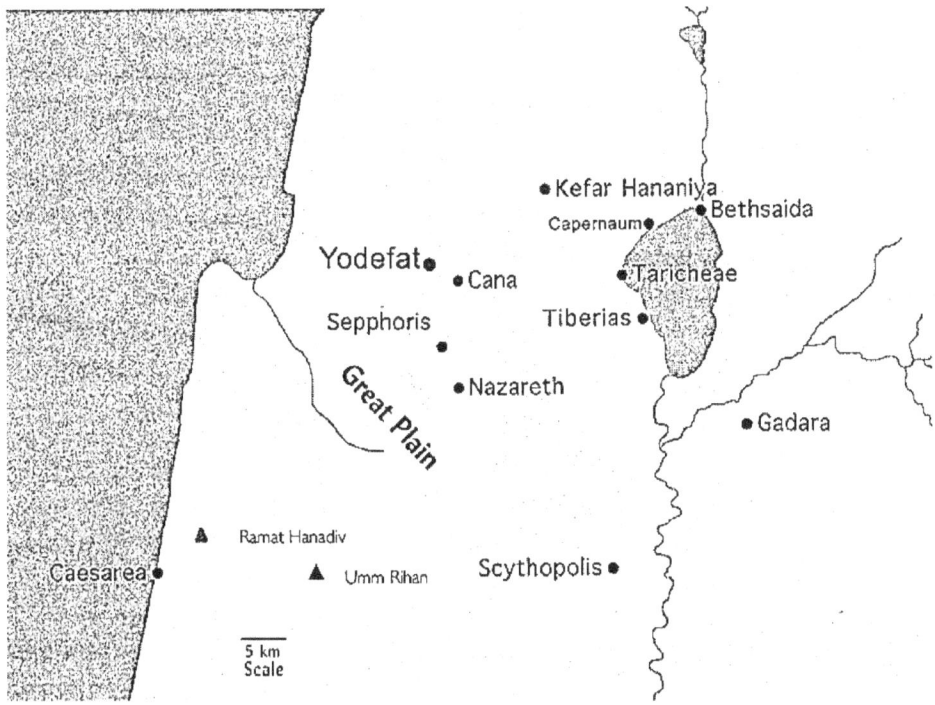

Map 4.1: Galilee and Northern Samaria

The Complex House

This architectural type, an expansion of the simple house, adds more rooms around the courtyard. Hirschfeld divides this type into urban apartment houses and rural farmhouses. The former appear to be phenomena mostly later than our period of concern, ranging in date from the second century CE to the seventh-eighth centuries CE.

The rural farmhouses as complex houses, however, were known in our period. In these cases, a farmhouse was simply gradually enlarged by adding more and more buildings to the compound. A farm house at Qalandiya, a few miles north of Jerusalem (see Chapter 7), which dates from the late Second Temple Period, illustrates this sort of house. The courtyard still dominates the domestic space but multiple rooms have been added over the years to the courtyard until the floor space of the rooms is more than the space of the courtyard. The house features northern rooms (for the family) and southern rooms for storage and for guest workers during harvest and other seasonal needs.[17]

---

17. Hirschfeld, *Palestinian Dwelling*, 52.

THE ARCHAEOLOGY OF DAILY LIFE

Courtyard Houses[18]

This building pattern is found in three forms: houses with side courtyards, houses with inner courtyards but no columns, and peristyle courtyards.

Side Courtyards

According to Peter Richardson,[19] this form of the courtyard house was the standard. It consisted of a roofed house which could be multistoried plus a small courtyard to one side of it. Examples of such houses are found from our period at small towns and villages such as Gamla, Yodefat, and Khirbet Qana (i.e. Cana). Houses with side courtyards could also be a feature in urban settings as the house known as "Insula IV" in Sepphoris.[20] This spacious house included residences, storage rooms, rooms for animals, and a courtyard.

Inner Courtyards

These were usually larger houses. They consisted of central courtyards with rooms on all sides. They have been found at Gamla, Yodefat, Khirbet Qana, Jerusalem, and Sepphoris. One such house in Jerusalem (see Figure 4.2 below and Chapter 2, Figures 2.3 and 2.4), often called the "Palatial Mansion," is a good illustration. It covered around 1,200 m^2 (13,000 sq. ft.), on two floors, surrounded its central courtyard with living rooms and other rooms (including a large "reception hall"), and held an in-door *miqveh*.[21] No houses of this size and grandeur have been found so far in Galilee or in the Judean hinterland.[22]

---

18. Hirschfeld, *Palestinian Dwelling*, 22, 57–85.

19. Richardson, "Typology" 60.

20. E. M. Meyers, "Roman-Period Houses," 487–99. Houses with side courtyards from our period have also been found in Jerusalem.

21. Avigad, *Discovering Jerusalem*, 95–120. The artist's construction of the reception hall is on p. 102. See also Hirschfeld, *Palestinian Dwelling*, 59–62; Richardson, "Typology," 60–61.

22. But see the mansion at Ramat ha-Nadiv NE of Caesarea Maritima, described below.

What Kind of House Would You Have Lived In?

Figure 4.2: The "Palatial Mansion" in Jerusalem, First Century CE[23]

Peristyle Houses

These houses are like those with inner or central courtyards but add roofed colonnades to the courtyard. Hirschfeld calls these house types "atrium houses."[24] They were an even more elaborate style of the central courtyard house. One such house was discovered at Sepphoris, the so-called "Villa" (see Figure 4.3). This was a partially two-story building with an interior, columned courtyard and a roof around three sides of the courtyard. The excavators estimate its size as around 500 m² (5,500 sq. ft).[25]

---

23. Photograph by the author of the model, Wohl Archeological Museum, Jewish Quarter, Old Jerusalem. For the interior of this house, see Figures 2.2 and 2.3.

24. Hirschfeld, *Palestinian Dwelling*, 85.

25. J. F. Strange, Longstaff, and Groh, *Excavations at Sepphoris* 73, 116–18.

The Archaeology of Daily Life

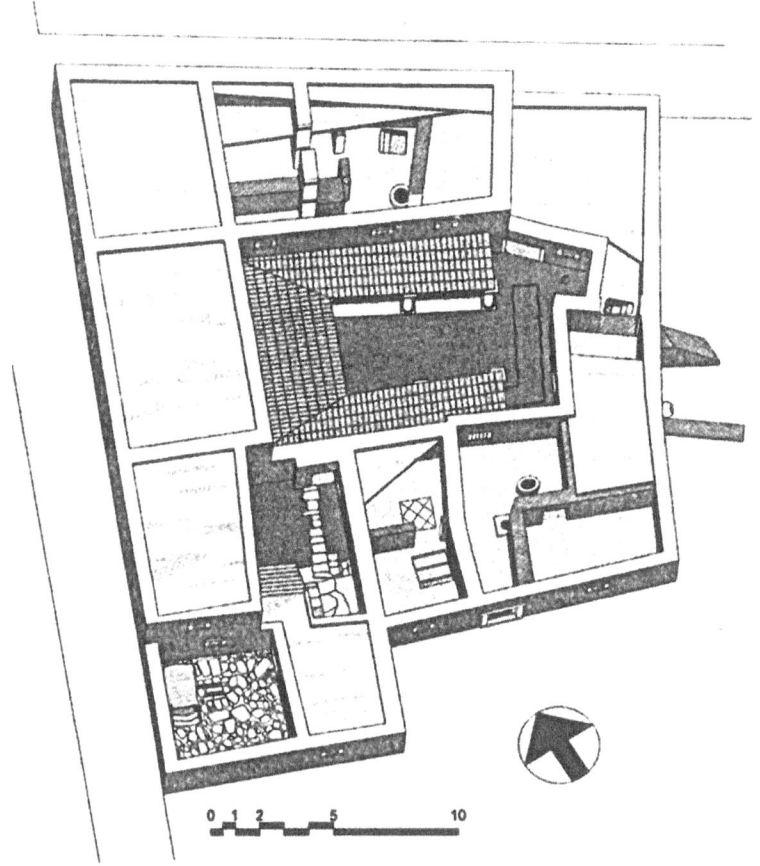

Figure 4.3: The "Villa," Sepphoris[26]

Terrace Houses

These houses were usually constructed without courtyards and were typical in villages and towns built on steep hillsides. In these constructions, the house up the hill used the roof of the lower house as a kind of patio or substitute courtyard. Examples are in Pella, Gamla, Yodefat, and Khirbet Qana.

The "Insula" (or Houses with Communal Courtyards)

In this arrangement several one-room or perhaps two-room houses surrounded a common courtyard. Some authors call these housing clusters *insulae* (Latin: "islands").[27]

---

26. J. F. Strange, Longstaff, and Groh, *Excavations at Sepphoris,* 117. Drawing by James Riley Strange. Used with permission.

27. Beebe, "Domestic Architecture", 96, defines what he calls *insulae*: "An architectural design requiring the construction of a group of buildings standing together in a block or square isolated by

Insulae have been discovered in Rome, Pompeii, Ostia, and other Italian sites.[28] The term has also been used of buildings in Palestine in the Roman period at sites such as Samaria,[29] Capernaum,[30] Meiron,[31] Arbel,[32] and in the Negev,[33] as well as at Dura-Europos in Syria.[34] It seems wisest here, however, to use Richardson's term "houses with communal courtyards"[35] to designate this housing type. Corbo calls these houses "clan dwellings."[36] *Insulae* proper were high-rise apartment buildings (up to seven stories high) in urban settings such as Rome. Villages with one-room houses clustered around a common courtyard do not seem to be the same architectural form.

Figure 4.4: Capernaum: House (allegedly Peter's) with Communal Courtyard[37]

Shimon Dar suggests that the village courtyard houses were originally built separately from each other, but as the villages grew and space became scarce, the buildings began

streets on four sides constitued (sic) the *insula* style of houses" Guijarro ("The Family" 55) defines *insulae* as high-rise apartments like those in Rome. Richardson ("Typology" 61) agrees.

28. For *insulae* in Rome see Carcopino, *Daily Life,* 22–44. On so-called *insulae* in Palestine, see also Bouquet, *Everyday Life,* 36–37.

29. See Crowfoot, Kenyon, and Sukenik, *The Buildings of Samaria,* 128, 137; also Dar, *Landscape and Pattern,* 42–46.

30. Corbo, *House of Saint Peter*; and Corbo, *Carfarnao I* . See also J. F. Strange and H. Shanks "House Where Jesus Stayed."

31. E. M. Meyers et al., *Excavations at Ancient Meiron,* 25–51.

32. Goodman, *State and Society,* 30.

33. Tsafrir and Holum "Rehovot."

34. Rostovtzeff, *Excavation in Dura-Europos.*

35. Richardson, "Typology" 61.

36. Corbo, "Capernaum," 867.

37. Copyright Balage Balogh/www.archaeologyillustrated.com. Used with permission.

to touch each other.³⁸ This suggestion might help explain the appearance of communal courtyards in several Palestinian villages and cities. At any rate, the development of communal courtyards in Palestine, perhaps due both to lack of space and to foreign influence, is a peculiarly Roman period phenomenon.³⁹

Miscellaneous Housing Styles

There were several types of housing that played a small role in the life of the ordinary Jewish village or urban dweller. Therefore, these houses are of least importance for our study but deserve a brief mention. Among these are the cave houses. References in the ancient literature to caves as houses usually have in mind hideouts for bandits or other revolutionaries.⁴⁰ But there are cave dwellings among contemporaneous traditional Palestinians as well.⁴¹ Traditional people use whatever natural resources are available for their housing. Therefore, not all cave dwellers were necessarily bandits or revolutionaries. Also included in this section are tents.⁴² Contemporaneous traditional villages still often leave open spaces for itinerant—or permanent—tent dwellers.⁴³ Monasteries might also be mentioned here. The only example of a monastery from our period of investigation would be Qumran.⁴⁴ Since the (presumably Essene) membership of this monastery was low, it had a relatively small influence on the Early Roman Palestinian people.

The final type of house we will discuss under the heading *Miscellaneous* is the rural mansion (sometimes referred to as a villa) and its related structure, the fortified palace. These were the huge dwellings of the very rich and the rulers of Palestine. One such mansion was located near Caesarea Maritima. This estate (Figure 4.5), on the Ramat Ha-Nadiv ridge (Map 4.1), controlled 2,500 acres according to Hirschfeld and was occupied in the Hellenistic-Roman periods. The most impressive ruins originate from the era that stretches from Herod the Great to the Great Revolt (37 BCE–66 CE). Hirschfeld speculated that this estate belonged to a member of the Herod family. On the estate were two complexes of buildings. The eastern complex, Horvat Eleq, had 150 rooms and was decorated in elaborate marble floor panels. The prominent feature of this mansion was its high tower which may have reached five stories. Hirschfeld

---

38. Dar, *Landscape and Pattern*, 83. On lack of space, see S. Safrai, "Home and Family," 730.

39. See the debate over whether Capernaum remains represent *insulae*: Murphy-O'Connor, *Holy Land*, 254 and Matilla, "Revisiting Jesus' Capernaum." Also see "Complex A" of single room houses at Chorazin in Yeivin, "Ancient Chorazin," which consists of fourteen one-room houses around a common central courtyard.

40. Richardson, "Typology" 55–56, 58; Richardson and Edwards, "Jesus and Palestinian Social Protest," 252.

41. Hirschfeld, *Palestinian Dwelling*, 135, 139, 146, 150–51.

42. Richardson, "Typology" 58 affirms that tents were being used in Galilee in antiquity.

43. Sweet, *Tell Toqaan*, 52–53.

44. Richardson, "Typology" 59. See also Magness, *Archaeology of Qumran*.

surmised that the tower was for defense against irate agricultural workers and bandits. The "manor" house of the estate was also equipped with a Roman bath and with a swimming pool. This was clearly the estate of a very wealthy person. The residents were evidently Jewish since there was an absence of pig bones and presence of stoneware vessels originating from Jerusalem. Again, we must point out that Ramat Ha-Nadiv is not located in Galilee or Judea and that no such country estates have so far been discovered in the Jewish regions of ancient Palestine/Israel.[45]

Figure 4.5: Artist's reconstruction of the mansion at Ramat ha-Nadiv.[46]
On the upper right is the mansion.
On the lower left are the swimming pool and bath house.

The mansion at Ramat Ha-Nadiv was fortified somewhat (the tower) but not effectively against an army. Other rural mansions were fortified heavily. These include the palaces of the Hasmonean and Herodian rulers at Masada, Herodium, Machaerus, and Jericho.[47]

---

45. See Hirschfeld and Feinberg-Vamosh, "A Country Gentleman's Estate," 18–19. See also Hirschfeld, "Early Roman Bath and Fortress," 28–55; Hirschfeld, *Ramat Hanadiv*.

46. Artist's reconstruction by Balage Balogh/www.archaeologyillustrated.com Used by permission.

47. For a summary of Herod the Great's building program, see Roller, *Building Program*, 125–238.

HOW DID THEY BUILD HOUSES?

When one builds a house in the western world today, he/she hires a contractor to do all the work. Occasionally, house owners may do a little of the work to save a bit of money, but most of the work is done by professional builders. But how did one acquire a house in late Second Temple Period Palestine/Israel?

Master Builders

Hirschfeld interviewed several residents in the Hebron hills in the course of his research for his monograph on Palestinian houses. He found that when they built a new house, they almost always employed a professional mason or "master builder." The actual work was done by the family to whom the house would belong, but the master builder supervised the work. The professional builder lived in the community and served the local needs. The master builder learned his profession from his father and grandfather. He used a standard plan (which he kept in his head) but could vary it somewhat according to the needs of the family.[48]

Hirschfeld also believed that most ancient houses in Palestine were built under the supervision of a master builder or stone mason.[49] The rabbinic literature refers to several builders/masons (carpenters?) by name and the rabbis held these builders in high regard. One story illustrates the work of such experts. Students are told to ask Abba Joseph, the builder, a question about the creation of the world. They went to ask him and found him standing on a scaffold. He responded to the students that he could not come down but would try to answer their questions from the scaffold.[50] The point is, the rabbis regarded master builders as very clever people.

Hirschfeld notes that these craftsmen/builders are often mentioned in the Greco-Roman literature and even depicted in wall paintings and sculptures. He assumes that the builders of ancient Palestine/Israel were similar to these.[51]

One is tempted to think of Jesus of Nazareth's family, said to have been carpenters (Mark 6:3; Matt 13:55). Did they function in the same way as master builders for the community? Perhaps they also traveled to other villages to supervise constructions.

Community-Built Houses

But in other areas in the Middle East the building of houses has traditionally been done exclusively by the extended family, rather like a barn-raising in the old American west.

---

48. Hirschfeld, *Palestinian Dwelling*, 113, 115, 120.
49. Hirschfeld, *Palestinian Dwelling*, 226–29.
50. Exod. R. quoted in Hirschfeld, *Palestinian Dwelling*, 228.
51. Hirschfeld, *Palestinian Dwelling*, 227. See his sketch of a mosaic from North Africa depicting a master builder (229) and of a relief sculpture from southern France depicting the architect (231).

Ethnographers report that in contemporary Middle Eastern cultures, each household builds its own house but that distant relatives and neighbors pitch in and help. This is especially true if someone has a special expertise or skill to contribute. In one village, it is the custom for everyone to assist the household and to finish the house building in only a few days.[52]

The house would be finished in only a few days and no one paid any money for the labor.[53] So, one's house could be built at no cost whatsoever, except for the land underneath it.[54]

Building Materials

The first task in building a house was to gather materials. The main materials were stone, mortar (clay soil mixed with water), and wood (for the roof). Builders of houses in contemporary traditional Palestinian villages will pile up the soil in huge heaps and bring in the quarried stones to stack in storage while waiting for the beginning of the construction. The stones may then be cut into "worked stones" (flat-surfaced blocks) or into "hammered" stones (hewn stones from a quarry that were not dressed or field stones with minimal dressing). The stones may also not be worked at all but merely picked up from the ground, especially from a wadi bed, and used as they are.[55]

Most houses in Herodian Palestine were made of stone, either the white limestone so abundant in much of Palestine or the black basalt found north and east of the Sea of Galilee. The exception was in the Sharon Plain and other lower lying areas where houses were built of mud brick.[56] The use of bricks in building houses seems to have been both a necessity for those living in certain regions where stones were

---

52. See Kramer, *Village Ethnoarchaeology*, 94, and Sweet, *Tell Toqaan*, 117. Clark, "Bricks," 38, maintains that it would take four men and a donkey around one month to construct a stone foundation story for a brick house.

53. As reported by Sweet, *Tell Toqaan*, 117. See also Amiry and Tamari, *The Palestinian Village Home*, 20, who write, "House building was a cooperative venture, and involved both men and women."

54. What would a house cost if one were to buy it completely finished? The prices preserved for us show varied costs. Ian Morris ("Archaeology," 126) notes that one could pay in fourth century BCE Greece from 230 drachmas to 5,300 drachmas for a house. Isaeus (2.35) stated that a small house in his day (fourth century BCE) cost 300 drachmas. Morris concludes that a poor, simple house would cost from 200 to 300 drachmas in fourth century BCE Greece. Daniel Sperber (*Roman Palestine*, 106) lists prices for two houses in Palestine in the era of 200 to 400 CE: 200 denarii and 250 denarii. These prices roughly coincide with Morris' price of a small and simple house. Richard Alston ("Houses and Households," 32) gives a table of house prices gleaned from the papyri. Urban houses in the first century CE averaged 853 drachmas; village houses averaged 488 drachmas. In the second century CE the prices were 1,200 drachmas and 500 drachmas respectively. Since the Egyptian drachma may have been worth less than the Greek drachma, these prices are not too far out of line with the other two sources.

55. Hirschfeld, *Palestinian Dwelling*, 217–19, 222.

56. Safrai "Home and Family," 732; and Hirschfeld, *Palestinian Dwelling*, 24. See m. Sotah 8:3 and m. B. Batra 1:1 for mud-brick houses. For the technology of ancient brick building, see Homsher, "Mud Bricks."

not readily available and also a local tradition as the following text from the Mishnah indicates.

> A place where people are accustomed to build with rough stones, hewn stones, rafters, or bricks, they build (that way). Everything is done according to the custom of the region.[57] (m. B. Batra 1:1).

According to Hirschfeld, the ancients used two types of brick: sundried and fired. By far, the most commonly used was the sundried. The disadvantage to this sort of construction was that after a heavy rain, there could be a great deal of damage to the construction. The house might even totally collapse.[58]

A. C. Bouquet also suggested that very poor peasants even in the Hill Country must have had huts built entirely of perishable material (branches, straw, and mud) so that no trace of them has survived.[59] In extreme cases, people may have had no houses at all, but merely wandered from place to place.[60] Homelessness was also known in antiquity.

The Building Process

They began the building by laying out the dimensions of the new house. Next came the excavation of the foundations down to the bedrock. The construction of the walls came next and then the cracks in the walls were filled in with mortar plaster. The houses were constructed of the stone from the area (limestone in Judea and Galilee, basalt in the Golan). They would plaster the interior of the walls next and then build the roof.

Canaan wrote that a new house in traditional Palestinian culture was considered unhealthy for the first year since it remained damp (because the walls were so thick). There was a saying among the peasants: "The first year (give your house) to your enemy, the second to your neighbor and the third (keep it) for yourself."[61] One can believe that the ancient houses were equally damp and unhealthy for the first year or so.

Underground Stables

L. E. Stager also suggests that livestock was usually brought into a room close to the living quarters at night, either underneath (in a dug cave) the living quarters or in a room next to it (see Chapter 6 of this volume). The practice was maintained in the

---

57. Translation from the Hebrew text in Mabratnora, *Six Orders*, II, 67.
58. Hirschfeld, *Palestinian Dwelling*, 221–22.
59. Bouquet, *Everyday Life*, 27.
60. M. Peah 8:7. See Goodman, *State and Society*, 39.
61. Canaan *Arab House*, 49.

Israelite period and is still done by Arabs today. He suggests that side rooms found at Capernaum with "fenestrated walls" actually contained not windows but storage niches for animals. If Stager is correct, then animals often slept on the ground floor or adjoining room to the living quarters.[62]

In addition, there were many houses with stables underground. If there was an excavated area under the floor of the house, it was often for the livestock. We know from excavations, especially in Nazareth (see, e.g., the so called "Grotto of St. Joseph", the underground area of an ancient house), that the ancients also utilized all available space, including the space under the floor of their house to give shelter to their livestock. The photograph below (Figure 4.6), illustrating an underground stable, is from the excavations beneath the courtyard of the Church of the Annunciation in Nazareth:

Figure 4.6: Underground Animal Stable, Church of the Annunciation, Nazareth[63]

---

62. Stager, "Archaeology of the Family" 11–14. For animals sleeping either in the living quarters of the family or under the living quarters, see Hirschefeld, *Palestinian Dwelling*, 120–34, 149, 158–59; Amiry and Tamari, *Palestinian Village Home*, 25–29.

63. Photograph by the author.

The Archaeology of Daily Life

The Roofs

The roofs in ancient Palestine—the more expensive ones[64]—were often made of limestone slabs like those in the traditional, contemporary Palestinian houses.[65] Such roofs were, for obvious reasons very strong but could only stretch a certain length without a support column on the first floor.

But those families of more modest means used wooden beams woven with smaller branches and then covered with plaster. These flat roofs are common in contemporary traditional sites in Israel today and were also the standard in ancient Palestine/Israel. For example, houses, such as those at Capernaum, apparently had roofs of wooden beams and smaller tree branches covered with mud-plaster and straw (cf. Mark 2:4).[66]

These waddle and daub roofs required continual maintenance especially during and just after the rainy season to keep the mud smoothed down. Since the mud-plaster has to be frequently smoothed down, in contemporary traditional houses there is a stone roller left in place on the roof to flatten it on occasion.[67] Undoubtedly the ancients had the same technique. Archaeologists have found stone roof rollers in some houses indicating the ancient method of maintaining their roofs was identical to the traditional Arab method.[68]

In traditional Arab villages where the roofing methods are still employed, the roof lasts on average seventy years.[69] One could evidently tell the house of a poor man by the height of his roof: that of the poor man was very low (b. Sanh. 100b).

The flat roofs often, when the walls were made strong enough to support it, held an upper room, either the full size of the room below or only as a partial second story.[70] There are numerous references to these second stories called עֲלִיָּה (ʿaliyyah) in the Hebrew Bible: Eglon sat in his ʿaliyyah when Ehud assassinated him (Judg 3:20). Elijah brought the dead boy to the ʿaliyyah (1 Kgs 17:19). Ahaziah fell through the lattice in his ʿaliyyah (2 Kgs 1:2). A woman of means made a room in the ʿaliyyah for Elisha

---

64. Krauss, *Talmudische Archäologie*, 1.27; Beebe, "Domestic Archecture," 101; Safrai, "Home and Family," 732; Yeivin, *Survey of Settlements*, XIV. Yeivin, "Ancient Chorazin," 25, describes the basalt roofs of ancient Chorazin.

65. Hirschfeld, *Palestinian Dwelling*, 120–34; Sweete, *Tell Toqaan*, 114–15; Thompson, *Land*, I.132, 386; II.434.

66. J.F. Strange and H. Shanks, "Where Jesus Stayed"; Corbo, *House of St. Peter*, 37.

67. Hirschfeld, *Palestinian Dwelling*, 120–34, 244; Canaan, *Arab House*, 48, 54–55; Sweet, *Tell Toqaan*, 114–15; and Thompson, *Land*, 1.132, 386; 2.434.

68. Dever, *Ordinary People*, 131; Borowski, *Daily Life*, 20; Wright, "Israelite Daily Life," 60.

69. Lancaster and Lancaster, "Jordanian Village," 39.

70. See S. Safrai, "Home and Family" 730; Krauss, *Talmudische Archäology*, 1.29; and Jdt 8:5; Mark 14:15; Acts 1:3; 20:8; m. Shabb. 1:4; m. B. Batra 2:2–3; m. Ned. 7:4. For an example of a flat roof, see E. M. Meyers et al., *Excavations at Ancient Meiron*, 40.

(2 Kgs 4:10).[71] The Greek equivalents were apparently ὑπερῷον ("upper room") and κατάλυμα ("guest room").[72]

Yeivin's survey found several ancient two-story houses still in use by Arabs.[73] The contemporary, traditional village dwellers in Palestine use the upper room for resting in private and for hosting guests and leaders of the clan.[74] The upper story was cooler in summer and perhaps in the winter helped the residents escape some of the barn odors emanating from below when the livestock were stalled there. The second story was especially used as a "wedding house" or "honey moon room" for a son and his wife. They will often live there as long as their family size allows. The upper room could also be for a widowed relative.[75]

In addition, the flat roofed house owners regard the roofs as extensions of the courtyard. One can use the roof for eating, praying, drying food, storing items, and for sleeping. It is a place apart from the noise of the rest of the household.[76] Was this the use of the guest room in Jerusalem that Jesus and his disciples borrowed for the Passover meal (Mark 14:14)?

Although flat roofs were much more common (and less expensive) in our period of concern in this monograph, the residents of ancient Palestine/Israel also sometimes built with vaulted stone roofs. Hirschfeld reports finding several such roofs from the third to the first centuries BCE. The stones were fitted together to form the vault in such a manner that no mortar was used or needed.[77]

Floors

The floors of Herodian period houses were most commonly packed earth. One can also find floors of stone slabs and plastered floors. The elaborate houses of the wealthy might have mosaic floors. Under the floors, people were accustomed to hide treasures, whether food or coins, usually stashed in clay jars. Hirschfeld reports that some houses in Jerusalem have been found that contained stone compartments under the floor, cut into the bedrock, that served as a kind of safe.[78]

---

71. See Stager, "Archaeology," 16.
72. Acts 1:13; 9:37, 39; 20:8; and Mark 14:14//Luke 22:11, respectively. See Danker, *Lexicon*.
73. Yeivin, *Survey of Settlements*, XIV.
74. Arabs in pre-modern times used the roofs of their one-story houses for summer sleeping. Often, according to Dalman (*Haus*, 58–59) they built a small hut on the roof for summer and for hosting guests.
75. Killebrew and Fine, "Qatzrin," 46.
76. Hirschfeld, *Palestinian Dwelling*, 246–47.
77. Hirschfeld, *Palestinian Dwelling*, 239–40.
78. Hirschfeld, *Palestinian Dwelling*, 270–72.

The Archaeology of Daily Life

THE COURTYARD

The courtyard (חָצֵר, *hatser* [Heb.]; αὐλή, *aule* [Greek]), has been especially important in both the ancient and contemporary (traditional) Palestinian houses. It was the place of both domestic work and leisure; the place to find privacy from the street and to meet and talk to neighbors and kinsmen. For most of the year the family ate in the courtyard and even slept there in the hot months. Krauss described the courtyard as follows:

> The courtyard was occasionally dug up and planted with decorative trees and fruit trees or vines. One walked around at leisure, ate, did the wash, and took care of all business necessary in life in the courtyard.[79]

As the archaeological remains and literature show, the courtyard often contained ovens, cisterns, toilets, millstones, gardens, ponds, chicken coops, dovecotes, and fruit trees.[80] Krauss suggests that many of these things were the common property of all sharing the courtyard.[81] The Mishnah refers to several uses of courtyards:

> He puts in the courtyard cattle, an oven, stoves, and a millstone; and he raises chickens and puts his compost in the courtyard … (m. B. Batra 3:5).[82]

Hirschfeld also emphasized that the courtyard was as important as the roofed portion of the house itself in the activities of the family. "It seems that the (roofed) house functioned primarily as a storehouse and pantry in the summer months, while the family lived outside in the courtyard both day and night."[83] That the traditional middle-eastern folk live mostly out of doors, except when weather forbids it, is commonly reported by local informants.[84]

Most courtyards appear to have been encircled with a wall at least two meters high (6½ ft.).[85] Hirschfeld observes that maintaining privacy was an important reason for the courtyard walls. The Mishnah refers to a courtyard in which a man is not ashamed to eat (m. Ma'as. 3:5), meaning a courtyard in which one can eat without

---

79. Krauss, *Talmudische Archäologie*, I.46. Krauss cites t. Ma'as. 2:8, 2:20, j. B. Batra 2.7, j. Shabb. 6.1

80. See Schwartz, "Realities," 435; Killebrew, "Village and Countryside," 199.

81. M. B. Batra 3:5, m. Pes. 1:1, m. 'Erub. 8:6, m. Ohol. 5:6, t. Ma'as. 3.8, 2:20. t. B. Batra 2:14, 2:16, 3:1. See Safrai, "Home and Family" 730; Krauss, *Talmudische Archäologie* I.46; Strange and Shanks, "Where Jesus Lived," 34; Yeivin, *Survey of Settlements*, XVII. For chicken coops and dovecotes see Hirschfeld, *Palestinian Dwelling*, 141, 142, 145, 153, 154–55.

82. Translation from the text of Mabratnorah, *Six Orders*, II, 75.

83. Hirschfeld, *Palestinian Dwelling*, 139.

84. See, e.g., Rihbany, *Syrian Christ,* 241–313.

85. S. Safrai, "Home and Family," 729; m. 'Erub. 7:1, m. B. Batra 1:4, t. 'Erub. 6:13–14. For archaeological evidence, see, e.g., Meiron in E. M. Meyers, J. F. Strange, and C. Meyers, *Excavations at Meiron*; and Corbo, *The House of St. Peter*. See also Krauss, *Talmudische Archäologie*, I, 45.

outsiders observing.⁸⁶ Courtyards, as in Meiron,⁸⁷ may have had flagstone pavements, or, more often, were simply packed dirt.

Some courtyards must have been quite small. The Mishnah (m. B. Batra 1:6) rules the smallest one can make a courtyard by dividing it up was 4 cubits or 2 meters (2 x 2 meters).⁸⁸ But most courtyards were much larger. The Tosephta (t. ʿErub. 7:9) refers to a courtyard of 10 cubits or 5 meters (i.e., 5 x 5 meters?) as "small." The courtyard in Meiron I was 7.5 x 5 meters (24 x 16 ft.).⁸⁹ A typical courtyard described by Dar for the village of Hirbet Buraq in Samaria was of similar size. Most of the ancient rural houses surveyed by Hirschfeld had rather large courtyards (see Figure 4.1).

Communal courtyards (see above for this type) appear, according to the Mishnah, to have had two to three houses. M. ʿArak. 9:6 describes a walled city as needing at least three courtyards with two houses in each.⁹⁰ M. B. Batra 6:7 has several rules for houses sharing a courtyard. One would think rules necessary for life that closely shared.

Dar found in Samaria that most courtyards contained five or six living quarters or houses, but notes that the later courtyard houses (Roman-Byzantine) tended to become smaller.⁹¹ Hirschfeld found houses (he calls them "apartments") in Hebron which shared courtyards.⁹² Yet at Capernaum and Chorazin, there were clusters of fourteen to fifteen one room houses sharing a courtyard.⁹³ The Tosephta refers to those sharing a common courtyard as "members of the courtyard" (t. ʿErub, 7:7, 14).

In addition to the living quarters which were attached to the courtyard, one could find other buildings used for crafts, for animals (cattle barns), straw sheds, wood sheds, and storage houses for wine and oil.⁹⁴ Krauss maintained that animals would have been kept in buildings behind the living quarters, or when there were two courtyards, in the second courtyard.⁹⁵

Thus, the courtyard was the main living area for a family. The indoors, for most families except the wealthy, were for escaping from inclement weather.

---

86. Hirschfeld, *Palestinian Dwelling*, 272.
87. E. M. Meyers, J. F. Strange, C. Meyers, *Excavations at Meiron*, 40.
88. Danby (*The Mishnah,* 366) understands the size to be 4 x 4 cubits.
89. E. M. Meyers, J. F. Strange, C. Meyers, *Excavations at Meiron*, 40.
90. Cf. m. ʿArak. 9:7; t. Maʾas. 2:20.
91. Dar, *Landscape*, 85.
92. Hirschfeld, *Palestinian Dwelling*, 273.
93. But see Matillah, "Revisiting," for an alternate view of Capernaum.
94. See E. M. Meyers et al., *Excavations at Ancient Meiron*, 33–37; Safrai, "Home and Family" 729; Yeivin, *Survey of Settlements*, XV; b. Pes. 8a; m. ʿErub. 8:4; m. B. Batra 2:2–3, 4:4.
95. Krauss, *Talmudische Archäologie* I.46. See b.Yoma 11a, b. Pes. 8a.

The Archaeology of Daily Life

Figure 4.7: Courtyard of first-century house excavated in Nazareth. Notice the cistern at bottom of the photo (photo by the author)

CONCLUSION

If you, the reader, had lived in Palestine/Israel in the late Second Temple Period (or ER I period), what sort of house would you probably have had? You would likely have lived in a house with stone walls, a dirt floor, and a flat waddle and daub roof. Your house would have been one room—possibly two rooms—and it would have shared a courtyard with other nuclear families, most likely your cousins. You would have built your house with materials you gathered locally at no cost: stones, wood, and clay soil for mortar. Your family would have provided the labor to build the house but you may have employed a master builder to supervise the work. Your family basically would have lived out of doors for most of the year in the courtyard. Your courtyard would have afforded you privacy from outsiders but still would have taken you out into the open air. Indoors would mainly have been used only for inclement weather and for storage. Your house may have had a cave beneath it for storage of food and for sheltering animals. If you lived in a village (which would be probable) your house, including courtyard, would have been around 300 m^2 (3,229 sq. ft.) in size.

5

What Would Your Family Dynamic Have Been Like?

THE FAMILY WAS THE most important social unit in the late Second Temple Period in Israel. What was it like to grow up in one of those families—for boys and for girls? How did one get married? What new information has archaeology brought to us recently that helps us envision the Jewish family of Palestine/Israel during the time of Jesus and the Gospels?

One must allow that families were not carbon copies of one another. As Miriam Peskowitz[1] has wisely cautioned, families took many forms. Some extended families lived in the same compound; others in adjacent compounds. Families may have been structured around males who worked away and traveled to find work; other families kept their men at home. Some families were well off enough to hire day laborers to assist them or even to own slaves. Some, undoubtedly, sent their sons off to learn a trade or even sold them into slavery for a while to enhance the family's financial situation. Some families were polygamous. We will try to note some of these nuances below but in a discussion of family in first-century Palestine/Israel one tends to generalize. What follows is mostly an abstraction from the sources with a few irregularities and variations noted as well.

CHILDREN

One of the first things one would encounter upon entering a typical house would have been, of course, the children. The book of Genesis makes it clear that God's people are supposed to "be fruitful and multiply" (Gen 1:28). The rabbis of the Mishnah took this commandment very seriously. They even prescribed how many children a couple

---

1. Peskowitz, "Family/ies," 14–15.

should have (minimally): two. The School of Shammai wanted two sons; the school of Hillel wanted a son and a daughter (m. Yebam. 6:6). The point was, no couple should refrain from producing children (abstain from sex) until they had met those minimal numbers. To postpone producing children was compared, in one text, to shedding blood because of the children one could have brought into the world and did not (b. Yebam. 63b).

Daughters

One could say that, in general, sons were more valued. The most striking statement to this effect comes to us in the book of Sirach, a sage who lived in Palestine in the early second century BCE. He writes:

- "when a daughter is born, (the family) is diminished" (22:3)[2]
- "a daughter secretly causes many sleepless nights to her father"[3] (42:9)

The preference for males is also found in Josephus' writings. In the place where he is explaining the "Water of Bitterness," which the wife suspected of adultery was made to drink (Num 5:11–31), he changes the text of the Bible by adding his own interpretation. He relates the straightforward text of the Bible that if the suspected adulteress drinks the water and it does not cause abdominal pain, she will be able to conceive children in the future. That means she is innocent. But then Josephus adds something to it: he says that she will be able to bear *male* children (*Ant.* 3.271) instead of females. In other words, where the biblical text simply promises that the innocent wife will be fertile (Num 5:28), Josephus promises that she will conceive male children as a kind of consolation for having been falsely accused.

At least two texts in the rabbinic literature repeat Josephus' explanation of this text (b. Ber. 31b; b. Sotah 26a). These texts promise to the woman proven to be innocent of the charge of adultery (by drinking the Water of Bitterness) that from then on, childbirth will be a dream: If she had previously born children in pain, she will now bear them easily; if she had previously given birth to dark-skinned children, now she will bear light-skinned children; if she had produced short offspring, she will now have tall ones; and *if she had been bearing females, she will now bear only males* (emphasis mine). In other words, included in this list of biased preferences for children is the prioritizing of male babies. The rabbi speaking in the Talmud (R. Ishmael) passes on Josephus' interpretation of (or spin on) the "Water of Bitterness" text from Numbers 5.[4]

In the rabbinic literature female children are often denigrated: "blessed is he whose children are male, and woe to him whose children are female" (b. B. Batra

---

2. My translation. Compare: "the birth of a daughter is a loss" (NRSV).
3. My translation. Compare: "a daughter is a secret anxiety to her father" (NRSV).
4. On this subject, see Archer, *Her Price*, 19.

16b = b. Sanh. 100b).⁵ They prayed for male babies to be born (m. Ber. 9:3). Further, anyone who does not have a son is as if dead (Gen. R. 45.2). If a man was told that his wife bore him a son he should say, "He that is good, does good" (evidently produces a son; b. Ber. 59a). Allegedly Abraham was blessed because he did not have daughters (t. Qidd. 5:17). The extra-Talmudic tractate, *Semaḥot* 8.7 (see Chapter 11), laments a man who died without a son. Finally, in the days of king David—as the rabbis tell the story—all the people were blessed because they bore only sons (b. B. Qama 9a).⁶ Clearly, families—well, maybe just the fathers—wanted sons.

On the other hand, these sources—from Sirach to the Talmud—come from wealthy and elite authors. We do not know positively how the ordinary people regarded the birth of girls. The literary sources we have show a marked favoritism for boys but they *may* not represent all levels of society. How would a poor family have received the birth of a girl? I surmise they would have thought similarly to the elite class. This speculation is re-enforced by contemporary Middle Eastern ethnographies. Canaan, for example, reports a saying current among the Palestinian Arabs of his day: "nothing will make men happy (lucky) except their (male) children" echoing the rabbinic texts cited above.⁷ Likewise, Tannous relates a saying in Arab culture: "May Allah give you a son." No one, Tannous continues, ever says may Allah give you a daughter.⁸ Nevertheless, our lack of sources here should make us cautious with our conclusions.⁹ We have no ancient texts from the lower classes or working classes that speak on this or any other topic, however.

Child Exposure

Although the literary sources that have survived evidence a preference for boys, there was allegedly no child exposure among Judaism as the pagans so often practiced (leaving unwanted babies—usually girls—along the roadside or in the woods to die, be eaten by animals, or picked up by strangers). Josephus writes that the Old Testament Law commands that a couple must raise all children and forbids any woman from an abortion (*Apion* 2.202). Philo, based on Exod 21:22 (LXX), argues that this scripture forbids exposing children (*Spec. Leg.* 3:110). Another Jewish work (Ps.-Phoc. 184–185) also teaches against both exposure and abortions: "Do not let a woman destroy the unborn babe in her belly, nor after its birth throw it before the dogs and

---

5. See Collins, "Marriage, Divorce, and Family," 142; trans. Neusner, *Babylonian Talmud*.
6. For these references, see Ilan, *Jewish Women*, 44–45.
7. Canaan, *Arab House*, 27.
8. Tannous, "Arab Village," 538.
9. Other cultures today devalue girls as well. The situation is grim in mainland China. See Cheung and Berlinger, "12 Year Old," who report on "blood mules" who carry blood samples to Hong Kong for sex testing. If the mother is pregnant with a girl, she will have an abortion. Infanticide is also common for girls.

the vultures as a prey."[10] Even Judaism's pagan critics admitted its strong objections to child exposure and abortion (Tacitus, *Hist.* 5.5 "it is a crime among [Jews] to kill any new born infant"; Diodorus Siculus 40.3.7: "[Moses] required [Jews] to rear their children").[11] Thus, one would think it a given that there was no child exposure among first-century Jews in Palestine/Israel.

And yet, there are challenges to this view. Catherine Hezser points out that foundlings—children abandoned on the streets—were assumed in the Mishnah. For example, see m. Qidd. 4:2: "an *asufi* . . . (is any child who) was picked up from the street and knows neither his father nor his mother" (see also m. Maksh. 2:7).[12] But if there are children abandoned on the streets, that certainly constitutes the Roman equivalent of *expositio*[13] or child exposure. The fact that the Mishnah casually refers to such children and their genealogical pedigree means that it was not an uncommon occurrence. There was, argues Hezser, child exposure in first-century Palestine/Israel even among the Jews.

If there was child exposure—abandoning children on the street or roadside—why all the strong testimony from both Jews and pagans alike that it did not happen among Jews? One would think that it was not as common among Jews as among Greeks and Romans. There was a forceful command—a strong taboo—against it. But no religious or social group ever has total compliance with mores and/or ethics. When times became critical economically, some families evidently compromised religiously and left their babies, perhaps even toddlers, alongside the road.

Selling Children

Further, there existed also the practice of selling children, especially girls. Whenever a family found itself in financial difficulty—from debt or famine—it would turn to whatever resources it had. The children might be seen in that case as a financial asset, something to be sold either for profit or to be traded for debt forgiveness. Exodus 21:7–11 tells about a man selling his daughter. Nehemiah 5:1–5 tells of selling children into slavery to pay taxes. The rabbinic texts agree that the father had the power—as *pater familias*—to sell his daughter (m. Ket. 3:8; m. Sotah 3:8; m. Qidd. 1:2). The only stipulation was that the girls must be sold before they reached puberty. Otherwise, their sale would be the same as prostitution.

10. Translation by van der Horst, "Pseudo-Phocylides."

11. See Safrai, "Home and Family," 750; R. S. Kraemer, "Jewish Mothers and Daughters"; and Hezser, "Exposure and Sale of Infants." Translation of Tacitus is Church and Brodribb, *Tacitus* and of Diodorus is Walton, *Diodorus of Sicily*.

12. See Hezser, "Exposure," 13–15. Translation from Danby, *Mishnah*. On this issue, see also Mayer, *Jüdische Frau*, 43. Mayer observes, based on the texts cited above, that exposing infants was "unthinkable." Yet, he adds: "Whether theory and practice agreed . . . is questionable" (43).

13. For the Greco-Roman practice of child exposure, see Bakke, *When Children Became People*, 110–51.

The sale of sons and daughters as debt slaves is highlighted in a parable in the Sifre on Deut 26. There a man owes a large wheat debt to a king. The king seizes all the children of the house and sells them off as repayment on the loan.[14] Childhood could be a time of horror for little ones in the ancient world.[15]

Naming

Children were usually named after their fathers or grandfathers (for boys) or after their mothers or grandmothers (for girls).[16] That tended to recycle the same names. The two most popular female names in the late Second Temple Period were Mariamme-Maria or Salome-Shelamzion (meaning "peace" and "peace of Zion" respectively), the two names accounting for nearly half of all. Thus, it was not uncommon to encounter a lot of women named Mary (as in John 19:25) even in the same family.[17] The most common boys' names were: Simon (or Simeon), Joseph (or Joses), Eleazar (or Lazarus), Judas (or Judah), John (or Yohanan), and Joshua (or Jesus).[18]

Childhood Stages

The sources describe the childhood of boys and girls differently indicating that the authors of the sources (undoubtedly males) thought of their development in very different ways. There is a text in the Mishnah[19] that lays out the progress for boys according to what a young man should be learning and doing in his life religiously. It compares interestingly with a somewhat similar text from the Dead Sea Scrolls from Qumran, the so-called "Charter for Israel in the Last Days"[20] or 1QSa. There are two texts in the Mishnah that also refer to the development of girls. But the contrast is striking. While

---

14. Hezser, "Exposure," 25. Cf. Matt 18:25.

15. Selling children still happens in the Middle East. See Walsh and Popalzai, "Mother Had 'No Other Choice.'" A six year old girl was sold in 2018 due to economic stress in her family. The buyer promised to make her the wife of his ten year old son.

16. But we know of at least one woman who was named after her father: Yohannah for her father Yohannan. See Hillel Geva, "Tombs," 756 for the inscription on her ossuary. Yohannan was son of the high priest Theophilus.

17. Reich, "Ossuary Inscriptions"; Ilan, *Jewish Women,* 54–55; and Mayer, *Jüdische Frau,* 41. Salome also appears in the New Testament (Mark 10:40, 16:1).

18. Reich, "Ossuary Inscriptions"; and Bauckham, *Jesus and the Eyewitnesses,* 85. Bauckham drew his lists from the New Testament, from Josephus, from the inscriptions on the ossuaries found in Palestine, and from the Judean desert texts. Other female names found frequently—though nowhere close to the female names given above—were Martha, Joanna, and Saphira (Bauckham, *Jesus and the Eyewitnesses,* 89).

19. See Schofer, "Different Life Stages." The Mishnah text is, according to Schofer, quite late but based on early synthesis of the "ways in which rabbis conceptualized the male life cycle from birth to death" (339).

20. This is the title given by Wise, Abegg, and Cook, *Dead Sea Scrolls,* 136. Another title is "Rule of the Congregation." See Schofer, "Life Stages," 330. The text dates from the first century BCE.

the Mishnah text and the Qumran text talk about boys growing in their understanding of religious obligations,[21] the Mishnah texts referring to girls focus on their growth into physical maturity in order to bear children. Here are the four texts:

Boys		Girls	
m. Avot 5:21	1QSa 1:7–8	m. Nidd. 5:7	m. Ket. 3:8
		The sages describe the girls' childhood as a parable:	The sages describe the penalty for raping a girl based on her age[22]
Age 5 years: for reading the Bible		She is like an unripe fig (only a child)	Under age twelve, she is a minor קְטַנָּה
Age 10 years: for learning Mishnah	Age 0–10 years: counted among the small children,[23] learns the Book of Hagi[24]		
		She is like a ripening fig (prepubescent girl)	Between ages twelve and twelve and a half, she is a girl נַעֲרָה
Age 13 years: for fulfilling the commandments (knows right from wrong)		She is like a ripened fig (fully ready to marry and bear children)	Past her girlhood, over age twelve and a half בֹּגֶרֶת
Age 15 years: for learning Talmud			
Age 18 years: for marriage			
Age 20 years: for pursuing a trade/business	Age 20 years: is enrolled in the ranks, can marry, knows right from wrong		

Table 5:1: Descriptions of Childhood Phases in Judaism

As the table illustrates, boys had to learn their religious responsibilities, how to make a living, and to take their place in the community. Girls just had to have babies. Of

---

21. Schofer, "Life Stages," 334: "the salient aspect of rabbinic thinking about young girls is their sexuality and potential for marriage and procreation." Schofer also refers to a rather silly list of life stages for boys in Eccl. R. 1.2 which compares their growth to various animals: age 1 year = a king on a litter (everyone makes a fuss); age 2–3 = a pig, always sticking their hands in the gutters; age 10 = a baby goat; age 20 = a horse, adorning his person and longing for a wife; after he marries = a donkey (working hard); after children come = a dog (brazen to supply food for the family); when he becomes old = an ape (no longer looks like a man).

22. See Archer, *Price is Beyond Rubies*, 44.

23. The word used here, טַף (*taph*), means a child so small in a wandering tribe that he/she is not "fit to march." Evidently, the smaller children rode animals when the tribes migrated. See W. Holladay, *Lexicon*, 125.

24. Is this a reference to the Torah or to some other wisdom book? See Schofer, "Life Stages," 331.

course, all four of these childhood development descriptions were written by males. How would a female have written them?

Childhood and Play

Did the children have a "normal" childhood full of play, games, and imagination? Well, probably not in the western, modern sense. The children probably started working at age five.[25] The younger children watered animals, gleaned in the fields, ran errands for their mother, helped care for elderly family members (if there were any; see Chapter 10), and gathered firewood (Jer 7:18).[26] The older children worked alongside adults, the girls making bread and watching the babies of the family; the boys out in the fields carrying rocks, plowing, planting, harvesting, and taking care of the sheep and goats.[27]

In addition, a father could hire out his children as day laborers, evidently at a very young age. Mishnah B. Metzia 7:6 gives the rules for compensation to the landowner should the laborer eat too much of the produce during his/her daily snack. The children must also agree to refrain from eating too much—if they are of an age to understand the agreement. Evidently, some were too young to comprehend. Thus, a man could hire out not only himself and his wife (m. B. Batra 7:6) but also his children to work the seasonal agricultural jobs.[28]

But these tasks would not have ruled out play entirely. The desire to play is a universal childhood phenomenon. Kristine Garroway has surveyed the types of play indicated in the literary sources and in archaeological remains. The types most relevant to our time period are:

1. Clay figurines of chariots and perhaps animals (though technically prohibited in the Torah)

2. Throw-away objects from the nearest garbage dump (old tools, broken pots, etc.; b. Shabb. 121 b)

3. Miniature clay vessels made by children. Archaeologists noticed finger prints on some tiny vessels and concluded that they were made by children perhaps in imitation of their parents' occupation.

---

25. C. Meyers, "Family," 27. But see *Rediscovering Eve,* 137, where she suggests age 6 as the start of work for children. Garroway, *Children,* 143, notes that some ancient Near Eastern legal texts refer to age 5 as the start of work for children (who have been sold as slaves) but opines that it really depended on the individual child. She suggests that somewhere between the ages of 4 and 6 a child was considered able to work. Naomi Steinberg (*World of the Child,* 78–80) found that age 4–5 was a transition in the Israelite life cycle. Lev 27:5–6 seems to make age 5 a turning point in childhood.

26. King and Stager, *Life in Biblical Israel,* 65; Garroway, *Children,* 45; C. Meyers, *Rediscovering Eve,* 52.

27. Ebeling, *Women's Lives,* 46.

28. Cf. Scheidel, "Real Wages"; and Garroway, *Children,* 155–58, for hiring out children in Roman Egypt and in the ancient near east respectively.

4. Village games such as shepherd/sheep/wolf in which one child plays the wolf and tries to steal away the sheep (a game still played in the Middle East).

5. They also played with pets such as birds, grasshoppers, and tame cattle (Job 4:29; m. Shabb. 9:7; t. B. Qama 2:2; b. B. Batra 20a)

6. They crafted tops and other spinning toys out of broken pieces of pottery.[29]

The presence of these toys in the material remains and the allusion to the games in the literature show that children, even those challenged by work burdens, will find a way to play. Did they play games as children do now? One would think that they must have but they also worked as much as they were physically capable in a day.[30] They must have played when they could, perhaps at the end of the day.

By age thirteen (or adulthood), children were doing a full day's work like an adult.[31] There was no youth as we know it (pre-teens and teens congregating for leisure). For most children, as a matter of fact, until modern times, their "youth" was one of work, either on a farm, in a shop, or (during our industrial age) in a factory.

One example of the youthful obligation, current in traditional Middle Eastern society, is watching livestock. Most adult men, if given the choice, will not tend to the sheep and goats in the Middle East as it is viewed as beneath them. Either boys are given that task or men of low class.[32]

So, was their childhood and youth "normal?" Yes, it was normal—for that day and place. But it was doubtless full of work just as soon as the child was capable to do any. Whether it was a magical time, as we try to make our children's youth, is highly doubtful.

Were Girls Slighted?[33]

Recently, some historians have made the controversial claim that girls were underfed and under-cared for. Nathan MacDonald, for example, suggests, based on a study of the skeletal remains of Tel Qiri (Persian period) in the Jezreel valley that Jewish women may have been underfed, at least in terms of the available meat. The women in

29. Garroway, *Growing Up*, 202–12, 215–18.

30. Children growing up in Mesopotamia also had toys. See Garroway, *Children*, 46.

31. C. Meyers, "Family," 27. But C. Meyers (*Rediscovering Eve*, 137) later decides that they begin at age 10 to work as an adult.

32. Fuller, *Buarij*, 45; Lutfiyya, *Baytin*, 28, 30. When grown men are forced by economic necessity to tend sheep and goats, they are often made fun of. In the country of Jordan today, the herders of sheep and goats in a village may often be Iraqi refugees. They are considered the lowest class. Even the boys do not like doing it evidently. Fuller (45) observed that the job was often given to a wayward son, to a dullard, or to an orphan. On the other hand, Borowski (*Every Living Thing*, 48) points out that the Bedouin (i.e. those not tied to a village) use young girls for tending the sheep and goats. The girls continue in this task until marriage. In the Hebrew Bible, one can find references both to unmarried girls tending goats (Rebecca, Rachel, and Leah) and to boys (David).

33. For a survey of the plight of young girls today, see Ahuja, "Day in the Life of a Girl."

this village were unusually shorter than the men. The physical anthropologist who examined the human skeletal remains suggested that the men ate meat and the women were not given meat. MacDonald seems inclined to accept this interpretation and to suggest that it applied also in other periods of Israelite history but does caution us that the sample size was only five males and three females.[34]

In my opinion, such a small sample size should be discarded. Even were the sample size a bit larger, it would not prove that the women were smaller because of the preferential feeding of males. Further, one must assume frequent meals of meat in the village of which the females were deprived. It may well be that the villagers seldom ate meat. Thus, even if the women were denied meat, it would not make much of a difference in their nutrition. There is thus no hard evidence, from the Tel Qiri excavation at least, that the women and girls were deprived of nutrition in favor of the men.

A similar suggestion was offered by Tal Ilan based on her analysis of skeletal remains from a first-century CE Jerusalem tomb and a first-fourth century CE tomb in Upper Galilee. She notes that in the Jerusalem tomb three children had died of starvation. She discounts "external political factors" (I take it the Jewish War which starved many persons) and then also suggests that the children were female (not indicated by the physical anthropologists who examined the remains) and that they were underfed by their parents. She next turns to the tomb at Meiron in Galilee and notes that of the eleven children between the ages of thirteen and eighteen that had died, ten of them were female and one was male. She suggests that the ten females died from malnutrition (but offers no specific pathological evidence from the skeletal remains).[35]

Both of these cases are highly dubious and not based on good historical method. It requires a great deal of speculation when several other causes (more reasonable) could be cited for the childhood deaths. Why discount "political factors" in the cases of the Jerusalem remains? Why does she opine that the skeletal remains are female? Why posit that the females in the Meiron tomb died from starvation?

Is it possible that girls were underfed and subsequently died from starvation? Many things are possible but we need positive evidence for such a conclusion. So far, there is none.

One can understand MacDonald's and Ilan's sensitivity to this culture. When one considers the culture of the contemporary Middle East—which may also have been the culture of late Second Temple Palestine/Israel in its valuation of women—one has little trouble imagining females eating after the males have eaten.

---

34. MacDonald, *Israelites Eat?*, 87.

35. See Ilan, *Integrating*, 205. See also Wells, "Obstetric Hazards," for a similar argument relevant to classical Greece: Greek girls were allegedly deprived of food, a claim also, in my opinion, based on speculation.

But such a possibility certainly does not mean that females were fed less or sometimes not fed at all. The Torah prohibited reducing the food of even a female *slave* let alone one's daughter.[36]

Further, rabbinic texts should cast doubt on the hypothesis that female family members were undernourished. Feeding a female family member was a priority in later Jewish law as represented by the Mishnah. In two almost identical texts, the female "maintenance" (food and clothing) take precedence over the male inheritance (m. Ket. 13:5//m. B. Batra 9:1). Even if the males had no inheritance at all these texts state, the female maintenance had to be, by law, honored. Another text (t. Ket. 4:8) states that "It is a religious duty to support the daughters, and one need not say, the sons. R. Yoḥanan b. Baroqah says, 'It is an obligation to support the daughters.'"[37] One gets no hint—even in the chauvinistic rabbinic literature—of starving females.

Finally, one of the texts from the Dead Sea area (Mur 115; see Table 5.3) requires maintenance of daughters. In this marriage contract, it stipulates that both the sons and daughters must be fed and clothed by the husband: "and of the children which (the wife) has and which she may have by him, sons and daughters . . . they will be nourished and clothed with the help of the goods of the same Eleaios. . . ."[38]

To be more cautious, perhaps one could surmise *at most* not that the women and girls were deprived of meat (or food) entirely but may have been deprived of the best cuts of meat. In such an understanding the choicest parts would go to the father, the second best went to his oldest son, and so forth. In this scenario, the women ate last but certainly still ate. The reader should remember that when a lamb, e.g., was butchered, it had to be eaten within a day since otherwise the meat would spoil. They needed everyone in the family to join in the feast. I find the hypothesis of female nutritional deprivation unconvincing.

MARRIAGE

The marriage of one's children is a huge event in the family. It symbolizes passing the torch to the next generation to continue the human race, to continue the family values, and to produce food and safety for the community. The event is probably equally important in every culture. But the way the event is done varies.

How Old Were They When They Married?

The girls were usually married off, in a rather business-like way, by their parents by the time they were thirteen years old. Sabine Huebner notes that throughout the

---

36. See Garroway, *Children*, 128, and Exod 21:10 for a prohibition of reducing a female slave's food.

37. Translation in Neusner, *Tosephta*. See also Hamel, *Poverty*, 41 who dates Yohanan b. Baroqa to early second century.

38. Translation in Archer, *Her Price Is Beyond Rubies*, 296.

Mediterranean world in antiquity (she lists specifically Rome, Athens, and Egypt) girls married in their mid-teens.³⁹ Thomas Gallant agrees that girls married in their mid-teens (ages 16–19) in ancient Greece, but perhaps late teens, in the first two centuries of the Roman imperial world.⁴⁰ The rabbinic texts indicate the same for the Jewish girls of Palestine. The texts demonstrate that a young girl (נַעֲרָה)—a virgin or prepubescent girl—would be betrothed at age twelve to twelve and a half and married about one year later (m. Ket. 5:2). A widow would be betrothed for thirty days (m. Ket. 5:2). The rabbis urged parents to marry their children close to their age of puberty.⁴¹ They cautioned strongly against waiting to marry both sons and daughters (b. Sanh. 76a). There were even cases of marrying girls younger than age thirteen—one rabbi suggested as young as age three!—but the reader never knows if these are exaggerations (b. Yebam. 100b).⁴²

These texts can be very unrealistic and theoretical. More in touch in reality would be actual examples of marriages. Tal Ilan has collected some data on marital ages of brides. In some cases, she had to calculate the ages but in others the ages were given. Berenice (daughter of Agrippa I) was probably married at age thirteen. Mariamme was around sixteen when she wed Herod the Great. Queen Salome Alexandra was twenty-seven when she married (quite old for that era). Some inscriptions from Israel offer even more evidence: One from the cemetery at Bet She'arim (Besara on Map 7.2) refers to a woman who died a virgin at age twenty-two. Three inscriptions at Nablus list girls that died at ages eighteen, fourteen, and twelve. Only the oldest of the three was married. We should at least go back one year and assume she was married at age seventeen, perhaps earlier. Finally, an inscription from Tiberias refers to a girl age twenty-two who was unmarried (though betrothed) at her death.⁴³ In our calculations below, we will not consider those who died unmarried since we cannot know if they ever would have married or, had they lived on and married, at what age.

Second, Günter Mayer has collected data from the classical literary sources as well as from inscriptions from Rome and from papyri from Egypt. He lists eight cases (one of which overlaps with Ilan's evidence), which we will incorporate in our table below.⁴⁴

Finally, there is the evidence of G. H. R. Horsley, also from the Jewish diaspora, who has collected data from Jewish tombstones in Rome. The tombstones indicate

---

39. See Huebner, "Mediterranean Family," 13.

40. Gallant, *Risk*, 18–19.

41. B. Yebam. 62b–63b//b. Sanh. 76b; b. Yebam. 100 b; m. Nidd. 5:6–8; b. Ned. 35b; b. Nidd. 45a

42. See Strack and Billerbeck, *Kommentar*, 2.373–375; Adams, *Social and Economic Life*, 71. Cf. also the peculiar text, b. Sanh. 55b, which speaks of betrothing a girl age three years and one day by intercourse.

43. Ilan, *Jewish Women*, 68–69.

44. Mayer, *Die Jüdische Frau*, 52.

the marital status at death of several young women.[45] The table below has been constructed based on the information of the above three scholars:

Age when married	12 years	13 years	14 years	15 years	16 years	17 years	18 years	20 years	23 years	25 years	27 years
Number in this category	3	7	2	6	2	5	1	1	1	1	1

Table 5.2: Age at marriage for Jewish girls in Palestine and the Diaspora (sample size 29)

Thus, the reader can discern that this society preferred to marry their daughters young. If we combine the women listed by Ilan, Mayer, and Horsley—a total of twenty-nine—we get the following results: twenty-four (83%) married by age seventeen and only five married after that. One died at age eighteen and was married; we do not know from the inscription how old she was at marriage (I calculated one year back). Four died from ages twelve to 22 unmarried and were not used in the table. The largest category by far is the age thirteen group (seven girls from the combined list). Thus, occasionally a woman might go until the late teens or even into her twenties before being given in marriage but parents preferred marrying off girls younger. There were some young women that died in their twenties unmarried.

What about the boys? Again, parents preferred to marry them young. The idealized text, m. Avot 5:21, recommended age eighteen. Other rabbinic texts suggested age twelve or around the time of puberty (Lam. R. 1.2; b. Yebam. 62b) like the girls. A passage in the Talmud asserts that if one is not married by age 20, God curses him (b. Qidd. 29b–30a). The Babylonian Talmud at one point (b. Sanh. 76b) says that a righteous man marries off his children close to the time of puberty. On the other hand, one text from the Qumran scrolls (1QSa 1:8–11, see above) wanted men to be at least twenty years old before marrying.[46] But this practice is an outlier among the rabbinic teachings. Thus, one would conclude that—contrary to the Qumran scrolls teaching—to marry young (while a teenager) was the common experience of Jewish boys in antiquity.[47] The preponderance of evidence shows that the males also married young, albeit not quite as young as the females did.

Why marry off your children so young? It helped them avoid sexual immorality. When one marries the children about the time sexual attraction begins, there is little time for immorality. But also, it allowed maximum time for reproduction. As our chapter on Mortality will stress (see Chapter 10), life spans were on average much

---

45. G. H. R. Horsley, *New Documents,* 4.221–23. None of Horsley's inscriptions overlap with Mayer's evidence.

46. See Schuller, "Women in the Dead Sea Scrolls," 131.

47. On this topic see also Ilan, *Jewish Women,* 65–69.

shorter than they are now in the western world. There was a small window to reproduce oneself. One needed to start as early as possible.

Whom Would They Marry?

The villages were probably endogamous.[48] Endogamy is the norm today in the Middle East;[49] it seems to have been the norm in the Old Testament; and there are indications that it was preferred in the late Second Temple Period. Günter Mayer suggests that these endogamous marriages were of two types: cousin marriage and uncle-niece marriage.[50]

The patriarchs in the Old Testament seemed to marry their cousins (Gen 28:2; 29:10). In the Second Temple period this custom continued. Philo as well, although not living in Palestine but in Egypt, preserved the Jewish affinity for marriage within family. He noted that marrying one's cousin was good for the dowry since it stayed in the family that way (*Spec. Leg.* 2.126). The Book of Jubilees[51] (4:15, 16, 20, 27, 28[52]) taught it as the rule. The Jewish work known as Pseudo-Philo[53] (2:5) has Enoch marrying in the family. In the book of Tobit, Tobias married his relative, Sarah (Tobit 6:13). Indeed, the book of Tobit emphasizes strongly the desirability of marriage to a relative (4:12–13; 7:10–11). Judith also married a relative (Jdt 8:2). Josephus reports several cousin marriages as well.[54]

Many rabbinic texts admonished men to marry their niece.[55] There are also examples, from both Josephus' narrative and from the rabbinic literature, of uncle-niece marriages.[56] Thus, most persons were related on several levels.

Therefore, from the village you found a spouse for your son or daughter who was a relative of some kind, probably a cousin but perhaps his niece/her uncle as the rabbis seem to have celebrated. Marrying your son or daughter to a relative insured,

---

48. C. Meyers, "Family," 36; Bendor, *Social Structure,* 84; Mayer, *Jüdische Frau,* 54–57; Hanson, "The Herodians and Mediterranean Kinship, Part II: Marriage and Divorce."

49. Endogamy seems to be the preference throughout the Middle East today in rural villages. See C. Kramer, *Village Ethnoarchaeology,* 21; Tannous, "Arab Village," 539; Lutfiyya, *Baytin,* 130. In the Jordanian village Lutfiyya reports on, they preferred to marry paternal cousins. Lancaster and Lancaster ("Jordanian Village," 39) report the same. Tannous, ("Arab Village," 539) reports that Muslims marry first cousins while Christian Arabs prefer second or third cousins.

50. Mayer, *Jüdische Frau,* 54–55.

51. Wintermute, "Jubilees."

52. Further references in Mayer, *Jüdische Frau,* 54.

53. Harrington, "Pseudeo-Philo."

54. See Mayer, *Jüdische Frau,* 54–55 and *Ant.* 15.23; 16.11,18, 133; 18.130; and *War* 1.563.

55. T. Qidd. 1:4, b. Yebam. 62b–63a; b. Sanh. 76b. On the other hand, the Qumran scrolls prohibited a man's marring his niece: CD 5:7–11, 11 QT 66:16–17. This prohibition can only be found among the sectarians and not in the general Jewish populace. See Archer, *Beyond Rubies,* 133.

56. *Ant.* 12.186–189; 19.277; *War* 1.563; b. Yebam. 15a; j. Yebam. 13; Gen. R. 17.3; m. Ned. 9:10 and Mayer, *Jüdische Frau,* 55.

scholars opine, that the marriage would be harmonious and it kept the wealth—both the dowry and the *ketubbah* (see below)—in the family.[57]

Polygamy or Monogamy?

The Hebrew Bible or Old Testament certainly allowed for polygamy. All of the patriarchs had more than one wife or concubine (a wife of lesser status). Many of the Hebrew kings had multiple wives and concubines.

Did this practice continue in the late Second Temple Period? The rabbis certainly thought it did. They speak of a priest having two wives (Lev. R. 4.5), of a man marrying a wife in front of his first wife (b. Abod. Zar. 55a), about a woman's husband and the other wife taking a trip (m. Yebam. 16:1), about a man who was married to two women and died (m. Ket. 10:1, 6), about a man who declares "I have two wives: one in Tiberias and one in Sepphoris"[58] (b. Sukk. 27ı), about another man having three wives (m. Ket. 10:4), and yet another with four wives (m. Ket. 10:5). The book of Sirach (second century BCE, 37:11) may refer to bigamy when it counsels against speaking to a woman about her rival (wife?). This text should be read alongside the many rabbinic references to "co-wives" (צָרָה).[59] Many of the Hasmonean princes and the Herodians had multiple wives (*Ant.* 12.186–189, 13.380, 17.18, 17.92). Josephus writes elsewhere that it was Jewish custom from ancient times to have several wives at the same time (*Ant.* 17.14; *War* 1.477). Philo criticizes the man who takes—apparently later in life—a second wife to the detriment of the first wife and her children (*Spec. Leg.* 2.135). And finally, lest one think that only persons of wealth and power took more than one wife, there is the case of Babatha, whose legal documents were found along the western coast of the Dead Sea (dating from the second century CE). According to these documents, she was the second wife of her husband.[60] Thus, it seems that there was no ethical objection to a man having multiple wives. Ilan suggests that only economic restraints (could one afford another wife or two?) dictated the number of wives.[61]

How did the wives feel about polygamy? We have no direct evidence to answer this question but there are interesting hints. Some of the marriage contracts found at the fifth century BCE Jewish colony at Elephantine in Egypt state that the husband will have no right to take a second wife. He must remain monogamous. Thus some of

---

57. See for endogamy in the Late Second Temple Period, Ilan, *Jewish Women,* 75–77; Adams, *Social and Economic Life,* 23–24; Archer, *Beyond Rubies,* 146–49; and Mayer, *Jüdische Frau,* 54–56.

58. Translation in Neusner, *Babylonian Talmud.*

59. See Lev 18:18; 1 Sam 1:6; m. Yebam. 1:1–4; t. Yebam. 1:10; b. Yebam. 15b. See Mayer, *Jüdische Frau,* 57–58.

60. See Ilan, *Women,* 85–88; and Instone-Brewer, "Marriage and Divorce."

61. Ilan, *Women,* 88. Herod the Great had nine wives (*Ant.* 17.19)

the brides—or their fathers?—found the idea of polygamy unpleasant and stipulated its prohibition in their marriage contracts, at least in the fifth century BCE.[62]

The exception to the general attitude of allowing polygamy, however, existed among the Qumran sectarians. Two texts from the Dead Sea community expressly prohibited taking more than one wife. It is even possible that one of these texts, the Damascus Document (CD), prohibited taking a second wife in the event that one's first wife died.

- 11QT 57:17–18: a king may not take a second wife but "she alone shall be with him as long as she lives."
- CD 4:20—5:2: the "Shoddy-Wall Builders (=Pharisees) . . . commit . . . fornication by taking two wives in their lifetimes."[63]

Thus, some communities were practicing and requiring monogamy. Some women—or their parents—were negotiating marriage contracts that forbade the husband from taking another wife. One might say that Judaism was trending toward monogamy. An interesting question to ponder is whether any of Jesus' disciples had more than one wife when they began to follow him? Did any of his close twelve disciples or more distant adherers have more than one wife? Did any of the female disciples (see Mark 15:40–41; Luke 8:2–3) come from polygamous marriages? What position did Jesus take on polygamy in light of Mark 10:6–9 (and parallels)? Would he have required his new disciples to divorce any second or third wives?

THE MARITAL PROCESS

The marriage process consisted of two steps: the betrothal (קִידּוּשִׁין) and the wedding itself (נְשׂוּאִין).[64] We will describe the betrothal process in some detail followed by a very brief account of what happened on the wedding day.

Betrothal: Three Stages of Development

We have a rather full accounting in the Mishnah, tractate *Ketubbot,* ("marriage documents"), of the process for marriage in the second century CE. We assume that at least most of these customs were in effect in the first century. What they did was far from the modern, western custom. We usually have, in Europe and North America, a courtship time followed by one of the parties' proposal of marriage (in the Hallmark movies, always the male on one knee). This is followed by a brief engagement period

---

62. On this topic, see Collins, "Marriage, Divorce," 115–16.
63. Translations in Wise, Abegg, and Cook, *Dead Sea Scrolls,* 55, 624.
64. Kehati, *Kiddushin,* 1–2; Kehati, *Ktubot,* 4; and Mayer, *Jüdische Frau,* 59–60.

which has no legal status but only a certain social recognition of the couple's intentions. A few months later the couple has a wedding that legalizes their relationship.

In the Mishnah, the whole thing is a business transaction (as also in Josephus[65]). The Mishnah indicates that there were three ways for a man to "acquire" a bride: by oral agreement before witnesses, by written document, and by sexual intercourse before witnesses (m. Qidd. 1:1; m. Ket. 4:4).[66] The parents negotiated a bride or groom for their child and sealed the deal before witnesses in one of the three ways.[67] The father of the bride agreed on a dowry that his daughter would bring into the marriage. The groom pledged a divorce settlement amount (or death benefit should he pre-decease her) to be paid to the bride should the marriage dissolve. This divorce settlement was a kind of delayed *mohar* or bride price. So much for the Mishnah. But was this always the case in Judaism?

Stage 1

There were three historical stages in the development of marriage arrangements in Judaism (as evidenced in b. Ket. 82b).[68] In the Old Testament period, the groom's family paid a "bride price" called in Hebrew a מֹהַר *mohar*.[69] In Gen 34:12 Dinah's family asked for a high bride price from Shechem's family. In Exod 22:16, a man must pay the customary bride price for a woman he has seduced and must marry her. In 1 Sam 18:25, Saul asks for a very unusual *mohar* from David.[70] Thus, we can discern that the family paid for the young lady for their son or grandson.[71]

The bride's father also would frequently give wedding gifts (a dowry) to the bride during this period (Gen 24:59, 61; 29:24, 29).[72] But these gifts were evidently not the main financial emphasis in the Hebrew Bible (in the First Temple period).

Why did they pay money for a bride? Was it because women were viewed as property like cattle?[73] So, just as a person must pay something to acquire a cow or

---

65. Josephus, *Apion* 2.200.

66. See Kehati, *Kiddushin*, 1–2; Kehati, *Ktubot*, 4; and Mayer, *Jüdische Frau*, 60. Kehati advises that the sexual intercourse before witnesses was simply a case of witnesses observing the couple entering a room alone.

67. Josephus (*Apion* 2.200) maintained that a man must arrange for marriage with the male head of the family. It must not be done for a high dowry; the prospective groom must not win over the bride by guile and deceit (woo her?); he must not take her by force.

68. Collins, "Marriage, Divorce," 114; and Hanson, "The Herodians and Mediterranean Kinship, Part II: Marriage and Divorce."

69. See Holladay, *Lexicon*. The RSV translates the word *mohar* "marriage present" and "bride-price."

70. He asks for one hundred Philistine foreskins.

71. Selling a daughter—requiring a *mohar*—still goes on today. One father in southern Sudan sold his daughter in 2018 on a Facebook auction for 500 cows, three cars, and $10,000. See, no author, "Facebook Fails to Save Child Bride."

72. See Instone-Brewer, "Marriage," 916.

73. Ilan, *Jewish Women*, 88.

The Archaeology of Daily Life

a goat from someone else, one paid for a woman as well? Or did they pay because the family needed to be compensated for the loss of a worker?[74] Without this young female assisting in baking the bread or tending the goats, the family is at a disadvantage, they might have reasoned. At any rate, at that time the groom's family bore the financial burden in the marriage process.

Stage 2

But after the exile, the financial responsibility switched to the bride's family. Now the bride's family continued to give the bride gifts to take into her marriage and these gifts, should she be divorced by her husband, had to leave with her. We have examples of the increased importance of dowry from the Elephantine texts (c. 459–420 BCE), from the Apocrypha, and from Josephus.

The Elephantine texts, produced by a Jewish colony in Egypt, developed its own twist on the bride price/dowry dynamic. There are seven marriage contracts that have survived (in Aramaic). They show that the dowry was an important part of the contract and that the groom added to the dowry. The contracts have the following order: groom requests hand of prospective bride; groom declares "she is my wife;" groom pays a *mohar* to bride's father (or slave master) consisting of five or ten shekels;[75] and the contract is written up listing details of bride's dowry. Although the groom pays a *mohar*, in reality, the father—to whom the bride price is paid—simply adds it to the bride's dowry.[76] The groom gave the bride price to the male in authority over the bride who then added it to the bride's dowry. Should the marriage be dissolved, she could take the dowry (plus the extra added to it from the groom) with her.[77]

For example, one document (459 BCE) stipulates that the father was giving his daughter, as dowry, a house when she married her first husband. One half the value of the house would return to the wife should the husband divorce her. He kept the other half as payment for his buildings attached to the house. Another contract for the same woman (between 446 and 440 BCE)—but with a different, third, husband—stipulated that the husband paid the wife five shekels in silver plus some clothing and household vessels which she added to her dowry.[78]

In another text (420 BCE), the groom states that he has paid "one *karsh* (= 10 shekels) of silver" for the bride and that she has added this to her dowry and brought into the marriage some cash, clothing, copper items, and vessels worth all together

---

74. Adams, *Social and Economic Life*, 30. See the discussion in Collins, "Marriage, Divorce," 113, 153.

75. Porten, *Archives*, 252–53, suggests ten shekels for a virgin and five shekels for a widowed or divorced bride.

76. See Collins, "Marriage, Divorce," 108, 114.

77. Collins, "Marriage, Divorce," 107, 113–14; Porten, *Archives*, 253; Porten, "Elephantine," 452.

78. Sayce, *Aramaic Papyri*, 38–43; Pritchard, *Ancient Near Eastern Texts*, 222.

seven *karsh* of silver. Thus, the dowry at this time consisted of cash, perhaps real property (houses), and movable property (jewelry, household items).[79]

The amounts of the dowries could vary widely. Several of the Elephantine texts indicate dowries of 12 shekels to 22 shekels, modest sums.[80] Two other dowries known from the Elephantine texts were 60-1/2 and 68-1/8 shekels. Porten[81] has calculated the value of these four dowries. He estimates that a day laborer (in Egypt in the fifth century BCE) could earn on average 12 shekels per month. According to his figures, the dowries would have the following values:

Dowry	12 shekels	22 shekels	60 ½ shekels	68 1/8 shekels
Value in days worked to earn it	1 month's pay	1-5/6 month's pay	5 months' pay	5-3/4 months' pay

Table 5.3: Values of dowries in fifth-century Elephantine

The last two are not fortunes, but are significant sums for the working class. Most could probably have afforded one month's pay but the dowries requiring almost one-half year's earnings would necessitate a fairly prosperous business person.

The Mishnah declared that a dowry equaling fifty denarii[82] in value was the minimum expected (m. Ket. 6:5), but this sum may only be the Mishnah's usual idealism. How could the rabbis dictate the sum of a daughter's dowry? One cannot command prosperity. We certainly have texts in which the sum of 50 denarii was not reached. As seen above, some of the Elephantine texts indicate smaller dowries than that and common sense would tell us that poor and working class persons could not come up with that sum.

We also have an interesting list of dowry objects in a late example of a marriage contract. It dates from 417 CE and comes also from Egypt. Although this date is quite late with respect to our period of interest, it is plausible that the practice of listing dowry objects was traditional and rather constant (it was done in similar manner in the Elephantine texts). This text is a Jewish marriage contract, written in Hebrew, between a groom named Samuel and a bride named Metra. In the document it lists the items the bride brings with her and the monetary value of each. The text lists various items of clothing, jewelry, and some pure gold. These items, they claimed, were valued at 11-½ denarii (not the minimum demanded by the Mishnah text cited above).[83]

---

79. See Pritchard, *Ancient Near East*, 2.84–86; Pritchard, *Ancient Near Eastern Texts*, 222–23; and Hanson and Oakman, *Palestine*, 38. For one *karsh* of silver equaling ten shekels, see Pritchard, *Ancient Near Eastern Texts*, 222.

80. See Yamauchi, "Marriage," 241.

81. Porten, *Archives*, 74–75.

82. The Roman denarius equaled around two shekels. Thus, this regulation was equal to 25 shekels dowry.

83. See Llewelyn, *New Documents*, 83–84.

Again, the text is quite late, but it may offer us an example of a rather modest dowry: a few items of clothing and jewelry. This list of dowry items seems more realistic for the ordinary people than the sometimes highly priced ones given in the Mishnah, in Josephus, and in the Dead Sea Scrolls (see below).

On the other hand, there are also texts indicating rich dowries, and not just among royalty either. In an era of conspicuous consumption, one should expect extravagant dowries. In Tobit 8:21, Sarah's father gives Tobias half of his possessions to marry her, potentially a fortune.

Whenever a prospective bride had a large and tempting dowry, many suitors would compete for her hand. Herod the Great gave his daughter a dowry of four hundred talents (= 2,400,000 denarii) in an attempt to make her an attractive bride. His prior offer of three hundred talents had been rejected (*War* 1.483, *Ant.* 16.228)![84]

Some of the documents recovered from the Dead Sea area (see Table 5.3 below) indicate dowries from 96 denarii to 2,000 denarii, the latter a huge sum. Doubtless the young lady's father with the second amount of dowry fended off many suitors.

A high dowry was intended to honor the bride—and attract desirable grooms. But marrying a woman for her dowry was condemned by the Jewish teachers. So, Sirach (Sir 25:21) counsels against taking a wife for her money (evidently referring to the dowry). Josephus also gives counsel about the dowry (Greek προίξ) and offers the same warning as Sirach: the Jewish Law commands Jews in taking a wife not to be influenced by her dowry (*Apion* 2.200).[85] The same warning is given in the Talmud which warns (b. Qidd. 70a) that men who marry for money will have bad children.

In addition to the moral restraints against marrying a woman for her large dowry, there were practical considerations, especially for someone uncertain about the future stability of his marriage. A large dowry could be a handicap to the husband wanting to divorce his wife. Rabbi Jose the Galilean (early second century CE), for example, allegedly married a cantankerous wife. He wished to divorce but her dowry was so large that he found it difficult to return it to her. His students took up a collection and paid for the dowry allowing Rabbi Jose to divorce (Gen. R. 17.3).

The dowry consisted of numerous items to enhance the bride's life and to give the groom a financial head start in the marriage. The groom controlled the dowry as long as they were married. But should the marriage be dissolved, the dowry had to leave with the wife—later also along with the penalty payment described below.

---

84. See Hanson and Oakman, *Palestine,* 40.
85. For other references to dowry in Josephus, see Adams, *Social and Economic Life,* 32–33.

Stage 3

But then another shift took place in the first century BCE. Then Simeon ben Shetach, great scribe and brother of Queen Salome Alexandra[86] (reigned 141–67 BCE), added the rule of the *ketubbah* (כְּתוּבָּה "marriage contract").[87] In this ruling—not at all hinted at in the Old Testament—if the husband divorced his wife, he paid her a kind of penalty.

Upon entering marriage, the husband promised that he would pay to the wife (in addition to returning to her the dowry), should he later divorce her, a stipulated amount of money. This was entirely a new concept, perhaps intended to reduce the number of divorces.[88] This divorce penalty or *ketubbah* became, in effect, a "delayed *mohar*" or delayed bride price. As Hannah Cotton has explained, "in time the *mohar* was transformed from an immediate payment (to the bride's father) into an endowed pledge, a divorce payment due to the wife upon dissolution of the marriage, and was written into the marriage contract."[89]

As we noted above, there is a rabbinic tractate entirely devoted to this process called, appropriately, *Ketubbot* "marriage contracts." In this tractate it stipulates that the standard payment for a divorced wife, who married as a virgin, would be two hundred denarii. The payment for a woman who married as a widow or divorcee would be half that amount (m. Ket. 1:2; 5:1). But there is one case referred to in which the husband had made a contract at their marriage to pay his wife four hundred denarii if the marriage dissolved. Later, even though he had fallen on hard times and only possessed that much wealth in totality at the time of divorce, the rabbis made him pay it (m. Ned. 9:5). A contract is a contract. The divorced or widowed wife was protected.[90] These are substantial sums and this penalty plus the bride's dowry would help insure the maintenance of the woman after the dissolution of the marriage.

Not only do we have a rabbinic tractate with rules and guidelines for this process, but now, we also have actual marriage contracts, some in Aramaic and some in Greek, from near our time period. These were discovered in caves on the west side of the Dead Sea and date from the early second century CE. Some have come from Wadi Muraba'at (about eleven miles south of Qumran), others from farther south yet, from the so-called "cave of Letters" located in Naḥal Ḥever (see below Map 5.1 and Table 5.4).

---

86. For Simeon ben Shetach, see: Bader, *Encyclopedia*, 72–78; Gilat/Wald, "Simeon ben Shetaḥ"; and Ilan, *Women*, 35.

87. See Instone-Brewer, "Marriage," 916 and t. Ket. 12:1. The word *ketubbah* could mean both the marriage contract or marriage document and the amount of the payment in the event of divorce or widowhood. See Danby, *Mishnah*, 794.

88. See Davidovitch, "Ketubbah." and Collins, "Marriage, Divorce," 115.

89. Cotton, "Cancelled Marriage Contract."

90. Cf. the complaint in the Talmud (b. Yebam. 63b) that there is nothing worse than a bad wife with a large *ketubbah*. The husband wants to get rid of the bad wife, but to do so will cost him too much, a dilemma.

The Archaeology of Daily Life

There are three Aramaic marriage contracts (Mur 20; Mur 21;[91] and 5/6 Ḥev 10[92]) in which the grooms promise to pay an amount of money. Some of the texts are fragmentary here and so we cannot tell how much the payment will be in the event the marriage ends in divorce. But one of the texts (5/6 Ḥev 10), that referring to the marriage of a woman named Babatha (mentioned above), promises to pay her four hundred denarii, a rather large sum. In addition, we presume she had brought a dowry with her into the marriage (it is referred to in the document), but the sum is no longer visible. Thus, she would take home in the event of divorce—or as it actually happened, the death of her husband—her dowry and the *ketubbah* settlement.[93] The wife would take the penalty payment along with her dowry in leaving the marriage.

On the other hand, the treasure trove of documents from the caves also yielded many texts in Greek. The three Greek marriage contracts[94] from Naḥal Ḥever and one of the two from Wadi Muraba'at exhibit a different emphasis from the Aramaic marriage contract of Babatha (5/6 Ḥev 10) and the two Aramaic contracts from Wadi Muraba'at (Mur 20 and Mur 21). Most of the Greek ones do not mention the *ketubbah* (or divorce settlement/delayed *mohar*) but stress the amount of the bride's dowry. They emphasize what the bride is bringing into the marriage in terms of wealth but do not mention a divorce payment to the bride from the groom in the event the marriage dissolves. Here is a summary of the contents of these eleven marriage/divorce texts:

Map 5:1: The Dead Sea Region Showing Sites Where Documents Were Found

---

91. Texts are in Fitzmyer and Harrington, *Manual of Palestinian Aramaic*, 140–43; and Benoit, Milik, and de Vaux, *Les Grottes des Muraba'at*.

92. Yadin, Greenfield, and Levine, *Hebrew, Aramaic, and Nabatean-Aramaic Papyri*, 118–41. This text = P. Yadin 10.

93. In general for the so-called "Babatha Archive" see Yadin, *Bar-Kokhba*, 222–53; Isaac, "The Babatha Archive"; Broshi, "Agriculture and Economy"; and Saldarini, "Babatha's Story."

94. See Lewis, *Documents from the Bar Kokhba Period*; and Cotton and Yardeni, *Aramaic, Hebrew, and Greek Documentary Texts*.

DOCUMENT[95]	DATE[96]	TYPE	LANGUAGE	DOWRY? (amount)	*KETUBBAH*? (amount)
Mur 19	111 CE	Divorce	Aramaic	Yes (unstated)	No
Mur 20	117 CE	Marriage	Aramaic	No	Yes (fragmentary, some denarii plus maintenance)
Mur 21	122–125 CE[97]	Marriage	Aramaic	Yes (unstated)	Yes (maintenance)
Mur 115	124 CE	Marriage	Greek	Yes (200 d.)	No
Mur 116	?	Marriage	Greek	Yes (2,000 d.)	?[98] (maintenance for as long as she wants after husband dies, dowry if she leaves)
5/6 Ḥev 10= P. Yadin 10	125–128 CE	Marriage	Aramaic	Yes (unstated)	Yes (400 d.)
XḤev/Se 13	134–135 CE	Receipt[99] for divorce document and *ketubbah*	Aramaic	No	Yes; receipt is evidently for *ketubbah*
5/6 Ḥev 18= P. Yadin 18	128 CE	Marriage Receipt for dowry?[100]	Greek	Yes (500 d. of which the future husband contributed 300 d.)	No (but husband gave bride 300 d. to add to her dowry)

95. I use the text abbreviations from Tov, *Texts*.

96. For these dates, see Benoit, Milik, and de Vaux, *Les Grottes de Muraba'at*; Lewis, *The Documents from the Bar Kokhba Period*; Yadin, Greenfield, and Levine, *Documents from the Bar Kokhba Period*.

97. Benoit, Milik, and de Vaux hesitated to date this one, but Cotton ("A Cancelled Marriage Contract") assigns the dates as 122–125 CE.

98. The text here is corrupt. The words "two thousand" are clearly visible but the words before these are not. Benoit, Milik, and de Vaux (*Les Grottes*) assumed the amount referred to the dowry mentioned in line six of this document. But Archer, *Beyond Rubies*, 297, believes the sum is in reference to the *ketubbah* that the wife would receive upon the death of the husband and her departure from the household. So, does Mur 116 refer to a dowry amount or to a *ketubbah* amount? Since the text has previously made reference to the dowry, I adopt the position of the previously mentioned editors over Archer.

99. This text has been debated. See Instone-Brewer, "Jewish Women"; Ilan, "Notes"; and Schremer, "Divorce." Ilan thinks the text is a divorce document written by the wife to the husband; Schremer thinks the document is merely the wife's quoting of the husband's divorce document; Instone-Brewer thinks that the document is a divorce document written on behalf of a woman to her husband using the Egyptian form of divorce. On the other hand, Cotton and Yardeni, (*Aramaic, Hebrew, and Greek Documentary Texts*, 65) maintain that this document is a receipt given by the wife to the husband acknowledging that she has received her dowry and *ketubbah* in full.

100. Hannah Cotton (private correspondence) does not stand behind the labelling of the Greek documents 5/6 Ḥev 18 and XḤev 65 as marriage contracts, and will discuss it in a future publication on speech acts and their language in Jewish law.

XḤev 65= 5/6 Ḥev 37= P. Yadin 37	131 CE	Marriage Receipt for dowry?	Greek	Yes (96 d.)	No
XḤev/Se 69	130 CE	Marriage	Greek	Yes (500 d.)	No
XḤev/Se 11	?	Marriage?[101]	Aramaic	fragmentary	fragmentary

Table 5.4: Summary of the Content of the Eleven Marriage/Divorce Documents

Why the difference? Hannah Cotton suggests that those writing a contract in Greek wanted to follow Roman law instead of Jewish law. They wanted to appear more Roman.[102] Hence, the absence of the provision regulated by the famous Simeon ben Shetach over two hundred years earlier. These people came from En-Gedi and other villages[103] around the Dead Sea area (and evidently fled to the caves to escape Romans in the early second century CE). Some of them, though evidently Jews, wanted a more cosmopolitan marriage contract.[104]

At any rate, we should presume that Jewish marriage in the late Second Temple Period, the period of Jesus and the early Jesus movement in Israel, was similar to the process evident from the Mishnah and the three Aramaic marriage contracts. When a couple entered a marriage, the groom wrote up a document and submitted it to the bride's family. In the document, the groom promised to pay the bride—in the event the marriage dissolved—a "delayed *mohar*" or dissolution penalty (the Mishnah says the minimum should be 200 denarii but this sum seems idealized). If the family approved the contract, the couple was betrothed. One year later, approximately (if the bride was a virgin), they consummated the marriage.

But a cursory glance at the monetary sums of both the dowries and the *ketubbot* causes us to ask if all these people were wealthy or did only the wealthy marry.[105] (One of the documents refers to a dowry of 2,000 denarii, an enormous sum.) In other words, how could a poor family afford a *ketubbah* of 200 denarii or a dowry of at least 50 denarii?

The answer is: they could not. As a later chapter will maintain (see Chapter 7) the average yearly income for a laboring family was around 250 denarii—unless the household hired out the wife and children as well as the father. In that economy coming

---

101. The content of this text is suggested by Cotton and Yardeni, *Aramaic, Hebrew, and Greek Documentary* Texts, 57 but the text is very fragmentary and uncertain.

102. Cotton, "Cancelled Marriage Contract."

103. According to Jackson-Tal ("Glass Vessel," 30), refuges came to these caves from En-Gedi, Herodium, Hebron, Jerusalem, Jericho, and from the eastern side of the Dead Sea.

104. But Collins, "Marriage, Divorce," 112, concludes that there were simply various ways to write up a contract and the strict rules of the Mishnah were not yet in force at this time.

105. Cf. Jackson-Tal, "Glass Vessel Use," 55: Many of the glass vessels in the Naḥal Ḥever caves were "luxury use" vessels. I.e. the owners of the vessels (and, evidently, of the contracts) were wealthy.

up with 50 denarii as a dowry would have been a major economic drain on the family and a 200 denarii *ketubbah* in the event of divorce would have been totally unrealistic. So, these documents only furnish us with the *form* of how marriage was conducted in the Mishnaic period (second century CE)—legally and in business fashion—but not the reality of the amounts of money changing hands for most of the lower-class folk, especially in the first century CE.[106] For that, we need hints from elsewhere.

There is evidence that even the poorest young man in antiquity could marry. A text in the Tosephta (t. Ket 6:8) states that if an orphan boy or girl wished to marry, they (evidently the rest of the village) would help them to wed. In the case of the boy, the village rents him a house and offers him a bed and afterwards a wife. The rabbis did stipulate, however, that they should help an orphan girl marry before they helped an orphan boy since her shame was worse (b. Ket. 67b). There was a village collection to assist grooms in affording marriage (t. B. Batra 10:7–9; b. B. Batra 144b).[107] The village poor fund would be used for a dowry of an orphan girl—not less than 50 denarii says the Mishnah (m. Ket. 6:5)—and if there was more in the fund than the minimally prescribed amount, they should give it too. Philo also refers to assisting poor brides to marry, especially in the event of the death of the father (Philo, *Spec. Leg.* 2.125). It appears from Philo's wording that the village leader would take charge of the betrothal and marriage commitments for the poor bride. In other words, the village would "pitch-in" to provide a poor boy or girl without family the means to marry.

The practice of making allowances for marriage for poor persons is also done in contemporary traditional societies in the Middle East. A recent ethnography of a Jordanian village noted that poor villagers commonly married without paying a bride price if a young man had a sister who could marry his bride's brother.[108] So, poor brothers/sisters married other poor brothers/sisters. In that case, they evidently ignored the bride price as well as the dowry.

We should probably think that this procedure was followed by most in first-century Palestine/Israel, the Palestine of the late Second Temple Period. The texts we now have—found in Wadi Muraba'at and Naḥal Ḥever, as well as the Mishnah—document the lives of rather well-to-do people. Should we even speculate that the poorest persons actually had no marriage document?[109] At least none of them has survived. But that the texts embody society's traditions as far as procedure seems to me a reasonable conclusion.

Some have argued that in Judea—but not in Galilee—they sometimes lived together in a sexual relationship before marriage. Tal Ilan, for example, argues for this

---

106. See Satlow, "Marriage and Divorce," who suggests that many in the first century and even later did not have a "written *ketubah*" but an unwritten agreement. Only families with property might actually have had a document.

107. See Safrai, "Home and Family," 757; Hanson and Oakman, *Palestine*, 40.

108. Lutfiyya, *Baytin*, 133.

109. Again, See Satlow, "Marriage and Divorce."

conclusion based mostly on a text, a marriage contract in Greek, from the Babatha archive which seems to indicate that the groom has already taken the betrothed to live with him before the actual marriage.[110] The contract dates from the early second century and this date makes such an argument a bit tenuous. Yet, there is also, as Ilan states, evidence from the Talmud for such a difference (b. Ket. 12a), also a late source.[111] Thus, it is possible that two different customs existed side by side: one for Judea and the other for Galilee with respect to when the couple cohabited.[112]

During the betrothal period, the exclusivity of the bride to the groom was the same as after the marriage had been consummated. The presumed situation we find in Matt 1:18–19 is supported by texts in both Philo and Josephus. Philo writes that for a betrothed girl to have sex with a man other than her future husband is adultery (*Spec. Leg.* 3.72). Josephus affirms that to violate a virgin betrothed to another was equal to seducing a married woman (*Apion* 2.201).[113] Thus, in spite of hesitation by some scholars as to the antiquity of the betrothal ritual,[114] the three texts given above seem to support it. Once a couple was betrothed, they were the same as married except for the marriage festivities and sharing a domicile.

The Wedding Day

The actual "ceremony" was more kinetic than in western societies. About one year after the betrothal,[115] after they had prepared the bride, she was carried to the groom's house. The rabbinic sources indicate that they usually did "five things" for a bride: wash her, adorn her, dress her up, dance before her, and take her to her husband's house.[116]

There were local customs that varied, of course, but the basic act was carrying the bride to the groom's house on a litter or carriage[117] while people applauded her, banged on drums, played other musical instruments, and perhaps danced in the streets (m. Sotah 9:14; m. Ket. 2:1; Pesikta Rabbati 20; Gen. R. 49.4). The bride evidently wore a "crown" of some sort (m. Sotah 9:14; Sem. 11.6). There might also be torches and/or

---

110. Ilan, "Premarital Cohabitation in Ancient Judea."

111. See Goodman, "Galilean Judaism and Judaean Judaism."

112. See m. Ket. 4:1 for different customs in Judea and Galilee with respect to betrothal. For "marriage by intercourse" see m. Qidd. 1:1. Collins, "Marriage, Divorce," 113 agrees with Ilan. Cotton and Yardeni, *Aramaic, Hebrew, and Greek*, 227–28 disagree with Ilan.

113. See Archer, *Beyond Rubies*, 53.

114. Satlow, "Marriage and Divorce," 349: "There is . . . almost no evidence that throughout the period of the Second Temple Jews practiced, or even knew of, betrothal as creating an inchoate marriage."

115. Strack and Billerbeck, *Kommentar, Johannes*, 374.

116. Avot de Rabbi Nathan 4. See translation in Neusner, *Classical Judaism*. Cf. also Eccl. R. 7.2 for adorning the bride.

117. She rides a horse in contemporaneous Arab villages. See Lutfiyya, *Baytin*, 139.

lamps carried by the procession (Matt 25:1).[118] Upon arriving at the groom's house, the groom and friends probably emerged with music (tambourines, drums, etc.; 1 Macc 9:39; m. Sotah 9:14).

There was a wedding feast associated with the action (John 2:1–10; Matt 22:1; 25:10; Luke 12:36; 14:8; Philo, *Spec. Leg.* 3.80; m. Keri. 3:7), given by the groom's family (m. Ḥall. 2:7),[119] which could last a week or more (Jos. Asen.[120] 21:8; Tobit 11:19; t. Ber. 2:10)[121] going well into the night (Luke 12:36).[122] Whether the couple stood under the canopy (*ḥuppah* חוּפָּה) in the first century is doubtful.[123] At some point, somebody uttered a benediction over the couple (m. Meg. 4:3). The "ceremony" was a huge event; the entire village celebrated, perhaps for several days.[124]

DIVORCE

Should the marriage break up, there was a procedure for that as well. The Old Testament seems to make provision only for the husband to initiate a divorce. Deuteronomy 24 states, "When a man takes a woman and possesses (marries) her . . . (and she displeases him) then he will write for her a document" (v. 1). Since the text did not say "a man or woman," the interpreters assumed that only a man could initiate divorce (*Ant.* 15.259; m. Yebam. 14:1). Nevertheless, the rabbis of the Mishnah made some exceptions. The exceptions were when a woman could bring her husband before a judge and the judge would force the husband to initiate a divorce: if the husband had a disgusting disease (boils or polypus) or if he practiced a disgusting and smelling trade (such as a tanner, coppersmith, or dog manure collector; m. Ket. 7:10). Thus, there were some humane exceptions.[125]

---

118. Ethnographically, see Jeremias, *Parables*, 173, who notes that Muslim Arabs in his day carried torches while Christian Arabs carried candles.

119. See Stauffer, "γαμέω, γάμος," 648. Also, Sifre Numbers on 15:21 which speaks of the master of the house who arranges the wedding feast for his son.

120. Burchard, "Joseph and Asenath."

121. We should probably think of a seven-day wedding feast as only for the wealthy. In contemporary Arab villages the feast might last one week as well. See Lutfiyya, *Baytin*, 135.

122. The situation envisioned by Matt 25:1–10 is unclear and debated. Jeremias, in his earlier publication (*Parables*, 173–74) maintained that the groom was negotiating his presents for the bride's family and the negotiations lasted into the night. But in a later work, ("νύμφη," 1100) he observed that there are textual differences (one group of mss reads in v. 1 "meet the groom," and the other "meet the groom and bride.") He offers explanations for each ms reading. The ten virgins are either going out to greet the groom and bride as they enter the wedding feast or to greet the groom as he comes to fetch the bride to take her to the feast.

123. Kehati argues for it but cites no early texts (*Kiddushin*, 1).

124. See Ilan, *Jewish Women*, 95; Safrai, "Home and Family," 758–59; Yamauchi, "Marriage," 242; Mayer, *Jüdische Frau*, 61.

125. See Ilan, *Jewish Women*, 143; Instone-Brewer, "Marriage," 917.

Naturally, one should expect that the rich and famous did not always adhere to Torah. Thus, there are noteworthy cases of wealthy women just leaving their husbands for various reasons (usually for greener pastures). Ilan and Mayer note several cases in the literature where Herodian women simply deserted their husband and married someone else. The examples below (except the last one) are from the Herod family:

- Salome divorced her husband, Costobar, even sending him a divorce document (*Ant.* 15.259);
- Drusilla left Azizus to marry the Roman procurator, Felix (*Ant.* 20.141–144);
- Berenice left her husband Polemo (*Ant.* 20.154–146);
- Mariamme left Archelaus (*Ant.* 20.147); and
- Josephus' first wife abandoned him (*Vita* 415)[126]

Of course, what the wealthy and entitled do should not be taken as standard behavior for the masses.

There was a famous debate among the two main Pharisaic schools, that of Shammai and that of Hillel. They debated the odd turn of phrase in Deut 24:1 עֶרְוַת דָּבָר *'ervat davar* "nakedness of a thing" or "indecency of a thing." Deuteronomy says, oddly stated, that if a man finds this quality in his wife, he may divorce her with a document. The school of Hillel said this meant that a man may initiate divorce for any reason whatsoever, even if the wife only burned a meal. But the school of Shammai said that this phrase refers only to sexual indecency and thus a man may only divorce if his wife has committed adultery (m. Gitt. 9:10). To complicate matters, the Qumran scrolls seem to refuse divorce for any reason. As we saw above, two texts from the Dead Sea community expressly prohibited taking more than one wife: 11QT 57:17–18 and CD 4:20—5:2. These texts seem to prohibit divorce for any cause, to prohibit polygamy, and, in one case, might even prohibit remarriage in case of the wife's death. So, there was a dispute as to the accessibility of divorce even for the husband during the late Second Temple Period. What was Jesus' position on it? The table below illustrates:

---

126. Ilan, *Jewish Women*, 145–46 and Mayer, *Jüdische Frau*, 79–80.

Most lenient					strictest
School of Hillel	School of Shammai	Jesus in Gospel of Matthew	Jesus in Gospels of Mark and Luke and in Paul	Qumran Temple Scroll	Damascus Document
Divorce for any cause whatsoever (m. Gitt. 9:10); presumably allowed polygamy	Divorce only for adultery by the wife (m. Gitt. 9:10); presumably allowed polygamy	Divorce only for adultery (Matt 5:32 and 19:9); no polygamy	No divorce for any cause (Mark 10:11–12; Luke 16:18; 1 Cor 7:10–11); no polygamy	No divorce for any cause; no polygamy (11QT 57:17–18)	No divorce and perhaps no second marriage if the wife died; no polygamy (CD 4:20—5:2)

Table 5.5: Views on Divorce/Remarriage and Polygamy in Late Second Temple Israel

Thus, there was a variety of views on the subject. Even in the New Testament, the Gospels represent Jesus' view on it a bit differently. Why do you think that is so? At any rate, the table indicates that this was one of the major contentions in the first century CE. Jesus' views as presented in the Gospels of Mark and Luke are like that of the Qumran Temple Scroll and in the Gospel of Matthew is like that in the school of Shammai. No view similar to that of the School of Hillel or to that in the CD was attributed to him.

As Deuteronomy regulates, a man must give a woman a divorce document. We now have a document—found in the same place as the two *ketubbot* described above—that has survived some two thousand years. It was found at Wadi Muraba'at (i.e. Mur 19, see Table 5.4 above) and dates to 111 CE. In the document the husband writes: "I, Joseph . . . divorce . . . you my wife, Miriam . . . I give you the dowry. . . ." The document does not mention the *ketubbah* payment. It stipulates, however, that if he has damaged any of her dowry, he would reimburse her four-fold.[127]

In addition, we have a kind of receipt from a wife to her husband acknowledging that she has received her divorce document and her *ketubbah*. This is XḤev/Se 13 (listed in Table 5.4 above) and dates from 134–135 CE. In this document, the former wife releases the husband from any further financial claims. She has evidently received her divorce-*mohar/ketubbah* and she has certainly received her divorce document. This text demonstrates that the former wife often granted a receipt to the husband for the transactions at divorce.[128]

Thus, when a young man or young woman married, they were in their teenaged years usually. They did not date each other for a while and then decide they had fallen in love; instead, their parents arranged the marriage. They usually married a relative: a cousin or an uncle/niece. They were betrothed with promises of dowry (following

127. See Fitzmyer and Harrington, *Manual*, 138–41.

128. But for an alternate interpretation of this text, see Cotton and Yardeni, *Aramaic, Hebrew, and Greek*, 65 n. 1. For the practice of granting the husband a receipt for the *ketubbah*, see m. B. Batra 10:3; m. Gitt. 8:8; and M. Ket. 9:9.

the bride into the marriage) and *ketubbah* payment (given to the bride if the marriage ended). If the marriage dissolved, there would be another document declaring that the wife was free to remarry. The wife would receive back her dowry plus the penalty-payment/delayed *mohar* agreed upon by the marriage contract. The wife would, then, give the former husband a receipt.

Although the marriage process might not make a good Hallmark movie, we should not think that they did not have meaningful relationships. It would be a western prejudice to think that only our customs produce happy marriages. It does not mean that husbands did not grow to love their wives nor wives their husbands. All the elements we think are necessary to make a romance may not actually be necessary. Marriage customs are a cultural given, not a biological or emotional necessity.

THE SIZE OF HOUSEHOLDS

We may surmise that most nuclear families had three children at any one time. Demographic studies of nuclear families (husband, wife, and their children) have indicated that there is an average of around five persons per family.[129] But, of course, family size was dynamic: There were births and deaths of children and parents, as well as marriages of female children (married male children tended to stay with the family for a while) that added and subtracted from the number. This information plus the mortality data offered in a Chapter 10 in this volume lead us to speculate that in, e.g., fourteen years of marriage, the wife will have suffered one or two miscarriages and given birth to five children, of which two will have died.

Scholars estimate roughly those same statistics: Carol Meyers estimates that each woman on average had eight pregnancies in her lifetime, giving birth to six children of which 50% survived.[130] Meyers further surmises that "if not infertile, women were pregnant or nursing for much of their adult life."[131] William Dever, suggests that the typical woman would give birth to "a dozen" children plus suffering numerous miscarriages and that only three or four of these twelve live births would survive childhood.[132] He does not state on what basis he makes these suggestions. Lawrence Stager, on the other hand, states that each family produced six children of which only two survived. Again, he does not indicate the evidence for his figures.[133] J. Lawrence Angel found in his data (based on only five individuals) that the average births per female in the Hellenistic Eastern Mediterranean world was 3.6 and the average survival of those live births was 1.6. One hesitates in this case to give Angel's otherwise valuable pioneering

---

129. See Laslett, "Mean Household"; and Hayami and Uchida, "Size of Household."
130. C. Meyers, "Family," 28; C. Meyers, *Rediscovering Eve*, 98–99, 109–10.
131. C. Meyers, "Archaeology," 77.
132. Dever, *Ordinary People*, 201.
133. Stager, "Archaeology," 18.

work too much credibility in light of such small sample sizes.[134] Carol Kramer reported that the average female in her studied village (western Iran) gave birth to 4.9 children.[135] Arieh ben-David[136] maintained that each family from our period contained 6 to 9 persons. He based his conclusions on Talmudic references to family tombs (usually with eight niches) and to villages sizes (e.g., a village of fifty persons with six houses). He also noted that the "Fellahin" of Palestine normally had families of 6 to 9 persons.

To these suggestions we may compare the data collected by Günter Mayer.[137] He has constructed a table—based on data drawn from Josephus, inscriptions, papyri, and the rabbinic literature—showing the number of children in known nuclear families. If we eliminate the non-Palestinian families listed in the table, we get a total of twenty-four mothers with seventy-seven children for an average of 3.2 children per nuclear family. If we include the diaspora families, known from the inscriptions and papyri, we have a total of one hundred three children and thirty-five mothers for an average of 2.9 children per nuclear family. The Palestinian families, then, tended to be a bit larger. Thus, Mayer's evidence corresponds fairly well with the suggestions of the historians given above. The typical nuclear family consisted of 5–6 members, assuming both parents were still living (an assumption one should not make too easily. See Chapter 10). We must caution, however, that Mayer's figures do not indicate the number of pregnancies a woman might have or the number of live births which later died.

We will see in Chapter 10 that, regardless of the average number of pregnancies or births, around 40% of children in Israel during our time period died before reaching adulthood. Thus, I arrive at the figure of five live births per couple of which two children, on average, tragically died.

THE STATUS OF WOMEN

Women for the most part shared the social status of their husbands. If the husband was a peasant farmer, chances are the wife held the same status. If the husband was an aristocrat, the wife enjoyed the same honor. In one case, however, a rich woman bought the high-priesthood for her future husband (m. Yebam. 6:4; b. Yebam. 61a; *Ant.* 20.213). Thus, sometimes the husband shared the social status of the wife. Most women, except for the aristocratic ones, probably did not think about and did not care about such a thing as social status. If their husband was a farmer, they probably grew up in a farming family themselves. If the husband was a craftsman, chances are they also came from a craft/artisan family. Their "standing" in our vernacular was just their natural self-identity.

---

134. Angel, "Ecology," 95.
135. Kramer, *Village Ethnoarchaeology*, 24.
136. Ben-David, *Talmudische Ökonomie*, 45.
137. Mayer, *Jüdische Frau*, 72.

The Archaeology of Daily Life

By some accounts, women in the patriarchal[138] Palestinian Jewish society lived according to strict rules of modesty and retirement. Women were for the most part under the power of either a father or a husband. Josephus wrote that women were in all ways inferior to men (*Apion* 2.201; cf. m. Ket. 4:4). Men were admonished in the Talmud not to talk much with women (m. Avot 1:5; cf. m. Qidd. 4:12; b. Ber. 43b). There were, evidently, too many temptations toward immorality when such conversations happened.

Joachim Jeremias[139] could write: "Eastern women take no part in *public life*." Women of means apparently were kept in seclusion, seldom venturing into public. Thus, a mother claims in a Jewish work written in our period that she was a chaste maiden and never left her father's house before she married (4 Macc. 18:7). Ben Sirach (c. 180 BCE; see 42:11) advised cloistering a daughter away in a room where there were no windows to look out onto the street. Philo, the Egyptian Jewish philosopher and Bible commentator (first century CE), warned against women exhibiting themselves in the street like some sort of vagabond (*Spec. Leg.* 171). They should only go out to go to the Temple and then during the low traffic hours.

There was a strong sense that inner-house life was appropriate to women and that public life was right for men.[140] Philo, again, maintained that the appropriate places for men were the market place, town councils, and law courts, places where large crowds were wont to congregate. But women, both married, mature women and "virgins" (i.e. not-yet-married women), should be at home with the two categories of women separated (Philo, *Spec. Leg.* 3.169). Philo claimed elsewhere that the married women as well as their "virgins" stayed in the inner chambers of the houses out of modesty (Philo *Flaccus* 89). The Talmud (b. Yoma 66b) stated that women only knew the wisdom that comes from running the spinning wheel.[141] Women stayed at

---

138. Here there is a debate over the extent to which ancient Israel was patriarchal, even in the Old Testament era. King and Stager, *Life in Biblical Israel*, 38 affirm that Israelite families were patriarchal and maintain that the oldest male was the *pater familias* like that of Roman culture who had power over the entire family, the wife, the children, and the slaves. (But King and Stager assert that the power of the Israelite father was not absolute since, for example, children were protected: Deut 21:18–21). C. Meyers, "Patriarchal," maintains that although Israelite families were patrilineal and patrilocal, they were not patriarchal. She further wants to regard him as the "senior male" and to conclude that he shared authority with the senior female of the extended family (private correspondence). Christine Garroway, on the other hand, follows the view of King and Stager and believes that Israelite families were patriarchal, referring to the head of the Old Testament era *bet 'av* ("household of the father") as the *pater familias* (*Children*, 134, 172, 174). The evidence seems to me overwhelming that the society was in both the Old Testament era (Iron Age through Persian period) and in the New Testament era (late Second Temple Period) more patriarchal than not. But that historians may have overlooked the influence of the mother is doubtless also correct, as Meyers has rightly pointed out.

139. See Jeremias, *Jerusalem*, 359–62. See also Strack-Billerbeck, *Kommentar*, 3:427–36; Witherington, "Women"; Stagg and Stagg, *Woman*, 15–54; Swidler, *Woman*, 114–25, 167–73.

140. See Mayer, *Jüdische Frau*, 85.

141. See Ilan, *Women*, 186.

home and did domestic tasks, if from poorer families, and oversaw such tasks among servants, if from wealthier families. Or, that is the usual story.

Further, women were sensitive about being veiled in public or at least about having their hair tied up on top of the head (Sus. 23; m. Shabb. 6:5; m. Ket. 2:1; m. Sotah 1:5; m. B. Qama 8:6). Showing the hair in public was considered quite shameful and nothing a self-respecting woman would do.

Yet some caution is in order in interpreting this evidence. In the first place, there was a Hasmonean queen, Salome Alexandra (*Ant.* 13.405–431), who ruled from 76 to 67 BCE (sister of the famous sage, Simeon ben Shetach, see above). She obviously had a public life and wielded power. Further, many of the Herodian women we meet in history do not at all seem shy and retiring. For example, Herod's mother-in-law, also named Alexandra, and the infamous Salome (*Ant.* 15.43–45; Mark 6:22) who danced at Antipas' birthday party, were anything but secluded. The wife of Pheroras—left unnamed by Josephus—attempted a political coup of sorts (*Ant.* 17.41-44) during the reign of Herod the Great. She obviously did not accept the cultural restraints of her day.[142] Women of wealth, then, could be quite the opposite of the stereotype we encounter in some of the sources.

But the women of the lower class probably did not usually fit the stereotype either. Common sense would indicate that they could not be cloistered away from the public but had to work beside their husbands producing and selling their wares or in the fields of their rural farms.[143] Since most of them lived in one or two-room houses that doubled as workshops, the life of the retiring and pampered elites in the back rooms of a mansion was impossible. Those who lived on farms had to help out with a multitude of tasks. Being shut up in a house all day is not an option for poor families.

But we need not simply appeal to common sense in this conclusion. Cynthia M. Baker[144] has collected several texts which represent women as out and about:

- m. Yebam. 5:2: women participate in the harvest
- m. ʿEd. 1:2: women are baking bread even during their menstrual period
- m. Ket. 1:8–10: a woman speaks to a man in the street; another goes to draw water
- m. Ket. 9:4: a woman is a shopkeeper
- m. B. Qama 8:6: a woman is in the street
- m. B. Metzia 7:6: a woman works as a day laborer
- t. Ket. 4:9 and t. Nidd. 6:17: women are in the market place

---

142. Cf. Mayer, *Jüdische Frau*, 87.

143. Jeremias makes this point (*Jerusalem,* 362). See also the interesting work of Prost in *History of Private Life,* 9-12, who points out that craftsmen from antiquity to fairly recent times opened their homes to the public. These were usually only one room residences. Thus women—who also helped produce the goods—could not have remained secluded. On the use of residences as workshops in ancient cities, see also MacMullen, *Roman Social Relations,* 48–87.

144. Baker, "Imagined Households," 117.

As Baker observes, the rabbis in their discussions assume that women are out in the open and in the public in fieldwork, in vending, in production of goods, and—just out (in the streets). The picture of women cloistered away is mainly a mischaracterization and perhaps a male ideal.

Were some women kept out of the public? Doubtless. The Talmud (b. Gitt. 90a) quotes a saying from a Palestinian sage that illustrates this point. The sage, R. Meir, indicates there are three types of men. One keeps his wife locked away; one allows her to converse with male relatives; the third, a base fellow, allows his wife to go out with her hair down and spin in the streets. Thus, there was a stereotypical behavioral pattern but women often lived in tension with the stereotype.

The documents relating to the above mentioned Jewish woman named Babatha, dating to the early second century CE, are informative. They are, it is true, from a period a little later than our primary focus, the late Second Temple Period (31 BCE—70 CE) but surely nonetheless provide insight into the role and status of women in this social world. The documents indicate that Babatha managed a considerable agricultural business yet needed a male representative in her contacts with authorities.[145] She was an independent woman in as much as one could be in her day. Yet, for legal transactions, she needed a male to represent her.

One can also certainly find misogynistic statements in the literature (e.g., Philo, *Hypoth.* 11.14). In the Jewish text called *Life of Adam and Eve* (first century CE), Eve takes all the blame for the sin in the Garden of Eden (*L.A.E.* 18:1–2[146]). In this retelling of the story, Adam is merely the innocent—and critical—bystander of the whole event. Some texts explain why women customarily precede the corpse in a funeral procession: because they are responsible for bringing death to the human race.[147]

Further, Josephus, in describing the Essenes, claims that they avoided women because they did not think any of them could be faithful to a husband (*War* 2.121). Historians rightly ask if this view is really the Essenes' view or Josephus' own view. Thus, one must read these negative statements warily.

Yet, there *are* some troubling attitudes. G. Mayer[148] has collected texts from various sources (mostly Josephus and Philo) that reflect a negative view of women. Women are said to be:

- Thoughtless (*Ant.* 4.219; b. Qidd. 80b)
- Frivolous talkers (*Ant.* 17.121; Gen. R. 45.5[149])
- Jealous (Philo, *Spec. Leg.* 1.108; *Virt.* 115; *Congr.* 180; Gen. R. 45.5)

---

145. On the Babatha collection, see Yadin, *Bar-Kokhba,* 222–53; Saldarini, "Babatha's Story," 28–37; Isaac, "The Babatha Archive," 62–75; and Broshi, "Agriculture and Economy," 230–40.

146. M. D. Johnson, "Life of Adam and Eve," 264.

147. See references in Oepke, "γύνη," 781: j. Sanh. 20b; 2 Enoch 30:17.

148. Mayer, *Jüdische Frau,* 45.

149. Gen. R. 45.5 states that women have four traits: greedy, eavesdroppers, slothful, and envious.

- Easily influenced or impressionable (Arist. 250[150])
- Weak (Arist. 250; *Ant.* 15.29)
- Unable to grasp the seriousness of a situation (Arist. 250; *Ant.* 4.219; 15.69)

This is quite a list of negative evaluations. Of course, the views come from men who had grown up in a rather misogynistic culture. Are they just mindless repetition of their culture or their actual feelings?

To this list one might add an interesting Talmudic discussion about "haughty women." The discussion begins with the statement that "Haughtiness is not appropriate for women."[151] One wonders at this point, is it appropriate in men then? The discussion continues to name the two arrogant women of the Hebrew Bible: Deborah and Hulda (b. Meg. 14b). Thus, two of the more heroic women of scripture become in this mindset the two immorally arrogant ones. Evidently, a strong woman—no matter how heroic—was also, to them, a haughty one.

We would conclude that although this society was patriarchal and at times misogynistic, we should not read too literally the statements of the Talmud and other sources. The practical necessities of living demanded that women often exceed customary expectations in public life and in independence. Second, many of these statements were written by the elite (Josephus, Philo, the rabbis) who tended to have an idealistic and privileged view of their situation. Third, even though legal stipulations might have required a male representative, some women probably found a way to assert themselves in business and in government. Finding a "front" for your activities can always be taken care of, as Babatha did. Yet, for some women at least, the societal expectations also probably described their daily life. Finally, there were some very unflattering attitudes and opinions about females but, again, these come from the elites. Did the working class men share these attitudes?

---

150. Shutt, "Letter of Aristeas."
151. Translation in Neusner, *Babylonian Talmud*.

6

What Would Be Inside Your House?

WE HAVE SURVEYED IN Chapter 4 the typical house in first-century Palestine. We find in the archaeological ruins varied sizes and styles. Examples of some of these styles are given in artists' reconstructions and site plans above. Now, in this chapter, we ask what went on inside the house and what would one see in the house. What did they eat in the main meal of the day, the evening meal?

THE CONTENTS OF THE HOUSE

Pretend you are invited to enter someone's first-century CE house in Palestine/Israel. What would you see there? The visitor to practically any house around the world expects to see furniture, decorative items (vases, pictures, etc.), and practical items (cooking ware, bedding, clothing, etc.). But how was it in Palestine/Israel in the late Second Temple Period? The following presentation of the inside of a typical village house is based on the archaeological remains and literary sources.

The Furniture

First, let us indicate what was *not* in the house. They had no furniture—or usually very little. These observations have been made for the Iron age or Old Testament period Israel: They usually had no bed or chair in their room[1] but rolled out mats at night for sleeping. Wealthier houses might have had a bed, a table, and a chair in the room (2 Kgs 4:10[2]) but the common rural folk living in a tiny village probably had few luxu-

---

1. Wright, "Israelite Daily Life," 61; Dever, *Ordinary People,* 169.
2. See Ps. 63:7 [Eng. 6], 132:3; and Job 17:13 for couches יָצוּעַ; and 1 Sam 19:13, 15–16; 2 Sam 4:7; 1 Kgs 17:19 for beds מִטָּה.

ries. For the ordinary houses from the Iron age or Old Testament period, nothing remains of furniture.

But was this true of ordinary persons in the late Second Temple Period? On the one hand, the New Testament often refers to persons sleeping in a bed and the rabbinic literature of the Mishnah refers to not only beds but other items of furniture in the houses. S. Safrai, for example—relying on rabbinic evidence—believed that a bed was essential to every house, that people reclined on couches as they ate their meals, and that sitting on the floor was "very uncommon."[3] On the other hand, the ethnographic informants lead us in another direction.

Not only do we have rabbinic texts giving information as far as the contents of a house in the Mishnaic period (second century CE), but also, we have the testimony of ethnographical studies (i.e. those studies of traditional Arab cultures). Until recent times, Arabs in the Palestine/Israel area owned little furniture. One sat on the floor on mats made of straw and other fibers. Somewhat wealthier households sat on rugs. There were no chairs or tables. Gustaf Dalman, for example, observed that mats in his day (from the late 19th through the early 20th centuries) in Palestine and Syria were made from papyrus, reed, rushes, and hemp. To have a rug instead of a mat, wrote Dalman, was a step up.[4]

Dalman wrote of one Arab house he visited (early 20th century): "Everything was done squatting, sitting, or lying on the bare floor." These people, wrote Dalman, were accustomed to the hard floors and seemed to need no chairs.[5] These informants lead us to suspect that the references to beds, tables, and chairs in the New Testament and rabbinic literature may not represent the typical household.

On the other hand, there is also a multitude of references to mats.[6] Rousseau and Arav suggest that the *kline* (κλίνη) of the Gospels (e.g., Matt 9:2; Luke 17:34) was like a modern stretcher and that the *krabbatos* (κράββατος) was a bag stuffed with straw.[7] Neither one would be a bed according to modern standards.

---

3. See S. Safrai, "Home and Family," 735–38. On the potential errors of using the rabbinic literature for a description of ordinary life, see the Introduction to this volume.

4. Dalman, *Haus*, 176. See also Canaan, *Arab House*, 48; Hirschfeld, *Palestinian Dwelling*, 120–34; Amiry and Tamari, *Palestinian Village*, 25–29; Sweet, *Tell Toqaan*, 131. These works observe that the Palestinian "peasants" or poor farmers had no furniture in their houses.

5. Dalman, *Haus*, 114, 176.

6. The Greek word κράβαττος (*krabattos*), the poor man's mat or bedroll, is referred to throughout the New Testament: Mark 2:4, 9, 11, 12; 6:55; John 5:8, 9, 10, 11; Acts 5:15; 9:33. For the rabbinic literature, see: m. Ket. 5:8; t. ʿErub. 11:12; Lev. R. 27.

7. Rousseau and Arav, *Jesus and His World*, 340. Danker (*Lexicon*) defines *krabattos* as a "mattress, pallet." It was the "poor man's bed."

The Archaeology of Daily Life

Figure 6.1: Inside Arab house at turn of last century.
Notice they sit and lie on a mattress on the floor.
© Bertelsmann Unternehmensarchiv. Used by permission[8]

The excavations of the Bar-Kokhba caves (at Naḥal Ḥever) and of Masada (see Map 5.1, Chapter 5) brought to light several mats and rugs. The mats were constructed of palm leaves—readily available at En-Gedi—and the rugs, made of wool, were surprisingly colorful. From three different dyes, they were able to produce thirty-four different colors.[9] One should probably imagine the floors of the ordinary persons of Israel in the late Second Temple Period as covered in such mats, although the colored rugs (as well as their clothes, see below) were probably for the more prosperous. Here is an inventory of the items found at these two sites that probably could have been found in the typical house in the Late Second Temple Period:

---

8. In Dalman, *Haus*, photo 91. The house was in the village of Nazareth circa 1900. The couple sit and lie on the floor, the husband on his sleeping mat.

9. Rousseau and Arav, *Jesus and His World,* 48.

Masada (73 CE)	Naḥal Ḥever (135 CE)
	Rugs (multicolored)
Tunics of wool	Tunics of wool, shirts of linen, woolen cloth and linen cloth
Baskets of palm leaves	Baskets of palm leaves and of willow (also mats)
	Mantles of wool
Ivory and bone objects (spindle whorls, egg spoons, spatula, dice)	
Bronze items (pan, jug)	Bronze items (jugs)
	Iron frying pan
Wooden comb	Wooden bowls
Stoneware (cups and bowls)	
Clay lamps, jars, and cooking pots	Clay jars and cooking pots
Leather sandals	Leather sandals
	Bags and water skins from goat hide
Cosmetic applicators	Powder box, glass cosmetic oil container, jewelry box, mirror, silver earring
	Glass bowls and plates
	Iron sickle, iron knives, iron keys

Table 6.1: Inventory of Items from Masada and the Bar Kokhba Caves at Naḥal Ḥever[10]

The suspicious items would be the ivory pieces at Masada and the very nice glass bowls and plates at Naḥal Ḥever. These Zealots at Masada may not have been poor any more than the refugees in the Bar Kokhba caves were (see the marriage documents in Table 5.4). Further, the stone cups and bowls went out of fashion only after the Bar Kokhba war (Chapter 12) when the zeal for ritual purity waned. But, there were none found in the Bar Kokhba caves. In general, these lists seem to give us a good impression of the contents of the average house: rugs and mats, baskets, clothing, lamps, some simple cups and bowls, and perhaps a couple metal pans. And, of course, in addition to these items there was—as at Masada—always an abundance of clay vessels.

There are references to beds being used in our period, although the beds seem to have been slept in by several persons at the same time as noted above. M. Nidd. 9:4–5 refers to three women sleeping in one bed (מִטָּה *mittah*). 1 Enoch 83:6 has the seer Enoch recounting a dream he had while sleeping with his grandfather.[11] Luke 11:7 narrates a parable in which the entire family is in the same bed (κοίτη *koitē*) asleep.[12] The tractate on mourning, *Semaḥot* (11.17; see Chapter 11) requires that while a family is

10. See Yigael Yadin, *Bar-Kokhba,* 66–81, 115–206; Yadin, *Masada,* 140–54. Cf. Safrai, "Home and Family," 744.

11. Though not explicitly in a bed. Cf. Eccl. 4:11.

12. This term for bed is to be distinguished from the Greek word κλίνη (*klinē*) "dining couch," "bier," or "stretcher" which could also be used for a bed (Danker, *Lexicon*). See Luke 17:34 for κλίνη as a bed and Rousseau and Arav, *Jesus and His World,* 340.

in mourning for a loved one they must turn their bed upside down. But the document also allows for those not having beds but who sleep on benches or "large basins." Thus, this text knew that not everyone could own a bed, however they imagined it. Perhaps there were more beds (mattresses or cots with mattresses) used in our time period than in the Iron age/Old Testament period. But to conclude that nearly every house had a bed—as did Safrai[13]—is suspect. That conclusion sounds like the elites' view of their own experience. So, how did, e.g., the famous house of Peter (at Capernaum) look inside? Did the occupants sit on chairs and couches or on mats and rugs?

Clothing

From the literary sources, we can say that the following fabrics were available: wool, linen, goat hair, camel hair, cotton, hemp, and silk.[14] Not all of these were common, however, to the ordinary person. Silk was a luxury, only purchased by the very rich. Linen was more expensive than wool but still, presumably, less expensive than silk. Wool, the cheapest fabric, could be made more expensive by dyeing the entire piece or by weaving in dyed designs. Let us see what the archaeological evidence reveals about how the ordinary people lived with respect to clothing.

Clothes were expensive—even the cheapest, undyed woolen ones. People wore both a tunic (Greek: χιτών *chitōn*) and a cloak (Greek: ἱμάτιον *himation*)[15] over the tunic in cold weather, the cloak doubling as a blanket a night. Bandits often robbed their victims of even their clothing.[16] Some people were so poor that they could not own a cloak in its entirety. So, they shared one: R. Judah b. Ilai and his wife shared a cloak; she wore it to the market and he to prayers (b. Ned. 49b[17]). Students often shared clothes: six disciples of Rabbi Judah ben R. Ilai covered themselves with one cloak (presumably at night; b. Sanh. 20a). Women often borrowed clothes from each other, taking turns wearing the same tunic (m. Nidd. 9:3[18]). Seven rabbis came together to intercalate the year. Whoever had no cloak, shared a cloak with someone else by cutting a cloak into two smaller pieces (j. Hag. 3.1[19]). Others regularly borrowed cloaks to go to a house of mourning or a house of rejoicing. A man was said to have borrowed

---

13. "(The) bed was considered an essential item." Safrai, "Home and Family," 735. But contrast Schwartz, "Realities of Jewish Life," 438: the bed was considered a status symbol.

14. Hamel, *Poverty,* 59 and m. Kil. 9:1–10. See also Mark 1:6 for camel hair.

15. See Danker, *Lexicon*. We find the Hebrew terms in m. Kel. 28:7: tunic: חָלוּק *ḥaluq*; cloak: טַלִּית *ṭalit*. See Hamel, *Poverty,* 60; Jastrow, *Dictionary*.

16. Luke 10:30; m. B. Qama 10:2.

17. The wife wore the cloak when she went to the market; the husband when he went for prayer.

18. I surmise they must have each had a ragged and patched tunic but perhaps borrowed a better looking one for going out of the courtyard.

19. Cf. the initial intentions of those at the cross of Jesus: John 19:23–24. They cut up his cloak into four parts, but not his tunic. For this, they cast lots.

clothes to visit his sick father and wound up having to tear the clothes because his father died (t. B. Metzia 8:28).[20]

These stories of sharing and borrowing become more poignant when we remember that most persons had but one set of clothing. Thus, to borrow a man's cloak meant he would have none for a time.[21] This makes Jesus' teaching (Luke 6:29//Matt 5:40) "do not prevent one who wants to take your cloak from also taking your tunic" even more striking. Likewise, the words attributed to Jesus (Matt 6:25//Luke 12:22): "do not (be anxious) about your body, what you will wear," come to us with new force. Some did not have clothes to wear, or at least, full ownership of clothes to wear.

We have now quite an inventory of clothing fragments from our period of time. O. Shamir and N. Sukenik have constructed a table based on the finds from twenty-five sites. These sites have yielded 1,727 fragments of cloth. We can, with caution, discover what kinds of clothing were available and what kind was most used. The caution is that most of these fragments have come from sites in the Judean wilderness or the Araba (south of the Dead Sea). This fact is to be expected since this area is the driest in Israel and, therefore, most likely to preserve perishable materials like cloth. Here is my summary of the table of Shamir and Sukenik:

Fabric	Number of fragments
Wool	1101
Linen	549
Goat hair	61
Camel hair	3
Mixed	13
Cotton	0
Silk	0
Hemp	0
Total	1727

Table 6.2: Clothing samples from the Roman period[22]

Based on the sheer numbers, one could say that the residents of Palestine/Israel in the late Second Temple Period preferred woolen clothing. It makes up nearly 64% of the total. Linen was more expensive than wool and required a longer process to manufacture. Therefore, one can—again, with caution[23]—conclude that most of the ordinary

---

20. Hamel, *Poverty*, 71–72 for these citations. See Chapter 11 for rending garments.

21. Some rabbis required men to own two cloaks, one for every day and one for Sabbath. But how realistic was this? See Hamel, *Poverty*, 72.

22. Adapted and summarized from Shamir and Sukenik, "Qumran Textiles," 215.

23. The cautions are: Most of these samples have come from the Dead Sea area; some of the samples are from Nabatean sites, not Jewish; some of the sites, e.g., Mo'a south of the Dead Sea, show a great deal of prosperity (see Shamir, "Textiles."); one of the sites, Qumran, had religious reasons for preferring linen exclusively (Shamir and Sukenik, "Qumran Textiles.").

folk would have worn woolen clothing. The Talmud states that Galilee was known for its linen and Judea for its wool production (m. B. Qama 10:9; b. B. Qama 119a). One must ask, then, if we would find these same percentages in Galilean sites were they to preserve cloth fragments.

Further, the clothing would have been usually undyed and undecorated. At the Mo'a site (near Petra, south of the Dead Sea), there were 141 woolen fragments undyed, 21 fragments dyed green, 10 brown, 18 red, and 1 blue.[24] Thus, even in this site of evidently prosperous people, the overwhelming majority of garments (74%) were undyed. Wearing dyed woolen clothing was a sign of wealth. The "Rich Man" in Jesus' parable wore "purple (wool) and fine linen,"[25] a combination showing extreme wealth. But we presume that the ordinary, working-class families predominantly wore woolen garments in their natural cream or beige color. Joan Taylor maintains that women tended to wear colored clothing more than men.[26]

Thus, we would say that the ordinary folk wore, in the main, undyed, woolen garments but that some of them had to share garments or borrow them when going to a specific event.

Other Guests

Second, there were other "guests" in the house: the animals (and I don't mean puppies and kittens!). Most archaeologists now think that the first floor in the Old Testament houses was used for stalling animals in the night (only in winter?) and for storage.[27] The side rooms would have been for the animals (donkeys, sheep, cattle) and the center room of the first floor for daily activities. The Upper floor was for the family to sleep, eat, and socialize.[28]

By the New Testament times, they were no longer building the standard "Four Room House" (which was as often as not only a three-room house) for an extended family but were living as nuclear families instead. Still the animals probably joined the family in-doors, especially in the winter, in some cases in a cellar under the main floor (see Chapter 4, Figure 4.6). Josephus writes about a prohibition of butchering animals which "take refuge in our houses" (*Apion* 2.213), evidently referring to these nocturnal guests. They became so close to the in-door animals that to kill and eat them seemed, at least to Josephus, unkind.

---

24. Shamir, "Textiles," 100.
25. Luke 16:19. I presume the tunic was linen and the cloak was woolen.
26. Taylor, *Jesus*, 175.
27. Dever, *Ordinary People*, 129; Stager, "Archaeology," 14; C. Meyers, "Family," 15; Netzer, "Domestic Architecture," 198 and n. 17.
28. Wright, "Israelite Daily Life," 60; C. Meyers, "Field Crops to Food," 71; Stager, "Archaeology," 11–13. Most of Stager's data seem to come from three excavations: ʿAi, Raddana, and Giloh (11). For grain storage pits, see Currid and Navon. "Iron Age Pits."

Further, this practice was still being done (and perhaps is continuing today in very traditional villages) up to the mid-twentieth century in the Middle East. Both anthropologists and travelers report that many traditional Arab houses brought the animals into the house at night, especially in the winter.[29] In most of these Arab houses, however, instead of two floors with animals on the first floor as in the Old Testament times, everyone was on the same floor with the animals on a lower level of the first floor and the family on a kind of upper bench.[30] The heat from the larger animals would elevate the temperatures of the entire house in winter and it would offer some protection against having one's animals stolen. Evidently, the animal odors would have been a matter of indifference to the human residents. As one local informant observed: "It seems that the idea of a separate barn has never taken root in that part of the world."[31]

Western travelers seem to have had a different opinion, however, as this famous quotation from Mark Twain shows:

> We could have slept in the largest of the houses, but there were some little drawbacks; it was populous with vermin, it had a dirt floor, it was in no respect cleanly, and there was a family of goats in the only bedroom, and two donkeys in the parlor.[32]

And one other western traveler from the same era was less generous if just as repulsed: "The houses are not fit to put pigs in, and every door-yard is full of mire and filth."[33] Well, mire and filth are evidently in the eyes of the beholder. Were the houses similarly filthy in first-century Israel? One would think so.

Togetherness

Third, the entire nucleated family slept in the same room. It seems improbable to westerners that the couple would sleep in the same room as the children but ethnographic studies from the Middle East show us that this is what traditional folk prefer.

---

29. See Dever, *Ordinary People,* 131; Stager, "Archaeology," 14; Borowski, *Every Living Thing,* 45.

30. Other ethnographic reports of the first floor of the house (or in many Arab houses, the lower level of the same room) being reserved for the livestock can be found in: Dalman, *Haus,* 121, 123, 129; Hirschfeld, *Palestinian Dwelling,* 120–34; Canaan, *Arab House,* 45; Fuchs, "Arab House," 158 (who calls the lower floor the "soiled area"); Kramer, *Village Ethnoarchaeology,* 106; Lutfiyya, *Baytin,* 20; Fuller, *Buarij,* 8; Bailey, *Jesus,* 28–29. Consider the words of Fuchs, "Palestinian Arab House," 163: "In the cottage it [the platform] is reserved for the use of the family while the lower portion of the room is occupied by the poultry and sometimes even the sheep and goats." Also note Bailey's observations *Jesus,* 29: "Each night into that designated area, the family cow, donkey and a few sheep would be driven."

31. Tannous, "Arab Village Community," 529.

32. Borowski, *Daily Life,* 130, note 29, quoting Mark Twain who traveled to Palestine in the nineteenth century.

33. Thompson, *Land,* 2. 544 (also from the nineteenth century).

They evidently wanted the entire family to be huddled together on their mats. We get this impression from several texts from the Gospels where the entire family is in one "bed" together on a cold night (Luke 11:7, 11:34). John Holladay cites ethnographic studies from western Iran that support this custom: "Each nuclear family had its own living room. There the family ate, slept, did indoor work, and entertained."[34] That is, they did all those things in the same room. The one room was their living room, dining room, and bedroom, all done on mats spread out on the floor. Other ethnographic studies confirm this observation.[35] The practice seems to be common throughout the Middle East.

The married couple lived a normal married life in spite of all the little eyes in the room. Y. Hirschfeld, in the course of his research on ancient Israelite housing, interviewed several traditional Arab villagers. He reports the response of one Arab *mukhtar* to the question, "How could the husband and wife have sex with everyone in the same room?" The *mukhtar* answered, "It was done by stealth."[36]

One might think that the frequency of marital relations would be considerably diminished under such circumstances but the Mishnah—if it is to be believed—argues otherwise. There, after reporting the opinions of the two main schools of interpretation (that of Shammai and that of Hillel) on how long one might abstain from marital sex in order to concentrate on prayer, the rabbis give a list of rules for marital frequency. They explain that the duty of marriage based on Exod 21:10 requires sex every day for those couples unoccupied, twice a week for laborers, once a week for donkey drivers, once a month for camel drivers, and once in six months for sailors (m. Ket. 5:6). These "schedules" seem to be based on the number of times the husband would be at home within a given time frame. In other words, the rabbis believed that frequent marital sex was the duty of every couple in spite of the crowded situation at home. The apostle Paul, in his first letter to the Corinthians, presented the rabbinic view as well (1 Cor 7:3–5). He expected married couples to maintain relations.

HOW MANY ROOMS?

The individual house (בַּיִת *bayit*) which held the nuclear family is the smallest social unit in the rural village. Many historians have concluded that most ancient Palestinian/Israeli folk lived in houses that were only one room.[37] This conclusion seems sup-

---

34. See Holladay, "House," 314.

35. Other ethnographers who refer to this practice are: Dalman, *Haus,* 77; Canaan, *Arab House,* 59; Hirschfeld, *Palestinian Dwelling,* 120–34; and Fuchs, "Arab House," 160. On the other hand, Dever, *Ordinary People,* 156–57 assumes that the married couples had a room separate from the children and that the extended family shared a large common room for dining and entertaining. His suggestions seem ethnographically uninformed.

36. Hirschfeld, *Palestinian Dwelling,* 134.

37. See e.g., Schwartz, "Realities of Jewish," 436; Killebrew, "Village and Countryside," 198.

ported by the common people of traditional villages today who live in such houses.[38] Yeivin estimates that, on average, the typical village house/room could accommodate five people.[39] Thus it is doubtful that anyone more than the nuclear family lived in a house/room under usual circumstances. Families with more than five people might be compelled to build a smaller upper room. Nevertheless, some evidence does exist that the extended families occasionally lived together in the same room (m. B. Batra 9:8–10. Mark. 1:29).[40]

Shimon Dar notes that the Mishnah describes a small house as 4.48 x 3.36 meters (15 m²) and a large house as 4.48 x 5/6 meters (22 m2/27 m2; m. B. Batra 6:4). Dar found these same measurements commonly in his survey of Samaria and, thus, he concludes they represent house sizes generally in Palestine in the Herodian period.[41] We must remember, however, that Dar means by "house size" the dimensions of the covered portions of the domestic area, not including the courtyard.

In the one room house, everything from eating, entertaining, and sleeping was done in the same place. At night they unrolled mats for sleeping. By day, the family sat on the floor for eating and entertaining.

Yizhar Hirschfeld maintains, however, that, though the residents today in traditional villages of Israel live in one room houses, it was not the case in the Roman and Byzantine eras. He has found that the houses of those periods usually contained two rooms: the טְרִיקְלִין (*triclin*) from the Latin *triclinium* (dining room) and the קִיטוֹן (*qiton*) from the Greek word κοιτών (*koiton*; bedroom).[42]

Hirschfeld's literary evidence is mostly Mishnaic and his archaeological examples of the two-room house as the most common are all from the Byzantine era (4th to 7th centuries CE). Yet, his argument does have some merit. Some of the houses, for example, at Khirbet Qana seem to have had more than a single room. Also, if some

---

38. Bouquet, *Everyday Life,* 28 notes that poor Arabs of Palestine still live in only one room. See also Amiry and Tamari, *The Palestinian Village Home,* 27; and Hirschfeld, *Palestinian Dwelling,* 120–34, 259.

39. Yeivin, *Survey of Settlements,* XV. Cf. Stager, "Archaeology of the Family," 18. This figure is close to the average family size (six) suggested by Ben-David, (*Talmudische Ökonomie,* 45. See also I. Finkelstein, "A Few Notes on Demographic Data," who estimated that the average house in pre-modern Palestine held 4.4 to 6 persons. But see also Hirschfeld, *Palestinian Dwelling,* 135, whose Table 5 gives much larger numbers for the houses he surveyed.

40. Safrai, "Home and Family" 733. That extended families lived in one house supports Hirschfeld's findings where as many as 25 persons lived in one house (which had 93 m²). See Hirschfeld, *Palestinian Dwelling,* 135. Alston ("Houses and Households" 34) gives a table of "House Occupancy and Household Sizes" (gleaned from tax records) in which he finds that the average number of people per house in ancient Philadelphia (Egypt) was 7–8. This number of people, he found, represented more than one household. Thus many houses in Egypt during our period of study were occupied by more than one household.

41. Dar, *Landscape and Pattern,* 85. Martin Goodman maintained (*State and Society,* 31) that the standard house sizes in the Mishnah are pure "theory."

42. Hirschfeld, *Palestinian Dwelling,* 260–61. Also Killebrew, "Village and Countryside," 199; and Schwartz, "Realities," 436, note references to these rooms in the rabbinic literature.

residents had a bed instead of sleeping on the floor on a mat, it *might* require two rooms.[43] Therefore, one may conclude that some two-roomed houses were known during our period (late Second Temple or the ER I period) although most were one-roomed. In that case, the Arab customs do not always picture for us the New Testament era but still offer us ethnographic comparisons. Whether the houses had one or two rooms, the family still slept together in the same room as the traditional societies do today.

FOOD

One of the main activities of the household was the evening meal. What they ate, typically, was based on varied considerations. Their food choices and opportunities emerged from climate, geography, technology, and economic standing. What foods would you typically eat were you a resident in Palestine/Israel in the late Second Temple Period? Would you have had enough to eat? Would you get "three squares" a day?

What Did They Eat?

What did the Jews of Late Second Temple Israel eat? We turn to four types of evidence to answer this question:

1. Literary evidence (supplemented by ethnographic informants): What does the literature from our period (mostly the Mishnah) reveal about the typical meals for a person of modest means?

2. The archaeological remains of food processing (wine presses, olive presses, grain grinders, threshing floors, *tabuns*, etc.): If they processed certain foods, we presume they must have eaten them.

3. The archaeological remains of food preparation (cooking ware): One changes the cooking ware to suit the type of food cooked.

4. The actual remains of food (seeds, fruit pits, fruit peels and husks, bones, etc.): Some sites have left behind carbonized or desiccated remains of plants and seeds. Bones of animals are also coming into light.

---

43. Depending on how we conceive of the "beds." See above and Rousseau and Arav, *Jesus and His World*, 340.

Literary Evidence

Let us turn to the first line of evidence. Several scholars[44] have compiled lists of foods from the Hebrew Bible, the New Testament, the Pseudepigrapha, the Qumran scrolls, and Rabbinic literature. Their combined list, gleaned from the literature, is as follows:

- Grains (comprised 50% of daily calories[45])
- Legumes (e.g., lentils, beans, chickpeas)
- Oil (almost exclusively from olives)
- Fruits and nuts (30 varieties; wine comprised one-fourth of daily calories for a male)[46]
- Vegetables (30 varieties)[47]
- Eggs
- Cheese, butter, milk
- Fish
- Meat
- Other items[48]

That is quite a menu as revealed in the literary sources. But the question one has is how available to the common person were all these types of food. Just because the literature refers to a food item does not mean that it was commonly eaten. In my culture, for example, I know about caviar but I do not eat it; I do not eat kale and do not intend to. The existence of a food item is not the same as the availability (or desirability) of a food item.

O. Borowski[49] published a well-known essay on the "Mediterranean Diet" that compared the Old Testament texts with the current Bedouin and Druze practices.

---

44. Hamel, *Poverty*, 9–21; Borowski, "Mediterranean Diet"; Broshi, *Bread, Wine*, 121–43; Rosenblum, *Food and Identity*, 17–20; Dar, "Food and Archaeology," 331; Kraemer, "Food," 405; Jacobs, "Diet." These authors glean references from wide ranging sources. Jacobs, e.g., offers as literary evidence: m. Kil. 1:1–3; m. Ma'as. 1:3; m. Sheb. 7:5; *War* 3.49, 7.296; Jdt. 10:5; *Ant.* 17:183; Matt 23:23; Luke 11:42; Mark 4:31; 11QT 43:3–9. Cf. also the text in Hab. 3:17 which lists figs, grapes, olives, grains (i.e. fields), sheep, and cattle as the basic food sources; and the celebrated "seven foods" in Deut 8:8.

45. A figure agreed upon by several scholars: Broshi, *Bread, Wine*, 121; McDonald, *Israelites Eat?* 9, 19, 23, 91; Dar, "Food," 74. McDonald even suggests that for some grains made up as much as 75% of their caloric needs. See also Hamel, *Poverty*, 22–23. The daily bread of the poorest families was from barley. Cf. John 6:9.

46. E.g., grapes, olives, figs, dates, pomegranates, carobs, apples, almonds, pears, peaches, plums, mulberries, walnuts, pistachios, and citrons. For wine as a quarter of a man's daily calories, see Broshi, *Bread, Wine*, 129.

47. E.g., onions, garlic, leeks, turnips, rapes, radishes, cabbages, black callah, kale, carrots, mangold, water melon, gourds, squash, lettuce, beets, parsnips.

48. E.g., salt, grasshoppers (m. Ber. 6:3; Mark 1:6), herbs, honey, spices.

49. Borowski, "Mediterranean Diet." Cf. King and Stager, *Life in Biblical Israel*, 68.

The Archaeology of Daily Life

He concluded that Israelites in the Iron Age rarely ate meat, but mostly ate fruits, vegetables, milk products (yogurt, cheese, and butter), and of course, grains (either as bread or as a porridge). When they did eat meat, only on special occasions maintained Borowski (i.e. when hosting a guest or at a festival), it was mostly mutton but perhaps some fowl. With these observations about the lack of meat, M. Broshi was in full agreement.[50]

There was a gradation of valued foods evidently, if we may trust one rabbinic text and this gradation may reveal common practices in dining. Broshi quotes a text which advises how to treat a guest so he will not stay too long:

> On the first day he feeds him fowl, on the second fish, on the third meat, on the fourth legumes. Thus he gives him less and less until he serves him vegetables.[51]

Evidently, fowl was considered the most valued dish and vegetables the least. The shrewd host feeds his guest less and less sumptuously until he takes the hint and leaves. But this graded list indicates that red meat, though highly desired, was not considered as desirable as fowl and fish.

Likewise a text from the Tosephta gives the ideal meal of a wealthy person: If a person has ten minas, he eats vegetables; if twenty, he eats vegetables and stew; if fifty minas, he eats vegetables, stew, and one litra of meat a week (on Sabbath); and if he has one hundred minas, he eats the vegetables, stew, and one litra of meat each day (t. Arak. 4:27). Thus, they valued meat but recognized that only the very wealthy could eat it every day.[52]

Borowski finished his essay with a dietary pyramid. The one below is my adaptation of his:

---

50. Broshi, *Bread, Wine*, 121, 132. See also Hamel, *Poverty*, 19.

51. Pesiqta Kehati 31. Translation in Broshi, *Bread, Wine*, 130.

52. Cited in Hamel, *Poverty*, 22, 24. Hamel maintains that the text is assuming the presence of bread and olive oil at the meal. The "mina" was a Greek monetary unit equivalent to 100 drachmas/denarii. Thus 100 minas would equal 10,000 denarii, a huge sum. The figures are, then, imaginary and hyperbolic. See Danker, *Lexicon*.

WHAT WOULD BE INSIDE YOUR HOUSE?

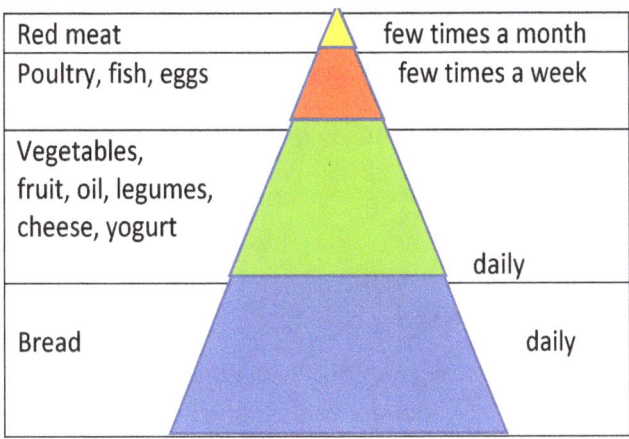

Figure 6.2: Dietary Pyramid Adapted from Borowski[53]

There is a listing in the Mishnah (m. Ket. 5:8) which gives the minimum weekly ration that a man must supply for his wife should he make a journey and leave her behind. The Mishnah passage demands that a man must feed his wife weekly wheat, barley, pulse of some sort (presumably beans, peas or lentils), olive oil, and fruit. S. Safrai opines that the food items given in the m. Ket. text were the standard fare on the weekly menu for most rural farming persons.

There is also passage in m. Peah 8:5 which lists food for the poor. These are the foods required by rabbinic law to help a poor person. Z. Safrai compares the two lists to gain confirmation of the basic diet of a rural working-class family:[54]

m. Peah 8:5 (food for a poor man)	m. Ket. 5:8–9 (rations for a wife)
Wheat	Wheat
Barley	Barley
Spelt (cheap grain)	
Fruit	Fruit
Wine[55]	
Oil (i.e. olives)	Oil (i.e. olives)
	Legumes

Table 6.3: Food rations according to the Mishnah

53. Borowski, "The Mediterranean Diet," 100. Borowski had a small segment for "sweets" and also considered rice and potatoes as a staple. These would not have been likely for the Second Temple Period. Potatoes are a new world food and hence not available in ancient Palestine. Rice was introduced during the Hellenistic age but needs a great deal of irrigation. It is unsuitable for growing in most of Israel according to Broshi, *Bread, Wine,* 126.

54. See S. Safrai, "Home and Family," 747; Z. Safrai, *Economy,* 124.

55. Why no wine for the wife? Both M. Broshi and Z. Safrai observe that lower class women did not drink wine. See *Bread, Wine,* 129; *Economy,* 130 (and j. Pes. 10, 37b).

Thus, the two Mishnah passages seem to have a rather common diet. In addition, take out the meat and poultry from Borowski's Mediterranean diet, and it is remarkably like the two Mishnah texts. One is inclined to conclude that this diet was more standard for poor persons than the food items first listed above. The other foods were known—and eaten regularly by the elites—but the ordinary persons probably found them seldom on their dinner plates.

Remains of Food Processing

Second, one should consider the food processing installations that have turned up in archaeological surveys and excavations. Nathan MacDonald has challenged Borowski's notion of a Mediterranean diet. Some of the items found in this diet (notably potatoes) were unknown to the Israelites. Even some of those items specifically referred to in the Bible were probably rarely seen by the average Israelite. The Old Testament speaks hyperbolically, maintains MacDonald, in describing a land flowing with milk and honey. The promises of extraordinary fertility and abundance (e.g., Deut 8:8) are metaphorical.[56]

The reality probably was, writes MacDonald, that the average Israelite ate a very narrow range of foods. Certainly the so-called "Mediterranean triad" (grain, olives, and grapes)[57] was regularly on the menu. The archaeological evidence for food processing (wine presses, olive presses, grinding stones, threshing floors, and ovens—or *tabuns*—for baking bread) makes it certain that these three (also well attested in the literary sources) were the main stays of the diet. But beyond that, the options were limited to mostly pulses and milk products, maintains McDonald. The average Israelite probably never ate pomegranates or nuts (so MacDonald). Dates would have been rather rare as well. Rather, their diet was centered on grains which supplied a huge portion of their daily caloric intake.[58] The reader will remember in a previous chapter (Chapter 3) that Table 3.4 indicates the installations of several villages. Most had wine presses, olive presses, grinding stones and/or *tabuns* for baking bread. The "triad" is well attested archaeologically—based on the food processing installations—in Palestine/Israel during the late Second Temple Period.

In addition, the clearing of land in three segments to accommodate these three crops further indicates their primacy. Many villages have their farms marked off for grains, grapes (indicated by towers), and olives.[59] Clearly, these were the main three crops in Israel, based on the processing and producing remains.

---

56. MacDonald, *Israelites Eat?* 6–8.

57. Further on the Mediterranean triad, see Dar, *Landscape and Pattern,* 74; Z. Safrai, *Economy,* 108.

58. MacDonald, *Israelites Eat?* 9, 19, 23, 91. See above for the percentage of 50% or higher for calories from grains.

59. Dar, *Landscape and Pattern,* 74.

What Would Be Inside Your House?

That they consumed milk products as Borowski maintained seems a safe conjecture in spite of a lack of direct archaeological remains. One would be hard pressed to think of a way milk processing into cheese, butter, and yogurt would leave a trace in the archaeological record. Their mention in the literature alerts us that they were eaten.[60] There is, however, *indirect* archaeological evidence of milk consumption in the animal bone remains. As we will discuss below, many sites preserve animal bones of sheep, goats, and large cattle. Excavators now have developed a reasonable argument to differentiate between animals used for meat and those used for milk-wool-pulling the plow. In the rural villages, animals were used more for repeated benefits; in the cities more for slaughter and meat consumption. Thus, milk products are attested archaeologically in an indirect way (see below).

Figure 6.3: Wine Press at Nazareth (Photograph by the author)

Remains of Food Preparation

Third, one can consider the food preparation vessels, namely the cooking pots and the so-called "casseroles." Andrea Berlin[61] has speculated on the food habits of a village in the tetrarchy of Philip (son of Herod the Great), named Tel Anafa (Map 1.1). She focuses on three types of clay vessels which turn up in the first-century CE pottery

---

60. For milk products and other foods such as fruits and grains, see Dar, "Food and Archaeology" 326–35.

61. Berlin, "What's For Dinner?"; Berlin, "Jewish Life." Cf. Balouka, "Roman Pottery," 32–33. It appears that the people of Sepphoris transitioned to the casserole style cooking a bit later.

assemblage: cooking pots (300 found, with round bodies and small mouths; Figure 6.4), casseroles (100 found, deep bowls with wide mouths; Figure 6.5), and pans (look like pie pans). The first vessels were used for soups (e.g., lentil soup and porridge); the second were used for stews with large chunks of both meat and vegetables; the third were used for quiche-like meals with meat, fruit, or vegetables swimming in raw eggs and then baked. One would conclude that they ate a variety of legumes, vegetables, meats, and fruits.

Figure 6.4: Cooking pots from Gamla (1st cent. BCE).
Photo by Danny Syon, Israel Antiquities Authority, used by permission.

In general, the people of Galilee and Golan began to manufacture more casserole style vessels in the first century BCE. In Gamla, for example, these vessels comprise one-third of the total assemblage during our time period (ER I period). Thus, we would conclude that the people in the northern regions began eating more stews (with meat, fish, and large vegetables such as cabbage) at this time but still mostly beans and soups.

Vessel type	Vessel shape	Vessel origin	Vessel function	Where found in Israel in late Second Temple Period
COOKING POTS	Round body with small opening (Fig. 6.4)	Ancient Near East and southern Levant	Soups and beans	Throughout accounting for most of the cooking vessels
CASSEROLES	With a large opening suitable for stews (Fig. 6.5)	Greece	Stews (meat, fish, and large chunks of vegetables such as cabbage)	Appears already in early-mid Second Temple times, beginning in the 3rd c. BCE, at sites on the coast (Ashkelon, Dor, Akko) and in the north (Kedesh). But it does not appear at sites with arguably Jewish populations until the early-mid 1st c. BCE in Lower Galilee and Golan. At Gamla they make up 1/3 of household's kitchen pottery. Widely used in Jerusalem in 1st CE
PANS	Like a modern pie plate or quiche dish: low and wide, with a flat bottom.	Italy	Baked dishes (quiche or frittata)	Mostly in upper class sites in Jerusalem (in the Upper City), and at Herodium, Masada, and Jericho (Herodian palaces). Not found in rural Judea.

Table 6.4: Cooking Vessels in the late Second Temple Period[62]

The third type of vessel, the ceramic pans, never caught on in Galilee, the Golan, or Judea but were used in Jerusalem (in the Upper City among the wealthy), and at the Herodian palaces at Jericho, Herodium, and Masada. The pans originated from Italy and, as indicated above, were used for baking dishes like quiche and frittata.[63] Thus, while the cooking pots at all sites in the north and south remained the favorite (indicating still a preference for thin, watery dishes like soup), the casserole with its large chunks of food became increasingly popular in the north.

---

62. Constructed from Berlin, "Jewish Life."
63. Berlin, "Jewish Life," 437–42.

The Archaeology of Daily Life

Figure 6.5: First-Century Casserole, Kibbutz Ginosar Museum
(Photograph by the author)

Food Remains

Fourth, an even better indicator of diet for our period of study (late Second Temple Period or Early Roman period) are the archaeological remains of food at several sites. We saw above that MacDonald challenges the broad menu of fruits and nuts in ancient Israel. He also opines that the Israelites ate more meat than Borowski and others have allowed in their studies of the ancient diet.

Faunal Remains

First, he looks at the faunal[64] remains from various archaeological sites. Although some of these bones may have been from animals (sheep/goats and cattle) used either for milking or for pulling the plow, some of them (most?) must have been the result of slaughtering young and thus used only for meat. The numbers of these faunal remains are too high to have been mostly used for secondary purposes (milk, wool, and

---

64. MacDonald, *Israelites Eat?* 25. MacDonald maintains that vegetables were not valued by the Israelites based on Prov. 15:17, a dubious conclusion. The study of bones is still in its infancy. Lev-Tov informs us that excavations have produced around thirty thousand bone pieces, most of which have yet to be studied. See "Diet," 298.

pulling the plow). It appears from the ratio, observes Macdonald, that they preferred to eat the sheep or goats over the cattle.⁶⁵

A better argument has been mounted by Sapir-Hen, Gadot, and Finkelstein based on the age at death of the animals. Their study looked at Iron II sites. They maintained that merely counting animal bones does not tell us whether the animals were used only as meat or for secondary uses (milk, wool, plowing). But these three scholars, based on the age in which the animals were slaughtered argue that in the urban areas (Jerusalem in their study) people tended to eat more meat. On the other hand, in the rural villages, the residents tended to use animals more for secondary purposes. This conclusion is based on the fact that the animals in the city were younger when slaughtered and larger. The animals' remains found in the villages indicated that they tended to be both smaller (thus probably females used originally for milking) and older (slaughtered only after milk production ended) when they were slaughtered.⁶⁶ Two further studies from the Iron II period have confirmed these conclusions.⁶⁷

The team of Guy Bar-Oz found similar results from a first-century garbage dump in Jerusalem. The team discovered that of the animals' bones recovered, 60% of the sheep and goats and 80% of the large cattle were less than twelve months old. This fact indicates that the animals were not used for secondary purposes (pulling the plow; wool, milk) but specifically for meat. Further, the team determined that the bones were of varying robustness—some being slender and others thicker—and that the teeth showed varying degrees of wear. Their conclusion was that the animals had been imported from all over Israel for their slaughter as meat (see Table 6.5 below).⁶⁸

Therefore, one could conclude that in the rural villages, they ate less meat than in the cities. Borowski, Broshi, and others may have been at least *partly* correct. They evidently did not eat meat for most meals in the rural villages, but maybe a bit more often than previously thought.⁶⁹

---

65. See also Firmage, "Zoology, (Fauna)," 1121–23 who gives a lengthy list of faunal remains from Israelite sites. For the Hasmonean-Roman Ages he lists nine occupation levels at six sites. These sites have bone remains of well over 1700 pieces. But do these remains represent slaughter of the animals after being used for years for milking, for wool production, and for pulling a plow or were most of these animals slaughtered young for their meat without any reference to secondary uses? I cannot find a reliable way to answer this question based in this data alone. But see below in the study of Sapir-Hen, Gadot, and Finkelstein, "Animal Economy."

66. See Sapir-Hen, Gadot, and Finkelstein, "Animal Economy."

67. These findings agree with those of Baruch Rosen at ʿIzbet Ṣarṭah ("Subsistence Economy"). Rosen found that, based on the bone evidence, only 6.8% of the sheep/goats were butchered young. Shafer-Elliott, *Food,* 111 agrees. She studied two rural farmsteads in comparison with two houses in cities and found evidence (based on the age at death and size of the faunal remains) that the urbanites used animals mostly for meat while the rural residents used them mostly for secondary purposes.

68. Bar-Oz, et al., "Holy Garbage."

69. Hamel, *Poverty,* 30, based entirely on literary evidence, had already suggested that the cities consumed more meat per capita than the villages. Kramer (*Village Ethnoarchaeology,* 40–44) observed in her village that a household of six to seven persons might eat one to four sheep/goats in the winter when the animals do not produce much milk. That rate of consumption does not seem like a lot of

Another study of faunal remains was done in Yodefat.[70] Excavators found in Yodefat 3075 bones of which 80% were cattle and sheep/goats; 6.8 % were chickens; 2.9% were partridges; and 2% were pigs. Clearly, the dietary preference was for the four-footed, kosher animals.

At Gamla (Map 7.2) both animal bones (sheep/goats and cattle) and fish bones have been recovered in excavations. They had a preference there for carp but also evidently ate catfish and drums.[71]

Bone evidence also comes from fish remains found both in cities like Jerusalem, Sepphoris, and Caesarea and in towns like En-Gedi. Excavators have extracted from the ruins fish bones in some locations which are not near a lake or ocean. We know that one of the major Galilean export items was fish. The Sea of Galilee contained many varieties of fish edible for both Jews and Gentiles (*War* 3.508, 520; m. Abod. Zar. 2:6). These fish were pickled or salted (Strabo 15.2.45; m. Abod. Zar. 2:6; m. Ned. 6:4) and then sold all over Palestine. Many were involved in this trade, from the fishermen—who could be day laborers (Mark 1:19–20)—to the owners of the fishing boats and the merchants who marketed the fish. Josephus could allegedly round up 230 boats on the Sea of Galilee (*War* 2.635). The Gospels also attest to a thriving fishing trade (Mark 1:16–17; Matt 4:17–22; Luke 5:11).[72] But in addition to the fish from the Sea of Galilee, there were fish transported also from the Mediterranean Sea and the Red Sea as the archaeological remains show.

The cities evidently consumed a lot of fish, even though they might be miles from either the Mediterranean Sea, the Red Sea, or the Sea of Galilee. Justin Lev-Tov[73] reports that fish bones become more frequent in Palestine in the Roman-era excavations, evidently an influence from the Roman dietary tastes. Many saltwater and freshwater fish were transported miles away from their sources. Towns like Tel Heshban (in modern Jordan) and En Boqeq (on the Dead Sea coast; Map 3.2) ate seabreams, tuna, mackerel, groupers, and mullets. En-Gedi, also on the western side of the Dead Sea, consumed a lot of tilapia from either the Jordan Valley (the Sea of Galilee and/or the Jordan River), or so the excavator opines, from nearby streams. En-Gedi also

---

meat-eating but perhaps is a greater consumption of meat than Borowski thought. Shimon Dar also has affirmed that the average resident of Palestine in our period ate more meat than historians have commonly assumed ("Food and Archaeology," 326–35).

70. Aviam, "Socio-Economic," 34.

71. See Lernau and Shemesh, "Fish Remains." They opine on the consumption of catfish in a Jewish town since it is not kosher. They suggest that the ancient Jews considered them kosher. For the cattle and sheep/goats, see Cope, "Butchering Patterns."

72. See Hoehner, *Herod Antipas*, 67; Wuellner, *Fishers of Men*, 45–63; K. W. Clark, "Sea of Galilee," 349; and K.C. Hanson, "Galilean Fishing Economy." For a glimpse of what archaeologists have found in one fishing town, Bethsaida-Julias, see Fortner, "Fishing Implements;" and Strickert, *Bethsaida*, 47–64.

73. Justin Lev-Tov, "Dietary Perspective."

consumed saltwater fish from either the Red Sea or the Mediterranean Sea.[74] We mentioned above that Gamla also yielded fish bones (carp, catfish, and drums).

Excavators in Sepphoris have discovered evidence of several different kinds of fish, imported both from the Mediterranean Sea (eighteen miles away) and from the Sea of Galilee. There are bones from grouper, mullets (both from the Mediterranean Sea) and Tilapia and Catfish from the Sea of Galilee. Obviously, on the table at Sepphoris was salted fish transported at some distance.[75]

Finally, a cesspit near a kiosk selling snacks to the circus-crowd in Caesarea Maritima, yielded over one thousand fish pieces. There were several species of salt water fish (Porgies, Herring, Sea Bass and European Bass, as well as Croakers) and three different fresh water species (Tilapia, Catfish, and Carp).[76] In the cities, therefore, fish became an important source of (imported) food, especially after the Romans began to influence the region.[77] The larger towns (En-Gedi and Gamla) also evidence fish consumption. One doubts if the small rural villagers ate much fish.

Garbage dump, 1st century CE Jerusalem	Yodefat food remains (1st century CE)	Gamla (1st BCE–1st CE)	En-Gedi (1st CE)	Fish bones at Sepphoris (ER–MR)	Fish pieces at Caesarea Maritima (ER–MR)
2,744 bones	3,075 bones				1431 pieces (bones and scales)
79% were sheep or goats (2 to 1 ratio of sheep to goats)	80% cattle, sheep/ goats	Sheep/goats and cattle			
9% cattle					
4% pigeons					
4% chickens	6.8% chickens				
	2.9 % partridges				
	2% pigs				
4% fish[78]					

74. Lernau, "Fish Remains."

75. Frakkin, "Long Distance Trade." In addition, there are quite a few mollusk shells in the soil at Sepphoris. Were these mollusks eaten (they would be unkosher and some are too small to be of any food value) or used as ornaments and utensils?

76. Lernau, "Fish Bones."

77. Lev-Tov, "Dietary Perspective," 435. Lev-Tov speculates that the Romans' love of seafood influenced a rise in this dietary item in Palestine.

78. The garbage dump also had some donkey bones, some rat and mice bones, and some bones from "perching birds." The authors do not give percentages but presume (I take it for religious reasons) that these animals were not eaten but lived around and on the dump. See Bar-Oz et al., "Holy Garbage," 5. The authors also point out that the dump is entirely absent of pig bones and that the fish bones are from kosher fish only.

The Archaeology of Daily Life

Garbage dump, 1st century CE Jerusalem	Yodefat food remains (1st century CE)	Gamla (1st BCE–1st CE)	En-Gedi (1st CE)	Fish bones at Sepphoris (ER–MR)	Fish pieces at Caesarea Maritima (ER–MR)
			Salt water fish[79]		
				Grouper	
Mullets				Mullets	
Porgies					Porgies
					Herring
					Sea bass
Mackerel/tuna					Croakers
		Drums			
Fresh water fish					
Tilapia			Tilapia	Tilapia	Tilapia
		Catfish		Catfish	Catfish
		Carp			Carp

Table 6.5: Early Roman–Late Roman Faunal Remains

We can conclude from Table 6.5 that in addition to mutton, the residents of many cities ate quite a lot of fish, especially Tilapia (from the Sea of Galilee or the Jordan river).

Plant Remains

We can also get an idea of the food people ate in our time period from remains of plants. There are eight excavations that can shed some light on the plant foods. As might be predicted, however, the evidence is tilted toward the Dead Sea area because these remains survive more easily in the arid climate. Thus, five of our eight excavations are in the Judean Wilderness area. Yet, this evidence is balanced somewhat by results from a Jerusalem garbage dump (featured above), from the excavation of Meiron in Upper Galilee, and from the excavation of Gamla in the Golan. First, are the plant remains from the garbage dump in first-century Jerusalem.[80] Second, from our era are the carbonized remains of food items found at Masada (destroyed 73 CE). Archaeologists discovered six different plant foods there.[81] Third, are desiccated remains found in the caves of Naḥal Ḥever under the excavation led by Yigael Yadin.[82] Fourth are the results of sifting "three pails" of dirt from the middle cave of the "Caves of the Spear" north of En-Gedi.[83] Fifth, are the remains from the En-Gedi excavations

---

79. The author (Lernau, "Fish Remains.") does not specify the species of the salt water fish.
80. Bar-Oz, et al., "Holy Garbage."
81. Yadin, *Masada*, 55.
82. Yadin, *Bar-Kokhba*, 211.
83. Simchoni and Kislev, "Relict Plant Remains."

What Would Be Inside Your House?

which found several seeds, pits, and hulls.[84] Sixth, are the remains on a mat covering the floor of a collapsed cave south of Khirbet Qumran.[85] Seventh, is the storage room in the so-called Patrician House at Meiron which dates a little after our time period (fourth century CE). This storage room revealed plant remains of eight different foods, many of which were also found at the other sites.[86] Eighth are the pollen remains, the charred wood remains, and the seed remains found at Gamla.[87] The table below presents these results:

Jerusalem Garbage dump, (1st CE)	Masada food remains (1st CE)	Naḥal Ḥever, Cave of Letters (2nd CE)	Naḥal Ḥever, Cave of Spears (2nd CE)	En-Gedi (1st CE)	Cave south of Qumran	Meiron storage room (4th CE)	Gamla (1st BCE —1st CE)
	Dates	Dates	Dates	Dates	Dates		
	Pomegranates	Pomegranates	Pomegranates				
Olives	Olives	Olives	Olives	Olives	Olives	Olives	Olives
	Walnuts	Walnuts	Walnuts	Nuts		Walnuts	
				Almonds		Almonds	
							Pistachios
Wheat	Grain		Wheat		Wheat	Wheat	Grain
			Barley		Barley	Barley	
Grapes			Grapes		Grapes	Grapes[88]	Grapes
			Pulses[89]			Beans	
				Peaches			
			Figs				
						Plums	
			Hackelberries				
				Jujube (Christ thorn)			

Table 6.6: Early Roman–Late Roman Plant Remains[90]

---

84. Liphschitz, "Archaeobotanical," (En-Gedi).
85. Kislev and Marmorstein, "Cereals and Fruits."
86. E. M. Meyers et al., *Excavations at Ancient Meiron*, 61, 273.
87. See Geyer, "Pollen Analysis"; and Liphschitz, "Archaeobotanical Remains," (Gamla).
88. Inferred from the wine amphoras.
89. Chickpeas, lentils, bitter vetch, and narbon vetch are identified.
90. For other archaeological studies of food in ancient Palestine, two based on the excavation of sites from the Iron II period and one spanning the ER-Ottoman periods (see Appendix B for dates), see: Cahill, et al., "It Had to Happen"; Weiss and Kisley, "Weeds and Seeds"; and Ramsay and Parker,

The reader will notice that olives appear on every list[91] and that wheat/barley are on six of the eight. Second, some crops, such as dates and pomegranates, seem to have been absent from lists 1, 7, and 8 out of regional necessities. Finally, one should observe that these remains are simply the accidents of history. That is, they somehow survived the ravages of time and later populations. There must have been other foods that did not. Therefore, we are left with those crops that somehow made it without decay. One should not think that the refugees at Naḥal Ḥever, for example, ate only those items on our list.

Returning to the ancient garbage dump dating from the first century CE in Jerusalem,[92] we discover some of the plant food sources of the Israelites in this period. The reader will discern from Table 6.6 that the residents of Jerusalem in the first century CE consumed the standard dietary triad of olives, grapes, and wheat. Did they also eat legumes and other vegetables? Common sense would say that they ate most of these things but they simply were not preserved in the garbage dump. Surprisingly, the excavators note, there are no fruit pits and no nuts in the garbage dump. These items should have survived in the remains if they were there in the first place (as they did at Meiron). The urbanites may have eaten less fruit than the villagers.

So what was on the Israelite table? Quite a variety of things according to these archaeological remains. The caveat is that these sites (Jerusalem, Masada, En-Gedi, the Qumran area cave in the first century; the Bar Kokhba caves—including the Cave of the Spears—in the early second century, Meiron in the fourth century, and Gamla from the first century BCE to the first century CE) only offer a snapshot of eating habits for each site. How representative are these samples for Israel as whole in the late Second Temple Period? Perhaps not very representative. These may have been rather well-to-do families or well-to-do neighborhoods and not good examples of the poor peasant's diet. Were these foods available all year long? Probably not. We wonder at the abundance of all the foods. The more modest variety of foods in the Mishnaic lists (Table 6.3) could be a better indicator of what most ordinary persons ate week by week.

And yet, a picture emerges. Those items frequently on the lists, both literary and archaeological, would probably—so common sense dictates—have been most frequently and commonly consumed. So, probably on the menu for a typical last meal of the day in the ER period in a Palestinian/Israelite household would have been:

"Diachronic." See also Killebrew and Fine, "Qatzrin," 51, who refer to an early Medieval Jewish poem which lists thirty-six foods common to Palestine. Many of these are on the above-mentioned three archaeological lists demonstrating that the food choices remained relatively stable.

91. There was no settlement in ancient Palestine "that did not have its olive press." Dar, "Food," 331. For olive cultivation in relation to climate in ancient Israel, see Finkelstein and Langgut. "Climate."

92. Bar-Oz, et al., "Holy Garbage."

- Daily: A milk-based food (cheese or yogurt), grains (either bread or porridge), and legumes. Olives and especially olive oil would also have been daily.[93]

- Several times a week: Fish and poultry would have been eaten along with the ubiquitous nuts we find in the remains. They would also have eaten whatever fresh vegetables and fruits that were in season along with preserved fruits and vegetables (e.g., dried fruit and wine).

- Once a month: Rather frequently (once a month?), mutton would have been on the dining-mat.

- Banquets: At the banquets of the wealthy, they would have served the grain-fattened cattle (Matt 22:4; Luke 15:23, 27, 30) plus, no doubt, a wide range of fruits and vegetables not usually available to the everyday life of the working-class persons. One should observe—with Gildas Hamel—that the feast of the "fatted calf" in Luke 15:32 was an "extraordinary festive meal that everyone in the village would enjoy and remember. . . ."[94] Such a feast would have been more significant for a villager than a city dweller.

Did They Eat Enough?

Further questions are: How healthy was their diet? Did they have enough to eat? The answers to these questions have been debated in the last decades. Some have tried to calculate the possible daily caloric intake per person based on the arable land available to the village and other factors.[95] Those engaging in this method of answering the questions usually have concluded that the Israelites had plenty to eat; there was no malnutrition. Shimon Dar, for example, calculates that during the Herodian period, they farmed 1.25 million acres and that only 50% of this arable land would have been necessary to support a population of 1.2–1.5 million.[96]

Douglas Oakman's study of conditions during our time period, however, answers the question in the negative. Oakman[97] asserts that the village farmers must have been chronically undernourished, that is below the 2500 calories per day for adults that he believes are required. A study by C. Clark and M. Haswell, however should invite caution in drawing conclusions about such an issue without proper information. They note that many people living in developing countries consume fewer calories than that per day and show no signs of malnutrition.[98] Oakman seems to assume that the

---

93. Compare with David Kraemer, "Food, Eating, and Meals," 405.
94. Hamel, *Poverty*, 25.
95. See MacDonald's survey in *Israelites Eat?* 45–57; and Dar, "Agrarian Economy," 307.
96. Dar, "Agrarian Economy," 307.
97. Oakman, *Economic Questions*, 58f. The author says that people need 794 grams of wheat per day (=2500 calories).
98. C. Clark and M. Haswell, *Subsistence Agriculture*, 1–22.

country people must have been undernourished since they could not possibly have had much of their harvest left over after paying taxes and/or rents.

There is slight archaeological evidence of malnutrition, even starvation from our time period but the evidence is ambiguous. First, there were three children in a tomb in Jerusalem from the first century CE that died from starvation (see Chapter 5). But there were also persons in the same tomb that died from violent attacks (mace, an arrow, execution by fire, and even crucifixion). It looks like these family members lived through the Jewish War and died from extreme circumstances. Thus, one would conclude that the three children did not die from poverty but simply from a war-time siege.[99]

Second, many of the skeletal remains in Palestine from our period—in burial caves ranging from Upper Galilee (Meiron) to Judea (En-Gedi)—showed signs of malnutrition and/or anemia (see below Chapter 9). This evidence was in the form of pits or porosities in their skulls. Usually, such skeletal evidence is taken to indicate that the persons did not have enough to eat. But the confusing part of this evidence is that sometimes (or often) the reason for the lack of nutrition was not lack of food but competition for the food by intestinal and other parasites. Chapter 9 will explain this further.

Thus, one cannot at this point say that there is good evidence the average Jewish person was undernourished. Doubtless finding enough food for a family was a constant challenge and during droughts it was very dangerous. But we should refrain from assuming or concluding that the people were chronically on the verge of starvation.[100]

The Dining Schedule

At the end of the day, the family gathered in the house for the meal. The largest and most important meal was the last meal of the day.[101] The first two were merely "snacks" in our terminology.[102] The wife and older daughters would have labored for hours to make the bread (see Chapter 7) and then in the afternoon put on the oven a pot of lentils or the like[103] with a few vegetables and herbs. They also would have eaten cheese which the wife had prepared some days before the evening meal and which was now ready to be eaten. The family would have gathered in their living/dining room, sitting on the floor around the large pot of stew placed beside the loaves of flat bread. There

---

99. See Haas, "Anthropological Observations."

100. Dar, "Food and Archaeology," 333, argues that most people had enough to eat.

101. King and Stager, *Life in Biblical Israel*, 67.

102. Sweet reports that in the village she studied (*Tell Toqaan*, 128) which was in Syria, they ate for breakfast tea and leftover bread (sometimes only tea); and for lunch bread, onions, and leftovers from last night's dinner.

103. נָזִיד See Holladay, *Lexicon*, 232. Lentils are mentioned in the Bible in the following places: Gen 25:29, 34; 2 Kgs 4:38; and Hag 2:13. For the Mishnah see: m. Ter. 10:1; m. Maas. 5:8; m. Orl. 2:7; m. Shab. 7:4, 21:5; m. Ned. 6:10; m. Maksh. 1:6; m. Teb. Yom 1:2.

were no forks or spoons with which to eat. Each one scooped food with his/her (right) hand or with the flat bread.[104] The men (father and older sons) knelt or squatted around the food items and the women and older girls stood to one side waiting for the men to finish. The women did not eat with the men ordinarily.[105]

Figure 6.6: Arab men enjoying a coffee get-together. Notice that they sit on the floor and that there are no women drinking coffee with them.[106]

After the men finished, the women and little children could eat what was left. There surely would have been bread and stew left (and meat when served but perhaps not the choicest cuts of the meat). The women cleaned up the cooking pot for the next day.

CONCLUSION

As one entered the typical village house, one would see woven mats on the floor for sitting. There might have been other mats rolled up and stacked in the corner for

---

104. King and Stager, *Life in Biblical Israel,* 67; Kraemer, "Food, Eating, and Meals,"409. Ethnographically, see Lutfiyya, *Jordanian Village,* 135.

105. King and Stager, *Life in Biblical Israel,* 67 n. 65, suggest that the women did not eat with the men but, like Arab households they were familiar with, stood by to serve or assist and, then, after the men were finished, ate. They suggest that the women were like Abraham in the story of the three visiting angels. Abraham is said to have stood by while the angels ate (Gen 18:8–9). For ethnographic support for this practice, see Sweet, *Tell Toqaan,* 131; Amiry and Tamari, *Palestinian Village House,* 28; Tannous, "Arab Village," 538, and Figure 6.6. C. Meyers disagrees with King and Stager on this issue and suggests (private correspondence) that segregating women from the evening meal is a later Muslim practice.

106. In Dalman, *Haus,* photo 74. The photograph is c. 1900. © Bertelsmann Unternehmensarchiv. Used by permission.

sleeping later at night. There might be a room under the house for animals—a donkey, some sheep and a few goats—to stay the night. The residents of the house would have had an array of plates, cups, pans, and cooking pots. They could have had some vessels made of bronze or iron. A few might have owned a glass vessel or two as well. Their clothing would have been woven from wool and probably not dyed. The ladies may have had—although I suspect only the wealthier ones—a cosmetic kit with jewelry, eye-makeup, and comb. They would have dined on olives, bread, cheese, and lentils (or chickpeas). Once a week they might have eaten meat of some kind. There is no hard evidence for widespread undernourishment.

7

What Would You Do for a Living?

To MAKE A LIVING in first-century Palestine/Israel, you would need to work in agriculture most likely. Possibly, you could earn your daily bread by the employment of a craft (making vessels of stone, pottery, or glass or making clothing). Your best road to security would be to combine the two.

FARMING

The first thing we should say about the ancient economy of Palestine/Israel, like that of every other economy of the ancient Mediterranean and Middle East, is that it was agrarian. This observation is so common as to be beyond dispute.[1] An agrarian economy was based on land ownership and farm production. Thus, most villages were supported by agriculture even though there were crafts and what we might today call "small industry." But what sort of farm would you work on?

Classes of Land Ownership

Shimon Dar[2] observes that there were three classes of land ownership in Palestine during our period:

---

1. Rostovtzeff, *Large Estate*; Finley, *The Ancient Economy*; Bedford, "The Economy of the Near East"; Malina and Rohrbaugh, *Social Science Commentary*, 3–6; Oakman, *Jesus and the Peasants*; J. K. Davies, "Hellenistic Economies"; Avi-Yonah, *Holy Land,* 188–89. Cf. also the results of the survey of the Golan by Urman, *Golan*, 93, who notes that most of the villages and towns had an agricultural economy. Cf. Lewis, *Life in Egypt*, 65.

2. Dar, "Agrarian Economy," 307.

161

The Archaeology of Daily Life

1. Small holdings farmed by free farmers
2. Large farms and villa estates farmed by the owners with help from day labor
3. Royal lands owned by the Herodian family and their elite associates. These lands were farmed by tenant farmers, day laborers, and slaves.

Let us look at each of these land ownership classes:

Small Holdings

There were two arrangements for the small freeholders to choose from in relation to their land. They could cluster in a village with other farmers and travel each day to their fields away from the village. Or, they could live on their field, in an isolated farmhouse.

Village Farms

When farmers huddled together in villages, they did not reside on their farm plot, but walked out to it from the village each day to work it. If Shimon Dar's findings in Samaria are typical, the individual farm plots (one for each nuclear family) were marked off in the fields surrounding the village. Examples of this arrangement can be seen in several villages in Samaria described by Dar in his important archaeological survey.[3] There the ruins of the villages and surrounding farm plots, marked off by stone walls, are still visible in many places. Several historians have informed us of other villages like these.[4]

The site plan of the farming village, Khirbet el-Buraq, in central Samaria, can illustrate how the farms were measured off and attached to the settlement. There were around twenty-five houses showing when Dar's team surveyed the village but he estimated that around sixty to seventy more houses were buried by the debris of time. The residential area covered 6.25 acres (25 dunams). Dar estimated the population of the village was 1,000 to 1,500.[5] By Broshi's method of calculation, the village would have had 1,000 persons. Here is the site plan as sketched by Dar:

---

3. Dar, *Landscape and Pattern*, 230–45.
4. E.g., see Ben-David, *Talmudische Ökonomie*, 49; and the maps of village farm allotments in Z. Safrai, *Economy of Roman Palestine*, 363–63.
5. Dar, *Landscape and Pattern*, 55.

What Would You Do for a Living?

Map 7.1: Plan of Khirbet el-Buraq (in the center).
Note how the farm plots are marked off on the land surrounding the village.[6]

Dar sketches the land divisions surrounding the village at one point in his report. He estimates that they farmed 411 acres which divide into around 73 households as follows:

- Vineyards: 1.28 acres for each household
- Olives: .8 acres for each household
- Grain: 1.68 acres for each household
- Common lands (for grazing animals): 1.88 acres for each household
- Total: 5.6 acres for each household

6. Dar, *Landscape and Pattern*, II, Figure 43. Used with permission. The small squares are vineyard towers. The plan also indicates wine presses, oil presses, lime kilns, cisterns, and threshing floors.

The Archaeology of Daily Life

Dar observes that this village cultivated a small area but also that they seem to have emphasized wine production judging by the number of winepresses nearby which could turn out seventy to eighty thousand liters of juice per year. He speculated that the village produced wine for export. Second, he reminds us that they often planted grains between the rows of vines and olives. Thus, each household had a total area for grain of around 3.75 acres.[7]

Buraq was a medium sized village with mostly a subsistence farming economy and perhaps some wine production for export. There was one very large house, "exceptionally well built," which evidently belonged to a wealthy family, a feature we saw frequently in other villages presented in Chapter 3 (Table 3.4). There were both rock-cut tombs in the area and cist graves. It was, in many ways, a typical Palestinian village.[8]

Isolated Farms

In Mark 6:56 we read, "Wherever [Jesus] went, into the villages, cities, or farms, they put the sick in the marketplace." Thus, not every farming family huddled together in a village, as archaeological surveys and excavations are now demonstrating. We saw in Chapter 3 that there were several tiers of villages and towns. In Table 3.2 of that chapter, some of the historians offered a category of rural residence which they called "isolated farm" or "farmhouse." These were family units that lived on their own land and in their own residence, separated from other people. Although most persons lived in a village in the late Second Temple Period, some lived on isolated farms. Hirschfeld has given a list of the known isolated farms. His list and map show eleven such farms in Judea, four in Samaria, two on the coastal plain, and one in Upper Galilee. He concluded that before the first Jewish War (66–73 CE), a significant minority of persons lived on isolated farms and that this phenomenon attests to the relative security of the time. After the war, however, these isolated farms began to disappear and almost everyone lived in a village.[9]

Avraham Faust has attempted to differentiate two sub-categories in this tier of residence: the farmstead (small farm) and the estate (larger farm). The former describes "isolated structures located in the midst of agricultural areas." The latter are farms that "extend over large areas and belong to the wealthy ... the residents may include servants, hired laborers, etc."[10] In general, the farmstead was smaller and was worked by the family. The estate was larger, had several buildings, and was worked by slaves, day laborers, and permanently hired hands.[11]

---

7. Dar, *Landscape and Pattern*, 74.

8. Dar, *Landscape and Pattern*, 55–59. The village evidenced dating from the Iron I and II periods, the Persian period, the Hell period, the LR, and the Byz period.

9. Hirschfeld, "Jewish Rural Settlement," 72–74.

10. Faust, "Farmstead," 91.

11. Faust, "Farmstead," 91.

We can describe an example of each tier of isolated farm. Our first example is a farmstead, the so-called "Ein Yalu" farm near Jerusalem. It was started sometime from the first century BCE to the first century CE and continued until the Byzantine period. It covered eleven acres and one of its notable features was its free use of terraces. The site includes a small house, terraced hillsides, and an open area for grazing sheep and goats.[12]

One could not farm very well in the highlands of Samaria and Judea if it were not for terraces. They built walls on the naturally outcropping stratification of limestone rock, leveling out a small strip of land on each level suitable for planting grains or trees. The first-century farm in Judea, which the excavators named the Ein Yalu farm, is a good example of a terraced farm. This eleven-acre plot was crossed with several terraced rows on a steep hill allowing for what would otherwise be an impossible piece of land for farming.[13] This was a farmstead of a small, isolated farm.

Figure 7.1: Terraces in the Judean Hill Country (photo by the author)

Large Farms and Villa Estates

In addition to the small holdings, there were farms notable by the size and architecture of their houses and complexes as well as by the extent of their land holdings. These were large farms with substantial industrial installations. Hirschfeld has made a list of such farms based on the size and architecture of the "manor house." He defines

---

12. Edelstein and Gibson, "Rural Food Basket."
13. Edelstein and Gibson, "Rural Food Basket."

a manor house, and subsequently a large farm, as having a wall around the compound, as having a defensive tower, as being located on an elevated spot, and as being near a main road.[14] Hirschfeld lists sixteen such farms identified solely by the presence of a "manor house." He finds one on Carmel, three in Samaria, four in Judea, seven in Idumea, and one in the Negev.[15]

An example of a large villa would be Figure 4.6, the manor at Ramat ha-Nadiv discussed in Chapter 4. This estate covered two thousand acres and was the residence and farm of a very wealthy family. There were a few of these large estates among the non-noble aristocrats but most of them were royal estates.

A good example of a more modest, yet still large, farm—even though it does not meet Hirschfeld's criterion of having a defensive tower in its compound—is the farm at Qalandiya (8 km—5 miles—NW of Jerusalem). This farm was devoted to viticulture and wine-making and must have employed at the harvest and wine-making season a substantial day-laborer force. The buildings included a North Complex, a South Complex, and a "hillock" in the middle of the two complexes that contained six winepresses, a small oil press, and a *mikveh*. The farm complex covered an area of 2.25 acres (9100 square meters). The buildings of the North Complex—built with finely dressed stones—offered residential quarters for the family. The rougher built South Complex was built for storerooms and also temporary housing for the seasonal laborers. If a farm needs to hire extra laborers, it is a fairly prosperous farm of at least middle-size.

This is an example of a larger isolated farm. The family must have owned several fields around the farm buildings, probably one hundred acres or more, to justify all the winepresses and buildings. Thus, the family would have owned a substantial ancient farm. It was not a "large estate" covering several thousand acres (as Ramat ha-Nadiv; Chapter 4) but a prosperous larger farm.

Royal Lands

The Herods and their elite associates inherited many royal lands from the Hasmoneans as well as expanding their holdings through conquest and annexation. These lands were probably (so opines Dar[16]) worked by tenant farmers, though one must also allow for day laborers and slaves as well (see below). Dar offers his own list of the locations of these royal estates: Jericho, Herodium, Jordan Valley, Jezreel Valley (Great Plain in Galilee), Sharon Plain, Samaria, Judea, and the Golan.[17]

---

14. Hirschfeld, "Fortified Manor," 200.
15. Hirschfeld, "Fortified Manor," 218.
16. Dar, "Agrarian Economy," 308.
17. Dar, "Agrarian Economy," 308. See also Fiensy, *Social History*, 21–73 for a discussion and map of these royal estates.

What Would You Do for a Living?

Had you lived in Palestine/Israel in the late Second Temple Period, you might have owned a small plot of ground. But you also may have worked as a day laborer for a well-to-do landowner.

The Annual Calendar

Farming requires accommodation to the weather and climate. Perhaps no other occupation so studies and depends on favorable weather. After a while, the farmer enters a kind of seasonal rhythm. Such a rhythm was understood centuries before our era of concern.

The Gezer Calendar is an inscription retrieved from the excavations of the biblical city of Gezer in Judah. It comes from the tenth century BCE.[18] It appears to have been a farmer's almanac or calendar of the cyclical tasks of life on the farm divided into twelve one-month periods. As the reader can see, there is no real down time according to this calendar. Every month is taken up with serious agricultural tasks. Although this artifact dates one thousand years before our focus in this monograph (c. 37 BCE—70 CE), it still records for us the agricultural responses to the climate of Palestine/Israel which must have remained fairly constant. I give the translation of the calendar below with the comments of Borowski:

Gezer Calendar[19]	Borowski's comments[20]	Time of year in Gregorian calendar[21]
His two months are (olive) harvest		Late August—late October
His two months are planting (grain)		Late October—late December
His two months are late planting	Planting legumes and vegetables	Late December—late February
His month is hoeing of flax	Hoeing weeds	March
His month is harvest of barley		Late April
His month is harvest and *feasting*	Harvesting wheat	Late April—late May
His two months are vine-tending	Grape harvesting	Late June—July
His month is summer fruit	Gathering fruit	Late July—late August

Table 7.1: Gezer Calendar and Commentary (It begins in late August)

Year after year, the farmer followed the dictates of the calendar—dry period or summer and then rainy season or winter. These realities informed his/her activities with respect to the crops. Ze'ev Safrai has published a suggested timetable for agricultural

---

18. King and Stager, *Life*, 87.
19. Translation in Pritchard, Ancient *Near East*, I.209.
20. Borowski, *Daily Life*, 28.
21. According Borowsky, *Daily Life*, 28.

The Archaeology of Daily Life

activities throughout the year which may with profit be compared to the Gezer Calendar above. Notice that his yearly cycle leaves a bit of rest time in the spring for the farmer. The following table summarizes a part of his table:

Month/crop	1	2	3	4	5	6	7	8	9	10	11	12
Grains					****	****			———	———	++++	++++
Legumes				****	****				———	———	++++	++++
Grapes						****	****	****	****			
Olives									****	****	****	****
Dates							****	****				

Table 7.2: The Agricultural Year[22] (beginning from the Hebrew month Nisan in late March–early April, which is the first month of the calendar).
Key: ——— = plowing; ++++ = sowing; **** = harvest

By the time of the late Second Temple Period, the first month of the year was in the spring, not in the fall. Hence, Safrai's calendar begins with Nisan (the first month of the Jewish calendar, which falls somewhere in late March or early April depending on the year) while the Gezer Calendar began with a month corresponding to our late August.

Figure 7.2: Basalt olive crusher, Capernaum (photo by the author)

22. Based on Safrai, *Economy,* 366. Cf. Rousseau and Arav, *Jesus and His World,* 9, for a calendar with differing details; and Hamel, *Poverty,* 110, for yet another calendar, again with different details.

As the reader can observe, there are three months (mid-March—mid-June) of "downtime" in the annual farming cycle according to Safrai. Yet, the two annual schedules match fairly well. There is usually something to harvest, plow, or plant. The schedule would be especially hectic in the ninth–twelfth months (roughly November to February) when the farmer must not only finish up the harvest of fruit (grapes and olives) that will rot quickly if not picked, but also plow and plant next year's grains and legumes. It was probably during these seasons that those farmers who could hired day laborers. But what did the day laborers do the rest of the year?

Of course, the crops, once harvested, must be processed. Olives were pressed into oil; grapes were made into wine; and grains were separated from the chaff by the process of the threshing floor and winnowing. Then it all had to be stored for use the rest of the year. So, while there seems to be "downtime" in the schedule of Safrai, because there is no planting or harvesting going on at those times, there would have been processing happening during part of that time.

Laborers

Someone had to work the land to reap its rewards. There were four options to the ancient landowner. He could settle semi-permanent tenant farmers on his land to work it and share its harvest. He could hire day laborers and pay them a daily wage. He could buy slaves and compel them to do the work. And he could, with his family, work the land himself, usually as a small freeholder.

Tenant Farmers

From the Mishnaic and Talmudic evidence one can see that tenants in Palestine from the second to the fifth century lived under about the same conditions as tenants elsewhere in the Roman empire. The sources refer to two kinds of tenants.[23] The first kind, the *ḥakhir* (חָכִיר), paid a set rent in kind; the second type of tenant, the *ʾaris* (אָרִיס), paid a percentage of the crop.[24]

The *ʾaris* paid a percentage that doubtless changed depending on the crop. The figures of one-half of the crop, one-third, and one-fourth as the standard percentages appear frequently in the rabbinic literature.[25] But there are also references to the landlord demanding two-thirds of the crop.[26]

---

23. Krauss, *Talmudische Archäologie*, 2.108.

24. Ben-David, *Talmudische Ökonomie,* 60; Krauss, *Talmudische Archäologie*, 2.109–10; Jastrow, *Dictionary.*

25. M. Peah 5:5; t. B. Metzia 9:11; j. Demai 6.1.

26. M. Peah 5:5.

Tenants appear to have had a written contract (m. B. Batra 10:4). The only example of such a contract for an *'aris* that we possess indicates that one-half of the produce went to the landowner:

> I shall plough, sow, weed, cut, and make a pile (of grain) before you, and you will then come and take half of the grain and straw. And for my work and expenses I shall take half.[27] (t. B. Metzia 9:13)

The parable in Mark 12:1–8, the Parable of the Wicked Tenants, pictures a landlord who demanded immediate and full payment. This relationship was evidently in the *ḥakhir* tenancy arrangement. In other words, they had to pay a set sum no matter how poor their harvest was. The relationship between landlord and tenants in this parable is mirrored in the examples given in de Ste. Croix of tenants being beaten and threatened unless they paid all that was due the lord.[28] A relationship of hostility and distrust may have been the usual.

Day Laborers

Day laborers (called פּוֹעֲלִים *po'alim* in the Mishnah and ἐργέται *ergetai* in the New Testament) were numerous in the ER I period.[29] There were landless inhabitants in Palestine even before the exile who hired themselves out especially at harvest time (Ruth 2:3). Whether this number increased during our period of concern is debated but at least one can say that they were a labor force in both the rural areas and the cities.

Types of Day Laborers

Of course, not all paid laborers were totally landless. Our sources inform us that there were two types of day laborers. The first type (פּוֹעֵל יוֹם) did not own any land at all and depended entirely on his daily wage to live.[30] These persons were perhaps the poorest of the land, except for the crippled and beggars. These workers had only their labor to live by. If they became ill or injured and unable to work, their situation could be very tenuous. This worker owned "neither the means nor the instrument of production . . ."[31]

---

27. Translation in Neusner, *Tosephta*.

28. De Ste. Croix, *Class Struggle*, 215f. The texts and translations of most of his inscriptions can be found in Frank, *Survey*, 4.96–98, 656–61.

29. Matt 9:37f=Luke 10:2; Matt 10:10=Luke 10:7; Matt 20:1,2,8; Luke 13:27; Jas 5:4; Luke 15:17, 19, 21; Mark 1:20; John 10:12.

30. Ben-David, *Talmudische Ökonomie*, 65; Krauss, *Talmudische Archäologie*, 2.102.

31. Kreissig, "Landwirtschaftliche Situation," 249.

Figure 7.3: Threshing floor with grain stalks piled nearby
(photo by the author)

The second type of day laborer (called a שָׂכִיר) owned a small piece of ground but found it necessary to supplement. They usually hired themselves out for a definite period of time (an hour, a day, a month, a year, or even up to seven years).[32] Klausner surmised that the younger sons of a farmer with a modest tract of land would not have received enough land as an inheritance to maintain them and thus must have resorted to working as a hired hand to supplement income from his tiny inheritance.[33] Other day laborers were probably simply poor small freeholders whose families were too large to be supported by their plot of ground (see below) and therefore were forced to supplement their income.

Types of Labor

The laborers could perform any number of jobs. Of course, there were craftsmen and other skilled laborers who were in a better economic situation than the unskilled laborers (see below). But these must have been a minority judging from the references in the rabbinic literature. The agrarian-oriented Mishnah often refers to the tasks of the day laborers. The following are mentioned frequently:[34]

---

32. See Ben-David, *Talmudische Ökonomie,* 66f; Krauss, *Talmudische Archäologie,* 2.105; and m. B. Metzia 9:11, t. Sheb. 5:21, t. B. Metzia 8:1, 10:2, t. Shabb. 17:27.

33. Klausner, "Economy of Judea," 190.

34. T. Maʿas. 2:13, 15; t. B. Metzia 7:5,6; m. B. Metzia 6:1, 7:4, 7:5, 7:6, 7:7, 8:8, 10:1; m. Maʿas. 5:5; m. Peah 5:5; m. Sheb. 8:5; m. Tohor. 10:1,3; m. Maʿas. 2:13; m. Shabb. 17:26–27. See also Krauss, *Talmudische Archäologie,* 2.105.

The Archaeology of Daily Life

- Plowing
- Weeding
- Harvesting grain
- Picking fruit
- Carrying burdens[35]
- Digging wells
- Barbering
- Working as a sailor
- Donkey driving
- Wagon driving
- Piping
- Flax laboring
- Watching over a field, a cow, or a child
- Pressing olives

Archaeological Evidence for Quality of Life

The life of a daily paid laborer must have been physically hard. Pathological examination of some skeletal remains from the ER I period has identified some examples of these workmen. For example, the remains from the Qumran cemetery, dating prior to 68 CE, contained the skeleton of a man who died at age 22 who had done hard physical labor with his hands from an early age and who had walked barefoot all his life. Another example was the skeleton of a man who had died at age 65 who had been a "laborer." This laborer had carried heavy weights on his shoulder much of his life so that his bone structure was permanently deformed.[36] A man who has never owned any sandals, whose bone structure indicates that he has done hard manual labor all his life (probably from age five; see Chapter 5), and who dies at a young age (22 years), has had a toilsome and sad life. The other man lived a long life for that day and time but had to carry heavy loads for his living. He had only his labor to keep him alive.

The Wages

Most historians agree that the average daily wage of the laborer was one denarius (or one drachma) per day, based mainly on the parable in Matt 20:2, 9, 13.[37] But there are

---

35. He might carry reeds, wood, harvested crops—even people. See Krauss, *Talmudische Archäologie*, 2.105. One story tells of five men who were paid to carry a polished stone from Galilee to Jerusalem to be used in the temple. See Ben-David, *Talmudische Ökonomie*, 294.

36. Steckoll, "Excavation Report." See also Table 8.1 below for these and other examples of workers.

37. Ben-David, *Talmudische Ökonomie*, 66f; Krauss, *Talmudische Archäologie*, 2.105; Grant,

other indications that one denarius was the average wage: Tobit 5:14, j. Sheb. 8:4, b. B. Batra 87a, b. Abod. Zar. 62a.

One must emphasize, however, that this wage was only the average. There could actually be a great variation in wages in ancient Palestine. The variation seems to have been based mainly on the type of task done rather than on inflation or recession. In general, the economy of Palestine was stable, except for times of famine, until the third century CE. So, although Hillel, the scholar, received one-half denarius as a woodcutter (b. Yoma 35b) another worker was paid one-sixth denarius to gather vegetables (m. Sheb. 8:4). Some persons received higher wages than one denarius, especially during harvest time. Work at harvest time might be worth four denarii per day (t. B. Metzia 6:15, b. B. Batra 87a) instead of the usual one denarius.

On the other hand, some wages recorded were paid per job, not per day. Wages for working a field of unspecified dimensions were ten *cors* of wheat and two hundred denarii (t. B. Metzia 5:13). The labor probably represented a full year's work. In addition, several sources indicate that the agricultural workers often ate some of the produce that they harvested (m. B. Metzia 7:2–5; t. B. Metzia 8:8). Thus, the payment in coins was not necessarily the full payment as was often the case of workers in Rome.[38] The table below gives the data we have on daily wages and compares Palestine with three other locations in the empire.

TYPE OF DAILY WORK	PALESTINE 1ST CENTURY CE[39]	EGYPT 1ST CENTURY CE[40]	GREECE 5TH AND 4TH CENTURIES BCE[41]	ROME/ITALY 1ST CENTURY CE[42]
Agriculture	1/6 denarius to 4 denarii (at harvest time)	1/3 to 1-1/2 drachma (Lewis)		
Soldier		2-1/2 to 3-1/3 drachmas (Lewis)		1/2 denarius
Unskilled laborer	1/6 denarius to 1 drachma/denarius	1 drachma (Scheidel)	1 drachma to 1-1/2 drachmas (Jevons)	1 denarius plus bread (at Pompeii; Scheidel)
Skilled laborer		1 drachma (Lewis)	2 to 2-1/2 drachmas	

Table 7.3: Daily Wages in the Roman Empire

Economic Background, 68; Jeremias, *Jerusalem,* 111; Klausner, "Economy of Judea," 191; Kreissig, "Landwirtschaftliche Situation," 236.

38. Ben-David, *Talmudische Ökonomie*; Fiensy, *Social History*; and Sperber, *Roman Palestine*.
39. Sperber, *Roman Palestine*; Ben-David, *Talmudische Ökonomie*; Fiensy, *Social History*.
40. Lewis, *Life in Egypt*; and Scheidel, "Real Wages."
41. Jevons, "Some Ancient Greek Pay-Bills."
42. Scheidel, "Real Wages"; Angela, *Day in the Life of Ancient Rome*.

The Archaeology of Daily Life

We can also compare annual incomes from many regions in the Roman Empire for a day laborer. One of the difficulties in such a comparison is the variation in the estimation of the number of work days for the average laborer. Ben-David estimates two hundred work days in Palestine; Jevons three hundred work days for Greece; and Scheidel estimates two hundred fifty work days for Egypt. Taking Scheidel's estimate as the average between the two extremes, we arrive at an annual income for the day laborer in Palestine in the late Second Temple Period of 250 denarii. One can see that skilled labor fared better financially than unskilled:

	ROMAN EMPIRE 1ST AND 2ND CENTURY CE[43]	EGYPT 1ST AND 2ND CENTURY CE[44]	PALESTINE 2ND CENTURY CE[45]	GREECE 4TH CENTURY BCE[46]
Unskilled labor	Lictor: 150 denarii	250 drachmas (= 250 days of work) for a man; 93 drachmas for a woman; 108 drachmas for a child	200 denarii/drachmas (= 200 days of work; Ben David)	450 drachmas (= 300 days of work at 1-1/2 drachmas per day)
Skilled labor	Scribe: 200 to 300 denarii (Andreau)			600 to 750 drachmas (skilled construction work)

Table 7.4: Annual wages for a day laborer

Could one live on the wages of an unskilled worker? Most ancient economists conclude that one could support a family of four persons but with no margin for error. They would have lived very simply and meagerly. But one economist, Scheidel, thinks that an unskilled worker could not support a family on his wages alone. He calculates that a family in Egypt needed three hundred and fifty-four drachmas but that the male head of household only earned two hundred and fifty. This worker could only earn seventy percent of the subsistence needed by a family of four. Therefore, he concludes, the wife and children must have worked as well to provide a "bare bones subsistence" for the family.

43. Dobson, "Comparison of Pay"; Millar, "Salarium"; Andreau, "Wages."
44. Scheidel, "Real Wages."
45. Sperber, *Roman Palestine*; Ben-David, *Talmudische Ökonomie*; Fiensy, *Social History*.
46. Jevons, "Pay Bills."

	PALESTINE 1ST AND 2ND CENTURIES CE[47]	**EGYPT 1ST CENTURY TO THE LATE 2ND CE**[48]	**GREECE 328 BCE**[49]	**ROME 1ST CENTURY CE**[50]
Bread	124 denarii	208 drachmas	112 drachmas ("food")	182 denarii

Table 7.5: Costs of Bread for Family of Four for One Year

We do not possess comparative data for all categories from our sources but Table 7.5 summarizes one of the important financial obligations: buying bread for one year for a family of four. There would have to be other food consumed beside bread (wine, meat, cheese, eggs, lentils, etc.). There must also have been a clothing allowance and a housing allowance. Finally, calculating food needs based on a family of four is unsound, in my opinion. A family of five seems more realistic (see Chapter 5). Thus, the actual costs must have been higher than these figures indicate but the cost of bread does help the historian get some idea of living expenses. A year's supply of bread for a family was rather uniform in cost—except for Egypt—throughout the Greco-Roman world.

Slaves

There were also certainly agricultural slaves. The New Testament alludes to them in several passages (Matt 13:27; Mark 12:2; Luke 15:22; 17:7). Thus, agricultural slavery does seem to have been practiced but as to what extent, we have no clear evidence. We discover as much evidence if not more that tenants and day laborers mostly worked the farms for the wealthy. One is led to conclude that although agricultural slavery was certainly employed in Palestine in the Herodian period, it never reached the extent of the great *latifundia* of Italy and Sicily which were worked mainly by slaves.

Freeholders

The main difference between small freeholders (those owning a small farm plot) and tenants was that the former were totally responsible for the harvest. As Finley has observed; "The freer the ancient peasant, in the political sense, the more precarious his position."[51] A tenant farmer might receive assistance during a drought from a beneficent (or shrewd) landlord and perhaps a relaxation of rent payments. But the freeholder, who farmed his own small plot, would have to fend for himself—or borrow from someone—to make it through the crisis.

47. Sperber, *Roman Palestine*.
48. Scheidel, "Real Wages."
49. Jevons, "Pay Bills."
50. Angela, *Day in the Life*.
51. Finley, *Ancient Economy*, 108.

Although there probably were some small freeholders who lived fairly comfortably, the farmer in general in the Greco-Roman world "was always at the margin of safety."[52] His/her main problem was the small size of the typical family farm. The following table indicates various estimates of the necessary land for a family of six:

Historian estimating	Necessary amount of land for family of six
Ben-David	16.8 acres
Oakman	16.5 acres
Dar	6 acres
Brunt	10.8 acres
White	More than 8 acres
Z. Safrai	5 acres

Table 7.6: Estimates of Necessary Farm Sizes in the Late Second Temple Period[53]

As the reader will observe, there is a significant disagreement as to how much land one needed to feed a family. We must bear in mind that the ancients let their land lie fallow every other year. Otherwise, it would soon be exhausted. Thus, one needs to multiply by two any calculations of food production. On the other hand, other historians have observed that because of the climate, farmers in Palestine can actually harvest twice in one year. Thus, the effects of fallowing land may have been somewhat blunted.[54]

Ze'ev Safrai surveyed several villages in Samaria and Galilee. The average size of the farm plots (marked off by stone walls) ranged from 1.2 acres to 3 acres. Safrai surmises that each family owned several plots.[55] What one cannot know is how many plots the average family of five persons owned. Common sense would suggest that a few families owned quite a few plots while others attempted to live on a very small farm.

Thus, one would likely need to supplement the farm produce by hiring out as a day laborer during part of the agricultural year. You could hire on to help pick the fruit or cut the wheat. Or you could learn a craft (weaving was a favorite) and engage in it during the few "downtimes" on the farm. Finally, one could send his/her children out as hirelings to bring home the daily wage (see Chapter 5).

INDUSTRY

But the agricultural base does not mean that there was no industry in late Second Temple Palestine. When we use the term "industry," however, we should not imagine

---

52. Finley, *Ancient Economy*, 107.

53. See Ben-David, *Talmudische Ökonomie*, 44; Oakman, *Economic Questions*, 64; Dar, *Landscape*, 262; Brunt, *Social Conflicts*, 35; White, *Roman Farming*, 336f; Z. Safrai, *Economy*, 355.

54. Jensen, "Climate."

55. Z. Safrai, *Economy*, 360.

the huge factories in the modern world. They were more like craft centers and food production centers for export. There may have been more industry in Lower Galilee than elsewhere in Palestine, except in Jerusalem, itself.

Stoneware Vessels

Y. Magen's work on stoneware production has brought to light several quarry workshops in Galilee and Judea, for example, the two in Lower Galilee—one in Bethlehem of Galilee (just southwest of Sepphoris) and the other in Kefar Reina (just east of Sepphoris; see Map 12.1). These were major producers of stone cups and other vessels. Stoneware has been discovered throughout Galilee (in several villages and cities).[56]

In addition, as we saw in Chapter 2, Jerusalem was a center for stoneware production. Stone vessels have been found distributed widely in Judea and Samaria as well. In every site identified as late Second Temple Period, excavators have found stone vessels (and ritual baths).[57] It was big business due to the changing religious environment.[58]

Pottery

There was also a vigorous trade in pottery in Galilee and the Golan in our period. This conclusion was first popularized by David Adan-Bayewitz. In a series of publications, he has highlighted the pottery industry of a small village in the middle of Galilee called Kefar Hananya. Adan-Bayewitz and I. Perlman have established that Kefar Hananya exported its common pottery up to 15 miles (24 km) away into Galilee and the Golan. The pottery manufactured in this village has shown up in Nazareth, Capernaum, Kafr Kanna, Tiberias, and Magdala/Taricheae in Lower Galilee, and in Meiron, Khirbet Shema, and Tel Anafa in Upper Galilee among other sites. It also appears in the ruins of Gentile cities such as Acco-Ptolemais, Hippos, Pella, and Scythopolis (or Bethshan).[59] They maintain that 75% of the first-century common table wares excavated at Sepphoris so far (cooking bowls) were made in Kefar Hananya.[60]

The process by which these conclusions were made is called neutron activation analysis. The scientific test allows the excavators to determine the chemical content of the clay used in making the pottery. The clay content of many of the wares found in the villages and cities of Galilee indicates that much of the pottery came from the area of Kefar Hananya and that many of the large jars came from the tiny village of Shikhin (1.5 kilometers from Sepphoris).

56. Magen, *Stone Vessel Industry*, 160.
57. Magen, "Land of Benjamin," 21–22.
58. See Chapter 12 of this volume.
59. Adan-Bayewitz and Perlman, "Socio-Economic and Cultural Ethos."
60. See Adan-Bayewitz, *Common Pottery*, 23–41, 216–36; Adan-Bayewitz, "Kefar Hananya"; Adan-Bayewitz and I. Perlman, "Local Trade of Sepphoris."

The Archaeology of Daily Life

Yet, now it appears that what they identified as "Kefar Hananya ware" was actually made in many sites in Galilee and not just in that one village center.[61] As a matter of fact, there have now been located six pottery production centers in the Golan from the first century and five in Galilee from the same time period. It appears, as Aviam has pointed out, that those villages where agriculture was challenged due to the terrain, learned to cope economically by initiating industry.[62] These excavations demonstrate that there was a vigorous trade of pottery in Galilee and in the Golan in the first century.

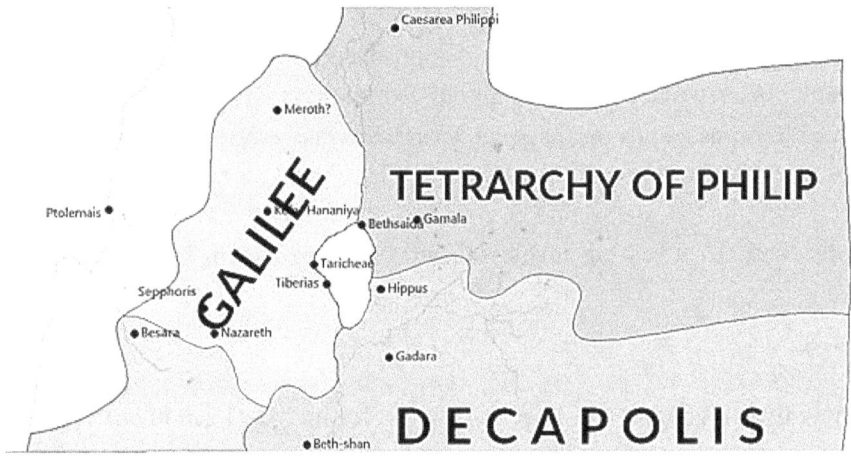

Map 7.2: Galilee and the Golan (i.e. Tetrarchy of Philip), including Meiron (i.e. Meroth),[63] Gamla, and Kefar Hananya
(Map created with Accordance)

Shikhin (Asochis) was located on a hill that covers 27 acres. Surely, however, the actual village was not that large. Based on surveys and seven seasons of excavations, it appears that the village lay toward the northern side of the hill. The pottery count so far indicates that the village reached its height during the Early Roman period. The abundance of pottery and pottery wasters indicate that the village, as celebrated in the Talmud, supported a major pottery-producing industry.

The survey team of Strange, Groh, and Longstaff concluded that 15% of the storage jars or kraters discovered thus far in Sepphoris originated in the nearby village of Shikhin (Map 12.1). The Shikhin storage jars, according to the three archaeologists,

---

61. Aviam, "Yodefat," 114; Aviam, "Kefar Hananya Ware."

62. Aviam, "Kefar Hananya Ware," 144. Four of the centers in Galilee listed by Aviam are Kefar Hananya, Shikhin, Karm er-Ras, and Yavor. But now it also appears, by chemical examination of the clays used in the pottery imported to Gadara, that Meiron (in Upper Galilee) also was a pottery producer and exporter. See Daszkiewics, Liesen, and Schneider, "Provenance."

63. I.e. on the map, Meroth. For Meroth in Josephus as Meiron, see E. M. Meyers et al., *Excavations at Ancient Meiron,* 3; and Josephus, *War* 3.39.

account for the majority of pottery of that type in Galilee.[64] Recent finds in Shikhin have also highlighted, especially, a lamp producing industry in this village (see Chapter 12).

Clearly, the residents of the village also engaged in agriculture since the implements of farming are readily observed: grinding stones, oil presses, and wine presses.[65] Yet they supplemented their farming with pottery production and export.

Cloth

One of the most important industries in Palestine/Israel was weaving cloth. Galilee was famous for its flax garments and Judea for its woolen garments. Certain cities and villages were known for their textile production. The cities and towns celebrated for flax production were Tiberias (b. Mo'ed Qat. 18b) and Arbel (m. Ket. 5:9). After cutting the flax in the fields, the workers needed to move through several time-consuming steps in order to bring it to a state suitable for weaving. This process was usually considered a female job. Thus, women supplemented the farming income by producing fibers that could be woven (m. B. Qama 10:9; t. Ket. 5:4; t. Qidd. 5:14).[66]

As we saw in Chapter 2 of this volume, the New City area of Jerusalem (Map 2.2) was, according to Josephus (*War* 5.331), the center for wool shops. They had many different dyes they could use to imbue color into the fabric. In Chapter 6 we described several woolen items discovered in the caves of Nahal Hever and presented Table 6.2, which lists clothing fragments found in Judea. Again, the making of woolen items was considered a female occupation. Thus, every farm and nuclear farming family might have been also a cottage industry on its own.

Five Villages: A Comparison

Further archaeological evidence as to the economies of the villages in Lower Galilee comes from the excavations of five villages. The first two villages, Khirbet Qana (believed to be the Cana of the New Testament) and Yodefat (or Jotapata) were somewhat more prosperous than the other three.[67]

Khirbet Qana

Khirbet Qana had a small industry: probably a wool-dyeing installation.[68] As we indicated in Chapter 6, dyed wool was a very expensive commodity. Thus, whoever

---

64. Strange, Groh, and Longstaff, "Excavations at Sepphoris."
65. J. R. Strange, "Report."
66. Safrai, *Economy,* 192–93; Rousseau and Arav, *Jesus and His World,* 314.
67. Richardson, *Building Jewish,* 57–71.
68. Richardson identifies the installation as a wool-dyeing industry. McCollough, "City and Village

Yodefat

Second, Yodefat also exhibits small industry, namely olive oil, clothing, and pottery production. Near Yodefat was a cave that had an "industrial-scale double press olive oil station". This installation would seem to indicate more olive oil production than simply for private use. There was, therefore, an olive oil business in Yodefat. Further, the numerous spindle whorls and loom weights found in and around the destroyed houses also attest to a "vigorous home industry of wool materials."[69] The most important industry in Yodefat, however, seems to have been pottery making since several kilns are evident among the ruins (see above).[70]

Jalame

Third, Jalame, located in western Lower Galilee was a glass manufacturing village. They invented glass blowing in the first century BCE making its dissemination throughout the empire, even to lower class persons, possible. Remains of glass factories have also turned up at Tiberias,[71] Hippos, and Beth-Shearim (or Besara). Glass was manufactured in two stages: First the glass slabs were created by heating sand, soda, and lime. Next the slabs were made (molded or blown) into glass vessels. The small vessels usually held liquids, perfumes, and ointments.[72] The larger ones included bowls, beakers, jugs, bottles, and jars.[73] There were also "luxury glass" vessels, that is, vessels whose manufacture would have taken considerable time and skill. But these fragments are small in number.[74]

En Boqeq

Fourth, let us move to the extreme south of Palestine/Israel to tiny En Boqeq situated on the western shore of the Dead Sea eight miles south of Masada (see Map 6.1). The

---

in Lower Galilee," 65 allows that it also could have been used for tanning or as a fullery.

69. M. Aviam, "People, Land, Economy, 27; Aviam, "Yodefat."

70. Richardson, *Building Jewish*, 57–71.

71. Rousseau and Arav, *Jesus and His World*, 229. The Palestinian Talmud declared that in its day (3rd -5th CE) the glass from Tiberias was the best. See j. Nidd. 2.

72. Leibner, "Arts and Crafts," 275. The small vials often were left behind in tombs. See Chapter 11.

73. See the glass assemblage in Jackson-Tal, "Glass Vessel Use," for vessels found in the Bar Kokhba caves.

74. See Jackson-Tal, "Glass Vessels," for a report of vessel fragments (5,000 in all) found at Gamla. She also reports that quite a lot of glass has been found in Jerusalem in first-century contexts (in the City of David, see Map 2.2, and in the Upper City).

village—more a hamlet really—was established during the time of Herod the Great in the late first century BCE and continued until Bar-Kokhba in the early second century CE. It was a center for the manufacture of pharmaceuticals, cosmetics, and perfumes. It was destroyed in the Jewish War (66–73 CE) but resumed for a season during the time of Bar-Kokhba. The "workshop" used the processes of drying, pressing, and boiling of aromatic plants, seeds, fruits, resins, twigs, and bark from the desert to produce their chemicals. The population must have been small, but amazingly it traded with far away towns and villages. Archaeologists have discovered seafood remains (bones and shells) from the Mediterranean Sea and Sea of Galilee in the ruins of the site (see Chapter 6).[75] This would probably have been a village devoted exclusively to industry.

Nazareth

Fifth (and finally), we might also compare the industrial villages named above with one other (see Table 3.4 in Chapter 3) where industry seems to have been non-existent: Nazareth. Nazareth was exclusively an agricultural village. Excavations in and around Nazareth have focused on six locations:

- under the Church of the Anunciation and under the Church of St. Joseph;
- at Mary's Well;
- in the area between Nazareth and Sepphoris (Naḥal Zippori);
- at the Nazareth Village Farm Project;
- at the International Marian Center;
- and under the Sisters of Nazareth Convent.[76]

So far, the excavations under the two churches in modern Nazareth (Church of St. Joseph and Church of the Annunciation) and on the Nazareth Village Farm have revealed granaries, pits, vaulted cells for storing wine and oil, wine presses, rock quarries, cisterns, silos, and oil presses.[77] Only slight traces of the houses have been left, leading one archaeologist to suggest that the houses must have been made of fieldstones and mud.[78]

Excavations at Mary's Well have revealed coins from the Hasmonean and Herodian times.[79]

The area between Nazareth and Sepphoris (north of Nazareth) has revealed "low-status" farms and very small villages. The area was apparently densely farmed during

---

75. Gichon, "Ein Boqeq."
76. See Jenks, "Historical Nazareth."
77. Bagati, "Nazareth, Excavations"; and Pfann, Voss, and Rapuano, "Nazareth Village Farm."
78. Reed, *Archaeology and the Galilean Jesus*, 132; Jenks, "Historical Nazareth."
79. Jenks, "Historical Nazareth."

the first century CE. The remains from the southside of the wadi (nearest Nazareth) are locally made pottery and stoneware vessels, indicating conservative Jewish occupation. On the northside of the valley (nearest Sepphoris), were found some fragments of ESA (imported) ware.[80]

The Nazareth Village Farm Project excavations (west of Nazareth) have discovered ancient terraces with ER pottery in them, thus dating the original construction of the terraces. The terraces and other farming installations such as wine presses (see Figure 6.3) indicate an agricultural community.[81]

One first-century house (see Figure 4.8) was recently excavated (across the street from the Church of the Annunciation at the International Marian Center). It yielded ER pottery and stoneware fragments. An additional first-century house was excavated under the convent of the Sisters of Nazareth (near the Marian Center). It was a typical first-century courtyard house yielding cooking ware, spindle whorls, and stoneware vessels. Also under the convent were two ER tombs.[82]

In addition, many of the houses were constructed around caves (that is, the caves were used for dwellings). These villagers do not seem to have been as prosperous as those at Yodefat and Khirbet Qana. Nor do they seem to have had any industry or way to make a living beyond farming.[83] Thus, one might conclude that if a villager from Nazareth did not own a significant amount of land, he might wander afar in seek of employment at certain times of the year. Many have speculated that the family of Jesus did exactly that.[84]

So, most residents of Palestine/Israel in the first century CE would have lived in an agricultural village with a few hundred to 2,000 inhabitants. But many would have been involved in industry, some exclusively, others as a supplement to their farming. It was not uncommon for entire villages to be devoted to one type of industry[85] such as the villages above devoted to pottery or stoneware vessels.

We should perhaps think of these village residents as existing in three categories: as "pure agriculturalists," as "mixed agriculturalists,"[86] and as purely industrialist villages. Kefar Hananya produced quite a lot of pottery that was exported. It may have been entirely industrial. Likewise, it is doubtful that the small settlement of En Boqeq, producing pharmaceuticals and perfumes, farmed in the hostile regions on the west shore of the Dead Sea. On the other hand, Nazareth seems to have been a purely

---

80. Jenks, "Historical Nazareth"; Dark, "Jesus' Nazareth House."
81. Pfann, Voss, and Rapuano, "Nazareth Village Farm"; Jenks, "Historical Nazareth."
82. Jenks, "Historical Nazareth"; Dark, "Jesus' Nazareth House."
83. See J. F. Strange, "Nazareth," (2015).
84. See Fiensy, *Christian Origins,* 23–33.
85. See Klausner, *Jesus of Nazareth,* 178; Avi-Yonah, *Holy Land,* 193.
86. These are the terms used by Halpern, *Serbian Village,* 71, to describe the residents of the village he studied.

agriculturalist village. Therefore, a carpenter family, ambitious for more business than making "yokes and ploughs"[87] would need to travel to nearby villages and cities.

But there were quite a few mixed agricultural villages. The mixed agriculturalists combined farming with a craft. It appears that several of the villages of Galilee—Kefar Reina, Bethlehem of Galilee, Khirbet Qana, Yodefat, Shikhin, and Jalame—were comprised of quite a large percentage of mixed agriculturalists. Those studying contemporary traditional villages have noted that the mixed agriculturalists generally fare better economically than the pure agriculturalists since they are not as dependent on luck and the weather.[88] The presence of so much industry in these villages might explain their apparent prosperity in comparison with Nazareth, purely devoted to farming.

WOMEN

Women averaged working ten hours per day.[89] The bread-making alone consumed two to five hours' time.[90] First, the women had to grind the raw wheat or barley on the grinding stones, which were probably stationed in their courtyard. Broshi has calculated that grinding enough flour for a family of six would require three hours each day.[91] The pre-pubescent girls in the villages were evidently put to work at the grinding stones.[92] Next they would sift the flour, then mix the flour with water and salt (perhaps leaven). Next they would knead it. They would let the dough rest, if it was leavened, roll it out and shape it, and, finally, they would gather sticks and animal manure to heat up the oven and would then place the dough in the oven.[93] Making bread for the evening meal, with some left over to snack on the next day, was one of the most important tasks of the female. Bread was their staple, their main source of calories. "No meal is considered complete without bread."[94]

Then women had to attend to the spinning and the weaving. To process flax required several stages of labor: harvesting the flax, sun-drying the fibers, soaking the fibers, re-drying them, crushing and winnowing them, spinning the fibers into thread,

87. See the discussion in Fiensy, *Christian Origins*, 25–29.

88. Halperin, *Serbian Village*, 95–96. The pure agriculturalist may boast of being such but his/her household "has no assured steady livelihood" (95).

89. C. Meyers' estimate ("Family," 25).

90. C. Meyers, "Family," 25, suggests bread-making took two hours a day (which she clarifies in *Rediscovering Eve*, 130, as just the grinding time). MacDonald, *Israelites Eat?*, 21, thinks it took three hours a day on average. Ebeling, *Women's Lives*, 48, offers that, based on her reading of ethnographies, bread-making took up to five hours each day.

91. Broshi, *Bread, Wine*, 123. Although Hamel (*Poverty*, 14) maintained that they did not grind grain daily, Rosenblum (*Food*, 26, following Dar, "Food and Archaeology," 330) observed that flour does not keep very long in Israel. Hence, the need to grind daily.

92. The Tosephta (t. Nidd. 6:9) noted that girls in the villages developed breasts earlier than girls in the cities because they ground the daily grain.

93. Rosenblum, *Food and Identity*, 26–28. For this sequence, see t. Ber. 6:2.

94. Tannous, "Arab Village," 534.

and weaving the linen.[95] To make woolen garments required them to shear the sheep, wash the wool, comb the wool, and then weave it.[96]

In addition to all this, she had to attend to cooking the supper and to the babies and toddlers (though an elder daughter probably also helped in that). She may also have had to care for an aging family member. She would tend to the garden and milk the sheep and goats (during the milking season of December–August).[97] Her life was in these tasks much like that of most other women in her era and in most other societies since civilization began.[98]

During harvest she and the children also work in the fields.[99] Yet, although the female's contribution to the agricultural process was in cooperation with the male's, it was probably in a different specific task. For example, in contemporary Arab cultures, during the olive harvest, the men will knock down the fruit using long poles to bang against the branches. Then the women and children will pick up the fruit from the ground. Likewise, the men press the oil from the olives; the women pickle some whole olives to be eaten later. These tasks, differentiated by gender, are rigidly observed.[100]

We also have some attestation from the ancient literature for the daily tasks of women. The table below lists the tasks as found in the Mishnah (and Gen. R.), the New Testament, and in the ethnographies mentioned above relative to our region:

Ethnographies[101]	m. Ket. 5:5[102] [Gen. R. 52.12]	New Testament[103]
Grinding wheat	Grinding wheat	Grinding wheat
Kneading dough		Kneading dough
Baking bread	Baking bread	
Preparing meals	Preparing meals	
Feeding babies/toddlers	Feeding children (nursing)	Nursing children
	Making the bed	
Spinning and weaving	Making woolen clothes	Making clothes

95. Shamir and Sukenik, "Qumran Textiles," 213.

96. Shamir and Sukenik, "Qumran Textiles," 218.

97. According to Borowski, *Every Living Thing*, 46, the milking season in Israel is from December/January to June/August.

98. C. Meyers, "Family," 25. See Prov 31:10–24. See also C. Meyers, "Women's Culture," 431; and Ebeling, *Women's Lives*, 46, who note that these work obligations for women are common in 185 societies examined around the world.

99. See C. Meyers, *Rediscovering Eve*, 51; and Ebeling, "Engendering," for some ethnographic and literary examples of women sharing the agricultural duties with men.

100. See Tannous, "Arab Village," 535.

101. See C. Meyers, "Family," 25; C. Meyers, "Women's Culture," 431; C. Meyers, *Rediscovering Eve*, 51; Ebeling, *Women's Lives*, 46; Ebeling, "Engendering"; Tannous, "Arab Village," 538.

102. See Ilan, *Women*, 185–86. The list of duties in Gen. R. is nearly identical to the one in the Mishnah, but Gen. R. adds "laundering."

103. Matt 24:41//Luke 17:35; Matt 13:33–34//Luke 13:20–21; Luke 15:8; Mark 13:17//Matt 24:19//Luke 21:23; Mark 16:1//Luke 23:55; Acts 9:39; and Ilan, *Women*, 185–86.

Ethnographies[101]	m. Ket. 5:5[102] [Gen. R. 52.12]	New Testament[103]
Washing clothes	Laundering	
		Sweeping floor
Caring for aging family member		
Pottering making		
Milking sheep/goats		
		Preparing the dead for burial
Helping with agricultural work in season		

Table 7.7: Women's Expected Tasks in Palestine/Israel in the Late Second Temple Period

Women, then bore the children, nursed them, and, in addition to these challenges to their strength, worked ten hours a day. These tasks, the rabbinic literature says, the wife "owes" the husband. One might ask what, then, the husband "owes" the wife? Gen. R. 52.12 responds: food, clothing, and marital privileges.

CONCLUSION

Had you lived in Palestine/Israel during our period of interest, you probably would have lived in a village with a population of a few hundred to as many as two thousand. You probably would have engaged in some type of farming, whether exclusively or partially, and may have also hired out as a day laborer or had a cottage industry in your home. If you had no land or almost no land, chances are your children would have to be hired out as well. Whether you farmed only part time or exclusively, your life centered on the annual calendar and the double seasons: seed time and harvest.

8

What Would Your Bones Tell Us?

I OFTEN TELL PEOPLE, "A good historian is just a very nosey person." By that I mean that a historian wants to know everything about the people of the past. The late twentieth century saw a transformation in the writing of history. No longer were historians only interested in the great men, the great battles, and the great nations of the past. They did not simply ask about the emperors, the generals, and the monuments. They began to ask what life was like for the ordinary men and women. What did they do for a living? What did they eat? How did they treat each other? Where did they live? What diseases did they suffer from? How long did they live? What did they think about certain issues? Was their life a misery? What would an ordinary day be like?

In this quest, historians have sought windows into the past in order to understand daily life. They are like surveillance police who watch people through their windows from a distance. Historians are in a sense "watching" the past. Just as the window tells only part of the story leaving the surveillance crew to infer the rest, so historians must extrapolate their window into a coherent story.

Sometimes the window is a papyrus text which describes the family situation of the person composing the document. For example, a text from Egypt dated to 13 BCE records a marriage agreement between bride and groom. The bride brings with her a dowry of two gold earrings and some silver drachmae and promises to fulfill her duties. The husband promises to treat the bride well and to provide for her, otherwise he must forfeit the dowry.[1] With this one text we get a brief look into the family situation of a young couple entering into legal marriage, presumably with all the hope and joy that newly married couples have experienced since time immemorial. But in case it does not work out, the family has protected their daughter with the dowry.

---

1. See the texts in C.K. Barrett, *New Testament Background,* 40.

Historians use whatever means are available—written texts such as the papyri and inscriptions, but also archaeological ruins—to recreate the lives of the ancient folk. The same interest is present in New Testament studies. As a result of asking questions about the ordinary persons, biblical scholars began to use methods and insights from sociology, cultural anthropology, and economics. From the pioneers in this field[2] until its more recent exponents,[3] the goal has been to put a face on the characters of the Hebrew Bible and the New Testament. They ask what it must have been like to live in the world of Palestine/Israel, in the ancient Near East, or in the Greco-Roman world. What were their values and their perceptions and how might knowing the answers to these questions help in understanding the biblical text of the Hebrew Bible or the New Testament? The rise of the social sciences in biblical interpretation was the result of a perceived need for a "sociological imagination" to understand the scenes and scenarios of scripture.[4] These interpreters maintain that merely collecting information is not enough to facilitate interpretation of the New Testament; one must have the means of, "envisioning, investigating, and understanding the interrelation of texts and social contexts."[5] The goal of the social science movement in interpretation has been to enable the interpreter to get to know the ordinary people for whom and largely by whom the texts were originally written.

In recent years, archaeologists of Israel and the Greco-Roman world have also begun to change their focus. Now they study not only the architectural features of the cities and the great monuments of antiquity (such as we looked at in Chapters 2–4 of this volume). As Justin Lev-Tov observed, the archeological study of Roman Palestine has largely been done like Classical Archaeology (that of Greece and Rome). These archaeological investigations engage in "massive excavations of Greek and Roman cities, studies of public architecture, sculpture and other ancient artistic endeavors. Economic studies of the classical era have focused on trade in luxury goods." Other items, maintains Lev-Tov, like bones, have been discarded as unimportant or uninteresting. But we need, he pleads, a "holistic approach."[6] A holistic approach considers all remains, not just the beautiful ones.

---

2. See, among others, Theissen, *Sociology of Early Palestinian Christianity*; Kee, *Christian Origins in Sociological Perspective*; Malina, *New Testament World*; Robert R. Wilson, *Sociological Approaches to the Old Testament*; and Lang, ed., *Anthropological Approaches to the Old Testament*.

3. Oakman, *Jesus and the Peasants*; Ekkehard W. Stegemann and Wolfgang Stegemann, *The Jesus Movement*; Blasi, Duhaime, and Turcotte, eds., *Handbook of Early Christianity*; Neufeld and Demaris, eds., *Understanding the Social World of the New Testament*; Elliott, *What Is Social-Scientific Criticism?*; Osiek, *What Are They Saying about the Social Setting of the New Testament?*; Rohrbaugh, ed., *The Social Sciences and New Testament Interpretation*; and Neyrey and Stewart, eds., *The Social World of the New Testament*.

4. See Elliott, *Social-Scientific Criticism*, 13.

5. Elliott, *Social-Scientific Criticism*, 13.

6. Lev-Tov, "Upon What Meat Doth This Our Caesar Feed?," 425–26. Lev-Tov elsewhere quotes in apparent frustration the words of Terry O'Connor: "the archaeology of the Roman Empire is typically finds-rich, and the reports are . . . often bones-poor." See Lev-Tov, "Diet," 297.

Likewise Tal Ilan laments that in the past when archaeologists found ossuaries (boxes for secondary burial, see Chapter 11), "bones in them have traditionally been swept away as an uninteresting and messy addition to a piece of fine craftsmanship."[7] But she argues that it is not just the workmanship of the stone ossuary that should be of interest, but also the contents: the skeletal remains. We are not just art historians but historians in general. We care about the people and not just the art they produced.

Who says bones are unimportant? In the next three chapters, I hope to demonstrate how important and how full of information bones—and other items—can be. Historians are looking for windows. Sometimes bones can give them to us; sometimes it takes other types of human remains (see Chapter 9) to find a window. We study not just texts and shiny objects buried in the dirt; we are not just interested in the lifestyles of the rich and famous; we are not merely awed by the monumental buildings of antiquity. We take the information wherever we find it; we want windows.

INTRODUCTION TO OSTEOARCHAEOLOGY

So, let us turn, in the next three chapters, to an examination of human skeletal remains. The skeletal remains are about as personal as we are ever going to get for the investigation of most of the ancient persons, the ordinary folk. The common man and woman, in the main, wrote nothing. But they did leave some of themselves behind: their physical remains.

We can meet these people in their skeletal remains and learn a great deal about the kind of lives they lived. We can find out: how tall they were, if they suffered from chronic illnesses, how long they lived,[8] if they were well nourished, to what ethnic group they belonged, whether they died of natural causes or violently, genetic affinities, the state of bodily development, wear and tear from labor, and social conditions.[9] The bones tell us many things.

The modern study of paleodemography through osteoarchaeology (or bone archaeology) began with the publications of J. Lawrence Angel,[10] who in 1947 collected 384 skeletal remains from Greece covering the Neolithic through the Byzantine eras. Although the sample size for each era was small, he nonetheless, produced some very interesting and innovative results for his time. The rates of infant mortality and life

---

7. Ilan, "Ossuaries," 64.

8. Grmek, *Diseases*, 383 n. 40: "The determination of age at death from these skeletal remains is based on tooth eruption, formation of long bones, cranial suture closure, metamorphosis of the public (sic. for "pubic") symphysis, radiographic translucency of proximal femur and humerus, dental wear, and a variety of minor indicators."

9. Patricia Smith, "Skeletal Analysis"; Eakins, "Human Osteology and Archeology"; Grmek, *Diseases*, 51; Nagar and Sonntag, "Byzantine Period Burials"; and Steckoll, "Preliminary Excavation Report."

10. Angel, "Length of Life."

expectancy rose and declined a bit as the eras changed but overall there was a very high rate of infant mortality and a very short life expectancy for adults.

Publications of analyses of skeletal remains from the Second Temple Period in Israel began in the 1960s.[11] There now—as the reader will see below—is quite a large database of osteological information out there.[12] At times, the bones are not very well preserved and so only the most basic information can be gleaned. At other times, the anthropologists seem to have been able to be quite precise in the age at death and general health of the individual.

I intend, in this chapter, in Chapter 10, and partly in Chapter 9 to survey reports of skeletal remains to get a clearer picture of the people of Palestine/Israel in the late Second Temple Period. The sites we will survey include[13] eleven tombs or tomb complexes in the vicinity of Jerusalem; one in Galilee; four sites (8 tombs) in Judea and southern Samaria; and four sites on the western shores of the Dead Sea including Jericho (130 tombs), cave 8 from Naḥal Ḥever, nine tombs at En-Gedi, and several collections[14] of the skeletal remains from the Qumran cemetery (see Map 5.1). The eleven tombs/tomb complexes in Jerusalem are: Giv'at ha-Mivtar, Mt. Scopus (twice), French Hill (both Hell II and ER tombs), the Caiaphas tomb, the Akeldama tombs, the Arnona tomb, the Abba cave, Wadi Ḥalaf, and an unpublished tomb described in a report on Jericho.[15] These tombs give us a total database of 1,598 individuals.

How does our database compare with that of other demographers studying the ancient world? Bagnall and Frier had 1,084 persons in their database. Russell had 813 persons in his Egyptian database, 2,345 persons from Asia, Greece and Illyricum, and 1,111 (males only) from Iberia.[16] Our sample size of evidence, then, is within their range.

To be sure, there are possible pitfalls in appealing to osteoarchaeology as one's main evidence. Walter Scheidel[17] lists two problems with this sort of evidence: First, he maintains that determining the precise age of adult bones is difficult. Thus, precision in establishing longevity models would be impossible.[18] Second, the skeletal remains might be skewed evidence since they might only witness to certain burial customs

11. See among the first: Nathan, "Skeletal Remains from Naḥal Ḥever."

12. Taylor, *Jesus*, 158 refers to a human osteological database maintained by the Israel Antiquities Authority.

13. Compare to Tal Ilan's list of skeletal remains in *Integrating Women*, 214.

14. For Qumran see Steckoll, "Preliminary Excavation Report"; Broshi and Eshel, "Whose Bones?" Röhrer-Ertl, "Facts and Results"; and Sheridan, "French Collection." Other reports (not useful for this study) of the skeletal remains at Qumran are: de Vaux, *Archaeology*; Bartlett, "Archaeology of Qumran"; and Bar-Adon, "Another Settlement."

15. Hachlili and Smith, "Goliath," 69.

16. See Frier "Pannonian Evidence," 335–36. On the other hand, Wells, ("Ancient Obstetric," 1235) reports a study done in 1959 using 24,848 epitaphs.

17. Scheidel, "Population and Demography," 3.

18. Scheidel, *Death on the Nile*, 122; and Scheidel, "Population and Demography." But Grmek, *Diseases*, 99, disagrees with this conclusion.

and might not inform us about migration. These are valid cautions. I would even add to it that the bones we find in tombs in Israel might belong to individuals that were somewhat elevated economically from the rest of the population. Less prosperous individuals might have been buried in trench graves instead of more costly tombs.[19] Thus, I recognize that there are difficulties but the evidence must, in my opinion, be considered. One can't simply ignore an area of evidence because there may be difficulties in using it.

Of course, the removal, examination, and publication of information about human skeletal remains is especially difficult in Israel. First, one must find a tomb that has not been already robbed and looted. Next, the bones in the tomb must be in good enough shape to be reliably analyzed; some are not. Finally, and most challengingly, the anthropologists must be allowed to study the bones. Because of religious conflicts, this is not always permitted, especially recently.[20] Nor is this issue only a problem in Israel. Other cultures wrestle as well with the conflict between respect for the bones of the ancestors and the desires of historical investigation.[21]

Nonetheless, it appears to me that osteoarchaeology is here to stay and that it will yield many exciting and interesting results in the future. There has been since 1991 a journal devoted exclusively to publishing its findings[22] and some universities offer master's degrees in this field (e.g., the University Edinburgh). The skeletal remains are an important line of evidence in the study of ancient demography.

On the other hand, demographers have noted that the other methods of studying populations, especially mortality, in the ancient world—tomb inscriptions, Ulpian's Life Table, and Egyptian census records preserved on papyrus—also have their problems. For example, people were in the habit of giving out false age-related information on tombstones and especially on tax documents. There are no problem free demographic data.[23] Thus, we need the osteological data from Palestine/Israel to supplement the other evidence from elsewhere in the Greco-Roman world. As classicist Tim

---

19. See C. Meyers, "Archaeology," 76, for the same caution with regard to Iron Age tombs. Did it require some means to own a family tomb in the Second Temple Period? The answer is debated. Magness (*Stone and Dung,* 156) answers "yes." Gibson (*Final Days,* 159–61) answers, "no." Gibson believes that even the poor could afford a tomb, probably one excavated by the family itself. See the discussion in Chapter 11 of this volume.

20. See, e.g., Siegel-Itzkovich, "Orthodox Jews"; C. Meyers, "Archaeology," 76; and Taylor, *Jesus,* 158.

21. See e.g., Seidemann, "Bones of Contention."

22. *The International Journal of Osteoarchaeology.*

23. The following are some of the cautions offered by paleodemographers: Some of the tomb inscriptions seem to exaggerate the age of the deceased, especially the age of an older person (Russell, *Late Ancient,* 23–24). Some of the census records exaggerate the age of maternity and paternity (Bagnall and Frier, *Demography,* 42). Some of them may want a middle-aged woman to appear younger and so subtract ten years or so from her age at death. Children do not usually even get a tombstone (Durand, "Mortality Estimates," 369–70). Further, the census documents from Egypt may give incorrect data because they want to hide those men turning 14 years to save tax money and likewise to exaggerate those in their 50s as being over 60 (Scheidel, *Death on the Nile,* 151, 156–57).

Parkin observes, "A skeleton cannot lie about its age.[24]" Further, for Palestine/Israel there really is very little demographic evidence except the osteological.

Moreover, one can offer a check or confirmation of the osteological evidence from Israel by comparing it with the evidence of the papyri, tomb stone inscriptions, and even skeletal remains from elsewhere in the Roman Empire. We will see that the data from the tombs of Israel from Hell II through ER II are similar to that obtained by the other means indicated above from elsewhere in the Empire.

Let us in this chapter first introduce some individual persons unknown to us before their remains were discovered. For some we can now even know their name. These are ordinary persons, people from the 99%, the working class. Then, second, we will make an indication of stature.

THE WORKING CLASS IN LATE SECOND TEMPLE ISRAEL/ PALESTINE: THE OSTEOLOGICAL EVIDENCE

We cannot read the diaries and literary works of the lower classes, but we can meet them in their remains. We will introduce the reader to ten individuals from this time period (some of them by name) completely unknown from any literary source. These forgotten persons represent the working class population. Some of them show evidence of this social stratification in the pathology of their bones. The table below will summarize our selection of individuals and then we will make a few observations.

#	Tomb/grave location	Sex	Age at death	Pathology	Inscription on the ossuary	Comments
1.	Jericho	F	20		"Miriame wife of Judah"	Bones of an infant also in ossuary
2.	Jericho	M	60+	Fused thoracic vertebrae		One of three in this tomb of 31 individuals with this condition
3.	Qumran	M	22	Bones in hands and feet thick and gnarled.		Did hard physical labor with his hands from an early age. Went barefooted all his life.
4.	Qumran	F	25			Buried with two-year-old toddler
5.	Qumran	M	65	Skeletal structure of shoulders and legs deformed.		Did hard labor. Carried heavy burdens on shoulders causing changes to skeletal structure of shoulders and legs.

24. Parkin, *Demography*, 43. See also K.K. Éry, "Investigations,": "The acquiring of factual knowledge concerning mortality conditions in the Roman era is to be expected therefore only from the demographic elaboration of the skeletal remains excavated from the cemeteries." (p. 62).

The Archaeology of Daily Life

#	Tomb/grave location	Sex	Age at death	Pathology	Inscription on the ossuary	Comments
6.	Giv'at ha-Mivtar	F	50–60	Lost most of her teeth. Well-developed muscles in left arm. Significant evidence of hard work.		Her head had been smashed by a blunt weapon such as a mace. 4'8" tall
7.	Giv'at ha-Mivtar	F	23–25	Osteoporosis, periodontitis. One leg 3 cm. shorter than the other. Very slight bones.	"Martha"	Perhaps had endocrine disorder. 4'9" tall
8.	Giv'at ha-Mivtar	M	50–60	Club foot. Many teeth missing.		Died from spike to head. 5'5" tall
9.	Giv'at ha-Mivtar	F	30–35	Deformed right side of the pelvis. Hunch backed. Full term fetus in pelvis. Unable to deliver child without help. Died in childbirth.	"Salome daughter of Saul who failed to give birth"	A mid-wife could have saved her and her baby. 4'11" tall.
10.	Giv'at ha-Mivtar	M	45–48	Bones well developed. Very strong hands. Robust and strong individual. Some arthritis.	"Simon builder of the Temple"	5'6" tall

Table 8.1: Ten individuals from the "ninety-nine percent."[25]

We have selected individuals from three burial sites (the "Goliath Family" tomb at Jericho, Qumran, and Giv'at ha-Mivtar in Jerusalem) because these remains had been pathologically examined. These three tombs and cemeteries will be featured further below in our investigation of the skeletal remains of ordinary people from the late Second Temple Period. Let us here make three observations:

First, individuals three, five, six, and ten demonstrate what it was like for the working class. They did hard labor—some from childhood (number 3; cf. Chapter 5)—and it shows in their bones. Individual five was evidently a day laborer who carried around heavy objects. It caused deformity to his skeletal structure. The left-handed lady (number four) worked at something requiring significant manual labor with one arm. Individual ten was a construction worker who worked on the building of the Temple in Jerusalem. These are the ordinary people who had only their labor to live from.

Second, a few of them had bone disorders: individuals two, seven, eight, and nine. A number of persons suffered from weak bones and teeth (numbers six and

---

25. Information gleaned from Hachlili and Smith, "Goliath Family Tomb," 68; Steckoll, "Preliminary Excavation," 335; Haas, "Anthropological"; and Naveh, "Ossuary Inscriptions."

eight). Were these conditions due to dietary deficiencies or inheritance? Would we find similar pathologies in other tombs?[26]

Third, some of these individuals died horrific deaths: number six who died from a blow to the head by a mace; number eight, who was killed by a massive blow to the head by a spike; and number nine who died in childbirth, unable to deliver because of her deformed pelvis. These were hard and violent times.

Each skeleton is a story about a human being who lived, loved, and suffered. There are, of course, many other stories we could tell based on the skeletal remains. These ten examples, however, give us an idea of the information that awaits us in the examination of the bones.

STATURE

Had you lived in Palestine/Israel in the late Second Temple Period, how tall would you have been? One easily answered question is the stature, on average, of these people. Often, physical anthropologists are able to determine stature from examination of the skeletal remains, measuring mostly the long bones of the leg. To find an average, we will simply note the average stature of individuals (male and female) from various tombs and then average these together. Our database is difficult to assess (300–500+). The reason is because some reports only give an average stature for the entire tomb complex or complexes and note that many of the individuals' remains were not measurable. Thus, the number of individuals they used to calculate their average is unknown. Nevertheless, one can gain some perspective on this question by looking at the averages submitted by these anthropologists. The table below has the results:

Site	Male Average Height	Female Average Height
Givʿat ha-Mivtar	165.5 cm	157 cm
Meiron	165.5 cm	148 cm
En-Gedi	166.9 cm	150.8 cm
8 tombs/Judea/Samaria	166 cm	147 cm
Mt. Scopus	166 cm	149 cm
Naḥal Ḥever	162 cm	154 cm
French Hill (Hell II)	167 cm	146 cm
Average	165.5 cm (5'5")	150 cm (4'11")

Table 8.2: Stature in the Hell II and ER I and II Periods in Israel[27]

26. Cf. Arensberg and Smith, "Appendix," 192–94. Out of a total of 185 individual skeletal remains in the tombs of Jericho they examined pathologically, thirteen had osteoporosis, osteophyles, or spina bifida (7%). The same bone diseases were also in evidence at Meiron. See Smith, Bornemann, and Zias, "Skeletal Remains."

27. The table is composed from information in: Zias, "Mount Scopus (Meiron, En-Gedi, and Mount Scopus)"; Haas, "Anthropological Observations (Givʿat ha-Mivtar)"; Nagar and Torgeé,

This figure agrees essentially with Joe Zias who affirms that the average height of Jewish males from the Hellenistic to the Roman-Byzantine periods was 166 cm and of females was 148 cm. Taylor maintains, based on her study of skeletal remains, that Jesus would have been between 164 and 168 cm (5'4" to 5'6").[28] Thus, my results based on an average of the averages of stature calculated from skeletal remains is consistent with two other studies.

Thus, the average male in this period living in Israel/Palestine was around five feet five inches tall and the average female was four feet eleven inches tall. The men and women of Palestine/Israel were a bit smaller than those attested for Greece in the Hellenistic period (Table 8.3). They were, however, about the same in stature as contemporary Sephardic Jews (see Table 8.4 below).

	Males	Females
Greece Classical period	169.8 cm	156.3 cm
Greece Hellenistic period	171.8 cm	156.6 cm

Table 8.3: Average stature in Greece[29]

Missing from these calculations, however, are the outlying data from a family buried in Tomb H in Jericho, sometimes called the "Goliath Family Tomb." As the name indicates, some of these persons were unusually tall in comparison with the others from their period. While we do not know exactly which ossuary belonged to the man nicknamed Goliath, the anthropologists surmise that one man in this three-generational family tomb measuring 188.5 cm (6'2"), was the one given this moniker.[30] We might compare "Goliath" at Jericho with a man 202 cm tall (6'7") found just north of Rome (from the 3rd cent. CE).[31] The anthropologists examining the Roman giant considered him abnormal and suffering from an endocrine disease. Thus, persons well over six feet tall were quite unusual in the ancient Mediterranean and Middle Eastern world.

It is also of interest to compare Table 8.2 above with data compiled by H. Nathan with respect to modern Ashkenazi and Sephardic Jews (including Samaritans). Has their average stature changed from antiquity? See Table 8.4 below.

		Male	Female
Ashkenazi Jews	Western Russia	161 cm	
	Poland	161	150.6
	Austria/Hungary	163.4	

"Biological Characteristics (8 tombs in Judea)"; Nathan, "Naḥal Ḥever"; and Arensburg and Rak, "Skeletal Remains (French Hill)."

28. Zias, "Appendix A: Anthropological Observations," 125; Taylor, *Jesus*, 159.
29. Grmek, *Diseases*, 109. Gallant, *Risk*, 69.
30. Hachlili and Smith, "Genealogy of the Goliath Family," 68.
31. Minozzi, et al., "Roman Giant"; and Dell'Amore, "Roman Giant."

Sephardi Jews	North Africa	165	
Samaritans		173	
Ancient Israel	Hell II–MR	165.5	150

Table 8.4: Jewish Stature, Ancient and Modern[32]

The reader will observe that the stature of antiquity is most like the modern Sephardi male Jews and is close to the Ashkenazi females of Poland. The Ashkenazi male Jews of today are on average a bit smaller than their ancestors. They average 162 centimeters (5'3 ½") compared to the 165.5 centimeters (5'5") of the ancient men. The women of today average almost exactly what their ancestors did.

Another way to picture the ancient Jewish people is to compare them with modern statures from various parts of the world. Tables 8.5 and 8.6 below compare the averages from our Table 8.2 with averages elsewhere in the world today. The smallest persons are the inhabitants of Bolivia and the tallest are the Danes.[33]

Bolivia 160 cm (=5'2")	Israel Antiquity 165.5 cm (=5'5")	U.S. 176.3cm (=5'9")	Denmark, 182.6 cm (=6')

Table 8.5: Scale of comparison (Men)

Bolivia 142.2 cm (=4'8")	Israel Antiquity 150 cm (=4'11")	U.S. 163.1 cm (=5'4")	Denmark, 168.7cm (=5'6")

Table 8.6: Scale of comparison (Women)

Knowing about the average stature in Israel at our time period helps us to imagine the story. We are accustomed to thinking about the New Testament characters as looking like Europeans. The Hebrew Bible (1 Sam 9:2) says that Saul was head and shoulders taller than the other Israelite men. We imagine him as six and one-half feet or more. The text also says the giant Goliath was six cubits and a span (or allegedly around 9 feet). All of this leaves the impression that most Israelite men must have been around six feet tall with Saul a bit taller and "giants" abnormally tall. Thus, we also assume that Jesus and the disciples were the same (perhaps Jesus was like Saul).

But the skeletal remains of many Jewish men from the late Second Temple Period argue otherwise. Jesus and the disciples did not look like our action heroes of today. They were not necessarily buff and did not tower over other persons (probably). Rather, they looked like most Middle Easterners look now. Jesus was probably around

---

32. This table is based on Nathan, "Naḥal Ḥever," 174.
33. No author, "Human Height."

five feet five inches tall and weighed around 140 pounds (see below). If King Saul was somewhat tall, we should think of him as around five feet eight inches (like the Samaritans in Table 8.4). Goliath was probably six feet six inches as some manuscripts represent him—still a giant to those people.[34] These results help us place those texts into the lives of real people. We can imagine the story more realistically.

If Jesus and his male disciples were average height (5'5"), there might, of course, also have been some of his followers that were a bit smaller or a bit taller. There certainly are remains of individuals whom the anthropologists would calculate as diverging from the average stature.[35] Joan Taylor notes that the male skeleton found in the caves of Naḥal Ḥever ranged from 5'2" to 5'8" and in the Giv'at ha-Mivtar tomb in Jerusalem from 4'11" to 5'11."[36] Likewise, Jesus' mother, Mary, was probably 4'11" tall, tiny by most contemporary societies' standards. But there were women a bit taller and smaller.[37] Thus, it is possible that Jesus (or Peter, John, Judas, etc.) was a bit taller than the average. Of course, it is also possible that he was below that stature. As historians, however, we should imagine the average and not insist on the unusual unless we have good reason to do so. To imagine Jesus and the disciples, both men and women, as Europeans and as having bodies that would seem attractive in today's cinema, would be a misrepresentation.

WEIGHT AND FACIAL TYPE

But what about the average weight? Joseph Zias has speculated in one publication on this issue. He opines, based again on skeletal remains, that the average male weighed between 62 and 67 kilograms (137 to 148 pounds). He further reasons that since Galilee had more food sources (agricultural plus the fish from the Sea of Galilee), the males there would tend toward the upper weight. The other regions such as Judea would have tended toward the lower. Those living in the desert, such as the Essenes at Qumran, would have been perhaps a little lower than the 137 pounds.[38]

Joan Taylor finds hints in Jesus' teachings that he was often hungry. This information plus the indication that he was an artisan—*tektōn*—means, to her, that Jesus was very slim with the "physique of someone who did manual craft." She does not offer what that physique would be.[39]

---

34. According to most Masoretic manuscripts, Goliath was over nine feet tall. But LXX (Codex Vaticanus) reads 4 ½ cubits (= 6 ½ feet); LXX (other mss) read 5 ½ cubits (= 8 ¼ feet); and 4QSam[a] reads 4 ½ cubits (= 6 ½ feet). See Abegg, Flint, and Ulrich, *The Dead Sea Scrolls Bible*, 229.

35. One young man, age sixteen years, was 4'11" tall. He was buried in the Giv'at ha-Mivtar tombs. On the other hand, Simon the Temple Builder, also buried in this tomb was 5'6" (see Table 8.1 above, individual 10). See Haas, "Anthropological Observations."

36. Taylor, *Jesus,* 158–59 gives other examples.

37. Again, looking only at the Givat ha-Mivtar tomb: one female was 4'8" and another 4'9". See Haas, "Anthropological Observations"; and Table 8.1 above, individuals 6 and 7.

38. Zias, "Appendix A."

39. Taylor, *Jesus,* 167. But the references to being hungry are dubious. Jesus blessed the poor and

After examining the archaeological evidence from the skeletal remains of Jewish men, after comparing first-century Jews with east Mediterranean people today, and after looking at ancient depictions of Jews (on late synagogue walls, on coins, and in literature), Taylor summarizes her picture of Jesus' appearance:

- 5'5" tall
- Slim
- "Reasonably muscular"
- Olive-brown skin
- Brown eyes
- Dark brown or black hair
- Short beard
- Short hair[40]

These features seem about right for most Jewish men from our period of time. Her idea that Jesus was unusually "slim" because he was frequently hungry, however, disagrees with Zias' view that the Galileans consumed more calories than elsewhere in Palestine.

A final issue regarding physique of the ancient Jewish people can be cleared up from the skeletal remains. What were their facial features? H. Nathan writes that the usual conclusion is:

> The original Jewish people is generally considered to belong to the basic Mediterranean dolichocephalic stock, much the same as their present Arab neighbors . . . Sephardini and oriental Jews have retained this original Mediterranean type.[41]

In other words, Jesus and his followers looked much like the Arabs of Palestine (and the Sephardic Jews) do today. They *probably* had brown skin—as Taylor maintained—and long-looking faces.[42] The Galilean men stood around 5'5" tall and weighed around 140 pounds. John the Baptist, however, was probably more in the 130 pound category since he had lived in the desert. The females from Galilee (Jesus' mother, Mary Magdalene, etc.) stood, on average, 4'11". The "Jesus characters" in most of the movies are just not realistic types.

---

hungry, to be sure, but does that mean that he was often without food himself?

40. Taylor, *Jesus,* 168.

41. Nathan, "Naḥal Ḥever," 173.

42. Yet, surprisingly, Nathan finds in the seventeen skulls from Naḥal Ḥever that they are more similar to the Ashkenazi Jews, assumed to have changed their look due to intermarriage with eastern Europeans in the diaspora. See Nathan, "Naḥal Ḥever,"174. Nathan further speculates that there were actually two populations—one dolichocephalic and the other brachycephalic—making up the ancient Jews. Thus, one cannot be definite about the facial features of Jesus and his disciples.

The next two chapters will make further use of the human skeletal remains to assess the morbidity of the folk in the late Second Temple Period (Chapter 9) and to calculate mortality and average life span (Chapter 10).

9

What Chronic Disease(s) Would You Probably Have Contracted?

IN THIS CHAPTER, I want to visit the ordinary people in their sickness and pain. For the biblical world was a time and place where daily suffering and horrible illness were taken for granted. If we can get a clearer view of the morbidity of the ancient persons who heard Jesus' parables and Beatitudes, for example, it might give us insight and nuance in our modern reading of these texts. We surely do not hear them now as the ancients did.

We saw in the Introduction to this monograph the three lists of important archaeological finds with respect to understanding the ministry of Jesus and the early Jesus Movement. Apart from the Shroud of Turin and the James ossuary, the three lists are rather similar. They want to use mostly large, monumental ruins to interpret the life and teachings of Jesus. We must not ignore these results; indeed Chapters 2–4 of this monograph have highlighted them. But are there other archaeological finds that can help?

As we observed in the previous chapter, the ordinary folk speak to us today not through their literature but through their bodily remains. They are speaking to us from the grave if we will listen. A careful analysis of their remains (bones, personal ornamentation, and even human waste) can tell us a great deal about their personal story.

As we also argued in the previous chapter—quoting Justin Lev-Tov[1]—we need a holistic approach, one that considers all the evidence, not just the shiny objects and not just the great works of art. Such an investigation may be, as recognized over a century ago, neither: "attractive nor cheerful . . . but it may not be labor altogether

---

1. Lev-Tov, "Upon What Meat."

useless."[2] By placing these finds in the context of what we already know from both literary sources and other archaeological discoveries, we will attempt to narrate an account of the health of ordinary persons in Israel in the first century CE.

What we will be considering in this chapter is morbidity, that is illnesses that were endemic and chronic in late Second Temple Israel. These were illnesses that, once you contracted them, stayed with you for years, perhaps even for life. Often, they were just something a person had to deal with. They would weaken one's immune system and make him/her more susceptible to other diseases and would be especially a problem in times of famine. They would affect children and their growth, both physically and mentally. They could be especially lethal to pregnant women. And, of course, they also could kill directly. While there are many diseases attested in the literature and one would expect to find everywhere heart diseases, flu, and so forth, and while there were seasons of plagues in the empire in the second century and later, the two chronic, ubiquitous (in the Roman Empire), and endemic (to Israel) diseases that troubled most ancient folk were parasitic: intestinal parasites and malaria (also caused by a microscopic parasite).

We will focus in this chapter on these two diseases and the archaeological evidence for them in ancient Israel. As stated above, there certainly were other illnesses as we know from several lines of evidence. In the first place, we have explicit evidence from the medical examination of "more than 8,000 mummies" from Egypt; in the second place we have the archaeological evidence from around the world; in the third place, we have the ancient Greek and Roman medical texts. Here are the major troublers of human health in the ancient world compared with one statistic from today:

Pathology from over 8,000 mummies[3]	Diseases featured in *the Archaeology of Disease*[4]	The major diseases in the ancient world according to the ancient literature[5]	The major causes of childhood mortality in the modern world[6]
TUBERCULOSIS	TUBERCULOSIS	TUBERCULOSIS	
Smallpox			
Skin infections			
LEPROSY	LEPROSY	LEPROSY[7]	

2. Merrins, "Deaths," 562.

3. Živanović, *Ancient Diseases*, 220; Mitchel, "Human Parasites," 52; Harrison, "Disease, Bible and Spade."

4. Roberts and Manchester, *The Archaeology of Disease*.

5. These diseases are discussed in the Greek and Roman medical texts as well as in the Talmud. See Reed, "Instability," 355; Salares, "Disease"; Grmek, *Diseases*, 131–51; Živanović, *Ancient Diseases*, 217–45; Preuss, *Talmudic Medicine*, 151–70; Touwaide, "Disease."

6. Roser, "Child Mortality"; Tyoalumun, "Prevalence."

7. Touwaide, "Disease," 547, explains that this (λέπρα in the Greco-Roman medical texts) was not leprosy in the modern sense but a skin disease. Yet the "leprosy" described in the mummy autopsies and in the archaeology of disease is really Hansen's disease or the modern meaning of the term "leprosy."

What Chronic Disease(s) Would You Probably Have Contracted?

Pathology from over 8,000 mummies[3]	Diseases featured in *the Archaeology of Disease*[4]	The major diseases in the ancient world according to the ancient literature[5]	The major causes of childhood mortality in the modern world[6]
INTESTINAL PARASITES[8]	INTESTINAL PARASITES	INTESTINAL PARASITES	
			Pneumonia
		DIARRHEA	DIARRHEA
MALARIA		MALARIA	MALARIA
	SINUS/EARS	SINUS/EARS	
	OSTEOMYELITIS	OSTEOMYELITIS	
	TREPONEMAL DISEASE[9]	SYPHILIS	
	Brucellosis[10]		
			Measles
			AIDS
		Typhoid Chickenpox Diphtheria Mumps Whooping cough Cancer Anemia Rickets Anemia Dysentery Scabies	

Table 9.1: Major Diseases in the Ancient World (those in all caps are in two or more lists)

8. See Jackson, *Doctors and Diseases*, 15 and 37: "As examination of mummies has made abundantly clear, intestinal and other parasites were widespread . . . in many places certain intestinal parasites were endemic."

9. This category includes syphilis.

10. This is a disease that mimics malaria but is caused by a bacterium instead of malaria's parasite. See No author, "Brucellosis."

The Archaeology of Daily Life

Interestingly, tuberculosis[11] and leprosy[12]—both of which are frequently in the evidence from the Egyptian mummies as well as in modern medical studies—were rare in ancient Israel. But these illnesses were certainly present in the rest of the ancient world[13] along with cancer, diphtheria, and others we know today. But we will not discuss any of the above diseases because many of them either do not show up in the archaeological remains (a disease must be chronic to leave traces in the bones) or were not common in Israel.[14] The two diseases we will highlight in this chapter were the bane of the ancient world, were endemic in Israel, and they show up in the archaeological remains in various ways.

THE BIBLICAL REFERENCES

When Jesus interacts with the elite persons in the Gospels—scribes, Pharisees, chief priests, and Sadducees—he engages in debate and intellectual dialogue. When he interacts with the non-elites, it is with teaching and healing. The poor came to him for comfort for their souls and bodies, not for disputation.

More often than not, the Gospels characterize illness as weakness.[15] Is this term used metaphorically—of course they are weak like any sick person—or literally? Is the only symptom or the main symptom many of these persons have simply weakness, lethargy, physical malaise, and acute weariness? If so, what sort of general illness could the Gospels be presenting here? Can archaeology help us answer this question?

---

11. See Zias, "Arnona." Zias notes that he has found only two cases of tuberculosis in the skeletal remains of Jews in antiquity and suggests that they had an "inherited immunity" (119). See also Zias, "Death and Disease," 152–53 for the same assertion. But Gibson, *Final Days*, 139–47, reports on a man with tuberculosis and three others in the same tomb (two were infants) dating to the first century CE. Thus, some Jews in our time period may have contracted tuberculosis. But it was, evidently, rare. The same man also suffered from Hansen's disease (modern leprosy). Yet, some archaeologists argue that the individuals in this tomb were not locals but Hellenistic Jews (who could have intermarried with gentiles in the diaspora). Some even maintain that they were not necessarily Jews. See Taylor, *Jesus*, 166; and Avni and Greenhut, "Resting Place," 41. Thus, finding one case of tuberculosis and Hansen's disease—see next note—may not alter the correctness of Zias' observation.

12. It is now commonly concluded that the Hebrew term צָרַעַת ṣaraʿat and the Greek λέπρα lepra did not refer to Hansen's Disease. See Hamel, *Poverty*, 53; Feder, "Polemic Regarding Skin Disease"; Kiuchi, "Paradox of the Skin Disease"; and, again, Zias, "Death and Disease," 149–50. But for a single case of actual leprosy from the first century CE, see Gibson, *Final Days*, 139–47; and no author, "DNA of Jesus-Era Shrouded Man." Again, see Taylor, *Jesus*, 166 for a challenge to the conclusion that this man was a local Jew or, for that matter, even a Jew at all. R. Krauss, "Kritische Bemerkung," challenges the common conclusion that ṣaraʿat was psoriasis.

13. See Grmek, *Diseases*; Preuss, *Biblical and Talmudic Medicine*.

14. But we will discuss anemia below.

15. From the Greek stem ασθεν—(*asthen-*). Matt 10:8, 25:36; Mark 6:56; Luke 4:40, 9:2; John 4:46, 5:3, 11:1; Acts 9:37; Matt 25:43; Luke 10:9; Acts 4:9, 5:15; Matt 8:17; Luke 5:15, 8:2, 13:11–12; John 5:5, 11:4. This term is the most commonly used designation for illness in the New Testament. See Stählen, "ἀσθενής," 492.

What Chronic Disease(s) Would You Probably Have Contracted?

Such characterization of illness in the Gospels bears similarity to diseases mentioned in the Hebrew Bible. An interesting text appears in the Old Testament book of Deuteronomy. In this verse, the Israelites are warned of coming diseases if they do not keep the covenant. We might presume that these diseases were the chronic and endemic maladies of the Israelite world in the late sixth century BCE and the text (Deut 28:21, 22b) seems to confirm this conclusion:

	Hebrew word	LXX[16]	NRSV	Borowski[17]	Sussman[18]	Tigay[19]	Nelson and Christianson[20]	Koehler/Baumgartner and Clines[21]
1	שַׁחֶפֶת	ἀπορία Discomfort from illness	Consumption	Consumption of the lungs	Emaciation from TB or parasites	Wasting, TB?		Emaciation, consumption
2	קַדַּחַת	πυρετός Malarial fever	Fever	High fever	Malarial semi-tertian fever	Malaria		Inflammation, fever
3	דַּלֶּקֶת	ῥίγος Shivering, chills	Inflammation	Inflammation	Malarial tertian or quartan fever	Fever		Flame, fever-heat, inflammation
4	חַרְחֻר	ἐρεθισμός Irritation	Fiery heat	Fever		Fever	Fever	Feverish heat, burning fever
5	חֶרֶב[22]	φόνος[23] murder	Drought[24]			Fever	Dehydration	Sword
6	שִׁדָּפוֹן	ἀνεμοφθορία Blight; damage by wind	Blight	Anorexia		Emaciation	fever	Scorching, burning, blight

16. Based on LSJM; Muraoka, *Lexicon*; and Goh and Schroeder, eds., *Dictionary*.
17. Borowski, *Daily Life*.
18. Sussman, "Sickness."
19. Tigay, *Deuteronomy*.
20. Nelson, *Deuteronomy*; Christiansen, *Deuteronomy*.
21. Koehler and Baumgartner, *Lexicon*; Clines, *Dictionary*.
22. The editors of *Biblia Hebraica Stuttartensia*, recommend either to read this word pointed as חֹרֶב horev "drought," as in the Vulgate, or follow the LXX manuscript Vaticanus and delete the word altogether.
23. This word is missing in the LXX Vaticanus manuscript.
24. Following the recommendation of *Biblia Hebraica Stuttartensia* editors and a host of older commentators, e.g., Driver, *Deuteronomy*, 308.

The Archaeology of Daily Life

	Hebrew word	LXX[16]	NRSV	Borowski[17]	Sussman[18]	Tigay[19]	Nelson and Christianson[20]	Koehler/Baumgartner and Clines[21]
7	יֵרָקוֹן	ῶχρα Paleness; yellow ocher; mildew	Mildew	Anemia or jaundice (Jer 30:6)	Anemia or jaundice (Jer 30:6)	Jaundice	Jaundice	Yellowness, paleness

Table 9.2: The List of Diseases in Deuteronomy 28:22

Although some older commentators[25] maintain that these seven plagues comprise four human diseases and three crop diseases, that is not at all certain. Max Sussman has suggested that the disease referred to as שַׁחֶפֶת (number one in our verse; cf. Lev 26:16) which was a "wasting disease" was actually emaciation caused by intestinal parasites. He believes the second and third items (קַדַּחַת and דַּלֶּקֶת) to be malarial varieties based on hints by the medieval rabbi Abraham ibn Ezra.[26] Tigay agrees, also being informed by the Medieval Hebrew commentators who were sensitive to the Arabic roots and their medical meanings.[27] Duane Christiansen[28] suggests that the word read as "sword" in the Hebrew Bible should be read as "drought" (following the Vulgate) and that this term can mean heat from the sun or from fever. Richard Nelson[29] suggests that numbers four and five could refer to fever and dehydration. Further, Oded Borowski and Tigay[30] opine that the next to last condition שִׁדָּפוֹן (shidaphon, number six) was anorexia, which often accompanies a severe intestinal parasitic infection. Finally, Sussman, Borowski, Tigay, and Nelson[31] affirm that number seven, יֵרָקוֹן (yeraqot), indicates anemia or jaundice, a condition caused by both parasitic intestinal infection and by malaria.[32]

If these identifications are correct, then the illnesses referred to in Deut 28:22 were all human and seem to point to two types of chronic[33] conditions. In sum, this warning of punishments through disease seems to emphasize—except for the word "sword," which either may not have been there originally or should be read as "drought"

25. See Driver, *Deuteronomy*, 308; Craigie, *Deuteronomy*, 342.
26. Sussman, "Sickness and Disease." See also Preuss, *Medicine*, 160–61, who agreed.
27. Tigay, *Deuteronomy*, 262, 396.
28. Christensen, *Deuteronomy*, 684.
29. Nelson, *Deuteronomy*, 331.
30. Borowsky, *Daily Life*, 76; Tigay, *Deuteronomy*, 262.
31. Nelson, *Deuteronomy*, 331.
32. Preuss, *Medicine*, 164–66, earlier had advocated for this position and argued for it at length. He affirmed that all seven diseases are human.
33. Merrill emphasizes that the diseases are chronic ("they will pursue you until they destroy you"). See *Deuteronomy*, 358.

or "fever" (see above[34])—two endemic and chronic diseases: intestinal parasites and malaria (a microscopic, blood parasite). Were these also the most common tormentors of the residents of Palestine/Israel in the late Second Temple Period? We are curious to find if these are especially indicated in the archaeology and in the literature.

EVIDENCE FOR UBIQUITOUS INTESTINAL PARASITIC INFECTION IN LATE SECOND TEMPLE ISRAEL

As one historian of disease (a palaeopathologist) has observed: in the Roman Empire, "intestinal parasites were endemic."[35] We will first describe the effects of this infection; then the direct archaeological evidence for it; present the indirect evidence; and, finally, offer literary references to this condition.

Intestinal Parasites and Their Effects

South Korean doctors were shocked in the fall of 2017 when they examined a North Korean defector.[36] Not only did he have four or five gunshot wounds, tuberculosis, and hepatitis B. He also was infected with an "enormous number" of intestinal parasites. The body of this twenty-four-year old man was, according to one physician, "a broken jar."[37] He was a walking pathology study. The most shocking sight was the nearly one foot long round worm, extracted from his intestines, photographed, and uploaded on the internet.[38]

I would say to those shocked by this man's maladies: welcome to the real world, the world inhabited by the majority of the populations on this planet. Indeed, one of the South Korean doctors, Dr. Choi Min-ho, who worked on the defector, surmised that at least one-half of the North Korean population was infected with intestinal parasites.[39] Throughout the rest of the "developing world," we find the same conditions.

It was also the world of the ancients, as archaeological excavations are now showing. The reader often assumes that when Isaiah wrote his fabulous poetry, he was reasonably comfortable. Or when Jesus delivered his parables, we assume that the audience listened in reasonable comfort, even as we do while reading them today.

---

34. But Tigay, Christiansen, and Nelson affirm that the Hebrew word *ḥerev* can be used as an equivalent for *ḥorev* "drought" and that, further, "drought" can also mean human fever. They, therefore, interpret the word *ḥerev* as a fever and not a sword. See Tigay, *Deuteronomy*, 262, 396; Christensen, *Deuteronomy*, 684; Nelson, *Deuteronomy*, 331.

35. Jackson, *Doctors and Diseases*, 37.

36. No author, "'Enormous Number.'"

37. Newton and Lee, "A Broken Jar."

38. But compare the man with the 5-½ feet long tapeworm from California in No Author, "Five-foot long tapeworm"; and the teenager who died of an acute tapeworm infection of the brain in Scutti, "Teen Dies of Tapeworm."

39. Westcott and Lee, "Worms in Defector."

We just presume that, aside from occasional illnesses, most persons in antiquity were fairly healthy even as they are in western societies today. But in this chapter, I intend to maintain that there was widespread infection of intestinal and malarial parasites in late Second Temple Israel. I maintain that a large percentage of the population of those following Jesus and the early church and of those attending the synagogues were infected as seriously as the North Korean defector. We can only then imagine how the message was received by such "broken jars."

There are two broad categories of parasites. There were/are ectoparasites such as fleas and lice and these have also shown up in the archaeological evidence.[40] Among the endoparasites, there were the helminth worms or intestinal parasites and the parasites causing three types of malaria.

The symptoms of the three most common intestinal parasites of late Second Temple Israel are as follows:

- Round worms:

  * In the lungs: coughing, gagging, vomiting worms, wheezing
  * In the intestines: nausea, vomiting, irregular stools, worms in the stool, weight loss
  * If a large infection: fever, fatigue, intestinal blockage (with severe pain) leading to death[41]

- Tape worms: nausea, weakness, diarrhea, abdominal pain, hunger or loss of appetite, weight loss, vitamin and mineral deficiencies[42]

- Whip worms: bloody diarrhea, painful or frequent defecation, abdominal pain, nausea, vomiting, weight loss, fecal incontinence[43]

The intestinal parasites were/are not in themselves usually *directly* fatal, but the problem was that they competed with the "host" for food. They might in times of plenty only cause a mild anemia and a feeling of weariness or weakness, especially in an otherwise healthy adult.[44] But if a person's diet was challenged, the parasites could cause many complications. Children would be especially vulnerable for their growth

---

40. Reinhard and Araújo, "Archaeoparasitology," 496; Zias, "Death and Disease," 159; and Borschel-Dan, "Bit Player."

41. No author, "Ascariasis." Compare these symptoms with those of a chronically infected man whose health was deteriorating for reasons he could not understand until doctors discovered the parasites in his body: Phillips, "His Health Had Been Failing."

42. No author, "Tape Worms."

43. No author, "Whipworm Infection." For these three infections, see also No author, "Ten Symptoms."

44. Cruz-Cruz, et al., "Stunting," note that sometimes the infection is a-symptomatic but usually announces itself with some sort of discomfort such as fever, lung inflammation, abdominal pain, and diarrhea.

would be stunted and their mental capacities and speech development reduced due to "vitamin deficiencies and impaired growth."[45] They would be underweight and underheight. The parasites could even cause anorexia. Chronic malnutrition would usually lead to deteriorating immune systems and therefore to susceptibility to other diseases. Therefore, the parasites often led *indirectly* to death.[46]

But in times of famine, a real crisis arises. Now the host of the parasites competes with the infestation for less and less food. Those so infected will feel the effects of starvation the quickest. Mitchell and Tepper observe grimly, "Those with the most parasites in their intestines . . . die from starvation first."[47] The indirect consequences of intestinal parasites range from anemia to starvation in times of famine.

But there can also be more *directly* lethal consequences of intestinal parasites. Extreme cases could lead to diarrhea, bowl blockages, malabsorption of food, and hence to death with extreme abdominal pain.[48] Although a minority of victims dies in this way directly from the infection, such cases in the developing world societies are, nevertheless, well known. They happen today and, one would presume, certainly happened in antiquity. As a matter of fact, there are apparently several instances of such outcomes narrated in the ancient literature (see below).

Because of these health dangers, two historians conclude: "Parasites are the major cause of ill health and early death in the world today."[49] If that is true today, one must presume that it was also true in antiquity. Their health consequences, especially for children, are/were significant and often lethal.

Direct Evidence of Intestinal Parasitic Infection: The Seven Sites in Israel

Let us first look at these infections from a *diachronic* perspective: evidence in Israel through the centuries. One way to establish the common infections of intestinal parasites is the examination of ancient fecal remains.[50] Archaeologists look for remains in

---

45. Mitchell and Tepper, "Intestinal Parasitic Worm Eggs," 93–94. See also Mitchel quoted in No author, "Human Parasites." Cruz-Cruz, et al., "Stunting," record the stunting problem in southern Mexico today in which one-third of the children are infected with parasites leading to "cognitive development failure," furthering the cycle of poverty.

46. See in this regard, especially Gutiérrez-Jiménez, Luna-Cazárez, and Vidal, "Malnutrition and Intestinal Parasites"; and Tyoalumun, et al., "Prevalence." In Nigeria, one study found that 37% of children were stunted, 29% were underweight, and 18% were "wasting" due to intestinal parasites (Tyoalumun, et al., "Prevalence," 147).

47. Mitchell and Tepper, "Intestinal Parasitic Worm Eggs," 94.

48. Mitchell and Tepper, "Intestinal Parasitic Worm Eggs," 94.

49. Reinhard and Araújo, "Archaeoparasitology," 495. Cf. the statement of Gutiérrez-Jiménez et al., "Malnutrition and Intestinal Parasites," who note that intestinal parasites are "some of the main causes of morbidity and mortality (in Mexico today)"; and that of Roberts and Manchester, *Archaeology of Disease,* 217: "infection by parasites is a cause of considerable morbidity."

50. Harter, et al., "Toilet Practices"; Mitchell and Tepper, "Intestinal Parasitic Worm Eggs";

ancient latrines, in cesspits, in coprolites, in fecal soil (i.e. areas where defecation took place), and in pelvic soil from burials.[51] The eggs from the helminth worms survive for thousands of years and thus are quite evident in these soils.[52] Thus, if excavators can get soil samples from these sources, they might find some parasite eggs. If there are parasite eggs in the soil, that means that the humans who "made the soil" were infected. That is precisely what happened at seven archaeological sites in Israel.

First, we will, as stated above, look at the evidence in Israel diachronically in sites ranging from the Iron II period to the late Arab period (see Appendix B). When investigated, the fecal remains of five latrines from five different eras and five different locations (see Maps 2.1 and 3.2), from one fecal area, and from one tomb yielded about the same results:

1. Iron II period Jerusalem (latrine)
2. Early Roman period Qumran (soil samples from fecal area[53])
3. Early Roman period Jerusalem (pelvic soil from a tomb)
4. Late Roman period Scythopolis (or Beth Shean; latrine)
5. Roman period[54] Caesarea (latrine)
6. Crusader period Acco (latrine)
7. Late Arab Jerusalem (coprolites in cesspit)

The remains of the latrines and cesspits were full of intestinal parasites, whipworms mostly but also tapeworms and roundworms. In the Iron Age Jerusalem sample, for example, each milliliter of organic residue had about 11,000 parasite eggs in it. 85% of the eggs were whipworm and 15% were tapeworm.[55] At the Qumran site, archaeologists found evidence of whipworm, tapeworm, pinworm, and roundworm.[56] Likewise, pelvic soil from a Herodian tomb in Jerusalem yielded the discovery of "two hollow, pebble-like artifacts" found in the abdominal cavity of an individual. The two objects turned out to be cysts of intestinal parasites.[57] Excavators found the fish tapeworm in latrines dating from the middle to late Roman Period at Beth Shan

---

Neufeld, "Hygiene Conditions"; Zias, "Death and Disease"; Cahill, et al., "Had To Happen"; Reinhard and Araújo, "Archaeoparasitology"; Geggel, "Medieval Parasite"; No author, "Human Parasites."

51. See Mitchell, "Human Parasites," 49.

52. Reinhard and Araújo, "Archaeoparasitology," 495.

53. The Qumran samples were not actually from a latrine or cesspit but from an area evidently used by the residents to defecate in shallow holes which were then immediately covered.

54. Le Bailly and Bouchet, "*Diphyllobothrium* in the Past," do not give dates for these samples but one assumes this era from the context.

55. Cahill, et al., "It Had To Happen."

56. Harter, Bouchet, Mumcuoglu, and Zias, "Toilet Practices"; Zias, Tabor and Harter-Lailheugue, "Toilets at Qumran"; No author, "Biblical Latrine." This is the first archaeologically attested evidence of pinworm in the ancient Near East.

57. Joseph Zias, "Death and Disease," 147–59.

(Scythopolis) and Caesarea Maritima.[58] The results from a cesspit in Acco were similar (whipworm and tape worm).[59] Finally, a latrine, located near the Church of the Holy Sepulcre in the Old City of Jerusalem and dating from around the fifteenth century CE, yielded twelve coprolites (fossilized feces) containing thousands of worm eggs. Although some of the eggs were from worms normally inhabiting northern Europe (causing speculation about travelers using the latrine when in Jerusalem) most were the common parasites of Israel: round worms and whip worms.[60]

The parasites were ingested, for the most part, as a result of either undercooked meat[61] or as the result of handling, and subsequently ingesting, fecal remains (e.g., on vegetables).[62] The presence of parasite eggs in the fecal remains of humans indicates a very poor hygienic environment (unclean hands) as well as undercooked meat and population crowding.[63]

But these are five different time periods and five different locations. Does this evidence show that people in the late Second Temple Period were mostly—or often—infected with such parasites? In addition to this direct evidence, we need to turn to more indirect evidence to make our case that a significant segment of society—fifty percent as the South Korean doctors estimate for North Korea?—was infected.

Indirect Evidence for Intestinal Parasitic Infection: Parasitic Infection Elsewhere in the Empire and Beyond

Now let us examine the remains *synchronically* by comparing Israel's findings with those roughly contemporaneous with our time period throughout the Roman Empire. Piers Mitchel has collected data on numerous excavations through the Roman Empire roughly from the time period of our focus in this monograph which we will supplement with other studies. He notes that intestinal parasites have been found in latrines and graves in ten European and Middle Eastern countries and that whip worm was the most frequently identified parasite, with round worm the second most common.[64] These two helminth parasites, along with two others, found in multiple sites in Israel from four different time periods, were also the most common in the Roman Empire in

---

58. Le Bailly and Bouchet, "*Diphyllobothrium*."

59. Mitchell and Tepper, "Intestinal Parasitic Worm Eggs."

60. Yeh, et al., "Human Intestinal Parasites," 75; Geggel, "Medieval Parasite"; and No author, "Human Parasites." Every coprolite contained roundworm and whipworm. Only a one or two also had eggs from beef/pork tapeworm, fish tapeworm, and two protozoa causing dysentery.

61. For the practice of eating raw meat in ancient Israel, see Hamel, *Poverty,* 19; and Broshi, *Bread, Wine,* 133.

62. Harter, et al., "Toilet Practices," surmise that the residents of Qumran also contracted the parasites by ritually bathing after an infected person (582).

63. Reinhard and Araújo, "Archaeoparasitology," 498.

64. Mitchel, "Human Parasites," 50–51.

The Archaeology of Daily Life

the late first and early second centuries CE with tapeworm also frequently occurring. We may summarize Mitchel's evidence (with supplements) as follows:

Species	Country
Tapeworm	Austria, France, Britain, Egypt, Germany, Israel, NW Iran
Fish tapeworm	Austria, Britain, France, Germany, Israel, Poland, Egypt
Roundworm	Austria, Britain, Germany, Israel, Netherlands, Poland, Greece, Turkey, NW Iran
Whipworm	Austria, Britain, France, Germany, Israel, Italy, Netherlands, Poland, Greece, NW Iran

Table 9.3: Findings of Helminth Parasites in the Early to Late Roman Empire[65]

The widespread infection gives us a *prima facie* case for presuming that they were also wide spread in Israel during this period. This condition, this disease was simply everywhere in the Greco-Roman world in our time period, the late Second Temple Period (37 BCE—70 CE). In every case where archaeologists have examined latrine remains, they have found the parasites. How many were infected? Was the percentage fifty as the South Korean doctor speculated for North Korea?

Literary Indications of Intestinal Parasitic Morbidity

Several persons have been described in the ancient literature as dying as the result of worm infections or dying amid worm infections. One commentator has alleged, implying that these tales are legendary, that to be eaten by worms is a typical death for one who despises God.[66] Yet, these references are not that numerous and are about what one should expect if this disease was ubiquitous in the ancient world.[67] Cassander (fourth century BCE) was allegedly filled with dropsy from which worms (εὖλαι) came (Pausanius 9.7.2–3). A woman named Pheretime "while yet living" festered with worms (Herodotus 4.205). A man named Pherecydes died with a multitude of worms (*serpentium*) erupting from his body (Pliny, *N.H.* 7.172). The Christian author, Papias (2nd century CE), described the death of Judas Iscariot, betrayer of Jesus, in which

---

65. Summary of table in Mitchel, "Human Parasites," 51; plus Le Bailly and Bouchet, "*Diphyllobothrium*"; Anastasiou, et al., "Infectious Disease"; Williams, et al., "Intestinal Parasites"; Nezamabadi, et al., "Paleoparasitological Analysis"; Searcey et al., "Parasitism of the Zweeloo Woman." The reader should also bear in mind the many studies of mummies from Egypt (more than 8,000) which show parasite infections. See Jackson, *Doctors and Diseases,* 15 who lists five species of intestinal parasites and Živanović, *Ancient Diseases,* 220.

66. Conzelman, *Acts,* 96–97. See also Wikenhauser, *Apostelgeschichte,* 143: "(it) is the typical punishment for the persecutor." Yet, the number of references to the disease in the literature is comparatively small. Many other bad persons' deaths are narrated without references to worms.

67. See Barrett, *Acts,* 591; Wikenhauser, *Apostelgeschichte,* 143; Conzelman, *Acts,* 96–97; and Lake and Cadbury, *Acts,* 140 for these references.

he was said to have discharged worms from his body.[68] Alexander the False Prophet died when his leg became gangrenous and produced maggots (σκωλήκων; Lucian, *Alexander the False Prophet*, 59). Tertullian (*To Scapula* 3) lists the fate of some of the persecutors of the church: one went blind, several had "troubles," and one had living worms. Eusebius tells of the death of the persecuting emperor, Maximin, who developed an ulcer on his genitals which became further infected and was eventually crawling with worms (*H.E.* 8.16.4). Finally, the imaginative Apocalypse of Peter (early 2nd century CE) pictures sinners in Hell having their entrails eaten by worms.

Some of these tales clearly do not describe intestinal helminth infections. The first, fifth, and seventh stories (Cassander, Alexander, and Emperor Maximin) given here are probably referring to maggots from flies which gathered in gangrenous members. The others, while told of "bad men" (and one woman), are not unrealistic tales, though the authors may have relished and embellished the details. If this disease was as prevalent as the archaeological evidence suggests, it certainly would not be uncommon for many people to show symptoms at death.

There are three notable references to persons from Second Temple Period Israel to abdominal maladies that remind one of severe—or "large"—intestinal parasitic infections. The first, narrated in 2 Macc 9:5-10, tells the story of Antiochus IV and his severe abdominal pain accompanied by a swarm of worms (σκώληξ) which led to his death. This condition could describe a severe intestinal parasitic infection.

The second, in Josephus (*War* 1.656/*Ant.* 17.169), tells about the end of Herod the Great who had, again, acute abdominal pain and fever and whose condition "generated worms (σκώληξ)." Again, he died a horrible death after many weeks of suffering.[69]

The last reference, in Acts 12:23 (cf. Josephus, *Ant.* 19.346-350), alleges that Agrippa I died from similar symptoms: acute pain in the abdominal area with signs of worms ("eaten of worms" σκωληκόβρωτας). The parallel description of Agrippa's death in Josephus does not mention worms but does emphasize acute abdominal pain that lasted five days:

Acts 12:23	*Ant.* 19.346-350
"The angel of the Lord struck him . . . and he was eaten of worms and died."	"He understood this (owl) to be a messenger (Gk. *angelos*) of bad things to come . . . then a pain shot through his heart. A violent suffering all at once gripped his stomach . . . Being worn out by five continuous days of abdominal suffering, he departed this life."

Table 9.4: Herod Agrippa I's death

These three stories seem to describe intestinal infections in their worst phase, the acute and overwhelming infection that leads to death (see above). In this phase, a

---

68. This account, given by Papias is quoted by Apollinarius of Laodicea, 4th century CE. See text in Holmes, *Apostolic Fathers*, 756-57.

69. Since Josephus refers to σῆψις *sepsis*, these worms may have been maggots and not intestinal parasites. But the Greek word is vague.

swarm of worms blocks the intestines causing extreme pain and leads to death. As one palaeoparasitologist has noted, the ancients must have known when they had worms.[70] They could see them in the stool; sometimes they coughed them up; occasionally the worms slithered out of the nose or mouth of the victim while sleeping.[71] The ancient medical texts (the Ebers Papyrus, the Hippocratic Corpus, and Galen[72]) talk about them and contemporaneous developing societies today are quite aware of their presence. Thus, the reports of worms being present in these three cases, along with abdominal pain, are not necessarily fabricated (i.e. "bad guys always die with worms"; these were bad men; *ergo*, they died with worms). These three cases would represent an extreme form of the infection but certainly would not have been an uncommon occurrence.[73]

Less dramatic is the reference in the Mishnah (m. Sheq. 5:1–2) about a certain priest in the days of the second temple who was in charge of "sickness of the intestines." The reference is in the context of listing the famous officers of the temple. One officer was over the seals, one over the drink offerings, one was over the casting of the lots, one over the bird offerings, one was a herald, one was over the gates, etc. These are then officers with important temple duties. Among this list of honored officers is Ahijah who was in charge of the bowel sickness. Evidently the priests ate undercooked or raw meat and contracted intestinal parasites.[74] To have a priest whose duties were devoted to bowel sickness suggests that the condition was widespread and serious.

The extra-Talmudic tractate, *Semaḥot* 3.11 (see Chapter 11), states that the Hasidim of old used to contract intestinal illnesses and die within twenty days. The Tosephta (t. Nidd. 9:16) observes that they used to burn incense for those that died of intestinal illnesses. Later they burned it for everyone. Evidently, dying from an intestinal disease was considered distinctive (especially horrible?). These ailments were so common that the above mentioned tractate, Sem. 12.10, gave a ruling: a man may only visit another man who has an intestinal disease while a woman may visit either a man or a woman (evidently because of the embarrassment of it). These intestinal diseases could be viruses but could also be overwhelming parasitic infections that were probably there for months or even years but finally erupted in a massive attack.

The rabbinic literature certainly was familiar with helminth worms. Their words קוֹקְיָאנֵ (tapeworms) and אַרְקְתָא (fluke worms)[75] were much discussed. They did not know how one contracted the infection (by eating old barley flour one rabbi thought)

---

70. Cox, "History of Human Parasitology."

71. See the story narrated in Preuss, *Biblical and Talmudic Medicine*, 185 about a Sadducee who had worms crawling out of his nose and subsequently died.

72. See e.g., Anastasiou, et al., "Infectious Disease"; Mitchel, "Human Parasites," 55; Cox, "History."

73. See Merrins, "Deaths"; Sussman, "Sickness and Disease"; and Harrison and Yamauchi, "Diseases and Plagues." Less certain would be New Testament texts such as 1 Timothy 5:23 (Timothy's stomach problems) and Acts 28:8 (the case of intestinal illness called by the author "dysentery").

74. See Eliav, "Medicine and Hygiene."

75. On the definitions of these terms, see Jastrow, *Dictionary*.

but offered several folk remedies. Thus, the malady was widespread and a bothersome reality in Talmudic age Israel.[76]

So how many persons were afflicted with intestinal parasites (we will investigate malarial parasites directly)? If the medical person's estimate for North Korea (see above) is anywhere near accurate for the ancient world—and the ubiquity of these remains in cesspits/latrines suggests that it is—then a large proportion of persons was infected. One parasitologist estimates that one billion persons on the earth today are infected with the intestinal parasite, round worm, like our Korean defector.[77] A recent study cited an estimate that 3.5 billion persons worldwide are infected with parasites of any kind.[78] Worldwide the estimate is that 250 million children are stunted due to parasites, 99 million are underweight, and 51 million are "wasted."[79] One recent study of Latin America found that an estimated 100 million persons were infected with whip worm, that 84 million were infected with roundworm, and that 50 million suffered from hookworm infections.[80] A recent study of school children in two Nigerian towns found that 21% were infected with intestinal parasites.[81] Studies in Mexico have revealed that 34% of children in the southern states are infected with round worms and that of those infected, one third are malnourished, feel weak, and are anemic. They are not mentally alert and not developing properly mentally. Further studies in central-east Mexico found that 60% were infected with whip worm which had led to low fertility rates and growth stunting.[82] Such percentages do not seem out of line with what Israel in the late Second Temple Period experienced.

Many (most?) children and even adults in late Second Temple Israel just never felt quite right, never felt well. Indeed, feelings of well-being in the majority of a population might be a modern phenomenon of developed countries. Some had emaciated children, sickly children and feared for their lives. If that was so, how might we re-imagine the reception of some of the biblical texts and events? What might petitions for healing have meant to these ancient sufferers? Before we answer these questions, let us look at the second most troublesome parasitic infection in the ancient world as in our contemporary developing world: malaria.

---

76. See Preuss, *Medicine*, 186–87; and b. B. Metzia 107b; b. Shabb. 109b; b. Gitt. 69a.
77. Cox, "History of Human Parasitology."
78. Tyoalumun, et al., "Prevalence," 147.
79. Tyoalumun, et al., "Prevalence," 147; Cruz-Cruz, et al., "Stunting," 1026; Sori, "Review." I interpret the term "wasted" to mean emaciated or anorexic. Sori defines it as: "acute malnutrition."
80. Gutiérrez-Jiménez, Luna-Cazárez, and Vidal, "Malnutrition and Intestinal Parasites."
81. Abah and Awi-Waadu, "Gastro-intestinal Helminthiasis." The children had mostly roundworm, but also hookworm, whipworm, and threadworm.
82. Gutiérrez-Jiménez, et al., "Malnutrition and Intestinal Parasites," 12.

EVIDENCE FOR UBIQUITOUS MALARIAL PARASITES IN LATE SECOND TEMPLE ISRAEL

Malaria may have changed the course of human history more than once. It may have helped destroy the Athenian empire and almost certainly was the cause of Alexander the Great's early death.[83] It was feared greatly by the ancient people, especially for their children and pregnant wives.

Malaria is a mosquito-borne illness caused by a microscopic parasite. The disease is spread in this manner:

> A mosquito bites an infected individual and draws out blood together with the parasites. When it bites another individual the parasites are transmitted to a fresh victim and immediately begin to multiply in the new organism. Parasites that penetrate into some organism may remain there for a long time, despite the recovery of the individual, and become resistant to various remedies, remaining dormant and awaiting the moment when the defensive forces of the organism slacken and there is an opportunity to break out once again.[84]

Symptoms include for "uncomplicated"[85] malaria:

- Intermittent fever and chills (flu-like symptoms)
- Headaches
- Nausea and vomiting
- General weakness/tiredness and body aches

For "complicated" malaria the symptoms include:

- Severe anemia
- Kidney failure
- Seizures and coma
- Cardiovascular collapse
- Low blood sugar
- Retinal damage
- Yellow skin
- Enlarged spleen and liver
- Still births in pregnant women as well as maternal death[86]

---

83. See Touwaide, "Malaria"; Freeman, *Alexander*, 320.

84. Živanović, *Ancient Diseases*, 219.

85. The distinction between uncomplicated and complicated malaria is made in No Author, "Malaria," *MedicineNet.com*.

86. For these symptoms, see No Author, "Malaria," *MedicineNet.com*; and No Author, "Malaria,"

What Chronic Disease(s) Would You Probably Have Contracted?

In the year 2016, according to estimates, 216,000,000 persons worldwide were infected with malaria and of that number it is calculated that from 400,000 to 800,000 died from causes directly related to the disease.[87] In parts of the Mediterranean in the nineteenth century, before the eradication of swamps and marshes, areas where malaria was endemic would see one fourth of the death toll directly caused by malaria.[88] Malaria is especially deadly in children and pregnant women.[89] It is the leading cause of death in Nigeria among children under five years old.[90]

In addition to deaths directly related to malaria, it can contribute to pneumonia which might make it an indirect cause. It might also cause chronic illness such as enlarged spleen or liver leading to a shorter life span. In Italy in 1925 in an area studied by Sallares, only eight percent of the deaths were caused *directly* by malaria. But all the children in the area had enlarged spleens. After malaria was eradicated, the death rate was cut in half (from 41 per 1,000 to 20 per 1,000). Evidently, malaria was a secondary cause of death for many.[91]

Indirect Evidence of Malaria in Israel in the Late Second Temple Israel, Part I: The Amulets

There is no *direct* archaeological evidence for malaria in Israel. That is to say, we do not have actual malarial parasites, their eggs, or their DNA from Israel in our time period that can indicate to us definitively that the ancients suffered from this disease (there is DNA evidence from Italy and Egypt from our time period; see below). We have only several lines of *indirect* evidence. The indirect evidence is not in this instance human remains. Rather it is a collection of metal-foil amulets discovered in tombs, synagogues, public buildings, and houses in Israel and dating from the fourth to the seventh centuries CE.[92] There are thirty-two such amulets of known provenance, fifteen of which have come from Israel. The amulets were inscribed with magical prayers which, the wearer hoped, would ward off a disease or a curse. Of the fifteen from Israel, six deal with fever, probably the fever of malaria:[93]

Wikipedia.

87. No author, "Malaria," *Wikipedia*; Piper, "Malaria."

88. See Sallares, *Malaria*, 116.

89. Boer, "Malaria." On malaria as a cause of maternal death, see Demand, *Birth, Death, and Motherhood*, 81–86.

90. Tyoalumun, et al., "Prevalence," 147.

91. Sallares, *Malaria*, 119, 136–40.

92. For a list of these amulets, see Eshel and Leiman, "Jewish Amulets."

93. In addition to the six named here, Naveh and Shaked, *Amulet* (55–62, 83–84, 102–4, and 224–29); and Naveh and Shaked, *Magic Spells* (142–43, 80–82), describe one from Aleppo, two from Egypt (one from the Cairo Geniza and one from Oxyrrhynchus), one from Mesopotamia (an incantation bowl), and two from an unknown provenance which seek to protect the wearer from malaria. A recently discovered amulet, from Khirbet Wadi Ḥamam (near the Sea of Galilee), is illegible but could

The Archaeology of Daily Life

- A copper amulet from Sepphoris in Galilee[94]
- A copper amulet from Western Galilee near ʿEvron[95]
- Two copper amulets from the village of Horvat Kanaf (north east of the Sea of Galilee)[96]
- A silver amulet from Tiberias[97]
- A bronze amulet from Horvat Kannah (on the north side of the Bet Netofah valley in Galilee)[98]

The amulets are made of silver, copper, or bronze foil. The metal foil is rolled up, attached to a string, and then worn about the neck.[99] All the amulets are in Aramaic (the one from ʿEvron is bilingual, in Aramaic and Greek). They invoke secret, magical formulae to protect persons from the fever and say the following:

- "amulet against fever protracted that burns and does not cease," (Sepphoris)[100]
- "let the fever be extinguished from (Casius) both the great (fever) and the slight (fever)." (Evron)[101]
- "Yahu, Yahu, Yahu, Yahu, Yahu, exorcise the fever and the chills."[102] (Horvat Kanaf)[103]
- "the angels that are [appointed] over fever and shivering, cure Ele[azar]." (Horvat Kanaf)[104]
- ""eradicate from the body of Ina daughter of Zeʾirti all hectic fever and illness and sickness in the name of Yhwh . . ." (Tiberias)[105]
- ". . . to expel the great fever and the tertian fever and the chronic fever and the semi-tertian fever . . . from the body of Simon, son of Kattia." (Horvat Kannah)[106]

---

plausibly have been a protection against malaria. See Leiman and Leibner, "Amulet."

94. See McCollough and Glazier-McDonald, "Magic and Medicine."
95. See Kotansky, "Copper Amulet from ʿEvron."
96. See Reed, "Instability"; Naveh and Shaked, *Amulets,* 45, 51; and No author, "Horvat Kanaf Amulet."
97. Naveh and Shaked, *Magic Spells,* 50–53.
98. Naveh and Shaked, *Magic Spells,* 60–63.
99. Eshel and Leiman, "Jewish Amulets."
100. McCollough and Glazier-McDonald, "Magic and Medicine," 146.
101. Kotansky, "Amulet," 82.
102. Fever and chills are diagnostic for malaria. They were especially feared in antiquity and often appear in texts written on magical amulets, bowls, and other documents. See Lincicum, "Greek Deuteronomy's 'Fever and Chills'"; and the Greek translation of words 2 and 3 in Table 9.2.
103. Naveh and Shaked, *Amulets,* 45.
104. Naveh and Shaked, *Amulets,* 51.
105. Naveh and Shaked, *Magic Spells,* 50–53.
106. Naveh and Shaked, *Magic Spells,* 60–63.

What Chronic Disease(s) Would You Probably Have Contracted?

In the amulets, in addition to praying for relief from fever, there are—to us—nonsensical syllables and sounds, which evidently were taken to have magical power. The invocations inscribed on the amulets were clearly about fevers and the great fear that people had of contracting them and dying from them. The amulet prayers describe the fevers as chronic ("does not cease"), severe ("great [fever]"), and intermittent—all characteristic of malaria. The sixth amulet even uses the Greek terms for malarial fever (see below), even though the amulets are all in the Aramaic language. Such descriptions, in regions near the Bet Netofa valley and the lake (see Map 9.1), lead one strongly to suspect malaria was a major problem. The presence of amulets[107] specifically for fever certainly suggests that malaria was a real danger for many persons in the region of Galilee.

Other evidence supports the conclusions drawn from the amulets. In the first place, ancient settlement patterns indicate a scarcity of habitation around the Lake Huleh. Josephus refers to the marshes (ἕλη) stretching from the city of Caesarea Philippi south past Lake Huleh (*War* 3.515, 4.3). As Zwickel's settlement map of the region from the Iron age to the Arab period shows, these marshes were not hospitable to settlement. In the Hellenistic period, there were no settlements at all west or east of the lake and none near the strip of land running nine miles north of it. In the Roman period, there was one settlement north-east of the lake. One is inclined to suggest that this pattern was due to the dangers of malaria.[108]

The ancients were unaware that the disease was caused by a microscopic parasite. They knew that certain regions were disease ridden but did not understand the actual cause. Thus, Josephus described the "air" around the Sea of Galilee as "pestilential" (νοσώδη; *War* 4.457). He writes that the Jordan Rift Valley is hot and dry in the summer and thus the air becomes conducive to sickness. The reader will learn (see below) that the summer months are when the mosquitoes emerge from their pupa states and also that this is the "season of death" in the Mediterranean world. In other words, malaria is at its worst during this season (see Table 9.4). This way of talking about the disease was common among the Romans who thought regions in Italy (near marshes and lakes) were pestilential because the air made people sick.[109] Thus, the region around the lake was known as malarial, to use our term.

Third, recent history of this region confirms this conclusion. Jonathan Reed argues that Galilee was malarial from the Huleh Valley south to Tiberias, then west over to and through the Bet Netofah Valley up to the early twentieth century. Nineteenth-century travelers noted that this area was malarial, writes Reed, and in the early

---

107. Pliny the Elder (*N.H.* 28.11.46) refers to another bizarre amulet many pagans used: hanging a nail or rope used in a crucifixion about one's neck to ward off malarial fevers. See Evans, *Remains*, 140 and Chapter 11.

108. See Zwickel, "Huleh Valley," 178, 180 for maps of the settlement in the Hellenistic and Roman periods. Farther north, around the ancient city of Dan (near Caesarea Philippi; see Map 2.1) was a very wet area which was also malarial. See Peirera, "Beautiful City."

109. Boer, "Malaria"; Cox, "History"; and Sallares, *Malaria*, 73, 212.

The Archaeology of Daily Life

twentieth century many Jewish settlers, who lived in these areas, died from malaria.[110] Early twentieth century scholarly works on Israel noted the problem of malaria in the areas of Caesarea Philippi, Lake Huleh, around the Sea of Galilee, the Jordan Valley, and the Shephelah.[111] In the 1920s there was a malaria epidemic in Israel.[112] Thus, until modern systems of irrigation, marsh drainage, and mosquito larval extermination controlled the standing water, these areas were pestilent.

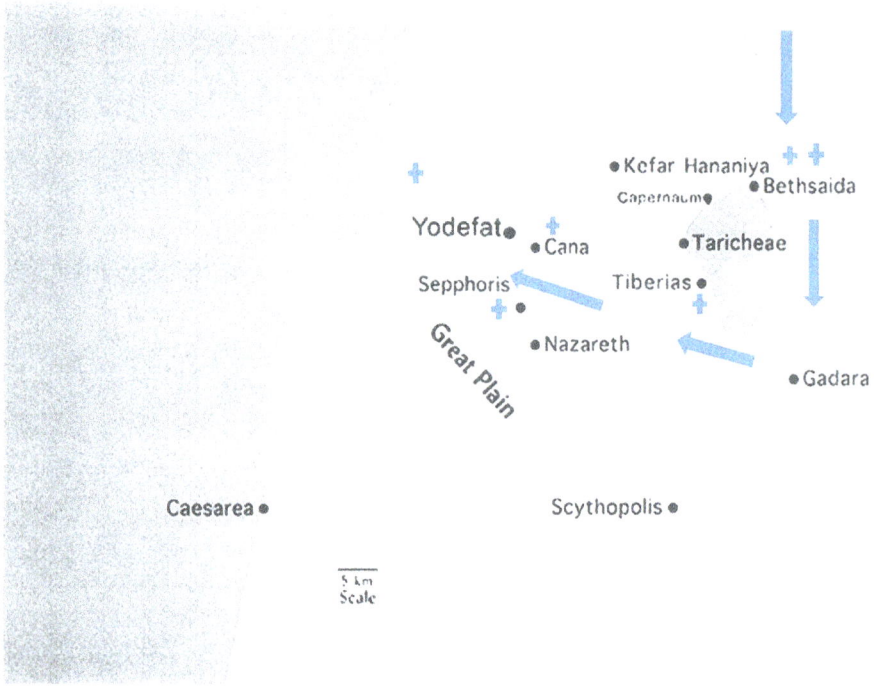

Map 9.1: Location of Amulets (+) and Malarial Areas (⇨)

In addition to the amulets from the Galilee/Golan area, there is other archaeological (and indirect) evidence elsewhere for malaria as an endemic disease. In the Naḥal Ḥever caves west of the Dead Sea,[113] archaeologists discovered several items of clothing from the early second century CE, preserved for nearly two thousand years due to the dry climate. Among these items was a tunic or shirt. From the size of the clothing, Yigael Yadin surmised that it was a tunic for a very small child. Attached to the bottom of the tunic or shirt were bags which Yadin suggested—based on Talmudic references—held herbs, spices, and/or seeds as protection against malaria. The text is b. Shabb. 66b: "For a daily fever [which would be semi-tertian fever, see below]

---

110. Reed, "Instability," 356; and see also Sussman, "Sickness," 8; and Karmon, "Settlement."
111. Macalister, "Fever." This encyclopedia article was written in 1915.
112. Leichman, "World Malaria." Malaria was obliterated in Israel sometime before 1948.
113. For this site, see also Chapters 5 and 6 and Map 5.1.

someone should (tie up items in a bag) and attach it to the neck... for a tertian fever, bring (other items) and attach them to the neck."[114]

Thus, the parents of this very small child, who had lived probably in En-Gedi, feared malarial infection for him/her. En-Gedi, as an irrigated village, would have had mosquitoes.[115] Malaria in children can be especially deadly. To ward off this dread disease, they attached pouches or cloth bags to the bottom of his/her tunic containing various—they hoped—magical items. One wonders if the child survived since the empty tunic was found.

There are references to the disease in the literature as well (see Josephus and the New Testament below). Thus, the known malarial nature of many parts of Galilee plus the references to it in the literature strongly argue that the "fever" in the amulets is from malaria.[116] Although the amulets date centuries after the late Second Temple Period, the time of Jesus and Antipas, they, nevertheless, attest to the nature of the geography which would not have changed until modern efforts to kill mosquitoes and control standing water. The amulets attempting to ward off fever, therefore, were probably trying to prevent malaria.

Indirect Evidence for Malaria in Israel Part II: Malaria in the Greco-Roman World

The historian of ancient diseases, Mirko Grmek wrote; "From the end of the fifth century, malaria was the disease *par excellence* in the Greek world."[117] It was one of the deadliest and the most widely spread maladies. The disease had existed since time immemorial but seemed to break out in Athens in an especially lethal strain. From then on, malaria was the bane of the Mediterranean world.[118] Although the ancients did not understand the disease—did not know that it was carried by mosquitoes—they knew that living near stagnant water was a cause of ill health.[119] Hippocrates, the celebrated Greek physician, described those living near still water as thin and intellectually weak. It was known that those living in those areas looked much older than they were.[120]

---

114. See Yadin, *Bar-Kokhba,* 79–81. Translation Neusner, *Babylonian Talmud.* For using herbs and roots in amulets as a prophylactic against illness, see also Preuss, *Biblical and Talmudic Medicine,* 146 and t. Shabb. 4:5, 9; j. Shabb. 8b.

115. See Chapter 3.

116. Reed, "Instability," 355, notes that malaria was one of the top three *directly* lethal diseases in the ancient world. The other two were tuberculosis and typhoid fever, but Jews, as stated above, seemed to have an immunity to tuberculosis. See Table 9.1.

117. Grmek, *Diseases,* 281.

118. Touwaide, "Malaria."

119. Cox, "History"; Sallares, *Malaria,* 282.

120. Grmek, *Diseases,* 281; Sallares, *Malaria,* 282.

The Archaeology of Daily Life

There are a few cases where DNA evidence has been extracted from mummies in Egypt[121] or bones in Italy[122] to show that malaria was prevalent in the Roman era. But for the most part, historians must infer the presence of the disease and its lethal effects. They infer its effects by looking at tombstones. Brent Shaw[123] published in 1996 his results from examining nearly four thousand tombstones in Rome dating mostly from the late fourth into the fifth century. These were graves of Christians who adopted the practice of recording the exact month and day of their death. Thus, one could compile a database to see if there was a particular time of the year that was deadly. His information can be summarized in the table below:

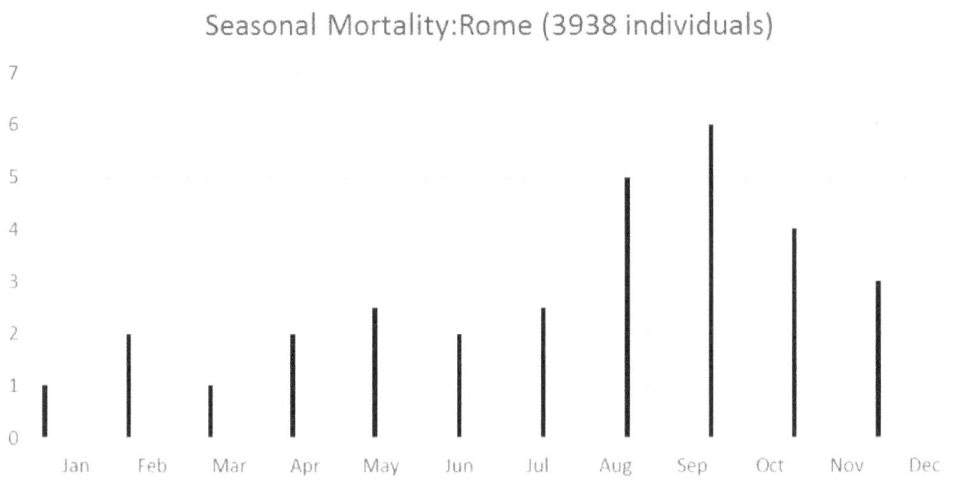

Table 9.5: Seasons of mortality (based on Shaw[124])

The reader can discern that the mortality rate begins to rise in August and reaches its peak in September. Shaw then looked at a few tombstones in northern and southern Italy, in Spain, in Gaul, in Germany, and in north Africa and found that they all had seasons in which mortality spiked and that the seasons were roughly the same as in Rome: July–October. In a recent essay, Roland Boer[125] has maintained that the peak season in the "Levant" (eastern Mediterranean area, including Israel) in antiquity was "summer and early autumn," the approximate times of the year identified in Shaw's table. This schedule coincides with the malarial season in the Mediterranean.

121. Mitchel, "Human Parasites," 52.

122. Scheidel, "Disease and Death." A skeleton was found in Umbria, a district in central Italy. Also Marciniak et al., "*Plasmodium falciparum* malaria," who found, from evidence extracted from teeth, two cases of *P. falciparum* in the area of Rome based on DNA; and Marciniak, et al., "Multi-Faceted," which found further DNA evidence for malaria in Italy.

123. Shaw, "Seasons."

124. Shaw, "Seasons," 115.

125. Boer, "Malaria." Macalister, "Fever," who observed Israel in 1915, also noted that the deadly season in his day was late summer and early autumn.

Mosquitoes breed in the spring in the wet season, pupate, and then emerge in the hottest time of the year.[126]

Shaw was reluctant to name a cause in the spike. He noted that many pointed to malaria as a seasonal disease and suggested that it was the cause of the increased deaths, but he, himself, hesitated to make the connection.

Walter Scheidel, however, followed by others,[127] has not hesitated. Adding data from first-century BCE cinerary urns (showing the same results) to the Christian tombstones cited by Shaw, he also noted that in nineteenth-century Rome, malaria peaked from August to October. He concluded that the spike in deaths must have been due to the most lethal strain of malaria: *plasmodium falciparum*. He supplemented his argument by appeal to the osteological evidence, namely the appearance of *cribra orbitalia* in the skulls (see below) and of enamel hypoplasia in the teeth. Both conditions, Scheidel maintains, could have been caused by chronic malaria.[128]

Likewise, Roberts and Manchester, in their groundbreaking study, report that researchers have sought to connect the findings of *porotic hyperostosis* (a similar condition to *cribra orbitlia*) in skeletons found in Greece, Cyprus, and Turkey—which were buried near marshy environments—to malaria. It makes good sense to them that the mosquito infested regions produced endemic malaria which in turn caused anemia, leaving its traces in the pitting of the skulls.[129] We will discuss these conditions below.

Thus, the wider evidence for malaria as a context for its appearance in northern Israel in the late Second Temple Period is found in Christian tombstones, pagan cinerary urns, and in the bones examined for the presence of abnormalities (given in the tables below), all found throughout the Greco-Roman world.

Literary References

None of the sources from Israel in the late Second Temple Period use the term that translates as malaria.[130] Indeed, there was no such word. Instead, the common people called the disease the "fever" (πυρετός[131]) or the "great fever." The Greek medical doctors called the disease "tertian fever," "semi-tertian fever," or "quartan fever."[132] There are four types of malaria of which only three were endemic in the Mediterranean area. The following table summarizes these malarial species:

    126. Sallares, *Malaria*, 212.

    127. See Sallares, *Malaria*; and Reed, "Instability."

    128. Scheidel, "Disease and Death." Enamel hypoplasia is the cessation of enamel development.

    129. Roberts and Manchester, *Archaeology*, 233.

    130. The word malaria is Italian for "bad air." It was first used, according to Sallares, in the fifteenth century (*Malaria*, 7).

    131. This Greek word came to mean malarial fever and not fever in general according to Grmek, *Diseases*, 280. This is the term used in the New Testament (see below). The plural of the term evidently indicates intermittent fever with chills, the symptoms of malaria. See Keener, "Fever."

    132. Grmek, *Diseases*, 280; Sallares, *Malaria*, 133, 222.

The Archaeology of Daily Life

Greek medical terms (πυρετός)	Latin medical terms (febris)	Modern medical terms	Duration	Outcome
τριταῖος	tertiana	plasmodium vivax	3–6 years	not fatal
τεταρταῖος	quartana	plasmodium malariae	many years	can be fatal
ἡμιτριταῖος	semi-tertiana	plasmodium falciparum	about 1 year	often fatal

Table 9.6: Malarial infections[133]

Of course, fever can arise from other causes but in an area near water where people were known to get sick with fevers one suspects malaria borne by mosquitoes as the illness. Further, the "periodicity of intense fever" that characterizes malaria makes the diagnosis as reported in the ancient texts certain.[134]

The Old Testament may refer to the disease. Sussman, and others[135] it may be remembered, suggests that the references in Lev 26:16 and Deut 28:22 to a קַדַּחַת (qadaḥat) "fever" as well as the דַּלֶּקֶת (daleqet) of Deut 28:22 (numbers two and three respectively in Table 9.2) were the tertian or quartan fever. Julius Preuss, in his classic treatment of Talmudic medicine, argued that the people of Israel, according to the Talmud, greatly feared fever and tried many remedies for a cure, especially the chronic fevers.[136]

Pliny the Elder referred to two men who suffered chronically with fevers, presumably malarial. Gaius Maecenas had perpetual fever. Pliny maintained that he got not even an hour's sleep the last three years of his life. Antipater of Sidon (a poet) used to have an attack of fever every year on his birthday (Pliny, *N.H.* 7.172). These sufferers had to cope with their malaria for many years.

One of the Hasmonean rulers succumbed to a form of malaria. Alexander Jannaeus labored from what Josephus called quartan fever (τεταρταῖος πυρετός). He suffered from the recurring fevers for many years and, exacerbating the disease with excessive drinking and exhausting military campaigns, finally died in 76 BCE (*War* 1.105; *Ant.* 13.398). Sallares diagnoses this as the *P. malariae* form of malaria.[137] One historian offers the same diagnosis for Alexander the Great.[138]

The New Testament gospels refer to fever in two passages. One passage narrates the healing of Peter's mother in law who was in bed with a fever (Mark 1:30–31//Matt

---

133. Based on information in Sallares, *Malaria*, 9–19; Celsus, *de Medicina* 3.3.2; Hippocrates, *Epidemics*, 1.11; and Galen 17A.222k.

134. Sallares, *Malaria*, 10.

135. See Table 9.2.

136. Preuss, *Medicine*, 160–61. Although Preuss gave a careful accounting of fever in the Talmud, he did not associate the fevers with malaria. Indeed, he thought malaria was spread by flies instead of by mosquitoes (see 348).

137. Sallares, *Malaria*, 133.

138. Freeman, *Alexander*, 320. Freeman observes that Alexander suffered for years from malaria, that he drank excessively, and that he endured unending military campaigns.

8:14–15//Luke 4:38–39). The Gospel of Luke describes it as a "great fever," perhaps wanting the reader to think of the disease we now call malaria. This story is set in Capernaum which is on the north shore of the lake. The second story (John 4:52) tells of the healing of an official's son who was also afflicted with fever. Again, the story is set in the village of Capernaum. The description (above) of Josephus of the region around the lake as pestilential plus the two narratives of persons afflicted with fevers and living in a village on the north shore of the lake argue together that this region was malarial. Therefore, we can say that the disease does appear in the New Testament.[139] Should we speculate that Galilee experienced in late summer–early fall a "season of death" from malaria as Rome did? Such speculation seems reasonable.

FURTHER INDIRECT EVIDENCE FOR BOTH INTESTINAL AND MALARIAL PARASITIC INFECTION: SKELETAL EVIDENCE OF ANEMIA

We will present this evidence here as indirect evidence for both intestinal and malarial infection. Another way to determine if persons were infected with parasites is to examine the skeletal remains for evidence of anemia. The hypothesis is that those so infected will exhibit signs of the problem in their skeletal remains, especially those of children. Parasitic infections and/or malaria, the reasoning goes, will cause anemia which will show up in certain conditions in the bones. The focus of such analyses has been the crania and the teeth.[140]

According to Piers Mitchel, anemia may be a hereditary condition caused by sickle cell, spherocytosis, or thalassemia. But it may also be acquired due to one of three conditions: dietary deficiencies, malaria, or intestinal parasites.[141] Thus, the argument is not that there is a one-for-one cause for the related conditions of *cribra orbitalia/porotic hyperostosis*. Not every person exhibiting such pitting or porosities in his/her skull had a parasitic infection necessarily. But many of them did.

One researcher has demonstrated that "the prevalence of parasitism co-varied with porotic hyperostosis prevalence" in ancient North American sites.[142] *Porotic hyperostosis* (and its similar condition, *cribra orbitalia*) is a form of a commonly observed disease in the crania of pre-modern people. These conditions are formed when there are "porosities (i.e. pitting) in the outer table of the cranial vault (*porotic*

---

139. Could one also speculate that another character in the New Testament had malaria? Did Epaphroditus come from Philippi in Macedonia to Rome to minister to Paul, arriving at the peak malaria season, and fall victim to this disease? See Phil. 2:26–27. Also, for the condition of Publius' father as malaria, see Keener, "Fever."

140. Although there is ample evidence from the crania excavated in Israel for anemia, there is, so far, no evidence based on the teeth of which I am aware.

141. Mitchel, "Pathology," 69.

142. Reinhard and Araújo, "Archaeoparasitology," 497.

hyperostosis) and orbital roof (*cribra orbitalia*)."[143] High incidences of *cribra orbitalia/porotic hyperostosis* are associated with anemia due to high infection of intestinal parasites and/or malaria.[144]

The presence of *cribra orbitalia* also correlates with high mortality rates, especially in children: "Conditions that caused cribra orbitalia greatly reduced chances of survival to maturity," writes Walter Scheidel. He found in a study of Nubian crania (gathered from the bones in two tombs) that 45% of the population in all had the condition and that 78% of the children that had died between the ages of four and six had it. At age four to six, life expectancy for children with *cribra* was 15.5 years lower than unaffected children. Clearly, skulls with signs of *cribra* were those of children that suffered from chronic illness, usually associated with anemia and assumed caused by malnutrition or parasitic infection.[145]

A study was done on a Jerusalem tomb containing the bones of sixty individuals and dating to the seventh century BCE. The physical anthropologists looked at the skulls (cranial vaults) of the individuals. The pathological results showed that almost one in three (31.5%) suffered from *cribra orbitalia* (or *porotic hyperostosis*).[146] Physical anthropologists also found a significantly high incidence of *cribra ortibalia* in children from the tombs of Meiron in Galilee. Almost 50% of the nearly two hundred individuals in the Meiron tombs were children under the age of eighteen and "most of the of the children's skulls" had signs of *cribra orbitalia*.[147] These tombs dated from the first century BCE to the fourth century CE. Studies done on burial caves near En-Gedi, one from the Hellenistic period and the other from the Early Roman Period, indicate that 33% of those buried from the former period exhibit signs of *cribra orbitalia* or *porotic hyperostosis* while 50% of those from the Roman period did so.[148] Nagar and Torgeé, who studied eight tombs in the area of ancient Judea and Samaria, noted that 10% of the individuals in the Samaritan tombs had pitting in their skulls.[149] The table below represents a *diachronic* look at the skull pitting diseases in Israel:

---

143. Walker, et al., "Causes of Porotic Hyperostosis and Cribra Orbitalia."
144. See Smith-Guzmán, "Cribra Orbitalia."
145. Scheidel, *Death on the Nile*, 139.
146. MacDonald, *Israelites Eat?* 82; Scheidel, *Death on the Nile*, 138–39.
147. Smith, Bornemann, and Zias, "Skeletal Remains." The authors also suggest that the lesions on the children's skulls could have come directly from diseases such as malaria. Contrast this evidence with that given by Aviam, "Socio-Economic," 36 where anthropologists examined (evidently in hurried fashion) 25 of the 2,500 individuals found at Yodefat. He reports that the anthropologists pronounced the people in "good health." They had no malnutrition and no diseases. But one must point out: 1) this was a small sample size (1% of the total); 2) the results of the examination are given in very unscientific language.
148. Goldstein, Arensburg, and Nathan, "Skeletal Remains, Pathology."
149. Nagar and Torgeé, "Biological Characteristics." The authors also note that none of the individuals buried in the Shephelah showed evidence of cribra obitalia. Further reports from Jerusalem in the Early Roman period also note an absence of cribra orbitalia/porotic hyperostosis. See Zias, "Mount Scopus tomb"; Zias, "Caiaphas tomb"; Smith and Zias, "French Hill Tomb." This leaves the

What Chronic Disease(s) Would You Probably Have Contracted?

Site	Jerusalem	En-Gedi	Samaria	En-gedi	Meiron	Jezreel
Percent of cribra	31	33	10	50	"most"	33
Date	7th BCE	Hell. II	Hell. II–ER	ER	1st BCE–4th CE	Crusader

Table 9.7: Skull pitting in Israel (diachronic look)[150]

The reader will observe that the appearance of this condition is fairly consistent in Israel and is found in both the southern part (Judea and Samaria) and the northern (Galilee and the Jezreel Valley).

For *synchronic* evidence, or evidence from outside Israel roughly contemporaneous to our period of study, we can again consider Piers Mitchel.[151] He cites a study done in Italy examining two tomb sites, one from the Imperial Period and one from the seventh century CE. Both sites had an incidence of 60 and 80% respectively of *cribra orbitalia* in the children buried there. Further evidence is available from three other excavations in Middle Eastern sites and from excavations done in England (see table below). These results suggest morbidity challenges which could be related to parasitic infection.

Site	Bahrain	Greece/ Asia Minor	Italy	Italy	Nubia	England	Egypt
Percent of cribra	56	24	60	80	45	23	43
Date	300 BCE—250 CE	150 CE	1st CE	7th CE	500–1500 CE	Roman era	Pre-historic to Christian

Table 9.8: Survey of Occurrences of *Cribra Orbitalia/Porotic Hyperostosis* (synchronic look)[152]

The condition known as *cribra orbitalia* and/or *porotic hyperostosis* is usually attributed to chronic anemia. Hence, physical anthropologists in the past have presumed

---

question as to why the incidence was so high in the 7th century BCE Jerusalem tomb and the En-gedi tombs. Perhaps the geographic conditions for the individuals buried in these tombs were better, thus avoiding malaria.

150. See Mitchell, "Palaeopathology of Skulls"; Mitchell, "Child Health"; and Smith, Bornemann, and Zias, "Skeletal Remains."

151. Mitchel, "Human Parasites," 50.

152. Adapted from Mitchel, "Child Health," with additions from Grmek, *Diseases,* 276; Nagar and Torgeé, "Biological"; Smith, Bornemann, and Zias, "Skeletal Remains"; McDonald, *Israelites Eat?* 82; Scheidel, *Death,* 139; Smith-Guzmán, "Cribra Orbitalia"; and Roberts and Manchester, *Archaeology,* 231. The table in Mitchell, "Child Health," 40, lists five sites outside of Israel. Scheidel, *Death on the Nile,* 138–40 cites two detailed studies from Egypt. See also Piontek and Kozlowsk, "Frequency of Cribra Orbitalis"; Facchini, Rastelli, and Brasili, "Cribra Orbitalia"; and Keenleyside and Panayotova, "Cribra Orbitalia," for studies from Poland in the Middle Ages, and Italy and the Black Sea area in antiquity.

malnutrition/anemia (either because of lack of food or because of competition with parasites) as the cause of *cribra orbitalia*. Where there was evidence of anemia in the skeletal remains, one had a strong suspicion that intestinal parasites or malarial parasites had caused the *cribra orbitalia/porotic hyperostosis* in the individual. Malaria—a blood parasite—can also cause anemia even when the victim has been fed adequately.[153]

Cribra orbitalia is, thus, very commonly seen in skeletal remains, not only in Israel in all periods but also widely in the Middle East and the Mediterranean world. Its presence in the skulls of the individuals buried in Jerusalem from the Iron Age, at En-Gedi in the Hellenistic and Roman periods, or in those buried in Meiron in the ER to LR (and in Jezreel in the Crusader period), is typical. Were most persons undernourished and/or infected with intestinal or malarial parasites until modern times? That conclusion seems to follow but only indirectly.

But we must give two cautions here: First, one might eat sufficient quantities of calories daily but not the correct balance providing protein, vitamins, and minerals. The cause of the anemia which left its traces in the skulls of these children (and adults) *could* have been improper (theoretically not even inadequate) nutrition and not intestinal parasites or malarial parasites (see Chapter 6). The evidence from the skeletal remains, by itself, is not sufficient to argue for widespread infections of parasites but it is a support to the more direct evidence, the fecal remains, and the indirect evidence of the fever amulets. The ubiquitous presence of *cribra orbitalia/porotic hyperostosis* is certainly suggestive.[154] Further, some studies have found a correlation between high rates of these conditions and high child mortality, as mentioned above.[155]

Second, the association of anemia with pitting in the crania has been challenged recently. One study[156] doubts that anemia causes this condition. But other research presents a more nuanced result than just a yes or no conclusion on the causes of cranial pitting. One study[157] of 333 individuals in the Sudan determined that of those cases with *cribra orbitalia*, 44% were the result of anemia and the rest were from various causes (including post-mortem decay). Further, studies done in the new world, in native American sites, have shown a positive *correlation* (not proof of cause-effect) of parasitism with *porotic hyperostosis*.[158] Thus, while the easy association of these pitting conditions in the crania with anemia (caused by malnutrition and exacerbated by parasitic infection or caused by malaria) is coming under scrutiny, there is still cause strongly to suspect parasitic infection. Again, we are not arguing for a one-for-one

---

153. For malaria as the cause, see: Mitchel, "Human Parasites," 49; and Smith-Guzmán, "Cribra Orbitalia." This suggestion was also noted in Reed, "Instability" 355; and Grmek *Diseases,* 282.

154. See Walker, et al. "Porotic Hyperostosis and Cribra Orbitalia." Although the association of cribra orbitalia and iron deficiency/nutritional deficiency is now being debated by some paleopathologists, most still support it.

155. Scheidel, *Death on the Nile,* 140.

156. Walter, et al., "Causes of Porotic Hyperostosis."

157. Wapler, Crubézy, and Schultz, "Is Cribra Orbitalia."

158. Reinhard and Araújo, "Archaeoparasitology."

cause of *cribra/porotic hyperostosis* from parasitic infection. Certainly not all cases of cranial pitting were caused by anemia/parasitic infection but a good portion of them probably were. Therefore, the skeletal evidence from the crania is a support for a widespread infection of parasites.

CONCLUSION

We have appealed in this chapter to humble objects: human fecal remains, old bones, magical amulets, and tombstones. No one will visit Israel or a museum to see those items. They will probably not be featured on the front cover—with glossy, color photographs—of an archaeological magazine. But from these remains we have attempted to meet the real folk.

In the Synoptic Gospels (Mark 10:13//Matt 19:13//Luke 18:15) parents bring children to Jesus so that he might "touch them" and bless them. We must imagine, in light of the above evidence, malnourished children, lethargic toddlers, anemic little ones, even anorexic children—in a word, very sick—among those coming for blessing. They were stunted and wasted (emaciated) children due to parasitic infections.[159] The children were not thriving, were not growing properly, were not as smart as the other children, and the parents did not know why. Many may have contracted strange diseases because they were already weakened by the parasites.

Many of the adults felt the same way but they were older and stronger and could more easily ignore the symptoms. And if one can scarcely remember what it feels like to be well, one does not miss wellness so much. Somehow they made it through the day fighting fatigue and weakness, perhaps fever as well. They no longer expected to get past their condition but they hoped that their children could.

Further, we begin to picture familiar scenes in a different way when we bear in mind the threat of malaria in the ancient world. Was the "season of death" already upon them when Jesus made his ministry/healing trips throughout Galilee? Maybe some of the children in the villages were already infected and running high temperatures. They seemed to know that when a pregnant woman contracted the "fevers" it was almost certain death. We must imagine, in light of the above evidence, feverish persons coming for healing. Perhaps the parents had already lost children to this horrible disease in previous years. If they survived the initial attack of the disease (perhaps the tertian or quartan fever), then they were thereafter spiking dangerous fevers on a regular basis. The parents could see their little lives flowing from their bodies. They lived in dread of the "fevers and chills" which caused death or became a chronic malady.

---

159. Titoria, Ponnusamy, and Mehra, "Undernutrition in Under Five Children." Stunting is being underheight for weight; wasting is being under weight for height. Both are measures for malnutrition in children.

So, they must have brought their loved ones to Jesus in the hope that something could be done. They were desperate and feared the worst. Perhaps they were already grieving the recent loss of children or spouses with similar symptoms. And, thus, they came, begging, "Please, bless my child." As Richard Rohrbaugh suggests, the children are "being brought by frightened mothers seeking healing or protection for their babies, many of whom will likely die."[160] Or, they brought their spouse—or, even, themselves—for healing. When we think of the crowds that followed Jesus, for example the "five thousand" (Mark 6:44), we must think of significant numbers of them (at least two thousand) as being very sick.

So, when they heard words like: "Come to me you who are weary . . . my burden is light . . . blessed are those that hunger now . . . blessed are those that weep now," what did they think and feel? The words must have been a balm, a comfort to "broken jars."

---

160. Rohrbaugh, "Introduction," 5.

10

How Long Would You Have Lived?

HOW LONG, ON AVERAGE, did people live in Israel/Palestine in the late Second Temple Period? What percentage of children died before reaching adulthood (youth mortality rate)? What was the average life span (from birth and from adulthood)? Were there very many old people back then? Did women, as they do now, live longer than men?

These are the kinds of questions demographers studying mortality ask. In more recent times, researchers could pore over records such as birth certificates, death certificates, and medical records. But these sorts of documents do not exist for the ancient world. What to do? We will look at what the skeletal remains tell us, the human bones, as we did in Chapter 8 and partly in Chapter 9. We will take the data we have, analyze it, and then compare it with the other demographic methods from elsewhere in the Roman empire (tombstone inscriptions, for example).

WHAT DO THE BONES SHOW US?

We will work from a total database of 1598 individuals. Of course, not every individual in the tombs can be factored into a given question since often the remains are too disintegrated to indicate more than a very rough age (not a precise age and not gender). To answer some queries, for example, we need only to know if the individual died in youth (before age 20; Table 10.3). Most of the skeletal remains (though not all even for this general question) can be used to formulate an answer to this investigation. But for other calculations (such as life expectancy by sex at adulthood, Table 10.6) we need a fairly accurate estimate of the age at death and a determination of the sex of the individual. Unfortunately, in some cases, this calculation is simply not possible due to the poorly preserved bones.[1] Therefore, Table 10.6 will have the smallest sample size.

---

1. For the accuracy in such determinations, see Smith, "Skeletal Analysis," 52–53

We will examine four considerations. We will look at child mortality (ages 0–5 years), youth mortality (0–19 years), average life-span from birth, and average life-span from adulthood.[2]

Let us say from the start that the study of demography has been going on among ancient historians and classicists for the last thirty or forty years. They have usually turned to the tombstone inscriptions for their information (with some profit also in searching the Egyptian papyri). They seem to agree on three observations:[3]

1. Infant mortality was shockingly high by today's standards.[4]

2. Even if one should reach the age of 20, the life expectancy was still pretty low (somewhere in the mid 30s to early 40s).[5]

3. There was a significant gap in the life expectancy of women and men.[6]

We will see if our findings agree or disagree with these earlier observations for the Greco-Roman world in general.

Child Mortality

One of the most telling statistics in any society is its child mortality rate. This data can be a good predictor of the prosperity of a society. If the child mortality (in our case ages 0–5[7]) is unusually higher than the surrounding societies, then chances are that Israel in the ER period was economically deprived relative to the surrounding regions. To figure child mortality, we will divide the total number of persons identified by the anthropologists as age 0–5 years at death by the total number of individuals in the tombs. The following table presents the evidence:

Tomb(s)	Number of individuals	Number of children (0–5 years old)
Jericho (Goliath, tomb H)	31	10
French Hill (ER)	64	10
French Hill (Hell II)	33	9
Meiron	197	70
Judea/Samaria (8 tombs)	227	54 (0–9 years)

2. For information on how anthropologists estimate age, see Brothwell, *Digging Up Bones,* 57–66; and Chapter 8, note 8 in this volume.

3. Parkin, *Demography,* 92; Burn, "Hic breve vivitur," 10; Grmek, *Diseases,* 104.

4. See e.g., Grmek, *Diseases,* 100; Parkin, *Demography,* 92–93.

5. See Grmek, *Diseases,* 106; Bagnall and Frier, *Demography,* 109.

6. See Grmek, *Diseases,* 100; Wells, "Ancient Obstetric."

7. The nomenclature changes from demographer to demographer. Usually infant mortality is measured on the basis of 0–1 year. The age at death for most skeletal remains of individuals from over two thousand years ago usually cannot be calculated that precisely. Thus, most physical anthropologists date within five years. We will use the term "child mortality" to designate those dying before age 5 and "youth mortality" to designate those dying before age 20.

Caiaphas	63	26
Giv'at ha-Mivtar	35	9
Arnona	41	14
Mt. Scopus	88	34
Har Haẓofim Observatory	147	54
Akeldama	115	45
Abba	4	1
Naḥal Ḥever	19	4
En-Gedi	164	49
Wadi-Ḥalaf	123	45[8]
Totals	1,351[9]	434

Table 10.1: Child Mortality in Hell II–ER II Israel[10] Child mortality: 32%

The table is a bit problematic because one of the sources only gives data for children from 0–9 years instead of 0–5 years as in all of the others. Still, this figure conforms rather well to other findings in other parts of the Mediterranean world. The average percentage results in a 32% child mortality rate for Israel in the Hell II through ER II periods.[11] The percentage is about six points lower than that of contemporary Greece (38%).[12] Thus, based on child mortality alone—although shockingly high by modern standards—one would not conclude that Palestine/Israel was worse economically than Greece in the Hell II through ER II periods.

Thus, 32% of the children born in Israel within our timeframe (expanded to Hell II to ER II) died before reaching age five. But can we be even more precise? We cannot from the data supplied in the reports used to construct Table 10.1. The bones were usually not in good enough condition to calculate the exact age at death.

8. This tomb (near Jerusalem) also included nine remains of fetuses. I have not used these remains in the calculation. How does one evaluate stillborn babies in mortality calculations?

9. Not all of the individuals in the total database can be used for this measure since the anthropologists could not always give a precise age for the children. Thus, if they only indicated that the skeletal remains were of a pre-adult or youth, we could use the data in the Table 10.3 but not for calculating child mortality for which we need an age range of from 0–5 years.

10. The table is produced by combined evidence in: Arieli, "Har Haẓofim Observatory"; Hachlili and Smith, "Goliath Family"; Arensburg and Rak, "French Hill"; Smith and Zias, "French Hill"; Haas, "Anthropological Observations," (Giv'at, ha-Mivtar); Nagar and Torgeé, "Biological Characteristics," (8 tombs); Smith, Bornemann, and Zias, "Skeletal Remains," (Meiron); Zias, "Caiaphas' Tomb"; ibid, "Mount Scopus"; ibid. "Anthropological Analysis," (Akeldama); ibid, "Human Skeletal Remains," (Arnona); Nathan, "Naḥal Ḥever"; Arensburg and Belfer-Cohen, "En-Gedi"; Smith, "Abba Cave"; Hadas, "En-Gedi"; and Kahana, "Wadi-Ḥalaf."

11. One of the French Hill tombs is Late Hellenistic as are the nine tombs at En-Gedi (see Hadas, "Nine Tombs"). The cemetery at Meiron dates from the first century BCE to the third century CE. Some of the tombs excavated by Nagar and Torgeé dated from the Late Hellenistic period; and finally, the remains from Cave 8 at Naḥal Ḥever are from the early second century CE which we have designated ER II (see Appendix B).

12. Hachlili, "Goliath."

The Archaeology of Daily Life

But a study from the Crusader village of Parvum Gerinum (in the Jezreel Valley or Great Plain; see Map 4.1) may at least offer some suggestions. Since the tomb is from a much later period (see Appendix B for "Crusader" period), we need to be somewhat cautious in concluding that these data would also represent the ER period. We would need to assume that the socio-pathological conditions remained essentially unchanged over one thousand years. Nevertheless, we present some data from this cemetery which seems to me to harmonize with the above Table 10.1.

Piers Mitchel has nicely summarized the evidence from the cemetery of this village. Only a part of the cemetery was excavated—the part used exclusively for children—and thus, he could not compare the children's mortality with the adults. But the comparison of the children among themselves is most instructive. Here is a summary of his data:

Age at death	Around birth	1 month to 1 year	1–2 years	2–3 years	3–4 years	4–5 years	5–18 years
Number in age rage	13	15	5	5	4	2	2

Table 10.2: Numbers (by age) in children's cemetery of Parvum Gerinum[13]

We may make the following observations:

1. 28% of the child deaths occurred around the time of birth.

2. 33% of children surviving childbirth died the first year of their lives.

3. The two classes together comprise 61%. Thus, six out of ten children died within the first year of life (including at or near birth). The first year of life was extremely dangerous.

Since the time of birth and the first year of life were the most dangerous times for children, might we assume that most of those in our Table 10.1 died during the same time frame? It seems warranted.

Although this child mortality rate is very high by our modern standards, it is not much different from what we can find recorded in recent, pre-modern history. Although child mortality (0–5 years old) is usually lower than 1% in wealthy countries today, in pre-modern times it ranged from 30% to 50%. In late nineteenth-century Germany as well as in India, Yemen, and Korea in 1800, the child mortality rate was over 50%. The healthiest countries had a rate of 30%. In 1800 the global average was 43%. (Now it is 3.4%). Thus, this child mortality rate for ancient Palestine/Israel is not high by pre-modern standards. It was toward the lower end of the range.[14]

---

13. Based on Mitchel, "Child Health," 38. There were also four fetuses in the tomb but I disregarded these numbers as irrelevant to our study.

14. See Roser, "Child Mortality." For the most lethal diseases for children in this age range, see Table 9.1.

Youth Mortality

Next we look at youth mortality. Here we want to know how many died before reaching adulthood (which we will define as age 20[15]). Tal Ilan,[16] from her database of 403 individuals, found a youth mortality rate of 44%. She wondered at the time if further results might move the number higher. Now, based on my much larger database, that question can be answered. We will look at our full sample size of 1,598 individuals to determine how many of them died before their twentieth birthday, calculating the same way we did to arrive at child mortality. Table 10.3 has the results:

Tombs	Total Individuals	Youths (0–19)
Jericho	185 (130 tombs)	54
French Hill ER	64	19
French Hill Hell II	33	9
Jerusalem (Unpublished)	65	28
Meiron	197	95
8 tombs in Judea/Samaria	227	73
Caiaphas	63	43
Giv'at ha-Mivtar	35	16
Arnona	41	21
Mt. Scopus	88	42
Har Haẓofim Observatory	147	81
Akeldama	115	55
Abba Cave	4	2
Naḥal Ḥever	19	12
Qumran	28	5
En-Gedi	164	77
Wadi-Ḥalaf	123	62
TOTAL	1,598	694

Table 10.3: Youth Mortality in Ancient Israel (Hell II through ER II periods)[17]

Average Youth Mortality: 43%

---

15. This age seems to be preferred by physical anthropologists as the biological age of adulthood. The socially determined age of adulthood in antiquity, however, was younger. See Chapter 5.

16. Ilan, *Integrating*, 201, 214.

17. Compiled from data in Arieli, "Har Haẓofim Observatory"; Arensburg and Smith, "Anthropological Tables"; Smith and Zias, "French Hill"; Arensburg and Rak, "French Hill"; Hachlili and Smith, "Goliath Family"; Haas, "Anthropological Observations," (Giv'at, ha-Mivtar); Smith, Bornemann, and Zias, "Skeletal Remains (Meiron)"; Nagar and Torgeé, "Biological Characteristics" (8 tombs); Zias, "Caiaphas' Tomb"; Haas, "Giv'at ha-Mivtar"; Zias, "Arnona"; Zias, "Mount Scopus"; Zias, "Anthropological Analysis (Akeldama)"; Nathan, "Naḥal Ḥever"; Smith, "Abba Cave"; Arensburg and Belfer-Cohen, "En-Gedi"; Hadas, "En-Gedi"; Kahana, "Wadi-Ḥalaf"; Steckoll, "Preliminary Excavation Report"; Broshi and Eshel, "Whose Bones?"; Röhrer-Ertl, "Facts and Results."

These results are almost exactly what Ilan found using a much smaller sample size. Further, we note the following observations: First, the Caiaphas tomb is unusually high in child mortality (68%). This family, presumably somewhat well-to-do, or at least of middling means to be able to afford a tomb and ornate ossuaries,[18] must have had a genetic tendency for youth mortality since we would assume that lack of nutrition would not have been the problem. On the other hand, the Jericho (29%) and French Hill Hell II (27%) cemeteries exhibit very low youth mortality for this period.

These outlying figures are even more striking when we compare them with those from Athens and Olynthus in the classical period and with Rome, the Italian countryside, and the eastern Mediterranean world in the Roman imperial period:

Location	Youth Mortality Percentage
Athens (classical)[19]	49%
Olynthus (classical)[20]	49%
Rome (Imperial)[21]	54%
Italian countryside (Imperial Period)[22]	42%
Eastern Mediterranean (Imperial Period)[23]	47%

Table 10.4: Youth Mortality in the Greco-Roman World

If we can assume that the cities of Athens and Rome were about average with respect to child mortality for the cities of the empire, we see how unusually high the Caiaphas tomb is and how incredibly low the two other above-mentioned tombs are. Over all, the tombs of Hell II, ER I, and ER II Israel exhibit a youth mortality rate that is 6% lower than Greece, 11% lower than that of the city of Rome, but about the same as that evidenced from other sites in Italy. How one explains this difference (the ritual washing of Judaism, simply better DNA, better nutrition, or the lack of sanitation in the cities) remains unclear. At any rate, one had a slightly better chance of growing to adulthood in Israel than in Athens or in Rome.

Meir Bar-Ilan[24] has arrived at a similar figure for Talmudic era Israel by using two methods: references in the rabbinic literature (especially to Tannaitic figures) and comparisons with pre-modern societies. He has conveniently organized all the

---

18. It is disputed as to whether this is the Caiaphas of the New Testament, the High Priest who condemned Jesus to death. Evans, "Excavating Caiaphas," doubts that this is the High Priest's tomb; Rousseau and Arav, *Jesus and His World*, 139–42, affirm that it is.

19. Reported in Hachlili, "Goliath."

20. Demand, *Birth*, 193 n. 117.

21. Hopkins, "Age Structure." Hopkins' figure for Rome was based on 8065 inscriptions; his figure for the Italian countryside was based on 5343 inscriptions.

22. Hopkins, "Age Structure."

23. Angel, "Ecology," 94.

24. Bar-Ilan, "Infant Mortality."

references in his collection in a table which lists 46 child deaths reported in the rabbinic literature, most of whom were males. But of the cases reported, nine of them happened to children of Tannaim. Since there were—so Bar-Ilan—around 100 Tannaim in all and since half of them are mentioned in the sources "only sporadically," he divides the 100 Tannaim by two. He then surmises that the deaths of females were seldom reported and thus multiplies the number of deaths by two. These calculations leave him with 18/50 deaths per Tannaitic family or "more than 30%" (36% to be exact). Thus he concludes that this percentage on average died before age fourteen. Bar-Ilan then confirms his hypothesis by looking at comparisons with pre-modern societies where he finds similar child mortality rates.

Some might question these mathematical steps in logic, but it is interesting that his figure is essentially in agreement with mine, which is based in skeletal remains. His percentage (36%) is somewhat lower than my 43%, but he only calculates for ages 0–14 while I calculate for ages 0–20. His figures and those of other demographers of the ancient world confirm that my estimates of child and youth mortality fall within the range of plausibility.

Life Expectancies

Another way of presenting the evidence is to assess life expectancies from birth and after reaching early adulthood. In addition to asking how many usually died before age five or age 20, we can ask what would be the average life expectancy of a person born in Hell II–ER II Israel calculating from birth and from adulthood. Some archaeologists and anthropologists have ventured such figures. I will first cite their calculations and then give mine based on my collection of the data.

Nagar and Torgeé, based on their excavation of the eight tombs in Judea in the Hell II and ER I periods, calculated that the average life expectancy from birth for all individuals was 24 years. Compare this figure with Greece (29 years)[25] and Egypt (24 years)[26] during this same period—based on funerary inscriptions (Greece) and based on papyrus census records (Egypt)—and with the Coale-Demeny Life Table West for females, which is, at birth, 22.5 years.[27] Frier states it was commonly accepted in scholarly circles at the time of his writing (1983) that a Roman life expectancy at birth was between 20 and 30 years.[28] So the results from the eight Hell II and ER I tombs in Judea/Samaria are rather typical for the Greco-Roman world during this period. Further, Frier maintains, based on his collection of evidence throughout the Roman Empire, that on average 66% of children born died before age 30.[29] In the eight

25. Grmek, *Diseases*, 106.
26. Bagnall and Frier, *Demography*, 109.
27. Bagnall and Frier, *Demography*, 35.
28. Frier, "Pannonian Evidence"; so also Durand, "Mortality Estimates," 372.
29. Frier, "Pannonian Evidence," 328, based on Ulpian's life table.

Judean/Samaritan tombs, however, according to the raw data they supply, 54% died before age 30.[30]

But we can compose our own life expectancy table from birth based on more data than just the eight tombs excavated by Nagar and Torgeé. We will gather information from ten different excavations consisting of hundreds of tombs and 1072 individuals. The average life expectancy calculated in this way should be more accurate than simply using the data of Nagar and Torgeé since the sample size is larger. Table 10.5 shows the data.

Site/tombs	Number of individuals	Total number of years lived
Caiaphas	51	540
Mount Scopus	70	949
Har Haẓofim Observatory	104	1,000
Arnona	25	309
Naḥal Ḥever	17	327
Jericho	192	6,335
French Hill (Hell II)	33	923
Giv'at ha-Mivtar	34	873
8 tombs in Judea/Samaria excavated by Nagar and Torgeé	121	2,363
Meiron	191	2,363
En-Gedi	149	2,579
Wadi-Ḥalaf	85	1,263
Totals	1072[31]	21,103

Table 10.5: Average Life Expectancy at Birth in the Hell II–ER II Periods in Palestine/Israel:[32] 20 years

These figures give us an average life expectancy from birth for both sexes of 20 years, somewhat lower than the calculations of Nagar and Torgeé as well as that of the Coale-Demeny Life Table West for females.

30. Nagar and Torgeé, "Biological Characteristics," 167. But in their mortality curve given below (Figure 10.1) they calculate 65.2% died before age 30. Their Mortality Curve is not the same as simply working with the raw data since they opine that many infants' remains were unreadable and thus that they were underrepresented in the sample size. To compensate for this assumed factor, they used "life-table methodology" in constructing a Mortality Curve.

31. The figures for total individuals in the tombs may differ from table to table because, as is the case here, the anthropologists were sometimes uncertain of the age of an individual. Hence, these remains cannot be used to calculate average life expectancy from birth.

32. The table is composed based on the data given in: Arieli, "Har Haẓofim Observatory"; Zias, "Caiaphas"; Zias, "Mount Scopus"; Zias, "Arnona"; Nathan, "Naḥal Ḥever"; Arensburg and Smith, "Jewish Population (Jericho)"; Smith and Zias, "French Hill"; Haas, "Giv'at ha-Mivtar"; Nagar and Torgeé, "Biological Characteristics (8 tombs)"; Smith, Bornemann, and Zias, "Skeletal Remains (Meiron)"; Arensburg and Belfer-Cohen, "En-Gedi"; Hadas, "En-Gedi"; Kahana, "Wadi-Ḥalaf."

Compare these life expectancies from birth with those today around the world: Japan (the highest) 82 years; United States 78 years; Sierra Leon (the lowest) 46 years.[33] Even the lowest life expectancy in today's world is more than twice that of the ancient Mediterranean person.

What about those reaching early adulthood? If one made it to age twenty, how long might one expect to live on average? There are two calculations given in the literature to which we may refer. Joe Zias[34] maintains that the average life span for the males examined at Qumran was 34 years. Nagar and Torgeé[35] calculated that the average life span for adults (both sexes) buried in the eight tombs of Judea/Samaria which they excavated was 38 years.

But, again, let us do our own calculation. We will add the total number of adult males and females in the Jerusalem tomb complexes,[36] in Meiron in Galilee, in the Goliath family tomb at Jericho (tomb H), in Cave 8 at Naḥal Ḥever, the nine Hell II tombs at En-Gedi, and in the few excavated graves at Qumran where these are identified by age and sex. To arrive at a life expectancy figure, we will then divide this number into the total number of years of life.[37] The cautions are that most of this evidence is from the Jerusalem area and has a much lower sample size[38] than the other two calculations: 161 males and 96 females.

	MEN	WOMEN
Caiaphas tomb	142 years /4 persons	40 yrs /1 person
Mt. Scopus	411/12	437/15
Giv'at ha-Mivtar	381/9	348/10
French Hill (Hell II)	429/10	308/8
Akeldama	89/3	73/3
Arnona	30/1	157/4
Jericho-Goliath (tomb H)	474/11	280/7
Meiron	745/21	842/25
Qumran	802/19	52/6
Abba Cave	33/1	

33. No author, "List of Countries by Life Expectancy." Compare No author, "Life Expectancies at Birth," *World Fact Book* (operated by the United States C.I.A.) which lists Monaco as having the longest life expectancy at 89 years and Chad as having the shortest at 49 years.

34. Zias, "Cemeteries of Qumran."

35. Nagar and Torgeé, "Biological Characteristics."

36. I.e. Giv'at; Caiaphas; Scopus; French Hill; Akeldama; Arnona; Wadi Ḥalaf; Har Haẓofim; and Abba.

37. See Frier, "Roman Life Expectancy," 219 for the method of computing average life expectancy. Also cf. Grmek, *Diseases,* 105.

38. Why is the sample size so small in comparison with the two previous tables? Other reports of tomb excavations in Israel could not be used since they did not give this much data. We need an approximation of age at death and the identification of the sex of the individual. Where the anthropologists gave a range of ages (e.g., 35–45), I gave the average (hence, 40) for the purposes of the table.

Naḥal Ḥever	159/4	91/3
En-Gedi	1630/47	
Har Haẓofim	120/4	200/6
Wadi-Ḥalaf	655/15	350/8
Totals	Average 6100/161 38 years	Average 3178/96 33 years

Table 10.6: Life Expectancy in Late Second Temple Israel from Adulthood (from age 20)[39]

We get the average of 38 years life expectancy for any male reaching adulthood and 33 years life expectancy for females reaching adulthood in Israel in the late Second Temple Period.

Compare these results with various calculations made by historians of Greece, Rome, and Israel given in Table 10.7:

HISTORIAN	AGE
Beloch[40]	Males: 36–37; Females: 30–31
Russell[41]	Males: 49.4; Females: 47.7
Angel[42]	Males: 42; Females 31
Angel[43] (25 years later)	Males: 40.2; Females: 34.3 (Roman Period) Males: 42.6; Females: 36.6 (Hellenistic Period)
Coale-Demeny Life Table West[44]	Females: 49.9
Gallant[45]	Males: 40; Females 38
Grmek[46]	Males: 40; Females 34

---

39. The table is compiled from Arieli, "Har Haẓofim Observatory"; Steckoll, "Preliminary Excavation Report" (Qumran); Sheridan, "French Collection" (Qumran); Broshi and Eshel, "Whose Bones?" (Qumran); Smith, "Skeletal Remains (Abba cave)"; Smith and Zias, "French Hill (LH)"; Hachlili and Smith, "Goliath Family"; Smith, Bornemann, and Zias, "Skeletal Remains (Meiron)"; Zias, "Caiaphas'"; Haas, "Giv'at ha-Mivtar"; Zias, "Arnona"; Zias, "Mount Scopus"; Arieli, "Har Haẓofim"; and Zias, "Anthropological Analysis (Akeldama)"; Nathan, "Naḥal Ḥever"; Arensburg and Belfer-Cohen, "En-Gedi"; Hadas, "En-Gedi"; Kahana, "Wadi-Ḥalaf." One is unable to use much of the osteoarchaeological data in this calculation due to: some publications did not calculate the ages beyond the most general observation: "child, adult, etc." (Arensburg and Rak, "French Hill" [ER] and Arensburg and Smith, "Jericho") and some did not give the sex of the individual (Nagar and Torgeé, "Biological Characteristics").

40. See Russell, *Late Ancient*, 25.
41. Russell, *Late Ancient*, 64.
42. Angel, "Length of Life," 20.
43. Angel, "Ecology," 94.
44. Bagnall and Frier, *Demography*, 35.
45. Gallant, *Risk*, 20.
46. Grmek, *Diseases*, 104.

HISTORIAN	AGE
Burn[47]	Males: 38; Females 33 (Carthage) Males: 40; Females 33 (Provinces of the Danube)
Zias[48]	Males: 34 years (Qumran)
Nagar and Torgeé[49]	All: 38 years (8 Judean/Samaritan tombs)
Mayer[50]	Females: 41.25 years (Palestine and Diaspora)

Table 10.7: Life expectancy at age 20—Various findings

The calculations above in Table 10.6, then, are a bit lower than most of those (but exactly the same as Carthage) based on evidence elsewhere in the Mediterranean world (Table 10.7) and obtained not only from osteoarchaeological methods but also from epigraphical.

One feature confronts us immediately from our calculation: There was a significant gender gap in life expectancy for those reaching early adulthood (also reported by most of the historians in Table 10.7). Wells affirmed that on average one could demonstrate a gap using both osteological and epigraphic evidence of five years life expectancy.[51]

Why the disparity in sexes? Most point to the dangers of childbirth in this non-medical age.[52] Demand maintains that childbirth, before the modern age, was absolutely perilous. The main causes of death in mothers before giving birth, during delivery, and also in the days after giving birth were puerperal fever, toxemia, hemorrhage, and malaria (for malaria, see above Chapter 9).[53]

Certainly, giving birth seems to have been feared by women in the ancient world. In Euripides, *Medea* (248–251) a woman states that she would prefer three times over to stand in a battle line than give birth once. S.R. Llewelyn gives the text of a letter (2nd century CE) from a husband to his wife who states how happy he is that is wife escaped the dangers of childbirth.[54]

The sages of the Mishnah noted the dangers in childbirth and offered three reasons why women died in giving birth: because the women neglected the laws about menstruation (Lev 15:19–30); because they neglected the law about dough offerings (Num 15:20); or because they did not properly light the lamp on Sabbath evening (m. Shabb. 2:6). Such tasks would be especially female obligations. These suggested causes

47. Burn, "Hic breve vivitur," 16.
48. Zias, "Cemeteries of Qumran."
49. Nagar and Torgeé, "Biological Characteristics."
50. Mayer, *Jüdische Frau*, 95–96.
51. Wells, "Ancient Obstetric," 1235.
52. Russell, *Late Ancient*, 35; Gallant, *Risk*, 20; Eakins, "Human Osteology," 95; and Stark, *Rise of Christianity*, 120 who emphasizes specifically inept abortions.
53. Demand, *Birth*, 76–86.
54. Llewelyn, *Greek Inscriptions and Papyri*, 57.

for the dangers of childbirth seem like males blaming the victim. Yet, they do illustrate that the ancients knew that giving birth was dangerous.

J. Naveh describes the ossuary of a young woman, found just north of Jerusalem and dating to the first century CE, which states, inscribed on one end, that she failed to give birth. Inside the ossuary were the bones of a woman with a fetus still in the birth canal. Her pelvis was curved and she was unable to deliver. Had she a midwife, Naveh opines, she would not have died.[55] Tal Ilan cites in addition five inscriptions that seem to indicate that mother and baby died in childbirth.[56] The archaeological data seem to support the textual.

Given the dangers of childbirth, it is no wonder that the midwife was an honorable and valued profession. The Mishnah refers to them (m. Shabb. 18:3; m. Rosh H. 2:5): the rabbis ruled that one could summon a midwife from anywhere (no matter how far away) on the Sabbath and on the New Year (*Rosh ha-Shanah*). The Talmud (b. B. Qama 59a) speaks about the fees for their service. They were often crucial in saving the lives of mother and child and thus the travel laws on the holy days could be ignored. Josephus identifies a zealot in the Jewish War as the son of a midwife (*Life* 185). Thus, his mother's profession seems to have been a high status.

Pagans valued midwives as well. G. H. R. Horsley cites the epitaph of a midwife from the early imperial period. In the epitaph, it states that she "saved" many women, saved in the sense of saved their lives in childbirth. The skills she knew were employed over the decades to save mother and child during and after birth. Horsley suggests that this is the sense of 1 Timothy 2:15 where it states that a godly woman will be saved in childbirth: saved in the sense of brought safely through it.[57]

Burn, however, finds a different cause for the discrepancy in life expectancy between males and females. He believes that female mortality was more about exhaustion. Giving birth, nursing infants, and doing all the daily required labor simply wore out the mothers (see Chapter 7, Table 7.7). Burn writes that the ancient mothers "combine in one organism the functions of the milk-cow and the draught ox."[58]

Third, Wells tried to establish that it was preferential feeding of boys over girls. The girls were undernourished and thus in young adulthood unable to survive (as discussed earlier in Chapter 5).[59] Whatever the cause,[60] in antiquity most men outlived women. Today, of course, that is reversed: women on average outlive men.

55. Naveh, "Ossuary Inscriptions." For the osteological information, see Haas, "Anthropological Observations." See Table 8.1, number 9 above for this information.

56. Ilan, *Jewish Women,* 118. These inscriptions may indicate—it is not always clear to me that they do—that the mother and baby died in childbirth.

57. G. H. R. Horsley, *New Documents,* 23.

58. Burn, "Hic breve vivitur," 12. His table on p. 16 lists average life expectancies of males and females from several different provinces in Africa and Europe. Grmek (*Diseases,* 89) agrees with Burn.

59. Wells, "Ancient Obstetric."

60. On the other hand, Durand ("Mortality estimates," 369) concludes that women did not usually die as young as their tombstones indicate since they, similar to our modern vanities, would have

We noted at the beginning of our presentation that there were three agreed upon results of the study of ancient demographics:

1. Infant mortality was shockingly high by today's standards (see Tables 10.1 and 10.2).
2. Even if one should reach the age of 20, the life expectancy was still pretty low (somewhere in the mid 30s to early 40s; see Table 10.6).
3. There was a significant gap in the life expectancy of women and men (see Tables 10.6 and 10.7).

Our own findings from the 1,598 individuals represented in the mostly Hell II and ER tombs of Israel confirm those results.

IMPLICATIONS FOR NEW TESTAMENT RESEARCH

What does all of this data mean in human terms? What must it have been like to live in such conditions? Walter Scheidel[61] gives a helpful overview of Greco-Roman population in antiquity:

1. Infant mortality was around 30% (for the first year of life; cf. our Table 10.2).
2. Half of all people died before they were old enough to bear or father children.
3. Death was as much a phenomenon of childhood as of old age.
4. Ancient populations were necessarily very young.

Such factors resulted, according to Scheidel, in the following socio-economic conditions:

1. Destabilization of families
2. Ubiquity of widows[62] and orphans
3. Disincentives to investment in education
4. Disruption of trust networks that sustain commerce.

These are very helpful conclusions for us to start with. I hope to expand on them a bit. I see the following five implications of the above data for our understanding of the New Testament: 1) There was mourning in every household over dead children. 2) There were many single-parent families. 3) There was a shortage of young workers. 4)

---

wanted to "appear young." So, their families would represent them as dying younger than they actually did and falsify the age at death on the tombstone. Angel, "Length of Life," 20–21, suggested that certain soil conditions might have skewed the evidence (viz. of the skeletal remains).

61. Scheidel, "Population and Demography."
62. Or, I would add, widowers.

There was pressure to marry and procreate early in life. 5) There was a lack of mentorship for the young.

A Household of Grief

Such high child mortality must have meant that death, mourning and sadness were a reality for every family almost constantly. We have a saying in the western culture, "No parent should have to bury a child." That saying would be meaningless in this society. What is a rather rare tragedy in our society—losing a child—was the experience of the overwhelming majority of families. And they did not lose just one child but several. This reality is presented to us frequently in the New Testament Gospels where families are often mourning a dead child or showing anxiety over the illness of a child.[63] There are references to sick children (Mark 9:17–18; Luke 8:42, 49; 9:42; John 4:49[64]) and to instances where young persons have died (Mark 5:35; Luke 7:12; John 11:14). We may have read these accounts in the past and regarded them as in our own life experiences, tragic but rare. From the skeletal evidence, however, we know these occurrences must have been, though still tragic, not at all rare. They were not the exception but the rule.

Based on my calculations above—and confirmed by those of others from elsewhere in the empire—if a couple gave birth to ten children (not at all an unusual occurrence), three of them would die before reaching age five and a fourth before age twenty. Of the remaining six children, three more would die before their mid-thirties. Only three of the ten could expect to live past age forty. Further, shortly after the birth of the tenth child, one would expect one of the parents to die leaving the surviving parent with six children to rear alone.

Single Parent Families

Second, a life expectancy, even for those reaching young adulthood, of mid- to late-thirties would mean that there would be small children still at home when one (or both) parents had died. Many families must have been missing parents from the nucleated family. If an Egyptian comparison may be offered here, it is telling: Bagnall and Frier[65] calculate—based on their mortality studies of the census records—that there was a one in four chance that one or even both of the parents would die within ten years of marriage. Where the census records show age at death of the spouse, they

---

63. Russell, *Late Ancient,* 35: "If a family had six children, it would have to expect that the first would die as a baby, the second by twenty, the third by thirty-five to forty, the fourth by forty-five to fifty, the fifth, by sixty and the sixth later." If anything, Russell's calculations are too optimistic. According to our calculations not two but probably three children would die before age twenty. Of the three left, one or two would die before age forty.

64. Compare the story in John with b. Ber. 34b.

65. Bagnall and Frier, *Demography,* 123.

indicate that the survivors were rather young (in their twenties and early thirties). Further, in the eight cases they looked at where the death of the spouse was expressly stated in the census report, only three of the men remarried while none of the women had remarried.[66]

Such conditions meant, surely, that there were many single parent families and that nucleated families were often forced to rely on the extended family for security. The nucleated family needed the extended family to rear the children and to provide a safety net. But in this period the *bet ʿav* probably no longer existed as it had in the Israelite period.[67] The safety net was no longer there. This would have meant that many children were reared by an aunt or uncle—or by an older sibling—since grandparents likely were not around either.[68] Doubtless, many children roamed the streets, unattended, like urchins or waifs. Perhaps this possibility changes our imagining the scene depicted in Mark 10:13-16 (Matt 19:14//Luke 18:16//Gos. Thom. 22) where Jesus announces that "to these waifs belongs the Kingdom of God."

Shortage of Young Workers

Further, there probably were not enough young men and women to do the farm work or craft work. That means children themselves must have done some of the work. One can imagine that people began laboring early in life and just never stopped (see Chapter 5). What we regard as a childhood—a time of leisure and imagination—did not happen to the majority of ancient children. They had to work, especially if one of the parents had died.[69] Hiring out one's child for wages (and even selling one's child into slavery) has a long history in the ancient Near East.[70] Needy families were often forced to utilize whatever resources were at their disposal and, unfortunately, the children were sometimes the only resource.

Pressure to Procreate Early in Life

Such short life spans also meant that people needed to marry young and procreate abundantly. In a world with such high child mortality, it takes at least six children per family to maintain the population. Two to three of the six children would die

---

66. Bagnall and Frier, *Demography*, 123. Incidentally, the same sort of remarriage rates held for divorces (p. 124): of the nine cases they sampled, only two of the nine males had remarried and none of the eight females. They also seemed to divorce young: Men: age 22, 31, 32, and 37—and some whose ages not given. Women: age 29 (2X) 33, 40, 49, and 57—and some whose ages were not given.

67. See Fiensy, *Social History*, 126-32; and Fiensy, *Insights from Archaeology*, 82-85.

68. See Reed, "Instability."

69. As Scheidel ("Real Wages") argues, even when there were both parents, the children often had to work to bring full subsistence to the family, especially if the parents were day laborers.

70. See Garroway, *Children*, 113-40 (debt slavery for children), 155-58 (hireling children). See also Chapter 5.

before reaching adulthood and at least one of the surviving three would die in his/her twenties.

The stress on the parents must have been intense. Living with the knowledge that your children could die in any given year—indeed that some of them almost certainly would die—would be scary.[71] The scripture quoted in Matthew and applied to the infants of Bethlehem (Matt 2:18, quoting Jer 31:15) might easily be a standing description of ancient villages throughout the Roman Empire. There would be mourning and weeping; a mother would be weeping for her children almost every day somewhere in the village.

So frequent was infant mortality that one passage in the Talmud (b. Mo'ed Qat. 24a) makes the following distinctions in burial customs: Infants under 30 days old are carried to the cemetery in their mother's arms. They do not "form a line of mourners" for this child and they do not recite the prayer for the mourners. Infants between the ages of 30 days and 12 months are carried to the cemetery in a small box. They do form the line of mourners and recite the benediction for the mourners. Infants over 12 months old are carried to the cemetery on a bier and the community can show public signs of grief. A poor child (since children are the sole pleasure of poor people) may be lamented after the age of three (or some rabbis said after age five). A wealthy child may be lamented only after age five (or some rabbis said after age six). Such rules, it seems, were designed to control the grief and lamentation which otherwise might be overwhelming.[72]

Anecdotal Evidence

Anecdotal evidence might help put a face on this data. Cornelia, (the mother of the Gracchi) bore 12 children. All survived their father but only three survived childhood (the two famous brothers and one sister).[73] Quintilian lamented the loss of his young wife and two young sons (who died at ages 4 and 9). Fronto and wife had 6 children but only one daughter survived. Marcus Aurelius and his wife Faustina had at least 12 children, of whom only one son, Commodus, lived to adulthood.[74] With child mortality that high, mourning entered every household almost every year.

The rabbinic literature also indicates a high child mortality. There are many references to children dying in the Talmudic and Midrashic literature. Especially tragic was the fact that often more than one child in the family died at nearly the same time,[75] evidently due to communicable diseases. Further, there are even references to

71. See Raaj K. Sah, "Child Mortality Changes." The "parental welfare" becomes better when child mortality decreases according to Sah.

72. See Garroway, *Children,* 243. Also see Chapter 11.

73. Plutarch, *Tib. Gracch.* 16.3.

74. Suetonius, *Gaius* 7; Quintillian, *Inst. Or.* 6; Parkin, *Demography,* 94.

75. See b. Moed Qat. 28b; b. Moed Qat. 21b; Midrash Mishlei 31:10; b. Taan. 13b; and Bar-Ilan, "Infant Mortality."

as many as ten of a family's children having died[76] before reaching adulthood. Losing that many children did not inoculate the parents from grief. The mourning would be very intense as one Talmudic story demonstrates.[77]

The Few Elderly

All of this is not, of course, to say that everyone died in his/her 30s or 40s. There are many alleged octogenarians and nonagenarians: Parkin and Grmek list several philosophers, political leaders, historians, poets, and rhetoricians who died in their 90s. They can even find a few (e.g., Democritus, age 104; Gorgias of Leontini, age 107) who eclipsed the century mark. Grmek notes that the oldest attested age on a Greek funerary inscription is 110 years.[78] In Christian tradition, we read of several elderly persons: A lady named Anna was 84 years old (Luke 2:37); Polycarp, the bishop of Smyrna, was said to have lived into his eighties before he died by martyrdom;[79] the Apostle John allegedly lived into the reign of Trajan,[80] which would have made him probably past ninety years old. But a few exceptions do not change the overall conditions. Very few lived to such an age.

Günter Mayer has included a study of tombstones in his work on the Jewish women. He lists 130 individuals in his study. Of these, fifty-one (39%; cf. Table 10.3 above) died before age nineteen. Fourteen (11%) lived past age sixty. Four were in their seventies when they died and six were in their eighties. The oldest was ninety-six.[81] Thus, there were elderly women in the ancient world. Mayer's table harmonizes with the following evidence from Nagar and Torgeé with respect to the survivals of elderly persons (not with respect to youth mortality).

The (rare) appearance of the elderly as reported in the literature is supported by the Mortality Curve of Nagar and Torgeé, based on the excavation of the Judean and Samaritan tombs dating from the Hellenistic to the Early Roman periods. They constructed their graph based on the data from two of their sites in Judea (comprising six tombs) to show the percentage of the population that died by age groups. The Mortality Curve below and Table 10.8 are calculated based on a "life-table methodology." They assumed that several infant remains (under one year old) were undeterminable and thus underrepresented. Hence to make the analysis more accurate they used the life table methodology, following Coal-Demeny Life Table West.[82]

---

76. As happened to R. Yehonan (b. Ber. 5a–b). See Bar-Ilan, "Infant Mortality."

77. See b. Sanh. 104b where one woman grieved so over the death of a child that R. Gamliel, her neighbor, wept in sympathy until "his eyelashes fell out." See Bar-Ilan, "Infant Mortality."

78. Parkin *Demography,* 107; Grmek, *Diseases,* 109.

79. *Martyrdom* IX.

80. Irenaeus, *Against Heresies,* 3.3.

81. Mayer, *Jüdische Frau,* 93–97. Mayer gleaned his data entirely from the *Corpus Inscriptionum Iudaicarum.*

82. Nagar and Torgeé, "Biological Characteristics," 167.

The Archaeology of Daily Life

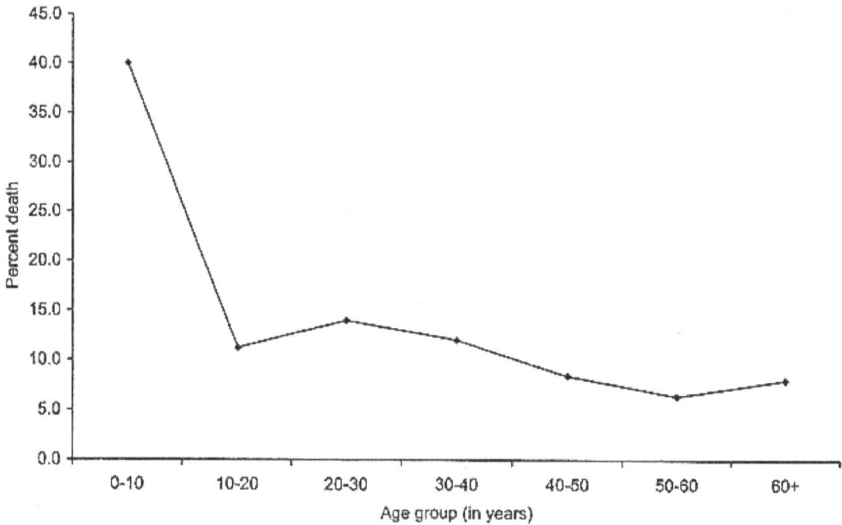

Figure 10.1: The Mortality Curve of Two Hellenistic-Early Roman Jewish Populations in Israel. Reproduced by permission of the *Israel Exploration Journal* and the authors.[83]

Their precise percentages for this population are as follows:

Age interval (years)	Percentage of deaths
0–9	40
10–19	11.2
20–29	14
30–39	12
40–49	8.4
50–59	6.4
60+	8

Table 10.8:[84] Population percentages

Notice the high mortality in the 0–9 years age-cohort. In this mortality curve, 40% of the children died before age 10, 11.2% more died by age 20, and a total of 65.2% died before age 30. This youth mortality rate (51.2%), then, is a bit higher than the average for Israel at this time according to our earlier calculations (43%).

The Mortality Curve gives us an overview of how many of the cohort in the two villages died every ten years and how many survived into their sixties and beyond. It offers a suggestion as to the life cycle and population profile of a typical Palestinian/Israeli village in this period. But since it is based on so little evidence (153 individuals),

---

83. Nagar and Torgeé, "Biological Characteristics," 167. The two populations were the villages of Tel Ḥadid and Shoham. They omitted the other two villages since their remains were difficult to assign ages to.

84. Adapted from Nagar and Torgeé, "Biological Characteristics," 166–67, Table 3.

we can only say at this point that it is suggestive. Still, it shows that some persons (8%) lived into old age. The point here is that there were not many over sixty years of age buried in the tombs, but there were a few.

The lack of mentorship from older men and women is a constant in societies with high child mortality rates. Patricia Smith observes that there is a correlation between high infant mortality and death in early adult life. Where infant mortality is high, very few adults survive past 50 years.[85] Smith offers several age group comparisons based on multiple tomb excavations in Israel. The two relevant for our purpose: En-Gedi and Jericho (because of their date) show a ratio of around 2 to 1 in terms of young adults (ages 20–49) to older adults (over 50). There would have been few older mentors or role models for young adults. As Jonathan Reed observes,[86] virtually no young man knew his grandfather and very few still had a living father. This situation created a restless class of (to us) younger men roaming about Galilee without "adult" supervision, exactly what we see in the Gospels.

This all makes one wonder about Jesus' family. Was Jesus in a single parent family? Was he reared by his mother? His father certainly disappears from the Gospels when Jesus is an adult. Did he start to labor early in life? Perhaps his "carpentry" began as a boy (Mark 6:3) and by the time we meet him, he has already been doing a full day's work for twenty-five years or more.

In light of such short life spans, Jesus' assigned age (by Luke 3:23[87]) of "about" 30 years does not really seem so young. It would be more in harmony with this data to envision Jesus and his disciples as, though rather young by our standards, middle aged. We often ask what happened to the rest of the Twelve Disciples not mentioned in the New Testament. Only Peter and John are featured (Gal 2:9; 1 Cor 9:5; James is said to have been martyred early; Acts 12:2) while the others disappear from the New Testament (though are featured in non-canonical literature).[88] The short answer is that most of them probably died early. When the average life expectancy of an adult male was 38 years, we cannot imagine that all of the Twelve, except those martyred, lived to old age.

---

85. Smith, "Approach," 5. The converse is also true. Where infant mortality is low, it is probable that the population will survive past age 50. ("Approach," 7).

86. Reed, "Instability."

87. Though if one calculates a probable birth for Jesus of between 6 and 4 BCE and takes the chronological note in Luke 3:1 seriously (that Jesus' began his ministry in the fifteenth year of Tiberius' reign), it makes Jesus more like 32 to 34 years old. Shimon Gibson, *Cave of John the Baptist,* 132, suggests that Jesus was 34 years old at the beginning of his ministry. Marshall, *Luke,* 162, thinks the reference in b Sanh. 106b to Balaam's age at death as 33 or 34 years is a coded reference to Jesus' age.

88. E.g., Thomas appears in many texts, especially of Syrian origin.

The Archaeology of Daily Life

Words of Comfort to the Grieving

Finally, what was it like for this company, where life was so brief and often so full of grief, to hear the words in the Gospels? The Beatitudes take on an enhanced meaning: "Blessed are those who mourn ... Blessed are those who hunger and thirst for justice...." (Matt 5:4, 6). How did the numerous promises of "rest" and "life" sound to them (e.g., Matt 8:28; John 10:10)? How did all those references to the "Kingdom of God" and to the "age to come" resonate? It reminds one of the twelfth century CE Christian hymn by Bernard of Morlaix:

Hic breve vivitur,	Brief life is here our portion,
hic breve plangitur,	Brief sorrow, short-lived care;
hic breve fletur.	The life that knows no ending,
Non breve vivere,	The tearless life, is there[90]
non breve plangere,	
retribuetur.[89]	

Brief lifetimes were the norm before the modern era in virtually every society. Such high child mortality and such brief adult life spans must have made the folk in the New Testament era—as also this hymn writer—that much keener to think about what lay beyond.

---

89. Text in Moorsom, *Historical Companion*, 124. Literally: "Here it is briefly lived; here briefly grieved; here briefly wept. Not to live briefly, not to grieve briefly, will be restored."

90. Bernard, *De Contemptu Mundi*; trans. J. M. Neale.

11

How And Where Would They Bury You?

THE HANDLING OF THE dead is one of the most important events in a family's life. There are social, kinship, and religious feelings to consider. The wider community wants the body to be removed to prevent contamination of any sort (see next chapter). The family wants to honor their dead relative. Friends want to comfort the family in their loss. Everyone wants to express their religious beliefs about death and the afterlife. Thus, a funeral is a big event for a village.

In this chapter, we will inform ourselves especially from a rabbinic text called *Semaḥot* (=Sem.). The name means, literally, "joys." This text, the name of which expresses at least euphemistically—but also, perhaps, apotropaically[1]—exactly the opposite of one's feelings at a funeral, is a Mishnaic era[2] (hence c. second–third century CE) work. Yet it seems to refer to old customs, many of which can also be found scattered in various texts from the first century (the New Testament, Josephus, Pseudepigrapha, Philo) as well as from the Mishnah and Tosephta. Hence, its information about the customs of funerals and burials in Palestinian Judaism is extremely valuable to us.

The duty to bury the dead was felt especially strongly in Judaism. To leave one's relatives unburied would be a grievous offense (Josephus, *Apion* 2.211). Even to ignore the burial of a stranger was considered a violation of taboo. On the other hand, to bury the poor and strangers was considered a distinctly virtuous act.[3]

---

1. Puech, "Inscriptions," 132, informs that there are inscriptions in many Jewish tombs from our period with names written backward evidently for a "magical and apotropaic meaning." Thus, one states the opposite of what one means.

2. See Zlotnick, "Semaḥot." Although many scholars date the final editing of this text to the 8th century, he dates it to the third century.

3. See Hengel, *Charismatic Leader,* 8–9; and Tobit 1:17–20; 4 Ezra 2:23–24; m. Sanh. 6:5; Sem. 4.16, 18, 19, 11.1; j. Ber. 3.1.

THE FUNERAL

As soon as an individual died, the family would tear their garments (Sem. 9.1–7; m. Moʾed Qat. 3:7), at least three fingers width, and then would light lamps at the head and feet of the corpse (m. Ber. 8:6).[4] They would then wash the corpse—women could wash both males and females, but men could only wash males (Sem. 12:10)—then wrap it in a body shroud and a head shroud.[5] They might add spices to the shroud and also perhaps sprinkle spices on the bier as it was being carried to the tomb.[6]

In the Jewish literature there are numerous references to the burial shroud.[7] In general, there was evidently a tendency to spend a lot of money on the shroud, perhaps due to the belief that the clothes one wore in burial would be the clothes one would also wear in the age to come (Sem. 9.23). The Test. Jud. 26:3[8] advises not to spend too much on the shroud, a tendency at the time, obviously. One rabbi allegedly exhorted his heirs to bury him in a cheap flax shroud (b. Ket. 8b).

In light of these texts, it is interesting that the single example of a first-century burial shroud that we now possess[9] is an imported, woolen cloth. It was found in a tomb near Jerusalem, a tomb evidently belonging to a wealthy family. The shroud was made of "good quality" sheep's or goat's wool. It was not one piece of cloth but four separate wrappings. Because of the type of weave, experts concluded that the body shroud was imported from Syria, Anatolia, Greece, or even Italy. This was not a simple, cheap burial shroud. The radio carbon dating confirmed that the cloth was from the early first century CE. In addition to the body shroud there was a linen facial shroud, reminiscent of John 11:44.[10] Thus, in spite of admonitions from the religious scholars, the wealthy still were buried in finer clothing.

Along this same line, the reference to Joseph of Arimathea's burying Jesus in a linen shroud (Matt 27:59//Mark 15:46//Luke 23:53) was evidently a sign of Joseph's respect. He wanted a distinctive burial for Jesus such as perhaps the aristocracy would have had. If Joseph really was a wealthy man (Matt 27:57), he evidently would have, himself, been buried in such a way, not unlike the "shrouded man" discovered by archaeologists and described in the preceding paragraph.

---

4. S. Safrai, "Home and Family," 774.

5. S. Safrai, "Home and Family," 776; Gibson, *Final Days*, 137–47. See m. Shabb. 23:4–5; John 11:44; 20:6–7; Acts 9:37; Matt 27:59.

6. S. Safrai, "Home and Family," 776. See John 19:39–40; Mark 16:1; Luke 24:1; *Ant.* 17.199//*War* 1.673; m. Ber. 8:6)

7. M. Kil. 9:4; m. Maʾas. S. 5:10; Sem. 12.10; John 19:40, 11:44; Acts 5:6.

8. Kee, "Testaments of the Twelve," 802.

9. Gibson, *Final Days*, 145 reports a fragment found in a burial cave at Jericho but there was, evidently, too little of it to examine.

10. Gibson, *Final Days*, 144–45. The shroud was wrapped around the man referred to in Chapter 9 who had died of leprosy and tuberculosis (146).

After shrouding the body, they would proceed to the tomb. They hired wailing persons and also flute players for the funeral procession.[11] In the rabbinic literature it appears that the professional wailers were always women[12] but men may also have been for hire at such events in the first century (see *War* 3.437; Matt 9:23[13]). The wailing involved screaming words of woe which communicated in their culture utter distress. In the Old Testament book of Amos, the prophet writes that:

> In all the streets they will say "*hô, hô*" (Heb. הוֹ הוֹ).
> Those with knowledge of lamentation will mourn.

The words *hô, hô* are often translated "Alas! Alas!"[14] Further, when Amos writes that "those with knowledge of lamentation will mourn," he seems to be referring to professional mourners like those alluded to in the Mishnah and the New Testament. Thus, Amos may offer us a window into the wailing practice. Professional mourners—those that could effect an emotional bout of lamentation—would shout the word "hô!" among other things.

The burial would be the same day as the death, usually (John 11; Acts 5:6, 10; m. Sanh. 6:5; Sem. 11.1), or barring that, as soon as possible.[15] The funeral procession would begin at the house of the deceased and move to the tomb with the family and friends in tow. The family accompanied the corpse "with tears" (Syr. Men. 465[16]). Some walked before the bier, others after it (Luke 7:12; Sem. 9.21–22, 10.5).

In the story in Luke 7:11–16, the dead son—evidently an unmarried teenager since he is called a "youth" (v. 14) and there is no mention of a wife and children—is being carried on a bier (v. 14) to the tomb or shaft grave outside the village of Nain. The mother is in the procession weeping (v. 13) and they are accompanied evidently by the entire village (v. 12). This description fits perfectly with the information in *Semaḥot*.

The procession might halt a few times along the way to allow for added mourning (m. Meg. 4:3; m. B. Batra 6:7; m. Ohol. 18:4) as the procession halted in the story in Luke 7:11–16 (v. 14).[17] The wailers and flute players made what must have been a loud racket on the way (Mark 5:38). They not only wailed and screamed, but sang

---

11. Mark 5:38; Matt 9:23; m. Ket. 4:4; m. Shabb. 23:4; t. Ned. 2:7; Sem. 14.7.

12. M. Mo'ed Qat. 3:9; t. Yebam. 14:7; t. Ned. 2:7; m. Ket. 4:4; and cf. Luke 23:27. See Ilan, *Jewish Women*, 189–90. This was one of the two acceptable occupations women could hold (along with the occupation of midwife). The Greeks also used women exclusively as wailers. See Lucian, *Funerals*, 12.

13. As S. Safrai ("Home and Family," 776) observed, the Greek terms in these texts are masculine plural.

14. Holladay, *Lexicon*.

15. McCane, *Stone*, 31.

16. T. Baarda, "Syriac Menander," 606.

17. McCane, *Stone*, 32. For a royal funeral procession with gem-encrusted bier, see Josephus description of Herod the Great's funeral (*War* 1.671–673).

dirges, clapped their hands,[18] and hit themselves in the chest (Matt 11:17; 24:30; Luke 8:52; 18:13; 23:27; Rev. 1:7; 18:9; *Ant.* 7.252).[19] Anyone who encountered the procession to the cemetery was obligated to join in and accompany the mourners (*Apion* 2.205; b. Ber. 18a).

As we informed in Chapter 10, they carried new-born infants to the tomb wrapped in a cloth; those infants between thirty days old and twelve months old in a small casket resting in one person's arms; and a child twelve months to three years old in a casket resting on the shoulders and in procession. Children three years old and older were carried on a bier like adults (Sem. 3.1–3).

At the tomb, after the family had placed the body inside, there would be a funeral oration/eulogy given and prayers (Sem. 8.13; m. Mo'ed Qat. 3:7). Some tombs' courtyards had benches on which the orator would sit to preach.[20] But there was a minimum age for these events. One had to be at least three years old if a poor child or four years old if a wealthy child (Sem. 3.4) to have a funeral oration. After the funeral oration, the grieving family would stand and friends and fellow villagers would form a line which filed past them to offer comfort (Sem. 10.8, 11.3, m. Mo'ed Qat. 3:7; b. Sanh. 19a; b. Ber. 16b).

THE TIME OF MOURNING

After the funeral, they observed a period of mourning—the time varied in accordance with the age of the deceased and the relationship of the survivors to the deceased—during which they refrained from certain activities and clothing. The rabbinic text, Lam. R. 1.1, lists the things mourners typically did:

- Hang sackcloth over their door
- Extinguish their lamps
- Turn over their couch
- Go barefoot
- Tear their garments
- Sit in silence
- Weep

There were three parts to the mourning calendar:[21]

18. M. Mo'ed Qat. 3:8;

19. For the Greek term κόπτω meaning "beat oneself in the chest" (i.e. in mourning), see Danker, *Lexicon;* and Stählin, "τύπτω," 262 n. 18. For beating the chest in mourning, see also Lucian, *Funerals,* 12 (along with rolling on the ground, beating one's head on the floor, tearing out the hair, and scratching one's cheeks bloody.)

20. McCane, *Stone,* 37.

21. See McCane, *Stone,* 38.

1. The first seven days after the death of the loved one
2. The first thirty days after the death
3. The first year after the death

Let us look at each of these periods of mourning. For seven days (see Gen 50:10; 1 Sam 31:13; Sir. 22:12; L.A.E. 51:1;[22] Ant. 17.200) after the death of the relative, the family would mourn by following certain prohibited activities. They stopped working—unless there was urgent need of work, for example in the grape harvest (Sem. 5.2)—they stayed at home, they refrained from bathing and anointing, they wore a head covering, and married couples refrained from sex (Sem. 5.1, 6.1, 11.11–17). In addition, they turned their bed upside down so that the legs of the bed were pointing upward. Those sleeping on other types of nighttime furniture (it mentions "benches" or a "large basin"?) must also turn them upside down (Sem. 11.17). Semaḥot does not mention mats but presumably one turned over the mat as well during the initial seven days of mourning.

All mourning was suspended during Sabbath and other religious festivals: "on the Sabbath ... a mourner is as if he were not a mourner"[23] (Sem. 7.1–2, 1.3). The festivals were for remembering other things and so, to mourn would be to disrespect the religious holiday.[24]

There are some persons listed in Semaḥot who should not be mourned: a fetus, a stillborn baby, a pagan slave, a suicide, and one executed by a Jewish court (Sem. 1.8, 10; 2.1, 6). The fetus and stillborn should not be mourned (of course no one can dictate how people feel) officially by the seven days' ritual because there were so many of them (see Chapter 10). Such mourning would be too much for the families. The pagan slave (unfortunately) was not considered important enough to mourn. The same was true of suicides and executed criminals. They had forfeited their right to be officially mourned in the minds of the religious leaders, again, an unfortunate ruling since their families felt the loss just the same. But, interestingly, a person executed by a Gentile court (the "state") may be fully mourned. That person may have been considered guilty of no real crime but a victim of oppressive occupiers.

After the initial seven days of mourning, Semaḥot prescribes an additional thirty days during which time one may work but may not cut the hair or nails, may not wear pressed clothing, may not engage in trade, and may not attend a banquet (Sem. 7.8, 10, 11; 9.14, 15). During the thirty day mourning, they might return to the tomb to check on the corpse (John 11:31; Sem. 8.1). This extended period was a time of less withdrawal from society but still a special honor paid to the dead.

---

22. M. D. Johnson, "Life of Adam and Eve," 294.

23. Translation in Zlotnick, Semaḥot, 73.

24. Is this regulation related—out of eschatological celebration—to Paul's similar admonition in 1 Cor 7:30?

For mourning the death of a parent, the prohibitions of the thirty days lasted a full year (Sem. 9.10, 15). Further, while one had to rend the garments to mourn for the dead and later mend them, tears in the garment for one's father and mother should never be mended (Sem. 9.19). This one year extended time of mourning seems to have applied, however, only for one's father and mother. At the end of the year, they practiced ossilegium in Judea, transferring the bones of the deceased into a bone box, usually made of stone but also sometimes of clay or wood (see below).

THE TOMBS

Families buried their dead in four types of tombs/graves.[25] The type of your tomb would depend on your family's finances and social standing. But also your burial type depended on changing social and religious conventions.

Interestingly, most of the rock-cut tombs found so far in the Jerusalem area are either north or south of the city. West of the city were the fewest tombs and none closer than one thousand cubits. Rousseau and Arav surmise that the ancients did not want the western breezes to blow the uncleanness of the dead onto the holy city.[26]

Monumental Tombs

First, they might use a monumental or "display" tomb. These have only been found so far in Jerusalem (less than forty are known). The first such tomb, according to the literature, was that build by Simon Maccabee who constructed a monument at his home village of Modi'in in Judea to honor his father and brothers. Simon added seven pyramids and colonnades (1 Macc. 13:27–29). Nothing of this tomb remains.[27]

Those that are visible today indicate that they were characterized by ashlar construction, columns, carved moldings, and decorated features (pyramidal or conical shapes, domes, etc.). These were monuments to the wealthy and powerful. The ordinary people were not laid to rest in such tombs. The New Testament may refer to some of these tombs in Matt 23:29: "they adorn monuments (μνημεῖα)[28] to the prophets and the righteous persons." Josephus seems to have disapproved of such displays of grandeur in one's burial when he wrote that the Torah does not provide for the dead to put up costly monuments (*Apion* 2.205).

---

25. Berlin, "Jewish Life," 454; Hachlili, *Jewish Funerary*, 30; Magness, *Stone*, 157.

26. Rousseau and Arav, *Jesus and His World*, 167–68. They report that 71.5% of the tombs are either to the north or the south of the city while 16.1% are east and 12.4% are west of the city. See their map of tombs on 168.

27. See Fine, "Death," 443.

28. The Greek term can mean both "monument" and "tomb." See Danker, *Lexicon*.

Several are clearly visible today east of the old city of Jerusalem (e.g., the tombs of Absalom and Bene Hazir; Map 2.2) and north (the tomb of Queen Helena of Adiabene).[29]

Loculus Tombs

Second, were the rock-cut tombs with *loculi* (Aramaic: *kokhim*) or niches for the bodies and later to receive the ossuaries. The *loculus* was "a long, narrow slot carved deep into the wall of the tomb" perpendicular to the wall.[30] Over one thousand *loculus* tombs have been found in the vicinity of Jerusalem with hundreds more located in Judea and Galilee (see Figures 11.1 and 11.3 below).[31] These human-made caves are characterized not only by the niches but also by a central chamber with benches for mourners. In front of the entrance to the tomb they would "seal" it with a rolling stone (see Fig. 11.5 below).[32]

Figure 11.1: Tomb niches (*loculi* or *kokhim*) in Church of the Holy Sepulcher, Jerusalem (photo by the author)

---

29. Berlin, "Jewish Life," 457; Evans, *Jesus and the Ossuaries*, 18–19. See photos of Jason's tomb, the tomb of Zachariah, the Cave of Jehoshaphat, and the Absalom monument in Raḥmani, "Ossuaries and *Ossilegium*"; and Fine, "Death," 444–45.

30. McCane, "Death and Burial," 263.

31. Gibson, *Final Days*, 156 for the count of rock-cut tombs.

32. Matt 27:6//Mark 15:46; Mark 16:3; Luke 24:2//John 20:1; m. ʿErub. 1:7; m. Sheq. 1:1; m. Moʿed Qat. 1:2. Or they might use a square stone to seal the tomb. See Evans, *Jesus and the Ossuaries*, 12.

THE ARCHAEOLOGY OF DAILY LIFE

Arcosolium Tombs

Third, were the *arcosolium* tombs: These were also hand-cut caves but without niches. They consisted of "a wide, shallow, arch-shaped niche carved along the wall of the burial chamber."[33] Since these tombs could only accommodate three or four persons, they tended to belong to the wealthy families while the *loculus* tombs were used more frequently by the lower classes. The corpse was then laid on a ledge under the arch or in a sarcophagus (stone coffin) on the ledge.

A family tomb could combine the *loculus* and *arcosolium* types of burials as in the Akeldama tombs. There were three cave tombs closely associated in this burial site, with multiple chambers for each cave. In cave 1, for example, chambers 1-A, 1-B, and 1-C were *loculus* burials but chamber 1-D was an *arcosolium* tomb with three bodies.[34]

According to Hachlili, the *arcosolium* tombs came into fashion toward the end of the late Second Temple Period.[35] So far, only about one hundred such tombs have been found.[36]

Figure 11.2: Inside "Herod Family Tomb" (west of the city; see Map 2.2). Note the benches for laying sarcophagi. In this more expensive tomb there are no niches.[37] (photo by the author)

33. McCane, "Death and Burial," 263.

34. Avni and Greenhut, "Resting Place," 37–40. The same pattern was found in Cave 3.

35. Hachlili, "Burials, Ancient Jewish," 790. See also Evans, *Jesus and the Ossuaries,* 12; McCane, "Death and Burial," 264.

36. Rousseau and Arav, *Jesus and His World,* 167.

37. The tomb had four chambers entered from a central hall. The walls of the chambers were faced

Trench Graves

Finally, there were trench graves, those dug into the ground as most modern people do. This was clearly the burial method of choice at Qumran, as the over 1,200 graves near the site of the ruin testify. Trench graves have also been found at En el-Ghuweir (just south of Qumran), East Talpiyot (south of Jerusalem); Beit Safafa (south of Jerusalem); and Horbat Egog (Judean Hills).[38] The questions for us are:

1. Did the Qumran people invent a new method of burial?
2. Did they revive an archaic method due to their religious conservatism and are the other shaft graves also Essene (i.e. Qumran-linked) graves?
3. Or did the Qumran people (and those of other sites) merely practice the common form of burial for poor persons?

Jodi Magness surmises that it was the last of these options. She maintains that rock-cut caves were expensive and that only the wealthy could have been buried in them. Most ordinary people she opines, were buried in "individual graves dug in the ground." She calls these trench graves and cist graves (stone lined pits). She points not only to the Qumran evidence but also to Luke 11:44: "woe to you! You are like unmarked graves ($\mu\nu\eta\mu\varepsilon\tilde{\iota}\alpha$) and people walk over (them). They don't know it." One would not probably "walk over" a cave tomb but could walk over a trench grave.[39] Magness further argues that the number of rock-cut tombs discovered so far—even were we to quadruple the total—could not hold all the population of Jerusalem from the mid-first century BCE to the mid-first century CE. She counts 900 rock-cut tombs in the Jerusalem vicinity[40] which could have held 18,900 bodies (21 per tomb). Even allowing four times that number in undiscovered tombs to date, there would not be enough tomb space for a large city like Jerusalem.[41]

Shimon Gibson, however, argues that most families dug their own burial caves into the rocky hills. The expense would not have been a factor for them, he affirms. He calculates that it would take about fifty or so hours of labor to carve out a cave with a

---

with very finely dressed ashlar stones. Several stone sarcophagi were in the tomb. See Avigad, "Jerusalem," 752. On sarcophagi, see the words of Fine, "Death," 446: "Those at the pinnacle of Jerusalem's social hierarchy were buried in stone sarcophagi, which were rare during this period." Was the tomb of Joseph of Arimathea like this one? On the other hand, Netzer, "Herod's Family Tomb," believed the Herodian tomb was north of the city (just opposite of the current Damascus Gate) instead of west of it near the current King David Hotel.

38. See Hachilil, "Jewish Life," 463. There were 17 shaft graves at En el-Ghuweir; 2 shaft graves at east Talpiyot; 53 cyst graves at Beit Safafa; and 7 shaft graves at Horbat Egog. Amos Kloner reported that he had discovered 83 "shaft and field burials," dating to the Second Temple Period, in his survey of Jerusalem. See Magness, "Disposing of the Dead," 121–22.

39. Magness, *Stone*, 157; Magness, "Disposing of the Dead," 125. Cf. Gudme, "Mortuary Rituals," 359, who agrees with Magness.

40. See above: Gibson, *Last Days*, 156 counts over one thousand tombs in the Jerusalem area.

41. Magness, "Disposing of the Dead," 119.

few niches. These were mostly do-it-yourself tombs, he maintains, and rich and poor alike chose this method of burial.[42]

How shall we conclude? On the one hand, there are references in the Mishnah and New Testament that seem most compatible with shaft/trench graves. In the first place are several references to "plowing up graves" in the rabbinic literature (m. Ohol. 17:1; 18:2; t. Ahil. 18:2[43]). One would not, it seems, plow up a grave that was a rock-cut cave. These references seem to point to trench graves. Further, the New Testament and the Mishnah note that at regular intervals, they "whited" (using lime) over graves to remind the village where people had been buried (Matt 23:27; m. Ma'as. S. 5:1; m. Sheq. 1:1; m. Mo'ed Qat. 1:2). This practice sounds more compatible with trench graves than rock-cut caves.

On the other hand, however, *Semaḥot* does refer to people digging their own rock-cut cave-tombs (Sem. 13.4) and there even seems to be an instruction manual for a do-it-yourself tomb in the Mishnah (m. B. Batra 6:8). Further, rock-cut tombs discovered in Galilean villages (see Figure 11.3) argue for a "working class" interest in either digging one's own family tomb or investing to pay professionals to do so. Third, some of the ossuaries in the Jerusalem tombs have inscriptions on them indicating that the occupants were working class persons, not aristocrats.[44] Thus, some families did, as Gibson hypothesized, excavate their own tombs out of a rocky hill or invest heavily (for them) in a professionally excavated one. We are left to conclude that some of these tombs were dug by working class persons wanting to imitate the elites.

Therefore, although the weight of evidence appears to fall in the direction of Magness' view (and others of like mind[45]), I do not think that rock-cut tombs were only for the wealthy and aristocracy. The working class sometimes also invested in a modest cave-tomb. Thus, I cannot accept either Magness' or Gibson's view entirely.

Perhaps the aristocracy began the custom but those that could (artisan-families and merchants) copied it. The very poor, however, buried the old way: dig a hole in the ground and place your loved one in it.

---

42. Gibson, *Final Days*, 160.

43. Magness, *Stone*, 159; Magness, "Disposing of the Dead," 124–25. The reference from the Tosephta describes the plow turning up a human skull in the field.

44. See Evans, *Jesus and the Ossuaries*, 56–57. Several ossuaries are occupied by artisans and day laborers, *pace* Magness, "Disposing of the Dead," 120. See Chapter 2 of this volume and Table 8.1 in Chapter 8.

45. Ilan, "Ossuaries," 64 agrees. She hypothesizes that very poor persons were buried in a potter's field or the like and cites Matt 27:7. See also Rousseau and Arav, *Jesus and His World*, 167: "these tombs belonged to the middle and upper classes, with the rest of the population buried in simple shallow pits. . . ."

HOW AND WHERE WOULD THEY BURY YOU?

Figure 11.3: *Loculus* or *Kokhim* Tomb (Khirbet Qana or Cana; Map 4.1)[46] (photo by the author)

OSSUARIES

Many first-century CE families living in Judea (but not Galilee) practiced secondary burial. On the one-year anniversary of the deceased person's death (see b. Qidd. 31b), they went to the tomb, gathered the bones, and placed them in a box, usually constructed of stone but sometimes of clay or wood.

How did ossilegium work? The oft quoted words of Rabbi Eleazar bar Zadok summarize the process: "My son, bury me at first in a fosse. In the course of time, collect my bones and put them in an ossuary."[47]

The tractate Mo'ed Qatan further discusses a complex situation: "A man may gather together the bones of his father or his mother (during mid-festival) since this is to him an occasion for rejoicing" (m. Mo'ed Qat. 1:5).[48] Thus, if the time for gathering the bones of one's parents falls on a festival, one may yet do it.

The Mishnah gives more details of the process: "When the flesh had wasted away, they gathered together the bones and buried them in their own place" (m. Sanh. 6:6).[49]

46. This tomb is on the north side of the site but there are also several tombs on the southside.
47. Sem. 12.9. Translation in Zlotnick, *Semaḥot*, 82.
48. Translation in Danby, *Mishnah*.
49. Translation in Danby, *Mishnah*. For texts in the Mishnah that refer to "gathering the bones," see m. Pes. 8:8; and m. Mo'ed Qat. 1:5.

The Archaeology of Daily Life

In Judea, beginning in the late first century BCE, they practiced secondary burial. In Jerusalem and Jericho, for example, families transitioned from primary burials for their loved ones in tombs in wooden coffins to secondary burials in ossuaries.[50] That is, they first placed the deceased in a tomb, either on a bench, in a niche, or in a coffin. Then, one year later, they collected the bones and put them into a box of some kind, usually stone (Fig. 11.4).

But although this change took place in Judea, it did not reach Galilee until the second century CE. To date no ossuaries from the first century have been found in Galilee.[51]

Why did Jews in Judea initiate the practice of secondary burial in ossuaries? The origin of this custom is something of a mystery. The following hypotheses are the main candidates to answer this query:

1. They initiated the practice because of the belief in the resurrection of the dead. They needed to keep the bones ready for the flesh to return on them at the resurrection. First the deceased is purged from sin by having his/her flesh decompose.[52] Then the individual is ready to receive the resurrection. The problem with this view is first of all, it appears that Sadducees also used ossuaries (and Sadducees according to both Josephus and the New Testament did not believe in the resurrection of the dead) and they sometimes placed the bones of more than one person in the same ossuary, especially of a parent and child. Thus, in the resurrection—following this logic—a mother might accidentally be given the thigh bone of a baby who had been placed in the ossuary with her.[53]

2. The practice is in imitation of the Roman use of cinerary urns (which look remarkably like the Jewish ossuaries). The Romans, after cremation, would put the ashes of their loved ones in ceramic box-shaped urns for keeping in the house or for burial. The use of ossuaries is the Jewish version of the Roman practice. Jews did not cremate but could still utilize the stone boxes for their family member's bones.[54]

3. The practice was intended to stress the importance of the individual (as opposed to the family as a unit). Thus, they buried each one individually in an ossuary. But, as noted above, they often placed the bones of more than one person in the same ossuary.[55]

4. Use of ossuaries was not really a new practice. It had been done in Israel (or Canaan) from the Bronze Age. They used stone ossuaries because there were

---

50. Hachlili, "Burial Practices," 449; Hachlili, *Funerary Customs,* 75, 94.
51. Aviam, "Distribution Maps," 125–26.
52. Rahmani, "Ancient Jerusalem's Funerary Customs," 110.
53. See Magness, *Stone,* 151; Rahmani, "Jewish Ossuaries," 30.
54. Magness, *Stone,* 152.
55. Hachlili, "Burial Practices," 450.

already expert stone cutters in Jerusalem to work on the Temple. The materials (limestone) and the craftsmen were at hand.[56]

Figure 11.4: Ossuaries from a tomb north of Jerusalem, near Dominus Flevit church. Notice the small one for a child. Some of them are decorated with rosettes.[57]
(photo by the author)

Whatever the origin, the use of ossuaries was across most class levels. Most of the ossuaries would have been cheaply made of soft limestone[58] and so affordable for the working class. There seems, then, to have been no correlation between the use of stone boxes to contain one's bones and wealth.[59] Thus, there was a kind of democratization

---

56. Evans, *Jesus and the Ossuaries,* 27–29; Rahmani, "Jewish Ossuaries," 31; Fine, "Death," 447–51.

57. For photographs of finely crafted, ornate ossuaries from our time period, see Varda Sussman, "A Jewish Burial Cave."

58. But there are a few hard limestone ossuaries in some of the tombs. According to Rahmani ("Jewish Ossuaries," 31–33) these would have been quite expensive and were the work of expert stone masons.

59. Magness, *Stone,* 151; Hachlili, "Burial Practices," 450. On the other hand, Ilan, "Ossuaries," 64

in burial, especially in Jerusalem and Jericho. Many wanted a rock-cut tomb, even those of modest (working class but not destitute poor) means, and they also wanted to use ossuaries in secondary burial. Why they turned to these customs, remains for us a mystery.

UNUSUAL CUSTOMS

It is almost a truism of history that the ordinary person was rarely "orthodox."[60] Theological orthodoxy was a luxury for the religious elite and archaeology is now bearing this out. James F. Strange wrote that on one end of the spectrum existed "orthodoxy"; on the other end was heresy; in between was where most persons lived and practiced their faith, sometimes practicing things of which the religious leaders did not entirely approve.[61] It is into this gray area, this middle ground, that we now step.

Items Left Behind in the Tombs

Excavators of tombs find things on the floor of the tomb, sometimes scattered about, sometimes in jars or bowls. Some of the items might have been used in the construction of the tomb and later in the inscriptions on the ossuaries. But most of them are a puzzle.

Coins

Excavators of tombs have found some surprises. One was a coin in the skull of certain individuals. In the Caiaphas tomb, there was such a coin in the skull of "Miriam."[62] Evidently, the coin had been placed in the mouth of the deceased when interred. The same phenomenon appeared "sporadically" elsewhere in Israel in our period of focus: at Jericho, at Mampsis, and at En Boqeq.[63] This practice was, one would presume, in

---

writes: "even the simplest ossuaries at our disposal do not represent the paupers of Jerusalem." As I wrote above, I conclude that the paupers were buried in the ground and did not practice secondary burial. Yet the working class, perhaps in imitation of the aristocracy, wanted a tomb and ossuary.

60. Fiensy, *Social History*, 2. See also the interesting essay by Neusner, "Babylonian Jewry," in which he compares the 7th century CE Rabbi Joshua b. Perahiah of the rabbinic literature (a legal expert) with the R. Joshua of the magical bowls (a magician) found in Nippur. The latter was, according to Neusner, the view of the common people. See also Berlinerblau, "Popular Religion," for a nuanced analysis of this phenomenon.

61. J. F. Strange, "Archaeology and the Religion," 667.

62. Evans, *Remains*, 143; Hachlili, *Funerary*, 438; Rousseau and Arav, *Jesus and His World*, 140.

63. See Hachlili and Killebrew, "Coin-on-Eye"; and Meacham, "Archaeological Evidence." The 2nd CE burial at Mampsis (Nabataean) may not have been Jewish. Likewise, the two coins placed over the eyes of an individual at En Boqeq in a second-century CE burial may not have been Jewish. At that period, En Boqeq was in the hands of Roman soldiers. Nor is it always clear where the coin(s) was/were placed originally (In the mouth? Over the eyes?).

imitation of the Greeks who put an obol into the mouth of their dead to pay for passage over the River Styx and thence into the underworld.[64] Some Jews, then, did this but it was rare.

But in many of the tombs several coins, at times even large hoards, have been found (stored in a jar, etc.). As many as 42 coins in one room of Jason's tomb in Jerusalem were discovered.[65] Why were coins put in the tombs? The family must have thought the dead needed them.

Figure 11.5: First-century rolling-stone tomb
(photo by the author)

Other Valuables

In addition to the coins, there were other items of value: earrings, pendants, bracelets, finger rings, and beads.[66] Excavators have additionally found non-valuables: spindle whorls, cosmetic applicators, bronze mirrors, sandals, iron keys, strigils (for scraping the skin), chisels, and shovels. Some of these items (e.g., chisels) may have been used in the tomb. But why the other objects? Many of these objects seem to have been those

---

64. See Segal, *Life after Death*, 211.

65. Hachlili, *Funerary*, 437. See her list of coins (402–34) found in numerous tombs. Many tombs had coins in them.

66. Hachlili, *Funerary*, 394–434. Her lists are drawn from tombs around Jerusalem, from Jericho tombs, and from En Gedi tombs.

used by the deceased persons. Did the relatives think the dead would still have need of them?

Nails

Another non-valuable item found frequently was nails. Their appearance is so odd that it merits a section of its own. Thus far, at least 138 iron nails have been found in tombs. Craig Evans[67] surmises that some of them may have been used to scratch the inscription on the ossuary. Not every ossuary has an inscription but a significant minority do, indicating the name of the individual whose bones are contained therein and occasionally the occupation or other distinguishing feature (see above and Chapter 2).

But Evans also believes that many of the nails were left behind to ward off evil spirits and to protect the dead. This practice would have been true especially in the case of nails previously used in a crucifixion. Both pagan (Pliny *N.H.* 28.11.46) and Jewish (m. Sanh. 6:5) sources refer to the magical power of crucifixion nails.[68] How do we know that some of these nails were removed from the corpses of crucified persons? Anthropologists examining the nails find bits of calcium adhering to them. Such traces of calcium have been found on nails from the Abba tomb and the Caiaphas tomb (see Chapter 10). Nails with calcium residue were probably not just used to scratch an inscription—so reasons Evans—on a stone ossuary.

Thus, one object found in several tombs was the common iron nail. But, of course, they were no longer common by the time they were left in a tomb. They had been—so the ancients reasoned—imbued with magical power. But one is left to wonder, what need have the dead to be protected by magical objects?

Ceramic and Glass Vessels

Archaeologists also frequently find containers of various sorts in the tombs: ceramic bowls, cooking pots, lamps, and unguentaria, as well as glass unguentaria (the ceramic ones seem to have been used for initial burial and the glass ones for the secondary burial). Interestingly, sometimes these objects were broken (intentionally?) at the time of interment.[69] Is there symbolic meaning in the broken vessels (brokenness=death)? Or were the vessels broken simply because they contracted corpse uncleanness (see chapter 12) and thus, by Torah regulation, had to be destroyed?

Why did they bring and leave these objects to the tombs? Hachlili suggests three main reasons:

---

67. Evans, *Remains*, 138–39.

68. Evans, *Remains*, 139–40. Evans also cites a magical text from a Cairo, Egypt, synagogue that indicates the power of the nail of a crucified person.

69. Hachlili, "Burials," 790; Hachlili, *Funerary*, 377–87; McCane, *Stone*, 47.

1. Some of the items were personal possessions of the deceased.
2. Some were items of everyday use. The survivors wanted to provide jewelry and food for the dead.
3. Some of the items were made and brought especially for the grave and funeral.[70]

Let us explore each of these suggested reasons. First, some of these items may have been personal possessions of the dead. Sem. 8.7 refers to a man being buried with his inkwell and pen and to another with his key and ledger. These objects may have represented what they did for a living. Sem. 9.23 refers to people being buried with their personal items: Some family members heap up too many of these items on the deceased. Other persons are thieves and break into tombs to steal the possessions. Thus, the tractate on mourning witnesses to the practice of burying objects of personal meaning to the deceased.

Second, scholars opine that the cooking pots, for example, might have been used to cook food for the dead or to hold commemorative meals for the dead.[71] Pagan mourners would host banquets at cemeteries in which they poured wine and food down pipes into the grave.[72] One Greek satirist[73] mocked this practice and the thinking behind it which was that the dead would ascend from the underworld for a moment to eat and drink the banquet. But the fact that he thought he needed to ridicule it witnesses to its being widespread. Sem. 8.4 refers to piping oil and wine for the dead.[74] Precisely how this worked—does it imply a shaft grave as opposed to a rock-cut tomb?—is not clear but it sounds like the pagan practice. The author of *Semaḥot* even finds it necessary to assure the reader that this is not a "heathen practice." Evidently, someone thought it was.

Third, the grave goods may have served a practical purpose:

- Cooking pots may have held hot water for washing one's hands or to wash the body
- Unguentaria (containing perfumes) were doubtless to deodorize the tomb
- Lamps were there simply to light up the tomb during the funeral proceedings (but also may have been used in a symbolic way. See Prov 20:27).[75]

The amount of grave goods or personal effects left at the tombs is curious. But people tend to be very conservative when it comes to burying their dead. Resorting to age-old practices gives comfort. Thus, most of these things were probably done without much thought or reasoning. They were just tradition.

---

70. Hachlili, *Funerary*, 376–77.
71. Hachlili, *Funerary*, 381; McCane, *Stone*, 47; Gudme, "Mortuary Rituals," 363.
72. Segal, *Life after Death*, 210.
73. Lucian of Samosata (*Charon*, 22).
74. Exactly as the pagans did. See Segal, *Life after Death*, 210.
75. Hachlili, *Funerary*, 381–82, 385, 388–89; McCane, *Stone*, 47.

Attitudes toward the Dead

Finally, we will look at a bit of evidence that may give us a window into the thinking of the first-century CE people about those that had passed on. First, we handle the unusual inscriptions in some tombs and then some curious burial and building practices in the vicinity of the tombs of famous holy men.

Apotropaic Inscriptions in Tombs

Emile Puech has made a collection of some unusual inscriptions occurring either on tomb walls or on ossuaries:

- Written on an ossuary lid in charcoal in a Jericho tomb were: the "beginning of the Greek alphabet followed by the (palaeo-) Hebrew letters *aleph* . . . and *qop*." He suggests that the aleph is an abbreviation for *'arur* ("cursed") and that the qoph is an abbreviation for *qadosh* ("holy"). These words, he opines, were there for apotropaic purposes.
- He also cites the benedictions and curses in the Khirbet el-Qom tomb
- Someone wrote on the tomb wall at the Tell Eitun tomb the Hebrew alphabet
- The amulets found in the tombs at Ketel Hinnom and Emmaus he surmises were also for apotropaic purposes.
- In one tomb he notes names and words are written backwards: *naduoI* for *Ioudan* (in Greek); *môlsh* for *shalom* (Hebrew); and *psôy* for *Yôseph* (Hebrew). The backward writing was, again, to protect the dead from evil.[76]

Again, the question arises: Why must one ward off evil from the dead using apotropaic inscriptions? Are they not now beyond harm? They apparently were not.

The Veneration of Tombs of Holy Men

James F. Strange observed in the Beth Shearim cemetery (Greek name: Besara; see Map 7.2), on the north side of the Plain of Esdraelon (or Great Plain, Map 4.1), a curious phenomenon. Evidence suggests that people venerated the graves of holy men. In particular, Catacombs 14 and 20 at Beth Shearim have small structures built over them. Inside the catacombs, around the stone sarcophagi, were pit graves. Excavators concluded that the pit graves were not family members but those wanting to be buried near an ancient sage who had been laid to rest in a sarcophagus. Strange hypothesized that they held meetings in the two structures built over the catacombs. They were venerating the tombs of holy men.[77]

---

76. Puech, "Inscriptions," 132.
77. J.F. Strange, "Archaeology and the Religion," 669.

Strange found literary support for the ancient practice in the book, Liv. Pro.⁷⁸ In this text the author is careful to point out where the prophets were buried (e.g., 1:2 Isaiah's burial; 6:3 Micah's burial;7:3 Amos' burial; 8:1 Joel's burial; etc.). Strange also suggested that Matt 27:52–53 hints at the veneration of tombs.⁷⁹

Figure 11.6: Façade of the Beth Sheʾarim Catacombs (Photograph by the author)

CONCLUSIONS

When you died in Palestine/Israel in the late Second Temple Period, they would wash your body, wrap you in a shroud, carry you to the grave (a tomb if your family possessed at least "working class" means, a trench grave if not) amid lamentation that would probably make our hair stand on end today, and then bury you. Then your kinsfolk would enter a period of mourning. The rabbinic materials seem very prescriptive as to how mourning must be done but we should probably take these instructions with a bit of a grain of salt. We cannot assume that every family followed them, even if they were actually in place in every village in Judea, Galilee, and the Golan in the first century CE. But the rabbinic evidence—much of it supported by the New Testament, Josephus, and other texts—gives us a fairly accurate picture of at least some of the practices of burial and mourning. Certainly, your family would feel an obligation to keep your memory alive by acts of mourning.

They would perhaps bury you with some of your peculiar possessions, those which might represent what you did in this life. They might leave behind food and

---

78. See the translation by Hare, "Lives." He assigns a date of first century CE to this text.
79. J.F. Strange, "Archaeology and the Religion," 667.

drink for your pleasure in the afterlife. The family might have fears for your soul's being attacked by evil spirits and, therefore, leave behind apotropaic symbols to ward off evil (and perhaps tomb robbers). If you had died a holy person, not just your relatives but also total strangers might venerate your place of burial. And finally, if you died in Judea (but not in Galilee and the Golan), they would return to your burial place one year later and place your bones in an ossuary.

12

How Would You Practice Your Religion?

THERE ARE MANY WORKS explaining the details of Jewish belief and practice in the late Second Temple Period.[1] We will not attempt a complete sketch of Jewish theology for our period in which we might write about covenant, eschatology, messianism, the restoration of Israel, various interpretations of the Torah, etc. We will limit our discussion in this chapter to the information given us in the archaeological remains and to the literary references helping us interpret the remains. We are primarily concerned with how religion affected the behavior of the common people and how this behavior is seen in the material remains. We hope to observe how daily activities were influenced—at times dictated—by core religious values.

Religion entered into every facet of life in the ancient world. They did not neatly compartmentalize their "secular" life from their religious; everything was religious to them. Now we are learning through archaeological finds how thoroughly their faith permeated their daily activities. Below we will survey the archaeological evidence of their religious practices supplemented by the literary interpretation of these remains. The practice of the Jewish religion in our time period has been called "Household Judaism"[2] by some and "Common Judaism"[3] by others. These designations refer to the life in faith lived by the ordinary people, the persons of the villages and cities who tried to live as closely to God as possible and to reflect this desire in their everyday practices. The question they faced daily was how does one live consistently with the Torah.

Our emphasis in this chapter will be on two core values: ritual purity and aniconic decorations. The period we call the late Second Temple Period or in a wider context,

---

1. See, e.g., Sanders, *Judaism*; McCready and Reinhartz, eds., *Common Judaism*.
2. Berlin, "Jewish Life"; Berlin, "Household Judaism."
3. Sanders, *Judaism;* McCready and Reinhartz, eds., *Common Judaism*.

The Archaeology of Daily Life

Hell II–ER II periods, witnessed changes in religious practices which are reflected in the material remains. The following table summarizes what we will present below:

RELIGIOUS PRINCIPLE	WHAT CHANGED			
Purity Concerns	ESA declines in Jewish regions	Use of stone ware rises in Jewish regions	Ritual baths appear in all Jewish regions	Jerusalem area lamps (and knock-offs) spread in popularity
Image Concerns	Tended to use Hasmonean coins with no images of humans and animals	Did not (usually) decorate houses with images	Did not (usually) decorate tombs and ossuaries with images	Lamps were plain

Table 12:1: Archaeological distinctives of "Household Judaism" or "Common Judaism" from 37 BCE to 135 CE[4]

RITUAL PURITY IN TEXTS AND IN MATERIAL REMAINS

To prepare us for the material remains, we will first introduce the Mishnah and its teaching on ritual purity, one of the driving religious ideas of the late Second Temple Period. The teachings on purity must be confused neither with moral purity nor with physical hygiene. As we will explain, ritual impurity describes a religious contagion that cannot be seen, smelled, or tasted. One only knows it is there because the Torah says it is.

A Brief Definition and Description of the Mishnah

Our main information on the subject of ritual purity—a major concern in our period—is the Mishnah. Although this collection of decisions and sayings was written down in the late second century CE, it reflects in places earlier thinking. As always, we will tend to give primary credence when the Mishnah runs parallel with texts directly from our period (e.g., Josephus, Philo, New Testament, Pseudepigrapha, and the Qumran scrolls).

The word Mishnah means repetition. This definition is a key to its method and its content. The rabbis of the Mishnah (and their Pharisaic forebears) conceived of it as being the distillation of centuries of oral law. The conception was that on Mount Sinai Moses received both written law and oral law. This oral law was passed on by word of mouth by being taught to other tradents throughout the generations. M. Avot chapters 1–4 contain sayings from this chain of tradition. Avot begins:

---

4. Adapted from Arbel, *Ultimate Devotion*, 139.

Moses received (the oral Torah) from Mt. Sinai. And he handed it down to Joshua, and Joshua to the elders, and the elders to the prophets, and the prophets to the men of the great synagogue. (1:1)

This chain of tradition continues in the Mishnaic tractate Avot from the time of the "great synagogue" on to the Pharisees of the pre-New Testament and New Testament periods and then through the second century sages (called Tannaim) of the Mishnah. Although m. Avot does not go further with the tradition, the rabbis of later generations conceived of the oral tradition as continuing up to the successors of the Mishnaic sages (called the Amoraim). The Mishnaic tractate m. Ḥag. 2:2 (and also t. Ḥag. 2:8) also gives a list of tradents. The Pharisees, the forerunners and associates of the scholars listed in the Mishnah, were well known for their adherence to oral law or "tradition" as Josephus (*Ant.* 13.297) and the Gospel of Mark (7:3) call it.

One should not dismiss the oral law concept as a pious legend to justify the Pharisaic viewpoint. There must have been procedures and interpretations that existed from the beginning side by side with the written canon. Thus, the story of an ancient oral tradition is not far-fetched. That the Mishnah is only oral tradition, however, is certainly not accurate.

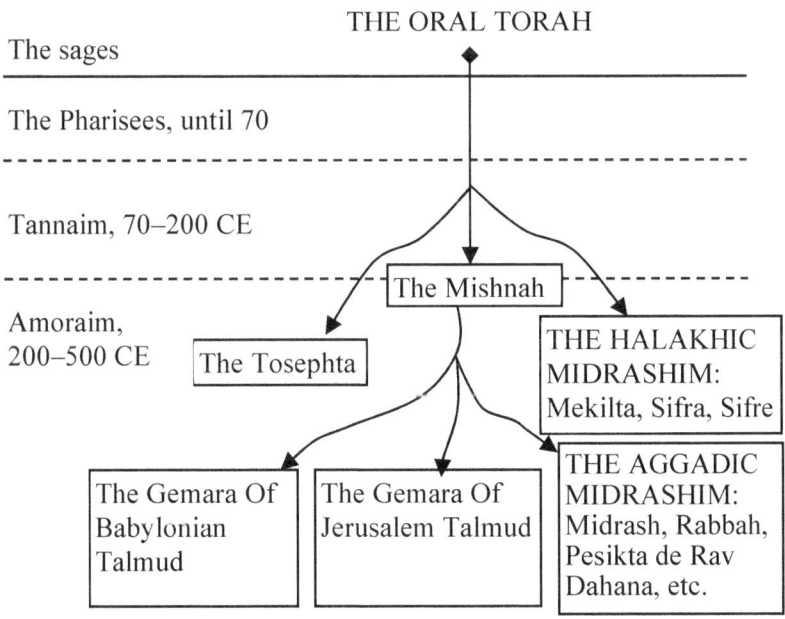

Figure 12.1: The Oral Torah[5]

To the outsider reading the Mishnah, the total work appears somewhat differently. The work appears to be the organization and interpretation of the many laws from

---

5. The table is based on Seltzer, *Jewish People*, 271.

the written Torah together with the way these laws were applied over the years. The laws of the Hebrew Bible are scattered throughout the Pentateuch. These have been gathered and arranged topically in the Mishnah so as to study them more precisely. To these laws from the Hebrew Bible others have been added to expand their application and make the laws more relevant.

E. E. Urbach[6] considered the sources of the Mishnah to be mainly three: 1) Many of the laws and regulations in the Mishnah have come from priestly circles. They tell how priests interpreted biblical laws concerning the Temple service. 2) Others have come from the houses of judgment, the courts. They are decisions about civil law. 3) Finally, still others are the result of expositions of the Bible.

Ritual Purity: What It Was and How It Worked

The rabbinic literature states at one point that in the late Second Temple Period "purity broke out"[7] (t. Shabb. 1:14; b. Shabb. 13b). That is, evidently, it became a point of emphasis. Purity (again, ritual purity, neither an absence of germs nor moral uprightness) became more of a daily obsession of ordinary Jews and not just of the priests or of the sectarians like the Essenes and Pharisees. Below, we will define and illustrate ritual purity as presented to us in the literature and its manifestations in the material remains in the late Second Temple Period. But the point is that concern for ritual purity was one of the main driving forces behind religious decisions of Jews in the late Second Temple Period (along with the rejection of iconic art).

Ritual Purity in the Torah

The rules of clean and unclean are found mainly in Lev 11–17 and Num 19. A good way to summarize these various rules is to identify the three main causes of uncleanness:

- Leprosy (of humans, clothes, and of buildings);
- Discharge from the sexual organs (a menstruating woman, a man or woman with a diseased flux, a seminal emission, and a woman after childbirth);
- Dead bodies (of animals or humans).[8]

To become unclean meant primarily that one was excluded from the temple until the process of purification could be completed. But there were some consequences of uncleanness that went beyond temple participation. First, in the case of leprosy,[9] the

---

6. Urbach, "The Mishnah."

7. Following Magen, *Stone Vessel,* 138. But see Jensen, "Purity and Politics," who offers some caution on this understanding and translation.

8. See Roth, et al., "Purity and Impurity," 1405.

9. For leprosy, see Chapter 9. This was not actually Hansen's disease but various skin conditions.

"unclean" leper or one suspected of having leprosy was shut away from the community until a decision could be reached about the leprosy and, if it was concluded that he/she had leprosy, the victim was excluded from the community and had to live outside the village. Second, a man was forbidden to have sexual relations with his wife during her days of menstruation. Third, food that became unclean, due to the corpse of a "creeping thing" (*sherets* שֶׁרֶץ, i.e., insects, mice, lizards, etc.), had to be discarded. Thus, even in the First Temple Period (or the period of the Hebrew Bible) uncleanness not only affected one's admissibility into the Temple but also had broader implications for daily life.

The book of Leviticus gives several different procedures for purification but they basically included bathing, sometimes washing one's clothes, and waiting until sunset (or longer for some impurities). Corpse uncleanness (that uncleanness contracted through contact with a human corpse) required seven days' wait, sprinkling twice with the water mixed with the ashes of the red heifer, and bathing. Uncleanness after childbirth required seven or fourteen days' wait, depending on whether the child was a boy or girl. Purification from leprosy required bringing two birds to the priest—one of which was killed and the other released—waiting seven days, shaving all of the hair from the unclean person's body, washing the clothes, bathing, and offering three lambs.

Not only could people become unclean, but utensils, clothes, food, and drink as well. The book of Leviticus gives instructions for the cleansing of some of these objects, but not for the purification of food and drink. Presumably unclean food simply could not be used for temple worship, but food made unclean by the corpse of a creeping thing was probably thrown away (Lev 11:20, 23, 29–30, 41–43). Even houses could be declared unclean from "leprosy." In these cases, the houses were destroyed. The following table summarizes the sources of uncleanness and the means of removing the uncleanness:

Impurity	Means of Purification
1. corpse uncleanness	7 days, red heifer, sprinkling
2. childbirth	7 to 14 days, then 33 to 66 days
3. menstruation	7 days

Impurity	Means of Purification
4. diseased discharge from the sexual organ (male) (female)	7 days, bathing, wash his clothes, sacrifices 7 days, sacrifices
5. semen	bathing and sunset
6. contact with what one who has a discharge sits, lies, or leans on (*midras* uncleanness); also with the spittle of such a person or touching or being touched by such a person	bathing, washing clothes, sunset

Impurity	Means of Purification
7. contact with what a menstruating woman sits, lies, or leans on	bathing, washing clothes, sunset
8. vessels which become unclean	Break, if fired clay; wash, if wooden (stone vessels, animal dung vessels, and unfired clay vessels cannot become unclean)
9. carcass of an unclean animal	for people—bathe, wash clothes, sunset; for vessels—break or wash; for food (only if also wet)—non use
10. leprosy in people, garments, and houses	long and complicated procedure

Table 12.2: Torah's Rule of Uncleanness (adapted from Sanders)[10]

Ritual Purity Defined

It might be helpful at this point to define what impurity was to the minds of first-century Jews. Mary Douglas' classic definition is that uncleanness is simply "matter out of place" and that it exhibits a lack of wholeness. Neusner similarly defines uncleanness as an imbalance in nature or what is disruptive of the economy of nature. F. Schmidt defines impurity as "mixture and disorder." Sanders explains it as a change of status.[11] Thus, given this definition, we would think of uncleanness as something that interrupts the accepted order.

But the above definition sounds more etic than emic. That is, it sounds more like an outsider's definition of uncleanness than the definition of one who believed in it and practiced it. Those societies for whom ritual purity was/is important conceive(d) of it as more than matter out of place or the like.

Cultures more primitive than that of the rabbis of the Mishnah treat(ed) impurity as a demonic presence or demonic force. W. R. Smith, in his description of the Semitic peoples of Arabia, distinguished between Semites and "savages." The Semites, he maintained, keep ritual purity taboos because uncleanness is hateful to God, but the savage avoids impurity taboos because dangerous spirits are associated with it.[12] The ancient Babylonians also associated ritual impurity with the presence of demons. To cleanse a house, for example, one had to drive out the demon.[13] Likewise, in the Zoroastrianism of Persia, uncleanness was considered demonic.[14]

---

10. This table is adapted and simplified from that given in Sanders, *Jewish Law*, 151. A helpful series of tables of purification procedures and effects is given in Milgrom, *Leviticus*, 986–91.

11. Douglas, *Purity and Danger*, 41; Neusner, *Purity in Rabbinic Judaism*, 92, 129; Schmidt, *How the Temple Thinks*, 91; Sanders, *Judaism*, 220.

12. Smith, *Religion of the Semites*, 447.

13. See Saggs, *The Greatness That Was Babylon*, 301–2. See also Milgrom, *Leviticus, 1–16*, 256 and 911.

14. Moore, *History of Religions*, I, 390.

In contemporary traditional cultures, uncleanness is more like an impersonal force and less like the presence of demons. Anna S. Meigs' study of the culture of New Guinea led to a definition of impurity which included decaying substances which threaten the body.[15] Likewise, in New Guinea, among the Hua people, the vital essence of another person (called nu), found in bodily fluids, pollutes (makes unclean) and can cause illnesses.[16] Among the Nuer folk of eastern Africa, uncleanness can jump from one person to another—entering the body through an open wound.[17] Thus, in ancient non-Jewish cultures and in contemporary "primitive" cultures, uncleanness is more than just matter out of place.

Even in the sophisticated teaching of the Mishnah it seems that uncleanness is conceived of as more than matter out of place. Neusner maintains that the Mishnah conceives of impurity as at times an invisible, "viscous liquid"; a "viscous gas"; a force something like what we would call radiation; a light; or a "nimbus."[18] Uncleanness squishes out if pressed upon, seeks to escape a vessel if not properly stopped, and radiates out into a tent where there is a corpse. Though invisible, the ancients knew it was there.[19] These similes of Neusner must not be taken too literally, but they do indicate that uncleanness was considered an unseen force, influence, or essence.

Concern for ritual purity was common throughout the Ancient Near East and the Mediterranean World. This concern was part of the cultural air that ancient persons breathed. Therefore, it would be quite anachronistic to attribute to the ancients a modern, western view about this topic. One did not just decide that one did not like purity concerns. They were assumed in Egypt, Mesopotamia, Asia Minor, Greece, and Rome.[20]

Further, as the cultural anthropologists inform us, many non-developed or traditional societies still have great concern for purity and pollution. These states are usually determined by matters related to corpses, menstruation, childbirth, the sexual organs and certain foods, much like those concerns in Leviticus and Numbers in the Hebrew Bible.[21] One of the best windows into the Hebrew Bible's teachings on purity is the study of these cultures.

15. Meigs, "Papuan Perspective," 313. This definition is accepted by Harrington, *Impurity Systems*, 23.

16. Meigs, *Food, Sex and Pollution*, 100–101.

17. Evans-Pritchard, *Nuer Religion*, 185 wrote that the uncleanness of an adulterous man and woman may enter the body of the wronged husband through an open wound.

18. Neusner, *Purity in Rabbinic Judaism*, 83, 87, 89.

19. How did they know impurity was present? By faith; the Torah told them it was.

20. This is widely recognized by those studying Jewish purity. See Milgrom, *Leviticus 1–16*, 763–64; Roth, et al., "Purity and Impurity," 1407; Sanders, *Judaism*, 230; Maccoby, *Ritual and Morality*, 30, 134. For authors on the Ancient Near East see: Hooke, *Babylonian and Assyrian Religion*, 52; Budge, *Osiris*, II, 176, 217–19.

21. See M. Douglas, *Purity and Danger*, 29–40; Meigs, *Food, Sex and Pollution*; Evans-Pritchard, *Nuer Religion*, 185; Buckser, "Purity and Pollution"; Smith, *Religion of the Semites*, 152–55, 446–54; Soper, *The Religions of Mankind*, 74; and Harrington, *Impurity Systems*, 22.

In considering this topic, the modern person must overcome a natural cultural revulsion. We must not think that everyone thinks about ritual purity the way we do. All of the talk in the Hebrew Bible and the Mishnah about bodily secretions may sound disgusting to those of us who grew up in the western hemisphere.[22] But what seems to us like a neurotic obsession with bodily dirt seems to them not only important but vital. It is their way of seeing the universe. Unless the interpreter can appreciate the supreme importance of ritual purity to these cultures, he/she will not grasp what was going on in Judaism in the late Second Temple Period.

Ritual Purity in the Mishnah

The Mishnah collects, organizes, explains, and expands the biblical texts. Sometimes the expansions are logical developments and sometimes the expansions are merely new decrees.

J. Neusner observes that the Mishnah wants to show:

1. the sources of uncleanness
2. the objects and substances susceptible to uncleanness
3. the modes of purification

In the Mishnah, the main topics of concern are corpse uncleanness, menstrual blood, and the diseased fluxes from the sexual organs of males or females.[23]

Both cleanness and uncleanness are more than changes of state and matter out of place (or in place). They are, in some way, real entities because one can be more unclean than another or, conversely, more holy. That is, some impurities were more impure than others. The Mishnah has a graded list of "the fathers of uncleanness" (*avot ha-tumah*). The expression, father of uncleanness, indicates any of the sources of uncleanness given in the Hebrew Bible (Table 12.2). These are distinguished from "offspring of uncleanness" (*toledot ha-tumah*) which is something made unclean by a father of uncleanness and which can, in turn, make something or someone else unclean to a lesser degree. Thus, a father of uncleanness imparts to a susceptible person or object first grade uncleanness; this person or object can impart second grade uncleanness and so forth. The Mishnah speaks of up to fifth grade uncleanness, which would be a very low grade of uncleanness.[24]

---

22. Douglas, *Purity and Danger*, 73–93. Douglas calls this mind-set "primitive." Smith, *Religion of the Semites*, 449 states: "From our standpoint the laws of uncleanness appear irrational."

23. Neusner, *Purity in Rabbinic Judaism*, 40, 66.

24. See Harrington, *Impurity Systems*, 149, 203, 240, 245, and 246. The author presents graphics to teach that the higher a person or object is on the purity scale, the more susceptible that person or object is to impurity. Thus, e.g., fourth grade impurity would not affect most objects but would render the sacrifices of the temple (the "holy things") unfit for temple use. Cf. also the "trees" of impurity contamination in Milgrom, *Leviticus 1–16*, 954–64. The trees are taken from the work of D. P. Wright.

M. Kel. 1:4, however, also makes distinctions even among the fathers of uncleanness. The gradations given are as follows:

WORST UNCLEANNESS	1. Corpse uncleanness
	2. Bones from humans
	3. A leper
	4. A woman who has a flux
	5. A man with a flux
	6. Whatever a man with a flux rides on
	7. The discharge of a man with a flux, his spittle, semen, and urine, and the blood of a menstruant
	8. One who has sexual intercourse with a menstruating woman
LEAST UNCLEANNESS	9. Carrion & sin offering water sufficient in quantity to sprinkle, dead creeping thing, male semen, person who has contracted uncleanness from corpse, leper in the days of reckoning, sin offering water too little to sprinkle

Table 12.3: Gradations of the Fathers of Uncleanness

But just as some uncleannesses were more unclean than others, some holinesses were holier than others. Again the Mishnah, with its love of organizing and presenting lists, gives a hierarchy of holy places (m. Kel. 1:6–9):

HOLIEST	1. The Holy of Holies of the Temple
	2. The Holy Place or Sanctuary of the Temple
	3. Between the Porch and the Altar of the Temple
	4. The Court of the Priests of the Temple
	5. The Court of the Israelites of the Temple
	6. The Court of Women of the Temple
	7. The Rampart of the Temple
	8. The Temple Mount
	9. Jerusalem
	10. Walled Cities in Israel
LEAST HOLY	11. The Land of Israel

Table 12.4: Gradations of Holiness

It was not a sin to contract uncleanness. As a matter of fact many of the unclean states in Judaism were the result of good and necessary actions.[25] It is a good thing to bury your dead relatives, to bear a child, and to have sexual intercourse with your spouse. Menstruation is natural and expected. But all of these processes would render one ritually unclean.

25. Cf. Sanders, *Jewish Law*, 142; Maccoby, *Ritual and Morality*, 149; H. K. Harrington, *Impurity Systems*, 32; and Schmidt, *How the Temple Thinks*, 91.

Further, other sources of uncleanness were unfortunate, but not morally bad: leprosy, diseased discharges, and carcasses of creeping things (insects, mice, lizards, etc.) in your food. These are not evil or sinful, but they must be remedied and purified.

Although there were uncleannesses such as idolatry, which were not permissible, in the main, it was failing to take purity seriously that was sinful, not the impurity *per se*. For someone to enter the temple or for a priest to attempt to undertake his duties in the temple in an unclean state, for example, would have been a terrible sacrilege (m. Sanh. 9:6). Of course, there were many different ideas in first-century Judaism about what it meant to take ritual purity seriously.

Finally, some holy objects or holy actions could leave the participant in a state of uncleanness. Those who officiated and handled the ashes of the red heifer were made unclean by the process (Num 19:7–8) and the holy scriptures made the hands unclean (m. Yad. 3:2). Such a—to us—peculiar phenomenon as a holy object making one unclean is known from other religions as well. W. R. Smith observed that, among the peoples of the Arabian Peninsula, there is sometimes doubtful ground between holy and unclean.[26]

Jewish Sects that Stressed Purity in the Late Second Temple Period

Pharisees

There were numerous Jewish sects that stressed ritual purity. First, there were the Pharisees. There is a sharp disagreement between J. Neusner and E. P. Sanders as to the extent to which the first-century ordinary Jews worried about ritual purity. Neusner has maintained that the Pharisees in general tried to live like priests in the temple creating a huge gulf between themselves and the ordinary people (called in the Mishnah *am ha-aretz*, "the people of the land"). Sanders, on the other hand, wants to shrink the gulf between the Pharisees and the ordinary people. Although the Pharisees were very concerned with ritual purity both in the temple and outside it, they did not try to live like priests performing duties in the temple, maintains Sanders, nor were the ordinary people as lax about ritual purity in everyday life as has been supposed.[27]

The evidence would seem to favor Sanders' position. A text from m. Ḥag., from which we will construct Table 12.7 below, does not indicate that the Pharisees were equal with the priests in purity but that they were certainly higher than the ordinary people. Further, as Sanders points out, nowhere in the Mishnah does it forbid a Pharisee to contract corpse uncleanness. If one was a priest, he was forbidden to contract corpse uncleanness except in the case of a close family member. The High

---

26. Smith, *Religion of the Semites*, 448–52. Cf. Frazer, *The Golden Bough*, 548–49.

27. Neusner, *From Politics to Piety*, 83; Neusner., *Idea of Purity*, 65; Sanders, *Jewish Law*, 173 and *Judaism*, 440. Some of Neusner's more recent publications seem to state the case in a modified form. See Neusner, *Purity in Rabbinic Judaism*, 70. For others who follow Sanders see: H. Maccoby, *Ritual and Morality*, 209–13; Dunn, "Jesus and Purity"; and Poirier, "Purity Beyond the Temple."

Priest could not contract it at all, meaning that he could not participate in the funeral services of his family (Lev 21:1–3,11). But the Pharisees are not forbidden to do this in the Mishnah. They could engage in the funeral rites of anyone but of course they would undergo purification afterward. Therefore, the Pharisees, although living in a higher level of ritual purity than the ordinary masses, did not think they should live like Temple priests.

Essenes

Second, the Essenes present us with another sect that was extremely meticulous about ritual purity. Both Josephus and the Dead Sea Scrolls attest to their emphasis on the purity of the group. In the first place, only members who had attained a high level of purity were allowed to share in the full meal of both solid food and liquids. L. Schiffman explains that there were three stages of purity at Qumran based on the three examinations done to novices (1QS 6:16–22). Only after the third examination, was the novice considered ritually pure and could not only eat the solid food of the community, but consume the liquids as well.[28] Not only were the novices kept from the communal meal of the members, but Josephus indicates that when a novice touched someone of a higher grade of purity the latter had to take a ritual bath (*War* 2.150).

The Essenes were especially scrupulous about liquids and evidently adopted the Pharisaic interpretation of Leviticus. Lev 11:34, 38 speak only of "water" predisposing to uncleanness. But the Mishnah interprets water to mean any one of seven liquids: water, dew, blood, milk, bee's honey, oil, or wine (m. Makhsh. 6:4). Thus, the Essenes were concerned to keep novices away from the liquids of the communal meal (e.g., wine). Further, although most people in that region would rub olive oil on their skin, as protection against the sun and wind, the Essenes refused to do so, evidently because they feared being more susceptible to uncleanness (*War* 2.123; CD 12:15–17). Finally, the Dead Sea document, called the Halakhic Letter (4QMMT), lists as one of the disputes between the Essenes and others the pouring of liquids from a clean container to an unclean container. The Essenes maintained that the uncleanness traveled up the unbroken stream of water to defile the clean container. The number of texts demonstrating that ritual purity was of supreme importance to the Essenes could be multiplied.[29] If anything, the Essenes were even more scrupulous about ritual purity than the Pharisees.

Perhaps the clearest evidence that the Essenes stressed ritual purity is the number of references to ritual baths and the actual baths found at Qumran. Josephus and

---

28. Schiffman, *Sectarian Law*, 162. See the Tohorot texts from Qumran cave 4 (4Q274–278).

29. See especially Vermes, *Dead Sea Scrolls*, 53–54, 102, 143, 180; VanderKam, *The Dead Sea Scrolls Today*, 81, 85–87; Milgrom, "Studies in the Temple Scroll"; Newton, *Concept of Purity*, 21–26; Harrington, *Impurity Systems*, 47–67; Poirier, "Purity Beyond the Temple" 247–265; and Magness, *Stone*, passim. See also CD 12, 11QT 45–48, 4QMMT.

The Archaeology of Daily Life

the Dead Sea Scrolls indicate that the Essenes bathed in cold water before each meal (*War* 2. 129; 1QS 5:13–14), that new members took the ritual bath (*War* 2. 138), and that, after defecation, they washed themselves as though ritually defiled (*War* 2.149). One Dead Sea document, the Damascus Document (CD 10:11), gives instructions on the proper kind of ritual bath. Several ritual bath installations have been found at Qumran.

Figure 12.2: *Mikveh* at Qumran (photo by the author)

Samaritans

Third, the Samaritans, for example, although considered by the Pharisees perpetually unclean, were actually very concerned about ritual purity. Epiphanius (*Haer.* 9.3) wrote that they took a ritual bath when they touched a stranger or a non-Samaritan and carefully avoided corpses if at all possible.[30]

Associates

Fourth, the rabbinic literature also makes reference to several pietist groups that were zealous to maintain ritual purity at all times. The so called "associates" (חֲבֵרִים *ḥaverim*) were supposed to refrain from giving their heave offerings and tithes to the *am ha-aretz* (the ordinary people), to protect their purity from the *am ha-aretz*, and to eat their ordinary food in a state of purity (t. Demai 2:2).[31]

---

30. See Büchler, "Levitical Impurity"; Büchler, "Law of Purification."

31. Were the *ḥaverim* the same as the Pharisees, a subgroup within the Pharisees, or a totally different group with some similarities to the Pharisees? Neusner (*From Politics to Piety*, 84, 87) seems

Morning Bathers

Fifth, the "morning bathers" (*tovlei shaharin*), who evidently took a daily ritual bath, regardless of any known defilement, were critical of the Pharisees because they did not (t. Yad. 2:20).[32]

Sadducees

Sixth, the Sadducees also took ritual purity very seriously and criticized the Pharisees because of their laxity in handling liquids (m. Yad. 4:7). Thus there were probably numerous sects the defining difference of which was the interpretation and the application of ritual purity. Concern—or hyper-concern—for ritual purity was a major feature in all Jewish sects.

Ritual Purity Important to Common Jews

Further, there is strong evidence that ritual purity was a concern for many Jews in the first century, not just for Pharisees, priests, Essenes, and other sectarians. Thus, we should not only lower the Pharisaic level of purity; we should raise the level of purity of the ordinary people. The peasants or ordinary persons were more scrupulous than we had thought. These conclusions are clear from a survey of the Mishnah (and Tosephta), Josephus, the Apocrypha, and especially of the material remains.

Additional Examples of Purity from the Literature

Ritual purity was increasingly important even to Jews that did not belong to a sect.[33] Probably most Jews of Palestine in the first century did not belong to a religious sect. It is to these ordinary persons that scholars give the designations "Household Judaism" or "Common Judaism." What sort of concerns would they have had about ritual purity apart from going to the temple? I offer eight cases from the literature:

First, Josephus writes that, when Antipas founded the city of Tiberias in Galilee (first century CE; see Chapter 2), he had trouble settling the city with Jews because there were so many graves in the area, and the Jews did not want to contract corpse impurity (*Ant.* 18.36–38). Tiberias is a long distance from Jerusalem and surely most

---

to equate the two. Sanders had previously suggested that the two were totally different religious sects (*Jesus and Judaism*, 187) but later expressed uncertainty about this conclusion (*Jewish Law* 250). Rivkin (*A Hidden Revolution*, 175) declares: "The *haberim* are not Pharisees." H. Maccoby (*Ritual and Morality*, 209) agrees. R. P. Booth believes the *haverim* were one of four sub-groups within Pharisaism: *haverim*, "extremist" Pharisees, ordinary Pharisees, and sages (*Jesus and the Laws of Purity*, 193).

32. Booth, *Jesus and the Laws of Purity*, 202 argues that the "morning bathers" were a pre-70 CE group since the text follows a pericope about pre-70 Boethusians who complain against the Pharisees.

33. Dunn, "Jesus and Purity" 455.

of those settling there were not intending to go to the temple every week. Yet, they did not want to live on or near a possible grave.

Second, he narrates the story of the opportunistic John of Gischala (first century CE) in which John sold cheap olive oil from Gischala for a high price to Jews in Caesarea Philippi because they did not want to buy oil from Gentiles, suspecting that their oil had contracted impurity from creeping things (*Life* 74–76=*War* 2.591; cf. *Ant.* 12.120). Thus the ordinary Jews of Caesarea Philippi did not want oil that might have been pressed or stored in an unclean state. There was no concern for using the oil in the temple. Rather, the oil seems to have been entirely for everyday use.

Third, the book of Judith (first century BCE) tells that Judith bathed each evening before eating dinner and, after the bath, remained in her tent to maintain purity (Jdt 12:7–9). Regular bathing before meals bespeaks a piety even beyond most of the Pharisees. Her habits were similar to the "morning bathers" and Essenes mentioned above.

Fourth, the men in the army of Judas Maccabeus (second century BCE) thought it necessary to undergo ritual purification before the Sabbath. But purification was not a Sabbath concern but originally only a temple concern. One purified himself/herself for participation in the temple cultus, not to celebrate the Sabbath. Thus they have by this time added further applications to ritual purity (see 2 Macc. 12:38).

Fifth, Tobit (Tobit 2:9; second century BCE), because he had had contact with a corpse, would not enter his own house in the evening. But the story makes no reference to his intending soon to enter the temple.

Sixth, two texts in the Jewish sections of the Sib. Or. 3.591–593 (second to first century BCE) and 4.162–166 (80 CE) refer to bathing in the morning before prayer, again similar to the "morning bathers."[34]

Seventh, both Arist. (written sometime between third century BCE and first century CE) and Josephus (first century CE) claimed that the translators of the Septuagint version washed their hands in the sea each day before working on the translation of the Bible (Arist. 305–306; *Ant.* 12.106). This too is an additional requirement to the Torah's regulations.

Finally, the Mishnah considers the ordinary people to be scrupulous about purity, at least in some respects. They would keep the second tithe from defilement and would not subject vessels left in their keeping to corpse impurity (m. T. Yom 4:5; m. Tohor. 8:2).[35] All of these cases indicate that ordinary people—not priests, not sectarians—were concerned about ritual purity, not just as it pertained to going to the temple. They preferred not to contract impurity if it could be avoided.

---

34. The dates are from Collins, "Sibylline Oracles," 355, 383.
35. See Sanders, *Judaism*, 434.

Figure 12.3: Ritual Bath in Yodefat (photo by the author)

Archaeological evidence of purity

In addition to the above literary evidence, the material remains of Palestine, from the late Second Temple Period, show that many people were concerned with ritual purity even when not going into the temple. Three kinds of material remains are important for this topic:

1. the ritual baths
2. the stoneware vessels
3. the oil lamps.

First, archaeologists have discovered many ritual bath installations throughout Israel. One might have concluded that taking a ritual bath was mostly a Pharisaic or a priestly requirement, since one of the tractates of the Mishnah (Mikv.) is wholly concerned with the regulations for it. But in recent years, over 1,000 installations,[36] identified as ritual baths (i.e. carved in bedrock, with steps, sometimes with a divider on the steps, a few with extra water tanks, with volume enough to immerse a person),

---

36. Adler, "Archaeology of Purity," counted 850 installations in his 2011 dissertation. But in private correspondence, he calculated that the number must by now be well over one thousand.

have been found in Israel.[37] These installations are in Jerusalem (at least 170 in the city and 40 near the southern gates of the Temple) as well as in other locations: Jericho, Masada, Herodium, Cypros, Qumran, Gezer, Gamla, Nazareth, Yodefat, Magdala, Sepphoris (around 41 baths), Qiryat Sefer, En-Gedi, and elsewhere in rural areas near oil and wine presses (430 in Judea and 100 in Galilee).[38] Since similar installations are absent in Gentile areas, these are surely Jewish.

The ritual baths or *mikva'ot* were placed especially in four types of locations:

1. in private houses
2. in public places, especially near synagogues and, in Jerusalem, near the Temple
3. near agricultural installations (wine presses and olive presses)[39]
4. near tombs[40]

In the town of Gamla, for example, we have examples of four different *mikva'ot*: One large *mikveh* was found in a house, perhaps the house of a wealthy person. Another one, a small one, was also in a private dwelling. The third one, a large one, was near the synagogue. Finally, there was a small *mikveh* near an oil press, evidently for the workers pressing the olive oil in case they acquired ritual impurity during the process.[41]

The baths begin appearing in the second century BCE and decline sharply in appearance after 135 CE. This window of time attests to the growing importance of ritual purity in the late Second Temple Period.[42] The baths in the Upper City of Jerusalem would probably have been used by Sadducees or the aristocratic priesthood. Those at Qumran we have already discussed above. The baths at Jericho, Herodium, and Cypros are in Herodian or Hasmonean palaces. But the rest were evidently used by ordinary people, far away from the Temple, who wanted to be ritually pure for harvest, for meals, or for prayer in the synagogue.

---

37. For examples, see Figures 2.5, 2.15, 12.2, 12.3, and 12.4.
38. Adler, "Archaeology of Purity"; and Jensen, "Purity and Politics," 17.
39. See especially, Adler, "Second Temple Period Ritual Baths."
40. Zissu and Amit, "Common Judaism."
41. Amit, "The Miqva'ot."
42. See R. Reich, "They *Are* Ritual Baths"; R. Reich, "Ritual Baths"; R. Reich, "Great Mikveh Debate"; R. Reich, *Miqwa'ot (Jewish ritual Immersion Baths)*; E. M. Meyers, E. Netzer and C. L. Meyers, *Sepphoris*, 28; Deines, *Jüdische Steingefässe*, 4–5; L. I. Levine, "Archaeology and the Religious Ethos"; Crossan and Reed, *Excavating Jesus,* 36, 168; Reed, "Galileans, 'Israelite Village Communities.'" See especially the maps in Reich, *Miqwa'ot*. The identification of some of these installations as ritual baths has been challenged in recent years. See B. W. Wright, "Jewish Ritual Baths," and especially the discussion in *BAR*: Eshel, "Pools of Sepphoris"; and E. M. Meyers, "The Pools of Sepphoris." See also E. M. Meyers, "Aspects of Everyday Life," esp. 211–15.

How Would You Practice Your Religion?

Figure 12.4: *Mikveh* (Ritual Bath), Jerusalem, west of the Temple.
Notice the divider. (photo by the author)

Second, among the material remains are the stoneware (or chalk) objects. Vessels made of stone, animal dung, or unfired clay could not become unclean according to the Mishnah (m. Kel. 4:4, 10:1, m. Ohol. 5:5, m. Parah 5:5, m. Yad. 1:2). While one would be required to break a fired clay pot if it became unclean (and this could be costly if one were really scrupulous about ritual purity), one would be exempt from that worry if the vessel were made of stone.

Stone vessels—cups, pots, bowls, and jars—have been found at more than 250 sites[43] in Palestine, especially in and around Jerusalem (concentrated in the City of David and Upper City; see Map 2.2[44]), in Galilee, and on the Golan, but also in the Jordan Valley, on the Coastal Plain, and in Perea. At Capernaum, each house from the first century contained stone vessel fragments.[45] At Gamla, numerous fragments of stone vessels have been excavated. They mostly consist of hand-carved cups or lathe-turned bowls but also include hand-carved bowls and lathe-turned goblets.[46] The residents of Gamla clearly imported a lot of stoneware. In the "land of Benjamin" area of Judea every Jewish site from the late Second Temple Period had stoneware vessels in its ruins (and also *mikva'ot*).[47] Aviam has recently published a map identifying the locations in Galilee and the Golan where stone ware vessels have been recovered in

---

43. Adler, "Archaeology of Purity"; and Jensen, "Purity and Politics," 13. Again, this is an old count. The total must be many more at this date.
44. Magen, "Stone Vessel Industry," 23.
45. Crossan and Reed, *Excavating*, 167.
46. Gibson, "Soft Limestone Vessels."
47. Magen, "Land of Benjamin," 22.

excavations. He lists twenty-five sites where the stone items were found.[48] There were several stone or chalk vessel workshops in Jerusalem and its environs and in Galilean villages (and the Golan).[49]

A recent analysis of one thousand fragments of stone ware in a first-century garbage dump in Jerusalem showed that the majority of the vessels were hand carved cups and small pitchers with a close second place to lathe turned bowls.[50] But they also made stone tables and large jars (like those in John 2:6. See Figure 2.2). Clearly the Jerusalem residents were using stone vessels freely.

Chalk vessels began to be popular in the first century BCE, continued to be commonly used in the first century CE, and on into the second century CE until the end of the Bar-Kokhba war (135 CE).[51] Thus, their popularity coincides with the building of ritual baths in Palestine.

The use of stone vessels also coincides with the decline of the ESA ceramic ware.[52] This imported pottery—made in Gentile cities—was coated with a red glossy substance and was very popular until around the late first century BCE. It continued to be used in gentile cities such as Tel Anafa, Dor, Ashdod, Ashkelon, and the predominantly gentile Caesarea. But in the first century CE it is almost completely absent from Judea and Galilee. It is not found, for example, in Bethsaida (in the Golan), in Capernaum, or in Yodefat (Galilee).[53] In general, the attractive ceramic ware declines in Jewish villages in our time period even though it continues in Gentile settlements. Excavators found some of this pottery in the houses of the wealthy in the Upper City of Jerusalem, however (see Chapter 2). Why did Jews start avoiding this type of Gentile pottery? Was it pure economics (cost of transporting it)? Were there religious reasons (the vessels might be impure since they were manufactured by Gentiles)? Adler opines that gentiles in this period were considered to have inherent impurity and so any vessel made by them must also be impure.[54] At any rate the decline of the important pottery and the rise of the stone vessels seem not to be a coincidence.[55]

---

48. Aviam, "Distribution Map," 119.

49. See the excellent survey of stone vessel remains in R. Deines, *Jüdische Steingefässe*, 71–165 (map on p. 165). See also Y. Magen, "Jerusalem as a Center," 244–56; Magen, "Ancient Israel's Stone Age," (also with map); Magen, *Stone Vessel Industry,* map for Galilee on 161; Reed, *Archaeology,* 44; Jensen, "Purity and Politics," 13; Berlin, "Jewish Life," 430.

50. Adler, "Quantitative Analysis." The same preference is evident at Gamla; see above.

51. Adler, "Archaeology of Purity."

52. Root, *Galilee,* 101. This type of pottery is also abbreviated ETS.

53. Berlin, "Jewish Life," 433; Adler, "Purity in the Roman Period," 247.

54. Adler, "Purity in the Roman Period," 247. Adler cites Josephus, *War* 1.229, 2.150, and Acts 10:28.

55. For differing view points see Adler, "Archaeology of Purity"; and Magness, *Stone,* 55. See Berlin, "Jewish Life," 445 who writes that the disappearance of the ESA ware at Jewish sites looks like "deliberate rejection."

The stone vessels seem not to have been merely a fashion but to have been used for religious reasons. This conclusion is supported by the fact that stone vessels have rarely been found in non-Jewish settlements (among Gentiles). Thus, they were not a phenomenon of the Gentiles. Further, many of them have been found in houses with ritual baths in Jerusalem, in rural villages, and on farms. Finally, they were used by rich and poor alike, by the aristocracy and the humble.[56] The widespread use of stoneware, evidently to avoid ritual impurity—both of the vessels and the contents of the vessels—testifies that the desire to maintain ritual purity, even in ordinary meals, was more widespread than simply among the Pharisees, the Essenes, and other sectarians.

Figure 12.5: Stoneware vessels (cups and a plate), Jerusalem (photo by the author)[57]

Third, a new kind of oil lamp emerged during our period. Beginning in the late first century BCE, lamp manufacturers in Jerusalem and its environs began making the wheel turned, knife-pared lamp (see photo). These lamps not only had a different sort of manufacturing technique (made on the potter's wheel instead of with a mold), but they *may* have taken on a sort of numinous quality when they were manufactured using clay from the city of Jerusalem and its immediate area.

---

56. See Jensen, "Purity and Politics," 15.
57. See also Figure 2.2.

The Archaeology of Daily Life

Figure 12.6: Herodian lamp (photo by the author)

The research of Adan-Bayewitz and associates has given us some very interesting conclusions. This team conducted an analysis on the chemical composition of the clay used in lamps sampled from three Jewish sites (Gamla, Yodefat, and Sepphoris) and from two Gentile sites (Dor and Scythopolis; see Maps 1.1 and 2.1). This analysis was then compared to the chemical analysis of clay from the Jerusalem area. The conclusion was that the overwhelming majority of lamps from the Jewish sites were made from Jerusalem area clay. At the Gentile sites, there were also some lamps made in Jerusalem from the clay of the region but they were a minority of the samples. Here are the results:

Jewish sites	SITE	SAMPLE SIZE	PERCENT FROM JERUSALEM AREA CLAY
	Gamla	57 lamps	96%
	Yodefat	39 lamps	95%
	Sepphoris	30 lamps	80%
Gentile sites	SITE	SAMPLE SIZE	PERCENT FROM JERUSALEM CLAY
	Dor	196 lamps	32 %
	Scythopolis	31 lamps	45%

Table 12.5: Results from chemical analysis of clay in lamps[58]

Thus one can conclude that the Jewish sites—especially the villages of Yodefat and Gamla where the Jewish population would be near 100%—strongly preferred the

---

58. Table constructed from information in Adan-Bayewitz, et al., "Preferential Distribution."

lamps manufactured in the area of Jerusalem. Sepphoris which had a minority of Gentiles living in it had a strong preference while the two Gentile cities (Dor and Scythopolis), although they still imported some Jerusalem lamps, had no preference for them.

Now excavators of the village of Shikhin (about one mile north of Sepphoris; Map 12.1) have done further analysis of lamps. Shikhin was also a lamp manufacturing center, although probably on a very limited basis.[59] One cannot at this time clearly date the lamp production at Shikhin; so, much is ambiguous. Yet, Anastasia Shapiro has examined the chemical analysis of lamps from several villages: Shikhin, Kh. Wadi Hamam, Tell Rekhesh, Yodefat, Gamla, Makberot Bʾnot Yaʾakov (north of the Sea of Galilee) Iʾbillin (in Lower Galilee) and Daburiay (also in Lower Galilee). She found that the residents of these villages widely used the Jerusalem lamps but also in some cases bought lamps manufactured in Shikhin. Here are her results:

Site	Shikhin	Makberot	Yodefat	Wadi Hamam	Rekhesh	Iʾbillin	Daburiyah	Gamla
Total number of lamps	15	2	1	4	1	5	3	2
Number from Jerusalem area clay	9	2	1	1	1			2
Number from Shikhin clay	6			3		5	3	

Table 12.6: Further Chemical analysis of lamps[60]

Some of these villages were content to use the Shikhin lamps. Again the dates are not yet clear (Late first century? Second century?[61]). But Shapiro notes that these lamps from Shikhin had the same look as the Jerusalem lamps. They used local clays—taken from an area southwest of the village of Shikhin—that resulted in a look much like the Jerusalem lamps.[62] So, one is tempted to surmise that the Galileans and Golani's preferred Jerusalem lamps. When they could not be obtained, perhaps because Jerusalem had by then been destroyed, they imported more locally made ones that looked a great deal like them.

---

59. Mordechai Aviam, private correspondence.

60. Based on information from Shapiro, "Petrographic Study." On the lamps in general, see J. R. Strange and Aviam, "Shiḥin Excavation Project."

61. Aviam, private correspondence.

62. Shapiro, "Petrographic Study," 103. She states that the Shikhin lamps are "similar in lithology" to the Jerusalem area lamps ((103); and opines that they used local Shikhin clays that would produce a "Jerusalem-like" lamp (105).

The Archaeology of Daily Life

Map 12.1: Lower Galilee showing the village of Shikhin

Why did the Jewish centers want lamps manufactured in Jerusalem? Adan-Bayewitz and his team surmise that they treasured them for lighting the Sabbath lights on Friday evenings. They suggest that Jerusalem pilgrims (attending the feasts) brought back supplies of them.[63] They would naturally tend to treasure these lamps and keep them for Sabbath purposes.

We might suggest another reason. The reader will review Table 12.4 above to learn that Jerusalem was considered holier than any other city. It was the location of the holiest site on earth: the Holy of Holies within the Temple. The Jerusalem lamps, either made from actual clay from the holy city or look-alike lamps from village sites such as Shikhin, were preferred because this was the center of the world for the Jewish believer in the late Second Temple Period. Anything from Jerusalem was holy.

The evidence given above from the Mishnah, Josephus, the Dead Sea Scrolls, and archaeology leads to the conclusion that ritual purity became increasingly important among most Jews in the first century CE until the defeat of Bar Kokhba in 135 CE. Some groups, such as the Essenes, Pharisees, and other sectarians, maintained a higher level of purity than ordinary folks, but the ordinary people were themselves certainly observant of ritual purity, even when not necessarily about to go into the temple.

Had you lived in Israel in the first century CE, which level of "cleanness" or purity would you have maintained? Probably that of the ordinary people. But bear in mind that in any society there are non-conformists. There would have been—and we encounter them in the literature—persons who were largely unobservant of the Torah

---

63. Adan-Bayewitz, et al., "Preferential Distribution," 75. On the other hand, see Magness, *Stone*, 220 n. 72, who opines that they did not buy the lamps in Jerusalem but the clay.

and its rules of purity. Thus, the lowest level of purity would be those persons who did not care about and did not observe purity laws.

The Mishnah, in its habit of making lists, has a listing of purity levels (m. Hag. 2:7). These are persons who maintain the strictest level of purity (priests) down to the common persons who maintained purity in some sense but not as fully as the priests. In between were the pietist sects like the Essenes. We can, based on this Mishnaic text, construct a scale of purity strictness in first-century Judaism as follows:

HIGHEST LEVEL	Priests Serving in the Temple
	Priests not Serving in the Temple
	Essenes, Other Pietists (e.g., *Haverim*)
	Pharisees
	Ordinary Persons
LOWEST LEVEL	Non-observant Persons

Table 12.7: Grades of Strictness in Purity in First-Century Judaism[64]

At this point, one might ask on which level of purity Jesus and the Jesus movement stood? Elsewhere I have argued that there was "no evidence that he and his disciples attempted to be as scrupulous as the Pharisees, Essenes, and other pietists. Thus, I would place Jesus on the same purity level as the ordinary observant Jews . . ."[65] He valued purity—how could he not since it is in the Bible?—but he did not maintain it as precisely as the Pharisees and certainly not as finely as the Essenes.

ANICONIC VESSELS AND DECORATIONS

The Torah prohibits making an idol or graven image. Exod 20:4 commands "you will not make for yourself an image or any likeness which is in the sky above, on the earth underneath, or in the sea."[66] The challenging part is to interpret these words. Are they an absolute prohibition against iconic art or simply a prohibition against worshipping images of birds, animals, and fish? In the late Second Temple Period, they apparently took it as an absolute prohibition of any images of humans or animals. Flowers and geometric patters were acceptable, however.

The change began with the Hasmonean rulers. During this period idolatry was the main religious problem of the Jewish people. Before this there were Persian coins with images of kings and queens, animals, and even pagan deities. But after the Hasmoneans, these images were avoided.[67] Israel entered an era of avoidance of any

64. Cf. Sanders, *Judaism*, 440; Sanders, *Jewish Law*, 205–7.

65. See Fiensy, *Jesus the Galilean*, 180.

66. See also Lev 26:1; Deut 4:15–19; and 27:15.

67. See Jensen, "Purity and Politics," 20; Lichtenberger, "Art," 57; Fine, *Art and Judaism*, 71. Fine prefers to use the term "anti-idolic" instead of aniconic (122).

THE ARCHAEOLOGY OF DAILY LIFE

sort of human or animal depiction as a breach of the second commandment. The Hasmoneans ruled with strict avoidance of statues and other depictions of humans and animals (1 Macc. 13:47). Josephus found it necessary to explain to his readers why Jews avoided statues in contrast to Greeks (*Apion* 2.75). Even the pagan, Roman historian, Tacitus, pointed out this—to them—peculiar trait: "(the Jews) call those profane who make representations of God in human shape out of perishable materials."[68]

Lamps

We see this prohibition in several types of material remains. Compare, for example the Herodian lamp pictured above (Figure 12.6) with these two below (Figure 12.7). Both lamps—roughly contemporaneous with the Herodian lamp above—depict persons, on the left in a gladiatorial combat, and on the right in a chariot race. In comparison, the Herodian lamp is quite plain and undecorated. Were the Jewish potters of Palestine/Israel unable to decorate their lamps? Certainly, they could. They have made a religious decision to avoid decoration with human and animal icons. The "pagan" lamps are attractive to the eye but offensive to the soul.

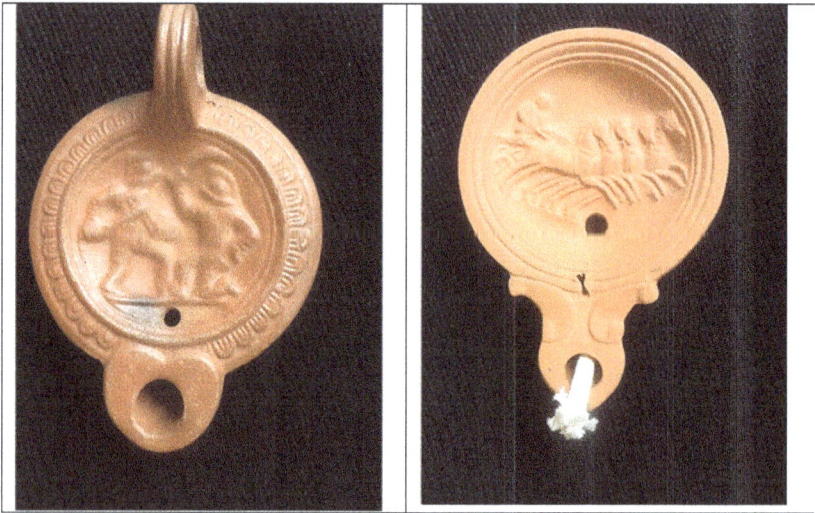

Figure 12.7: Replica lamps contemporaneous to the Herodian lamp above.
Left, from first-century Ephesus. Right from first-century Britain (photo by the author)

Synagogues

The avoidance of human and animal figures also prevailed in the synagogues of this period. The reader can see in the photograph of the Magdala synagogue below (Figure 12.8) how modest and plain everything was. The same is true of every other synagogue

68. *Hist.* 5.5. Translation in Church and Brodribb, *Tacitus*. See further, Lichtenberger, "Art," 57.

from our time period (compare the Gamla synagogue, Figure 3.2). They avoided frescoes and mosaics that depicted humans, animals, and pagan deities. The same was true of the Temple, itself, in Jerusalem. Excavations of the interior vaults of the Hulda gates (southside of the Temple mount) have shown that they were decorated with geometric patterns.[69]

Figure 12.8: Interior of the Magdala synagogue with a replica of the "stone table" (photo by the author)

On the other hand, synagogues from later periods show little restraint in this area. For example, the synagogue from Hamath-Tiberias (the village and hot bath just south of Tiberias) dating to the 4th century CE, had as one of its floor mosaics a center panel with the pagan god Helios surrounded by animal and human representations of the twelve signs of the zodiac. On the four corners of the mosaic were female figures representing the four seasons.[70] Another example is the late Roman synagogue at En-Gedi which had a mosaic of birds.[71] Another is the Torah ark from the synagogue

---

69. Fine, *Art and Judaism*, 78. But see Japp, "Decorative Art," 243 who notes that Herod the Great put the image of an eagle over the entrance to the Temple.

70. See Dothan, "Hamath-Tiberias"; Savage, "Hamath Tiberias."

71. Hirschfeld, *En-Gedi II*, Plate II. For other examples, see Harrison and Yamauchi, "Art," 97.

at Nabratein in Galilee. The large stone fragment, dating from the third or fourth century CE, has two lions sculpted on it.[72]

The contrast with the synagogues of the late Second Temple Period and the later synagogues is striking. Obviously, in a later era, devout Jews did not consider depicting these images—evidently as long as one did not worship them—as idolatrous.[73] There was a "radical disjunction" at the LR-Byz era from the ER I (or late Second Temple Period). During our time period, even to have the image was considered idolatry.[74]

House and Tomb Decorations

The same is true of even private decorations. The reader may want to look again at the mosaic floor of the house of a wealthy family in Jerusalem (Figure 2.2) where there is a geometric pattern but no animal or human representations. Even the upper class of Jerusalem, probably priestly, *usually* avoided any human or animal depictions. The aniconic value was not just a lower class conservative conviction. Likewise, the same sensitivity existed in Galilee (Yodefat) and the Golan (Gamla). There houses of the wealthy were decorated with frescoes and stucco but without images.[75]

One should not think, however, that forbidden images are totally absent. Steven Fine has collected a list of these found here and there among the ruins. Many were in the houses of the wealthy in the Upper City (a fish carved on a table, a bird depicted on a table top, animals in stucco, etc.). Yet, these are rare exceptions to the general picture.[76]

Even Herod the Great, who was not clearly a Jew at heart, refrained—for the most part—from breaching the Second Commandment. Archaeologists have found a few depictions of humans, animals, and mythological characters in his palaces (Herodium and Cypros) and in his gentile cities (Caesarea Maritima and Sebaste) but for the most part, he seems to have been sensitive to this issue, especially in Jewish cities. No where on his coins was his image ever depicted. Where a region was populated mostly by Jews, he was observant of the commandment; where gentiles predominated, he was less so. Herod borrowed decorative designs from the Romans but limited these mostly to geometric and floral patterns in Jerusalem, Maresha, and Masada. In other words, he remained in these centers aniconic.[77]

---

72. The ark fragment is in the Art Museum on the campus of Duke University.

73. Lichtenberger, "Art," 58.

74. Fine, *Art and Judaism*, 86.

75. See Arbel, *Ultimate Devotion*, 133; Farhi, "Stucco Decorations," 176 (Gamla); Aviam, "Socio-Economic," 31 (Yodefat).

76. Fine, *Art and Judaism*, 77–78.

77. See Japp, "Decorative Art"; Peleg-Barkat, "Fit for a King." The reader is reminded, however, of the three cities Herod the Great founded, each with a pagan temple to Augustus and Roma (with statues). See Chapter 2.

His grandson, Agrippa I, was apparently much like Herod the Great. He is said to have had statues (ἀνδριάντας) of his three daughters erected (in his palace?), a deed considered quite offensive and which was, after his death, reproached with obscene behavior on the part of some (*Ant.* 19.357). Perhaps he had busts of the three girls stationed in his palace gardens or entryway in imitation of wealthy Romans. Thus, Agrippa I followed the Herodian family practice of appearing piously Jewish in Jewish cities but assimilated elsewhere. The fact that the people took such great offense at his statues, however, shows the Jewish sensitivity to such icons.

Likewise, on the ossuaries in Figure 11.4 there are rosettes but no images of the deceased or the like. The families did not always decorate their bone boxes (ossuaries) but when they did, they used flowered symbols, rosettes, and geometric patterns. There is almost no iconic art in Jewish tombs from this period.[78] Contrast this with the paintings in the Egyptian tombs from this period where an image of the deceased often decorated the tomb wall. The same was true for many Roman sarcophagi.

Coins

The same can be observed in the Jewish preference for coins. Bradley Root[79] makes two observations based on the coin assemblage from Galilee in the ER I period. First, the Phoenician coins dropped significantly in this period. Second, when the locals minted coins, they avoided images of people or animals. One could also add another observation to these two: Jewish centers treasured use of the old Hasmonean coins. Let us talk about each of these items.

During our time period (ER I), in the tetrarchy of Herod Philip in the Golan area (towns with greater Gentile population), in the coastal area, and in the expressly Gentile cities of the Decapolis, the offensive coins with their idolatrous images are still common. At Bethsaida, for example, a town in Philip's tetrarchy, many iconic and pagan coins have been discovered but only a few "Jewish" coins.[80] Philip struck five coins, four with his image on it (along with the emperor), and one with just the emperor and the imperial temple.[81] Agrippa I struck his own portrait coin in Caesarea Philippi in 41 CE and his son, Agrippa II, struck one with the god Pan on it in 88

---

78. See Hachlili, *Funerary Customs,* 129–55. But see 133 where she describes a tomb in Jericho with birds on its wall, a rare exception. Fine, *Art and Judaism,* 78 reports on a lead sarcophagus in the tomb of Helena of Adiabene which had carved in it a sphinx and a dolphin. Avni and Greenhut ("Resting," 41) describe the head of a horned animal (bull?) carved on an ossuary from the Akeldama tombs in Jerusalem.

79. Root, *Galilee,* 105.

80. According to Jenks, "Coins," out of his total of 139 coins reported (many of which were illegible), 70 were pagan and iconic but only 21 were Jewish (either Hasmonean, Herod the Great, Agrippa I, or Tiberias). The Jewish coins were all aniconic.

81. Rousseau and Arav, *Jesus and His World,* 64–65. The coins were minted in 1 BCE, 8 CE, 30 CE, and 33 CE. One coin has no date.

The Archaeology of Daily Life

CE.[82] In the north, among the pagan centers, the Herodian heirs—like their dynasty founder, Herod the Great—had little hesitation in appealing to both the use of images and to pagan beliefs.

When Herod the Great and his son Antipas minted coins in Jewish regions (and even when Roman procurators minted them), they avoided such images.[83] For example, the bronze coins of the city of Tiberias (established by Antipas somewhere between 19–21 CE) have an inscription on one side and a floral motif (reed, palm branch, date cluster) on the other. Of the five series of coins Antipas minted, none has figural images.[84]

Further, archaeologists have noted the differences between Sepphoris coins from the first century and coins from the same city in the second century. A coin minted in the first century, intended to flatter Emperor Nero, has his name in an inscription but not his image. But coins minted in the second century depict both Trajan and Antoninus Pius. By the second century, Sepphoris had more Gentiles living in the city.[85] Root informs that they minted ten series of bronze coins in Galilee in the ER I period (Antipas, Agrippa II, and Roman magistrates). All series avoided images of humans, animals, and deities.[86] Finally, they stopped using the Tyrian sheqel to pay the Temple tax during the Jewish revolt. The Tyrian sheqel had images of pagan deities and monarchs. During the revolt, they minted their own silver coins with images of vessels from the Temple.[87]

But in Jewish villages and cities there is a tendency to use the old Hasmonean coins evidently to avoid the images. Jewish coins from the Persian period—pre-Hasmonean—had images. But none appear on Hasmonean coins.[88] These aniconic coins apparently became favored in Jewish population centers. Aviam[89] reports in his study that in the Jewish parts of Galilee and the Golan, sixty-five sites have Hasmonean coins frequently in the ruins. When they do use newly minted coins, they prefer coins minted in Tiberias (mostly issuing from Antipas).[90] At Gamla, for example, of the 5892 identifiable coins, 3964 were Hasmonean (67%).[91] That means that the coins

---

82. J. F. Wilson, *Caesarea Philippi,* 59, and Figures 9, 12, and 15. On the obverse of the Pan coin was depicted Titus and Domitian, the former and current emperors.

83. See Aviam, "Distribution Maps," 117–18; Jensen, "Purity and Politics," 21; Root, *Galilee,* 104–5; Arbel, *Ultimate Devotion,* 124; Rousseau and Arav, *Jesus and His World,* 60.

84. Weiss, "Josephus and Archaeology," 392; Jensen, "Antipas."

85. Chancey and Meyers, "Sepphoris," 24, 28.

86. Root, *Galilee,* 105.

87. Arbel, *Ultimate Devotion,* 125.

88. Arbel, *Ultimate Devotion,* 124. Cf. the coin map in Syon, "Galilean Mints," 57. The Galileans and Golanis also preferred coins minted in Tiberias to those minted in Phoenicia.

89. Aviam, "Distribution Maps," 117–18.

90. Syon, "Galilean Mints," 58.

91. Syon, "Coins."

most frequently used at Gamla—a Jewish town in Philip's tetrarchy—in the first century CE were over a hundred years old.

CONCLUSIONS

Had you lived in Palestine/Israel in the late Second Temple Period, you would have been very concerned with matters of ritual purity. Even when not intending to enter the Temple anytime soon, even if living in far away Galilee or the Golan, you would have wanted to maintain a certain level of purity by bathing in a *mikveh* and by using stone vessels (and avoiding the pagan ESA ware). You would have ordered your daily life around such matters. If you acquired impurity in the field or wine press, you would adjourn to the bath. If your clay vessel acquired uncleanness, you would break it—but if it was made of stone you would need not worry. And on the Sabbath, you would prefer to use a "semi-sacred" lamp made with clay from the holy city (If not an actual Jerusalem lamp, then a cheap imitation made from a local pottery village like Shikhin).

Further, you would want to avoid even the slightest hint of idolatry. Therefore, you would want lamps without decoration, kitchen ware simply made, and houses and synagogues with no fancy art. Among the wealthy even—with rare exceptions—there would be a tendency to use geometric patterns or rosettes as decorations since even they avoided the images so hated by Jews at this time. Thus, your ordinary daily activities—your eating, your food production, the coins your spent, your household decoration—stressed to yourself and to your family who you were.

Archaeology, therefore, informs us about the daily religious activities and values of the common folk. The scholars studied Torah intensely but the ordinary people tried to live the Torah as best they could in their mundane lives.

Summary

So, what would your daily life have been like if you had lived in Palestine/Israel in the late Second Temple Period? The answer depends somewhat on the place you lived, assuming you were a working-class person. You probably would live in a village of less than two thousand in population (90% did). You probably would have had a house made of undressed stones, coated with mud plaster, and sitting under a waddle and daub roof. You probably would have gotten married as a teenager and would have married a relative, as arranged by your parents. That said, geography would play a large role in your everyday experiences.

If you had lived in Meiron, e.g., in Upper Galilee (Map 7.2), you would have known forty inches of rain a year and would have experienced average temperatures of 75 degrees Fahrenheit. Your village would have rested on mountains 3,900 feet above sea level and would have had a population of under two thousand people.

But if you had lived in En-gedi—a village of similar size—on the west coast of the Dead Sea (Maps 3.2 and 5.1), you would have received less than five inches of rain each year and would have known average temperatures of 88 degrees Fahrenheit. And in striking contrast to Meiron, your village's elevation would be 1300 feet *below* sea level. Yet, in En-gedi, you would not have wanted for water since you would have enjoyed the ten springs that fed the village.

If you have lived at Meiron, you would have likely been engaged in farming one or both of their main crops: olives and grains. At En-gedi, your farming labor—enabled by the ten springs—would have been toward raising dates and balsam.

You also could have been involved at Meiron in industry or craft, namely in the cooperage or pottery trades. Your products might have been a supplement to your farming or perhaps were your sole income. So far, no similar industry has been identified at En-gedi.

Your food at Meiron would have included plums, almonds, olives, walnuts, barley, wheat, beans, and grapes (Table 6.5). At En-gedi, you would have eaten dates, olives, almonds, nuts, peaches, and jujube (Table 6.5). Both villages ate olives (and olive oil), evidently imported at En-gedi, and both consumed nuts as part of their diet.

Summary

En-gedi villagers also ate a lot of fish (imported or caught locally in the ten springs; Table 6.4).

At Meiron, one of the chronic diseases that plagued the villagers was malaria. One would expect malaria to be a problem in so wet a region and the skeletal remains seem to support this hunch. The anthropologists found in many of the skeletal remains from the Meiron tomb that they studied, "thick diploe and hyperplastic sternae, two conditions that occur as a response to . . . malaria."[1]

Likewise, at En-gedi, malaria was greatly feared as seen in the child's tunic found in the cave in Naḥal Ḥever (Map 5.1) probably belonging to a refugee from nearby En-gedi (Chapter 9). The tunic—the reader will recall—was attached to small bags of spices and herbs, evidently as a protection against disease. The Talmud speaks of such bags for protection from malaria (b. Shabb. 66b).

The dangers to your children were about the same in Meiron and En-gedi, perhaps due to the prevalence of malaria. The average youth mortality in Palestine/Israel as a whole, according to our calculations in Chapter 10, was 43% (Table 10.2). That is, 43 out of 100 children died before age twenty. But the rate at Meiron was 48% and at En-gedi it was 47%. Both villages were more dangerous for children than the average village in Palestine/Israel.

Were you a female, we can speculate that, after marrying as a teenager, you might have eight to ten pregnancies, five live births, and lose two of the five children in childhood. Either you or your husband would likely die before age thirty. The average life expectancy for men at both Meiron and En-gedi, if they reached adulthood, was 35—three years less than the average for Palestine/Israel as a whole (Table 10.5). Women at Meiron had a life expectancy equal to elsewhere in Palestine/Israel. There is no data for women at En-gedi (Table 10.5).

Thus, was daily life back then. It was brief and filled with disease, suffering, and loss. It was occupied with labor, family, and religion. Were they happy? Were they content? In spite of such challenges, there is no good reason to conclude that people were generally gloomy. One does not need modern conveniences to be happy. One may not even need a widely experienced longevity to find a measure of happiness. Doubtless, they were exploited by the aristocracy and abused from time to time by Roman occupiers. They may have known hunger at certain periods in the late Second Temple Period. Yet, the overall picture one sees is of having essential needs met.

But one should not compare their experiences with ours. Life still held its pleasantries, its loves, and its religious euphoria. These people knew the joys of marriage, of parenthood, and of a loving home. They felt the security of being accepted in an extended family. They could still have been happy with their life.

---

1. Smith, Bornemann, and Zias, "Skeletal Remains," 117).

Appendix A
Why Did Jesus Not Marry?

IN THE LAST FORTY years, the pendulum has swung completely the other way. When I was in my Ph.D. program, one almost had to apologize for any curiosity about the historical Jesus. Although the so-called New Quest was well underway and the Third Quest just beginning, the vestiges of the Bultmannian attitude were still present, especially in the minds of the older faculty members. But now we hear of scholars and amateurs who want to know (and often claim to know) even the intimate parts of Jesus' life. There are "researchers" who claim to know *that* Jesus married, *to whom* he was married, how many children he fathered, and what the names of the children were! Therefore, before we can suggest reasons as to why Jesus did not marry, we perhaps had better briefly examine the hypothesis that he did marry.

HYPOTHESES CONCERNING JESUS' MARITAL STATUS

To William Phipps (in 1970) belongs the claim of being the first scholar to offer a sustained argument for a married Jesus.[1] To be sure, others had mentioned Jesus' sexuality: The Mormons had taught for years that Jesus married three women: Mary and Martha of Bethany and Mary Magdalene.[2] John Erskine in 1945 had argued that Jesus had been married prior to his ministry but that he and his wife had not gotten along and thus were estranged.[3] Hugh Montefiore offered in 1969 that Jesus had had homosexual inclinations (and therefore was not the marrying kind) but also affirmed that Jesus had never acted on those inclinations.[4] And, of course, Dan Brown's *Da Vinci Code* was not the first novel to handle the question of Jesus' sexuality. The controversial *The Last Temptation of Jesus* by Nikos Kazantzakis, published in 1960, pictured a Jesus being tempted to take Mary Magdalene as his wife but not acting on

1. Phipps, *Was Jesus Married?*
2. Phipps, *Was Jesus Married*, 9.
3. Erskine, *Human Life of Jesus*, 27–28.
4. Montefiore, *For God's Sake,* 182.

Appendix A: Why Did Jesus Not Marry?

the temptation.[5] So, when Phipps came to his task in 1970, he had a few allies already at hand.

His main line of argument was Jewish custom. Fathers found brides for their sons while their sons were still quite young. This was the pattern, as Phipps quite rightly indicates, throughout the ancient Near East and the Greco-Roman world.[6]

Rabbinic Texts on Marriage

Here are the pertinent rabbinic texts on marrying one's children:

> ... at eighteen [one is fit] for the bride-chamber ... (m. Avot 5:21; trans. Danby[7])

> Someone twenty years of age and not married spends his whole day in sin ... Once [a man] reaches the age of twenty and has not married, he says, "Blast be his bones" ... While your hand is still on your son's neck, marry him off, that is, between sixteen and ... twenty-four. (b. Qidd. 29b-30a; trans. Neusner[8])

> ... he who raises up his sons and daughters in the right path, and he who marries them off close to the time of their puberty—of such a one, Scripture says, "And you shall know that your tabernacle shall be in peace and you shall visit your habitation and you shall not sin." (b. Sanh. 76b; trans. Neusner)

> What is a commandment pertaining to the father concerning the son? To circumcise him, to redeem him [if he is kidnapped], and to teach him Torah, and to teach him a trade, and to marry him off to a girl. (t. Qidd. 1:11; trans. Neusner[9])

In Chapter 5 of this volume, we even expanded on Phipps' evidence. There we listed several texts—rabbinic texts—that showed a decided inclination to marry boys in their teenage years. But what the rabbis deemed "normal" or desirable practice might not always have had purchase among the common folk of the villages. Even if these *were* the common practices, however, a historian always has to make room for the uncommon. After all, people are not robots; they think and act independently sometimes.

---

5. Kazantzakis, *The Last Temptation of Christ*.

6. Phipps, *Was Jesus Married?*, 22. Phipps cites in support of his contention the code of Hammurabi (#166). And see more recently Phipps, "Itinerating Wives," where he once again stresses that Joseph would "probably have arranged marriage for Jesus" (396). In the latter work, Phipps cites b. Qidd. 29a [=t. Qidd. 1:11]. For another author who follows the same line of argument, see Padovano, "Possible That Jesus Was Married?"

7. Danby, *The Mishnah*.

8. Neusner, *The Babylonian Talmud*.

9. Neusner, *The Tosephta*.

Appendix A: Why Did Jesus Not Marry?

If one married, he would probably have married young. But what if one did not marry? That was rare according to the rabbis. The necessity of marriage for men was a widespread conviction in rabbinic Judaism. Again, the rabbis state: He who has no wife is not a proper man (b. Yebam. 63b; b. Pes. 113b; Gen. R. 172). Only one devoted to the intense study of the Torah could be excused from marriage (b. Yebam. 63b; b. Sotah 4b; Gen. R. 31.14; t. Yebam. 8:14). Rabbi Ben-Azzai responded to criticism for not being married: "What am I supposed to do? My soul lusts only after Torah. Let others have children" (b. Yebam. 63b; translation Neusner).

Additionally, one totally given over to one's work, even if not Torah, could be excused for postponing marriage (Test. Iss. 3:5[10]). Other than for work or study, young people were expected to marry. It was one of the important duties of fatherhood to find a son a wife and a daughter a husband (b. Qidd. 30a; t. Qidd. 1:11).

Rabbinic Texts on Bachelors

Yet there were bachelors. R. Safra was a bachelor (b. Pes. 113b). Another Talmudic passage praises two bachelors, R. Hanina and R. Oshaya, who were shoemakers in Jerusalem and had a shop on the same street as the brothels and yet remained righteous (b. Pes. 113b). The Yalkut lists seven classes of righteous men in paradise, among them the bachelors who remain sinless.[11] The Mishnah lists three brothers and indicates that only two of them were married (m. 'Ed. 4:9). Further, Tal Ilan argues that Agrippa II was a bachelor.[12] R. Aqiba, the great early second-century scholar, lived as a bachelor for 24 years before he married (b. Ket. 63a). Here are some of the texts referring to unmarried males:

> Over three does the Holy One, blessed be He, issue a proclamation every day: a single man who lives in a big city without sin . . . R. Safra was a single man living in a big city. (b. Pes. 113b; trans. Neusner)

> R. Hanina and R. Oshayya (bachelors) were cobblers in the Land of Israel, who lived on Whore Street and made shoes for the whores and went to them. The whores looked at them, but they wouldn't raise their eyes to look at them, and the whore's oath was "by the life of the holy rabbis of the Land of Israel." (b. Pes. 113 b; trans. Neusner)

> If there were three brothers, two married to two sisters, and one unmarried . . . (m. 'Ed. 4:9; trans. Danby)

---

10. Issachar on his death bed remembers that he was only married at age thirty-five. Kee, "Testaments," 803.
11. See Montefiore and Loewe, *A Rabbinic Anthology*, 598.
12. Ilan, *Jewish Women*, 63.

> In paradise there are seven classes of the righteous ... The sixth class consists of the bachelors who have remained sinless all their lives. (Yalkut; trans. Montefiore and Loewe[13])

But we must remember that these are rabbinic sources. Both Philo and Josephus describe the Essenes (at least part of them) as eschewing marriage (Philo, *Hypoth.* 11.14; Josephus, *War* 2.120). We would also suppose that John the Baptist was not married. Jesus even refers to those who were "eunuchs" by choice in Matt 19:12. Was he alluding to the Essenes or were there others in the late Second Temple period who refused marriage due to religious devotion?

At any rate, there were unmarried men in Palestine in Jesus' time. It is inadequate to argue that Jesus must have been married because that is what Jewish boys did. There were exceptions to this practice.

Who Was Mary Magdalene?

Second, Phipps readily accepted the church's identification of Mary Magdalene, Mary of Bethany, and the "sinful woman" of Luke 7. Thus, the woman in Luke was the (at that time) sinful Mary Magdalene who was converted by Jesus and later married him.[14] Although Phipps' identification of these three figures was not presented with a compelling argument (and even if true would not necessarily indicate that Jesus married this woman!), and although some feminist scholars today complain of the identification of Mary Magdalene with a prostitute as a slander, one increasingly finds this conclusion assumed.

The idea that Mary Magdalene was a former prostitute or adulteress is certainly not in the New Testament. She is rather a witness to the crucifixion of Jesus (Matt 27:56; John 19:25), to the burial (Matt 27:61), and to the empty tomb (Matt 28:1; Luke 24:10; John 20:1). She also is the first, or one of the first, to see the risen Lord (John 20:10–18). The Gospel of Luke characterizes her as a former demoniac (Luke 8:2). But there is no trace of a sinful past.

The idea that Mary Magdalene had been a sinful woman first arose in the sixth century when Gregory, in a sermon, synthesized the story in Luke 7 of the sinful woman with the references to Mary Magdalene.[15] Thus, the picture of Mary Magdalene as a prostitute/adulteress is late and unbiblical.

Further, why must we think Mary Magdalene was a youthful woman? Since she is usually presented as the leader of a group of women, we might think of her as older. In a society where few women lived into their fifties or sixties, a woman of that age would be looked up to as a person of wisdom. Perhaps she was twenty or thirty years

---

13. Montefiore and Loewe, *A Rabbinic Anthology*, 598.
14. Phipps, *Was Jesus Married?*, 64.
15. See Pearson, "Did Jesus Marry?," 36–37; R. Collins, "Mary."

older than Jesus, hardly the stuff of a Hallmark movie. The idea of a romance between the two of them seems to me a western fantasy.

Popular Views

Today the view that Jesus and Mary Magdalene were husband and wife is popular especially among the sensationalist authors. Baigent, Leigh, and Lincoln, in *Holy Blood, Holy Grail*, the book that inspired Dan Brown, write that Jesus was certainly married since an unmarried rabbi was forbidden.[16] Further, they maintain that the wedding at Cana (John 2) was Jesus' own wedding and that Jesus' wife was either Mary Magdalene or Mary of Bethany.[17] Barbara Thiering[18] added her name to the list of those who believe that Jesus was married to Mary Magdalene and of course the famous *Da Vinci Code*'s Dan Brown made his case as well.[19] Even the Jesus Seminar concluded that Jesus "had a relationship with Mary Magdalene," i.e. that he was not celibate.[20]

Those who insist that Jesus was married to Mary Magdalene rely mostly—besides circumstantial evidence such as that Mary Magdalene first saw the risen Christ—on the third century CE Gospel of Philip. This text states that Mary Magdalene was Jesus' "companion" and also that Jesus used to "kiss her [often] on her [mouth]."[21] To these statements some add the reference in the second century Gospel of Mary that Jesus loved Mary Magdalene more than he loved the other disciples.

Here are the main texts usually cited:

Nag Hammadi Texts

> There were three who always walked with the Lord: Mary his mother and her sister and Magdalene, the one who was called his companion (Gos. Phil., *NH* II, 3, 59; trans. Isenberg)

> And the companion of the [Savior is] Mary Magdalene. [But Christ loved] her more than [all] the disciples [and used to] kiss her [often] on her [mouth]. (Gos. Phil., *NH* II, 3, 63; trans. Isenberg)

> Assuredly the Savior's knowledge of her is completely reliable. That is why he loved her more than us. (Gos. Mary; trans. King[22])

---

16. Baigent, Leigh, and Lincoln, *Holy Blood*, 331. They cite Phipps, *Was Jesus Married?*, as evidence for this statement. This use of Phipps is, in my judgment, an exaggeration.
17. *Holy Blood*, 332–338. It is erroneous to assert that "an unmarried rabbi was forbidden."
18. Thiering, *Jesus and the Riddle*, 87–88.
19. Dan Brown, *The Da Vinci Code*, 246–47.
20. Funk and Hoover, *Five Gospels*, 221.
21. Translation is from Isenberg, "The Gospel of Philip," 136, 138. Notice that the word "mouth" is in brackets indicating that this is a hypothetical restoration.
22. See the translation of Karen L. King, *Mary of Magdalen*, 21.

Yet Birger A. Pearson, a noted expert on Gnosticism and one of the translators of the Nag Hammadi scrolls, disagrees. First, he notes that neither of these texts claims that Jesus was married to anyone. Second, the words translated "companion" in the Gospel of Philip—ΚΟΙΝΩΝΟC (*koinōnos*) a Greek loanword, in one instance and *hotre*, a Coptic word, in the second—can be translated business partner, fellow member, perhaps a paramour, or sharer in something but never "spouse." Third, Jesus' kissing Mary is a reference to the liturgical kiss that is mentioned several other times in the Gospel of Philip and is common in both the New Testament and other Nag Hammadi texts. For example, Pearson notes that in the Second Apocalypse of James, Jesus kisses his brother James on the mouth.[23] Fourth, he adds, why should we believe what a third century text tells us about the historical Jesus?[24]

This might be the appropriate place to report briefly on the sensational "Gospel of Jesus' Wife" papyrus text brought to light in 2012 and published in 2014.[25] The tiny fragment read at one point, "Jesus said to them, 'My wife . . .'" Those words alone were enough to create a stir in the academic and ecclesiastical communities. Yet the text was received with wariness from the start. The same publication that presented the text carried also an article challenging its authenticity.[26] This summary rejection of its authenticity was followed by an almost entire issue of *New Testament Studies* one year later that was devoted to this text. In this issue, four authors[27] unambiguously rejected the authenticity of the fragment and one examined again the evidence for Jesus' having been married, finding that it is lacking.[28] Thus, this new fragmentary text is of no help in our determination.

Conclusion on Jesus' Marital Status

So, was Jesus married? I would not deny it on theological grounds. That is to say, it does not offend my theology to think of Jesus as married. To me it would not be diminishing of his deity, for those who are Trinitarian in theology, if he had been married to a nice Jewish girl and had a few children. To be offended at the idea of Jesus' being married would be to view sexuality *per se* as sinful. My theology rejects that notion.

---

23. See *Nag Hammadi Library*, 253.
24. Pearson, "Did Jesus Marry?"
25. See K. King, "New Coptic Papyrus."
26. Depuydt, "Alleged Gospel." The author of this article states that it is "out of the question that the so-called *Gospel of Jesus' Wife* . . . is authentic."
27. Askeland, "Lycopolitan"; Bernard, "Gospel"; Jones, "Jesus' Wife"; Robinson, "Papyrus Fragment."
28. Gathercole, "Gospel." He looks at evidence in the Gospel of Philip, in the Gospel of Thomas, and in Epiphanius, *Pan.* 49.1.2–3. He states that Jesus is never said to be married but is depicted in somewhat intimate ways as granting revelation.

APPENDIX A: WHY DID JESUS NOT MARRY?

Yet, as a historian, I would argue that Jesus was not married for three reasons: First, no gospel writer (or any other ancient source for that matter) ever wrote that Jesus had a wife or mistress. We can plead all we want based on what "would have been" appropriate for a Jewish young man. People are not rubber stamps of one another. It is a naïve and simplistic historiography that disallows exceptions to customs.

Second, there seems to have been a trajectory of celibacy among some of the devoted followers of Jesus on into middle and late first century. Paul indicates that neither he nor Barnabas was married though some of the apostles were (1 Cor. 9:5). Philip had four unmarried daughters that prophesied (Acts 21:9). The book of Revelation celebrates the 144,000 male virgins (14:4).[29] The question is, who started this trajectory? I suggest that Jesus did and that Matt 19:12 ("there are those who have made themselves eunuchs for the kingdom of heaven.") witnesses to the beginning of the trajectory.

Third, Jesus took what must have looked like a rather anti-family stance for himself and his closest group of disciples:

> And his mother and brothers standing outside (the house) sent word to him and summoned him. And there was a crowd seated around him and they said to him, "Look, your mother and brothers outside are seeking you." He answered and said to them, "Who is my mother and (who are) my brothers?" And he looked around at those sitting about him and said, "See, my mother and my brothers. For whoever does the will of God is my brother, my sister and my mother." (Mark 3:31–35 and par.; Gos. Thom. 99; Gos. Ebion.; 2 Clem. 9:11)

> And it came to pass when he had said these things that a certain woman from the crowd lifted up her voice and said, "Blessed is the womb which bore you and the breasts which nursed you." But he said, "Blessed are those who hear the word of God and keep it." (Luke 11:27–28; Gos. Thom. 79)

> If anyone comes to me and does not hate his father, mother, wife, children, brothers, and sisters, yes, even his own life, he cannot be my disciple. (Luke 14:26 and par.; Gos. Thom. 55; cf. Gos. Thom. 101; and Mark 10:29–30)[30]

> "A prophet is not without honor except in his hometown, among his kinsfolk and in his own house." (Mark 6:4 and par.; John 4:44; Gos. Thom. 31; POxy 1.30–35)

One could certainly get the impression from these texts that Jesus has separated from his family. He is, if not estranged from them, at least not performing the expected familial obligations. In the first text, Jesus explains that his family now is his followers. He has created a new, fictive family. In the second text, Jesus deflects praise for his

---

29. See Amy-Jill Levine, "The Word Becomes Flesh."

30. See Stein, "Luke 14:26," who notes that this text also meets the criteria of dissimilarity and coherence (cf. Mark 10:29–30; 13:12–13). Wright (*Jesus*, 401f) adds to these texts about family Mark 10:29–30, Jesus' promise of reward for those who have left houses and family.

mother (which is indirect praise for himself) by praising those who keep the word of God. In the third text, Jesus actually advises his followers to "hate" their kinfolk, an absolute horror for first century Jewish persons, an example of Semitic hyperbole.[31] In the last text, we infer that Jesus' family does not honor him.

On the other hand, Jesus is also found affirming care for parents, which seems out of place in one who has abandoned his family (Mark 7:9–12; 10:19; John 19:26–27) and he disallows divorce (Matt 5:31–32//Luke 16:18; Mark 10:2–12//Matt 19:3–12; see Table 5.4 above). How can we explain someone who seems both anti-family and pro-family at the same time?

E. P. Sanders suggests that Jesus had three groups of followers: 1) Close disciples 2) Slightly more remote followers 3) Still more remote sympathizers or supporters. In group one were the Twelve. In group two were Levi, the tax collector; the women of Galilee (especially Mary Magdalene); and the 120 persons in the Upper Room (Acts 1:14). In group three were people such as Simon, the Pharisee; Zaccheus; Joseph of Arimathea; and Mary and Martha of Bethany.[32] Group three comprised the "sympathizers" who stayed at home, kept their families, and supported his ministry with their finances. Groups one and two were the radical followers who left everything (possessions and families) to follow him. Thus, for his sympathizers there is marriage without divorce. But for his close followers there was no marriage. I do not think that Jesus would have divorced his wife, if he had had one, in order to practice his itinerant prophetic ministry and then disallowed others to divorce. And I think he would have required the same lifestyle for himself as he did for his intimate group of disciples. Thus, it seems to me that he did not have a wife at the time of his ministry and never had one (but it is possible he had a wife as a younger man and that she had died. See Chapter 10.)

WHY DID JESUS NOT MARRY?

If Jesus had never married, why, therefore, was Jesus not given a wife as a teenager? At least three answers have been proposed for these questions? We may call these suggestions:

1. The Economic

---

31. I.e. "hate" in the metaphorical sense of "not prefer." Cf. Deut. 24:3; Mal. 1:2–3. In the parallel passage in Matt. 10:37, the language is less hyperbolic (and less Semitic): "The one loving father or mother more than me is not worthy of me; the one loving son or daughter more than me is not worthy of me."

32. Sanders, *Historical Figure of Jesus*, 123–126. Cf. Wright, *Jesus*, 300; Meye, *Jesus and the Twelve*, 118–124; and especially Theissen and Merz, *Historical Jesus*, 217, 378, who suggest that concentric circles formed around Jesus: a staff of secondary charismatics (the Twelve) and a wider circle of sympathizers who did not leave their homes. Those who have accepted the view of Theissen and Merz include: Duling, "Jesus Movement;" and Crossan, "Itinerants and Householders," who suggests two groups for the early (post-Easter) Jesus movement: itinerants and householders.

2. The Ascetic

3. The Charismatic

The Economic View

The economic explanation for Jesus' celibacy is simply that he was too poor to afford a wife. This is the view offered by John Dominic Crossan. Crossan argues that, unlike John the Baptist who was an ascetic and would have refused a wife, Jesus would probably have gladly accepted one if his family could have afforded it. Jesus was no ascetic (Matt 11:18–19//Luke 7:33–34). Rather, Jesus was not married because he was a "dispossessed peasant." He and his family were not skilled carpenters. To be a τέκτων meant to be a "manual laborer." Jesus never had a chance to marry because of the extreme poverty of his life. He never married because of "injustice."[33]

I would make two arguments in response to Crossan's suggestion: First, I do not agree that Jesus' family was that poor. Crossan has only assumed this level of poverty and has not responsibly handled the word τέκτων.[34] Second, there is evidence that even the poorest young man in antiquity could marry (See Chapter 5). A text in the Tosephta (t. Ket. 6:8) states that if an orphan wished to marry, they would rent him a house and offer him a bed and afterwards a wife. In other words, the village would "pitch-in" to provide a poor boy without family the means to take a wife. The practice of making allowances for marriage for poor persons is apparently done in contemporary traditional societies in the Middle East. A recent ethnography of a Jordanian village noted that poor villagers commonly married without paying a bride price if a young man had a sister who could marry his bride's brother.[35]

The Ascetic View

The ascetic explanation for Jesus' refusal to marry takes at least two forms. The first form of this explanation has been offered by G. W. Buchanan. It suggests that Jesus and his group of disciples formed a monastic community like the Essenes.[36] This community was celibate, communistic, male, and dispossessed of family ties and personal possessions. Buchanan places the most emphasis on the celibacy of the community, as he sees it, by organizing and understanding all of the other features of his monastic construction around that feature. The celibacy was necessary, he opines, to avoid ritual defilement from women (from menstruation and from sexual relations).[37]

33. Crossan, "Why Didn't Jesus Marry?"
34. See Fiensy, *Jesus the Galilean*, 66–83.
35. Lutfiyya, *Baytin*, 133.
36. Josephus, *War* 2.120 says that the Essenes spurned marriage
37. Buchanan, "Jesus and Other Monks." Others have also suggested that Jesus' marital practices

Yet, Buchanan's argument fails, it seems to me. There are references to women being a part of Jesus' ministry (Luke 8:1–3; Mark 15:40-41). Thus, they must have been in the company of Jesus and the Twelve. Further, impurity from menstruation is contracted not only by sexual relations—which were taboo at any rate during menstruation (Lev. 15:24)—but also, for instance, by sitting where a menstruating woman has sat (Lev. 15:20). Just being near women could lead to impurity from menstruation. Buchanan seems to assume that contracting ritual impurity was sinful, which was not the case (see Chapter 12). Thus, it does not appear that Jesus organized his lifestyle around celibacy in order to avoid ritual impurity from female menstruation.

The second form of the ascetic explanation comes from Dale Allison.[38] He has proposed the view that Jesus' behavior was based on millennarian asceticism. When groups become millennarian enthusiasts (swept up in fervor over the coming new age or millennium), they often quit their jobs, engage in fasting, and forgo marriage. Allison points to the life of poverty and the celibacy of the early Jesus movement as evidence that it was an ascetic movement motivated by the imminent coming of the kingdom of God.

Millennarian enthusiasm as the reason for the "asceticism," however, is a problem.

The problem is that if eschatological enthusiasm was the cause of the asceticism, it seems that Jesus would have asked everyone to sell off the farm and leave his/her family instead of just a select group. Clearly, several of Jesus' disciples surrendered their possessions and left their extended families in order to follow him. They either abandoned their houses, fishing boats, tax tables and families, or they sold off their possessions in order to follow him.

But, surprisingly, the Gospels and Acts also refer to persons who still owned property and had families as among those who believed in him and helped him. These references are scattered across several sources, indicating that this theme is not the work of an editor:

- **There are several named who still own their houses**: Luke 10:31–42 (Mary and Martha; cf. John 11:20, 12:1–2); Luke 14:1 (a rich Pharisee); Mark 13:15 (some will possess houses when the tribulation comes); Mark 14:14–15 (the Upper Room of the Last Supper); Acts 9:36 (Tabitha); and 12:12 (Mary of Jerusalem)

- **There are several who give alms**: Matt 6:3–4 (=Luke 6:34–35); Acts 11:27–30.

(or lack of them) came from the influence of the Essenes. Those affirming that Jesus was influenced by the Essenes at least regarding their views of wealth are: Flusser, *Judaism and the Origins of Christianity*, 153, 169, 196; Charlesworth, "Dead Sea Scrolls," 18, 38; Charlesworth, *Jesus within Judaism*, 59–61; Broshi, *Bread, Wine*, 253, 258; Broshi, "What Jesus Learned," 32; Braun, *Spaetjuedisch-haeretischer und fruechristlicher Rakikalismus*, II, 73. But J. Murphy-O'Connor, who also notes a close comparison between the attitudes of Jesus and the Essenes on wealth, rejects direct dependence as do F. G. Martinez and J. T. Barrera. See for O'Connor, "Qumran and the New Testament," 58; for Martinez and Barrera, *People of the Dead Sea Scrolls*, 207.

38. Allison, *Jesus of Nazareth*, 172–215.

- **Jesus is the guest of rich persons. He seems to accept their food without reproaching them for being wealthy**: Mark 2:15; Luke 7:36; 11:37; 19:5-7.
- **There are some rich persons who come to Jesus' aid**: Luke 8:1-3 (the rich Galilean women; cf. Mark 15:40-41); and Mark 15:43 (Joseph of Arimathea).[39]
- In addition to associating with wealthy friends, **Jesus is also found affirming care for parents**, which also seems out of place in one who has abandoned his family (Mark 7:9-12, 10:19; John 19:26-27) and forbidding divorce.

As we reported above, E.P. Sanders[40] suggests that Jesus had three groups of followers. This suggestion makes eminently good sense to me. Jesus' closest disciples (category one) were called upon to abandon their homes and livelihoods and follow him. Those in category three were not urged to do that.

Thus, the Jesus movement had at least two tiers of obedience. Those in the bottom tier would have been summoned to believe in and await the kingdom of God but not to follow him around. They would have supported Jesus' ministry with their resources but would not have given away all of their possessions or left their families. Thus, the presence of disciples with wealth and families seems to me to refute the idea that Jesus was unmarried because he was an ascetic. Some of his disciples perhaps were like him but not all.

The Charismatic View

We need an explanation that accounts for both Jesus' renunciation of possessions and his breaking family ties for himself and some (but not all) of his disciples. Further, we must explain why he required these harsh measures for some, but not for others (the sympathizers). I would like to suggest that the third view—that Jesus was a charismatic—is the most helpful model and the one that explains all of the information the best. Scholars, that have investigated this type in history, use somewhat differing terminology (Holy Man, Charismatic, Spirit Person),[41] but mean essentially the same thing.

The classic statement, about this historical type, is by Max Weber. Weber used the term charismatic in a very broad sense of military leaders, leaders of the hunt, healers, shamans, "berserks," those with legal wisdom, and prophets. We will focus on the last manifestation of this type.

---

39. See van Campenhausen, *Tradition and Life*, 95; Johnson, *Sharing Possessions*, 16-22; Mealand, *Poverty*, 105-106; and Hengel, *Property and Riches*, 27-28.

40. Sanders, *Historical Figure of Jesus*, 123-126.

41. See Hengel, *Charismatic Leader*, 16-18; Borg, *Conflict, Holiness, and Politics*, 88, 240-241; Vermes, *Jesus the Jew*, 58-77; Theissen and Merz, *Historical Jesus*, 215; P. Brown, "Holy Man in Late Antiquity," 80-100.

APPENDIX A: WHY DID JESUS NOT MARRY?

Weber explained that there were essentially three types of authority: There are first the Rational Grounds of authority, (which rest on the belief that those in power have been elevated to it by approved legal means). Second, there are Traditional Grounds of authority, (which are based on an established belief in the sanctity of traditions). Finally, there is charismatic authority, which rests on "devotion to the exceptional sanctity, heroism or exemplary character of an individual person."[42]

According to Weber, "charisma" is applied to persons:

1. Who were considered endowed with supernatural, superhuman, or at least exceptional powers
2. Who called disciples based on the charismatic qualifications of those summoned
3. Who, along with his disciples, took no salary and who tended to live communally by means of the voluntary gifts of sympathizers.[43]

Weber writes:

> Pure charisma is specifically foreign to economic considerations.[44]

> In order to live up to their mission the master as well as his disciples and immediate following must be free of the ordinary worldly attachments and duties of occupational and family life. Those who have a share . . . in charisma must inevitably turn away from the world.[45]

Martin Hengel[46] has reminded us of this type of prophet in his groundbreaking work. After Elijah summoned Elisha to the prophetic, charismatic life (as Elisha was plowing the fields with one of his twelve teams of oxen), Elisha turned back, slaughtered all twenty-four oxen (thus repudiating any economic security) and followed Elijah (1 Kgs 19:19–21). It was a radical break with his past and with society.

Likewise, Jeremiah was forbidden to take a wife and have a family (Jer 16:1–4), to mourn the dead (vv. 5–7), and to attend banquets and feasting (vv. 8–9). He displayed "anti-social behavior" as a sign to Israel. He lived the life of a charismatic man which meant living often as an outsider, as one who renounced the social norms of his day.

Finally, Ezekiel was not allowed to mourn the death of his wife, a symbol of the coming profanation of the temple (Ezek. 24:15–18), as a sign to Israel. He gave up

---

42. Weber, *Economy and Society*. 1.215.

43. Weber, *Economy and Society*, 1.241–245. Weber defines charisma as follows: "The term 'charisma' will be applied to a certain quality of an individual personality by virtue of which he is considered extraordinary and treated as endowed with supernatural, superhuman, or at least specifically exceptional powers or qualities" (p. 241).

44. Weber, Economy and Society, 1.244.

45. Weber, *Economy and Society*, 1.244–245. Quote in 3.1113–1114. Weber considered both Buddha and Francis of Assisi examples of charismatic leaders. They also renounced possessions and family to live a life of homelessness and poverty.

46. Hengel, *Charismatic Leader*, 11–16.

what was a very strong obligation of society (and the heart, Chapter 11) to live the life of a charismatic prophet.

I would like to propose that Jesus' renunciation of possessions and family be understood within this historical type. Jesus' miracles and exorcisms; his renunciation of possessions, home, family, and occupation; and his calling of disciples to behave in the same way certainly suggest that Jesus fits this type. Jesus' authority was charismatic in the sense that Weber explained. Charismatics live apart from the world. They cannot become bogged down in the normal ways of life. They do not hold down a regular job, receive a salary, or otherwise engage in ordinary life. They are exceptional persons, living by the grace of God and by the contributions of adherents. They do not necessarily renounce all possessions—except in certain situations—but they do always renounce entanglements in society.

Thus, Jesus as a charismatic leader renounced his possessions and family and lived the life of an itinerant, teacher, demanding also that his closest disciples—at least temporarily[47]—do the same.[48] The Weberian type explains why Jesus considered it necessary to renounce family, home, occupation, and possessions. His mission took precedence as it did for Elisha, Jeremiah, and Ezekiel. He could not stay in the village and remain with the family.

This explanation further suggests that Jesus as a teenager refused a wife, that he already knew of his special calling. Did he receive a call like those of Elisha, Jeremiah, and Ezekiel? One can certainly surmise that he did.

---

47. We assume that negation of family was viewed by disciples, such as Peter, as temporary, since years later he is said to have had a wife (1 Cor 9:5).

48. Wright, *Victory*, 400, who explains Jesus' demand for renunciation of possessions as follows: "I am suggesting . . . that Jesus was an eschatological prophet, announcing the kingdom"; Davies and Allison, *Matthew*, 2.57: "[P]rophets (such as Jeremiah and Ezekiel) transgress custom in order to proclaim through unusual actions the coming judgment of God"; L. Goppelt, *Theology of the New Testament*, 1.83; R. Schnackenburg, *Moral Teachings*, 142; Hengel, *Charismatic Leader*, 16–18; Guijarro, "Family in the Jesus Movement."

Appendix B
Archaeological Periods Of Palestine[1]

ARCHAEOLOGICAL PERIOD	ABBREVIATION	DATES
Iron IA		1200–1150 BCE
Iron IB		1150–1000 BCE
Iron IIA		1000–925 BCE
Iron IIB		925–720 BCE
Iron IIC		720–586 BCE
Persian		586–333 BCE
Hellenistic I	Hell I	333–152 BCE
Hellenistic II	Hell II	152–37 BCE
(Hasmonean 125–63 BCE)[2]		
Early Roman I (=Late Second Temple Period)	ER I	37 BCE—70 CE
Early Roman II	ER II	70–135 CE[3]
Middle Roman	MR	135–250 CE
Late Roman	LR	250–363 CE
Byzantine I	Byz 1	363–451 CE
Byzantine II	Byz 2	451–640 CE
Early Arab		640–1099 CE
Crusader and Ayyubid		1099–1291 CE
Late Arab		1291–1516
Ottoman		1516–1917

1. Table composed from dates in Mazar, *Archaeology*, 30; Fiensy and Strange, *Galilee I*, ix; and Levy, *Archaeology of Society*, xvi.
2. Following Root, *Galilee*, 7, in further delineating the Hellenistic II period.
3. Again, following Root, *Galilee*, 7.

Bibliography

Abah, A. E., and G. D. B. Awi-Waadu. "Gastro-intestinal Helminthiasis among School Children in Gokana and Khana Local Government Areas of Rivers State, Nigeria." *Primary Health Care* 8/4 (2018). Online: file:///E:/Documents/Daily%20Life/articles/Gastro-intestinal_Helminthiasis_among_Sc.pdf.

Abegg, Martin, Jr., Peter Flint, and Eugene Ulrich. *The Dead Sea Scrolls Bible.* New York: HarperCollins, 1999.

Adams, Samuel L. *Social and Economic Life in Second Temple Judea.* Louisville: Westminster John Knox, 2014.

Adan-Bayewitz, David. "Kefar Hananya, 1986." *IEJ* 37 (1987) 178–79.

———. *Common Pottery in Roman Galilee.* Ramat-Gan: Bar-Ilan University Press, 1993.

Adan-Bayewitz, David and I. Perlman. "The Local Trade of Sepphoris in the Roman Period." *IEJ* 40 (1990) 153–72.

———. "The Socio-Economic and Cultural Ethos of the Lower Galilee in the First Century: Implications for the Nascent Jesus Movement." In *The Galilee in Late Antiquity,* edited by Lee I. Levine, 53–91. New York: Jewish Theological Seminary, 1992.

Adan-Bayewitz, David, and Mordechai Aviam. "Iotapa, Josephus, and the Siege of 67: Preliminary Report on the 1992–1994 Seasons." *Journal of Roman Archaeology* 10 (1997) 131–65.

Adan-Bayewitz, D., F. Asaro, M. Wieder, and R. D Giauque. "Preferential Distribution of Lamps from the Jerusalem Area in the Late Second Temple Period (Late First Century B.C.E.—70 C.E.)." *BASOR* 350 (2008) 37–85.

Adler, Yonatan. "The Archaeology of Purity: Archaeological Evidence for the Observance of Ritual Purity in Erez-Israel from the Hasmonean Period until the End of the Talmudic Era (164 BCE—400 CE)." Ph.D. diss., Bar Ilan University, 2011.

———. "Purity in the Roman Period." In *OEBA* 2:240–49.

———. "A Quantitative Analysis of Jewish Chalk Vessel Frequencies in Early Roman Jerusalem: A View from the City's Garbage Dump." *IEJ* 66 (2016) 202–19.

———. "Second Temple Period Ritual Baths Adjacent to Agricultural Installations: The Archaeological Evidence in Light of the Halakhic Sources." *JJS* 59 (2008) 62–72.

Aharoni, Yohanan. *The Land of the Bible: A Historical Geography.* Philadelphia: Westminster, 1979.

Ahuja, Masuma. "What's a Day in the Life of a Girl Look Like in 10 Countries? Meet Jennifer in Nigeria, Sophie in the United States, Anjali in India and Girls From Seven Other Countries." *The Lilly* September 27, 2018 Online: https://www.thelily.com/whats-a-day-in-the-life-of-a-girl-look-like-in-10-countries-sign-up-for-the-lilys-girlhood-around-the-world-for-a-look.

Alexandre, Yardenna. "Karm er-Ras Near Kafr Kanna." In *GLSTMP* 2:146–57.

Alföldy, Géza. *Die Römische Gesellschaft: Ausgewählte Beiträge*. Heidelberger althistorische Beiträge und epigraphische Studien 1. Stuttgart: Steiner, 1986.

———. *Römische Sozialgeschichte*. Wiesbaden: Steiner, 1975.

———. *The Social History of Rome*. Translated by David Braund and Frank Pollock. London: Croom Helm, 1985.

Alkier, Stefan and Jürgen Zangenberg. "Zeichen aus Text und Stein—Einladung zu einem interdisciplinären Gespräch." In *Zeichen aus Text und Stein: Studien auf dem Weg zu einer Archäologie des Neuen Testaments*, edited by Stefan Alkier and Jürgen Zangenberg, x–xvi. Tübingen: Francke, 2003.

Allison, Dale. *Jesus of Nazareth*. Minneapolis: Fortress, 1998.

Alston, Richard. "Houses and Households in Roman Egypt." In *Domestic Space in the Roman World: Pompeii and Beyond*, edited by Ray Laurence and Andrew Wallace-Hadrill, 25–39. Portsmouth, RI: Journal of Roman Archaeology, 1997.

Amiry, Suad, and Vera Tamari. *The Palestinian Village Home*. London: British Museum, 1989.

Amit, David. "The Miqva'ot." In *Gamla II: The Architecture, The Shmarya Gutmann Excavations, 1976–1989*, edited by Danny Syon and Zvi-Yavor, 193–96. Jerusalem: IAA, 2010.

Amorai-Stark, Shua, and Malka Hershkovitz. "Jewelry." In *Gamla III: The Shmarya Gutmann Excavations 1976–1989 Finds and Studies. Part 2*, edited by Danny Syon, 97–189. Jerusalem: IAA, 2014.

Anastasiou, Evilena et al. "Infectious Disease in the Ancient Aegean: Intestinal Parasitic Worms in the Neolithic to Roman Period Inhabits of Kea, Greece." *Journal of Archaeological Science* (2017), online: https://www.academia.edu.

Andreau, Jean. "Wages: Classical Antiquity." In *BNP* 15:542–44.

Angel, J. Lawrence. "Ecology and Population in the Eastern Mediterranean." *World Archaeology* 4/1 (1972) 88–105.

———. "Length of Life in Ancient Greece." *Journal of Gerontology* 2 (1947) 18–24.

Angela, Alberto. *A Day in the Life of Ancient Rome*. New York: Europa, 2009.

Applebaum, S. "The Zealots: The Case for Reevaluation." *JRS* 61 (1971) 155–70.

———. "Economic Life in Palestine." In *The Jewish People in the First Century*. Edited by S. Safrai and M. Stern, 631–700. Compendia Rerum Iudicarum I/2. Assen: Van Gorcum, 1976.

———. *Judaea in Hellenistic and Roman Times: Historical and Archaeological Essays*. Studies in Judaism in Late Antiquity 40. Leiden: Brill, 1989.

———. "Judea as a Roman Province: The Countryside as a Political and Economic Factor." In *ANRW* II.8 (1978) 355–96.

———. "The Problem of the Roman Villa in Eretz Israel." *Eretz Israel* 19 (1987) 1–5.

———. "The Settlement Pattern of Western Samaria from Hellenistic to Byzantine Times." In *Landscape and Pattern: An Archaeological Survey of Samaria 800 B.C.E.—636 C.E.*, edited by Shimon Dar, 255–69. BAR International Series 308. Oxford: BAR, 1986.

Arav, Rami. "Bethsaida Excavations: Preliminary Report, 1994–1996." In *Bethsaida*, edited by Rami Arav and Richard Freund, 2:3–113. Kirksville, MO: Truman State University Press, 1999.

Arbel, Yoav. *Ultimate Devotion: The Historical Impact and Archaeological Expression of Intense Religious Movements*. Approaches to Anthropological Archaeology. London: Equinox, 2009.

Archer, Léonie J. *Her Price Is Beyond Rubies: The Jewish Woman in Graeco-Roman Palestine*. JSOTSup 60. Sheffield: Sheffield Academic, 1990.

Arensburg, B., and Y. Rak. "Skeletal Remains of an Ancient Jewish Population from French Hill, Jerusalem." *BASOR* 219 (1975) 69–71.

Arensburg, B., and Anna Belfer-Cohen. "Preliminary Report on the Skeletal Remains from the ʿEn Gedi Tombs." *Atiqot* 24 (1994) 12–14.

Arensburg, B., and Patricia Smith. "Anthropological Tables." In *Jericho: The Jewish Cemetery of the Second Temple Period*, edited by Rachel Hachlili and Ann E. Killebrew, 192–94. Jerusalem: Israel Antiquities Authority, 1999.

———. "Appendix: the Jewish Population of Jericho 100 BC—70AD." *PEQ* 115 (1983) 133–39.

Arieli, Rotem. "Human Remains from the Har Haẓofim Observatory Tombs (Mt. Scopus, Jerusalem)." *Atiqot* 35 (1998) 37–42.

Askeland, Christian. "A Lycopolitan Forgery of John's Gospel." *NTS* 61 (2015) 314–34.

Aviam, Mordechai. "Distribution Maps of Archaeological Data from the Galilee: An Attempt to Establish Zones Indicative of Ethnicity and Religious Affiliation." In *Religion, Ethnicity, and Identity in Ancient Galilee: A Region in Transition*, edited by Jürgen Zangenberg et al., 115–32. WUNT 210. Tübingen: Mohr/Siebeck, 2007.

———. "Economy and Social Structure in First-Century Galilee: Evidence from the Ground—Yodefat and Gamla." Paper presented at the annual meeting of the Society of Biblical Literature, Boston, November 2008.

———. "Galilee: The Hellenistic to Byzantine Periods." In *NEAEHL* 2:453.

———. *Jews, Pagans and Christians in the Galilee: 25 Years of Archaeological Excavations and Surveys, Hellenistic to Byzantine Periods*. Rochester, NY: University of Rochester Press, 2004.

———. "'Kefar Hananya Ware' Made in Yodefat: Pottery Production at Yodefat in the First Century AD." In *Roman Pottery in the Near East: Local Production and Regional Trade*, edited by Bettina Fischer-Genz et al., 139–46. Oxford: Archaeopress, 2014.

———. "People, Land, Economy, and Belief in First-Century Galilee and Its Origins: A Comprehensive Archaeological Synthesis." In *The Galilean Economy in the Time of Jesus*, edited by David A. Fiensy and Ralph K. Hawkins, 5–48. Early Christianity and Its Literature 11. Atlanta: Society of Biblical Literature, 2013.

———. "Socio-Economic Hierarchy and Its Economic Foundations in First Century Galilee: The Evidence from Yodefat and Gamla." In *Flavius Josephus: Interpretation and History*, edited by Jack Pastor et al., 29–37. Journal for the Study of Judaism Supplements 146. Leiden: Brill, 2011.

———. "The Synagogue." In *Magdala of Galilee: A Jewish City in the Hellenistic and Roman Period*, edited by Richard Bauckham, 127–34. Waco: Baylor University Press, 2018.

———. "Yodefat." *Hadashot Arkhedogiyot* 112 (2000) 18–19.

———. "Yodefat-Jotapata." In *GLSTMP* 2:109–26.

Avigad, Nahman. "The Burnt House Captures a Moment in Time." *BAR* 9 (1983) 66–72.

———. "A Depository of Inscribed Ossuaries in the Kidron Valley." *IEJ* 12 (1962) 1–12.

———. *Discovering Jerusalem*. Oxford: Blackwell, 1980.

———. "Jerusalem Flourishing—a Craft Center for Stone, Pottery and Glass." In *Archaeology and the Bible: Volume Two*, edited by Hershel Shanks and Dan P. Cole, 78–95. Washington, DC: BAS, 1990.

———. "How the Wealthy Lived in Herodian Jerusalem." *BAR* 2 (1976) 22–35.

———. "Upper City." In *NEAEHL* 2:729–35.

Avi-Yona, Michael. *The Holy Land*. Grand Rapids: Baker, 1966.

———. *The Madaba Mosaic Map*. Jerusalem: Israel Exploration Society, 1954.

Avni, Gideon, and Zvi Greenhut. "Resting Place of the Rich and Famous." *BAR* 20/6 (1994) 36–46.

Baarda, T. "The Sentences of the Syriac Menander." In *OTP* 2:583–606.

Bader, Gershom. *The Encyclopedia of Talmudic Sages*. London: Aronson, 1988.

Bagati, B. "Nazareth, Excavations." In *NEAEHL* 3:1103–5.

Bagnall, Roger S., and Bruce W. Frier. *The Demography of Roman Egypt*. Cambridge: Cambridge University Press, 1994.

Baigent, M., R. Leigh and H. Lincoln. *Holy Blood, Holy Grail*. New York: Dell, 2015.

Bailey, Kenneth E. *Jesus Through Middle Eastern Eyes*. Downers Grove, IL: IVP Academic, 2008.

Le Bailly, Matthieu and Françoise Bouchet. "*Diphyllobothrium* in the Past: Review and New Records." *IJP* 3 (2013) 182–87.

Baker, Cynthia M. "Imagined Households." In *Religion and Society in Roman Palestine: Old Questions, New Approaches*, edited by Douglas R. Edwards, 113–28. New York: Routledge, 2004.

Bakke, O. M. *When Children Became People: The Birth of Childhood in Early Christianity*. Minneapolis: Fortress, 2005.

Balogh, Balage. *Archaeology Illustrated*. http://www.archaeologyillustrated.com.

Balouka, Marva. "Roman Pottery." In *The Pottery from Ancient Sepphoris*, edited by Eric M. Meyers and Carol L. Meyers, 13–129 Winona Lake, IN: Eisenbrauns, 2013.

Bar-Adon, Pessaḥ. "Another Settlement of the Judean Desert Sect at ʿEn el-Ghuweir on the Shores of the Dead Sea." *BASOR* 227 (1977) 1–25.

Bar-Ilan, Meir. "Infant Mortality in the Land of Israel in Late Antiquity." In *Judaism and Jewish Society*, edited by Simcha Fishbane and Jack N. Lightstone, 1:3–25. 2 vols. Montreal: Concordia University Press, 1990. https://faculty.biu.ac.il/~barilm/articles/publications/publications0024.html.

Bar-Oz, Guy, Ram Bouchnik, Ehud Weiss, Lior Weissbrod, Daniella E. Bar-Yosef Mayer, and Ronny Reich. "'Holy Garbage': A Quantitative Study of the City-Dump of Early Roman Jerusalem." *Levant* 39 (2007) 1–12.

Barrett, C. K. *The Acts of the Apostles*. Vol. 1. Edinburgh: T. & T. Clark, 1994.

———. *The New Testament Background*. San Francisco: HarperSanFrancisco, 1987.

Bartlett, John R. "The Archaeology of Qumran." In *Archaeology and Biblical Interpretation*, edited by John R. Bartlett, 67–94. London: Routledge, 1997.

Batey, Richard A. "Is not This the Carpenter?" *NTS* 30 (1984) 249–58.

———. *Jesus & the Forgotten City: New Light on Sepphoris and the Urban World of Jesus*. Grand Rapids: Baker, 1991.

———. *Jesus and the Poor*. New York: Harper & Row, 1972.

———. "Sepphoris: An Urban Portrait of Jesus." *BAR* 18 (1992) 50–62.

Bauckham, Richard. *Jesus and the Eyewitnesses: The Gospels as Eyewitness Testimony*. Grand Rapids: Eerdmans, 2006.

———, ed. *Magdala of Galilee: A Jewish City in the Hellenistic and Roman Period.* Waco: Baylor University Press, 2018.

———. "Magdala as We Now Know It: An Overview." In *Magdala of Galilee: A Jewish City in the Hellenistic and Roman Period*, edited by Richard Bauckham 1–67. Waco: Baylor University Press, 2018.

Bedford, P. R. "The Economy of the Near East in the First millennium BC." In *The Ancient Economy: Evidence and Models*, edited by J. G. Manning and Ian Morris, 58–83. Social Science History. Stanford: Stanford University Press, 2005.

Beebe, H. Keith. "Domestic Architecture and the New Testament." *BA* 38 (1975) 89–104.

Ben-Ami, Doron, and Yana Tchekhanovets. "The Lower City of Jerusalem on the Eve of Its Destruction, 70 C.E.: A View from Hanyon Givati." *BASOR* 364 (2010) 61–85.

Ben-David, Arieh. *Talmudische Ökonomie.* Hildesheim: Olms, 1974.

Ben-Dov, M. *In the Shadow of the Temple: The Discovery of Ancient Jerusalem.* New York: Harper & Row, 1985.

Bendor, S. *The Social Structure of Ancient Israel: The Institution of the Family (Beit ʿAb) from the Settlement to the End of the Monarchy.* Jerusalem Biblical Studies 7. Jerusalem: Simor, 1996.

Benoit, Pierre, Josef T. Milik, and Roland de Vaux. *Les Grottes de Muraba'at.* Discoveries in the Judaean Desert II. Oxford: Clarendon, 1961.

Berlin, Andrea M. "Household Judaism." In *GLSTMP* 1:208–15.

———. "Jewish Life before the Revolt: The Archaeological Evidence." *JSJ* 36 (2005) 417–70.

———. "What's for Dinner? The Answer Is in the Pot." *BAR* 25/6 (1999) 46–55, 62.

Berlinerblau, J. "The 'Popular Religion' Paradigm in Old Testament Research: A Sociological Critique." In *Social-Scientific Old Testament Criticism*, edited by David J. Chalcraft, 53–76. Biblical Seminar 47. Sheffield: Sheffield Academic, 1997.

Bernard, Andrew. "The Gospel of Jesus' Wife: Textual Evidence of Modern Forgery." *NTS* 61 (2015) 335–55.

Bernard of Morlaix. "De Contemptu Mundi." Translated by J. M. Neale. In *Hymns of the Christian Church.* Harvard Classics. 1909–14. http://www.bartleby.com/45/2/114.html.

Blanton, Thomas R., IV. "Archaeology and the Historical Imagination: The Corinthians Eucharist in Architectural Context(s)." In *Archaeology and the New Testament World: New Discoveries and New Frontiers*, edited by James Riley Strange and Tom McCollough, Atlanta: Society of Biblical Literature, Forthcoming.

Blasi, Anthony J. et al., eds. *Handbook of Early Christianity: Social Science Approaches.* New York: Altamira, 2002.

Bliss, F. J. and A. C. Dickie. *Excavations at Jerusalem.* London: Palestine Exploration Fund, 1898.

Boer, Roland. "Malaria in the Ancient World." *Political Theology Today* (April 17, 2016). http://www.politicaltheology.com/blog/malaria-the-ancient-world.

Bonnie, Rick. "How 'Urban' Was Tiberias in the First Century CE?" In *Essays in Honor of James F. Strange*, Kinneret, Israel: Ostracon, Forthcoming.

Bonnie, Rick, and Julian Richard. "Building D1 at Magdala Revisited in the Light of Public Fountain Architecture in the Late-Hellenistic East." *IEJ* 62 (2012) 71–88.

Booth, Roger P. *Jesus and the Laws of Purity: Tradition History and Legal History in Mark 7.* Journal for the Study of the New Testament Supplements 13. Sheffield: JSOT, 1986.

Borg, Marcus J. *Conflict, Holiness, and Politics in the Teachings of Jesus.* Harrisburg: Trinity, 1998.

Borowski, Oded. *Daily Life in Biblical Times*. Archaeology and Biblical Studies 5. Atlanta: Society of Biblical Literature, 2003.

———. "Eat, Drink and Be Merry: The Mediterranean Diet." *NEA* 67/2 (2004) 96–107.

———. *Every Living Thing: Daily Use of Animals in Ancient Israel*. Walnut Creek, CA: AltaMira, 1998.

Borschel-Dan, Amanda. "A Bit Player in Human History, The Mighty Louse Is Important—and Here to Stay: From the Migration of Early Hominids to Jewish Rebels at Masada, The Perfectly Adapted Parasite Is a Portal in Time to Shed Light on Even the Smallest of Mysteries." *The Times of Israel*, September 25, 2018. https://www.timesofisrael.com/a-bit-player-in-human-history-the-mighty-louse-is-important-and-here-to-stay.

Botha, Pieter J. J. "Houses in the World of Jesus." *Neotestamentica* 32 (1998) 37–74.

Bouquet, A. C. *Everyday Life in New Testament Times*. London: Batsford, 1953.

Bovon, François. *Luke 1: A Commentary on the Gospel of Luke 1:1—9:50*. Translated by Christine M. Thomas. Hermeneia. Minneapolis: Fortress, 2002.

Braemer, Frank. *L'Architecture Domestique du Levant a L'Age du Fer*. Cahier / Editions Recherche sur les civilisations 8. Paris: Recherche sur les civilisations, 1982.

Braun, H. *Spätjüdisch-Häretischer und Frühchristlicher Radikalismus: Jesus von Nazareth und die Essenische Qumranseckte*. Beiträge zur historischen Theologie 24. Tübingen: Mohr/Siebeck, 1957.

Brody, Aaron J. "The Archaeology of the Extended Family: A Household Compound from Iron II Tell En-Nasbeh." In *Household Archaeology in Ancient Israel and Beyond*, edited by Assaf Yasur-Landau et al., 237–54. Culture and History of the Ancient Near East 50. Leiden: Brill, 2011.

Broshi, Magen. "Agriculture and Economy in Roman Palestine: Seven Notes on the Babatha Archive." *IEJ* 42 (1992) 230–40.

———. *Bread, Wine, Walls and Scrolls*. Journal for the Study of the Pseudepigrapha. Supplements 36. Sheffield: Sheffield Academic, 2001.

———. "Estimating the Population of Ancient Jerusalem." *BAR* 4/2 (1978) 10–15.

———. "Excavations in the House of Caiaphas, Mt. Zion." In *Jerusalem Revealed*, edited by Y. Yadin, 57–60. Jerusalem: Israel Exploration Society, 1975.

———. "The Population of Western Palestine in the Roman-Byzantine Period" *BASOR* 236 (1979) 1–10.

———. "What Jesus Learned from the Essenes." *BAR* 30/1 (2004) 32–35.

Broshi, Magen, and Hanan Eshel. "Whose Bones?" *BAR* 29/1 (2003) 26–33, 71.

Brothwell, Don R. *Digging Up Bones: The Excavation, Treatment and Study of Human Skeletal Remains*. 2nd ed. London: British Museum, 1972.

Brown, Dan. *The Da Vinci Code*. New York: Doubleday, 2003.

Brown, Peter. "The Rise and Function of the Holy Man in Late Antiquity." *JRS* 61 (1971) 80–101.

Brown, Raymond E. *The Gospel according to John*. 2 vols. Anchor Bible 29, 29A. Garden City, NY: Doubleday, 1966, 1970.

Bruce, F. F. *Commentary on the Book of Acts*. Grand Rapids: Eerdmans, 1954.

Brunt, P. A. *Social Conflicts in the Roman Republic*. New York: Norton, 1971.

Buchanan, George Wesley. "Jesus and Other Monks of New Testament Times." *Religion in Life* 18 (1979) 136–42.

Büchler, Adolf. *Economic Conditions of Judaea after the Destruction of the Second Temple*. Jews' College Publications 4. London: Oxford University Press, 1912.

———. "The Law of Purification in Mark vii.1–23." *Expository Times* 20 (1909) 34–40.
———. "The Levitical Impurity of the Gentile in Palestine before the Year 70." *JQR* 17 (1926–27) 1–81.
———. *The Political and Social Leaders of the Jewish Community of Sepphoris in the Second and Third Centuries*. Jews' College Publications 1. London: Jews College, 1909.
———. "Die Schauplätze des Bar-Kochbakrieges" *JQR* 16 (1904) 143–205.
Buckser, A. S. "Purity and Pollution." In *Encyclopedia of Cultural Anthropology*, edited by David Levinson and Melvin Embers, 3:1045–49. New York: Holt, 1996.
Budge, E. A. Wallis. *Osiris: The Egyptian Religion of Resurrection*. 1911. Reprint, New Hype Park, NY: University Books, 1961.
Bull, Robert J. "Caesarea Maritima—The Search for Herod's City." In *Archaeology and the Bible, Volume Two: Archaeology in the World of Herod, Jesus and Paul*, edited by Hershel Shanks and Dan P. Cole, 106–23. Washington, DC: BAS, 1990.
Bullard, Reuben G. "Geological Studies in Field Archaeology." *BA* 33/4 (1970) 98–132.
Bultmann, Rudolf. *History of the Synoptic Tradition*. Translated by John Marsh. Oxford: Blackwell, 1963.
Bunimovitz, Shlomo, and Avraham Faust. "Ideology in Stone: Understanding the Four Room House." *BAR* 28/4 (2002) 32–41, 59–60.
———. "Reconstructing Biblical Archaeology: Toward an Integration of Archaeology and the Bible." In *Historical Biblical Archaeology and the Future: The New Pragmatism*, edited by Thomas E. Levy, 43–54. London: Routledge, 2010.
Burchard, C. "Joseph and Asenath." In *OTP* 2:177–248.
Burn, A.R. "Hic Breve Vivitur: A Study of the Expectation of Life in the Roman Empire." *Past & Present* 4 (1953) 2–31.
Cahill, Jane, et al. "It Had to Happen—Scientists Examine Remains of Ancient Bathrooms." *BAR* 17 (1991) 64–69.
Campenhausen, Hans von. *Tradition and Life in the Church: Essays and Lectures in Church History*. Translated by A. V. Littledale. Philadelphia: Fortress, 1968.
Canaan, Taufik. *The Palestinian Arab House: Its Architecture and Folklore*. Jerusalem: Syrian Orphanage Press, 1933.
Carcopino, Jerome. *Daily Life in Ancient Rome*. New Haven: Yale University Press, 1968.
Carter, Charles E. "Ethnoarchaeology." In *OEANE* 2:280–84.
Center for Online Judaic Studies. "Horvat Kanaf Amulet: Incantation Against Fever and Pain." *Center for Online Judaic Studies*. http://cojs.org/horvat_kanaf_amulet-_incantation_against_fever_and_pain.
Chancey, Mark A. "The Cultural Milieu of Ancient Sepphoris." *NTS* 47 (2001) 127–45.
———. *The Myth of a Gentile Galilee*. Society for New Testament Studies Monograph Series 118. Cambridge: Cambridge University Press, 2002.
Chancey, Mark A., and Eric M. Meyers. "How Jewish Was Sepphoris in Jesus' Time?" *BAR* 26/4 (2000) 18–33, 61.
Charlesworth, James H. "Archaeology, Jesus and Christian Faith?" In *What Has Archaeology to Do with Faith?*, edited by James H. Charlesworth and W. P. Weaver, 1–22. Faith and Scholarship Colloquies. Philadelphia: Trinity, 1992.
———. "The Dead Sea Scrolls and the Historical Jesus." In *Jesus and the Dead Sea Scrolls*, edited by James H. Charlesworth, 1–74. New York: Doubleday, 1992.
———. "Jesus Research and Archaeology: A New Perspective." In *Jesus and Archaeology*, edited by James H. Charlesworth 11–63. Grand Rapids: Eerdmans, 2006.

———. *Jesus within Judaism: New Light from Exciting Archaeological Discoveries.* New York: Doubleday, 1988.

Charlesworth, James H., and Mordechai Aviam. "Reconstructing First-Century Galilee: Reflections on Ten Major Problems." In *Jesus Research: New Methodologies and Perceptions. The Second Princeton–Prague Symposium on Jesus Research, Princeton, N.J. 2007*, edited by James H. Charlesworth, 103–37. Princeton–Prague Symposia Series on the Historical Jesus 2. Grand Rapids: Eerdmans, 2014. https://www.academia.edu/5838233/Reconstructing_First_Century_Galilee_Reflections_on_Ten_Major_Problems.

Cheung, Eric, and Joshua Berlinger. "12-Year-Old Blood Mule Caught Trying to Transport 142 Samples into Hong Kong." *CNN*, March 29, 2019. https://www.cnn.com/2019/03/29/asia/blood-mule-shenzhen-intl/index.html.

Christiansen, Duane L. *Deuteronomy 21:10—34:12.* Word Biblical Commentary 6B. Nashville: Word, 2002.

Christus Rex (website). "Capernaum: The Town of Jesus." http://www.christusrex.org/www1/ofm/sites/TScpvill.html.

Church, Alfred John, and William Jackson Brodribb. *Tacitus.* New York: Modern Library, 1942.

Clark, Colin, and Margaret Haswell. *The Economics of Subsistence Agriculture.* New York: St. Martins, 1966.

Clark, Douglas R. "Bricks, Sweat and Tears: The Human Investment in Constructing a 'Four-Room' House." *NEA* 66 (2003) 34–43.

Clark, K. W. "Sea of Galilee." In *IDB* 2:348–50.

Clines, David J. A., ed. *The Dictionary of Classical Hebrew.* 9 vols. Sheffield: Sheffield Academic, 1993–2012.

Coale, Ansley, and Paul Demeny. *Regional Model Life Tables and Stable Populations.* New York: Academic, 1983.

Collins, John J. "Marriage, Divorce, and Family in Second Temple Judaism." In *Families in Ancient Israel*, edited by Leo G. Perdue, et al., 104–62. Louisville: Westminster John Knox, 1997.

———. "Sibylline Oracles." In *OTP* 1:317–472.

Collins, John J., and Daniel C. Harlow. *The Eerdmans Dictionary of Early Judaism.* Grand Rapids: Eerdmans, 2010.

Collins, Raymond F. "Mary." In *ABD* 4:579–81.

Conzelmann, Hans. *Acts of the Apostles: A Commentary on the Acts of the Apostles.* Translated by James Limburg et al. Hermeneia. Philadelphia: Fortress, 1987.

Coogan, Michael D. "The Geography of the Bible." *Oxford Biblical Studies Online.* http://www.oxfordbiblicalstudies.com/article/book/obso-9780195288803/obso-9780195288803-chapter-10.

Cope, Carole. "Butchering Patterns." In *Gamla III: The Shmarya Gutmann Excavations 1976–1989 Finds and Studies. Part 2*, edited by Danny Syon, 331–42. Jerusalem: IAA, 2014.

Corbo, Virgilio C. "Capernaum." In *ABD* 1:866–69.

———. *Cafarnao I.* Jerusalem: Franciscan, 1975.

———. *The House of Saint Peter at Capharnaum.* Translated by S. Saller. Jerusalem: Franciscan, 1972.

Cotton, Hannah. "A Cancelled Marriage Contract from the Judean Desert." *JRS* 84 (1994) 64–86.

Cotton, Hannah M., and Ada Yardeni. *Aramaic, Hebrew, and Greek Documentary Texts from Naḥal Ḥever and Other Sites with an Appendix Containing Alleged Qumran Texts (the Seiyal Collection II)*. Oxford: Clarendon, 1997.

Cox, F. E. G. "History of Human Parasitology." *Clinical Microbiology Reviews* 15 (2002) 595–612. https://www.ncbi.nlm.nih.gov/pmc/articles/PMC126866.

Craigie, Peter C. *The Book of Deuteronomy*. New International Commentary on the Old Testament. Grand Rapids: Eerdmans, 1976.

de Ste. Croix, G. E. M. *The Class Struggle in the Ancient Greek World*. Ithaca, NY: Cornell University Press, 1981.

Crossan, John Dominic. *The Birth of Christianity: Discovering What Happened in the Years Immediately after the Execution of Jesus*. San Francisco: Harper, 1998.

———. "Itinerants and Householders in the Earliest Jesus Movement." In *Whose Historical Jesus?*, edited by William E. Arnal and Michel Desjardins, 5–24. Studies in Christianity and Judaism 7. Waterloo, ON: Wilfrid Laurier University Press, 1997.

———. "The Relationship between Galilean Archaeology and Historical Jesus Research." In *The Archaeology of Difference: Gender, Ethnicity, Class and the "Other" in Antiquity, Studies in Honor of Eric M. Meyers*, edited by Douglas R. Edwards and C. Thomas McCollough, 151–62. Boston: American Schools of Oriental Research, 2007.

———. "Why Didn't Jesus Marry?" *Committee for the Scientific Review of Religion Review* 1/1 (2006) 5–7.

Crossan, John Dominic, and Jonathan L. Reed. *Excavating Jesus: Beneath the Stones, Behind the Texts*. San Francisco: HarperSanFrancisco, 2001.

———. *In Search of Paul*. San Francisco: HarperSanFrancisco, 2004.

Crowfoot, J. W., et al. *The Buildings of Samaria*. London: Palestine Exploration Fund, 1942.

Cruz-Cruz, Carolina, et al. "Stunting and Intestinal Parasites in School Children From High Marginalized Localities at the Mexican Southeast." *Journal of Infection in Developing Countries* 12/11 (2018) 1026–33.

Currid, John D., and Avi Navon. "Iron Age Pits and the Lahav (Tell Halif) Grain Storage Project." *BASOR* 273 (1989) 67–78.

Cytryn-Silverman, Katia. "Tiberias, from Its Foundation to the End of the Early Islamic Period." In *GLSTMP* 2:186–210.

Dahood, Mitchel. *Psalms I: 1–50*. Achor Bible 16. Garden City, NY: Doubleday, 1966.

Dalman, Gustaf. *Arbeit und Sitte in Palästina*. Vol. 7, *Das Haus, Hühnerzucht, Taubenzucht, Bienenzucht*. Gütersloh. Bertelsmann, 1942.

Danby, H. *The Mishnah*. Oxford: Oxford University Press, 1933.

Danker, Frederick W. et al. *A Greek-English Lexicon of the New Testament and Other Early Christian Literature*. 3rd ed. Chicago: University of Chicago Press, 2000.

Dar, Shimon. "The Agrarian Economy in the Herodian Period." In *The World of the Herods*, edited by Nikos Kokkinos, 305–11. Stuttgart: Steiner, 2007.

———. "Food and Archaeology in Romano-Byzantine Palestine." In *Food in Antiquity*, edited by John Wilkins et al., 326–35. Exeter: University of Exeter Press, 1995.

———. "The History of the Hermon Settlements." *PEQ* 120 (1988) 26–44.

———. *Landscape and Pattern: An Archaeological Survey of Samaria 800 B.C.E.—636 C.E.* With a historical commentary by Shimon Applebaum. BAR International Series 308. Oxford: BAR, 1986.

Dark, Ken. "Has Jesus' Nazareth House Been Found?" *BAR* 41/2 (2015) 54–63.

Daszkiewicz, Malgorzata, Bern Liesen and Gerwulf Schneider. "Provenance Study of Hellenistic, Roman and Byzantine Kitchen Wares from the Theatre-Temple Area of Umm Qais/Gadara, Jordan." In *Roman Pottery in the Near East: Local Production and Regional Trade*, edited by Bettina Fischer-Genz et al., 147–58. Oxford: Archaeopress, 2014.

Davidovitgch, David. "Ketubbah." In *EncJud2* 12:93–98.

Davies, J. K. "Hellenistic Economies." In *The Cambridge Companion to the Hellenistic World*, edited by G. R. Bugh, 73–92. Cambridge: Cambridge University Press, 2008.

Davies, W. D., and Dale Allison. *The Gospel according to St. Matthew*. International Critical Commentary. Edinburgh: T. & T. Clark, 1988–1997.

Deissmann, Adolf. *Light from the Ancient East*. 2nd ed. 1927. Reprint, Eugene, OR: Wipf & Stock, 2004.

Deines R. *Jüdische Steingefässe und Pharisäische Frömmigkeit*. WUNT 2/52. Tübingen: Mohr/Siebeck, 1993.

Dell'Amore, Christine. "Ancient Roman Giant Found—Oldest Complete Skeleton with Gigantism." *National Geographic*. (2012). http://news.nationalgeographic.com/news/2012/11/121102-gigantism-ancient-skeleton-archaeology-history-science-rome.

Demand, Nancy. *Birth, Death, and Motherhood in Classical Greece*. Ancient Society and History. Baltimore: Johns Hopkins University Press, 1994.

Depuydt, Leo. "The Alleged Gospel of Jesus Wife: Assessment and Evaluation of Authenticity." *HTR* 107 (2014) 172–89.

Dever, William G. *The Lives of Ordinary People in Ancient Israel: Where Archaeology and the Bible Intersect*. Grand Rapids: Eerdmans, 2012.

———. *Recent Archaeological Discoveries and Biblical Research*. Seattle: University of Washington Press, 1990.

———. *What Did the Biblical Writers Know and When Did They Know it? What Archaeology Can Tell Us about the Reality of Ancient Israel*. Grand Rapids: Eerdmans, 2001.

Dobson, B. "Legionary Centurion or Equestrian Officer? A Comparison of Pay and Prospects." *Ancient Society* 3 (1972) 193–207.

Donaldson, Terence L. "Rural Bandits, City Mobs and the Zealots." *JSJ* 21 (1990) 19–40.

Dothan, Moshe. *Hamath Tiberias*. Jerusalem: Israel Exploration Society, 1983.

———. "Hamath-Tiberias." In *NEAEHL* 2:573–77.

Douglas, Mary. *Purity and Danger*. London: Routledge, 1966.

Driver, S. R. *Deuteronomy*. International Critical Commentary. Edinburgh: T. & T. Clark, 1902.

Duling, Dennis C. "The Jesus Movement and Social Network Analysis." *BTB* 30 (2000) 3–14.

Dunn, James D. G. "Jesus and Purity: An Ongoing Debate." *NTS* 48 (2002) 449–67.

Durand, John D. "Mortality Estimates from Roman Tombstone Inscriptions." *American Journal of Sociology* 65 (1960) 365–73.

Eakins, J. Kenneth. "Human Osteology and Archeology." *BA* 43 (1980) 89–96.

Ebeling, Jennie R. "Engendering the Israelite Harvests." *NEA* 79 (2016) 186–94.

———. *Women's Lives in Biblical Times*. New York: T. & T. Clark, 2010.

Edelstein, Gershon, and Shimon Gibson. "Ancient Jerusalem's Rural Food Basket." *BAR* 8/4 (1982) 46–54.

Edwards, Douglas R. "First Century Urban/Rural Relations in Lower Galilee: Exploring the Archaeological and Literary Evidence." *SBL 1988 Seminar Papers*, 169–82.

———. "Identity and Social Location in Roman Galilean Villages." In *Religion, Ethnicity, and Identity in Ancient Galilee*, edited by Jürgen Zangenberg et al., 357–74. WUNT 210. Tübingen: Mohr/Siebeck, 2007.

———. "Khirbet Qana: From Jewish Village to Christian Pilgrim Site." In *The Roman and Byzantine Near East*, 3:101–32. JRA Supplementary Series 49. Portsmouth, RI: Journal of Roman Archaeology, 2002.

———. "The Socio-Economic and Cultural Ethos of the Lower Galilee in the First Century: Implications for the Nascent Jesus Movement." In *The Galilee in Late Antiquity*, edited by in Lee I. Levine, 53–74. New York: Jewish Theological Seminary, 1992.

Edwards, James R. "Archaeology Gives New Reality to Paul's Ephesus Riot." *BAR* 42/4 (2016) 24–32, 62.

Ehrenberg, Victor. "Polis." In *OCD* 851–52.

Eliav, Yaron Z. "Medicine and Hygiene." In *Dictionary of Early Judaism*, edited by John J. Collins and Daniel C. Harlow, 929–31. Grand Rapids: Eerdmans, 2010.

Elliott, John H. *What Is Social-Scientific Criticism?* Guides to Biblical Scholarship: New Testament. Minneapolis: Fortress, 1993.

Engels, Donald W. *Roman Corinth: An Alternative Model for the Classical City*. Chicago: University of Chicago Press, 1990.

Erdemgil, S., et al. *Ephesus*. Istanbul: Cemberlitas, 2000.

Erskine, John. *The Human Life of Jesus*. New York: Morrow, 1945.

Éry, K. K. "Investigations on the Demographic Source Value of Tombstones Originating from the Roman Period." *Alba Regia* 10 (1969) 51–67.

Eshel, Hanan. "The Pools of Sepphoris: Ritual Baths or Bathtubs?" *BAR* 26/4 (2000) 42–45.

Eshel, Hanan, and Rivka Leiman. "Jewish Amulets Written on Metal Scrolls." *Journal of Ancient Judaism* 1 (2010) 189–99.

Evans, Craig A. "Excavating Caiaphas, Pilate, and Simon of Cyrene: Assessing the Literary and Archaeological Evidence." In *Jesus and Archaeology*, James H. Charlesworth, 323–40 Grand Rapids: Eerdmans, 2006.

———. *Jesus and the Ossuaries*. Waco: Baylor University Press, 2003.

———. *Jesus and the Remains of His Day: Studies in Jesus and the Evidence of Material Culture*. Peabody, MA: Hendrickson, 2015.

Evans-Pritchard, E. E. *Nuer Religion*. Oxford: Clarendon, 1956.

Facchini, F., et al. "Cribra Orbitalia and Cribra Cranii in Roman Skeletal Remains from the Ravenna Area and Rimini (I–IV century AD)." *IJO* 14/2 (2004) 126–36.

Falconer, Steven E. "Village Economy and Society in the Jordan Valley: A Study of Bronze Age Rural Complexity." In *Archaeological Views from the Countryside: Village Communities in Early Complex Societies*, edited by Glenn M. Schwartz and Steven E. Falconer, 121–42. Washington, DC: Smithsonian Institution, 1994.

Farhi, Yoav. "Stucco Decorations from the Western Quarter." In *Gamla II: The Architecture. The Shmarya Gutman Excavations 1976-1989*, edited by Danny Syon and Zvi Yavor, 175–87. Jerusalem: IAA, 2010.

Faust, Avraham. *The Archaeology of Israelite Society in Iron Age II*. Winona Lake, IN: Eisenbrauns, 2012.

———. "The Farmstead in the Highlands of Iron Age II Israel." In *The Rural Landscape of Ancient Israel*, edited by Aren m. Maeir et al., 91–104.Oxford: BAR, 2003.

———. "The Rural Community in Ancient Israel during Iron Age II." *BASOR* 317 (2000) 17–39.

Faust, Avraham, and Shlomo Bunimovitz. "The Four Room House: Embodying Iron Age Israelite Society." *NEA* 66 (2003) 22–31.

Feder, Yitzhaq. "The Polemic Regarding Skin Disease in 4QMMT." *Dead Sea Discoveries* 19 (2012) 55–70.

Fiensy, David A. *Christian Origins and the Ancient Economy*. Eugene, OR: Cascade Books, 2014.

———. "The Galilean House in the Late Second Temple and Mishnaic Periods." In *GLSTMP* 1:216–41.

———. "The Galilean Village in the Late Second Temple and Mishnaic Periods." In *GLSTMP* 1:177–207.

———. *Insights from Archaeology: Reading the Bible in the Twenty-First Century*. Minneapolis: Fortress, 2017.

———. *Jesus the Galilean: Soundings in a First Century Life*. Piscataway, NJ: Gorgias, 2007.

———. *The Social History of Palestine in the Herodian Period: The Land Is Mine*. Studies in the Bible and Early Christianity 20. Lewiston, NY: Mellen, 1991.

Fiensy, David A., and Ralph K. Hawkins, eds. *The Galilean Economy in the Time of Jesus*. Early Christianity and Its Literature 11. Atlanta: Society of Biblbical Literature, 2013.

Fiensy, David A., and James Riley Strange, eds. *Galilee in the Late Second Temple and Mishnaic Periods*. Vol. 1: *Life, Culture, and Society*. Minneapolis: Fortress, 2014.

———. *Galilee in the Late Second Temple and Mishnaic Periods*. Vol. 2: *The Archaeological Record from Cities, Towns, and Villages*. Minneapolis: Fortress, 2015.

Fine, Steven. *Art and Judaism in the Greco-Roman World: Toward a New Jewish Archaeology*. Cambridge: Cambridge University Press, 2005.

———. "Death, Burial, and Afterlife." In *OHJDL* 440–62.

Finkelstein, L. "The Pharisees: Their Origin and Their Philosophy." *HTR* 22 (1929) 185–261.

———. *The Pharisees*. Philadelphia: Jewish Publication Society of America, 1962.

Finkelstein, Israel. "A Few Notes on Demographic Data from Recent Generations and Ethnoarchaeology" *PEQ* 122 (1990) 47–52.

Finkelstein, Israel and Dafna Langgut. "Climate, Settlement History, and Olive Cultivation in the Iron Age Southern Levant." *BASOR* 379 (2018) 153–69.

Finley, M. I. *The Ancient Economy*. Berkeley: University of California Press, 1985.

Firmage, Edwin. "Zoology (Fauna)." In *ABD* 6:1109–67.

Fitzmyer, Joseph A., and Daniel J. Harrington. *A Manual of Palestinian Aramaic Texts: Second Century B.C.—Second Century A.D.* Biblica et Orientalia 34. Rome: Biblical Institute Press, 1978.

Flusser, David. *Judaism and the Origins of Christianity*. Jerusalem: Magness, 2009 [1988].

Foerster, Gideon. "Beth-Shean at the Foot of the Mount." In *NEAEHL* 1:223–35.

———. "Herodium." In *NEAEHL* 2:618–21.

———. "Tiberias: Excavation South of the City." In *NEAEHL* 4:1470–73.

Fortner, Sandra. "The Fishing Implements and Maritime Activities of Bethsaida–Julias (et-Tell)." In *Bethsaida*, edited by Rami Arav and Richard Freund, 2:269–80. Kirksville, MO: Truman State University Press, 1999.

Fox News. "'Enormous Number' of Parasites in North Korean Defector's Body, Doctors Say." *Fox News*, November 17, 2017. http://www.foxnews.com/world/2017/11/17/enormous-number-parasites-in-north-korean-defectors-body-doctors-say.html.

Fradkin, Arlene. "Long Distance Trade in the Lower Galilee: New Evidence from Sepphoris." In *Archaeology and the Galilee: Texts and Contexts in the Graeco-Roman and Byzantine*

Periods, edited by Douglas R. Edwards and C. Thomas McCollough, 107–16. SFSHJ 143. Atlanta: Scholars, 1997.

Frank, Tenney. *Economic Survey of Ancient Rome*. 6 vols. Baltimore: Johns Hopkins University Presss, 1936–1938.

Frankel, R. N. et al. *Settlement Dynamics and Regional Diversity in Ancient Upper Galilee*. Publications of the Israel Antiquities Authority: IAA Reports 14. Jerusalem: Israel Antiquities Authority, 2001.

Frazer, James G. *The Golden Bough: Abridged Edition*. New York: Macmillan, 1960.

Freedman, H., and Maurice Simon. *Midrash Rabbah*. London: Soncino, 1939.

Freeman, Philip. *Alexander the Great*. New York: Simon & Schuster, 2011.

Freedom United. "Facebook Fails to Save Child Bride from Auction." *CNN*, November 20, 2018. https://www.freedomunited.org/news/facebook-fails-to-save-child-bride-from-auction.

Frey, J. B. *Corpus Inscriptionum Iudaicarum*. 2 vols. Sussidi allo studio delle antichità cristiane 1 and 3. Rome: Pontificio Instituto di Archeologia Cristiana, 1936–1952.

Freyne, Seán. "Archaeology and the Historical Jesus." In *Archaeology and Biblical Interpretation*, edited by John R. Bartlett, 117–44. London: Routledge, 1997.

———. *Galilee from Alexander the Great to Hadrian 323 BCE to 135 CE*. Edinburgh: T. & T. Clark, 1980.

———. "Town and Country Once More: The Case of Roman Galilee." : *Texts and Contexts in the Graeco-Roman and Byzantine Periods*, edited by Douglas R. Edwards and C. Thomas McCollough, 49–56. SFSHJ 143. Atlanta: Scholars, 1997.

Frick, Frank S. "Palestine, Climate of." In *ABD* 5:119–26.

Frier, Bruce. "Roman Life Expectancy: The Pannonian Evidence." *Phoenix* 37 (1983) 328–44.

———. "Roman Life Expectancy: Ulpian's Evidence." *Harvard Studies in Classical Philology* 86 (1982) 213–51.

Fry, Evan. "Cities, Towns, and Villages in the Old Testament." *Bible Translator* 30 (1979) 434–38.

Fuchs, Ron. "The Palestinian Arab House and the Islamic 'Primitive Hut.'" *Muqarnas* 15 (1998) 157–77.

Fuller, Anne H. *Buarij: Portrait of a Lebanese Muslim Village*. Cambridge: Harvard University Press, 1963.

Funk, Robert W. *Honest to Jesus: Jesus for a New Millennium*. San Francisco: HarperSanFrancisco, 1996.

Funk, Robert W. and Roy W. Hoover. *The Five Gospels: The Search for the Authentic Words of Jesus: New Translation and Commentary*. New York: Macmillan, 1993.

Gallant, Thomas W. *Risk and Survival in Ancient Greece*. Stanford: Stanford University Press, 1991.

García Martínez, Florentino, and Julio Trebolle Barrera. *The People of the Dead Sea Scrolls*. Translated by Wilfred G. E. Watson. Leiden: Brill, 1993.

Garroway, Kristine. *Children in the Ancient Near Eastern Household*. Winona Lake, IN: Eisenbrauns, 2014.

———. *Growing Up in Ancient Israel: Children in Material Culture and Biblical Texts*. Archaeology and Biblical Studies 23. Atlanta: SBL Press, 2018.

Gathercole, Simon. "The Gospel of Jesus' Wife: Constructing a Context." *NTS* 61 (2015) 292–313.

Geggel, Laura. "Medieval Parasite-Filled Poop Found in Jerusalem Latrine." *Life Science.com* March 30, 2015. https://www.livescience.com/50268-jerusalem-latrine-parasites.html.

Geyer, Patrick Scott. "Pollen Analysis." In *Gamla III: The Shmarya Gutmann Excavations 1976–1989 Finds and Studies. Part 2*, edited by Danny Syon, 351–62. Jerusalem: IAA, 2014.

Geva, Hillel. "Jerusalem: the Second Temple Period." In *NEAEHL* 2:717–29.

———. "Tombs." In *NEAEHL* 2:747–57.

Gibson, Shimon. *The Cave of John the Baptist: The First Archaeological Evidence of the Historical Reality of the Gospel Story*. New York: Image, 2004.

———. *The Final Days of Jesus: The Archaeological Evidence*. New York: HarperCollins, 2009.

———. "Soft Limestone Vessels." In *Gamla III: The Shmarya Gutmann Excavations 1976–1989 Finds and Studies. Part 2*, edited by Danny Syon, 49–81. Jerusalem: IAA, 2014.

Gichon, Mordechai. "Ein Boqeq." In *NEAEHL* 2:395–99.

Gilat, Yitzak Dov and Stephen G. Wald. "Simeon ben Shetaḥ." In *EncJud2* 18:600–601.

Goh, Madelein, and Chad Schroeder, eds. Franco Montanari. *The Brill Dictionary of Ancient Greek*. Leiden: Brill, 2015.

Goldstein, M.S., B. Arensburg, and H. Nathan. "Skeletal Remains of Jews from the Hellenistic and Roman Periods in Israel: II. Non-metric Morphological Observations." *Bulletins et mémoires de la Société d'anthropologie de Paris XIII* 8 (1981) 279–95.

———. "Skeletal Remains of Jews from the Hellenistic and Roman Periods in Israel: III. Pathology." *Bulletins et mémoires de la Société d'anthropologie de Paris XIII* 8 (1981) 11–24.

Goodman, Martin. "The First Jewish Revolt: Social Conflict and the Problem of Debt." *JJS* 33 (1982) 414–27.

———. "Galilean Judaism and Judaean Judaism." In *The Cambridge History of Judaism*. Vol. 3: *The Early Roman Period*, edited by William Horbury et al., 596–617. Cambridge: Cambridge University Press, 1999.

———. *The Ruling Class of Judea*. Cambridge: Cambridge University Press, 1987.

———. *State and Society in Roman Galilee*. Totowa, NJ: Rowman & Allanheld, 1983.

Goppelt, Leonhard. *Theology of the New Testament*. Translated by John E. Alsup. Edited by Jürgen Roloff. Grand Rapids: Eerdmans, 1981.

Govier, Gordon. "Biblical Archaeology's Top Ten Discoveries of 2013." *Christianity Today*, December, 2013. http://www.christianitytoday.com/ct/2013/december-web-only/biblical-archaeologys-top-ten-discoveries-of-2013.html.

Grant, F. C. *The Economic Background of the Gospels*. London: Oxford University Press, 1926.

Grey, Matthew J., and Chad S. Spigel. "Ḥuqoq in the Late Hallenistic and Early Roman Periods." In *GLSTMP* 2:362–78.

Grmek, Mirko D. *Diseases in the Ancient Greek World*. Baltimore: Johns Hopkins University Press, 1989.

Groh, Dennis. "The American Field School and the Future of Biblical Archaeology." In *A City Set on a Hill: Essays in Honor of James F. Strange*, edited by Daniel A. Warner and Donald D. Binder, 128–60. Mountain Home, AR: BorderStone, 2014.

Grünewald, Thomas. *Bandits in the Roman Empire: Myth and Reality*. London: Routledge, 1999.

Gudme, Anne Katrine de Hemmer. "Mortuary Rituals." In *The Oxford Handbook of Early Christian Ritual*, edited by Uro Risto et al., 353–69. Oxford Handbooks. Oxford: Oxford University Press, 2018.

Guijarro, Santiago. "The Family in First-Century Galilee." In *Constructing Early Christian Families: Family as Social Reality and Metaphor*, edited by Halvor Moxnes, 42–65. London: Routledge, 1997.

Gurtner, Daniel M., and Loren T. Stuckenbruck, eds. *T&T Clark Encyclopedia of Second Temple Judaism*. London: Bloomsbury T. & T. Clark, 2020.

Gutiérrez-Jiménez, Javier, Lorena Mercedes Luna-Cazárez, and Jorge E. Vidal. "Malnutrition and Intestinal Parasites: Mexico Perspectives." *Academia*, pp. 1–18 (4). https://www.academia.edu/34590130/Malnutrition_and_Intestinal_Parasites_Mexico_Perspectives.

Gutman, Shmaryahu. "Gamala." In *NEAEHL* 2:459–63.

Haas, N. "Anthropological Observations on the Skeletal Remains from Giv'at ha-Mivtar." *IEJ* 20 (1970) 38–60.

Haas, N. and H. Nathan. "Anthropological Survey of Human Skeletal Remains from Qumran" *RevQ* 6/3 (1968) 345–52.

Haber, Susan. "Common Judaism, Common Synagogue? Purity, Holiness, and Sacred Space at the Turn of the Common Era." In *Common Judaism: Explorations in Second-Temple Judaism*, edited by Wayne O. McCready and Adele Reinharts, 63–77. Minneapolis: Fortress, 2008.

Hachlili, Rachel. "Burials, Ancient Jewish." In *ABD* 2:798–94.

———. "Burial Practices." In *The Eerdmans Dictionary of Early Judaism*, edited by John J. Collins and Daniel C. Harlow, 448–452. Grand Rapids: Eerdmans, 2010.

———. "The Goliath Family in Jericho: Funerary Inscriptions from a First Century A.D. Jewish Monumental Tomb." *BASOR* 235 (1979) 31–65.

———. *Jewish Funerary Customs, Practices and Rites in the Second Temple Period*. Leiden: Brill, 2005.

Hachlili, Rachel, and Ann Killebrew. "Was the Coin-on-Eye Custom a Jewish Burial Practice in the Second Temple Period?" *BA* 46/3 (1983) 147–153

Hachlili, Rachel, and Patricia Smith. "The Genealogy of the Goliath Family." *BASOR* 235 (1979) 67–71.

Hadas, Gideon. "Abstract: Nine Tombs of the Second Temple Period at 'En-Gedi." *Atiqot* 24 (1994) 1–8.

———. "En-Gedi." In *NEAEHL* 2:1723–24.

Haenchen, Ernst. *Die Apostelgeschichte*. Göttingen: Vandenhoeck und Ruprecht, 1957; ET *The Acts of the Apostles*. Oxford: Basil Blackwell, 1971.

Halpern, J. M. *A Serbian Village*. New York: Columbia University Press, 1958.

Hamel, Gildas. "Poverty and Charity." In *OHJDL* 308–24.

———. *Poverty and Charity in Roman Palestine, First Three Centuries C.E.* Berkeley: University of California, 1990.

Hamilton, Victor P. "Marriage, Old Testament and Ancient Near East." In *ABD* 4:559–69.

Hanson, K. C. "The Galilean Fishing Economy and the Jesus Tradition." *BTB* 27 (1997) 99–111.

———. "The Herodians and Mediterranean Kinship, Part II: Marriage and Divorce." *BTB* 19 (1989) 142–51.

———. "The Herodians and Mediterranean Kinship, Part III: Economics." *BTB* 20 (1990) 10–21.

Hanson, K. C., and Douglas E. Oakman. *Palestine in the Time of Jesus: Social Structures and Social Conflicts*. 2nd ed. Minneapolis: Fortress, 2008.

Hardin, James W. *Lahav II: Households and the Use of Domestic Space at Iron II Tell Halif: An Archaeology of Destruction.* Winona Lakee, IN: Eisenbrauns, 2010.

———. "Understanding Houses, Households, and the Levantine Archaeological Record." In *Household Archaeology in Ancient Israel and Beyond*, edited by Assaf Yasur-Landau et al., 9–25. Culture and History of the Ancient Near East 50. Leiden: Brill, 2011.

Hare, D. R. A. "The Lives of the Prophets." In *OTP* 2:379–99.

Harper, M. "Village Administration in the Roman Province of Syria." *Yale Classical Studies* 1 (1928) 105–68.

Harrington, Daniel J. "Pseudo-Philo." In *OTP* 2:297–378.

Harrington, Hannah K. *The Impurity Systems of Qumran and the Rabbis.* SBL Dissertation Series 143. Atlanta: Scholars, 1993.

———. "Purity." In *The Encyclopedia of the Dead Sea Scrolls*, edited by Lawrence H. Schiffman and James C. VanderKam, 2:724–28. Oxford: Oxford University Press, 2000.

Harrison, R. K. "Disease, Bible and Spade." *BA* 16/4 (1953) 88–92.

Harrison, Roland K., and Edwin M. Yamauchi. "Art." In *DDL* 1:91–99.

———. "Diseases and Plagues." In *DDL* 2:63–84.

Harter, S., F. Bouchet, K. Y. Mumcuoglu, and J. Zias. "Toilet Practices among Members of the Dead Sea Scroll Sect at Qumran." *RevQ* 21 (2004) 579–84.

Hayami, Akira and Nobuko Uchida. "Size of Household in a Japanese County Throughout the Tokugawa era." In *Household and Family in Past Time: Comparative Studies in the Size and Structure of the Domestic Group over the Last Three Centuries in England, France, Serbia, Japan and Colonial North America, with Further Materials from Western Europe*, edited by Peter Laslett, 473–516. Cambridge: Cambridge University Press, 1972.

Health.Facty.com (website). "Ten Symptoms of Parasites." health.facty.com/ailments/body/10-symptoms-of-a-parasite.

Healthline (website). "Ascariasis." https://www.healthline.com/health/ascariasis#symptoms.

———. "Whipworm Infection." https://www.healthline.com/health/whipworm-infection.

Heichelheim, F. M. "Roman Syria." In *Economic Survey of Ancient Rome*, edited by Frank Tenney, 4:121–257. Baltimore: Johns Hopkins University Press, 1938.

Hengel, M. *Between Jesus and Paul.* London: SCM, 1983.

———. *The Charismatic Leader and His Followers.* New York: Crossroad, 1981.

———. *The Hellenization of Judaea in First Century after Christ.* Philadelphia: Trinity, 1989.

———. *Property and Riches in the Early Church.* Philadelphia: Fortress, 1974.

Heritage Daily (website). "Human Parasites Found in Medieval Cesspit Reveal Links between Middle East and Europe." N.d. https://phys.org/news/2015-03-human-parasites-medieval-cesspit-reveal.html

Herr, Larry G. "Israel, Geography of." In *New Interpreter's Dictionary of the Bible*, edited by Katharine Doob Sakenfeld, 3:101–15. Nashville: Abingdon, 2008.

Herr, Larry G., and Gary L. Christopherson. *Excavation Manual: Madaba Plains Project.* Berrien Springs, MI: Andrews University Press, 1998.

Hezser, Catherine. "The Exposure and Sale of Infants in Rabbinic and Roman Law." In *Jewish Studies between the Disciplines: Papers in Honor of Peter Schäfer on the Occasion of His 60th Birthday*, edited by Klaus Herrmann et al., 3–28. Leiden: Brill, 2003.

———, ed. *The Oxford Handbook of Jewish Daily Life in Roman Palestine.* Oxford: Oxford University Press, 2010.

Hirschfeld, Yizhar. "Architecture and Stratigraphy." In *En-Gedi Excavations II: Final Report 1996–2002*, edited by Yizhar Hirschfeld, 23–156. Jerusalem: Israel Exploration Society, 2007.

———. "The Early Roman Bath and Fortress at Ramat Hanadiv Near Caesarea." In *The Roman and Byzantine Near East: Some Recent Archaeological Research*, edited by J. H. Humphrey, 28–55. JRA Supplemental Series 14. Ann Arbor, MI: Journal of Roman Archaeology, 1995.

———. "En-Gedi." In *NEAEHL* 5:1718–22.

———. "Fortified Manor Houses of the Ruling Class in the Herodian Kingdom of Judaea." In *The World of the Herods*, edited by Nikos Kokkinos, 197–226. Stuttgart: Franz Steiner, 2007.

———. "Jewish Rural Settlement in Judaea in the Early Roman Period." In *The Early Roman Empire in the East*, editedi by Susan E. Alcock, 72–88. Oxford: Oxbow, 1997.

———. *The Palestinian Dwelling in the Roman-Byzantine Period*. Jerusalem: Franciscan, 1995.

———. *Ramat Hanadiv Excavations*. Jerusalem: Israel Exploration Society, 2000.

———. *Roman, Byzantine, and Early Muslim Tiberias: A Handbook of Primary Sources*. Jerusalem: Israel Antiquities Authority, 2005.

———. "Tiberias." In *NEAEHL* 4.1464–70.

———. "Tiberias—Preview of Coming Attraction." *BAR* 17/2 (1991) 44–51.

Hirschfeld, Yizhar, and Miriam Feinberg-Vamosh. "A Country Gentleman's Estate: Unearthing the Splendors of Ramat Hanadiv." *BAR* 31/2 (2005) 18–31.

Hirschfeld, Yizhar and Katharina Galor. "New Excavations in Roman, Byzantine, and Early Islamic Tiberias." In *Religion, Ethnicity and Identity in Ancient Galilee: A Region in Transition*, edited by Jürgen K. Zangenberg et al., 207–30. WUNT 210. Tübingen: Mohr/Siebeck, 2007.

Hoehner, H.W. *Herod Antipas*. Cambridge: Cambridge University Press, 1972.

Hoglund, K.G. and E.M. Meyers. "The Residential Quarter on the Western Summit." In *Sepphoris in Galilee: Crosscurrents of Culture*, edited by Rebecca Martin Nagy et al., 38–42. Winona Lake, IN: Eisenbrauns, 1996.

Holladay, John S., Jr. "House, Israelite." In *ABD* 3:308–18.

Holladay, William L. *A Concise Hebrew and Aramaic Lexicon of the Old Testament*. Grand Rapids: Eerdmans, 1988.

Holmes, Michael W. *The Apostolic Fathers: Greek Texts and English Translations*, 3rd edition. Grand Rapids: Baker, 2007.

Holum, Kenneth. "The Combined Caesarea Expedition Excavations." In *NEAEHL* 5:1665–68.

Homsher, Robert S. "Mud Bricks and the Process of Construction in the Middle Bronze Age Southern Levant." *BASOR* 368 (2012) 1–27.

Hooke, S. H. *Babylonian and Assyrian Religion*. Norman: University of Oklahoma, 1963.

Hopkins, David. *The Highlands of Canaan: Agricultural Life in the Early Iron Age*. Social World of Biblical Antiquity 3 Sheffield: Almond, 1985.

Hopkins, Keith. "On the Probable Age Structure of the Roman Population." *Population Studies* 20 (1966) 245–64.

Hoppe, Leslie J. "Caesarea Maritima." In *IDB (New)* 1:516–17.

———. *What Are They Saying About Biblical Archaeology?* New York: Paulist, 1984.

Horsley, G. H. R. *New Documents Illustrating Early Christianity.* Marrickville, NSW: Macquarie University Press, 1987. [AQ: vol. ?]

Horsley, Richard A. *Archaeology, History, and Society in Galilee: The Social Context of Jesus and the Rabbis.* Valley Forge, PA: Trinity, 1996.

———. *Sociology and the Jesus Movement.* New York: Crossroad, 1989.

Horsley, Richard A., and John S. Hanson *Bandits, Prophets, and Messiahs: Popular Movements at the Time of Jesus.* New York: Harper & Row, 1985.

Horst, P. W. Van der. "Pseudo-Phocylides." In *OTP* 2:565–82.

Huebner, Sabine R. "A Mediterranean Family? A Comparative Approach to the Ancient World." In *Mediterranean Families in Antiquity: Households, Extended Families, and Domestic Space*, edited by Sabine R. Huebner and Geoffrey Nathan, 3–26. Oxford: Wiley-Blackwell, 2016. https://www.academia.edu/26034682/_A_Mediterranean_Family_A_Comparative_Approach_to_the_Ancient_World_in_Sabine_R._Huebner_and_Geoffrey_Nathan_eds._Mediterranean_Families_in_Antiquity_Households_Extended_Families_and_Domestic_Space._Oxford_Wiley-Blackwell_2016_3-26.

Ilan, Tal. *Integrating Women into Second Temple Judaism.* Peabody, MA: Hendrickson, 1999.

———. *Jewish Women in Greco-Roman Palestine.* Peabody: MA: Hendrickson, 1996.

———. "Notes and Observations on a Newly Published Divorce Bill from the Judean Desert." *HTR* 89 (1998) 195–202.

———. "Ossuaries of the Herodian Period." In *The World of the Herods*, edited by Nikos Kokkinos, 61–69. Stuttgart: Steiner, 2007.

———. "Premarital Cohabitation in Ancient Judea: the Evidence of the Babatha Archive and the Mishnah ('Ketubbot' 1.4)." *HTR* 86 (1993) 247–64.

Instone-Brewer, David. "Jewish Women Divorcing their Husbands in Early Judaism: the Background to Papyrus Şe'elim 13." *HTR* 92 (1999) 349–57.

———. "Marriage and Divorce." In *The Eerdmans Dictionary of Early Judaism*, edited by John J. Collins and Daniel C. Harlow, 916–917. Grand Rapids: Eerdmans, 2010.

Isaac, B. "The Babatha Archive: A Review Article." *IEJ* 42 (1992) 62–75.

Isenberg, W. W. "The Gospel of Philip." *NH*, 131–151.

Jackson, Ralph. *Doctors and Diseases in the Roman Empire.* London: British Museum, 1988.

Jackson-Tal, Ruth Eve. "Glass Vessels." In *Gamla III: The Shmarya Gutmann Excavations 1976–1989 Finds and Studies; Part 2*, edited by Danny Syon, 1–47. Jerusalem: IAA, 2014.

———. "Glass Vessel Use in Time of Conflict: The Evidence from the Bar Kokhba Refuge Caves in Judaea, Israel (135/136 C.E.)." *BASOR* 376 (2016) 29–62.

Jacobs, Naomi. "Diet among Second Temple Jews in the Eastern Levant." In *The T. & T. Clark Encyclopedia of Second Temple Judaism*, edited by Daniel Gurtner and Loren T. Stuckenbruck, 202–204. London: T. & T. Clark, forthcoming.

Japp, Sarah. "Public and Private Decorative Art in the Time of Herod the Great." In *The World of the Herods*, edited by Nikos Kokkinos, 227–246. Stuttgart: Steiner, 2007.

Jastrow, Marcus. *Dictionary of the Targumim, Talmud Bavli, Talmud Yerushalmi and Midrashic Literature.* New York: Judaica, 1971.

Jenks, Gregory C. "Bethsaida Excavations Project: Coins from the 2001–2012 Seasons." (December 26, 2013). Online: https://www.academia.edu/3988826/2001-2012_Bethsaida_Coin_Report?auto=download.

———. "The Quest for the Historical Nazareth." https://www.academia.edu/3988852/The_Quest_for_the_Historical_Nazareth?email_work_card=view-paper.

Jensen, Morton Hørning. "Antipas: The Herod Jesus Knew." *BAR* 38/5 (2012) 42–46.

———. "Climate, Droughts, Wars, and Famines in Galilee as a Background for Understanding the Historical Jesus." *JBL* 131 (2012) 307–24.

———. "Political History in Galilee from the First Century BCE to the End of the Second Century CE." In *GLSTMP* 1:51–77.

———. "Purity and Politics in Herod Antipas's Galilee: The Case for Religious Motivation." *JSHJ* 11 (2013) 3–34.

———. "Rural Galilee and Rapid Changes: An Investigation of the Socio-Economic Dynamics and Developments in Roman Galilee." *Bib* 93 (2012) 43–67.

Jeremias, Joachim. *Jerusalem in the Time of Jesus: An Investigation into Economic and Social Conditions during the New Testament Period*. Translated by F. H. Cave and C. H. Cave. Philadelphia: Fortress, 1969.

———. "νύμφη, νυμφίος." In *TDNT* 4:1099–106.

———. *The Parables of Jesus*. Translated by S. H. Hooke. New York: Scribner, 1963.

Jevons, F. B. "Some Ancient Greek Pay-Bills." *Economic Journal* 6/23 (1896) 470–75.

Johnson, L. T. *Sharing Possessions*. Philadelphia: Fortress, 1981.

Johnson, M. D. "Life of Adam and Eve." In *OTP* 2:249–96.

Jones, A. H. M. *The Greek City From Alexander To Justinian*. Oxford: Clarendon, 1940.

———. "The Urbanization of Palestine." *JRS* 21 (1931) 78–85.

Jones, Christopher. "The Jesus Wife Papyrus in the History of Forgery." *NTS* 61 (2015) 368–78.

Kahana, Tzipi. "Human Skeletal Remains from Wadi-Ḥalaf (Near Khirbat Ras Abu Ma'aruf), Jerusalem." *Atiqot* 48 (2004) 83–90.

Karmon, Y. "The Settlement of the Northern Huleh Valley since 1838." *IEJ* 3/1 (1953) 4–25.

Kautsky, J. H. *The Politics of Aristocratic Empires*. Chapel Hill: University of North Carolina Press, 1982.

Kazantzakis, Nikos. *The Last Temptation of Christ*. New York: Simon & Schuster, 1960.

Kee, Howard Clark. *Christian Origins in Sociological Perspective: Methods and Resources*. Philadelphia: Westminster, 1980.

———. "Early Christianity in the Galilee: Reassessing the Evidence from the Gospels" In *The Galilee in Late Antiquity*, edited by Lee I. Levine, 3–22. New York: Jewish Theological Seminary of America, 1992.

———. "Testaments of the Twelve Patriarchs." In *OTP* 1:775–828.

Keener, Craig S. "Fever and Dysentery in Acts 28:8 and Ancient Medicine." *BBR* 19 (2009) 393–402.

Keenleyside, A. and K. Panayotova. "Cribra Orbitalia and Porotic Hyperostosis in a Greek Colonial Population (5th to 3rd centuries BC) from the Black Sea." *IJO* 16/5 (2006) 373–384.

Kehati, Pinhas. *Mishnah Kiddushin*. Jerusalem: Elinar Library, 1994.

———. *Mishnah Ktubot*. Jerusalem: Elinar Library, 1994.

Killebrew, Ann E. "Village and Countryside." In *OHJDL* 189–209.

Killebrew, Ann and Steven Fine. "Qatzrin-Reconstructing Village Life in Talmudic Times." *BAR* 17/3 (1991) 44–56.

King, Karen L. *The Gospel of Mary of Magdalen*. Santa Rosa, CA: Polebridge, 2003.

———. "Jesus Said to Them: 'My Wife . . .': A New Coptic Papyrus Fragment." *HTR* 107 (2014) 131–59.

King, Philip J. "Jerusalem." In *ABD* 3:753.

King, Philip J., and Lawrence E. Stager. *Life in Biblical Israel.* Library of Ancient Israel. Louisville: Westminster John Knox, 2001.

Kislev, Mordechai E., and Mina Marmorstein. "Cereals and Fruits from a Collapsed Cave South of Khirbet Qumran." *IEJ* 53 (2003) 74–77.

Kiuchi, Nobuyoshi. "A Paradox of the Skin Disease." *ZAW* 113 (2001) 505–14.

Klassen, William. "Judas and Jesus: A Message on a Drinking Vessel of the Second Temple Period. " In *Jesus and Archaeology*, edited by James H. Charlesworth, 503–520. Grand Rapids: Eerdmans, 2006.

Klausner, J. "The Economy of Judea in the Period of the Second Temple." In *The Herodian Period: The World History of the Jewish People; First Series: Ancient Times Volume 7*, edited by M. Avi-Yona, 180–205. London: Allen, 1975.

———. *Jesus of Nazareth.* New York: MacMillan, 1925.

Koehler, Ludwig and Walter Baumgartner. *The Hebrew and Aramaic Lexicon of the Old Testament.* Leiden: Brill, 1994.

Kokkinos, N. "The Location of Tarichaea: North or South of Tiberias?" *PEQ* 142 (2010) 7–23.

Kotansky, R. "An Incised Copper Amulet from 'Evron." *Atiqot* 20 (1991) 81–87.

Kraemer, David. "Food Eating and Meals." In *OHJDL* 403–19.

Kraemer, Ross S. "Jewish Mothers and Daughters in the Greco-Roman World." In *The Jewish Family in Antiquity*, edited by Shaye J. D. Cohen, 89–112. Atlanta: Scholars, 1993.

Kramer, Carol. *Village Ethnoarchaeology: Rural Iran in Archaeological Perspective.* New York: Academic, 1982.

Krauss, Rolf. "Kritische Bemerkung zur Erklärung von Ṣāra'at als schuppende Hautkrankheit, inbesondere as Psoriasis." *Biblische Notizen* 177 (2018) 3–24.

Krauss, Samuel. *Talmudische Archäologie.* Hildesheim: Olms, 1966.

Kreissig, H. "Die Landwirtschaftliche Situation in Palästina vor dem Judäischen Krieg." *Acta Antiqua* 17 (1969) 223–54.

Lake, Kirsopp and Henry J. Cadbury. *The Beginnings of Christianity, Part I: The Acts of the Apostles. VOLUME IV, English Translation and Commentary.* Grand Rapids: Baker, 1979.

Lancaster, William, and Fidelity Lancaster. "Jordanian Village Houses in their Contexts, Growth, Decay and Rebuilding." *PEQ* 129 (1997) 38–53.

Lance, H. Darrell. *The Old Testament and the Archaeologist.* Philadelphia: Fortress, 1981.

Lang, Bernhard, ed. *Anthropological Approaches to the Old Testament.* Philadelphia: Fortress, 1985.

Laslett, Peter. "Mean Household Size in England Since the Sixteenth Century." In *Household and Family in Past Time*, edited by Peter Laslett and Richard Wall, 125–158. Cambridge: Cambridge University Press, 1972.

Lawrence, Paul, et al. *The IVP Atlas of Bible History.* Downers Grove, IL: IVP Academic, 2006.

Leap, Dennis. "Archaeology Proves Bible History Accurate." *The Trumpet* (December 2005). https://www.thetrumpet.com/1912-archaeology-proves-bible-history-accurate.

Leibner, Uzi. "Arts and Crafts, Manufacture and Production." In *OHJDL* 264–96.

———. "Khirbet Wadi Hammam in the Early and Middle Roman Periods." In *GLSTMP* 2:343–61.

———. *Settlement and History in Hellenistic, Roman, and Byzantine Galilee: An Archaeological Survey of the Eastern Galilee.* Texte und Studien zum antiken Judentum 127. Tübingen: Mohr/Siebeck, 2009.

Leichman, Abigail Klein. "World Malaria Experts Look to Israel's Past for Future Solutions." *Israel 21C: Uncovering Israel*. December 17, 2013. https://www.israel21c.org/world-malaria-experts-look-to-israels-past-for-future-solutions.

Leiman, Rivka Elitzur, and Uzi Leibner. "An Amulet from Khirbet Wadi Ḥamam." *IEJ* 66 (2016) 220–31.

Lenski, Gerhard E. *Power and Privilege: A Theory of Social Stratification*. New York: McGraw-Hill, 1966.

Lernau, Omri. "Fish Bones from a Cesspit Adjacent to Herod's Circus." In *Caesarea Maritima I: Herod's Circus and Related Buildings Part 2: The Finds*, edited by Yosef Porath, 203–216. Jerusalem: Israel Antiquities Authority, 2015.

———. "Fish Remains from En Gedi." *Atiqot* 49 (2005) 49–56.

Lernau, Omri, and Aharon Shemesh. "Fish Remains." In *Gamla III: The Shmarya Gutmann Excavations 1976–1989 Finds and Studies. Part 2*, edited by Danny Syon, 343–50. Jerusalem: IAA, 2014.

Lev-Tov, Justin. "Diet, Hellenistic and Roman." In *OEBA* 1:296–302.

———. "Upon What Meat Doth This Our Caesar Feed . . . ? A Dietary Perspective on Hellenistic and Roman Influence in Palestine." In *Zeichen aus Text und Stein Studien auf dem Weg zu einer Archäologie des Neuen Testaments*, edited by Stefan Alkier and Jürgen Zangenberg, 420–46. Tübingen: Francke, 2003.

Levine, Amy-Jill. "The Word Becomes Flesh: Jesus, Gender, and Sexuality." In *The Historical Jesus in Recent Research*, edited by James D. G. Dunn and Scot McKnight, 509–23. Winona Lake, IN: Eisenbrauns, 2005.

Levine, Lee I. "Archaeological Discoveries From the Greco-Roman Era." In *Recent Archaeology in the Land of Israel*, edited by Hershel Shanks and Benjamin Mazar, 75–88. Washington, DC: Biblical Archaeology Society, 1984.

———. "Archaeology and the Religious Ethos of Pre-70 Palestine." In *Hillel and Jesus*, edited by James H. Charlesworth and L. John, 110–120. Minneapolis: Fortress, 1997.

———. "'Common Judaism': The Contribution of the Ancient Synagogue." In *Common Judaism: Explorations in Second Temple Judaism*, edited by Wayne O. McCready and Adele Reinhart, 311–43. Minneapolis: Fortress, 2008.

———. "The Synagogues of Galilee." In *Galilee in the Late Second Temple and Mishnaic Periods Volume 1: Life, Culture, and Society*, edited by David A. Fiensy and James Riley Strange, 129–150. Minneapolis: Fortress, 2014.

Levy, Thomas E., ed. *The Archaeology of Society in the Holy Land*. London: Leicester University Press, 1995.

Lewis, N. *The Documents from the Bar Kokhba Period in the Cave of the Letters*. Vol. 1, *The Greek Papyri*. Jerusalem: Israel Exploration Society, 1989.

———. *Life in Egypt under Roman Rule*. Oxford: Clarendon, 1983.

Lichtenberger, Achim. "Art, Hellenistic and Roman Period." In *OEBA* 1:57–66.

Lincicum, David. "Greek Deuteronomy's 'Fever and Chills' and Their Magical Afterlife," *Vetus Testamentum* 58 (2008) 544–49

Liphschitz, Nili. "Archaeobotanical Remains." In *Gamla III: The Shmarya Gutmann Excavations 1976–1989 Finds and Studies. Part 2*, edited by Danny Syon, 363–69. Jerusalem: IAA, 2014.

———. "Archaeobotanical Remains from the En-Gedi Excavations (1996–2002)." In *En-Gedi Excavations II: Final Report 1996–2002*, edited by Yizhar Hirschfeld, 595–603. Jerusalem: Israel Exploration Society, 2007.

Lipschits, Oded, Yuval Gadot, Benjamin Arubas, and Manfred Oeming. "Palace and Village, Paradise and Oblivion: Unraveling the Riddles of Ramat Rahel." *NEA* 74 (2011) 2–49.

Llewelyn, S. R., ed. *A Review of the Greek Inscriptions and Papyri Published in 1986–97: New Documents Illustrating Early Christianity, Volume 9*. Grand Rapids: Eerdmans, 2002.

Loffreda, S. "Capernaum." In *NEAEHL* 1:292.

London, Gloria. "Ethnoarchaeology and Interpretations of the Past." *NEA* 63 (2000) 2–8.

Longstaff, Thomas R.W. and Tristram C. Hussey. "Palynology and Cultural Process: An Exercise in the New Archaeology." In *Archaeology and the Galilee: Texts and Contexts in the Graeco-Roman and Byzantine Periods*, edited by Douglas R. Edwards and C. Thomas McCollough, 151–62. SFSHJ 143. Atlanta: Scholars, 1997.

Luca, F. Massimo. "Kafr Kanna (The Franciscan Church)." In *GLSTMP* 2:158–66.

De Luca, Stefano and Anna Lena. "Magdala, Taricheae." In *GLSTMP* 2:280–342.

Lutfiyya, Abdulla M. *Baytin: A Jordanian Village*. London: Mouton, 1966.

Mabratnora, Obadiah. *The Six Orders of the Mishnah*. Jerusalem: Eschol, n.d.

Macalister, Alexander. "Fever." In James Orr, ed., *International Standard Bible Encyclopedia*. 1915. https://www.bible-history.com/isbe/F/FEVER.

McCane, Byron R. "Death and Burial, Hellenistic and Roman Period, Palestine." In *OEBA* 1:262–70.

———. *Roll Back the Stone: Death and Burial in the World of Jesus*. Harrisburg: Trinity, 2003.

Maccoby, H. *Ritual and Morality*. Cambridge: Cambridge University Press, 1999.

McCollough, C. Thomas. "City and Village in Lower Galilee: The Import of the Archeological Excavations at Sepphoris and Khirbet Qana (Cana) for Framing the Economic Context of Jesus," In *The Galilean Economy in the Time of Jesus*, edited by David A. Fiensy and Ralph K. Hawkins, 49–74. Early Christianity and Its Literature 11. Atlanta: Society of Biblbical Literature, 2013.

———. "Khirbet Qana." In *GLSTMP* 2:127–45.

McCollough, C. Thomas, and Beth Glazier-McDonald. "Magic and Medicine in Byzantine Galilee: A Bronze Amulet From Sepphoris." In *Archaeology and the Galilee: Texts and Contexts in the Graeco-Roman and Byzantine Periods*, edited by Douglas R. Edwards and C. Thomas McCollough, 143–49. SFSHJ 143. Atlanta: Scholars, 1997.

McCown, C. C. "The Density of Population in Ancient Palestine." *JBL* 66 (1947) 425–36.

MacDonald, Nathan. *What Did the Ancient Israelites Eat?* Grand Rapids: Eerdmans, 2008.

McGarvey, J. W. *Lands of the Bible*. Nashville: Gospel Advocate, 1966.

Mack, Burton. *A Myth of Innocence*. Philadelphia: Fortress, 1988.

McCready, Wayne O., and Adele Reinhartz, eds. *Common Judaism: Explorations in Second-Temple Judaism*. Minneapolis: Fortress, 2008.

MacMullen, Ramsay. *Enemies of the Roman Order*. Cambridge: Harvard University Press, 1966.

———. *Roman Social Relations*. New Haven: Yale University Press, 1974.

McRay, John. *Archaeology and the New Testament*. Grand Rapids: Baker, 1991.

Magen, Y. "Ancient Israel's Stone Age." *BAR* 24/5 (1998) 46–52.

———. "Jerusalem as a Center of the Stone Vessel Industry during the Second Temple Period. " In *Ancient Jerusalem Revealed*, edited by H. Geva, 244–56. Jerusalem: Israel Exploration Society, 1994.

———. "The Land of Benjamin in the Second Temple Period." In *The Land of Benjamin*, edited by Yitzhak Magen et al., 1–28. Jerusalem: Israel Antiquities Authority, 2004.

———. "Qalandiya—A Second Temple-Period Viticulture and Wine-Manufacturing Agricultural Settlement." In *The Land of Benjamin*, edited by Yitzhak Magen et al., 29–144. Jerusalem: Israel Antiquities Authority, 2004.

———. "The Stone Vessel Industry during the Second Temple Period." In *Purity Broke Out in Israel (Tractate Shabbat 13b)*, 7–27. Haifa: Reuben and Edith Hecht Museum, 1994.

———. *The Stone Vessel Industry in the Second Temple Period*. Jerusalem: Israel Exploration Society, 2002.

Magen, Yitzhak, Yoav Tzionit, and Orna Sirkis. "Khirbet Badd'isa—Qiryat Sefer." In *The Land of Benjamin*, edited by Yitzhak Magens et al., 179–242. Jerusalem: Israel Antiquities Authority, 2004.

Magness, Jodi. *The Archaeology of Qumran and the Dead Sea Scrolls*. Grand Rapids: Eerdmans, 2002.

———. "Disposing of the Dead: An Illustration of the Intersection of Archaeology and Text." In *"Go Out and Study the Land" (Judges 18:2): Archaeological, Historical and Textual Studies in Honor of Hanan Eshel*, edited by Aren M. Maeir et al., 117–132. JSJSup 148. Leiden: Brill, 2012.

———. *Stone and Dung, Oil and Spit: Jewish Daily Life in the Time of Jesus*. Grand Rapids: Eerdmans, 2011.

Magness, Jodi, et al. "The Huqoq Excavation Project: 2014–2017 Interim Report." *BASOR* 380 (2018) 61–131.

Malina, Bruce J. *The New Testament World: Insights from Cultural Anthropology*. Atlanta: John Knox, 1981, 2001.

Malina Bruce J., and Richard L. Rohrbaugh. *Social Science Commentary on the Synoptic Gospels*. Minneapolis: Fortress, 1992, 2003.

Marciniak, Stephanie, et al. "*Plasmodium falciparum* Malaria in 1st–2nd Century CE Southern Italy." *Current Biology* 26/23 (2016) 1220–22.

Marciniak, Stephanie, D. Ann Herring, Alessandra Sperduti, Hendrik N. Poinar, Tracy L. Prowse. "A Multi-Faceted Anthropological and Genomic Approach to Framing *Plasmodium Falciparum* Malaria in Imperial Period Central-Southern Italy (1st–4th c. CE)." *Journal of Anthropological Archaeology* 49 (2018) 210–24.

Marshall, I. Howard, *The Acts of the Apostles*. Tyndale New Testament Commentaries. Leicester, UK: InterVarsity, 1980.

———. *The Gospel of Luke: A Commentary on the Greek Text*. New International Greek Testament Commentary. Grand Rapids: Eerdmans, 1978.

Martin, Dale B. "Slavery and the Ancient Jewish Family." In *The Jewish Family in Antiquity*, edited by Shaye J.D. Cohen, 113–29. Atlanta: Scholars, 1993.

Matillah, Sharon Lea. "Capernaum, Village of Nahum, from Hellenistic to Byzantine Times." In *GLSTMP* 2:217–57.

———. "Revisiting Jesus' Capernaum: A Village of Only Subsistence-Level Fishers and Farmers?" In *The Galilean Economy in the Time of Jesus*, edited by David A. Fiensy and Ralph Hawkins, 75–138. Early Christianity and Its Literature 11. Atlanta: Society of Biblical Literature, 2013.

Mayer, Günter. *Die Jüdische Frau in der Hellenistische-Römischen Antike*. Stuttgart: Kohlhammer, 1987.

Mazar, Amihai. *Archaeology of the Land of the Bible: 10,000–586 B.C.E.* New York: Doubleday, 1990.

———. "The 1997–1998 Excavations at Tel Rehov: Preliminary Report." *IEJ* 49 (1999) 1–42.

Mazar, Benjamin. "Herodian Jerusalem in the Light of Excavations South and South-West of the Temple Mount." *IEJ* 28 (1978) 230–37.

———. *The Mountain of the Lord.* Garden City, NY: Doubleday, 1975.

Meacham, William. "On the Archaeological Evidence for a Coin-on-Eye Jewish Burial Custom in the First Century A.D." *BA* 49/1 (1986) 56–59.

Mealand, D. L. *Poverty and Expectation in the Gospels.* London: SPCK, 1980.

MedicineNet.com (website). "Malaria." *MedicineNet.com.* https://www.medicinenet.com/malaria_facts/article.htm.

Meigs, A. S. *Food, Sex and Pollution.* New Brunswick, NJ: Rutgers University Press, 1984.

———. "A Papuan Perspective on Pollution." *Man* 13 (1978) 304–318.

Merrill, Eugene H. *Deuteronomy.* Nashville: Broadman & Holman, 1994.

Merrins, M. "The Deaths of Antiochus IV, Herod the Great, and Agrippa I." *Bibliotheca Sacra* 62 (1904) 561–62.

Meye, R. P. *Jesus and the Twelve.* Grand Rapids: Eerdmans, 1968.

Meyers, Carol. "Archaeology—A Window to the Lives of Israelite Women." In *Torah*, edited by Irmtraud Fischer et al., 61–108. Atlanta: Society of Biblical Literature, 2011.

———. "The Family in Early Israel." In *Families in Ancient Israel*, edited by Leo G. Perdue, et al., 1–47. Louisville: Westminster John Knox, 1997.

———. "From Field Crops to Food: Attributing Gender and Meaning to Bread Production in Iron Age Israel." In *The Archaeology of Difference: Gender, Ethnicity, Class and the 'Other' in Antiquity*, edited by Douglas R. Edwards and C. Thomas McCollough, 67–84. Boston: American Schools of Oriental Research, 2007.

———. "Material Remains and Social Relations: Women's Culture in Agrarian Households of the Iron Age." In *Symbiosis, Symbolism, and the Power of the Past: Canaan, Ancient Israel, and Their Neighbors form the Late Bronze Age through Roman Palaestina*, edited by William G. Dever and Seymour Gitin, 425–444. Winona Lake, IN: Eisenbrauns, 2003.

———. *Rediscovering Eve: Ancient Israelite Women in Context.* Oxford: Oxford University Press, 2013.

———. "Was Ancient Israel a Patriarchal Society?" *JBL* 133/1 (2014) 8–27.

Meyers, Carol L., and Eric M. Meyers. "Sepphoris." In *OEANE* 4:531–32.

Meyers, Eric M. "Aspects of Everyday Life in Roman Palestine with Special Reference to Private Domiciles and Ritual Baths." In *Jews in the Hellenistic and Roman Cities*, edited by J. R. Bartlett, 193–219. London: Routledge, 2002.

———. "The Bible and Archaeology." *BA* 47 (1984) 36–40.

———. "The Cultural Setting of Galilee: The Case of Regionalism and Early Judaism." In *ANRW* II.19.1 (1979) 686–702.

———. "The Emergence of Early Judaism and Christianity in the Light of Second Temple Diversity and Qumran Sectarianism." In *One Hundred Years of American Archaeology in the Middle East*, edited by Douglas R. Clark and Victor H. Matthews, 97–113. Boston: American Schools of Oriental Research, 2003.

———. "Galilean Regionalism as a Factor in Historical Reconstruction." *BASOR* 221 (1976) 93–101.

———. "Jesus and His Galilean Context." In *Archaeology and the Galilee: Texts and Contexts in the Graeco-Roman and Byzantine Periods*, edited by Douglas R. Edwards and C. Thomas McCollough, 57–66. SFSHJ 143. Atlanta: Scholars, 1997.

———. "Jesus and His World: Sepphoris and the Quest for the Historical Jesus" In *Saxa Loquentur: Studien zur Archäologie Palästinas/Israels: Festschrift für Volkmar Fritz zum*

65. *Geburtstag*, edited by Cornelus G. den Hertog et al., 185–97. Alter Orient und Altes Testament 302. Münster: Ugarit-Verlag, 2003.

———. "The Problems of Gendered Space in Syro-Palestinian Domestic Architecture: The Case of Roman-Period Galilee." In *Early Christian Families in Context*, edited by David L. Balch and Carolyn Osiek, 44–69. Grand Rapids: Eerdmans, 2003.

———. "Roman-Period Houses from the Galilee: Domestic Architecture and Gendered Spaces." In *Symbiosis, Symbolism, and the Power of the Past: Canaan, Ancient Israel, and Their Neighbors from the Late Bronze Age through Roman Palaestina*, edited by William G. Dever and Seymour Gitin, 487–499. Winona Lake, IN: Eisenbrauns, 2003.

———. "Roman Sepphoris in Light of New Archaeological Evidence and Recent Research." In *The Galilee in Late Antiquity*, edited by Lee I. Levine, 321–338. New York: Jewish Theological Seminary, 1992.

———. "The Pools of Sepphoris: Ritual Baths or Bathtubs: Yes, They Are." *BAR* 26/4 (2000) 46–49, 60–61.

Meyers, Eric M., and Carol Meyers. "Digging the Talmud in Ancient Meiron." *BAR* 4/2 (1978) 32–42.

———. "Holy Land Archaeology: Where the Past Meets the Present." *Buried History* 50 (2014) 3–16.

———. "Introduction." In *The Pottery from Ancient Sepphoris*, edited by Eric M. Meyers and Carol L. Meyers, 1–12. Winona Lake, IN: Eisenbrauns, 2013.

Meyers, Eric M., Carol L. Meyers, and Benjamin D. Gordon. "Residential Area of the Western Summit." In *GLSTMP* 2:39–52.

Meyers, Eric M., and James F. Strange. *Archaeology, the Rabbis and Early Christianity*. Nashville: Abingdon, 1981.

Meyers, Eric M., et al. *Excavations at Ancient Meiron, Upper Galilee, Israel 1971–72, 1974–75, 1977*. Cambridge, MA: ASOR, 1981.

———. "The Meiron Excavation Project: Archeological Survey in Galilee and Golan, 1976." *BASOR* 230 (1978) 1–24

———. "Second Preliminary Report on the 1981 Excavations at en-Nabratein, Israel" *BASOR* 246 (1982) 35–54.

———. *Sepphoris*. Winona Lake, IN: Eisenbrauns, 1992.

Milgrom, Jacob. *Leviticus 1–16*. AB 3. New York: Doubleday, 1991.

———. "Studies in the Temple Scroll." *JBL* 97 (1978) 501–523.

Millar, Fergus Graham Burtholme. "Salarium." In *OCD* 945–46.

Miller, Shulamit. "Tiberias." In *OEBA* 2:429–37.

Minozzi, S., W., et al. "The Roman Giant: Overgrowth Syndrome in Skeletal Remains from the Imperial Age." *IJO* 25 (2015) 574–84.

Mitchell, Piers D. "Child Health in the Crusader Period Inhabitants of Tel Jezreel, Israel." *Levant* 38 (2006) 37–44.

———. "Human Parasites in the Roman World: Health Consequences of Conquering an Empire." *Parasitology* 144 (2017) 48–58. https://www.cambridge.org/core/services/aop-cambridge-core/content/view/S0031182015001651.

———. "The Palaeopathology of Skulls Recovered from a Medieval Cave Cemetery near Safed, Israel (Thirteenth to Seventeenth Century)." *Levant* 36 (2004) 243–250.

———. "Pathology in the Crusader Period: Human Skeletal Remains from Tel Jezreel." *Levant* 26 (1994) 67–71.

Mitchell, P. D., and Y. Tepper. "Intestinal Parasitic Worm Eggs from a Crusader Period Cesspool in the City of Acre (Israel)." *Levant* 39 (2007) 91–95.

Montefiore, Hugh. *For God's Sake*. Philadelphia: Fortress, 1969.

Montefiore, C.G. and H. Loewe. *A Rabbinic Anthology*. New York: Schocken, 1974.

Moore, G. F. *History of Religions*. New York: Scribners, 1947.

Moorsom, Robert Maude. *A Historical Companion to Hymns Ancient and Modern*. London: Clay, 1903.

Moreland, Milton C., et al. "Introduction: Between Text and Artifact." In *Between Text and Artifact: Integrating Archaeology in Biblical Studies Teaching*, edited by Milton C. Moreland, 1–10. Atlanta: Society of Biblical Literature, 2003.

Morris, Ian. "Archaeology, Standards of Living and Greek Economic History." In *The Ancient Economy*, edited by J.G. Manning and Ian Morris, 91–126. Stanford: Stanford University Press, 2005.

Muraoka, T. *A Greek-English Lexicon of the Septuagint*. Louvain: Peeters, 2009.

Murphy-O'Connor, Jerome. *The Holy Land*. Oxford: Oxford University Press, 2008.

———. "Qumran and the New Testament." In *The New Testament and Its Modern Interpreters*, edited by E. J. Epp and G. W. MacRae, 55–74. Atlanta: Scholars, 1989.

Nagar, Yossi, and Hagit Torgeé. "Biological Characteristics of Jewish Burials in the Hellenistic and Early Roman Periods." *IEJ* 53 (2003) 164–71.

Nagar, Yossi, and Flavia Sonntag. "Byzantine Period Burials in the Negev: Anthropological Description and Summary." *IEJ* 58 (2008) 79–93.

Nakhai, Beth Alpert. "Embracing the Domestic." In *40 Futures: Experts Predict What's Next for Biblical Archaeology*, 37. Washington: Biblical Archaeology Society, 2015.

Nathan, H. "Skeletal Remains from Naḥal Ḥever." *Atiqot* 3 (1961) 165–75.

Naveh, J. "A New Tomb Inscription from Giv'at at Hamivtar." In *Jerusalem Revealed*, edited by Y. Yadin, 73–74. Jerusalem: Israel Exploration Society, 1975.

———. "The Ossuary Inscriptions from Givat ha-Mivtar," *IEJ* 20 (1970) 33–37.

Naveh, Joseph, and Shaul Shaked. *Amulets and Magic Bowls: Aramaic Incantations of Late Antiquity*. Leiden: Brill, 1985.

———. *Magic Spells and Formulae: Aramaic Incantations of Late Antiquity*. Jerusalem: Magness, 1993.

Nelson, Richard D. *Deuteronomy*. Louisville: Westminster John Knox, 2002.

Netzer, Ehud. "Domestic Architecture in the Iron Age." In *The Architecture of Ancient Israel*, edited by Aharon Kempinski and Ronny Reich, 193–201. Jerusalem: Israel Exploration Society, 1992.

———. "Herod's Family Tomb in Jerusalem." *BAR* 9/3 (1983) 52–59.

———. "Jericho." In *NEAEHL* 5:1798–800.

———. "Masada." In *NEAEHL* 3:973–85.

———. "The Promontory Palace: Description and Stratigraphy." In *Excavations at Caesarea Maritima 1975, 1976, 1979—Final Report*, edited by Lee I. Levine and Ehud Netzer, 149–160. Jerusalem: Hebrew University Press, 1986.

Netzer, E. and Z. Weiss. *Zippori*. Jerusalem: Israel Exploration Society, 1994.

Neufeld, Dietmar and Richard E. Demaris, eds. *Understanding the Social World of the New Testament*. London: Routledge, 2010.

Neufeld, Edward. "Hygiene Conditions in Ancient Israel (Iron Age)," In *The Biblical Archaeologist Reader IV*, edited by E. F. Campbell Jr. and D. N. Freedman, 151–79. Sheffield: Almond, 1983.

Neusner, Jacob. "Archaeology and Babylonian Jewry." In *Near Eastern Archaeology in the Twentieth Century*, edited by James A. Sanders, 331–343. Garden City, NY: Doubleday, 1970.

———. *The Babylonian Talmud*. Peabody, MA: Hendrickson, 2005.

———. *Classical Judaism: Torah, Learning, Virtue; An Anthology of the Mishnah, Talmud, and Midrash*. Vol. 3, *Virtue*. Frankfurt: Lang, 1993.

———. *From Politics to Piety*. Englewood, NJ: Prentice Hall, 1973.

———. *The Idea of Purity in Ancient Judaism*. Leiden: Brill, 1973.

———. *Introduction to Rabbinic Literature*. New York: Doubleday, 1994.

———. *Purity in Rabbinic Judaism: A Systemic Account*. Atlanta: Scholars, 1994.

———. *The Tosephta*. Hoboken, NY: Ktav, 1977–1986.

Newton, M. *The Concept of Purity at Qumran and in the Letters of Paul*. Cambridge: Cambridge University Press, 1985.

Newton, Paula, and Taehoon Lee. "North Korean Soldier: Surgeon Says Defector 'Was Like a Broken Jar.'" *CNN* December 5, 2017. http://www.cnn.com/2017/12/04/health/north-korea-defector-doctor-intl/index.html.

Neyrey, Jerome H., and Eric C. Stewart, eds. *The Social World of the New Testament*. Peabody, MA: Hendrickson, 2008.

Nezamabadi, M. et al. "Paleoparasitological Analysis of Samples from the Chehrabad Salt Mine (Northwestern Iran)." *IJP* 3/3 (2013) 229–33.

No author. "Ascariasis." *Healthline*. https://www.healthline.com/health/ascariasis#symptoms.

No author. "Biblical Latrine: Ancient Parasites Show that Cleanliness May Have Been Next to Sickliness." *Science Daily* November 13, 2006. https://phys.org/news/2006-11-ancient-parasites-cleanliness-sickliness.html.

No author. "Brucellosis." *Wikipedia*. https://en.wikipedia.org/wiki/Brucellosis.

No author. "Capernaum: the town of Jesus." http://www.christusrex.org/www1/ofm/sites/TScpvill.html.

No author. "DNA of Jesus-Era Shrouded Man in Jerusalem Reveals Earliest Case of Leprosy." *Science Daily* (December 16, 2009). https://www.sciencedaily.com/releases/2009/12/091216103558.htm.

No author. "'Enormous Number' Of Parasites In North Korean Defector's Body, Doctors Say." *Fox News* (November 17, 2017). http://www.foxnews.com/world/2017/11/17/enormous-number-parasites-in-north-korean-defectors-body-doctors-say.html.

No author. "Facebook Fails to Save Child Bride from Auction." *CNN* (November 20, 2018). https://www.freedomunited.org/news/facebook-fails-to-save-child-bride-from-auction.

No author. "Five-foot long tapeworm came 'wiggling out' of man's body after he ate sushi." https://www.youtube.com/watch?v=OADHIBgRwKA.

No author. "Horvat Kanaf Amulet: Incantation Against Fever and Pain." *Center for the Online Judaic Studies*. http://cojs.org/horvat_kanaf_amulet-_incantation_against_fever_and_pain.

No author. "Human Height." *Wikipedia*. https://en.wikipedia.org/wiki/Human_height.

No author. "Human Parasites Found in Medieval Cesspit Reveal Links Between Middle East and Europe." *Heritage Daily*. https://phys.org/news/2015-03-human-parasites-medieval-cesspit-reveal.html.

No author. "Life Expectancy at Birth." *World Fact Book*. https://www.cia.gov/library/publications/the-world-factbook/rankorder/2102rank.html.

No author. "List of Countries by Life Expectancy." *Wikipedia*. https://en.wikipedia.org/wiki/List_of_countries_by_life_expectancy.

No Author. "Malaria." MedicineNet.com. https://www.medicinenet.com/malaria_facts/article.htm.

No Author. "Malaria." *Wikipedia*. https://en.wikipedia.org/wiki/malaria.

No author. "Tape worms in Humans." *WebMD*. https://www.webmd.com/digestive-disorders/tapeworms-in-humans#1.

No author. "Ten Symptoms of Parasites." https://facty.com/ailments/body/10-symptoms-of-a-parasite.

No author. "Whipworm Infection." *Healthline*. https://www.healthline.com/health/whipworm-infection.

Oakman, Douglas E. *Jesus and the Economic Questions of His Day*. Studies in the Bible and Early Christianity 8. Lewiston, NY: Mellen, 1986.

———. *Jesus and the Peasants*. Matrix 4. Eugene, OR: Cascade Books, 2008.

Oepke, Albrecht. "γύνη." In *TDNT* 1:776–89

Oliver, J. H. *The Sacred Gerusia*. Baltimore: American School of Classical Studies, 1941.

Onn, A., S. Wexler-Bdolah, Y. Rapuano, and T. Kanias. "Khirbet Umm el-ʿUmdan." *Explorations and Surveys in Israel* 114 (2002) 64*–68*.

Osiek, Carolyn. *What Are They Saying About the Social Setting of the New Testament?* New York: Paulist, 1992.

Overman, J. Andrew. "Jesus of Galilee and the Historical Peasant." In *Archaeology and the Galilee: Texts and Contexts in the Graeco-Roman and Byzantine Periods*, edited by Douglas R. Edwards and C. Thomas McCollough, 67–73. SFSHJ 143. Atlanta: Scholars, 1997.

———. "Who Were the First Urban Christians?" *SBL Seminar Papers* (1988) 160–68.

Padovano, A. T. "Is It Just Possible That Jesus Was Married?" *National Catholic Reporter* 32/24 (1996) 12–15.

Parkin, Tim G. *Demography and Roman Society*. Baltimore: Johns Hopkins, 1992.

Patrich, Joseph. "Chapter 1. The Excavations 1993–1998, 2000–2001." In *Archaeological Excavations at Caesarea Maritima, Areas CC, KK and NN Final Reports, Volume I: The Objects*, edited by Joseph Patrich, 1–11. Jerusalem: Israel Excavation Society, 2008.

———. "Caesarea." In *OEBA* 1:147–57.

———. "The Combined Caesarea Expedition Excavations." In *NEAEHL* 5:1673–80.

Pearson, Birger A. "Did Jesus Marry?" *Bible Review* 21/2 (2005) 32–39, 47.

Peleg-Barkat, Orit. "Fit for a King: Architecture Décor in Judaea and Herod as Trendsetter." *BASOR* 371 (2014) 141–61.

Pereira, Sydney. "A Beautiful City in the Bible Was Ravaged by Disease and Chaos Because of Climate Change." http://www.newsweek.com/city-bible-ravaged-disease-chaos-climate-change-724633.

Peskowitz, Miriam. "Family/ies in Antiquity: Evidence from Tannaitic Literature and Roman Galilean Architecture. In *The Jewish Family in Antiquity*, edited by Shaye J. D. Cohen, 9–36. Brown Judaic Studies 289. Atlanta: Scholars, 1993.

Pfann, Stephen, Ross Voss, and Yehudah Rapuano. "Surveys and Excavations at the Nazareth Village Farm (1997–2002): Final Report." *BAIAS* 25 (1997) 19–79.

Phillips, Kristine. "His Health Had Been Failing for Years. Then He Saw Something Crawling in His Eye." News. To Your Health. *Washington Post*, August 9, 2018. https://www.

washingtonpost.com/news/to-your-health/wp/2018/08/09/an-artist-found-a-parasitic-worm-in-his-eye-and-turned-it-into-art/?noredirect=on&utm_term=.2fa072c4bd49.

Phipps, William E. "Itinerating Wives and Mary Magdalene." *Currents in Theology and Mission* 33 (2006) 394–96.

———. *Was Jesus Married? The Distortion of Sexuality in the Christian Tradition.* New York: Harper & Row, 1970.

Piontek, J., and T. Kozlowsk. "Frequency of Cribra Orbitalia in the Subadult Medieval Population from Gruczno, Poland." *IJO* 12 (2002) 202–8.

Piper, Kelsey. "Malaria is among the world's biggest killers of children. Now there's a vaccine." *Vox*, April 24, 2019. https://www.vox.com/future-perfect/2019/4/24/18514577/malaria-vaccine-malawi-pilot-program.

Poirier, J. C. "Purity beyond the Temple in the Second Temple Era." *JBL* 122 (2003) 247–65.

Porath, Y. "Caesarea: Israel Antiquities Authority Excavations." In *NEAEHL* 5:1656–65.

———. *Caesarea Maritima I: Herod's Circus and Related Buildings Part 1: Architecture and Stratigraphy.* Jerusalem: Israel Antiquities Authority, 2013.

———. "Herod's 'Amphitheatre' at Caesarea: A Multipurpose Entertainment Building." *JRA Supplemental Series* 14 (1995) 15–27.

———. "Vegas on the Med." *BAR* 30/5 (2004) 24–35.

Porten, Bezazel. *Archives from Elephantine: The Life of an Ancient Jewish Military Colony.* Berkeley: University of California Press, 1968.

———. "Elephantine Papyri." In *ABD* 2:445–55.

Preuss, Julius. *Biblical and Talmudic Medicine.* New York: Sanhedrin, 1978.

Pritchard, James B. *Ancient Near Eastern Texts Relating to the Old Testament.* Princeton: Princeton University Press, 1955.

———. *The Ancient Near East.* Vol. I: *An Anthology of Texts and Pictures.* Princeton: Princeton University Press, 1958.

———. *The Ancient Near East.* Vol. II: *A New Anthology of Texts and Pictures.* Princeton: Princeton University Press, 1975.

Prost, A. and G. Vincent, eds. *A History of Private Life.* Cambridge: Harvard University Press, 1991.

Puech, Emile. "Palestinian Funerary Inscriptions." In *ABD* 5:126–35.

Rahmani, L. Y. "Ancient Jerusalem's Funerary Customs and Tombs: Part Four." *BA* 45 (1982) 109–19.

———. "Jewish Ossuaries." In *Purity Broke Out in Israel (Tractate Shabbat 13b)*, 28–36. Haifa: Reuben and Edith Hecht Museum, 1994.

———. "Ossuaries and *Ossilegium* (Bone-Gathering) in the Late Second Temple Period." In *Ancient Jerusalem Revealed*, edited by Hillel Geva and Joseph Shadur, 191–205. Jerusalem: Israel Exploration Society, 1994.

Rainey, Anson F., and R. Steven Notley. *Carta's New Century Handbook and Atlas of the Bible.* Jerusalem: Carta, 2006.

———. *The Sacred Bridge: Carta's Atlas of the Biblical World.* Jerusalem: Carta, 2006.

Rajak, T. "Justus of Tiberias." *Classical Quarterly* n.s. 23 (1973) 345–68.

Ramsay, Jennifer H. and S. Thomas Parker. "A Diachronic Look at the Agricultural Economy of the Red Sea Port of Aila: An Archaeobotanical Case for Hinterland Production in Arid Environments." *BASOR* 376 (2016) 101–20.

Reed, Jonathan L. *Archaeology and the Galilean Jesus.* Harrisburg: Trinity, 2000.

———. "Galileans, 'Israelite Village Communities' and the Sayings Gospel Q." In *Galilee though the Centuries*, edited by Eric M. Meyers, 87–108. Winona Lake, IN: Eisenbrauns, 1999.

———. "Instability in Jesus' Galilee: A Demographic Perspective." *JBL* 129 (2010) 343–365.

Reich, Ronny. "The Great Mikveh Debate." *BAR* 19/2 (1993) 52–53.

———. "Miqwa'ot (Jewish Ritual Immersion Baths) in Eretz Israel in the Second Temple and the Mishnah and Talmud Periods." PhD diss., Hebrew University, 1990.

———. "Ossuary Inscriptions of the Caiaphas Tomb." In *Ancient Jerusalem Revealed*, edited by Hillel Geve, 223–225. Jerusalem: IES, 1994.

———. "Ritual Baths." In *OEANE* 4:430–31.

———. "They Are Ritual Baths: Immerse Yourself in the Ongoing Sepphoris Mikveh Debate." *BAR* 28/2 (2002) 50–55.

Reich, Ronny, and Marcela Zapata-Meza. "The Domestic Miqva'ot." In *Magdala of Galilee: A Jewish City in the Hellenistic and Roman Period*, edited by Richard Bauckham, 109–25. Waco: Baylor University Press, 2018.

Reinhardt, Wolfgang. "The Population Size of Jerusalem and the Numerical Growth of the Jerusalem Church." In *The Book of Acts in Its Palestinian Setting*, edited by Richard Bauckham, 237–65. Grand Rapids: Eerdmans, 1995.

Reinhard, Karl J., and Adauto Araújo. "Archaeoparasitology." In *Encyclopedia of Archaeology*, edited by Deborah M. Pearsall, 494–501. Amsterdam: Elsevier, 2008.

Rey-Coquais, Jean Paul. "Decapolis." In *ABD* 2:116–21.

Richardson, Peter. *Building Jewish in the Roman East.* Waco: Baylor University Press, 2004.

———. "Khirbet Qana (and Other Villages) as a Context for Jesus." In *Jesus and Archaeology*, edited by James H. Charlesworth, 120–44. Grand Rapids: Eerdmans, 2006.

———. "Towards a Typology of Levantine/Palestinian Houses" *JSNT* 27 (2004) 47–68.

———. "What Has Cana to Do with Capernaum?" *NTS* 48 (2002) 314–31.

Richardson, Peter, and Douglas Edwards. "Jesus and Palestinian Social Protest: Archeological and Literary Perspectives." In *Handbook of Early Christianity*, edited by Anthony J. Blasi et al., 247–66. New York: Altamira, 2002.

Rihbany, Abraham Mitrie. *The Syrian Christ.* Boston: Houghton Mifflin, 1916.

Rillinger, R. "Moderne und zeitgenössische Vortellungen von der Gesellschaftsordnung der römischen Kaiserzeit." *Saeculum* 36 (1985) 299–329.

Rivkin, E. *A Hidden Revolution.* Nashville: Abingdon, 1978.

Roberts, Charlotte, and Keith Manchester. *The Archaeology of Disease.* Gloucestershire, UK: History, 2010.

Robinson, Gesine Schenke. "How a Papyrus Fragment Became a Sensation." *NTS* 61 (2015) 379–94.

Rohrbaugh, Richard L. "Introduction." In *The Social Sciences and New Testament Interpretation*, edited by Richard. L. Rohrbaugh, 1–15. Peabody, MA: Hendrickson, 1996.

———. "The Pre-Industrial City in Luke–Acts: Urban Social Relations." In *The Social World of Luke–Acts*, edited by Jerome H. Neyrey, 125–49. Peabody, MA: Hendrickson, 1991.

———. ed. *The Social Sciences and New Testament Interpretation*. Peabody, MA: Hendrickson, 1996.

Röhrer-Ertl, Olav. "Facts and Results Based on Skeletal Remains from Qumran Found in the *Collectio Kurth*: A Study in Methodology." In *Qumran: The Site of the Dead Sea Scrolls; Archaeological Interpretations and Debates; Proceedings of a Conference Held at Brown*

University, November 17–19, 2002, edited by Katharina Galor et al., 181–93. Studies on the Texts of the Desert of Judah 57. Leiden: Brill, 2006.

Rösel, H. "Haus." In *Biblisches Reallexikon*, edited by Kurt Galling, 138–41. Tübingen: Mohr/Siebeck, 1977.

Roller, Duane W. *The Building Program of Herod the Great*. Berkeley: University of California Press, 1998.

Root, Bradley W. *First Century Galilee: A Fresh Examination of the Sources*. WUNT 2/378. Tübingen: Mohr/Siebeck, 2014.

Rosen, Baruch. "Subsistence Economy of Stratum II." In *'Izbet Ṣarṭah: An Early Iron Age Site Near Rosh Ha'ayin, Israel*, edited by Israel Finkelstein et al., 156–85. Oxford: BAR, 1986.

Roser, Max. "Child Mortality." *OurWorldInData.org*. http://ourworldindata.org/data/population-growth-vital-statistics/child-mortality (2015).

Rostovtzeff, M. I. *Excavation in Dura-Europos*. New Haven: Yale University Press, 1943–1968.

———. *A Large Estate in Egypt in the Third Century B.C.* Madison: University of Wisconsin Press, 1922.

Roth, C., et al. "Purity and Impurity." *EncJud1* 13:1405–14.

Rousseau, John J., and Rami Arav. *Jesus and His World: An Archaeological and Cultural Dictionary*. Minneapolis: Fortress, 1995.

Russell, J. C. *The Control of Late Ancient and Medieval Population*. Philadelphia: American Philosophical Society, 1985.

———. *Late Ancient and Medieval Population*. Philadelphia: American Philosophical Society, 1958.

Safrai, Samuel. "Home and Family." In *The Jewish People in the First Century: VOLUME 2*, edited by S. Safrai and M. Stern, 728–292. Philadelphia: Fortress, 1976.

Safrai, Ze'ev. "Agriculture and Farming." In *OHJDL* 246–63.

———. *The Economy of Roman Palestine*. London: Routledge, 1994.

Saggs, H. W. F. *The Greatness That Was Babylon*. New York: Mentor, 1962.

Sah, Raaj K. "The Effects of Child Mortality Changes on Fertility Choice and Parental Welfare." *Journal of Political Economy* 99 (1991) 582–606.

Saldarini, Anhony J. "Babatha's Story: Personal Archive Offers a Glimpse of Ancient Jewish Life." *BAR* 24/2 (1998) 28–37.

Sallares, Robert. *Malaria and Rome: A History of Malaria in Ancient Italy*. Oxford: Oxford University Press, 2002.

———. "Disease." In *OCD3* 486.

Samovar, Larry A., Richard E. Porter. *Communication between Cultures*. Stamford, CT: Thomson Learmomg, 2001.

Sanders, E. P. *The Historical Figure of Jesus*. London: Penguin, 1993.

———. *Jewish Law from Jesus to the Mishnah*. London: SCM, 1990.

———. *Jesus and Judaism*. Philadelphia: Fortress, 1985.

———. *Judaism: Practice and Belief: 63 BCE—66 CE*. London: SCM, 1992.

Sapir-Hen, Lidar, et al. "Animal Economy in a Temple City and Its Countryside: Iron Age Jerusalem as a Case Study." *BASOR* 375 (2016) 103–18.

Satlow, Michael L. "Marriage and Divorce." In *OHJDL* 344–61.

Savage, Carl E. "Hamath Tiberias." In *GLSTMP* 2:211–16.

Sayce, A.H. *The Aramaic Papyri Discovered at Assuan*. London: Moring, 1906.

Scheidel, Walter. *Death on the Nile: Disease and the Demography of Roman Egypt*. Leiden: Brill. 2001.

———. "Disease and Death in the Ancient City of Rome." *Princeton/Stanford Working Papers in Classics* (2009). https://www.ancient.eu/article/257/disease-and-death-in-the-ancient-city-of-rome.

———. "Population and Demography." *Princeton/Stanford Working Papers in Classics*, (2006). https://www.princeton.edu/~pswpc/pdfs/scheidel/040604.pdf.

———. "Real Wages in Early Economies: Evidence for Living Standards from 1800 BCE to 1300 CE" *Princeton/Stanford Working Papers in Classics* (2009). http://www.princeton.edu/~pswpc/papers/authorMZ/scheidel/scheidel.html.

Schiffman, L. H. *Sectarian Law in the Dead Sea Scrolls*. Chico, CA: Scholars, 1983.

Schloen, J. David. *The House of the Father as Fact and Symbol: Patrimonialism in Ugarit and the Ancient Near East*. Winona Lake, IN: Eisenbrauns, 2001.

Schmidt, F. *How the Temple Thinks*. Sheffield: Sheffield Academic, 2001.

Schnackenburg, R. *The Moral Teachings of the New Testament*. Freiburg: Herder, 1965.

Schofer, Jonathan. "The Different Life Stages: From Childhood to Old Age." In *OHJDL* 327–43.

Schremer, Adriel. "Divorce in Papyrus Ṣe'elim 13 Once Again: a Reply to Tal Ilan." *HTR* 91 (1998) 193–202.

Schürer, Emil, Geza Vermes, and Fergus Miller. *The History of the Jewish People in the Age of Jesus Christ (175 B.C.-A.D. 135)*. Volume 1. Edinburgh: T. & T. Clark, 1973.

Schuller, Eileen. "Women in the Dead Sea Scrolls." In *The Dead Sea Scrolls after Fifty Years*, edited by Peter W. Flint and James C. Vanderkam, 117–144. Leiden: Brill, 1999.

Schumer, Nathan. "The Population Size of Sepphoris: Rethinking Urbanization in Early and Middle Roman Galilee." *Academia* Online: https://www.academia.edu/33894484/The_Population_Size_of_Sepphoris_Rethinking_Urbanization_in_Early_and_Middle_Roman.

Schwartz, Joshua J. "Realities of Jewish Life in the Land of Israel, c. 235–638." In . In *The Late Roman-Rabbinic Period*, edited by Steven T. Katz, 431–456. Cambridge: Cambridge University Press, 2006.

Science Daily. "Biblical Latrine: Ancient Parasites Show that Cleanliness May Have Been Next to Sickliness." *Science Daily*, November 13, 2006. https://phys.org/news/2006-11-ancient-parasites-cleanliness-sickliness.html.

———. "DNA of Jesus-Era Shrouded Man in Jerusalem Reveals Earliest Case of Leprosy." *Science Daily* (December 16, 2009). https://www.sciencedaily.com/releases/2009/12/091216103558.htm.

Scutti, Susan. "Teen Dies of Tapeworm Egg Infestation in Brain." *CNN*, March 28, 2019. https://www.cnn.com/2019/03/28/health/brain-parasites-case-study/index.html.

Searcey, Nicole, et al. "Parasitism of the Zweeloo Woman: Dicrocoeliasis Evidenced in a Roman Period Bog Mummy." *IJP* 3/3 (2013) 224–28

Segal, Alan F. *Life after Death: A History of the Afterlife in the Religions of the West*. New York: Doubleday, 2004.

Seidemann, Ryan M. "Bones of Contention: A Comparative Examination of Law Governing Human Remains from Archaeological Contexts in Formerly Colonial Countries." *Louisiana Law Review* 64 (2004) 545–88.

Seltzer, R. M. *Jewish People, Jewish Thought: The Jewish Experience in History*. New York: Macmillan, 1980.

Sevenster, J. N. *Do You Know Greek?* Leiden: Brill, 1968.

Shafer-Elliott, Cynthia. *Food in Ancient Judah: Domestic Cooking in the Time of the Hebrew Bible*. Sheffield: Equinox, 2013.

Stählin, Gustav. "ἀσθενής." In *TDNT* 1:490–93.

Shamir, Orit. "Textiles, Basketry, Cordage and Whorls from Mo'a (Moje Awad)." *Atiqot* 50 (2005) 99–152.

Shamir, Orit and Naama Sukenik. "Qumran Textiles and the Garments of Qumran's Inhabitants." *Dead Sea Discoveries* 18 (2011) 206–25.

Shanks, Hershel. *Judaism in Stone*. Jerusalem: Steinmatzky, 1979.

Shapiro, Anastasia. "A Petrographic Study of Roman Ceramic Oil Lamps." *BAIAS* 35 (2017) 101–14.

Shaw, Brent. "Seasons of Death: Aspects of Mortality in Imperial Rome." *JRS* 86 (1996) 100–138.

Sheridan, Susan Guise. "Skeletal Remains from the Cemetery of Qumran: The French Collection." (2002). http://www3.nd.edu/~qumran/QumranBrown.pdf.

Sherwin-White, A. N. *Roman Society and Roman Law in the New Testament*. Oxford: Oxford University Press, 1963.

Shiloh, Yigal. *Excavations at the City of David I, 1978–1982*. Jerusalem: Hebrew University Press, 1984.

———. "The Four-Room House: Its Situation and Function in the Israelite City." *IEJ* 20 (1970) 180–90.

———. "The Population of Iron Age Palestine in the Light of a Sample Analysis of Urban Plans, Areas, and Population Density." *BASOR* 239 (1980) 25–35.

Shogan, Gary. "My Favorite New Testament Archaeological Discoveries in Recent Years." blog: https://openoureyeslord.com/2017/03/31/my-favorite-5-new-testament-archaeology-discoveries-in-recent-years.

Shutt, R. J. H. "Letter of Aristeas." In *OTP* 2:7–34.

Siegel-Itzkovich, Judy. "Orthodox Jews Demand University Bury Its Bones." *British Medical Journal* (May 5, 2001). http://www.ncbi.nlm.nih.gov/pmc/articles/PMC1773291.

Simchoni, Orit and Mordechai E. Kislev. "Relict Plant Remains in the 'Cave of the Spear.'" *IEJ* 59/1 (2009) 47–62.

Sjoberg, G. *The Preindustrial City*. Glencoe, IL: Free Press, 1960.

———. "The Preindustrial City." In *Peasant Society: A Reader*, edited by J. M. Potter, et al., 15–24. Boston: Little, Brown, 1967.

Smith, Patricia. "An Approach to the Paleodemographic Analysis of Human Skeletal Remains from Archaeological Sites." In *Biblical Archaeology Today: Proceedings of the Second International Congress on Biblical Archaeology; Pre-Congress Symposium, Population, Production and Power, Jerusalem, June 1990, Supplement, Volume 2*, edited by Joseph Aviram and Allen-Paris Siddur, 2–13. Jerusalem: Israel Exploration Society, 1993.

———. "The Human Skeletal Remains from the Abba Cave." *IEJ* 27 (1977) 121–124.

———. "Skeletal Analysis." In *OEANE* 5:51–56.

Smith, Patricia and Joseph Zias. "Skeletal Remains from the Late Hellenistic French Hill Tomb." *IEJ* 30 (1980) 109–15.

Smith, Patricia, et al. "The Skeletal Remains." In *Excavations at Ancient Meiron, Upper Galilee, Israel 1971–72, 1974–75, 1977*, edited by Eric M. Meyers et al., 110–20. Cambridge: ASOR, 1981.

Smith, W. R. *Lectures on the Religion of the Semites*. London: Black, 1927.

Smith-Guzmán, Nicole E. "Cribra Orbitalia In The Ancient Nile Valley And Its Connection To Malaria." *IJP* 10 (2015) 1–12.

Sofaer, Joanna R. *The Body as Material Culture: A Theoretical Osteoarchaeology.* Cambridge: Cambridge University Press, 2006.

Soper, E. D. *The Religions of Mankind.* New York: Abingdon, 1921.

Sori, Ermias Alemu. "Review on Child Malnutrition Status in Ethiopia." *Nursing and Health Care* 3/1 (2018) 76–79.

Sperber, D. "Costs of Living in Roman Palestine I." *Journal of the Economic and Social History of the Orient* 8 (1965) 248–71.

———. *Roman Palestine 200–400: Money and Prices.* Ramat-Gan, Israel: Bar-Ilan University Press, 1974.

Stagg, Evelyn, and Frank Stagg. *Women in the World of Jesus.* Philadelphia: Westminster, 1978.

Stählin, Gustav. "τύπτω." In *TDNT* 8:260–69.

Stager, Lawrence E. "The Archaeology of the Family in Ancient Israel." *BASOR* 260 (1985) 1–35.

Starbuck, Scott R.A. "Why Declare the Things Forbidden? Classroom Integration of Ancient Near Eastern Archaeology with Biblical Studies in Theological Context." In *Between Text and Artifact: Integrating Archaeology in Biblical Studies Teaching*, edited by Milton C. Moreland, 99–113. Atlanta: Society of Biblical Literature, 2003.

Stark, Rodney. *The Rise of Christianity.* San Francisco: Harper, 1996.

Stauffer, Ethelbert. "γαμέω, γάμος." In *TDNT* 1:648–57.

De Ste. Croix, G. E. M. *The Class Struggle in the Ancient Greek World: From the Archaic Age to the Arab Conquests.* Ithaca: Cornell, 1981.

Steckoll, S. H. "Marginal Notes on the Qumran Excavations." *RevQ* 7 (1969) 33–40.

———. "Preliminary Excavation Report in the Qumran Cemetery." *RevQ* 6 (1968) 323–44.

Stegemann, Ekkehard, and Wolfgang Stegemann. *The Jesus Movement: A Social History of Its First Century.* Translated by O. C. Dean Jr. Minneapolis: Fortress, 1999.

Stein, Robert H. "Luke 14:26 and the Question of Authenticity." *Forum* 5/2 (1989) 187–92.

Steinberg, Naomi. *The World of the Child in the Hebrew Bible.* Sheffield: Sheffield University Press, 2013.

Stern, M. "Aspects of Jewish Society: The Priesthood and other Classes." In *The Jewish People in the First Century*, edited by S. Safrai and M. Stern, 561–630. Compendia Rerum Iudaicarum ad Novum Testamentum I/2. Amsterdam: Van Gorcum, 1976.

———. "The Herodian Dynasty and the Province of Judea at the End of the Period of the Second Temple." In *The Herodian Period: The World History of the Jewish People; First Series: Ancient Times Volume 7* M. Avi-Yona, 124–178. London: Allen, 1975.

———. "The Province of Judea." In *The Jewish People in the First Century*, edited by S. Safrai and M. Stern, 308–76. Compendia Rerum Iudaicarum ad Novum Testamentum I/1. Amsterdam: Van Gorcum, 1974.

Stewart, Edward C., and Milton Bennett. *American Cultural Patterns A Cross Cultural Perspective.* Rev. ed. Yarmouth, ME: Intercultural Press, 1991.

Strack, Hermann L., and Paul Billerbeck. *Kommentar zum Neuen Testament aus Talmud und Midrasch.* 4 vols. Munich: Beck, 1924.

Strange, James F. "Archaeology and the Religion of Judaism in Palestine." *ANRW* II.19.1 (1979) 646–85.

———. "The Eastern Basilical Building." In *Sepphoris in Galilee*, edited by Rebecca M. Nagy et al., 117–121. Winona Lake, IN: Eisenbrauns, 1996.

———. "Enigmatic Bible Passages: 2 Corinthians 10:13–16 Illuminated by a Recently Published Inscription." *BA* 46 (1983) 167–68.

———. "First Century Galilee from Archaeology and from the Texts" In *Archaeology and the Galilee: Texts and Contexts in the Graeco-Roman and Byzantine Periods*, edited by Douglas R. Edwards and C. Thomas McCollough, 39–48. SFSHJ 143. Atlanta: Scholars, 1997.

———. "Nazareth" In *ABD* 4:1050.

———. "Nazareth." In *GLSTMP* 2:167–80.

———. "The Sayings of Jesus and Archaeology." In *Hillel and Jesus*, edited by J. H. Charlesworth and L. L. Johns, 291–305. Minneapolis: Fortress, 1997.

———. "Sepphoris: The Jewel of the Galilee." In *GLSTMP* 2:22–38.

———. "The Sepphoris Aqueducts." In *GLSTMP* 2:76–87.

———. "Six Campaigns at Sepphoris." In *The Galilee in Late Antiquity*, edited by Lee I. Levine, 311–43. New York: Jewish Theological Seminary of America, 1992.

———. "Some Implications of Archaeology for New Testament Studies." In *What Has Archaeology to Do with Faith?*, edited by James H. Charlesworth, 23–59. Philadelphia: Trinity, 1992.

———. "Tombs, the New Testament, and the Archaeology of Religion." *RevExp* 106 (2009) 399–419.

Strange, James F., D. E. Groh, and T. R. Longstaff. *Excavations at Sepphoris*. Leiden: Brill, 2006.

———. "Excavations at Sepphoris: The Location and Identification of Shikhin." *IEJ* 44 (1994) 216–27; 45 (1995) 171–87.

Strange, James F., Thomas R. Longstaff, Dennis E. Groh, and James Riley Strange. *The Excavations at Shikhin: Manual for Area Supervisors*. Birmingham, AL: Samford University Press, 2013.

Strange James F., and H. Shanks. "Has the House Where Jesus Stayed in Capernaum been Found?" *BAR* 8/6 (1982) 26–37

Strange, James Riley. "Report of the 2011 Survey and 2012 Excavation Seasons at Shikhin." American Schools of Oriental Research Annual Meeting 2012, Chicago, Illinois. http://www.samford.edu/uploadedFiles/2012_AS_Shikhin/ASOR_Shikhin2012.pdf.

Strange, James Riley, and Mordechai Aviam. "Shikhin Excavation Project: Oil Lamp Production at Ancient Shikhin." *BAIAS* 35 (2017) 63–100.

Strickert, F. *Bethsaida*. Collegeville, MN: Liturgical, 1998.

Syon, Danny. "The Coins." In *Gamla III: The Shmarya Gutmann Excavations 1976–1989 Finds and Studies. Part 1*, edited by Danny Syon, 109–231. Jerusalem: IAA, 2014.

———. "Gamla: Portrait of a Rebellion." *BAR* 18/1 (1992) 20–37, 72.

Syon, Danny, and Zvi Yavor. "Galilean Mints in the Early Roman Period: Politics, Economy, and Ethnicity." In *Judaea and Rome in Coins 65 BCE–135 CE*, edited by David M. Jacobson and Nikos Kokkinos, 51–64. London: Spink, 2012.

———. "Gamala." In *NEAEHL* 5:1739–42.

———. *Gamla II: The Architecture. The Shmarya Gutman Excavations 1976–1989*. Jerusalem: IAA, 2010.

Sweet, Louise E. *Tell Toqaan: A Syrian Village*. Ann Arbor, Mich.: University of Michigan, 1974.

Swidler, L. *Women in Judaism: The Status of Women in Formative Judaism.* Metuchen, NJ: Scarecrow, 1976.

Sussman, Max. "Sickness and Disease." In *ABD* 6:6–15

Sussman, Varda. "A Jewish Burial Cave on Mount Scopus." In *Ancient Jerusalem Revealed*, edited by Hillel Geva, 226–230. Jerusalem: IES, 1994.

Tannous, A.I. "The Arab Village Community of the Middle East." *Annual Report of the Board of Regents of the Smithsonian Institution* (1944) 523–43.

Taylor, Joan E. "Missing Magdala and the Name of Mary 'Magdalene.'" *PEQ* 146 (2014) 205–23.

———. *What Did Jesus Look Like?* London: Bloomsbury, 2018.

Tessler, Yitzhak. "Ancient synagogue discovered in Galilee." *ynetnews.com.* August 14, 2016. https://www.ynetnews.com/articles/0,7340,L-4841308,00.html.

Theissen, Gerd. *Sociology of Early Palestinian Christianity.* Philadelphia: Fortress, 1977.

Theissen, Gerd, and Annette Merz. *The Historical Jesus: A Comprehensive Guide.* Minneapolis: Fortress, 1998.

Thiel, Winfried. "Jehu." In *ABD* 3:670–73.

Thiering, Barbara. *Jesus and the Riddle of the Dead Sea Scrolls.* San Francisco: Harper, 1992.

Thomsen, Peter. "Die lateinischen und griechischen Inschriften der Stadt Jerusalem" *Zeitschrift des deutschen Palästina-Vereins* 44 (1921) 90–168.

Thompson, William M. *The Land and the Book.* 1877. Reprint, Hartford, Conn.: Scranton, 1910.

Tigay, Jeffrey H. *Deuteronomy.* JPS Torah Commentary. Philadelphia: Jewish Publication Society, 1996.

Titoria, Reena, Prabhu Ponnusamy, and Sunil Mehra. "Identification of Undernutrition in Under Five Children: Z Score or a Composite Index of Anthropometric Failure?" *International Journal of Community Medicine and Public Health* 6/7 (2019) 3150–55.

Touwaide, Alain. "Disease." In *BNP* 4:543–54.

———. "Malaria." In *BNP* 8:195.

Tov, Emanuel. *The Texts from the Judean Desert: Indices and an Introduction to the Discoveries in the Judean Desert Series.* DJD XXXIX. Oxford: Clarendon, 2002.

Trebilco, Paul. "Asia." In *The Book of Acts in its Graeco-Roman Setting*, edited by D. S. J. Gill and C. Gempf, 291–362. Grand Rapids: Eerdmans, 1994.

———. *The Early Christians in Ephesus from Paul to Ignatius.* Grand Rapids: Eerdmans, 2007.

Tsafrir, Y. and K. G. Holum "Rehovot in the Negev: Preliminary Report, 1986." *IEJ* 38 (1988) 117–27.

Tsuk, Tsvika. "The Aqueducts of Sepphoris." In *Galilee through the Centuries*, edited by Eric M. Meyers, 161–76. Winona Lake, IN: Eisenbrauns, 1999.

———. "Bringing Water to Sepphoris" *BAR* 26/4 (2000) 34–41

Tyoalumun, Kpurkpur, Sani Abubakar, and Nongu Christopher. "Prevalence of Intestinal Parasitic Infections and Their Association with Nutritional Status of Rural and Urban Pre-School Children in Benue State, Nigeria." *International Journal of MCH and AIDS* 5/2 (2016) 146–52.

Tzaferis, V. "Jewish Tombs at and near Giv'at ha-Mivtar, Jerusalem." *IEJ* 20 (1970) 18–32.

Ulama, M. L. *Jerash.* Amman: Feras, 1996.

United States Central Intelligence Agency. "Life Expectancy at Birth." *World Fact Book.* https://www.cia.gov/library/publications/the-world-factbook/rankorder/2102rank.html.

Urbach, E. E. "The Mishnah." *EncJud1* 12:93–109.

Urman, D. *The Golan.* Oxford: BAR, 1985.

Vale, Ruth. "Literary Sources in Archaeological Description: The Case of Galilee, Galilee and Galileans." *JSJ* 18 (1987) 209–26.

Vann, Lindley. "Herod's Harbor Construction Recovered Underwater." In *Archaeology and the Bible, Volume Two: Archaeology in the World of Herod, Jesus and Paul*, edited by Hershel Shanks and Dan P. Cole, 130–31, 134. Washington, DC: BAS, 1990.

VanderKam, J. C. *The Dead Sea Scrolls Today.* Grand Rapids: Eerdmans, 1994.

Vaux, Roland de. *Archaeology and the Dead Sea Scrolls.* Schweich Lectures 1959. London: Oxford University Press, 1973.

Vermes, Geza. *The Dead Sea Scrolls: Qumran in Perspective.* Cleveland: Collins-World, 1977.

———. *Jesus the Jew.* Philadelphia: Fortress, 1973.

Walker, P. L., R. R. Bathurst, R. Richman, T. Gjerdrum, and V. A. Andrushko. "The Causes of Porotic Hyperostosis and Cribra Orbitalia: a Reappraisal of the Iron-deficiency-anemia Hypothesis." *American Journal of Physical Anthropology* 139/2 (2009) 109–25. http://www.ncbi.nlm.nih.gov/pubmed/19280675.

Walsh, Nick Paton, and Masoud Popalzai. "Mother Had 'No Other Choice' But to Sell Her 6-Year-Old Daughter." *CNN.* https://www.cnn.com/2018/11/22/asia/afghan-child-sales-intl/index.html.

Walton, Francis R., trans. *Diodorus of Sicily.* LCL. Cambridge: Harvard University Press, 1933–1967.

Wapler, Ulrike Eric Crubézy, and Michael Schultz. "Is Cribra Orbitalia Synonymous with Anemia? Analysis and Interpretation of Cranial Pathology in Sudan." *American Journal of Physical Anthropology* 123/4 (2004) 333–39.

Weber, Max. *Economy and Society: An Outline of Interpretive Sociology.* 3 vols. Edited by Guenther Roth and Claus Wittich. Translated by Ephraim Fischoff et al. New York: Bedminster, 1968.

WebMD, s.v. "Tape Worms in Humans." https://www.webmd.com/digestive-disorders/tapeworms-in-humans#.

Weiss, Ehud, and Mordechai E. Kisley. "Weeds and Seeds" *BAR* 30/6 (2004) 32–37.

Weiss, Zeev. "Josephus and Archaeology on the Cities of the Galilee." In *Making History: Josephus and Historical Method*, edited by Zuleika Rodgers, 385–413. JSJSup 110. Leiden: Brill, 2007.

———. "From Galilean town to Roman City, 100 BCVE-200 CE." In *GLSTMP* 2:53–75.

———. "Theatres, Hippodromes, Amphitheatres, and Performances." In *OHJDL* 623–40.

Weiss, Zeev, and Ehud Netzer. "Hellenistic and Roman Sepphoris: The Archaeological Evidence." In *Sepphoris in Galilee: Crosscurrents of Culture*, edited by Rebecca Martin Nagy et al., 29–37. Winona Lake, IN: Eisenbrauns, 1996.

Wells, Calvin. "Ancient Obstetric Hazards and Female Mortality." *Bulletin of the New York Academy of Medicine* 51 (1975) 1235–41.

Westcott, Ben and Taehoon Lee. "What Parasitic Worms In Defector Reveal about Conditions In North Korea." CNN November 23, 2017. http://www.cnn.com/2017/11/22/health/north-korea-defector-parasites-health/index.html.

White, K. D. *Roman Farming.* London: Thames & Hudson, 1970.

White, L. "Die Ausbreitung der Technik 500–1500." In *Europäische Wirtschaftsgeschichte: Mittelalter*, edited by C. M. Cipolla and K. Borchardt. Stutthgart: Fischer, 1978. English Translation: "The Expansion of Technology 500–1500." In *The Fontana Economic History of Europe: The Middle Ages,* edited by C. M. Cipolle and K. Borchardt, 1:143–74. London: Collins, 1993.

Wikenhauser, Alfred. *Die Apostelgeschichte*. Regensburg: Pustet, 1961.

Wikipedia, s.v. "Brucellosis." https://en.wikipedia.org/wiki/Brucellosis.

———, s.v. "Human Height." https://en.wikipedia.org/wiki/Human_height.

———, s.v. "List of Countries by Life Expectancy." https://en.wikipedia.org/wiki/List_of_countries_by_life_expectancy.

———, s.v. "Malaria." https://en.wikipedia.org/wiki/malaria.

Wilkinson, J. "Ancient Jerusalem, Its Water Supply and Population." *PEQ* 106 (1974) 33–51.

———. *Jerusalem as Jesus Knew It*. London: Thames & Hudson, 1978.

Williams, Faith W. et al. "Intestinal Parasites from the 2nd-5th Century AD Latrine in the Roman Baths at Sagalassos (Turkey)." *IJP* 19 (2017) 37–42.

Wilson, John Francis. *Caesarea Philippi: Banias, the Lost City of Pan*. London: Tauris, 2004.

Wilson, Robert R. *Sociological Approaches to the Old Testament*. Philadelphia: Fortress, 1984.

Wintermute, O. "Jubilees." In *OTP* 2:35–142.

Wise, Michael O., et al. *The Dead Sea Scrolls: A New Translation*. San Francisco: HarperSanFrancisco, 2005.

Witherington, Ben, III. "Top Ten New Testament Archaeological Finds of the Past 150 Years: How do shrouds, boats, inscriptions, and other artifacts better help us understand the Christ of the Ages?" *Christianity Today* (September 1, 2003). http://www.christianitytoday.com/ct/2003/septemberweb-only/9-22-21.0.html.

———. "Women, New Testament." In *ABD* 6:957–61.

Wright B. W. "Jewish Ritual Baths—Interpreting the Digs and the Texts: Some Issues in the Social History of Second Temple Judaism." In *The Archaeology of Israel*, edited by N. A. Silberman and D. Small, 190–214. Sheffield: Sheffield Academic Press, 1997.

Wright, C. J. H. "Family." In *ABD* 2:761–69.

Wright, George E. "Israelite Daily Life." *BA* 18 (1955) 50–79.

———. "What Archaeology Can and Cannot Do." *BA* 34 (1971) 70–76.

Wright N.T. *Jesus and the Victory of God*. Christian Origins and the Question of God 2. Minneapolis: Fortress, 1996.

Wuellner, Wilhelm H. *The Meaning of "Fishers of Men."* New Testament Library. Philadelphia: Westminster, 1967.

Yadin, Yigael. *Bar Kokhba: The Rediscovery of the Legendary Hero of the Second Jewish Revolt against Rome*. New York: Random House, 1971.

———. *Masada: Herod's Fortress and the Zealots Last Stand*. New York: Random House, 1966.

Yadin, Yigal, Jonas C. Greenfield, and Baruch A. Levine. *The Documents from the Bar Kokhba Period in the Cave of the Letters*. Volume 2, *Hebrew, Aramaic, and Nabatean-Aramaic Papyri*. Jerusalem: Israel Exploration Society, 2002.

Yamauchi, Edwin M. "Marriage." In *DDL* 3:221–49.

Yamauchi, Edwin M., and Marvin R. Wilson, eds. *Dictionary of Daily Life in Biblical and Post Biblical Antiquity*. 3 vols. Peabody, MA: Hendrickson, 2014.

Yavor, Zvi. "The Architecture and Stratigraphy of the Eastern and Western Quarters." In *Gamla II: The Architecture. The Shmarya Gutman Excavations 1976–1989*, edited by Danny Syon and Zvi Yavor, 13–112. Jerusalem: IAA, 2010.

Yeh, Hui-Yuan et al. "Human Intestinal Parasites from a Mamluk Period Cesspool in the Christian Quarter of Jerusalem: Potential Indicators of Long Distance Travel in the 15th Century AD." *IJP* 9 (2015) 69–75.

Yeivin, Z. "Ancient Chorazin Comes Back to Life." *BAR* 13/5 (1987) 22–36.

———. "On the Medium-Sized City." *Eretz Israel* 19 (1987) 59–71.

———. "Survey of Settlements in Galilee and the Golan from the Period of the Mishnah in Light of the Sources." PhD diss., Hebrew University, 1971.

YouTube (website). "Five-foot long tapeworm came 'wiggling out' of man's body after he ate sushi." https://www.youtube.com/watch?v=OADHIBgRwKA.

Zangenberg, Jürgen. "Archaeology and the New Testament. In *The HarperCollins Study Bible*, edited by Harold Attridge, lxii–lxvi. New York: HarperCollins, 2006.

Zapata-Meza, Marcela. "Domestic and Mercantile Areas." In *Magdala of Galilee: A Jewish City in the Hellenistic and Roman Period*, edited by Richard Bauckham, 89–108. Waco: Baylor University Press, 2018.

Zias, Joseph. "Anthropological Analysis of Human Skeletal Remains." In *The Akeldama Tombs*, edited by Gideon Avni and Avi Greenhut, 117–21. Jerusalem: Israel Antiquities Authority, 1996.

———. "Appendix A: Anthropological Observations." *Atiqot* 19 (1990) 125.

———. "The Cemeteries of Qumran and Celibacy: Confusion Laid to Rest?" In *Jesus and Archaeology*, edited by James H. Charlesworth, 444–71. Grand Rapids: Eerdmans, 2006.

———. "Death and Disease in Ancient Israel." *BA* 54 (1991) 147–59.

———. "Human Skeletal Remains from the Caiaphas' Tomb." *Atiqot: English Series* 21 (1992) 78–80.

———. "Human Skeletal Remains from the Mount Scopus Tomb." *Atiqot: English Series* 21 (1992) 97–103.

———. "Human Skeletal remains from a Second Temple-Period Tomb in Arnona, Jerusalem." *Atiqot: English Series* 54 (2006) 117–20.

Zias, Joe E., James D. Tabor, and Stephanie Harter-Lailheugue. "Toilets at Qumran, the Essenes, the Scrolls, New Anthropological Data and Old Theories." *RevQ* 22 (2006) 631–40.

Zissu, Boaz and David Amit. "Common Judaism, Common Purity, and the Second Temple Period Judean Miqwa'ot (Ritual Immersion Baths)." In *Common Judaism: Explorations in Second-Temple Judaism*, edited by Wayne O. McCready and Adele Reinhartz, 47–62. Minneapolis: Fortress, 2008.

———. "Two Herodian Dovecotes: Horvat Abu Haf and Horvat 'Aleq." *Roman and Byzantine Near East* 1 (1995) 56–69.

Zissu, Boaz, and A. Ganor. "Horbat 'Ethri." *Hadashot Arkheologiyot: Excavations and Surveys in Israel* 113 (2001) 101–4.

Živanović, Srboljub. *Ancient Diseases: The Elements of Palaeopathology*. New York: Pica, 1982.

Zlotnick, Dov. "Semaḥot." *EncJud2* 18:273–74.

———. *The Tractate "Mourning" (Semaḥot): (Regulations Relating to Death, Burial, and Mourning)*. New Haven: Yale University Press, 1966.

Zwickel, Wolfgang. "The Huleh Valley from the Iron Age to the Muslim Period: A Study in Settlement History." In *Religion, Ethnicity, and Identity in Ancient Galilee: A Region in Transition*, edited by Jürgen Zangenberg et al., 163–192. WUNT 210. Tübingen: Mohr/Siebeck, 2007.

Subject Index

Agrippa I, 108, 211, 295
Agrippa II, 23, 295, 296, 303
Amulets, 215, 216, 217, 218, 219, 226, 227, 266
Anemia, 158, 201, 202, 204, 206, 207, 214, 221, 223, 224, 225, 226, 227
Aniconic, 269, 291, 294, 295, 296
Annual wage, 174
Antipas, 2, 43, 47, 48, 49, 50, 51, 55, 129, 219, 281, 296
Apotropaic, 249, 266, 268
Aqueduct, 23, 35, 41, 48, 49, 50, 73
Aramaic language, 12, 42, 52, 114, 117, 118, 119, 120, 216, 217, 255
Asceticism, 310
Ashlar stones, 67, 71, 254, 257
Associates (*haverim*), 280
Augustus, 35, 37, 40, 42, 294

Bachelors, 303, 304
Balsam oil, 72, 75, 298
Bar Kokhba, 71, 134, 135, 156, 180, 181, 286, 290
Barley, 143, 145, 155,, 156, 167, 183, 212, 298
Basilica(l), 48, 49, 68, 73
Bath, hygienic, 23, 53, 73, 87, 253, 293
Bath, ritual (also *mikveh, mikva'ot*), 3, 5, 27, 33, 44, 47, 68, 71, 74, 75, 177, 209, 270, 273, 274, 279, 280, 281, 282, 283, 284, 285, 286, 287, 297
Bethsaida, 3, 54, 286, 295
Betrothal, 112, 121, 122
Bones, Animal, 47, 53, 87, 142, 147, 150, 151, 152, 153, 154, 181, 187
Bones, Human, 2, 3, 4, 5, 8, 30, 31, 186, 188, 189, 190, 191, 192, 193, 199, 202, 220, 221, 223, 224, 227, 229, 231, 240, 254, 259, 260, 261, 264, 268, 277, 302

Boys, 98, 100, 102, 103, 104, 105, 109, 240, 302, 304
Bricks, 89, 90
Burial, 8, 67, 71, 158, 185, 188, 189, 192, 208, 224, 244, 249, 250, 251, 254, 256, 257, 258, 259, 260, 262, 264, 266, 267, 268, 304
Burnt house, 3, 27
Byzantine Period, 35, 59, 62, 66, 69, 80, 95, 141, 165, 188, 194

Caesarea (Maritima), 2, 3, 10, 16, 21, 22, 34, 35, 36, 37, 39, 40, 41, 43, 47, 48, 50, 57, 58, 64, 73, 82, 86, 152, 153, 154, 208, 209, 294
Caesarea Philippi, 21, 35, 37, 61, 217, 218, 282, 286, 295
Caiaphas, 2, 3, 4, 189, 231, 233, 234, 236, 237, 262, 264
Calendar, 167, 168, 185
Cana (Khirbet Qana), 3, 59, 63, 65, 67, 69, 70, 72, 73, 74, 75, 77, 82, 84, 141, 149, 180, 182, 183, 259, 305
Capernaum, 59, 61, 64, 65, 70, 72, 74, 75, 77, 85, 86, 91, 92, 95, 136, 168, 177, 223, 285, 286
Cardo, 37, 48, 49, 51, 52, 53, 73
Casseroles, 147, 148, 149, 150
Cave, 10, 71, 79, 86, 90, 97, 117, 118, 120, 134, 135, 154, 155, 156, 158, 179, 180, 182, 189, 196, 218, 224, 231, 233, 237, 250, 255, 256, 257, 258, 299
Celibacy, 307, 309, 310
Cellar (*see* Underground animal stables)
Ceramics (*see* pottery), 12, 28, 30, 42, 44, 75, 80, 105, 147, 149, 161, 177, 178, 179, 180, 182, 183, 286, 297, 298

355

Subject Index

Charismatic, charisma, 308, 309, 311, 312, 313
Cheese, 30, 143, 144, 147, 157, 158, 160, 175
Chemical analysis, 288, 289
Child birth, 99, 192, 193, 232, 239, 240, 272, 273, 275
Child exposure (*expositio*), 100, 101
Child mortality, 226, 230, 231, 232, 233, 234, 235, 242, 243, 244, 247, 248
Children, 5, 32, 98, 99, 100, 101, 102, 103, 104, 105, 106, 107, 108, 109, 111, 116, 120, 126, 127, 128, 139, 140, 158, 159, 175, 176, 184, 185, 190, 200, 206, 207, 213, 214, 215, 219, 223, 224, 225, 226, 227, 228, 229, 230, 231, 232, 235, 241, 242, 243, 244, 245, 246, 251, 252, 299, 301, 302, 303, 306, 307
Church of the Holy Sepulcher, 3
Circus (*see* Hippodrome)
City of David, 31, 33, 180, 285
Climate, 7, 9, 10, 19, 20, 142, 154, 156, 167, 176, 218
Clothing, cloth, 8, 55, 107, 114, 115, 116, 132, 134, 135, 136, 137, 138, 160, 161, 175, 179, 180, 185, 218, 219, 250, 252, 253, 272, 273, 274
Coastal plain, 9, 10, 11, 15, 18, 164, 285
Coins, 47, 58, 67, 71, 93, 173, 182, 197, 262, 263, 270, 291, 294, 295, 296, 297
Common Judaism (*see* Household Judaism)
Cooking pots, 135, 147, 148, 149, 160, 264, 265
Corpse, 130, 250, 251, 253, 256, 264, 273, 275, 276, 277, 278, 280, 281, 282
Courtyard, 27, 44, 66, 67, 78, 79, 80, 81, 82, 83, 84, 85, 86, 91, 93, 94, 95, 96, 97, 136, 141, 182, 183, 252
Craftsmen, 28, 29, 31, 88, 129, 171, 261
Cribra orbitalia, 221, 223, 224, 225, 226
Crusader Period, 208, 225, 226, 232

Daily wage, 169, 170, 173, 174, 176
Dates (fruit), 72, 75, 143, 146, 155, 156, 296, 298
Daughters/female children, 36, 99, 100, 101, 102, 107, 108, 109, 110, 113, 114, 115, 116, 126, 128, 158, 184, 186, 192, 216, 244, 295, 302, 303, 307, 308

Day laborers, 30, 53, 98, 104, 152, 162, 164, 166, 169, 170, 171, 175, 243, 258
The Dead, 185, 249, 253, 254, 260, 263, 264, 265, 266, 279, 312
Dead Sea, 5, 11, 14, 16, 17, 18, 19, 20, 26, 53, 63, 72, 76, 107, 111, 112, 116, 117, 118, 120, 124, 137, 138, 152, 154, 181, 183, 189, 218
Decumanus, 37, 45, 48, 49
Demographics, 5, 241
Desert, 9, 14, 15, 18, 19, 20, 102, 181, 196, 197
Diaspora, 23, 31, 32, 33, 34, 108, 109, 127, 197, 202, 239
Diseases, 5, 8, 20, 186, 193, 200, 201, 202, 203, 204, 205, 207, 212, 219, 224, 227, 232, 244, 299
Divorce, 112, 113, 114, 116, 117, 118, 119, 120, 121, 123, 124, 125, 243, 308, 311
Dolichocephalic, 197
Dowry, 110, 111, 113, 114, 115, 116, 117, 118, 119, 120, 121, 125, 126, 186
Dyeing, 30, 70, 75, 136, 179, 181

Early Roman Period, 23, 57, 62, 86, 150, 154, 155, 178, 208, 224, 245, 246
Economics, 187, 286
Elderly persons, 104, 245
Elephantine, 111, 114, 115
Emic, 274
En Boqeq, 20, 53, 75, 76, 152, 181, 183, 262
Endogamy, 110–11
En-Gedi, 62, 63, 72, 75, 76, 120, 134, 152, 153, 154, 155, 156, 158, 189, 193, 219, 224, 225, 226, 231, 233, 236, 237, 238, 247, 263, 284, 293, 298, 299
ESA, 27, 182, 270, 286, 297
Essenes, 5, 72, 130, 196, 272, 279, 280, 281, 282, 287, 290, 291, 304, 309, 310
Ethnography, ethnographic, 7, 57, 64, 89, 100, 121, 123, 133, 139, 140, 142, 159, 183, 184, 185, 309
Etic, 274
Expositio (*see* child exposure)

Famine, 101, 173, 200, 207
Farm sizes, 176

356

Subject Index

Fever, 203, 204, 205, 206, 211, 214, 215, 216, 217, 218, 219, 221, 222, 223, 226, 227, 239
Fish, 17, 19, 20, 40, 53, 55, 143, 144, 148, 149, 152, 153, 154, 157, 196, 208, 209, 210, 291, 294, 299, 310
Floors, 27, 28, 44, 49, 51, 55, 73, 81, 82, 86, 91, 92, 93, 96, 133, 134, 138, 139, 140, 141, 142, 158, 159, 185, 252, 293, 294
Food, 8, 19, 40, 42, 93, 97, 103, 106, 107, 142, 143, 144, 145, 146, 147, 149, 150, 153, 154, 155, 156, 157, 158, 159, 175, 176, 177, 185, 196, 197, 206, 207, 226, 265, 267, 273, 274, 275, 278, 279, 280, 297, 298, 311
Fountains, 53, 319
Freeholders, 162, 171, 175, 176
Fresco(es), 27, 28, 44, 55, 67, 68, 293, 294
Fruit, 20, 30, 94, 142, 143, 144, 145, 147, 148, 156, 157, 167, 169, 172, 176, 181, 184
Funeral, 249
Furniture, 30, 132, 133, 253

Galilee, 3, 10, 11, 12, 13, 15, 16, 17, 19, 21, 22, 28, 42, 43, 44, 45, 46, 47, 52, 53, 54, 57, 58, 59, 60, 61, 62, 63, 64, 68, 69, 70, 72, 74, 75, 79, 81, 82, 86, 87, 89, 90, 106, 121, 122, 138, 148, 149, 152, 153, 154, 158, 164, 166, 172, 176, 177, 178, 179, 180, 181, 183, 189, 196, 197, 215, 216, 217, 218, 219, 223, 224, 225, 227, 237, 247, 255, 259, 260, 267, 268, 281, 284, 285, 286, 289, 290, 294, 295, 296, 297, 298, 308
Galilee boat, 2, 3, 65
Gamla, 2, 3, 63, 67, 68, 69, 70, 71, 72, 73, 75, 77, 82, 84, 148, 149, 152, 153, 154, 155, 156, 178, 180, 284, 285, 286, 288, 289, 293, 294, 296, 297
Gate, 3, 25, 30, 51, 52, 68, 72, 73, 212, 257, 284, 293
Gezer calendar, 167–168
Girls, 98, 100, 101, 102, 103, 104, 105, 106, 107, 108, 109, 159, 183, 240, 295
Glass, 30, 55, 75, 120, 135, 160, 161, 180, 264
Golan, 3, 54, 58, 59, 60, 61, 62, 63, 64, 72, 73, 79, 90, 148, 149, 154, 161, 166, 177, 178, 218, 267, 268, 285, 286, 289, 294, 295, 296, 297

Goliath, 192, 194, 195, 196, 230, 237
Gospel of Jesus' Wife, 306
Gospel of Mary, 305
Gospel of Philip, 305, 306
Gradations of holiness, 277
Gradations of uncleanness 277
Grapes, 74, 143, 146, 156, 169, 253, 298
Great Plain (Jezreel), 10, 11, 12, 13, 77, 105, 166, 225, 226, 232, 266
Greece, 23, 89, 106, 108, 149, 174, 187, 188, 189, 194, 210, 221, 225, 231, 234, 235, 238, 250, 275
Greek language, 12, 31, 32, 35, 37, 42, 48, 52, 53, 58, 93, 94, 116, 117, 118, 119, 120, 122, 125, 133, 135, 136, 141, 144, 202, 211, 216, 217, 219, 221, 222, 245, 251, 252, 254, 266, 306
Grinding stones/millstones, 94, 146, 179, 183
Gymnasium, 47, 48, 73

Hebrew language, 12, 13, 30, 32, 42, 90, 105, 113, 115, 136, 168, 202, 203, 204, 205, 266
Hellenistic Age, 31, 32, 42, 47, 59, 62, 66, 73, 79, 86, 126, 145, 194, 202, 217, 224, 226, 231, 238, 245, 246
Herod the Great, 2, 5, 23, 25, 34, 35, 37, 41, 51, 86, 87, 108, 111, 116, 129, 147, 181, 211, 251, 293, 294, 295, 296
Herodium, 2, 3, 65, 76, 77, 87, 120, 149, 166, 284, 294
Hill country, 9, 11, 13, 14, 15, 18, 21, 90, 165
Hippodamian Grid, 35, 37, 48, 49, 53, 64, 70, 73
Hippodrome (Circus), 35, 38, 39, 40, 47, 48, 53, 73, 153
House
    Simple, 79–81
    Complex, 81
    Courtyard, 82–84
    Terrace, 84
Household Judaism (also Common Judaism), 269, 270, 281
Huleh Valley/Lake Huleh, 15, 16, 19, 217, 218

Iconic, 54, 272, 291, 295
Impurity (ritual), 270, 273, 274, 275, 276, 278, 281, 282, 284, 286, 287, 297, 310

Subject Index

Industry, 53, 71, 75, 77, 161, 177, 178, 179, 180, 181, 182, 183, 185, 298
Infant mortality, 188, 189, 230, 241, 244, 247
Inscriptions, 3, 4, 12, 27, 29, 30, 31, 32, 39, 40, 102, 108, 109, 127, 167, 170, 187, 190, 191, 192, 229, 230, 234, 235, 240, 245, 249, 258, 262, 264, 266, 296
Insula (ae), 79, 82, 84, 85, 86
Iron Age, 128, 132, 133, 136, 144, 190, 208, 217, 226
Isolated farms, 63, 162, 164, 165, 166

Jalame, 180, 183
James ossuary, 3, 4, 199
Jericho, 14, 28, 32, 65, 72, 75, 76, 77, 87, 120, 149, 166, 189, 191, 192, 193, 194, 230, 233, 234, 236, 237, 247, 250, 260, 262, 263, 266, 284, 295
Jerusalem, 2, 3, 13, 14, 15, 21, 22, 23, 24, 25, 26, 27, 28, 29, 30, 31, 32, 33, 34, 37, 42, 43, 44, 54, 55, 57, 58, 68, 71, 73, 77, 81, 82, 83, 87, 93, 106, 120, 149, 151, 152, 153, 154, 155, 156, 158, 165, 166, 172, 177, 179, 180, 189, 192, 196, 208, 209, 224, 225, 226, 231, 233, 237, 240, 250, 254, 255, 257, 258, 260, 261, 262, 263, 270, 277, 281, 284, 285, 286, 287, 288, 289, 290, 293, 294, 295, 297, 303, 310
Jewelry, 30, 42, 115, 116, 135, 160, 265
Jewish sects, 278, 281
Jezreel Valley (*see* Great Plain)
Jordan rift, 9, 217
Judea, 3, 12, 13, 15, 17, 19, 34, 35, 36, 39, 59, 60, 62, 63, 64, 72, 77, 87, 90, 121, 122, 138, 149, 158, 164, 165, 166, 177, 179, 189, 193, 196, 224, 230, 233, 235, 236, 237, 245, 254, 255, 259, 260, 267, 268, 284, 285, 286

Ketubbah, 111, 117, 118, 119, 121, 125, 126
Kefar Hananya, 177, 178
Khirbet Karqush, 63, 66, 67, 70
Khirbet Qana (*see* Cana)
Kokhim (*see* tomb, *loculus*)

Lamp, 40, 54, 123, 135, 179, 239, 250, 252, 264, 270, 283, 287, 288, 289, 290, 292, 297

Large Estates/farms, 26, 162, 165, 166
Late Roman Period, 154, 155, 208, 293
Latin language, 35, 39, 42, 84, 141, 213, 222
Legumes (also pulses), 143, 144, 145, 146, 148, 156, 157, 167, 168, 169
Leprosy, 200, 202, 250, 272, 273, 278
Life expectancy, 189, 224, 229, 230, 235, 236, 237, 238, 239, 240, 241, 242, 247, 299
Linen, 135, 136, 137, 138, 184, 250
Lower City (Jerusalem), 17, 25, 31, 32, 33, 34

Magdala (Taricheae), 12, 19, 20, 22, 23, 42, 43, 44, 48, 52, 53, 54, 55, 57, 58, 64, 72, 73, 74, 77, 284, 292
Malaria, 19, 200, 201, 204, 206, 213–27, 239, 299
Mansion, 3, 27, 28, 34, 44, 55, 69, 79, 82, 83, 86, 87
Marriage, 107–22
   Age at, 107–10
   Process, 112–22
   To whom, 110–11
Mary Magdalene, 55, 197, 301, 304, 305, 308
Masada, 2, 18, 20, 65, 76, 77, 134, 135, 149, 154, 155, 181, 284, 294
Meiron, 75, 85, 94, 95, 106, 154, 155, 156, 177, 178, 193, 224, 225, 226, 230, 231, 233
Menstruation, 239, 273, 275, 277, 310
Merchants, 26, 28, 29, 30, 31, 152, 258
Middle Roman Period, 62
Mid-wife, 240, 251
Mikveh, mikva'ot (*see* Bath, ritual)
Mixed agriculturalists, 182–83
Mohar, 113, 114, 117, 118, 120, 125
Morning bathers, 281–82
Mosaics, 27, 28, 44, 49, 55, 88, 93, 293, 294
Mosquitoes, 214, 217, 218, 219, 221, 222
Mourner (professional), 251
Mourning (time of), 135, 136, 252, 253, 254
Mummies, 200, 201, 202, 210, 220
Mutton, 144, 154, 157

Nails, 217, 253, 264
Names (of children), 102
Nazareth, 3, 12, 59, 62, 72, 75, 78, 91, 96, 134, 147, 177, 181, 182, 183, 284

Subject Index

Naḥal Ḥever, 117, 118, 120, 121, 134, 135, 154, 155, 156, 179, 189, 193, 197, 218, 231, 233, 236, 238
Negev, 10, 15, 85, 166
New City (Jerusalem), 24, 25, 30, 31, 34, 179
Nuts, 143, 146, 150, 155, 156, 157, 298

Oil (Olive), 30, 66, 71, 72, 95, 143, 145, 157, 163, 166, 169, 179, 180, 181, 184, 265, 279, 282, 283, 284, 287, 298
Olives, 30, 68, 70, 74, 75, 142, 143, 144, 145, 146, 155, 156, 157, 160, 163, 164, 167, 168, 169, 172, 184, 284, 298
Opus sectile, 51
Ossuary (ies), 2, 3, 4, 5, 29, 30, 31, 32, 188, 191, 194, 199, 234, 240, 255, 258, 259, 260, 261, 262, 264, 266, 268, 270, 295
Osteoarchaeology, 188–90
Oven, 94, 158, 183

Palace, 32, 35, 38, 40, 50, 51, 55, 65, 75, 79, 86, 87, 149, 284, 294, 295
Palaestra, 48, 53, 73
Palatial Mansion (Jerusalem), 27, 44, 82–83
Paleopathology, 226
Papyrus (i), 4, 89, 108, 127, 133, 186, 187, 190, 191, 212, 230, 235, 306
Parasites (intestinal), 200–213
Pater familias, 101, 128
Persian Period, 43, 105, 128, 164, 296
Pharisees, 5, 112, 271, 272, 278, 279, 280, 281, 282, 287, 290, 291, 308, 310
Philip the Tetrarch, 37, 147, 178, 295
Plasmodium
    Falciparum, 221–222
    Malariae, 222
    Vivax, 222
Plaster, 51, 78, 90, 92, 93, 98
Play (of children), 104–5
Polis, 22, 23, 42, 58, 64
Polygamy, 98, 111, 112, 124, 125
Pontius Pilate, 3, 4, 39
Population, 4, 6, 12, 21, 23, 31, 34, 35, 37, 41, 45, 46, 50, 52, 53, 54, 55, 58, 59, 60, 61, 62, 63, 66, 70, 71, 72, 157, 162, 181, 185, 190, 191, 205, 206, 209, 213, 224, 241, 243, 245, 246, 247, 257, 258, 288, 295, 296, 298

Porotic hyperostosis, 221, 223, 224, 225, 226, 227
Pottery (*see* ceramics)
Priests, 6, 26, 27, 28, 29, 30, 32, 102, 111, 202, 212, 234, 272, 277, 278, 279, 281, 282, 291
Proselyte, 30–32
Pulses (*see* legumes)
Purity (ritual), 8, 27, 47, 135, 269, 270, 272, 274, 275, 276, 278, 279, 280, 281, 282, 283, 284, 285, 287, 290, 291, 297

Qalandiya, 81, 166
Quartan fever, 203, 221, 222, 227
Qiryat Sefer, 62, 63, 67, 71, 75, 284
Qumran, 2, 86, 102, 103, 109, 110, 112, 117, 125, 137, 143, 155, 156, 172, 189, 191, 192, 208, 233, 237, 238, 257, 270, 279, 280, 284

Rabbis, 6, 30, 31, 88, 98, 99, 100, 102, 110, 111, 115, 116, 117, 123, 130, 136, 137, 140, 204, 212, 240, 244, 250, 259, 262, 271, 274, 302, 303, 305
Rainfall, 10, 13, 14, 15, 16
Romans, 2, 3, 68, 101, 120, 153, 217, 260, 294, 295
Roof, 34, 78, 80, 83, 89, 92, 93, 94, 96, 298
Rooms, 27, 28, 40, 49, 60, 69, 71, 79, 80, 81, 82, 86, 91, 96, 129, 138, 141, 142
Royal lands, 162, 166

Sadducees, 202, 212, 260, 281, 284
Samaria, 13, 17, 19, 21, 37, 58, 59, 62, 63, 66, 72, 81, 85, 95, 141, 162, 164, 165, 166, 176, 177, 189, 193, 224, 225, 230, 233, 235, 236, 237
Samaritan (s), 13, 66, 194, 195, 196, 224, 236, 239, 245, 280
Sea of Galilee, 10, 16, 17, 19, 52, 53, 54, 68, 74, 89, 152, 153, 154, 181, 196, 215, 216, 217, 218, 289
Semi-tertian fever, 203, 216, 218, 221, 222
Sepphoris, 2, 4, 5, 12, 21, 22, 23, 35, 42–50, 53, 54, 55, 57, 58, 59, 61, 62, 64, 68, 73, 82, 83, 84, 111, 147, 152, 153, 154, 177, 178, 179, 181, 182, 216, 284, 288, 289, 296
Settlement categories, 63
Shikhin, 75, 178, 179, 183, 289, 290
Shroud, 3, 4, 199, 250, 267
Siloam Pool, 25, 32, 33

359

Subject Index

Skeletal remains, 106, 158, 188–98, 202, 223, 226, 229, 230, 231, 235, 241, 299
Slaves, 33, 50, 98, 102, 104, 107, 114, 128, 162, 164, 166, 169, 175, 253
Small landholdings, 162, 165
Social Groups/classes, 26, 41, 43
Sons, 98, 99, 100, 102, 107, 108, 159, 171, 244, 302
Stadium, 43, 51, 73
Stages (of childhood), 102–4
Stature, 8, 20, 191, 193–96
Stoa, 53
Stoneware vessels, 5, 30, 72, 87, 135, 177, 182, 285, 287
Survey (archaeological), 12, 57–59, 62, 63, 93, 141, 146, 161, 162, 164, 178, 179, 257
Synagogue(s), 3, 30, 32, 36, 51, 64, 65, 68–72, 75–77, 197, 206, 215, 264, 271, 284, 292–94

Taricheae (*see* Magdala)
Temperature, 10, 13, 17, 18, 139, 227, 298
Temple
    Caesarea Maritima, 37, 39, 40, 42
    Sebaste, 37
    Caesarea Philippi, 37
Temple Mount (Jerusalem), 2, 24, 25, 227, 293
Tenant farmers, 162, 166, 169, 170, 175
Tent, 34, 60, 68, 76, 79, 86, 275, 282
Terraces, 72, 165, 182
Tertian fever, 203, 216, 219, 221, 222, 227
Theater, 23, 35, 36, 38, 39, 40, 41, 43, 46, 48, 49, 51, 52, 73
Tiberias, 2, 12, 21, 22, 35, 42–48, 50–55, 57, 58, 61, 64, 73, 108, 111, 177, 179, 180, 216, 281, 293, 295, 296
Tombs
    Arcosolium, 256
    Loculus (*kokhim*), 67, 70, 255, 256, 259 Monumental, 32, 254–55
    Trench, shaft, cyst, 70, 190, 251, 257, 258, 267

Top Archaeological Finds, 2, 3
Tuberculosis, 200, 202, 205, 219, 250

Ulpian's Life Table, 190
Underground stable (also Cellar), 91, 138
Unguentaria, 264, 265
Upper City (Jerusalem), 24–27, 30, 31, 33, 34, 149, 180, 284, 286, 294
Upper room, 92, 93, 141, 308, 310

Veneration of tombs, 266, 267
Villa, 27, 44, 48, 63, 79, 83, 84, 86, 162, 166
Village farms, 162–64, 181, 182
Virgin, 108, 114, 117, 120, 122, 123, 128, 307

Wadi Muraba'at, 117, 118, 121, 125
Wailer, 251
Weaving/cloth production, 29, 30, 55, 135–38, 176, 179, 184, 185, 219, 250, 252
Wedding, 122–23
Weight (human), 196, 206, 227
Wheat, 102, 145, 155, 156, 157, 167, 176, 183, 184, 298
Widow, 93, 108, 114, 117, 241
Wilderness, 11, 14, 15, 17, 26, 72, 137, 154
Wine, 44, 71, 75, 95, 143, 145, 157, 164, 166, 169, 175, 181, 265, 279
Wine press, 71, 72, 146, 147, 163, 179, 181, 182, 284, 297
Women
    Status of, 127–31
    Tasks of, 183–85
Wool, 30, 70, 75, 134–38, 147, 150, 151, 160, 179, 180, 184, 185, 250
Worms, 17, 205, 206, 208–13
Yodefat, 2, 59, 62, 67, 70, 73, 75, 82, 84, 152, 153, 154, 180, 182, 183, 224, 284, 288, 289, 294
Young workers, 241, 243
Youth mortality, 229, 230, 233–35, 245, 246, 299

Scripture Index

OLD TESTAMENT

Genesis

1:28	98
8:22	19
18:8–9	159
24:59, 61	113
25:29, 34	158
28:2	110
29:10	110
29:24, 29	113
34:12	113
50:10	253

Exodus

20:4	27, 51, 291
21:10	107, 140
21:22	100
21:7–11	101
22:16	113

Leviticus

11–17	272
11:7	47
11:20	273
11:23	273
11:29–30	273
11:41–43	273
11:34	279
11:38	279
15:19–30	239
15:20	310
15:24	310
18:18	111
26:1	291
26:16	204

Numbers

5:28	99
19	272
19:7–8	278

Deuteronomy

4:15–19	291
8:8	143
11:13–17	19
24:1	124
27:15	291
28:22	204, 222

Judges

3:20	92

1 Samuel

1:6	111
9:2	195
18:25	113
19:13	132
19:15–16	132
24:1	72
31:13	253

2 Samuel

4:7	132

1 Kings

17:19	132
19:19–21	312

2 Kings

1:2	92
4:10	93, 132
4:38	158

1 Chronicles

9:13	29

Nehemiah

11:10–14	29

Job

4:29	105
17:13	132

Psalms

63:7 (6)	132
132:3	132

Isaiah

40:7	19

Jeremiah

7:18	104
16:1–4	312
16:5–7	312
16:8–9	312
30:6	204
31:15	244

Ezekiel

24:15–18	312

Amos

5:16	251

Habakkuk

3:17	143

Haggai

2:13	158

Malachi

1:2–3	308

NEW TESTAMENT

Matthew

1:18–19	122
2:18	244
4:17–22	152
5:4	248
5:6	248
5:31–32	308
5:32	125
5:40	137
6:3–4	310
6:25	137
8:14–15	223
8:17	202
8:28	248
9:2	133
9:23	251
9:37–38	170
10:8	202
10:10	170
10:37	308
11:16	68
11:17	252
11:18–19	309
13:27	175
13:33–34	184
13:55	88
18:25	102
19:3–12	304, 307
19:9	125
19:13	227
19:14	243
20:1	170
20:2	30, 170, 172
20:3	68
20:8	170
20:9	30, 172
20:13	30, 172
22:1	123
22:4	157
23:7	68
23:23	143
23:27	258

23:29	254	10:40	102
24:19	184	12:1–8	170
24:30	252	12:2	175
24:41	184	12:28	68
25:1	123	13:12–13	307
25:10	123	13:15	310
25:36	202	13:17	184
25:43	202	14:14–15	310
27:6	255	14:14	93
27:7	258	14:15	92
27:52–53	267	15:21	32
27:56	304	15:40–41	112, 310, 311
27:57	250	15:43	311
27:59	250	15:46	250, 255
27:61	304	15:47	55
28:1	55, 304	16:1	55, 102, 184, 250
		16:3	255

Mark

1:6	136, 143	**Luke**	
1:16–17	152	1:39	28
1:19–20	152	2:37	245
1:20	170	3:1	247
1:29	141	3:23	247
1:30–31	222	4:38–39	223
2:4	133, 142	4:40	202
2:9	133	5:11	152
2:11	133	5:15	202
2:12	133	6:29	137
2:15	311	6:34–35	310
3:31–35	307	7	304
4:31	143	7:11–16	251
5:35	242	7:12	242, 251
5:38	251	7:32	68
6:3	88, 247	7:33–34	309
6:4	307	7:36	311
6:22	129	8:1–3	310, 311
6:44	228	8:2	55, 202, 304
6:55	133	8:32	112
6:56	68, 164, 202	8:42	242
7:3	271	8:49	242
7:4	68	8:52	252
7:9–12	308, 311	9:2	202
9:17–18	242	9:42	242
10:2–12	308	10:2	170
10:6–9	112	10:7	170
10:11–12	125	10:9	202
10:13–16	243	10:30	136
10:13	227	10:31–42	310
10:19	308, 311	11:7	135, 140
10:29–30	307	11:27–28	307

Scripture Index

Luke (continued)

11:34	140
11:37	311
11:42	143
11:43	68
11:44	257
12:22	137
12:36	123
13:11–12	202
13:20–21	189
13:27	170
14:1	310
14:21	56
14:26	307
15:8	184
15:17	170
15:19	170
15:21	170
15:22	175
15:23	157
15:27	157
15:30	157
15:32	157
16:18	125, 308
16:19	138
17:7	175
17:34	133, 135
17:35	184
18:13	252
18:15	227
18:16	243
19:5–7	311
21:23	184
22:11	93
23:27	251, 252
23:53	250
23:55	184
24:1	250
24:2	255
24:10	55, 304

John

2	305
2:1	69
2:1–10	123
2:6	286
4:44	307
4:46	202
4:49	242
4:52	223
5:3	202
5:5	202
5:8	133
5:9	133
5:10	133
5:11	133
6:9	143
6:23	50
9:7	32, 33
10:10	248
10:12	170
11	251
11:1	202
11:14	242
11:20	310
11:31	253
11:44	250
12:1–2	310
19:23–24	136
19:25	102, 304
19:26–27	308, 311
19:39–40	250
19:40	250
20:1	55, 255, 304
20:2	55
20:10–18	304
20:11–18	55

Acts

1:3	92
1:13	93
1:14	308
4:9	202
4:36	32
5:6	250, 251
5:10	251
5:15	133, 202
6	32, 36
6:1	32
6:5	32
6:9	32
8:40	36
9:33	133
9:36	310
9:37	93, 202, 250
9:39	184
10	36, 42
10:28	286
11:27–30	310

12:2	247
12:12	310
12:23	211
18:22	36
20:8	92–93
21:8–9	36
21:8	36
21:9	307
23–27	36
23:35	38
24:27	38
28:8	212

1 Corinthians

7:3–5	140
7:10–11	125
7:30	253
9:5	247, 307, 313

Galatians

2:9	247

Philippians

2:26–27	223

1 Timothy

2:15	240
5:23	212

James

1:11	19
5:4	170

Revelation

1:7	252
14:4	307
18:9	252

www.ingramcontent.com/pod-product-compliance
Lightning Source LLC
Chambersburg PA
CBHW081148290426
44108CB00018B/2478